# Essential LightWave® 3D [8]

## The Fastest and Easiest Way to Master LightWave

## Timothy Albee and Steve Warner with Robin Wood

**Wordware Publishing, Inc.**

**Library of Congress Cataloging-in-Publication Data**

Albee, Timothy.
    Essential lightwave 3D 8 / by Timothy Albee and Steve Warner with Robin Wood.
      p.  cm.
    Includes index.
    ISBN 1-55622-082-0 (pbk., companion CD-ROM)
    1.  Computer animation.   2.  Computer graphics.   3.  LightWave 3D.
    I.  Warner, Steve, 1970-   II.  Wood, Robin, 1953-   III.  Title.
    TR897.7.A4215 2005
    006.6'96--dc22
                                     2004029130
                                        CIP

ISBN 1-55622-082-0
10 9 8 7 6 5 4 3 2 1
0412

All inquiries for volume purchases of this book should be addressed to Wordware Publishing, Inc.,
at the above address. Telephone inquiries may be made by calling:

(972) 423-0090

## Dedication

To the memory of my grandfather, Winston Hudson: automotive designer, actor, director, singer, violinist, and luthier. His life was a continuous example that all things are possible for the dedicated heart and the creative mind.

Timothy Albee


To my parents, Charles and Dorothy, who didn't flinch when I told them I wanted to be an artist. The greatest gift a child can receive is the unwavering love and support of his parents. You provided that in spades. Thank you.

Steve Warner

# Contents

# Contents

# Contents

# Contents

# Introduction

What you have in your hands is, quite simply, a collection of tools and techniques that many professional LightWave artists use every single day doing what we do in our various fields. The tools and techniques explored in this book are essential to creating the caliber of imagery that you see on film and television and in print and video games.

While this book contains no "secrets," per se, it does strip away the techno-babble that plagues so many technical documents and reveals easy-to-follow, industry-proven techniques. These are techniques that you would eventually pick up on your own, as did the rest of us. However, the average learning curve for "discovering" them on your own is estimated at between five and eight years (much less if you find yourself hired into a studio where you are working on actual productions).

The information in this book is designed to get you up and running with the software as quickly as possible. The first few chapters will orient you to LightWave's unique interface. The next several chapters focus on lighting and surfacing techniques. Subsequent chapters develop your modeling skills and teach you the basics of animation. The final chapters show you how to add "pizzazz" to your work with special effects and dynamics simulations. The files for the tutorials discussed in this book can be found on the companion CD-ROM. When

available, both PC and Mac versions have been included.

Obviously, the information contained in this book may seem overwhelming, especially if this is your first foray into 3D. In the immortal words of Douglas Adams, "Don't panic!" This book will provide you with a solid foundation in LightWave. It comes from those with many years of experience who still have the passion of those newly introduced to the art form!

From this foundation you will discover new things, find better solutions, and generally raise the bar for us all. Show us the dreams you've got in your head, the things that you wished you could always see but didn't know quite how to bring to life. Share those dreams that were so exciting they kept you awake at night. Share these things with the rest of us, post them on forums, feature them on web sites, and show them in film festivals. Help to inspire the rest of us by sharing what moves you in ways words can never relay!

Welcome to the path! May your journey be one that fills you with wonder and excitement, far exceeding what you barely dare to dream possible.

—Timothy Albee
http://Timothy.ArtistNation.com

—Steve Warner
http://stevewarner.com

# Chapter 1

# Playing in Three Dimensions

Before we get really deep into the nuts and bolts of the major LightWave tools, we've got to make sure everyone is on the same page about understanding the core concepts of 3D. Math and geometry figure heavily in these core concepts, but they come into play in such a way that they're fun. (This is probably because when working in 3D, math no longer represents abstract, almost arcane, concepts. In 3D, math and geometry are almost tangible. They give you immediate gratification with imagery that looks awesome when you solve whatever problem you're working on.)

## Note

If kids were taught math and geometry with 3D (making movies or exporting animations into a public domain game engine), you couldn't keep them away from it.

Using 3D, you not only see an immediate use for all that nifty trigonometry, geometry, tensor calculus, and algebra, but you also have a lot of fun *playing* with it (yes, *playing*)! So, as you explore this, keep in mind that the whole objective is to have fun, explore, and play. If you keep that focus in mind, the nuts and bolts will be almost effortless.

## 3D "Space"

To measure any three-dimensional object, whether it be in "real" space or the "virtual world" of a computer, you need to attribute to that object three dimensions. In the real world, these three dimensions are most commonly thought of in terms of length, width, and depth.

So, a "dimension" is really just a *vector* (a line that extends infinitely in each direction from its origin, never turning and never stopping) laid along a specific *axis* (the angles that define the vector's orientation). Height is a dimension, just as width and depth are. But the labels "height," "width," and "depth" are too subjective to be used with any certainty within the precise areas

of mathematics, drafting, or computer-aided design. Certain *conventions* (agreements that, to make things easier for everyone, a certain *symbol* will always represent a certain *concept*) were brought into play for the defining of these three dimensions as they exist within the conceptual space of a computer.

In three-dimensional space, up and down are defined as parts of the Y axis. The area above the *ground plane* (defined where $Y=0$) is measured with *positive values* (like $Y=5$). Below the ground plane, the Y axis is measured with *negative values* (like $Y=-5$). Left and right are measured along the X axis. Space to the left of $X=0$ is measured

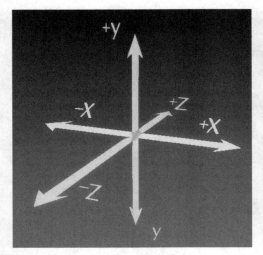

*Figure 1-1: The convention for defining three-dimensional space.*

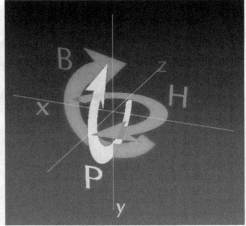

Figure 1-2: Heading (H) rotates around the Y axis. Pitch (P) rotates around the X axis. Bank (B) rotates around the Z axis.

with negative values, and space to the right of X=0 is measured with positive values. Space "away from you" is measured with positive values of the Z axis, and space "toward you" is measured with negative values of the Z axis.

Bear in mind that like the image in Figure 1-1, your *viewport* (your window into this "virtual world," of which you may have more than one open) may be offset from what the computer considers "world-space." *World-space* is easy to think of as LightWave's "handle" on its reality. No matter how you spin an object, no matter how you rotate a viewport, LightWave will always keep X=0, Y=0, and Z=0 *exactly* where it always has been (and forever will be). So, like in Figure 1-1, the viewport can be rotated counterclockwise a bit and tilted up just a bit so you can see the axes all nicely laid out before you, but LightWave's

handle on where +X becomes –X will never vary.

For keeping track of how an object is rotated within three-dimensional space, LightWave has taken its labels for the rotation axes from what you'd think of while flying a plane: **H**eading, **P**itch, and **B**ank.

Figure 1-2 is probably confusing. Let me take a different angle on the concept.

If you think of your hand like an airplane (I know it's simplistic, but bear with me), heading is the axis that would change your compass direction, pitch is the axis that would raise and lower the nose of the airplane, and bank is the axis that would get the plane to roll on its side. It may seem silly, but for the first couple of years that I worked in 3D, I still did the "my-hand-is-an-airplane" thing to figure out rotation axes. (Hey, if it works, don't knock it!)

*Figure 1-3: LightWave's rotation axes — think of your hand like a plane.*

## Objects

Behind every slick render — hidden under the fur, buried within the volumetrics, deep within the polish of the texturing — is an object. At its core, the *object* is made up of a meshwork of lines that define triangles, quadrangles, or other variously shaped *polygons*.

The quickest way to understand the concept of what 3D is all about is to think of

*Figure 1-4: Beneath the 3D fur (generated with Worley Labs' Sasquatch) is a model made up of thousands and thousands of triangles.*

papier-mâché laid over a chicken-wire mesh. The papier-mâché *surface* may have all sorts of paint and whatnot on it (giving it the appearance of anything from flesh to rock), but at its core is a carefully planned-out *wireframe* structure. That structure is what we would consider the object.

LightWave has very few limitations as to what it can "conceptualize" as an object. If you wanted to have a single polygon (a closed plane bounded by straight sides) defined by 500 points, you could. (Many other programs restrict the user to building only with triangles.) LightWave also allows you to build using *splines* (spatial-lines, originally thought up for designing cars) and a wonderful hybridization of splines and polygons known as *sub-patches* (also known as "subdivision surfaces" in other software packages).

The toolset that this combination of polys, splines, and sub-patches offers means you can create extremely complex geometric or organic shapes with amazing speed. We get into using each one of these different tools in a bit. But how can you see what you've built without light?

*Figure 1-5: The same sphere can look completely different with different surfacing treatments.*

# Virtual Lights

Without *light*, we would see nothing. The same applies to the virtual world within LightWave. In order to "see" anything in LightWave, you must (in essence) use one of LightWave's lights to send a "wavicle" (a wave/particle of light) scattering off the surface of an object and into the lens of LightWave's camera. (When you think of your eyes as cameras, this is exactly the way things operate in real life.)

Each of the lights within LightWave has a real-world counterpart. A *distant light* is like a light that is so far away that its rays all behave as if they are parallel to one another. This is like sunlight or moonlight or nondescript "bounced" lighting. Distant lights can cast shadows, but they only cast hard-edged *ray-traced* shadows (shadows that are perfect in every detail except that they are also perfectly sharp).

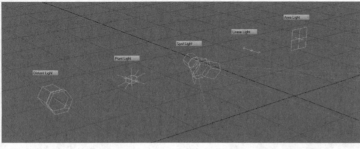

*Figure 1-6: The different kinds of lights available to a LightWave artist.*

*Figure 1-7: Distant light.*

*Figure 1-8: Point light.*

Distant lights give a flat, almost "spacey" kind of feeling. They're great for when you want to imply that light has traveled great distances to impact the objects (like from the sun, moon, or distant stars). Distant lights that don't cast shadows are also great for precisely suggesting *ambient* light (more on this in Chapter 4).

*Point lights* are like candles or non-frosted "globe" lightbulbs. Like distant lights, point lights can cast only hard-edged, ray-traced shadows.

Point lights cast their light from a single point. Notice how you don't actually see the light itself but only the impact of the light's waves. (If you wanted to see a light "bulb," you would build a model of one and "attach" the light to the lightbulb object.)

*Spotlights* are like the klieg lights used on live-action productions. They cast a cone of light in only one direction and can fade that light gently from the light's "hot spot" to the edge of its cone. Spotlights can cast hard-edged, ray-traced shadows, and they can also cast soft-edged (but technically imperfect) *shadow-mapped* shadows, which are much quicker to calculate than ray-traced shadows. These are the most commonly used light. They're fast, predictable, and versatile.

*Linear lights* are like fluorescent tubes. They cast only ray-traced shadows, but these shadows are soft-edged. The amount of softness in the shadows from linear lights is determined by how long the "fluorescent tube" is and how far away it is from the objects casting or receiving shadows (just like a "real" fluorescent light). These lights give a soft, gentle glow. Their shadows take longer to calculate than shadows from distant, point, or spotlights, but not as long as shadows from area lights.

*Figure 1-9: Spotlight.*

*Area lights* are a little like spotlights in that they cast light in roughly a cone shape. But this cone lacks the controls given to spotlights, and light is given off *both* in the direction the light is facing and directly behind it. Area lights most closely simulate real-world lights and shadows. They are slow to render, even when they are not casting shadows, so use them sparingly.

*Figure 1-10: Linear light.*

As LightWave has progressed from version to version, its lights and *renderer* (the complex engine that calculates how everything looks) have been updated to allow light to behave more and more like light in the real world. Light can now bounce off surfaces (giving the same

*Figure 1-11: Area light.*

kind of red hint when an apple is placed right next to a white wall). And light can now obey the laws of *caustics*, meaning that light "wavicles" will be *refracted* (focused) through transparent objects (like sunlight through a magnifying glass) and *reflected* off shiny objects (like a gold ring throwing a bit of brightness onto the stone plinth that holds it).

So, the important thing to remember when lighting your scene in LightWave is to think, "How would I light this in real life?" (Those of you who have studied photography or directed live-action film or theater have a distinct advantage in understanding lighting. When a room is lit for a production, it is lit differently than how it would be lit for general use. Studying how theatrical and cinematic lighting is accomplished could not be more strongly recommended.) As you walk around your world, always look for how the environments you are moving through are lit. Then think about the slight changes to the real-world lights that you'd have to make to get the same effect within LightWave.

## Virtual Camera

LightWave's "cameras" are the windows through which your audience will see your final product (you can have up to 100 cameras in a scene). All of LightWave's other windows are aids in *constructing* your work; the camera's viewport is the one window where you will showcase your work.

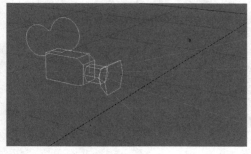

*Figure 1-12: The camera icon serves as a visual representation for the camera's position and rotation within three-dimensional space. It also reflects the camera's field of view, its focal distance (what will be in focus when using depth of field), and where objects begin to disappear into LightWave's fog.*

When you tell LightWave to render, whatever the camera is "seeing" will be fair game for the renderer to draw. The camera can be moved and rotated along all axes. It can track to items in the scene and inherit its motion directly from other items (it could be "parented" to the wingtip of a plane if you wanted). There are more settings on the LightWave camera than most of us will ever need — though it is wonderful to know that they're there, just in case we ever do.

Figure 1-13 has Show Safe Areas active, which gives me two sets of lines running around the outside edge of the renderable area. Even modern televisions cut off much of the picture. The outer line is known as "Action Safe" and shows where you can safely assume that any important action won't be cut off by a viewer's TV set. The inner line is known as "Title Safe" and marks the extents of where important text or logos should go — just in case the viewer's TV is really old and crops that much off the picture.

The partially gridded cross that looks like it could be in a submarine's range finder is what's known as a *field chart*. For traditional animators, a field chart helps calculate *panning* shots (shots where the background is moving), but for 3D, it is

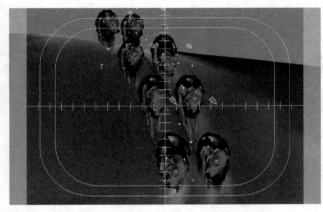

*Figure 1-13: The Camera view. The areas shaded with tan on the left and right of the viewport are indications of what is outside the camera's 640x480 field of view.*

used mostly as a reference guide for element placement.

"If you nail together two things that have never been nailed together before, some schmuck will buy it from you."
— George Carlin

Note

While LightWave's camera has, literally, no strings attached and though you could do things with that camera that would be impossible with a real camera, just keep in mind that audiences have built up almost 100 years of experience watching the results of real cameras. I find that unless there's a darn good reason to have a "flying" camera, the story you're telling is served much better with the camera handled as if it were on a virtual tripod.

• • •

With those basic concepts, that's about all there is to 3D! Everything else is just about finding new ways of putting things together.

Your greatest assets are creativity, problem-solving skills, and a darn good sense of humor.

# Chapter 2

# LightWave Dissected

I'd like to take a moment to point out that while this book may cover a great many things, it isn't trying to be the LightWave manual. Its focus is that of being a "kick-bootie" introductory course that will be a bit like a "rail-gun" in getting you some serious momentum on your way to becoming one of the great LightWave jockeys.

There are quite a few commands, tools, and windows that I don't cover at all (some because they should be self-explanatory once you get the hang of things, and others because in an introduction to LightWave, they're just too much information). There are others I go through step by step, explaining all the whys and wherefores that you need to not just be parroting my actions; you'll learn how LightWave "thinks."

Once you understand how to correctly phrase the question, the answer almost completes itself.

Some of the real "gold" in this book is the collection of secrets, tips, tricks, and techniques I've discovered over the years. (A few of these are new discoveries I've put together over the past few weeks — Light-Wave is *always* showing you new things *if you're willing to see*. No matter how good you *think* you are, remember that you are always and only just scratching the surface of the power contained within LightWave.)

LightWave makes use of the idea of "separation of power" better than any other 3D package I've used. In Modeler, you sculpt your objects; in Layout, you lay them out to create your scene.

If you've worked with 3D packages in which you have to fight with modeling the details on an object while it is encroached upon on all sides by other items in a scene, modeling in one environment and animating in another might seem almost too easy. But the first time you have to tweak an object buried within a packed scene, you will love the fact that Modeler lets you isolate that object in its rest position without anything else (objects, deformations, or the like) getting between you and the exact shape that you're looking for.

When "dissecting" LightWave, it can first be separated into two major elements: Modeler and Layout.

- **Modeler** is where objects are "sculpted" using a set of comprehensive tools. For almost anything you need, Light-Wave's Modeler seems to have a tool that does just that, as there are many tools to explore. Play with them all and get to know them so that when you need something, you know where to look.

- **Layout** is where the objects that you've sculpted are lit, animated, and ultimately rendered for their final presentation.

LightWave also integrates other programs that support both Layout and Modeler. We touch on each of these as we go through this chapter.

- The **Hub** conducts the flow of information between Layout and Modeler.

- **Plug-ins** are separate programs that attach to LightWave, "LEGO®-like," and boost the functionality of Layout and Modeler.

- **LScript** is the scripting language through which the end user *has complete control over every aspect of LightWave*.

- **LWSN** is LightWave's ScreamerNet, the *free* network renderer that allows you to use nearly every computer in your establishment to help render your animations.

So, in its simplest sense, you model in Modeler, and lay out the models in Layout. Though both Modeler and Layout have been crafted and refined over the years to be the optimal environment for doing what they each need to do, they are both startlingly similar in many respects. Everything else pretty much functions behind the scenes; you could spend an entire career with LightWave and never do more than add plug-ins you find freely available over the Internet (mondo thanks to the wonderful, supportive, and blisteringly intelligent LightWave user/support base out there). But should you want to "pop the hood" and "trick her out," with LScript and LightWave's open-ended functionality, there is, quite literally, no limit to what you can do.

# Modeler

Modeler's default tool/window layout features four viewports (Top, Perspective, Back, and Right), a collection of commands and information readouts on the bottom of the screen, a set of tools on the left-hand side of the screen, and a series of tabs that offer different sets of these tools.

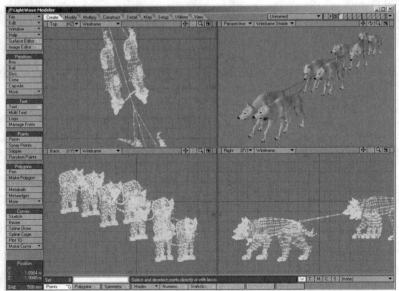

*Figure 2-1: LightWave's Modeler (as seen from a screen resolution of 1024x768). Modeler houses all the tools you need to build the objects you will animate in Layout.*

# Viewports and Viewport Controls

Each window that shows a different angle on the model that you're sculpting is known as a *viewport*. Each viewport is completely customizable, as is the number of viewports and their relationship to one another. By referencing your work at different angles, you can be assured that you will always be able to isolate the exact point or poly you want to manipulate, even amid a complex model like the one shown in Figure 2-1.

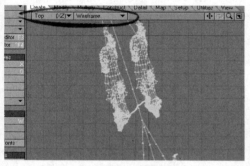

Figure 2-2: The View settings, located in the upper-left corner of each viewport, let you quickly set that viewport's angle and display type.

## Newbie Note

A *pop-up menu* in LightWave is indicated by a small downward-pointing triangle next to a tool or button. (You can see two next to Top (XZ) and Wireframe in Figure 2-2, the first pertaining to the viewport angle (or view angle) and the second being a separate control that lets you choose the level of real-time rendering the viewport should display.) These triangles let you know that there are more options than what is shown. Clicking on a pop-up menu presents you with a list of other options from which you can choose.

Clicking on the View Angle pop-up menu lets you choose which kind of view you want that viewport to display. In Figure 2-3, you see that Top (XZ) is highlighted, showing that it is the active choice.

The pop-up menu to the right of the View Angle pop-up menu lets you choose what level of real-time rendering you wish to apply to that viewport. In Figure 2-3, you can see that Wireframe is highlighted, reiterating that the viewport's current display type is Wireframe.

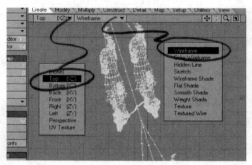

Figure 2-3: The View settings pop-up menus.

Figure 2-4: The Color Wireframe display type reflects the polygons' Sketch Color attribute.

Figure 2-5: The Hidden Line display is similar to Wireframe; however, only the polygons facing the Perspective view's camera are displayed. Other polys are hidden, making it easier to edit the object.

**10**

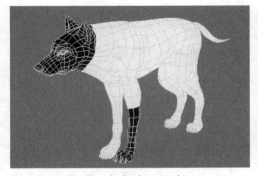

Figure 2-6: The Sketch display type lets you see your object as a solid, wireframed object that doesn't show any kind of lighting or surfacing attributes. Sketch does, however, show polygons' Sketch Color attribute.

Figure 2-9: Smooth Shade shows your model with all its surface smoothing settings considered. (I've activated the sub-patches, which bring into play a complex smoothing algorithm on the model's geometry itself. More on sub-patches in Chapter 7.)

Figure 2-7: Wireframe Shade is a lot like Sketch in that you see the polygons outlined in their respective Sketch Color. However, Wireframe Shade also shows surface coloring and the rudimentary lighting that Modeler uses to help you figure out the direction each poly is facing.

Figure 2-10: The Weight Shade display type shows the effect that weight maps will have on your model. Here, we're looking at the weight map for the husky's head; the bright red that indicates 100% influence dissipates into "circuit-board green" that indicates 0% influence.

Figure 2-8: Flat Shade shows your model as a solid object without any kind of smoothing going on between polygons; that is, each poly comes to a sharp edge when it meets its neighbor, regardless of its smoothing settings. (More on smoothing in Chapter 3.)

Figure 2-11: The Texture display type loads in any image-based textures you may have applied to your model and maps them accordingly. This husky is sporting a simple UV texture map. (See Chapter 4 for more on texture mapping.)

Figure 2-12: Textured Wire display combines Texture and Wireframe Shade displays, giving you the best of both worlds. Your object will show image-based textures and rudimentary lighting along with wireframes rendered according to each polygon's Sketch Color.

In addition to the controls that change the viewport's angle and its display type, the top of every viewport has four control buttons that let you move, rotate, zoom, and minimize or maximize the view.

Figure 2-13: These tools control the position, rotation, zoom, and size of the viewports.

Clicking and dragging on the Pan button scrolls the viewport around so you can center in on different things. (All viewports that do not have Independent Center checked under **Modeler | Options | Display Options** will also move when you pan Modeler's center about. More on this later in the "Modeler Display Options" section.)

Clicking and dragging on the Rotate button *orbits* a Perspective viewport around its center. (This button is inactive in non-perspective views.)

Clicking and dragging on the Zoom button *zooms in* and *zooms out* on the view's current center (as with Pan, all viewports without Independent Zoom selected will respond). Drag to the left to zoom out, and drag to the right to zoom in.

 Figure 2-14: Pan button.

 Figure 2-16: Zoom button.

Figure 2-15: Rotate button.

Figure 2-17: Min/Max button.

Clicking and dragging on the Min/Max button toggles the viewport in and out of full-screen mode.

> **Note**
>
> *Hot keys* (or keyboard shortcuts) let you get the job done as quickly as possible, with an absolute minimum of mouse-clicking and hoop-jumping.
>
> When I mention the hot keys I use (almost without thinking anymore), I'll set them off in a special "Hot Key Block," as follows.
>
> (Remember that LightWave's hot keys are *case sensitive!* If you're having trouble, check to make sure that Caps Lock isn't on.)

## Hot Key Block

**Viewports**

**<g>** centers your view around the current location of the mouse. You can use this to cover great distances (like when you're in close working on your character's foot and want to zip to his shoulder without having to zoom out, recenter, and zoom back in).

**<,>** (comma) zooms out by a factor of 1.

**<.>** (period) zooms in by a factor of 1.

**<Shift>** + **<,>** zooms out by a factor of 2.

**<Shift>** + **<.>** zooms in by a factor of 2.

**<Ctrl>** + **<Alt>** and dragging in a viewport zooms in and out, just like clicking and dragging on the Zoom button (Figure 2-16).

**<Alt>** and dragging in an orthogonal viewport (any view that isn't a Perspective view) scrolls that viewport in the direction you drag the mouse.

**<Alt>** and dragging in a Perspective viewport orbits the view around its center.

**<Shift>** + **<Alt>** and dragging in a Perspective viewport scrolls (pans) it in the direction you drag the mouse. (In an orthogonal view, this works just the same as **<Alt>** dragging.)

# Current Object

In the upper right-hand corner of Modeler's screen is a set of controls that perform various tasks. The first control that we will discuss is the Current Object pop-up menu.

Figure 2-18: LightWave keeps a running list of all objects open in both Modeler and Layout. The current object's filename is shown in the Current Object pop-up menu.

Unnamed *
F:\3dProjects\YukonQuest2003\Objects\Final\BG\Ground_F.lwo
F:\3dProjects\YukonQuest2003\Objects\Final\SledDog\SledDog.lwo
F:\3dProjects\YukonQuest2003\Objects\Final\SledDog\SledDog_Eye.lwo
F:\3dProjects\YukonQuest2003\Objects\Final\SledDog\SledDog_EyeLenses.lwo

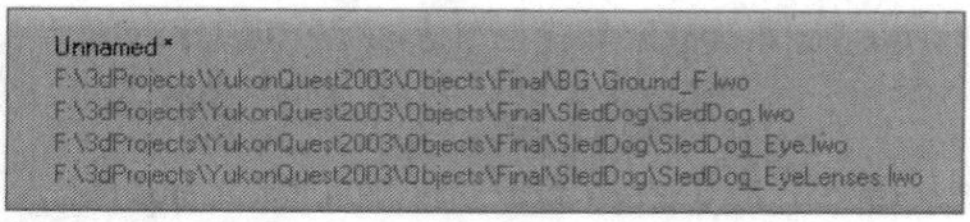

Figure 2-19: Clicking on this pop-up menu shows the list of objects currently open in Layout and Modeler.

Objects open in Modeler are shown in black (as is Unnamed in the above figure). Objects open in Layout but not currently open in Modeler are shown in gray (all the others). Objects that have been modified in Modeler or Layout but not saved are shown with an asterisk (*) after their name (just as Unnamed is).

# Layers

One of the most versatile tools that LightWave offers is its ability to support *layers*. With layers, you can break up a mind-numbingly complex model into small, manageable "bite-sized" pieces, reference another object in the same 3D space as you work without worrying about accidentally mangling your reference material, and perform complex modeling functions such as Booleans, drilling, and lofting.

Figure 2-20: The Layer controls are simple and easy to understand, but this outward simplicity is a veneer, cleverly concealing their awesome power.

Layers really have only four possible options to them:

- A layer can have something in it, you can see its contents, and you can directly manipulate what you see. (This is considered a layer in the *foreground*.)

- A layer can have something in it and you can see its contents, but you *cannot* directly manipulate what you see. (This is considered a layer in the *background*.)

- A layer can have something in it, but its contents are not visible. (This is like keeping something in the attic that you can't quite find a use for, but it just might come in handy one day.)

- A layer can be empty (like a vacant storage locker in a vast "U-Stor-It").

A layer whose contents are shown in the foreground is rendered in that viewport's current display type. The contents of a

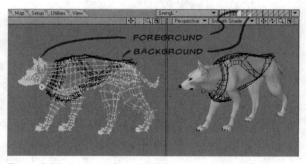

Figure 2-21: Layers with contents have a little "divot" in the upper-left corner of the Layer icons (like Layers 1 through 3, numbered from left to right). Layers in the foreground have their entire Layer icon highlighted, as does Layer 1. Layers in the background have only the bottom half of their Layer icon highlighted, like Layer 3.

background layer are shown in black wireframe.

There are 10 Layer icons visible at any one time, but you can have up to 99 "banks" of these sets of 10 layers. That's 990 separate layers per object!

*Figure 2-22: The number to the left of the "layer bank" shows which set of Layer icons you are currently perusing. The "<" and ">" buttons shift you up and down through the "banks."*

Layers are saved with the object they comprise. When you load in an object that has content on different layers, each layer is exactly where it was in relation to the other layers when you last saved the object — *even blank layers!* (Say I was to cut and paste the dog's nose to Layer 98, save the SwingL object, and shut down the computer for the night. A week later when I reloaded SwingL, I'd still have content on the first three layers (as in Figure 2-21), and I'd still have his nose on Layer 98.) Each layer is

handled as its own, separate object. In the case of the SwingL object, the dog on Layer 1 could be manipulated as a completely separate item from his harness on Layer 3.

LightWave has a quick and easy way of navigating through the different layers of your object: the Layer Browser. You can access the Layer Browser from **Window | Layers Panel**.

### Newbie Note

When you have two items, and you want one implicitly linked to the other (like having SwingL's harness move when he's moved), you have to establish the *hierarchy* for the objects. In 3D terminology, this is considered a "parent" and "child" relationship.

Child items *inherit* (follow implicitly) the motion applied to their parent items (which can, in turn, be children of other items). Child items can themselves be moved as well, but whatever happens to their parent item will always affect the child item, no matter how great the distance may be between them.

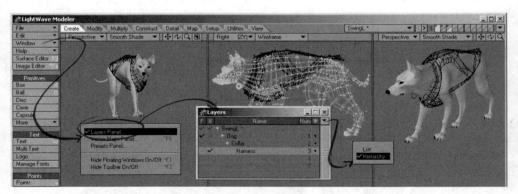

*Figure 2-23: The Layer Browser shows all objects currently open in Modeler, each layer of that object, and the hierarchy of the layers if the Hierarchy view is selected from the pop-up menu in the upper right of the Layer Browser window. (See the Newbie Note on this page if you're not quite sure what "hierarchy" means in the world of 3D animation.)*

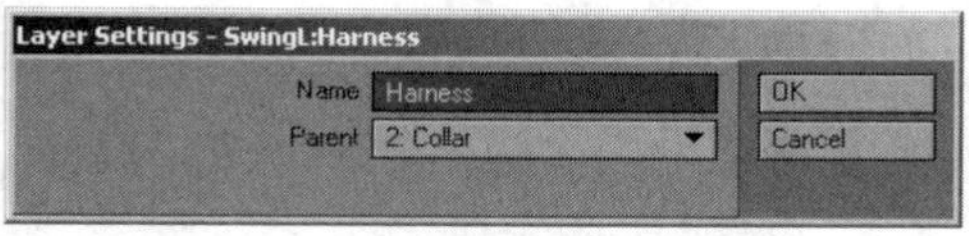

Figure 2-24: Layer names can be assigned and changed by double-clicking on the layer name in the Layer Browser. A layer's parent can also be set in this window.

Foreground layers have a check under the "F" column in the Layer Browser; layers in the background have a check under the "B" column. If you have Hierarchy view active (as in Figure 2-23), you can assign a layer's parent by clicking and dragging it onto the desired parent layer.

## Linking to Layout

When you are running Modeler with the Hub active (more on the Hub later in this chapter), you have a "conduit" open between the two interfaces. The pop-up menu without a label in the upper-right corner of Modeler is the direct link to that conduit. (When you are running LightWave with the Hub disabled, this pop-up menu isn't visible.)

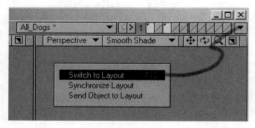

Figure 2-25: The Layout Link pop-up menu lets you switch your focus to Layout (Switch to Layout). It can make doubly sure that Layout has the most recent changes that you've made in Modeler (Synchronize Layout). Or it can send a model that you've just sculpted (or just loaded into Modeler) directly into Layout (Send Object to Layout).

## Vertex Mapping

In the lower-right corner of Layout are the primary VMap selectors. The following are LightWave's main VMaps:

- **Weight maps** define areas of influence. They affect bones and sub-patch details and can be referenced by Texture, Bump, and Displacement maps in Layout.

- **Texture maps** assign UV maps to your model, so you can "unwrap" it — that is, lay out your model *exactly* how it would be easiest for you to paint its texture maps in a 2D paint package.

- **Morph maps** ("endomorphs") allow you to store specific, referential deformations with your object. You can use endomorphs for facial animation or to power joint-driven morphing (so bending a forearm *automatically* bulges the bicep into the shape you've sculpted!).

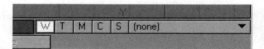

Figure 2-26: Weight, Texture, Morph, Color, or Selection may be chosen. Then the appropriate map can be selected or created from the pop-up menu on the right.

- **Color maps** allow you to apply color to individual points. Unlike the color applied to an object's surface (which is assigned to polygons), Color maps are applied to points and can utilize falloff to provide a soft, feathered edge. Color maps are most useful when used in conjunction with surface colors and Texture maps to provide localized color "boosts."

- **Selection maps** enable you to store point sets that can be recalled for later use. When modeling, Selection can be used to recall parts of an object that require frequent modification (such as the upper eyelid of a character). When animating, selection sets allow you to restrict Dynamics functions to particular parts of your object.

# Adjustment Windows

There are four adjustment windows you'll find yourself using on a regular basis. The Numeric, Statistics, Info, and Surface buttons allow you to access these windows.

## Hot Key Block

**Adjustment Windows**

**<n>** opens the Numeric window for the tools in LightWave (creation, modification, or otherwise).

**<w>** opens the Statistics window, giving you information about the points and polygons in your object.

**<i>** opens the Info window, which gives you detailed information about the selected points or polygons.

**<q>** opens the Change Surface window, allowing you to assign surfaces to the polygons in your object.

## Numeric

The Numeric window allows you to adjust the properties for many of Modeler's tools. The options displayed in the Numeric window are context sensitive to the currently selected tool.

*Figure 2-27: The Numeric window.*

## Statistics

The Statistics window gives you general information about the points or polygons in your object. We'll take a more detailed look at the Statistics window in Chapter 3.

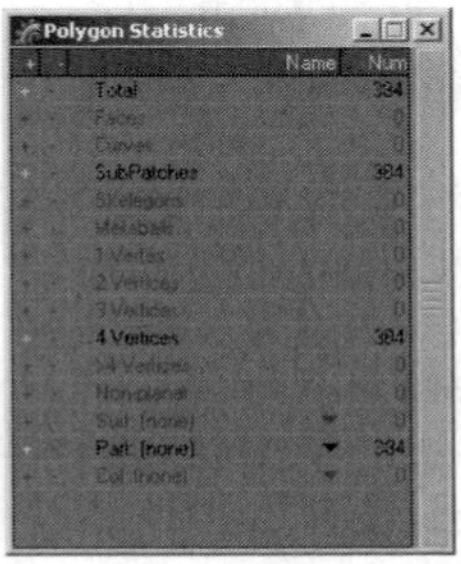

*Figure 2-28: The Statistics window.*

## Info

The Info window gives specific information about the points or polygons in your object. You must first select some points or polys in order to use this window.

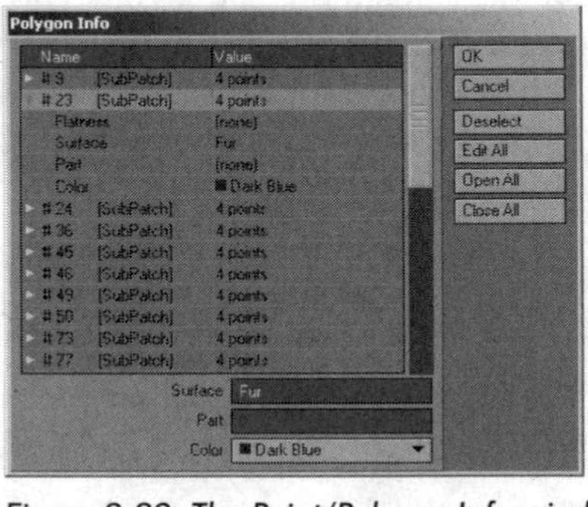

*Figure 2-29: The Point/Polygon Info window.*

## Change Surface

The Change Surface window allows you to assign a new surface to the currently selected polygons. If no polygons are selected, the surface will be assigned to all polys in the currently selected layer.

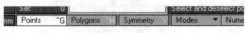

*Figure 2-30: The Change Surface window.*

# Selection/Action Modes

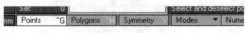

*Figure 2-31: The selection and action modes.*

LightWave lets you select and manipulate specific elements of your geometry depending upon the active selection mode. There are tools that work only with polygons and tools that work only with points. There are times when selecting and moving individual points will get you the result that you're looking for, and times when you will want to manipulate polygons in the same manner. Each selection mode gives you a different angle to get at those hard-to-reach places.

---

### Hot Key Block

**Selection/Action Modes**

`<Ctrl>` + `<g>` selects and/or modifies points.

`<Ctrl>` + `<h>` selects and/or modifies polygons.

`<Ctrl>` + `<j>` selects and/or modifies volumes (everything that falls within a lassoed area).

`<Space>` toggles between the Points and Polygons selection modes.

`<Y>` activates/deactivates Symmetry mode.

`<Return>` deselects your current Geometry Creation tool (Box, Ball, Sketch, etc.), accepting its current settings.

`</>` drops your current selection and deselects your current Geometry Creation tool. (If you were creating geometry, like a box, ball, or whatever, what you were creating goes away.)

---

### Note

**Selecting and Deselecting**

• With nothing selected, to select elements (points or polygons, depending on selection mode), left-click on the elements (or right-click to "lasso" elements) you wish to select.

• When you have elements selected, to *remove* elements from your selection, simply left-click on the elements (or right-click and "lasso" elements) you wish to deselect.

• When you have elements selected, to *add* elements to your selection, hold down `<Shift>` while left-clicking on them (or right-click, "lassoing" elements).

• To completely deselect everything you have selected, press `</>` (or left-click on the "reset area," the area between the buttons, as in Figure 2-32).

*Figure 2-32: Clear the current selection by clicking here.*

---

## Symmetry

The Symmetry action mode is one of the handiest things to come along in LightWave since its integration of OpenGL. With Symmetry active, what you do to the right side of your model is *automatically mirrored* to its left side!

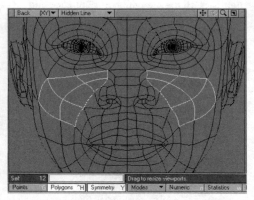

Figure 2-33: With the Symmetry action mode active, selecting the polygons on the right side of the model's nose automatically selects their counterparts on the left side. Any tweaking of the polygons on the right will automatically be mirrored on the left.

---

Note

Symmetry is a great tool, but to use it, you must be immaculate in your modeling skills. Symmetry only works when what is to the left of X=0 is *an exact mirror* of what is on the right of X=0 — just being close won't do a darn bit of good. (You can always mirror your model if things get really out of whack. There are also free "symmetry fixers," but they still require a fair amount of attention to get things back on track.)

If you are planning to make something that is symmetrical, start out with your base form perfectly centered along the X axis, and always make sure you have Symmetry active when you are sculpting.

An odd thing about the Symmetry function is that with it active, if you move something with your mouse's focus to the left of X=0, its effect along the X axis will be "backward."

## Action Centers

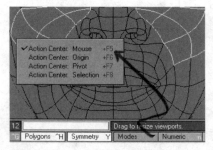

Figure 2-34: Under the Modes pop-up menu are selections to tell Modeler where you want your actions to be centered.

It's easiest to understand action centers when thinking about rotating something that you have selected.

- **Action Center: Mouse** — Wherever your mouse is positioned becomes the pivot around which your selection is rotated.

- **Action Center: Origin** — When you rotate your selection, the rotation will be centered around X=0, Y=0, Z=0.

- **Action Center: Pivot** — Your selection will be rotated around where you have set that layer's pivot point to be.

- **Action Center: Selection** — The rotation will be centered right in the middle of your selection.

## Quick-Info Display

In the lower-left corner of Modeler is a readout that quickly lets you know the exact position of your mouse, how many elements you have selected, and how much area each grid square represents.

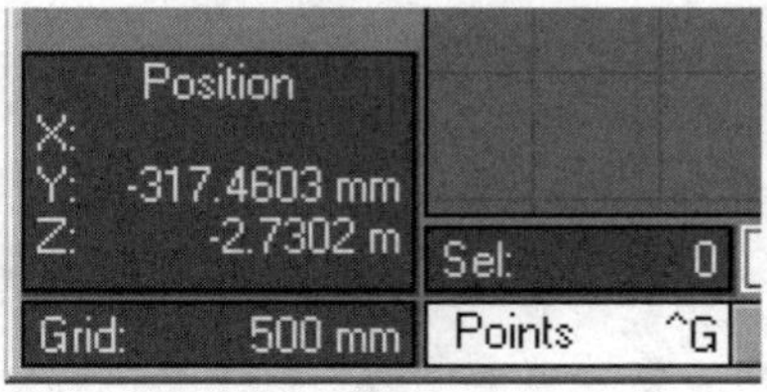


*Figure 2-35: Modeler's Quick-Info display.*

## Modeler Toolsets

On the left-hand side of Modeler are the toolsets. These toolsets are directly linked to the tabs at the top of Modeler's window.

When the Create tab is active at the top of the screen, the toolset shown is LightWave's primary set of tools geared for the creation of geometry.

> **Note**
>
> Anytime you see a pop-up menu with "More" on it, that means there are additional tools that aren't being displayed because of the screen size; you can access these tools through the pop-up menu.

It's a pretty simple way to think about it, but you *create* "stuff" with the tools under the Create tab (Figure 2-36) and you *modify* that "stuff" with the tools under the Modify tab. With these tools, you can move, rotate, drag, bend, twist, size, and stretch elements and generally "push points."

> **Note**
>
> I imagine that it's because of the vast array of tools LightWave has in its arsenal that it refrains from showing you pictures of spheres, capsules, boxes, and metaballs. Clicking on any one of these tools and then click-dragging in the viewports will create the geometry associated with that tool.
>
> Remember that even though we'll be getting into more detail with some of these tools in later chapters and exercises, the best way to get to know these (and all of LightWave's tools) is to play around with them. If you're wondering what a metaball is, try it out; you're not going to break anything by having a few metaballs floating around on your screen.
>
> The key is to have fun building "riffs" that you can call on later when the need arises. It may be years before you find a need for a specific, rather arcane tool, but when that need comes around, you can remember, "Oh yeah, I think I saw something like that..." and be able to zero in on it much more quickly than paging through a manual (or decrypting strange, iconic representations of abstract concepts).

The Modify tab (Figure 2-37) contains a collection of tools that *modify* existing geometry.

The Multiply tab (Figure 2-38) holds the tools that take existing geometry and make more of it (cloning or extruding, for example).

The Construct tab (Figure 2-39) houses tools that are useful as you continue to refine and construct your geometry (such as Booleans and point/polygon reduction).

The Detail tab (Figure 2-40) holds the tools that focus on the more detail-oriented bits of modeling. You can assign a sketch color, fuse (weld) two vertices into one, and add, remove, and reduce the edges of your object.

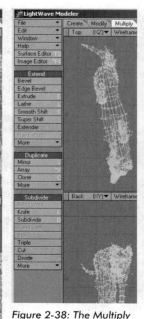

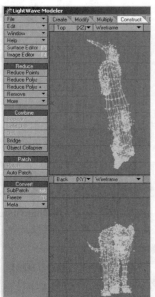

Figure 2-38: The Multiply tab.

Figure 2-39: The Construct tab.

Figure 2-36: The Create tab.

Figure 2-37: The Modify tab.

The Map tab (Figure 2-41) houses most of the tools that you use to modify and refine your VMaps. Using the tools in this tab, you can create textures, morph targets, and weight (influence) maps that will give you tremendous control over your character animation.

The Setup tab (Figure 2-42) contains the tools you'll need to set up and modify a character's skeleton (used for character animation) as well as adding *gons* (polygons that can be converted to various objects such as lights in Layout).

The Utilities tab (Figure 2-43) allows you to add plug-ins and launch custom scripts (known as LScript commands). The Utilities tab also features a "catch-all" pop-up menu called "Additional." The

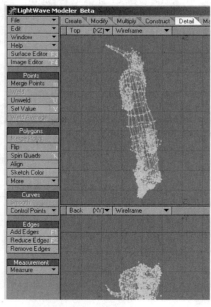

Figure 2-40: The Detail tab.

third-party plug-ins you bring into Modeler will appear under this menu item.

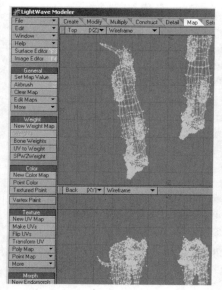

Figure 2-41: The Map tab.

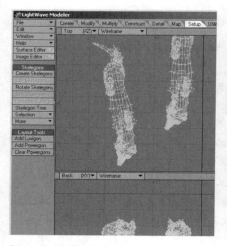

Figure 2-42: The Setup tab.

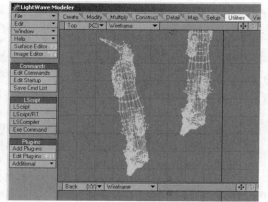

Figure 2-43: The Utilities tab.

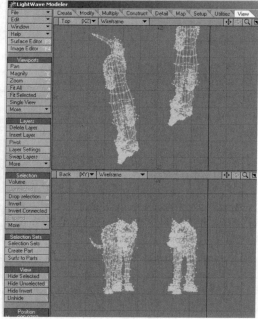

Figure 2-44: The View tab.

The View tab (Figure 2-44) controls zooming and panning. It lets you hide and unhide selected elements and group polygons and points to quickly zero in on tight areas of complex models. The View tab also features several Layer tools to add, delete, and merge the layers of your object.

# Modeler General Options

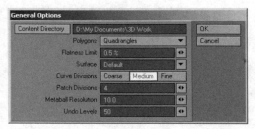

*Figure 2-45: Modeler's General Options window.*

LightWave's Modeler keeps its options in two separate locations. It has display options (which we'll get to in just a moment) and general options. The General Options window can be found under **Edit | General Options**.

---

### Hot Key Block

**General Options**

**<o>** brings up Modeler's General Options window.

---

The options in the General Options window include:

- **Content Directory** — This tells LightWave the default root path to where its models and scenes are kept.

- **Polygons** — This tells LightWave what base shape to use in geometry creation whenever possible. Quadrangles work best when creating sub-patch surfaces for high-resolution models, while triangles work best for many game engines.

- **Flatness Limit** — This is a setting you will probably never need to change (I've never touched it in all my years of using LightWave). It tells Modeler how much deviation is acceptable among the points that define a flat, planar polygon before it is considered non-planar. (See Figure 3-6.)

- **Patch Divisions** — This tells LightWave how much of its geometric smoothing algorithm to use when displaying subpatches. Higher numbers yield smoother surfaces but are much slower to work with.

- **Undo Levels** — This tells LightWave how many levels of "Undo" to keep in memory. (The default is 8. But I like a high level so I can feel free to explore what might turn out to be a blind alley and still be able to get back to where I was when I started that particular exploration without having to revert to a saved version of my object.)

The other options are fairly self-explanatory, so I'll let the LightWave manual cover them — these are just the ones I've found to be not really intuitive.

# Modeler Display Options

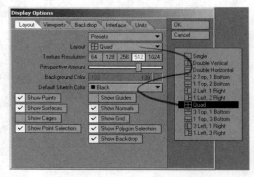

*Figure 2-46: Modeler's Display Options window.*

The Display Options window is accessible through **Edit | Display Options**.

---

### Hot Key Block

**Display Options**

**<d>** opens Modeler's Display Options window.

---

Modeler offers a lot of customization for tailoring itself to how you want your work presented to you. When the Display Options window is first opened, the Layout tab is shown. With this tab, you set the general display options for all windows, unless a window is specifically freed from these generalizations under the Viewports tab.

One important thing to make note of is that LightWave Modeler's familiar "quad"-style layout can be changed here by selecting another style from the Layout pop-up menu. Don't get locked in to just using the Quad layout out of habit. The other layouts can be quite helpful.

> **Note**
>
> LightWave's Viewport layout can be further tweaked by clicking and dragging on the bars that separate the viewports, resizing them to your exact needs.

Figure 2-47 shows my personal preferences for the Perspective viewport (located at the top right by default).

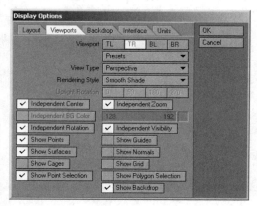

*Figure 2-47: Changing display options for individual viewports.*

- **Independent Center** and **Independent Zoom** let me pan and zoom around my Perspective viewport without disturbing the other viewports that I might have centered in on some important details.

- **Independent BG Color** has been changed from LightWave's hallmark gray to dull blue. I almost never use that particular shade of blue in my work, so my models stand out against it.

- **Independent Rotation** means that any other Perspective viewports aren't linked to this one's rotation. (This kind of linkage can be helpful when you've got one Perspective viewport showing the model in Wireframe and the other in Smooth or Weight Shade.)

- **Independent Visibility** lets me see what I want, when I want. Cages (the polygonal base of sub-patches) get in my way when working in shaded views, as do their "guides." Polygon normals also tend to get in my way, so I've turned them off for this view as well. I intermittently turn on and off Show Point Selection and Show Polygon Selection when it suits the detail work I'm doing on a model.

The Backdrop tab (Figure 2-48) lets you put a loaded image into the background of any orthogonal viewport. This is helpful when you're building a model that references a photograph or drawing. (We go through the steps to do this in Chapter 10.)

The Interface tab (Figure 2-49) lets you make some customizations to how Modeler's interface looks. (I touch on how you can really rework LW's interface in just a moment.)

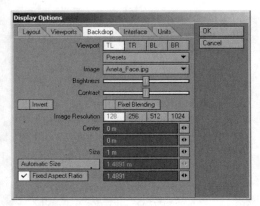

Figure 2-48: The Backdrop tab.

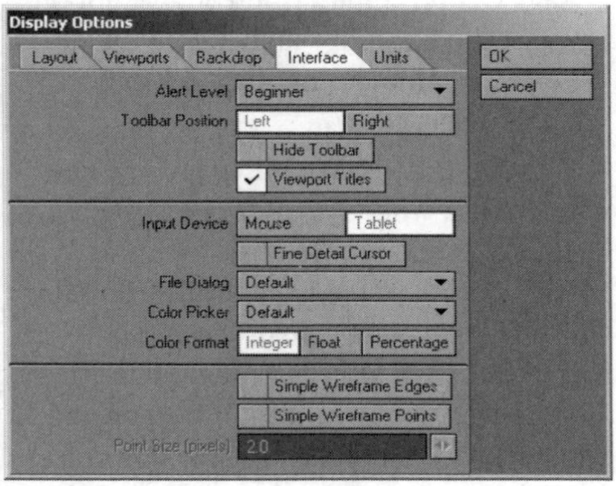

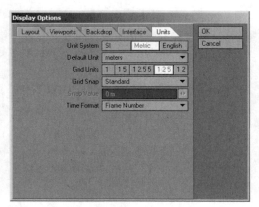

Figure 2-49: The Interface tab.

Figure 2-50: The Units tab.

## Note

To be honest, the only changes I've ever made to the Interface tab are to set Input Device to Tablet and to change the Alert Level. The Alert Level lets you set how urgent an alert must be in order for it to ask you to press OK to continue. (We get into how Alert Level affects workflow later on in the chapters on modeling.)

If you haven't tried modeling with a tablet device (Wacom is my personal favorite for durability and precision), I highly recommend it. When you're dragging points around, your motions are a lot like drawing. You simply touch the stylus tip down on a point and drag and bring the stylus up off the pad when the point is where you want it to be. I find it to be so much *faster* than clicking a mouse and a lot less painful. (And because holding a "pencil" is more of a natural position than holding a mouse, I imagine that a tablet could be a help to people worried about carpal tunnel syndrome — though this is only a guess.)

The Units tab (Figure 2-50) is the tab I use most frequently in the Display Options window in Modeler. In this tab, you can tell LightWave whether you want to work in metric units or English units. More importantly, this tab is where you activate and adjust Grid Snap.

LightWave's quick and variable Grid Snap is another one of those things that you'll wish every 3D program had. Its settings are as follows:

- **Standard** lets you quickly position objects with respect to decent-sized (one-tenth) segments of Modeler's visible grid.

- **Fine** breaks Modeler's Standard snap into even smaller units for precise positioning, still respecting units of its visible grid.

- **Fixed** lets you specify *exactly* what interval to which you wish to adhere your movements, regardless of the visible grid.

- **None** lets you move objects in utter, minute detail.

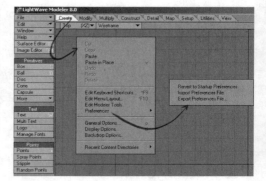

Figure 2-52: The Edit pop-up menu.

## The File Menu

In the upper-left corner of Modeler is the File pop-up menu. Here, you will find the Load, Save, Import, and Export commands.

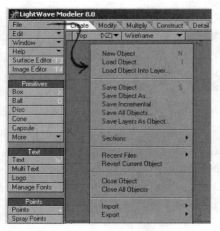

Figure 2-51: The File pop-up menu.

## The Edit Menu

The Edit pop-up menu, located just below the File pop-up menu, provides traditional edit functions (cut, copy, paste, etc.) as well as access to the commands through which you can customize almost every aspect of Modeler. With the saving and loading of preferences, keyboard shortcuts, and menu layouts, you can take your personal customizations with you wherever you go.

## The Window Menu

Just below the Edit menu is the Window pop-up menu. Here you'll find access to three additional panels that let you adjust layers, modify VMaps, and manage surface presets. You can also use this menu to hide any floating windows and turn on and off the toolbar.

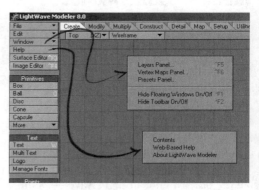

Figure 2-53: The Window and Help pop-up menus.

**Note:**

If you turn off the menu toolbar and find later that you don't know how to turn it on again, don't panic! You can restore the toolbar by using the <Alt> + <F2> keyboard shortcut or by unchecking the Hide Toolbar button on the Interface tab of the Display Options panel (shortcut <d>).

*Figure 2-54: <Shift> + <Ctrl> + left-click brings up this menu.*

## The Help Menu

When you run into trouble or have questions about a particular aspect of the software, the Help menu (Figure 2-53) is the first place to turn. The Help menu links you to the online and web-based documentation. Completely rewritten for LightWave 8, these files contain a wealth of useful information to aid in your understanding of the software.

*Figure 2-55: <Shift> + <Ctrl> + right-click brings up this menu.*

## Modeler Quick Menus

The LW manual calls these "contextual pop-ups." I prefer the term "quick menu" because that's exactly what they are. You hold <Shift> + <Ctrl> while left-, right-, or middle-clicking in your workspace, and these menus appear. (See Figures 2-54 to 2-56.) They let you do all sorts of things you would normally have to sift through a few layers of pop-up menus to get at. (These menus are fully customizable, as are all the other menus in LightWave — pointers on how to customize menus follow in a moment.)

*Figure 2-56: <Shift> + <Ctrl> + middle-click brings up a quick menu that covers just about everything else Modeler has a command for.*

# Hot Key Customization

What if you come to LightWave already accustomed to certain hot keys doing certain things? No problem. You can assign and reassign every command, script, macro, etc., to a hot key!

If I wanted to assign Close All Objects to the hot key <Ctrl> + <F12> (as in Figure 2-57), I would do this:

1. Choose **Edit | Edit Keyboard Shortcuts** to bring up the Configure Keys window, as shown in Figure 2-57.

2. Search through the commands in the left-hand column (or use the **Search** button on the right side of the window), expanding the drop-down lists.

3. When you've found the command you want to assign to the hot key, click on it, highlighting it.

4. Scroll through the hot key list until you've found the key you want to assign.

5. Click on the desired hot key, highlighting it.

6. Click on **Assign** to assign the command to the hot key. (Clicking on

**Unassign** removes the command from the key.)

7. Repeat as desired.

8. Click on **Save** and back up your hot keys for those "CYA" kind of happenings.

9. When you're finished, click **Done**.

## Note

Under the Presets pop-up menu are the default hot key mappings, so you can go crazy with your assignments if you like and can always get back to the defaults should you need to.

However, as nifty as interface customization is (hot keys or menu layouts), it makes it really hard to use someone else's version if you ever get together with friends and work on a film together. I found this out the hard way starting my own studio. From being an independent contractor, I had my own license of LW so "tricked out" that the first time I sat down at a new hire's version, I was almost completely lost with the default hot keys and menu layouts.

A solution to this is to have your configuration files where you can access them from the Internet, or carry them around on one of those keychain USB drives. But remember to save your host's configurations before you load yours, and restore his configs when you're done.

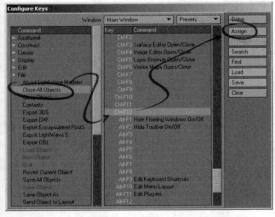

*Figure 2-57: **Edit | Edit Keyboard Shortcuts** brings up the Configure Keys window.*

# Menu Layout Customization

If you want to completely rework LightWave's menus or make a new plug-in easily accessible as a button, you can do this just as easily as assigning hot keys. You can add, delete, and reorder the menu tabs across the top of Modeler, keeping all your favorite tools just a mouse-click away.

In Figure 2-58, you can see that the Ball Tool command, located under the Create drop-down list, has been given a menu position just under Box (and renamed to just Ball) under the Primitives group. By

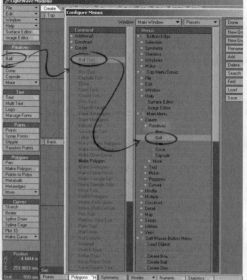

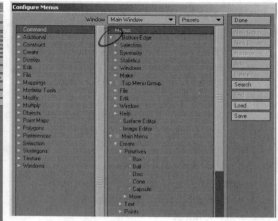

Figure 2-59

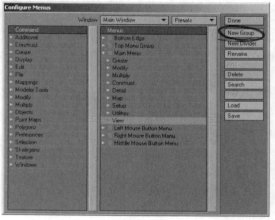

Figure 2-58: **Edit | Edit Menu Layout** brings up
the Configure Menus window.

comparing the actual menu and the Configure Menus window, you can see how
each tool, group, tab, and menu is
configured.

This may be a bit confusing, so here's
an exercise for you to get more of a handle on menu customization. Let's add a
temporary menu and assign some tools
to it:

1.  Activate the Configure Menus win-
    dow (**Edit | Edit Menu Layout**).

2.  Collapse all the drop-downs except
    the one for Main Menu. (You do this
    by clicking on the little downward-
    pointing triangles next to each main
    group, circled in Figure 2-59.)

3.  Select the View sub-group under
    Main Menu, and click on **New
    Group**. See Figure 2-60.

Figure 2-60

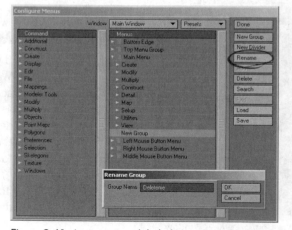

Figure 2-61: A new group, labeled New Group, is created
directly below the previously highlighted group.

A new group, labeled New Group, is created *directly below* the previously highlighted group.

4. Select **New Group**, and click on **Rename**. Name this group anything you like (Figure 2-61).

5. Find the Ball Tool under the Create commands. Highlight it and the new group you've just created and renamed, and click on **Add**.

A new instance of the Ball Tool now appears under the Deleteme tab, as shown in Figure 2-63. (It doesn't disappear from where it was under the Create | Primitives Tab/Group. It just can now *also* be found here, under this new tab we've created.)

6. To organize your new menus, you create groups and sub-groups. With **Ball** in your new menu tab selected, click on **New Group** (Figure 2-64).

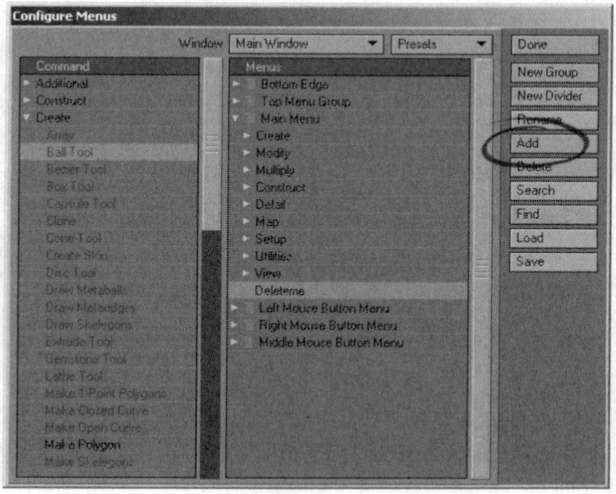

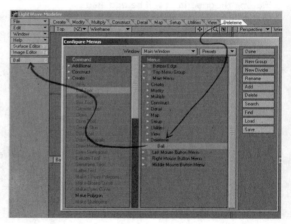

*Figure 2-62*

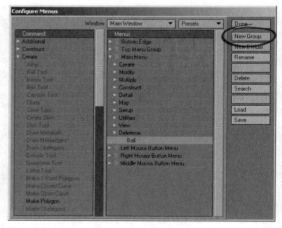

*Figure 2-63*

*Figure 2-64*

**29**

7. Highlight **New Group**, which is created *directly below* the item previously selected, and click on **Rename** to change its name to whatever you'd like. (See Figure 2-65.)

8. You can then drag the new tool, Ball, *onto* the new group (which I named Kemu) to assign it to that group. (See Figure 2-66.)

> **Note**
>
> Notice that in Figure 2-66, there is a blue line just below and slightly shorter than Kemu. This line means that the dragged item will be *attached* to the item directly above the line. If the blue line were to reach all the way to the left side of the word "Kemu," that is LightWave's indication that the item being moved will simply be *shuffled below* the item directly above the line.

*Figure 2-65*

You have now created the Ball Tool under the Kemu group in the new Deleteme menu tab.

*Figure 2-66*

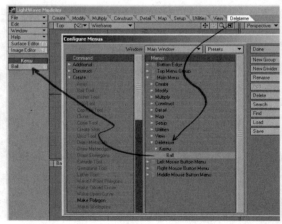

*Figure 2-67*

# Layout

Layout is where you bring everything together to create those incredible master-works you have in you. Layout is where you position your objects, hang your lights, and set your objects moving (if you're animating). After LightWave takes a moment or so to render, out comes this slick image for you to show off in e-mails to all your friends (or print and tape to your refrigerator, if that's your kind of thing).

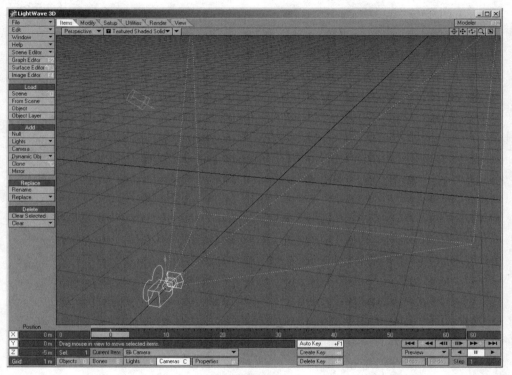

*Figure 2-68: Layout has a lot in common with Modeler. The tabs, menu styles, viewport controls, and Quick-Info display readout are all pretty much the same. The differences between Layout and Modeler are so intuitive, you'll get the hang of them without even realizing it.*

# Viewport Styles

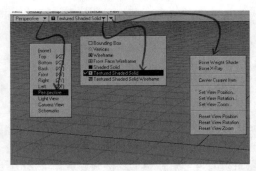

Figure 2-69: Layout's viewport settings and display type, called Maximum Render Level here, are almost identical to Modeler's.

Figure 2-71: Layout's Vertices Maximum Render Level shows only the points in the objects.

Figure 2-72: Layout's Wireframe and Front Face Wireframe are similar to Modeler's Wireframe and Hidden Line display types. Front Face Wireframe speeds refresh rates (how quickly LightWave is able to redraw the screen) and decreases clutter by not bothering to draw any polygon facing away from the viewport (knowing which way a poly is "facing" is explored in Chapter 3 in the section on normals).

The biggest differences between Modeler and Layout viewports are that in addition to viewing orthogonal and perspective projections, you can also set the view to see what any of your cameras or lights are seeing or view the contents of your scene as presented in a Schematic layout. Because bones figure so heavily in character animation, Layout also adds two bone-specific display types: Bone Weight Shade and Bone X-Ray, which we touch on in just a moment.

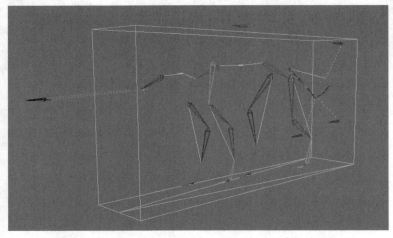

Figure 2-70: Layout's Bounding Box Maximum Render Level display does away with all but the simplest geometry. Objects are represented only by a bounding box that encompasses the object's volume. (Bones, lights, cameras, and other "iconic" items are shown normally.)

*Figure 2-73: Layout's Shaded Solid and Textured Shaded Solid (not shown) are a little prettier than Modeler's because Layout's takes into account up to eight lights in its OpenGL rendering.*

*Figure 2-76: Bone Weight Shade shows the effect your object's bones have on its mesh. Colors are determined by the bone's color, and the blending shows the effect of the various bone weight maps that limit the bone's influences.*

*Figure 2-74: Layout's Textured Shaded Solid Wireframe is similar to Modeler's Textured Wire view type.*

## Viewport Controls

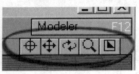

*Figure 2-77: Layout's viewport controls.*

The viewport controls in Layout are almost exactly the same as Modeler's. Move (Pan), Rotate (Orbit), Zoom, and Min/Max all do exactly the same thing. The one change to the viewport controls is the addition of the little symbol on the left that looks like a registration mark. That symbol is a toggle button that activates Center Current Item. When active, LightWave will center that viewport in all three dimensions around your current item's pivot point.

*Figure 2-75: Bone X-Ray lets you see the bones that might be hidden by the object's geometry.*

### Note

You can activate Center Current Item to find an item and then deactivate it, moving your view around to bring in things on the periphery.

It's easy to forget you've got Center Current Item active when you get into noodling details. If Center Current Item is active when you switch to another item, that new item will then be centered in that viewport.

Note

**Moving and Rotating in Perspective Viewports**

LightWave has established a convention about moving things in Perspective viewports that doesn't require you to have one hand on the keys and the other on the mouse.

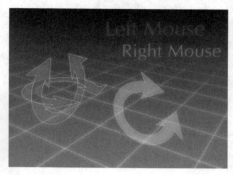

Figure 2-79

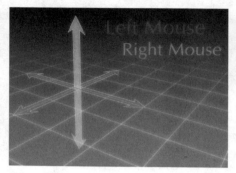

Figure 2-78

Moving an item or panning a viewport while holding down the left mouse button constricts movement to the X/Z plane. Holding the right mouse button constricts movement to the Y axis.

Rotating an item or orbiting a viewport while holding down the left mouse button rotates in heading and/or pitch. Holding down the right mouse button rotates in bank only.

In addition to using the viewport controls, remember these quick ways of moving about, identical to what we mentioned for Modeler's Perspective viewports:

• To *orbit* about a Perspective viewport's center, hold <Alt> while dragging the mouse in the viewport that you wish to examine (still following the above rules for left and right mouse buttoning).

• To *scroll* (pan) the view in a Perspective viewport, just as in Modeler, hold <Shift> + <Alt> while dragging your mouse in the viewport you wish to explore (still following the above rules for left and right mouse buttoning).

# Linking to Modeler

Layout's link to Modeler is the Modeler button in the upper-right corner of the window. (This button is only visible when running LightWave with the Hub active.) When you click on this button, you are taken to Modeler, and your most recently selected object will be open and ready for you to modify.

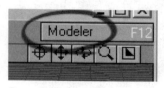

Figure 2-80: The Modeler button.

# The Frame Slider

The Frame Slider is like a ruler for measuring time. The little thing that looks like the shooter from Space Invaders is the slider that controls which frame you are currently viewing.

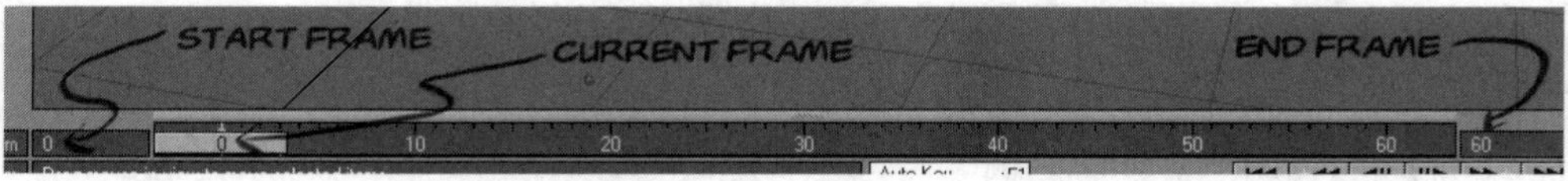

*Figure 2-81: The Frame Slider is at the bottom of Layout's viewport(s), sandwiched between input fields for the start frame and end frame. (You can click in these fields and change how long your scene is; negative numbers are okay.)*

> **Note**
>
> The slider part of the Frame Slider always shows the current frame. It can be set to show that frame in frames (fractional and whole), SMPTE time code, feet and frames (film key code), and the scene's time in seconds.
>
> You can find out how to set the Frame Slider later in this chapter in the "Layout General Options" section.

# Frame Controls

*Figure 2-82: The Frame controls.*

In the lower right-hand corner of Layout is a set of controls that you might find on a high-end VCR. These controls let you play your scene immediately (without having to render anything), forward or backward, in all viewports, respecting each viewport's Maximum Render Level.

*Figure 2-83: The Previous Key and Next Key buttons.*

You may not have seen Previous Key and Next Key before. Keyframes are discussed in Chapter 15, but for the moment, think of a keyframe as telling the computer, "As you move this item, make absolutely sure it passes through this specific point and/or this specific rotation."

At the bottom of Figure 2-82 is the Step input field. You can click in this area and tell LightWave to play every frame (Step=1), every *other* frame (Step=2), every *third* frame (Step=3), etc. Increasing the Step can improve playback performance on complex scenes at the cost of playback accuracy.

At the left side of Figure 2-82 is the (Animation) Preview pop-up menu. Building and playing animation previews is discussed in Chapter 15, so just store this info away for later.

At the bottom of Figure 2-82, you'll find Layout's Undo/Redo buttons. The number of Undos available can be set in the General Options panel (more on that later).

## Key Creation/Deletion

*Figure 2-84: The Create Key and Delete Key buttons.*

Just to the left of the frame controls are the buttons that let you create and delete keyframes for your items.

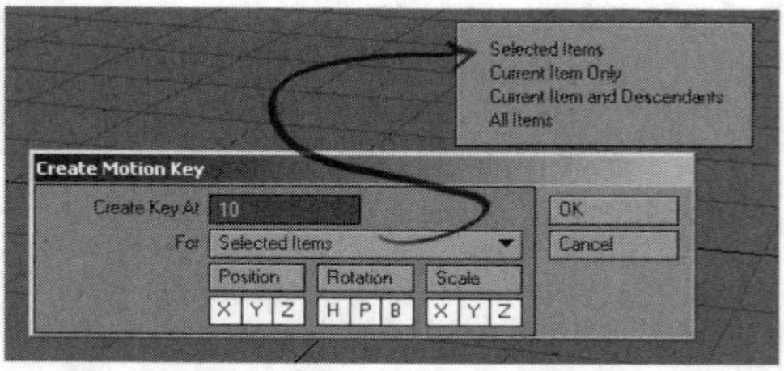

*Figure 2-85: Create Key brings up a window where you can tell LightWave to remember the position, rotation, and/or scale along any axis for your choice of items.*

Delete Key works the same as Create Key (only it deletes keyframes, rather than creating them).

---

### Hot Key Block

**Time Controls**

**<Left Arrow>** steps to the previous frame of your scene. (At the first frame of your scene, the Frame Slider "wraps around" to the last frame of your scene.)

**<Right Arrow>** advances to the next frame of your scene. (Again, at the end of your scene, the Frame Slider "wraps around" to the beginning.)

**<Shift> + <Left Arrow>** jumps to the previous keyframe of the currently selected item.

**<Shift> + <Right Arrow>** jumps to the next keyframe of the currently selected item.

**Undo/Redo**

**<Ctrl> + <z>** and **<z>** respectively undoes and redoes what can be undone and redone.

---

### Note

You can enter any frame in the Create Key At box. (You aren't limited to creating keyframes only on your current frame.)

For looping animations, I make sure the scene's "head" and "tail" match up by creating a keyframe for all items on the last frame of my scene, referencing the position of everything on the first frame.

To do this, you move the Frame Slider to the first frame of your scene, click on Create Key, type in the number of the last frame of the scene in the Create Key At box, and choose All Items in the For pop-up menu.

The Auto Key button (see Figure 2-84), when active, will automatically create keyframes for any item you move, rotate, or resize. This is a great thing for newcomers to animation because it frees you from having to remember to create a keyframe for your modified items before moving on to the next frame or exiting Layout.

## Note

The Auto Key function is actually a two-part system. Auto Key will not work unless both parts are active.

In addition to having the Auto Key button active, you must also tell LightWave on which channels (axes) you wish to create keys — only the ones you've modified or all channels.

You set this additional information in Edit | General Options | Auto Key Create.

(I touch on this again later in this chapter when we go over Layout's general options and when we work with animation in Chapter 15.)

## Item Selection

*Figure 2-86: Just to the left of the key creation/ deletion buttons are the controls that tell Layout whether you want to manipulate the scene's objects, bones, lights, or cameras.*

To help you navigate through scenes where you have hundreds of objects (with a few of those objects perhaps having a couple hundred bones), tens or hundreds of lights, and two or more cameras, Layout automatically "filters" that information for you.

When you have the Objects button active, only objects will appear in the Current Item pop-up menu. When you have the Bones button active, only the bones of the most recently selected object will appear in the Current Item pop-up menu. Similar rules apply to the Lights and Cameras buttons.

## Note

I'm going to skip over the Properties button right now. Because there are so many varied properties for each kind of item, it is best to explore them in the chapters where we actually use these properties in the exercises.

Directly above the Current Item pop-up menu is a line of information that Layout uses to keep you on top of what's going on. Information about using the current tool can be found here, like "Drag mouse in view to move selected items." Error messages also appear here. If something has you stumped, take a peek here — there might be a clue to unraveling your mystery quietly sitting there.

## Quick-Info Display

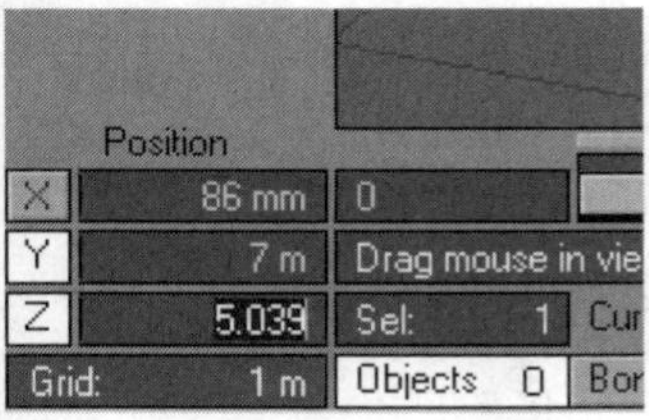

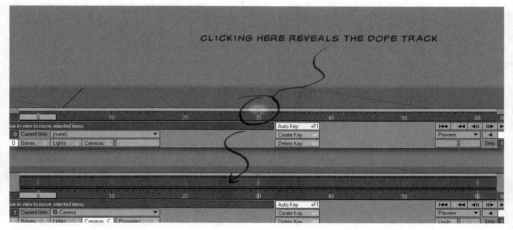

Figure 2-87: Layout's Quick-Info display.

Just like in Modeler, Layout includes a read-out of important information, such as position, rotation, scale, how many items you have selected, and how much area each grid square represents, in the lower-left corner of the window. (What is currently shown as position information changes to show rotation and scaling, etc., when Layout's active tool is changed.)

The one big difference between Layout's Quick-Info display and Modeler's is that Layout's is interactive. You can enter data into each of the X, Y, and Z fields, as is being done with the Z axis in Figure 2-87.

You can also click on each individual X, Y, or Z axis button (normally white with black text) to protect it from accidental manipulation. This will deactivate the button, giving it a blue background with colored text, as is the case for the X axis in Figure 2-87. This means that with the X axis protected, if I were to left-click and drag to move my selection, it would move only along the Z axis, not along both the X and Z axes.

## The Dope Track

Just above the Frame Slider but below the viewport window lies a small gray bar. Clicking the center of this bar will pop up the Dope Track. (No giggles from the peanut gallery, please!) The Dope Track is an adjustment tool that can be used to quickly create and modify your keyframes. We'll talk more about the Dope Track and its cousin, the Dope Sheet, in Chapter 15.

Figure 2-88: The Dope Track.

# Layout Menu Tabs

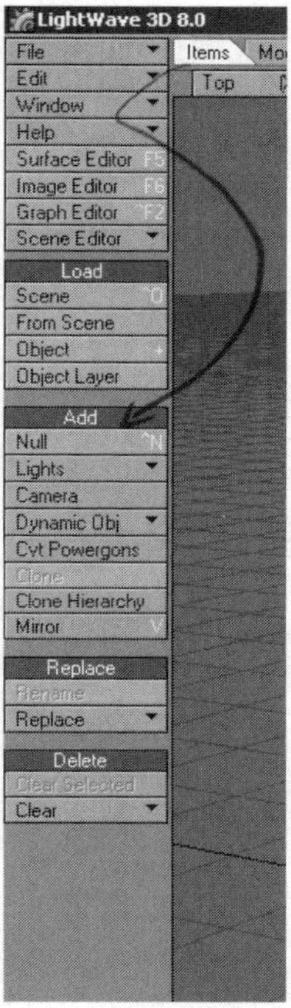

*Figure 2-89: The Items menu tab.*

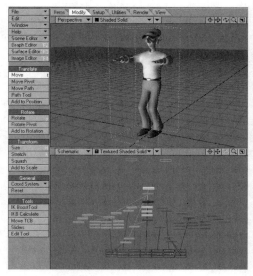

*Figure 2-90: The Modify menu tab.*

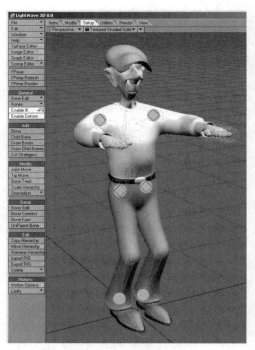

*Figure 2-91: The Setup menu tab.*

With the Items menu tab (Figure 2-89) selected at the top of the window, you are presented with tools that let you load, add, replace, and delete the different items in your scene.

As with the other menu tabs in Layout, I get into the more important pop-ups, windows, and tools as we use them in later chapters. Just be aware that all this stuff is here and waiting for you.

The Modify menu tab (Figure 2-90) contains tools to move, rotate, and resize the objects in your scene. You'll also find tools to adjust keyframes and unleash the power of LightWave's Inverse Kinematics on your characters (more on that in Chapter 16).

The Setup menu tab (Figure 2-91) gives you access to LightWave's powerful character rigging tools. If you've ever rigged a character in another package, you know what a pain it can be. But these tools make it a breeze to create, edit, adjust, and save a character's skeleton. We'll be taking a closer look at these tools in Chapter 16.

> **Note**
>
> The bottom viewport in Figure 2-90 shows a Schematic view of all the items in the scene. Schematics are covered in depth in *Light-Wave 3D 8 Character Animation* (Wordware Publishing). In short, they help to break your scene into bits and pieces that conform to your personal preferences for visual organization.

The Utilities menu tab (Figure 2-92) allows you to add and remove plug-ins as well as run your own custom scripts. The Utilities menu in Layout is virtually identical to the one in Modeler. (Easy, huh?) You'll find the tools here to do everything from writing your own particle dynamics simulation engines to crafting custom shaders, should you ever feel so inclined. (There's even a robotic chess game and a Tetris clone someone wrote using LScript — they both play right inside Layout.) The Additional

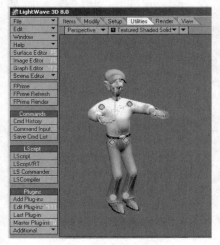

*Figure 2-92: The Utilities menu tab.*

pop-up menu here functions just like its counterpart in Modeler and houses the third-party plug-ins you've loaded into Layout.

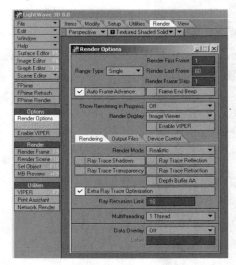

*Figure 2-93: The Render menu tab.*

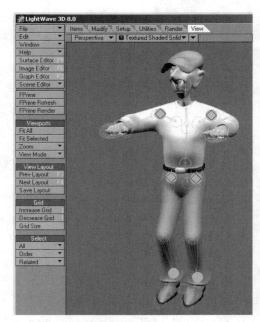

*Figure 2-94: The View menu tab.*

The Render menu tab (Figure 2-93) lets you change settings in the Render Options window (such as turning on raytracing and choosing an output format for your animation). You'll also find tools to render individual objects, single frames, or full animations, and the ability to activate LightWave's Versatile Interactive Preview Render (VIPER), which lets you see changes to your surfaces in real time. Talk about power!

The View menu tab (Figure 2-94) gives you the ability to change your viewport setup, adjust the grid, and make complex selections.

## The File Menu

The File menu in Layout has many of the same functions as it does in Modeler. Rather than repeat that information here, I'll touch on the more esoteric functions:

- **Load Items From Scene** loads the objects (and lights, if you wish) and all their motions into the scene on which you are currently working. This is a great way of combining a complex scene for "in-camera"

rendering if you have broken it apart into small, bite-sized pieces to work on it more easily.

- **Load Object Layer** lets you load just a single layer from an object rather than loading all its layers at once (which is what Load Object will do).

- **Save Trans(formed) Object** is something I use a lot when I want to "freeze" an object's deformations, position, orientation, and scale into a single object I can use in a background layer for reference while sculpting a model that will interact with it in an animation. (This is what I did with the sled-dog models in earlier illustrations.)

- **Save Motion File** will save all of an item's movement, rotation, and scaling into a single file, which you can then load onto any other item.

- **Content Manager** is a tool used to consolidate the items in your scene and gather all the resources used into one central location. This can be a lifesaver when you need to share your complex scenes with others or simply need to port the scene between work and home.

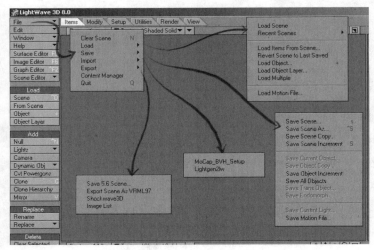

*Figure 2-95: The File menu.*

## The Edit Menu

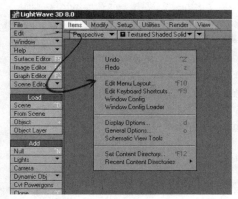

*Figure 2-96: The Edit menu.*

Like its counterpart in Modeler, the Edit menu houses most of Layout's customization functions.

## The Window and Help Menus

The Window menu provides access to many of Layout's floating palette windows. The Help menu offers local and web-based support options.

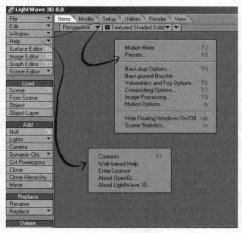

*Figure 2-97: The Window and Help menus.*

## Layout Quick Menus

*Figure 2-98: <Shift> + <Ctrl> + left-click opens a menu that gives you instant access to many of Layout's most frequently used commands.*

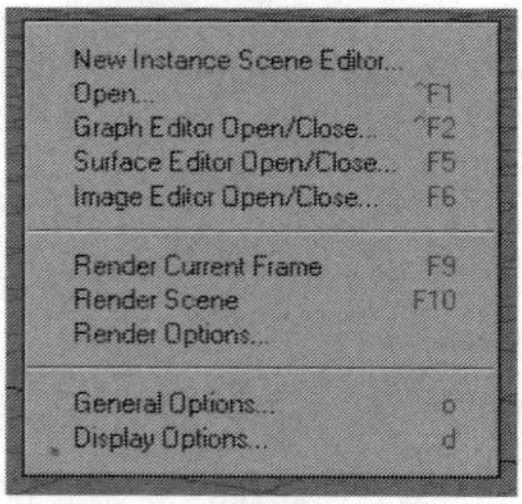

*Figure 2-99: <Shift> + <Ctrl> + right-click brings up a menu that lets you quickly launch different editing windows and select from various rendering options.*

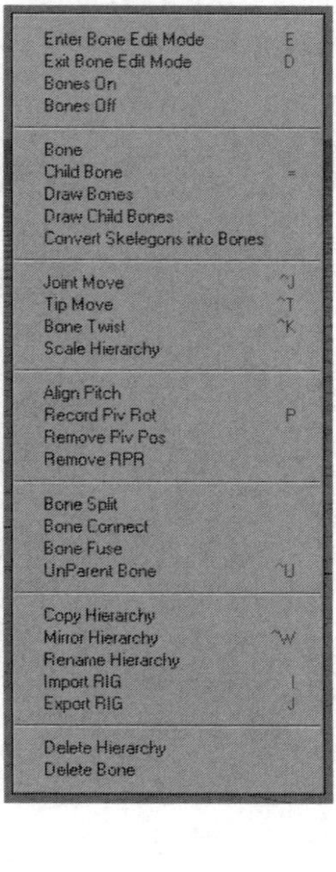

*Figure 2-100: <Shift> + <Ctrl> + middle-click gives you quick access to a plethora of character rigging tools.*

# Layout General Options

Layout's General Options tab is where you'll find the other half of the two-part Auto Key Create system. Notice that Auto Key Create is currently set to create keys on just those channels that have been modified.

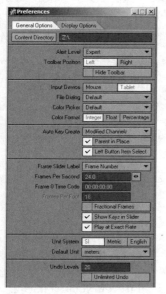

*Figure 2-101: Layout's General Options tab.*

**Edit | General Options** opens Layout's Preferences window, which contains the General Options tab. A few of the less obvious commands are discussed below.

Even though we haven't gotten into how to assign hierarchy in Layout yet, Parent in Place is something I'd like you to start thinking about. When Parent in Place is active, when you "attach" one item to another (by assigning another item as its parent), the child item appears to stay exactly where it was before the operation. (With Parent in Place inactive, if the child was at X=0, Y=0, Z=0 and the parent item was at Y=1, the moment you parented the child, it would instantly inherit the parent's

positioning, appearing to be moved instantly to the parent's location of Y=1.)

> ### Note
>
> I use Parent in Place a lot to copy an item's position, rotation, and scaling to another; with Parent in Place inactive, I assign the item I want to move to be the child of the item whose position I want to copy. Then I activate Parent in Place and unparent the child item.
>
> With Parent in Place active when unparenting the child item, it stays exactly where it was while it was parented. In effect, it has been quickly "moved" to the exact position, size, and rotation of its once-parent item!

- **Left Button Item Select** means that you can left-click on an item to select it. (Layout doesn't use the same selection rules as Modeler, so clicking on an item to select it can sometimes be tricky.)

- **Frame Slider Label** tells Layout what time format you want to see in the Frame Slider (Frames, SMPTE, Feet/Frames, or Seconds). I do most of my work at 24 frames per second (the current value in the Frames Per Second input box in Figure 2-101). If I needed to render to the NTSC Television frame rate of 29.97 FPS, I would change this value, and my animation would automatically be stretched to fit the new frame rate. If I were to do this, expanding my animation by a factor of 1.25, a lot of my keyframes might fall on fractional frames. In order for me to then get at those frames (if, heaven forbid, the client should want another "minor change"), I would have to activate Allow Fractional Current Frame.

- **Show Keys in Slider** makes the keyframes for the current item appear as yellow "tick-marks" in the ruler-like portion of the Frame Slider. (I've never found a reason to not show keyframes in the slider, but I once accidentally deactivated this setting, and it took far too long for me to figure out how to get them back.)

- **Play at Exact Rate** is a setting that applies only to the real-time playing of your scene through the frame controls in Layout. With this active, Layout will make sure the playback is at exactly the FPS you have set in your Frames Per Second option, skipping frames if necessary if your scene is too complex for your video card to handle at real time.

## Layout Display Options

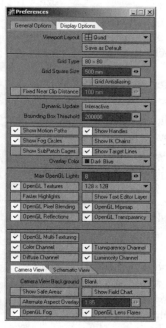

*Figure 2-102: Layout's Display Options tab.*

Following are some of the options available in Layout's Display Options tab.

- **Viewport Layout** lets you choose all sorts of combinations of viewport numbers and arrangements.

- **Grid Type** is where you can turn off Layout's grid if you need to. You can also

specify how large it is (anywhere from 10x10 to 100x100).

- **Grid Square Size** is where you manually type in how much area you want each grid square to represent.

---

**Hot Key Block**

**Layout's Grid Size**

<[> decreases Layout's grid size, effectively zooming in on all but Light and Camera viewports.

<]> increases Layout's grid size, effectively zooming out on all but Light and Camera viewports.

---

- **Grid Antialiasing** makes the distant grid squares look nicer (but it slows my video card down — not a lot, but enough for me to notice).

- **Fixed Near Clip Distance** forces Layout to draw things it may be leaving out because it thinks they're "too close" (determined by some mysterious referencing of the Grid Square Size).

- **Dynamic Update** lets you tell Layout to hold off updating the viewports until you're done making adjustments. When LightWave first offered dynamic updating (move a slider and see the results immediately in the viewports), it could be pretty darn sluggish in certain areas. With LW 8, however, every aspect of dynamic updates (that I've found, at least) is lightning-fast. I've yet to see a reason to change this from Interactive in the recent versions of LW.

- **Bounding Box Threshold** tells LightWave how many polygons an object has to have before it substitutes a bounding box for it while you're manipulating it. (It shows the object in all its Maximum Render Level glory when it's done redrawing it.) In Figure 2-102, you can see that my own preference for this cutoff point is 200,000 polygons. With my current processor speed and GL graphics accelerator, I find I get about a 24 FPS refresh rate when animating my characters that have less than 200,000 polys (using sub-patches, this figure can be dialed up or dialed down on demand — more on this in Chapter 7). If I'm working with a character that has many more than 200,000 polys, I find that things begin to slow down past the point where things are fun. (When an object gets temporarily replaced with a bounding box, I can still see the bones that "drive" him as I work. It's just his mesh that gets temporarily substituted.)

- **Show Motion Paths** displays the currently selected item's path in the viewports. Keyframes are shown with large ticks, while inbetween frames are shown with smaller ticks.

- **Show Fog Circles** draws dotted circles (in the Overlay Color) around the camera, indicating where objects begin to be affected by LW's fog and where they disappear completely into it.

- **Show SubPatch Cages** shows a ghosting of the polygonal mesh that is the base for your sub-patch object.

- **Show Handles** turns on the little arrows and rings that show translation, rotation, and scaling axes for the currently selected items. (You can click directly on a handle and manipulate the item in only that one clicked axis; this overrides the left and right mouse button conventions mentioned earlier.)

- **Show IK Chains** draws a line from an IK chain's root to its goal.

- **Show Target Lines** draws a dashed line between, for instance, a camera or a light and the item it is targeting.

---

### Advanced Note

I've noticed that when an item is being moved about in LightWave's default parent coordinate system, the handles of "protected" axes are ghosted. You can't click on the ghosted handles, so you can't accidentally manipulate an item on a protected axis.

If you change your preferred coordinate system to Local or World, protected axes are no longer ghosted; they can be clicked on and manipulated.

For my own projects, I create some very complex nested character riggings. Moving some referential controls that aren't meant to be touched can really bugger an animation. When handing these riggings off to less-experienced animators, I'll often disable Show Handles to remove the possibility of them accidentally moving one of those referential controls while they are working away in world- or local-space coordinate systems.

---

- **Max OpenGL Lights** tells LightWave how many lights you want it to factor in when shading its OpenGL viewports. Eight is the current maximum number of lights; each extra light will slow your system slightly.

- **OpenGL Multi-Texturing** allows you to preview the effects of multiple textures right in your OpenGL display.

- **Camera View Background** shows the background image (still image, image sequence, or movie) you are compositing your LightWave render onto when looking through a Camera View viewport. (You assign the background image using **Window | Compositing Options | Background Image**.)

# Plug-ins

Plug-ins are separate little bits of program code that LightWave calls on to do special things. For instance, you may want to use the Coffee shader, which changes the color and opacity of transparent objects based on their thickness. LightWave doesn't do this by default, so some clever folks wrote a shader for LightWave that does. That shader (Coffee.p) is a tiny piece of code (only 17 KB) that Layout filters information through when it renders an object that has that shader applied to one of its surfaces.

But shaders are only a small part of what plug-ins can do. Plug-ins have complete access to every part of LightWave, and a lot of tools we think of as a standard part of LightWave, like loading Wavefront OBJ files into Modeler, are, in actuality, plug-ins.

Plug-ins can be added through **Utilities | Plug-ins | Add Plug-ins** (or **Edit Plug-ins**).

You can examine plug-ins that Light-Wave has integrated in the Edit Plug-ins

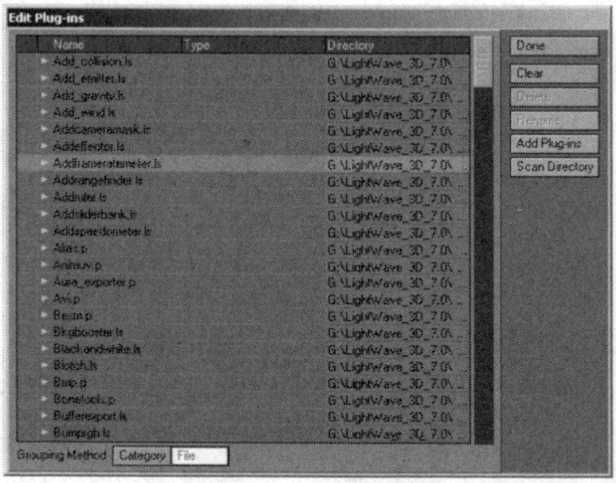

*Figure 2-103: One method of adding plug-ins is to use the Edit Plug-ins window by selecting **Utilities | Plug-ins | Edit Plug-ins**.*

window, grouped either by category or by file. You can carefully remove any plug-ins that may not be doing for you what you had hoped they might by making totally sure you've selected the correct plug-in and clicking on Delete. (The plug-in isn't deleted from your hard disk — only from being integrated into LightWave.)

# The Hub

What is the Hub? NewTek calls the Hub a "message board." I think of it like a conduit. This little icon in the taskbar is all most PC folks ever see of it, while the Mac crowd always sees it "expanded," as the PC folks do when the icon is double-clicked.

The Hub is a separate process that is called by default whenever Layout or Modeler is started. It acts as a bit of a "client" and a bit of a "server," and in truth, it is quite a bit of both.

Whenever you switch between Layout and Modeler (with the Link buttons in either program or using <Alt> + <Tab>), the Hub makes sure both programs are on

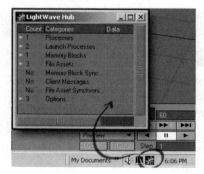

*Figure 2-104: The Hub.*

the same "page," with the most up-to-date versions of objects, surfaces, and all the other bits of information LightWave as a whole uses to get its job done.

Would you ever want to run LightWave without the Hub? Oh yeah.

The Hub, because of all that it does, makes starting up or switching to Layout or Modeler significantly slower. If either Layout or Modeler crashes (thankfully, this is a rare-ish thing), the Hub often "gasps" for resources if you try to restart the crashed program, really bringing things to a crawl.

The best thing to do at times like this is to make sure you save a revision of your work (or zip up an archive of your files before saving over them — just in case) and reboot your machine. But sometimes when a reboot is impractical or you really need to be running Layout or Modeler solo, you can disable the Hub.

### Note

Since the Hub acts as both a client and a server, it can cause red flags in certain firewall software. Don't be alarmed if you see this happen. *LightWave does not contain spyware!* The Hub is simply sending data back and forth between the two principal applications.

### PC-Specific Info

*Figure 2-105*

To disable the Hub, create a copy of your Layout or Modeler icon (here, called LightWave-NoHub). Then, tack on a " –0" (space, minus, zero) after the name of the executable in the Target line.

### Mac-Specific Info

To disable the Hub on a Macintosh, enter the Programs folder in the LightWave folder, and then edit the Modeler cmdLine (or Layout cmdLine) file in your favorite text editor. (This file may or may not already have stuff there.) Enter " –0" as the first line of the document, and then save the file.

When you run Modeler with " –0" added to the first line of Modeler cmdLine, you will run without the Hub active! (You can keep a folder somewhere to hold different versions of your *cmdLine files so you can alternate between using the Hub and not using the Hub almost as quickly as running on a PC.)

### Note

When running multiple instances of LightWave, only the first will run connected to the Hub (if that instance is started from a Hub-enabled icon). All subsequent instances will run without the Hub active until you close the instance that is already connected.

# LightWave ScreamerNet

LightWave ScreamerNet is a stand-alone program that does nothing but render. Through discipline, focus, and binary-level programmatic optimization, the coders at NewTek have managed to condense LightWave's awesome might at creating the incredible; they have distilled all that awesome rendering power until it fits into the 528 KB space of a little command-line program that would leave room to spare on a floppy disk.

*Figure 2-106: As simple as it may look, this little thing has all the power of LightWave's renderer at its command.*

Using LWSN and a local area network, you can expand your rendering capabilities to almost any machine on your LAN. (Don't throw out that old 366 laptop! Hook it up and use it as part of your render-farm!)

> **Note**
>
> Because of the way networks generally handle filenames, never have spaces in the names for your objects or scenes if you plan on rendering over a network. Even if you don't immediately think you'll be rendering across multiple machines, not using spaces in your LightWave names is just a good habit to get into. (That's why you see all of the names in this book divided with underscores (_) instead of spaces.)

> **Note**
>
> LightWave was first built on the Amiga platform, back when its 1 MB of internal memory was seen as ludicrously large by the PC and Apple crowds. Back then, memory was precious (even as late as 1994, an 8 MB SIMM could cost almost $1,000).
>
> Even though memory and hard disk space prices have fallen below where any of us "old-guard geeks" could ever have hoped, and a simple word processor can require up to 500 MB of space to run, the programmers at NewTek seem to remember the old days when space was limited. Why is this important? Optimization means speed!
>
> (Take a look at how much our old video game favorites were able to do in the space and with the hardware that an electric toothbrush of today would find constrictive. Most of them, like Ms. Pac Man, Defender, Stargate, and Star Wars, are less than 40 KB worth of information!)
>
> The larger a program is, the longer it takes to get a memo from one end of it to the other (just like in any other bureaucracy or corporation). LightWave has not expanded to fill the gaps left by cavernous memory and blistering processor speed but remains streamlined, leaving you more space for complex objects, surfaces, and FX and resulting in one of the fastest, most reliable renderers, period!

• • •

All of this is LightWave ... and we have just barely scratched its surface.

# Chapter 3

# Modeling 1: Foundation Material

"You gotta learn to walk before you can fly," the old saying goes.

This is the chapter where you will learn the foundation material of modeling from which all your other modeling skills will grow. In this, as well as every aspect of *all forms of art*, the foundation materials give you the rules to follow to get something done quickly, easily, and reliably. After you know the "rules" like the back of your hand, you cast them to the wind and explore as far and as wide as you can. Remember the paths explored by the great artist/scientists before you: Nikola Tesla, Max Plank, Copernicus, Albert Einstein. They could have explored the same well-traveled trails everyone else at their level had hashed and rehashed. Instead, armed with granite understandings of their respective foundation materials, they in essence said, "I've already been down that road. I know where it leads. Aaah now, this path over here ... *this* looks like fun."

> "Some rules may be bent... others may be broken."
> — Morpheus, *The Matrix*

## Points (Vertices)

**point** *n.* **1.** A mark formed by or as if by the sharp end of something. **2.** *Mathematics.* A dimensionless geometric object having no property but location. (*The American Heritage Dictionary*)

**ver•tex** *n.* The point at which the sides of an angle intersect. (*The American Heritage Dictionary*)

Points exist within three-dimensional space, having X, Y, and Z position information. They take up no "space," and until being assigned as a part of a polygon they *do not*, themselves, render (show up) in Layout's finished drawings or movies (see Figure 3-1).

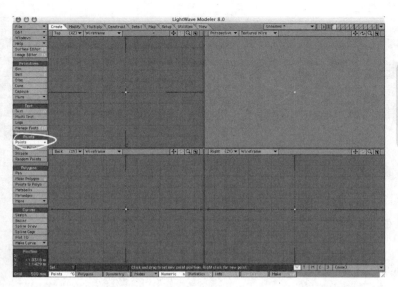

Figure 3-1: The point is your most basic tool for creating geometry. Points are created using **Create | Points | Points**.

**Note**

Points, in 3D lingo, are also referred to as *vertices* or *vertexes*.

When you left-click in the viewport with the Create Points tool active, you get a point that you can drag around until it is in the place you want it.

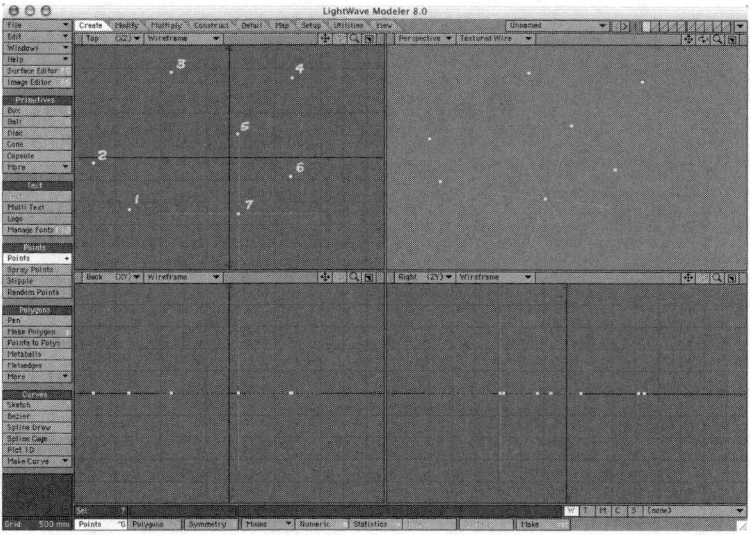

Figure 3-2: Right-clicking accepts the position of the point you were working with, giving you a new point to position and leaving the other points you have created selected in the order in which they were created.

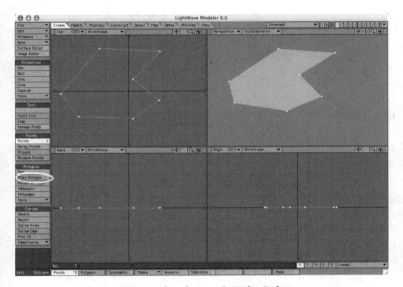

*Figure 3-3: Clicking on* **Create | Polygons | Make Polygon** *creates a polygon from the points you have just created by deselecting the points and adding the polygon that was just created to the current polygon selection.*

Note

The *order* in which points are created is very important. LightWave "connects the dots" when you make a polygon. Changing the *point order* can drastically change the shape of the polygon.

If, for whatever reason, you realize that the order in which you're creating the points isn't quite right, you can press <Return> to keep the position of your most recently created point (or press </> to remove your most recently created point) and deselect the points you've created. Then, you can reselect the points in the order you want them to "outline" the polygon to be created (just like a connect-the-dots puzzle)!

Note

The Pen tool in Modeler (under **Create | Polygons | Pen**) combines the acts of making points and connecting the dots to make a polygon into one easy tool.

# Polygons

**pol•y•gon** *n*. A closed plane figure bounded by three or more line segments. (*The American Heritage Dictionary*)

Polygons are the second-most-basic building block for creating objects in LightWave (second only to the point). The most common polys you'll be working with will have three or four vertices and three or four sides (tris and quads). But in LightWave, you aren't limited to tris and quads. You can make polygons with up to 1,023 points, while single-point polygons are often used in creating the stars in space scenes.

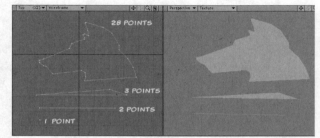

Figure 3-4: Polygons in LightWave can be made up of as many as 1,023 points or as few as a single point.

## Note

The key to doing anything in 3D is to find the most elegant way of doing something. By "elegance," I mean to use the absolute minimum to get the job done.

When you're building a polygon, use the smallest number of points you need to hold that shape in place.

Sure, you can see flat spots on the back of the dog's ear at this distance in Figure 3-4, but if he were *intended* to only be viewed at half that size (or from twice that distance), the viewer wouldn't notice those flat spots. It is only when the object is going to be brought close to the camera that you nail in a lot of detail and then only in the areas on which the camera will be focusing.

Polygons are the most elemental piece of geometry that shows up in LightWave's renderer because polygons have *surfaces*. (More on surfaces, how to assign them, and how to change them later on in this chapter.) When you make a polygon, LightWave assigns it a default surface (initially a light gray). Once LightWave has a surface from which to scatter its light, its camera can "see" it.

But in order for LightWave's camera to see a surface, it has to know which direction the surface is pointing. In LightWave, that direction is defined by a *surface normal*.

# Normals

**nor•mal** *adj.* **4.** *Mathematics* **a.** Being at right angles; perpendicular. (*The American Heritage Dictionary*)

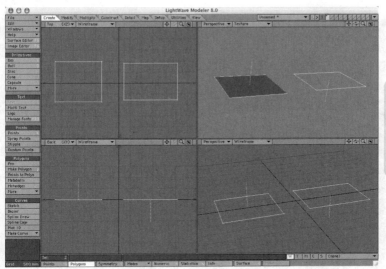

> "Abby...someone ..."
> "Abby who?"
> "Abby... Normal."
> — Igor and Dr.
> Frankenstein,
> *Young Frankenstein*

*Figure 3-5: The direction a polygon is facing is indicated by the dashed line rising perpendicular from its surface. This dashed line is known as the surface normal.*

Surface normals tell LightWave which direction a polygon is facing. If a polygon is facing *away* from its viewer, it is treated as "invisible," like the polygon on the right in the shaded Perspective window in Figure 3-5.

You can tell the specific surface on a polygon to be visible from either side by setting its Double Sided surface attribute (**Surface Editor | Double Sided**). The reason this attribute isn't active by default is that most objects are really only seen from one side, the *outside* — like a basketball or a jet fighter. So LightWave *culls* the back side of its surfaces by default to speed

its displays and its rendering. (*Elegance* — If you aren't going to see something, don't bust your chops on it!)

## Note

You can use the fact that unless you specifically tell a surface to be treated as *double sided*, it is "invisible" from its back side when rendering interior sets. You won't be limited to placing your camera inside the set. You can have your camera positioned outside your set, facing in, and if the walls of your set aren't double-sided, you'll be able to see right through them!

# Planar vs. Non-Planar

**pla•nar** *adj.* **1.** Of, relating to, or situated in a plane. **2.** Flat: *a planar surface.* (*The American Heritage Dictionary*)

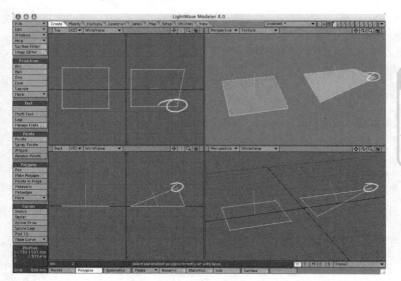

**Note**

Triple turns all selected polys into tris, regardless of whether they are non-planar.

Figure 3-6: One point on the quad on the right was moved upward, making it fall outside the plane defined by the quad's other three points. This polygon is now non-planar.

With power comes responsibility. And with LightWave allowing us to have as many as 1,023 points defining a polygon, we have to take it upon ourselves to make sure that all these points *lay within a flat plane*.

Non-planar polygons are a big deal because, even though LightWave does a good job of "guessing" which way the poly is facing, it doesn't know for sure. When rendering a non-planar polygon, it may appear to strobe, flash, or do other unacceptable things.

In even a moderately complex model, trying to isolate an offending point or points and move them back into a plane described by the other points can be a real headache.

(You can assign a specific X, Y, or Z value to a selection using **Detail | Points | Set Value**, which would make a non-planar planar once again.) The easiest thing to do, other than try to make sure your polys remain planar, is to convert non-planars into three-sided polygons using **Multiply | Subdivide | Triple**.

---

### Hot Key Block

**Triple**

**<T>** triples the polys you have selected. (This is the capital letter "T.")

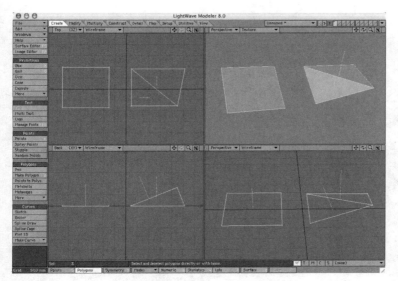

*Figure 3-7: The non-planar polygon on the right was tripled, turning it from a quad into a set of two tris, which are always planar.*

## Note

Tripling non-planars may be easy, but I find it's far better to just be aware of my axes when I'm moving a single point of a polygon that has more than three points. Tripling can create a whole lot of geometry that can slow things down, especially if you triple a polygon that has a lot of points.

Use tripling as a last resort.

When you've got a sizable model, how can you tell if there are polys that have gone non-planar? LightWave has a Statistics window that is absolutely invaluable for modelers.

# Statistics Windows

Can you tell *if*, let alone *how many*, non-planar polys are in the sword in Figure 3-8? With the Polygon Statistics window, you can.

The Statistics window is a heads-up display that tells you pretty much anything you need to know about the selection type you have active (points, polygons, or volumes — more on this in just a moment). You access the Statistics window through the

Statistics button found at the bottom of Modeler's interface.

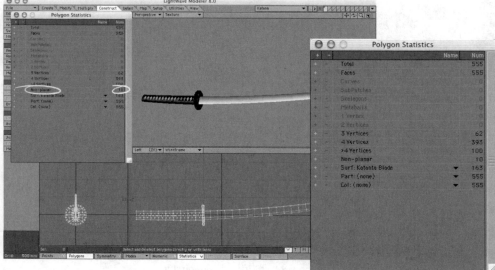

Figure 3-8: The Polygon Statistics window.

Figure 3-9: A detail of the Polygon Statistics window from Figure 3-8.

Here's what the Polygon Statistics window tells me about the Katana object:

● **Total** — There are 555 total poly items in the model.

● **Faces** — Of these 555 total poly items, 555 of them are faces (standard polygons).

● **Curves** — The object has no curves as part of its geometry.

● **SubPatches** — There are no sub-patches in this object either.

● **Skelegons** — There are none of Modeler's bone-placement icons, known locally as *skelegons*.

● **Metaballs** — There are no instances of metaballs, a type of digital clay.

● **1 Vertex** — There are no polygons that have only one vertex.

● **2 Vertices** — There are no polygons that are made up of only two vertices.

● **3 Vertices** — There are 62 tris in this model.

● **4 Vertices** — There are 393 quads in this model.

● **>4 Vertices** — There are 100 polys with more than four vertices in this model.

● **Non-planar** — Of all these polys, 10 of them are non-planar.

● **Surf: Katana Blade** — 163 of these polys have the Katana Blade surface applied to them. (This and the remaining items in the Polygon Statistics window are pop-up menus that display lists of the surfaces, parts, or sketch colors you've created for your object.)

● **Part: (none)** — All 555 of the poly items in this object belong to the part None (that is, no polys have been assigned to any part; this is just a way of grouping polys so you can easily sift through them later).

● **Col: (none)** — None of the 555 polygon items have been assigned a sketch color (yet another way of keeping your polys separate).

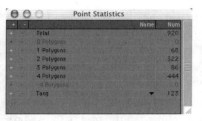

Figure 3-10: The Point Statistics window.

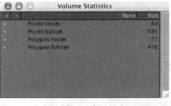

*Figure 3-11: The Volume Statistics window.*

Changing the selection mode to Points makes the Statistics window display point statistics.

The Point Statistics window for the Katana object tells us:

● **Total** — There are 920 total points in this object.

● **0 Polygons** — There are no points that don't belong to any polygons (usually leftovers or mistakes, though there are times when you will want to have a point without a poly).

● **1 Polygons** — There are 68 points that belong to only one polygon each.

● **2 Polygons** — There are 322 points that are shared between two polygons.

● **3 Polygons** — There are 86 points that are shared among three polys.

● **4 Polygons** — There are 444 points that are shared among four polys.

● **>4 Polygons** — There are no points that are shared among more than four polys.

● **Tang** — There are 123 points that belong to the point selection group Tang. (This is a pop-up menu that lists all the point selection sets you've created for the object.)

The Volume Statistics window tells you how many points and polys fall inside and outside the (right-click-lassoed) selection area when the selection mode is set to Volume.

> **Note**
>
> The easiest way to understand the difference between Include and Exclude Volume selection mode is to lasso only part of your model and, using the "+" and "–" buttons in the Volume Statistics window, add and remove polygons from your selection.
>
> • **Exclude** — A polygon that has some points inside *and* some points *outside* the Volume Selection Area is *not* considered part of the selection.
>
> • **Include** — A polygon that has some points inside *and* some points *outside* the Volume Selection Area *is* considered part of the selection.

The Statistics window also shows information about the items you currently have selected.

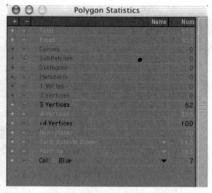

Figure 3-12: The Polygon Statistics window.

When you have geometry selected, the categories into which items in your selection fall are shown in light gray text. For Figure 3-12, I have selected four polygons somewhere on the sword. The Polygon Statistics window tells me the following about the polygons I have selected (from top to bottom, only listing the *highlighted* headings that polygons in my selection fall under). *The numbers on the right-hand side don't change; they reflect the totals for each category.*

- **Total** — Total is highlighted because the polys I have selected are part of the total polygon count (kind of a no-brainer).

- **Faces** — My Katana object consists of only faces, so the fact that the Statistics window shows my selection to contain faces isn't surprising either.

- **4 Vertices** — Of the different possible numbers of vertices polys can have, my selection falls only under the category of polys with four vertices. (The 4 Vertices category is the only vertex-number category that is highlighted.)

- **Non-planar** — My selection of four polygons contains at least one of the ten non-planar polys.

- **Surf: Katana Blade** — Since I have the Katana Blade surface selected in this pop-up menu, it being highlighted tells me that my selection contains at least one poly with that surface.

- **Part: ha** — My selection also contains at least one poly from the part of the sword I have grouped and named "ha."

Figure 3-13: Detail from the Statistics window.

The Statistics window does more than just show you information. You can use it to add and remove points and polys from your selection. Clicking on the + or − in the columns at the window's left *adds* or *subtracts* all the polys from that category, respectively.

Using this, I could triple all the non-planar polygons I've got in the Katana, turning them into triangles so they render without the worry of them flickering during an animation. To do this:

1. I would first make doubly sure that I've got nothing else selected, so I know I'm *only* tripling the non-planars. (Check the Quick-Info display in the lower-left corner of Modeler, and click in the reset area or press </> to drop any polys I might have selected; see Chapter 2.)

2. Click on the "+" in the Polygon Statistics window's *Non-planar* line. (This *adds* all ten non-planar polys that this object has to my selection.)

3. Press <T> to triple the selected polygons.

# Grouping Polygons (Parts) and Point Selection Sets

Getting at a tight area of an object has always been an issue for modelers as they work. Fingers, if modeled so they touch each other, can be tricky, as can the surface detail of a vehicle or weapon. Grouping the lower part of a character's facial "mask" separately from the upper part is integral to quickly creating the "endomorph" targets that drive facial animation. (In grouping for facial animation, you'll also want to establish separate groups for upper and lower "inner" mouth parts, such as the jaw/teeth masses, in addition to groups for left and right brows, upper and lower eyelids, and cheeks.)

You create a polygon group (a *part*) or a point selection set anytime you want to quickly isolate a part of your object that you'll want to get at later.

The Grouping controls can be found under **View | Selection Sets**. With the polys selected that you wish to add to, remove from, or reassign to a grouping (a part), choose the **Create Part** button.

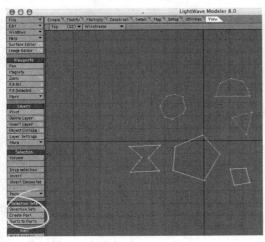

Figure 3-14: The Grouping controls.

## Note

In the "old days," modelers had to assign separate surfaces to groups of polys that they wanted to get at quickly. Though this is still very much a viable option, the addition of groups and point selection sets makes life much easier when you want to have easy access to a model covered in a lot of the same surface.

To *add* the selected polys to a part or *change* the part the polys are associated with, type in the name of the part or select it from the pop-up menu that lists all currently assigned parts.

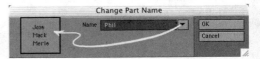

Figure 3-15: The Change Part Name window.

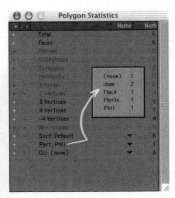

Figure 3-16: The Part heading in the Polygon Statistics window now lists stats for the parts you've created in its pop-up menu.

To remove a poly selection from a part, simply leave the Name box blank in the Change Part Name window.

**Note**

A polygon may only belong to *one part at a time*. When you change the part assigned to a poly, it no longer is a part of the group to which it previously belonged.

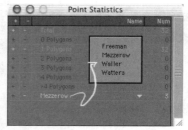

Figure 3-18

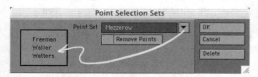

*Figure 3-17*

Assigning a selection of points to a *point selection set* works exactly the same way as assigning a poly to a part.

Once a point has been assigned to a selection set, that set appears under the Point Statistics window's point selection set pop-up menu (Figure 3-18).

*Figure 3-19*

A point may belong to more than one selection set at a time. To remove it from a set, you must choose the set's name from the Point Set pop-up menu, check Remove Points, and then click OK.

# Selection "Tricks"

This section lists Modeler tools for manipulating your selection that "hard-core" modelers couldn't live without.

Modelers new to LightWave who aren't used to these kinds of tools in their old programs may not at first notice these quiet, unassuming tools in their perusings of the LW manual. But once they've been clued in to what they do, these new LW converts can't get enough of them!

### Hot Key Block

**Selection "Tricks"**

<]>   Select Connected

<">   Invert Selection

<}>   Expand Selection

<{>   Contract Selection

<=>   Show *Only* Selection (Hide Unselected)

<\>   Show All

<->   Hide Selection

<|>   Invert Hidden

# Select Connected

Select Connected (**View | Selection | Connected**) *adds* to your selection *every polygon* directly "connected" (that has points shared by its neighbor) to the poly(s) you currently have selected.

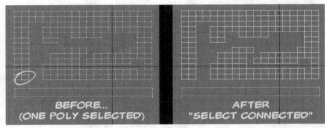

Figure 3-20: Using Select Connected.

With one polygon selected, and using Select Connected, you can instantly select an entire subset of a complex object. You can also use Select Connected with points.

The concept is the same as it is with polys, except that points are selected instead of polygons.

# Invert Selection

Invert Selection (**View | Selection | Invert**) "flip-flops" what you've currently got selected with what is currently not selected.

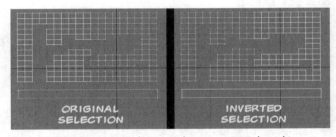

Figure 3-21: After Invert Selection, what was once selected is now unselected and vice versa.

# Expand/Contract Selection

Expand/Contract Selection (**View | Selection | Expand** and **View | Selection | Contract**) *adds* or *removes* the outermost row of connected polys or points to your current selection.

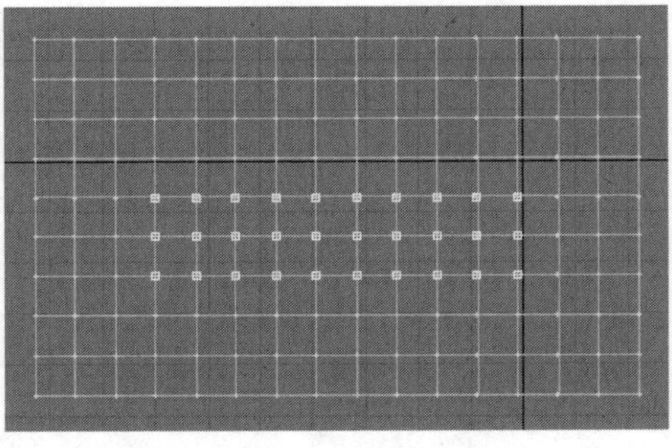

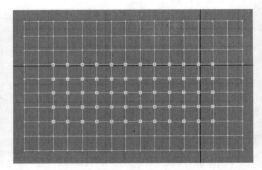

Figure 3-22: A nice neat grouping of points selected.

Figure 3-23: After Expand Selection, the current selection now encompasses the row of points that bounded the original selection.

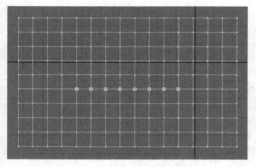

Figure 3-24: From the original selection in Figure 3-22, after Contract Selection, the points on the border of the original selection are no longer selected.

## Select Loop

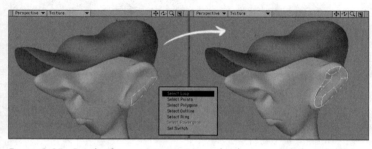

Figure 3-25: Bands of consecutive points and polys can easily be selected with the Select Loop tool.

The Select Loop tool (**View | Selection | More | Select Loop**) allows you to select bands of points or polygons that follow a set path along your geometry. In the case of polygons, this path is defined by a string of quadrilaterals. In the case of points, it is defined by the edge between strings of quadrilaterals. That sounds complicated, but it simply means that if you've got a sequence of quads or a sequence of points attached to quads, you can select them easily with this tool. You'll probably find yourself using this tool quite a bit (I know I do) so it's worth assigning a keyboard shortcut for it.

Select any two adjacent points or polys and run this tool to quickly select the entire band. The selection will stop when it reaches a non-quad polygon or winds its way around and loops back on itself. Additional bands can be selected by holding the Shift key, selecting two more adjacent points or polys, and running the tool again.

## Select Points/Polygons

Imagine that you've got a fairly complex selection of polygons and you want just the points from those polygons to be selected. The **View | Selection | More | Select Points** tool will let you do just that. Conversely, **View | Selection | More | Select Polygons** will change your point selection back into a polygon selection.

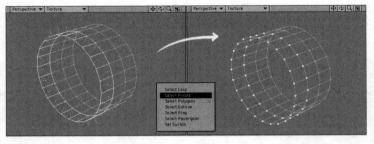

*Figure 3-26: The Select Points tool converts your polygon selection into a point selection.*

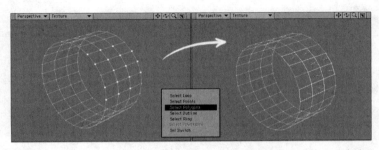

*Figure 3-27: Switching points back to polygons can quickly be done with the Select Polygons tool.*

> **Note**
>
> In order for a polygon to be selected with the Select Polygons tool, all of the points that make up that polygon must be selected. For example, with a simple box, all four points must be selected in order for the Select Polygons tool to select it.

## Show/Hide Selection

With the Show Selection and Hide Selection tools, you can use your ability to select groups of points or polys and temporarily remove from view all but the geometry you want to zero in on.

Having already assigned the polys of the eyelids to separate parts while building the mesh, using the Polygon Statistics window I first select the polys of the lower eyelid, then add to that selection the polys of the upper eyelid. (See Figure 3-29.)

With just the eyelids selected, using **View | View | Hide Unselected** will get your view to "equal" only what you've got selected (its hot key is <=>). (See Figure 3-30.)

When you want to bring all your hidden geometry back into view, **View | View | Unhide** will do just that.

If you have polys selected and you want to hide them, **View | View | Hide Selected** will "subtract" what you've got selected from your

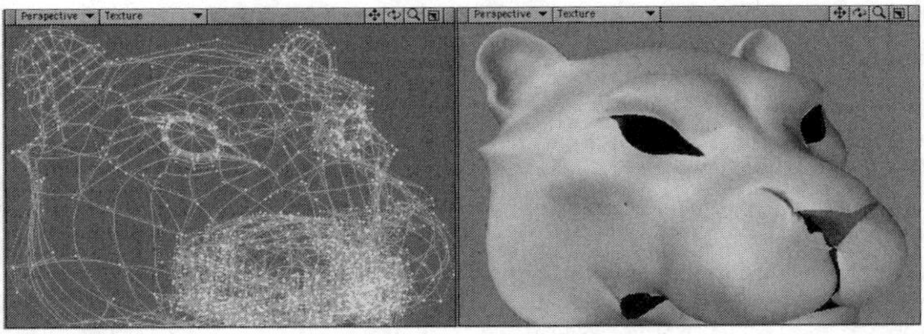

*Figure 3-28: If I wanted to just get in and work on the shape of this tiger's eyelid, it would be easiest to do without the other geometry getting in my way.*

view (its hot key is <->). (See Figure 3-31.)

**View | View | Hide Invert** will "flip-flop" what you have hidden with what you have visible.

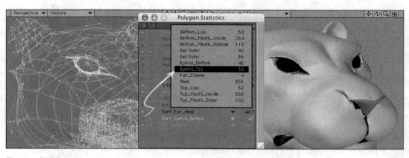

Figure 3-29

Figure 3-30

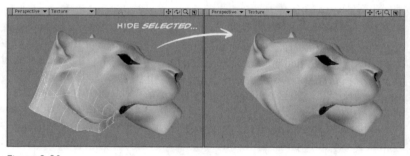

Figure 3-31

# Primitives

**prim•i•tive** *adj.* **1. a.** Of or pertaining to an earliest or original stage or state. **b.** Archetypal. **2.** *Math.* A form in geometry or algebra from which another form is derived. (*The American Heritage Dictionary*)

LightWave's Modeler gives you quick access to a slew of simple objects created from mathematical formulae. Balls, boxes, discs, cones, capsules, donuts, even gemstones are among these quickly accessible items.

Selecting **Create | Primitives | Box** and click-dragging one viewport will create a plane constrained by the two dimensions represented within that particular viewport. Click-dragging in *another viewport* or two will "flesh out" your primitive into a fully three-dimensional object. (Figure 3-32 shows the Box primitive segmented and with the Numeric window open as well.)

---

### Hot Key Block

**Primitive Segmentation**

While creating primitives, you can press the **Left**, **Right**, **Up**, and **Down Arrow** keys to add or remove additional segments. *What each key does is dependent upon the viewport the mouse is currently over.*

---

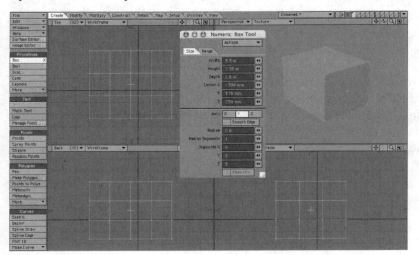

*Figure 3-32*

---

### Note

Most of the other primitive object tools located under the Create menu tab are easy to understand after playing with them a few times. I'm showing the Box tool because in Chapter 7 when we get into sub-patch modeling, a simple box like the one shown in Figure 3-32 will become the base from which you will "grow" your detailed sub-patch models.

You can get a tiny taste of what sub-patch modeling is like by pressing <Tab> or choosing **Construct | Convert | SubPatch** to turn any selected four-sided polygons into subpatches; remember that with nothing selected, Modeler treats everything in the foreground as being selected.

# Text

Making text in LightWave is a two-part process that isn't immediately obvious. To save memory space, LightWave's Modeler doesn't load in all the *fonts* (typefaces) you have on your computer. You have to specifically tell Modeler which fonts you wish to use.

You add fonts to Modeler's Font List through **Create | Text | Manage Fonts** (Figure 3-33). Here you can add either your operating system's TrueType fonts or a PostScript Type-1 font (several of which are included with LightWave).

Clicking on Add True-Type brings up an OS-specific font requester. Highlighting a font and clicking OK returns you to the Edit Font List window, now with the selected font appearing in the Font pop-up menu (Figure 3-34).

Having accepted the changes to the font list made in Figure 3-34, you can then activate **Create | Text | Text** and click in any viewport, typing the text you want to create and pressing <**Return**> to "make" your text.

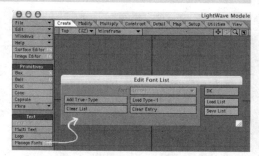

Figure 3-33: Using **Create | Text | Manage Fonts**.

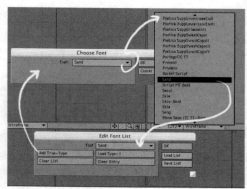

Figure 3-34

Figure 3-35

---

## Note

Because LightWave limits a polygon to having a maximum of 1,023 points, you may run into problems with extremely ornate fonts. (Notice that in Figure 3-35, each letter's contiguous shape is a single polygon.)

The workaround for this, albeit not a perfect one, is to change Curve Divisions to Coarse under **Modeler | Options | General**

**Options**. This slightly reduces the number of points created as the curve data that TrueType and PostScript fonts are made of are converted into polygons.

You can do this for the entire line of text you are creating or just certain letters that are heavily ornate.

# Surfacing

Of all the 3D packages I've used, Light-Wave has the quickest, most powerful, and most intuitive surfacing model. In this section, we just scratch the surface of what it can do. It'll be enough to give you a piton for the more advanced techniques we go into in the next chapter.

To assign a surface to a polygon, you simply select the polys to which you want the surface applied and choose the Surface button found at the bottom of the interface. You can choose from your already created surfaces, enter a new name, change a surface's color, and set other simple attributes.

Figure 3-36: The Change Surface window.

Figure 3-37: Shaded viewports show GL versions of the surfaces you've applied to each polygon. (You can have an unlimited number of surfaces on your objects and in your scenes.)

## Hot Key Block

**Surfacing**

<q> brings up the Change Surface window.

The real power of LightWave's surfacing is glimpsed through the Surface Editor, which is identical in Layout and Modeler. Each surface is listed under the object to which it belongs. Selecting that surface from the list (such as the surface named Shoe in Figure 3-38) shades the default sphere in the Surface Editor window with that surface. You can explore the LW manual for in-depth descriptions of what each setting, button, and pop-up menu does; let's focus on getting familiar with the most basic of basics right now.

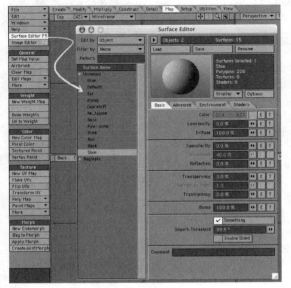

Figure 3-38: The Surface Editor.

The Color box is used to change the color of the surface. You can click on the Color box to open a color picker. Alternately, you can click and drag left or right on any of the three numbers, which represent red, green, and blue values (0 to 255). Right-clicking on these numbers will toggle between RGB and HSV modes. Dragging in HSV mode allows you to alter the hue, saturation, and value (brightness) of the color.

*Figure 3-39*

The Luminosity setting reflects how perfectly lit the surface will appear, even if it is in shadow (Figure 3-40).

Diffuse is the channel that controls the degree to which light *scatters* across a surface. Paper has a high level of diffuseness, while metal, which reflects most of the light that falls on it, has a low level of diffuseness.

*Figure 3-40*

Specularity is a measure of *how much* of a hot spot lights produce on a surface.

Glossiness is a measure of *how big* the hot spot will be. Higher numbers (like the value in Figure 3-43) give a small, tight hot spot, as on glass or water, while low numbers (like in Figure 3-42) give a wide, soft hot spot, as on paper or snow.

*Figure 3-41*

Reflection is the channel that controls how much of the *environment* is "thrown back" by the surface. (Under the Environment tab of the Surface Editor, you can set whether the surface truly reflects its environment, which is computationally intensive, or uses a *reflection map* to give a quick but convincing *illusion* of reflecting the world around it.)

Transparency is a measure of how much the surface can be "seen through" (Figure 3-45).

Refraction Index is a measure of how much light "wavicles" are "bent" as they pass through the transparent surfaces of an object. (There is a chart in the LightWave 8 manual that lists materials from air to iodine crystal and their respective refraction indices.)

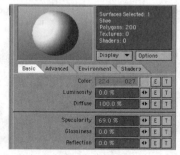

*Figure 3-42*

Translucency is a measure of how much light passing through an object will be "seen" on its other side (think of leaves glowing when back-lit by the sun).

Bump tells LightWave what percentage of the textures active on this channel (accessible through the little "T" button, shown active in Figure 3-48) to apply to the surface. Negative numbers and numbers over 100% *are* allowed. (We get more into textures in Chapter 4.)

*Figure 3-43*

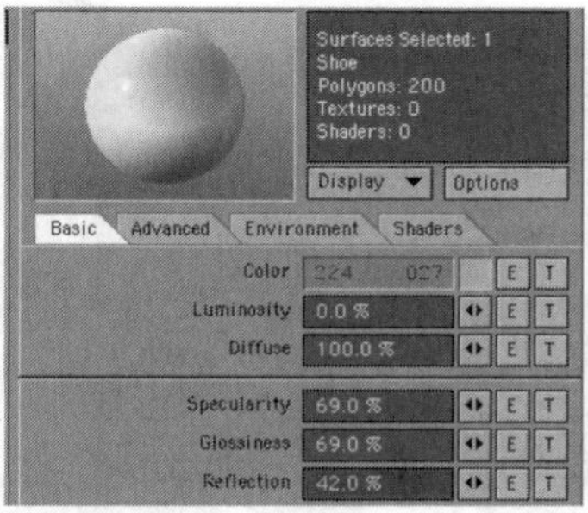

Figure 3-44

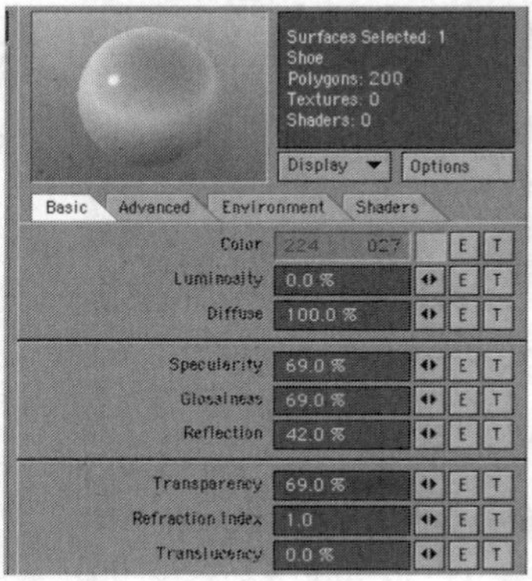

Figure 3-45

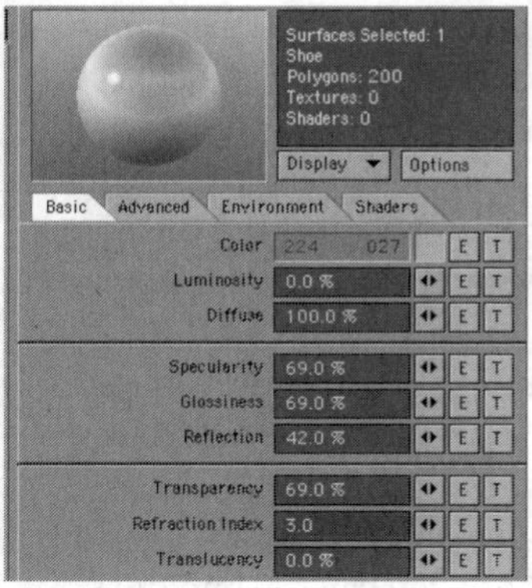

Figure 3-46

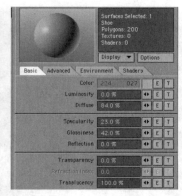

Figure 3-47

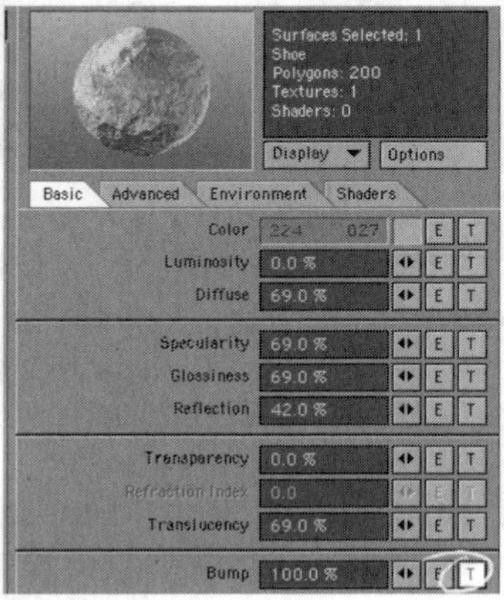

Figure 3-48

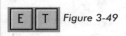

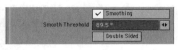

Figure 3-50

## Note

Figure 3-49

The little "E" button means you can assign an envelope for that setting to change over time. The "T" button opens up the Texture Editor where you can assign painted or procedural (mathematical) textures.

To quickly get rid of an envelope or a texture (if you've clicked on the buttons just to see what they brought up and are now wondering how to deactivate the button), simply hold <Shift> while clicking on the button.

Smoothing tells LightWave to look to the Smooth Threshold when shading the joining of two polygons. In Figure 3-50, if two polys meet at an angle of 89.5° *or less*, those polys are shaded as if they were one smooth surface. If polys meet at 89.6° *or more*, there would be a sharp "crease" visible where they join.

The Double Sided setting is also shown in Figure 3-50. Activate this to make a planar polygon visible from either side, regardless of which way its surface normal is facing.

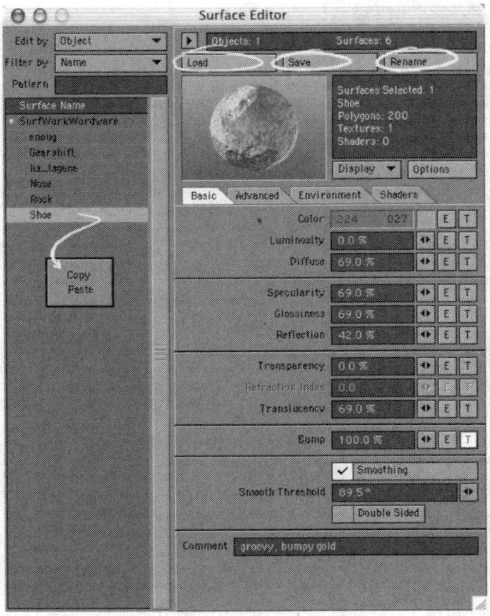

Figure 3-51

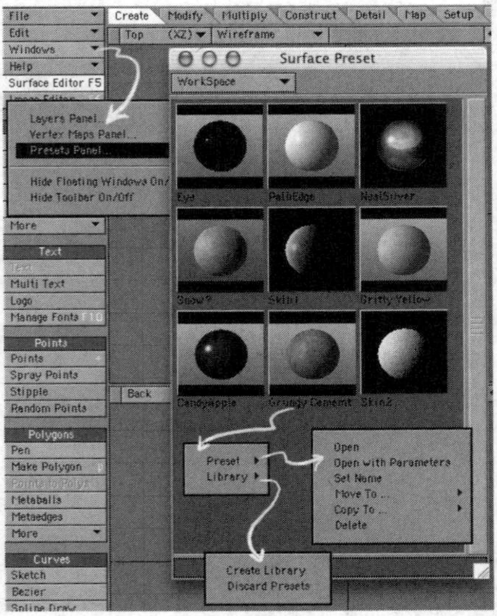

Figure 3-52: The Surface Preset window.

You can right-click on a surface's name and copy and paste all of those surface's attributes to another surface. Using the buttons at the top of the Surface Editor, you can load, save, and rename a surface you may find a use for later.

> ## Note
>
> As you're exploring surfacing settings, just playing around and having fun, you're bound to come across some cool combinations that you may find a use for later.
>
> Remember the old saying, "The palest ink is better than the strongest memory."
>
> If you stumble across something that looks even remotely neat, save those settings in a directory for later use. Surface setting files are small, disk space is cheap, and you never know when something will come up where you will find a use for "Gritty Yellow" or "Grungy Cement."

Another way to get quick access to your favorite surfaces is through the Surface Preset window. This window gives you quick, visual access to a whole slew of stock settings provided by NewTek that range from Rocks to Raw Umber and just about everything in between. The presets are separated into different libraries, selectable through the pop-up menu at the top of the window (showing the WorkSpace library in Figure 3-52).

Double-clicking on a preset will load that preset's settings onto the currently selected surface in the Surface Editor.

Right-clicking on a preset will open a menu tree where you can rename the preset, delete it, move it to another library, or create and manage libraries of your own.

If you want to add the surface you're working on to your currently active preset library, just press <s> when the Surface Editor window is active. A preset will be created with an icon of the current sample sphere named the same as your currently active surface.

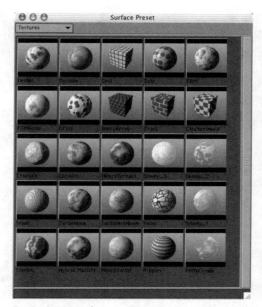

> **Note**
>
> When you want to really be blown away by the power of how LightWave's surfaces can be layered and how each channel can, through the Gradient function, reference another, load in Rock_1, Rock_2, and/or Lava from the Rock library of the surface presets. (Picking apart these surface presets will really start your mind rolling as to just what can be done — *simply* and *elegantly* — with the LightWave surfacing settings.)

*Figure 3-53: As they say, "A picture is worth a thousand words." But an example you can pick apart is worth a thousand pictures.*

One of the surface preset libraries that LightWave ships with is called Textures. Here you will find examples of how each of those procedural textures *can* be used (meaning this is *not* the *only* way it can be used; creativity bordering on being a "smart-ass" is often highly rewarded in the realm of texturing, especially when dealing with procedurals).

So explore and pick apart each one of these surface presets and figure out how setting changes affect the way they look.

# Move, Rotate, and Scale

Move, Rotate, and Scale are the basic tools of point pushers around the world.

Let's say we were doing one of those monochromatic still life drawing assignments from Drawing 101. We've got a bunch of primitives laid down and now we've got to get them into their proper places. (See Figure 3-54.)

1. First, let's set the ground plane to Y=0 by following these steps:

   a. Select one of the ground plane's points. Then choose **Select Connected** (press <]>) to select the rest of the points in the ground plane polygon.

   b. Choose **Detail | Points | Set Value** to bring up the Set Value window.

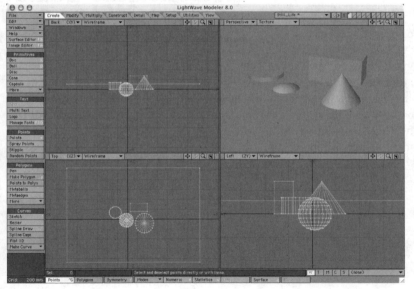

*Figure 3-54*

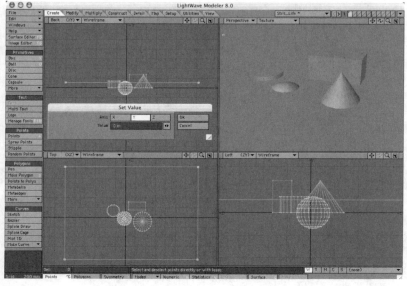

Figure 3-55

c. Enter **0** for the Y axis, and click **OK**. (Meters is assumed by Modeler when you don't add "mm" or the like after the numeric value. This is because the default unit, set under **Display Options | Units**, is meters.)

2. Next, I'm going to move the sphere behind the cylinder and box.

a. Select a few polygons of the sphere. Then choose **Select Connected** to select the rest of the polys that make up the sphere.

b. **Modify | Translate | Move** activates the move mode where you can then click and drag the selected polys around in the viewports.

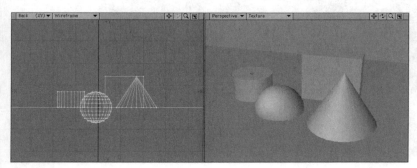

Figure 3-56

3. After moving the sphere behind the cylinder and box, select the **Rest On Ground** tool, which is under the More pop-up menu of the Translate submenu.

   a. Make sure that Rest Axis is set to **Y**.

   b. Uncheck all the boxes for centering the selection on the X, Y, and Z axes. (With these checked, the tool will center the selected polys, as well as "rest" them as a unit on the "ground," which is defined by Rest Axis=0).

   c. Make sure that + is selected for the Sense buttons. (This will "rest" the selection *above* Y=0, whereas having it set to – would "rest" the selection *below* Y=0). Click **OK**.

4. Next, I want to stretch the box to make it more like a cube.

   a. Select the cube and choose **Modify | Transform | Stretch**.

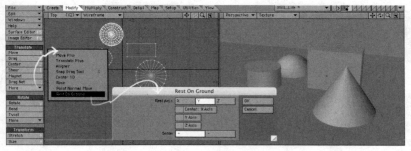

Figure 3-57

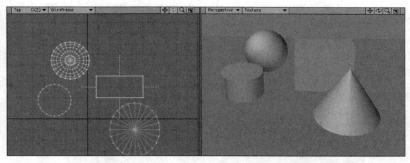

Figure 3-58: Rest On Ground positions the selected sphere so that its bottommost point falls on Y=0.

b.  In a Top view, drag left to *reduce* the X dimension (drag right to *increase* its X dimension), and drag up to *increase* its Z dimension (dragging down would *decrease* its Z dimension).

5.  I want the cube angled a bit, so leaving it selected, I choose **Modify | Rotate | Rotate**. Clicking and dragging in a Top view rotates my selection around where I clicked my mouse.

6.  I want the sphere to be *exactly* 1.5 times bigger than it is and to stay in roughly the same spot. I select the center points of the sphere from a Top viewport and activate the Point Info window (via the button located at the bottom of Modeler's interface or by pressing <**i**>).

Note

With the Point Info window open and points selected, the window tells me every detail of each point I have selected. It even labels the points in the viewports so I know which point is #1 and which point is #266.

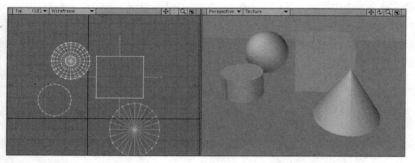

Figure 3-59

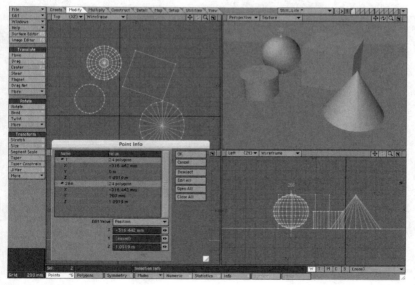

Figure 3-60

75

a. Make a note that the sphere's center points are at *roughly* X=–316 mm and Z=1.09 m.

7. After choosing **Select Connected** and activating the Size tool (**Modify | Transform | Size**) I could just click and drag in the viewports to resize the sphere, watching my Quick-Info readout in the lower-left corner to find out when I've reached 150% of the sphere's original size. But going for *precision*, I press the Numeric button at the bottom of Modeler's interface (keyboard shortcut <**n**>) to open the Numeric window for the Size tool.

Figure 3-61

8. Enter **150%** in the Factor box, and enter the center coordinates jotted down from above (leaving the Y axis at 0 so the size effect will have its origin at ground level). Click **Apply**.

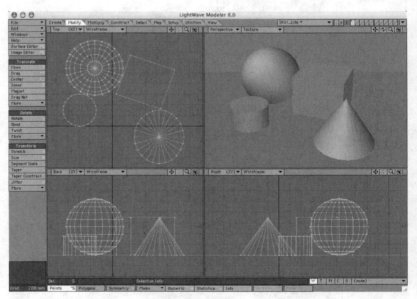

Figure 3-62: Having deselected the sphere's points, the modeling for the still life is now finished.

# Extrude

**ex•trude** *v.* **1.** To push or thrust out. **2.** To shape by forcing through a die. (*The American Heritage Dictionary*)

If you're going to be doing any sort of "flying logos," you're going to get real cozy with Extrude. It's a quick way to add dimension to planar polys.

As shown in Figure 3-63, make some text by clicking your Text tool in a viewport showing a *back* view, and let's get started.

1. Just to keep everything "tight," I'm going to make sure the text I've typed is centered on all axes. To do this, press <F2> and choose **Modify | Translate | Center.**

> ### Note
>
> Modify | Rotate | Bend will bend your object as if you were grabbing the end of a fencing foil sticking straight out on the axis that you are "looking" at. So, to bend an object *around* an axis, you must look at that axis from the "side" and bend *straight up* or *straight down*.
>
> With complex polys like text, Bend can quickly create non-planars if you bend a complex poly on any axis other than one that will keep all its points still lying along a single plane. (In the case of our text, *all* its points *must* remain at Z=0.)
>
> Having Grid Snap set to Standard will help when mousing with the Bend tool.

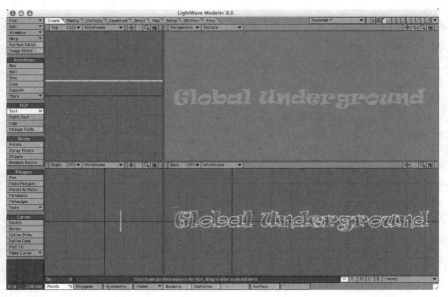

Figure 3-63

I want to give the text a nice curve so it doesn't look quite so boring. Enter the Bend tool.

2. Click at Y=0, Z=0 in a Side viewport, and drag *straight down* along the Y axis. This bends your text *around* the Z axis (see Figure 3-64).

3. Having bent your text, rotate it so that it is level again (see Figure 3-65).

Figure 3-64

Figure 3-65: Looking more like a logo. We're just about there!

4. Center your text again (see step 1).

5. Select **Multiply | Extend | Extrude** to activate the Extrude tool.

6. With the Extrude tool active, click and drag in a line along the +Z axis on either a Right or Top viewport (basically, anything that isn't Perspective or where you're looking at the letters head-on will do). The more you drag, the more the text will be extruded.

7. Press <**Return**> to accept the effects of the Extrude tool (see Figure 3-66).

**Note**

Depending on which direction the surface normals of your polys to be extruded are facing, dragging one way will create the new geometry with their normals facing "out" (which is what you want most often) or "in" (which means you're seeing "through" the outer surface of the object, seeing only the "insides," which can be cool for faking the effect of volumetric lighting).

Save this text you've created, as we use it in an upcoming example on using one layer of your object to modify another.

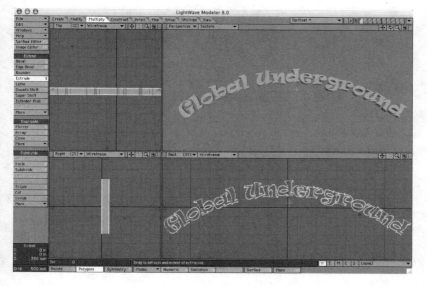

*Figure 3-66*

# Extender Plus

**ex•tend** *v.* **1.** To spread or stretch forth. **6a.** To cause to be of greater area or volume. (*Merriam-Webster Online Dictionary*)

What Extrude is to polygons, Extender is to points. Specifically, it expands the geometry around the selected points.

Let's use Extender Plus to make a simple bowl.

1. Activate the **Ball** tool and drag out a circle in the Top view. The exact size doesn't really matter. Now, holding the <**Ctrl**> key (or the middle mouse button), drag in the Back view to create a perfectly round sphere. For this

example, I've increased the number of sides and segments to provide a very smooth surface. Now hit <**F2**> to center the ball.

2. Using your right mouse button, drag out a lasso selection around the top half of the sphere including the band of polys just below the center.

3. Press the <**Delete**> key to remove these polygons. This leaves us with a nice simple bowl shape. As you can see, however, the bowl has no interior. We'll use the Extender Plus tool to remedy this.

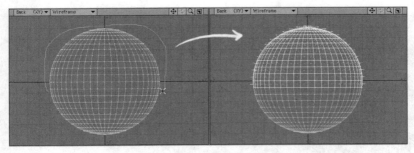

*Figure 3-67: Deleting the top half of the ball leaves us with a generic bowl shape.*

4.  Select a couple of points along the open edge of the bowl, then activate the **Select Loop** tool. With all of the points along the edge selected, go to the **Multiply | Extend** menu and select **Extender Plus**.

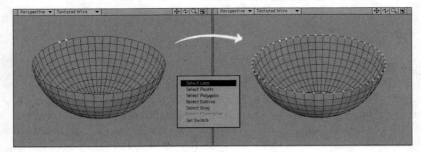

*Figure 3-68*

Looking at your geometry, it will appear as if nothing has happened. On the contrary, Extender Plus has actually expanded the edge of the ball. The only problem is that this new edge lies directly on top of the old one. Therefore, in order to see the effect of the Extender Plus tool, we must modify the new geometry by moving, rotating, or sizing it.

5.  Select the **Modify | Transform | Size** tool and scale the selection in slightly. You'll see the lip of the bowl "magically" appear.

> **Note**
>
> If your selection does not scale inward evenly, make sure the Modes button at the bottom of the interface is set to Action Center: Selection.

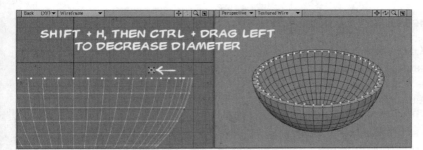

Figure 3-69

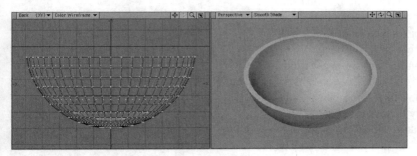

Figure 3-70: The final bowl with a smooth surface.

6. With the edge points still selected, click on the **Extender Plus** tool again. Then activate the **Move** tool. Holding the <Ctrl> key down (or using the middle mouse button), drag down slightly to form the initial inside edge of the bowl.

7. Click on the **Extender Plus** tool again, followed by the **Move** tool. Move the new edge down slightly. Then use the **Size** tool to shrink the selection so that the points are inside the bowl. Repeat this process again, moving the points and sizing them so that they're not poking through the outside polys of the bowl. Continue this process several more times until you've reached the bottom of the bowl.

8. Finally, click on **Extender Plus** once more. Click on the **Weld Average** tool from the **Detail | Points** menu. This will weld all of the points together at their averaged center.

# Booleans and Solid Drilling

**Bool•e•an** *adj.* Of or pertaining to an algebraic combinatorial system treating variables, such as propositions and computer logic elements, through the operators AND, OR, NOT, IF, THEN, and EXCEPT. [After George Boole (1815-1864).] (*The American Heritage Dictionary*)

With Booleans and solid drilling, you can use parts of your object to "carve out" spaces in other parts of your object. This is powerful computing, and you've got to make sure your prep work for these kinds of operations leaves LightWave with as clean a start as possible. (Non-planar polys are a surefire way to generate errors.) But when you're thinking ahead and planning your modeling tasks as if you were playing a strategy game or solving a puzzle, these tools can be incredible allies.

| Hot Key Block |  |
| --- | --- |
| **Booleans and Solid Drilling** | |
| **<B>** | Boolean |
| **<C>** | Solid Drill |
| **<m>** | Merge Points |

In a nutshell, with both Booleans and solid drilling, you're using an object in a *background layer* to modify an object in a *foreground layer*. The following exercises show how to use these tools.

Let's start with the objects shown in Figure 3-71 — a white cube on Layer 3 and an orange sphere on Layer 4.

1. To use the sphere to "carve out" a section of the cube, we put the sphere into the background layer and leave the cube in the foreground.

2. **Construct | Combine | Boolean** brings up the Boolean window (Figure 3-73). Since we are going to

be *subtracting* the volume of the object in the background layer, we choose **Subtract** and click **OK** (see Figure 3-74).

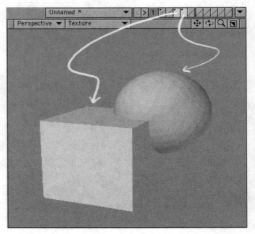

Figure 3-71

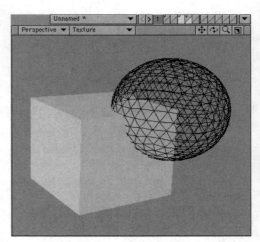

Figure 3-72

Figure 3-73

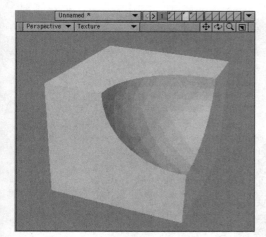

*Figure 3-74*

Showing only the foreground layer after the Boolean operation, we see the "bite" taken out of the cube by the volume of the sphere. *Notice how the sphere's orange surface is now the color for the "bitten" polys!*

With Solid Drill, you don't "carve out" bits of an object like you do with Booleans.

Instead, you use layers to "cut holes in" or "stencil" shapes into other object layers.

For the next exercise, I've created a simple white plane (a two-dimensional box) and use the text we created in the Extrude exercise to "stencil" the shape of the text onto the plane (see Figure 3-76).

### Note

You should notice that the plane to be stenciled in Figure 3-76 has five width segments and three height segments. This is because the text I wish to stencil has 2,876 points on its face polygons. Trying to stencil this would be asking LightWave to try to have many more than its maximum number of points per poly in the resultant white plane that bound the letter shapes.

I've helped LightWave by breaking this plane up into segments, so the maximum point-per-poly limit won't be pushed by any one poly. (After the Solid Drill operation, using the information window for all polys, I was told that the largest number of points any poly had was 428.)

### Note

When you do a Boolean operation, the points of the "bitten" polys aren't "stitched" directly to the points of the original object — this gives a nice, sharp edge when both surfaces have Smoothing active. This can cause a problem if you do a lot of selecting with the Select Connected tool because the two pieces aren't really connected; they're only laying *exactly* on top of each other, which *isn't* the same thing.

*Figure 3-75*

To connect the "bitten" part of a Boolean operation with its original object, you must use **Detail | Points | Merge Points**.

- **Automatic** "fuses" multiple points into one point only if the points are laying *exactly* in the same space, with not even a micrometer difference between their *exact* position. This is what you use to fuse the pieces after a Boolean operation.
- **Fixed** lets you decree "all points that are within 'X' mm of each other shall now become one," and so forth.

After you've merged points, especially if you've just merged with the Fixed option, it's a good idea to peruse the Point and Polygon Statistics windows. Merging points gets rid of points, not the poly information tacked to those points. You need to check to see if you have any "0 Point" or "2 Point" polygons (or points that don't belong to any polygons at all) that you don't specifically want.

After merging points, you may have to adjust the smoothing angle of your surfaces so they still give you a nice, sharp edge where they meet.

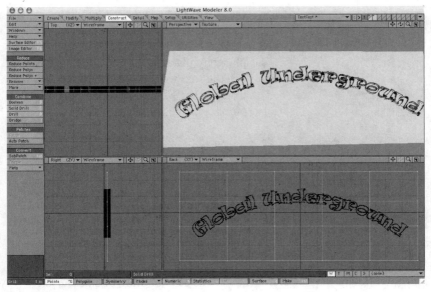

*Figure 3-76*

Like with Booleans, the object in the background layer is the "cutter," and the object in the foreground layer is the object to be cut. The "cutter" must pass *through* the "cuttee."

*Figure 3-77*

1. I want to use the text to stencil a new surface into the white plane, so I choose **Solid Drill**, which brings up the Solid Drill window and activates the Surface box where I can type in a new surface name or select an existing one from the pop-up menu.

### Note

If you don't see the effect of the Solid Drill function, make sure that you are viewing the object in one of the wireframe display types (such as Textured Wireframe). If your drilled surface is the same as the object it's drilled into, it won't be visible in Smooth Shaded or Textured view types.

### Note

- **Core** leaves just the polys of the foreground layer in the shape of where the two objects *intersect*.
- **Tunnel** "cuts a hole" in the polys of the foreground layer with the shape of the object in the background.
- **Stencil** cuts the polys of the foreground layer and assigns a new surface to them.
- **Slice** cuts just the polys of the foreground layer, leaving them with their original surfacing.

Figure 3-78

2. The **Construct | Combine | Solid Drill** operation leaves me with the text that was in the background layer "stenciled" onto the plane. (Unlike a Boolean operation, all these polys *are* connected — there is no need to merge points.)

Before we move on to beveling and smooth-shifting, there is one more cool thing I want to show you how to do with Booleans.

With the Bend tool, we got our text to bend around the Z axis. But if we had also wanted our text to bend around the Y and/or X axes, Bend would have made all our letters non-planar, which Triple may or may not have been able to make sense out of (because a poly in the shape of a letter is so very complex).

However, if we want our flying logo to look even cooler than it already does, we can use one of the Boolean operations to add some curve to our text. (Light scatters so much better off a subtle curve than it does off a flat plane. This is part of knowing how to make something look professional.)

1. To do this we need a bit more depth in our letters as we work (see Figure 3-79). So, dragging using the right mouse button (<**Command**> + **mouse-button** on a Mac with a one-button mouse) will let you lasso the polys you want selected. Grab the rear polys of your text and move them back a bit to give us some room.

2. Next, as in Figure 3-80, bring up an empty foreground layer, and put your text into the background as a reference as you create a highly tesselated sphere, the surface of which will represent the curve of our text's new face.

Figure 3-79

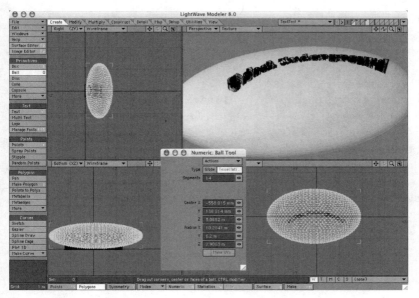

Figure 3-80

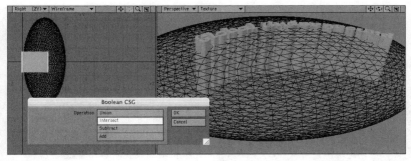

*Figure 3-81*

3. With our text in the foreground layer and the sphere in the background, activate Boolean again, but this time choose **Intersect**. The end result will create an object that consists of only the area where the two volumes are "inside" one another.

The letter faces now catch the light in a much more interesting way than they did when they were all flat, even, and ever so slightly boring. There are exactly *no* non-planar polygons. (After doing the Boolean, the points of the back of the logo were moved forward to a place where they looked good.)

Save what you've got here. We're going to do some cool things with it in future chapters.

*Figure 3-82: The finished Boolean operation.*

## Note

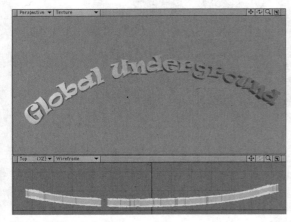

If you wanted to have all the letters the same thickness and not get thicker toward the center of the logo, as is the case in Figure 3-82, you could jump back to where things were at Figure 3-81. Instead of doing a Boolean, do a **Solid Drill | Core**, then **Extrude** the results, and resurface the sides of the letters to their original surface. You'd then have something like Figure 3-83.

*Figure 3-83*

# Bevel and Smooth Shift

Bevel and Smooth Shift are two of the most frequently used modeling tools. They do almost the same thing, except Bevel affects *every polygon individually*, while Smooth Shift treats all contiguous selections as a *single unit*.

| Hot Key Block |
| --- |
| **Bevel and Smooth Shift** |
| <b>      Bevel |
| <F>      Smooth Shift |

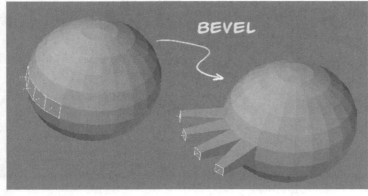

With four of this sphere's polys selected, **Multiply | Extend | Bevel** "pushes" each poly out separately. Dragging *up* "pushes" the polys out from their original position, and dragging *left* makes the polys smaller.

*Figure 3-84*

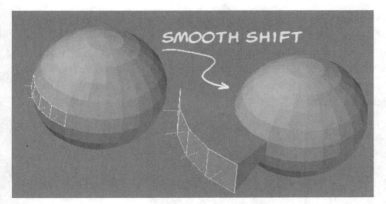

*Figure 3-85*

With four of the sphere's polys selected, **Multiply | Extend | Smooth Shift** pushes and/or pulls the polys, but Smooth Shift treats them as a single unit. Drag *left* to "suck them into" their originating volume; drag *right* to "push" them out, away from their original volume.

## Edge Bevel and Super Shift

The last two modeling tools we'll look at are Edge Bevel and Super Shift. As you might have guessed, these are variations of the Bevel and Smooth Shift tools mentioned above.

Edge Bevel is useful anytime you need to create geometry between two or more adjacent polygons. When we talk about edges in this case, we're referring to more than just the geometry along the perimeter of your object. Edges occur at the boundaries of every single polygon.

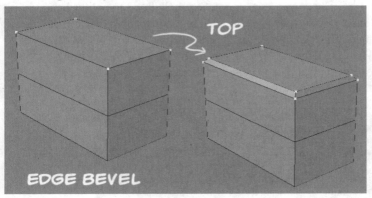

*Figure 3-86*

By edge beveling the top of this box, we create the same basic effect as if we had used the traditional Bevel tool. However, if we select the edge around the center of the box, we can "open" it to create an additional band of polygons. Dragging to the right makes the bevel larger, while dragging to the left makes it smaller. Edge Bevel is particularly helpful when working on characters, where beveled edges can be used to create wrinkles in the character's skin.

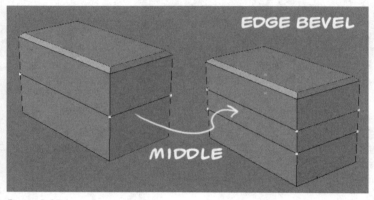

Figure 3-87

Super Shift is a handy alternative to the traditional Smooth Shift tool. While Smooth Shift allows you to push and scale groups of polygons, it does not give you independent control over either process. Super Shift, however, does, thus enabling you to perform a "group bevel" on your polygons. In addition, Super Shift automatically generates polygons with zero offset and a Maximum Smoothing Angle of zero simply by activating the tool. (While the benefits of that may not make sense now, they will later when we talk about sub-patch modeling.) For now, let's take a quick look at the differences between Smooth Shift and Super Shift.

When pushing these polys out of the ball using Smooth Shift, Modeler looks at each individual polygon's normal to determine how it should move and scale the entire group. Super Shift, on the other hand, averages the group's normals. What that means in practice is that Super Shift won't "puff up" the polys on a curved surface as it pushes them out.

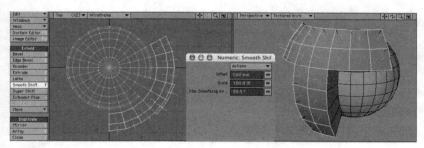

Figure 3-88

Super Shift also scales your polys using a local inset, which is similar to how the Bevel tool operates. Moving your mouse to the left scales the group in. Moving your mouse to the right scales it out. Moving your mouse up pushes the polygons out. Moving your mouse down pulls the polygons in.

When used on an irregular selection, the differences between Smooth Shift and Super Shift become apparent. As you can see, the "T" that was pushed into the ball using Super Shift maintained its shape much better than the "T" using Smooth Shift.

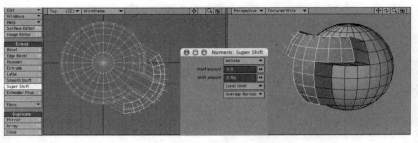

Figure 3-89

• • •

That concludes our discussion of a respectable number of modeling tools. A modeler could almost go his entire career and never use more than these, but in later chapters on modeling, we add to this repertoire of yours so you'll be able to handle just about anything a client cares to put into your capable hands. Remember, even all the tools explored in the more advanced chapters are *still* only just scratching the surface.

You will reach your fullest potential by pushing, peeking, and playing. If you view 3D as a puzzle, game, or toy through which all things are possible with the "right" pattern of patience, exploration, observation, and retention, there will be no limits as to what you can do.

## Note

To this end, I'd like to take a moment to point you toward one of the programs available on the companion CD. Sherlock is a game that trains your mind to see even the most seemingly complex tasks as *simply a process of elimination*.

"...When you have eliminated the impossible, whatever remains, however improbable, must be the truth..." — Sherlock Holmes

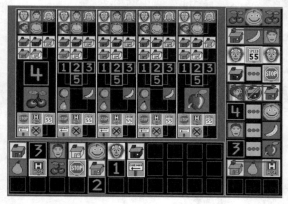

*Figure 3-90: Sherlock*

Sherlock (PC only) by Everett Kaser (http://www.kaser.com) is a "game" where, like LightWave, you are given all the clues you need to do what you need to do. In this case, it is to find the locations for each icon within a grid from 3x3 to 8x8, with as much

(or as little) help and as many (or as few) hints as you need.

I hesitate to call Sherlock a game, even though it is a fun and rewarding way to pass the time. Part of this is that often in computer games, from the moment you click "Go," the computer will do everything in its power to keep you from reaching your goal, whatever it happens to be — and I, for one, find this to be a waste of my time. Sherlock, on the other hand, gives you all the resources you need to solve the puzzle — and unlike solitaire, your winning is *not* dependent upon chance. Your success, or lack thereof, rides entirely upon your shoulders (think about it). Success in Sherlock, as in Light-Wave, feels like an *achievement*, not a fight.

The other reason I hesitate to call Sherlock a game is that it is much *more* than just an enjoyable way to pass the time. It is *training* for your mind. ("Use it or lose it.") Exploring this kind of training, you begin to become accustomed to seeing the whole picture as patterns of interrelated subsets and steps. When temporarily stumped in either LightWave or Sherlock (or life), you become able to take a step back and see the *next step* toward the solution, sometimes just sitting there in plain sight, patiently waiting for you to take notice of it.

# Chapter 4

# Layout 1: Foundation Material

One of the best ways to think about the whole process of 3D is to equate it to building scale models and then photographing them. All the different parts of the process are the same. You've got to sculpt the pieces that you'll eventually turn the camera on, sometimes "kit-bashing" free models found on the Internet or cannibalizing old pieces laying around in an attic-like part of your hard drive.

If you were working with *practical* ("real") models, you'd paint the models so they looked just the way you wanted, from whatever camera angle you were going to shoot them. You'd find a private stage to set them up. You'd get lights to shine on them and bounce off of diffusing boards and screens. You'd look through your camera or director's viewfinder and see what needs to be touched up on the models, placement, or lighting. You'd possibly add some smoke or wind and, making sure exposure, filters, and camera speed are all correct, you'd let the cameras roll!

The best-looking work I've seen from 3D artists is from people who were thinking as though they were "doing this in real life." 3D is just a tool to give you rent-free, unlimited soundstage space. Once you get beyond the fact that you can't really "hold" what you're working on, becoming good in 3D is mostly a matter of finding out how what you know about your physical, *practical* "reality" translates into the tools you use to manipulate this *virtual* "reality."

> ### Note
>
> Some of the most impressive work to come out of *Babylon 5* was from a guy in his late 40s who, until he was hired, had never worked in 3D CGI before. He was a photographer, and as such, *he understood how light behaved.* After he got the knack of Light-Wave's controls, his 3D work began to reflect how he would light and shoot an event in "real life."
>
> Being a computer whiz has very little to do with being good at 3D. After you know your way around the tools, it's all about what you choose to focus your camera on and how you choose to showcase that environment. *Anyone*, given the time, can learn the tools — possibly one of the most liberating things about working in 3D.
>
> There are no limits!

# LightWave's Camera

If you were to go out and look at a 35mm motion picture camera or even a professional-level 35mm single-lens reflex, you'd see a whole lot of settings that you can play with. LightWave does a lot to pattern its camera's adjustments after its "real-world" counterpart, so if you come to LightWave knowing how to use a film camera, the transition will be very smooth. Even if the most

- The **Resolution** pop-up menu lets you choose from a list of presets that define the "base" size of your rendering.

- **Resolution Multiplier** is a pop-up menu that lets you *scale* your image (a multiplier of 50% on a resolution of 640x480 would yield a rendered image of 320x240) while still letting any special post-processing filters that calculate on a per-pixel basis think in terms of the "base" size set under Resolution. (See the following note if this is confusing.)

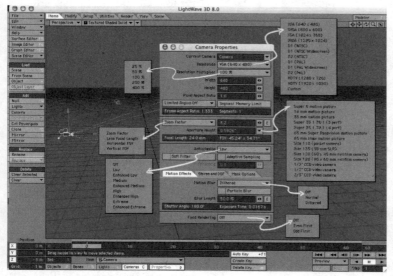

*Figure 4-1: The Camera Properties window.*

- **Width** and **Height** change to reflect the combination of the resolution and its multiplier. You can enter values here directly if you need to render to unique-sized formats.

- **Pixel Aspect Ratio** is an input field that changes

you've done to study photography is take a night course at a local college, you'll notice things like shutter speed and F-stop that at the very least should sound familiar.

LightWave's Camera Properties window, accessible by clicking **Properties** while the camera is selected, gives you access to many of the settings that control how your output will look.

- The **Current Camera** pop-up menu lists all the cameras you have in your scene; each camera can have its own, separate settings.

automatically when you select a (base) resolution from its pop-up menu. Pixel Aspect Ratio takes into account the fact that the pixels (picture elements) for PAL and NTSC aren't perfect squares, as they are on a computer monitor. Both PAL and NTSC, and their regular and wide-screen modes, each have separate aspect ratios. Because this field is automatically updated when you change the resolution to one of these television formats, you'll probably never have to worry about this value. But here it is, just in case.

## Note

One of my favorite post-process filters is Glow Effect, which we get into in Chapter 17. The way its settings work tell it how many pixels out from a "glowing" surface to spread the glow's effect.

With Resolution Multiplier, I can do a test render with a multiplier of 25% to save time. If the "base" resolution of my render was 640x480, it would then be reduced to 160x120, meaning that LightWave would only have to figure out the colors of 19,200 pixels, not 307,200 pixels. Because Resolution Multiplier is used (instead of manually setting the image size), the pixel-based setting in Glow Effect is *also* scaled.

Once I get the look I want in my test render, I can return the multiplier to 100%, knowing the effect I saw in the tiny, quick test will be the same in the full-size render.

● **Limited Region** is a pop-up menu that allows you to specify a smaller portion of the frame to render. It can only be adjusted while looking through the Camera view. Limited Region Borders will render full-sized frames; however, everything outside the limited region area will be masked off in black. Limited Region No Border will crop the area normally masked out by the

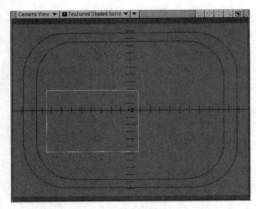

*Figure 4-2: Pressing <l> while looking through a Camera viewport both activates Limited Region and allows you to adjust it by clicking on the dotted yellow line that appears and dragging it to resize.*

Borders option, thereby giving you an image whose dimensions are exactly the size of your limited region.

## Note

Limited Region is useful when you've got an intense scene that takes minutes to render and you are working on tweaking one small area of that scene. You could also use Limited Region if you wanted to render a "wide-screen" format and a "TV" (1:1.333) version without destroying your composition by "panning and scanning." (You'd be doing the same thing that some directors do when they choose to shoot on super 35mm when they know their work will be seen on both the silver and small screens.)

● **Segment Memory Limit** opens a panel where you can specify the amount of memory that LightWave sets aside for the rendering of each piece of the finished frame. The default of 8 MB is large enough to render a 640x480 frame in a single segment.

Small Segment Memory Limit settings are helpful when you have a limited amount of physical memory on your computer or on a render node. It is almost always faster to render an image in a single segment than it is to have a frame split up into several segments. What you want to do is find a setting for your computer that is as large as you need it to be to render your average work in a single segment without causing your machine to "dig too deeply" into virtual memory resources. (Disk access will always be slower than RAM.)

## Note

Some plug-ins require you to render your scenes in a single segment. So, if you're getting weird results in your renders when things looked just fine in your tiny test render, try upping the Segment Memory Limit.

• **Frame Aspect Ratio** is a readout that tells you about the ratio of your frame's width to its height. In Figure 4-1, Frame Aspect Ratio reads "1.333" because, with a Pixel Aspect Ratio of 1.0 (1 to 1) when you divide width by height, you get 1.333. (The industry officially calls this "1 to 1.333," or "1:1.333.")

• **Segments** tells you how many segments LightWave will need to render an image the size you've asked for with the amount of memory allocated under Segment Memory Limit.

• The **Zoom Factor** menu allows you to choose how you want to change LightWave's camera's zoom. Zoom Factor, Lens Focal Length, Horizontal FOV (Field of View), and Vertical FOV change the input field to the right to reflect that particular way of thinking about camera zoom.

> **Note**
>
> Notice the little "E" button to the right of the input field. You can access LightWave's Graph Editor through this button to envelope this setting to change over time.

• **Aperture Height** changes the size of the "gate" inside LightWave's virtual camera. It is a measure, in inches, of just how tall the exposed frame of film would be were it a real-world camera. You use this when you are matching your rendered imagery to be composited onto film that has been shot with a real camera. It affects how LightWave's camera calculates Depth of Field and Lens Focal Length. Aperture Height defaults to the height of a frame of 35mm motion picture film. Many other presets are available through the pop-up menu to the field's right.

• **Focal Length** and **FOV** (Field of View) are readouts that give you

information about the current settings based on Zoom Factor and Aperture Height.

• The **Antialiasing** pop-up menu gives you a list of settings from Off to Enhanced Extreme that specify how many passes LightWave makes to take the "jaggies" out of a picture. (See Figure 4-3.)

*Figure 4-3: Here's the text we created in the last chapter. The top version was rendered without antialiasing. You can see the sharp edges, especially where the light text meets the dark background. The bottom version was rendered with Enhanced Low antialiasing. Notice how much smoother those areas are.*

> **Note**
>
> The difference between Low, Medium, High, and Extreme antialiasing settings in LightWave is the number of passes used to "explore" the detail areas of a piece. Low makes *five* passes, Medium makes *nine* passes, High makes *seventeen* passes, and Extreme makes *thirty-three* passes. With each pass, LightWave is able to figure out more and more details that are smaller than a pixel.

• **Adaptive Sampling** is normally used when smoothing an image. This means that after it renders a pass, it goes around and finds all the pixels that differ a certain amount from their neighbor. (This level of acceptable difference is set in the **Threshold** input box.) LightWave then re-renders *only* those pixels, letting everything else stay as it is.

Using Adaptive Sampling, you can get a very good-looking image in a fraction of the time it would take to render and antialias on most other rendering engines. Without Adaptive Sampling, LightWave re-renders everything in the entire frame for each pass. This is good for when you have tiny surfacing details or intricate texturing with detail smaller than a single pixel of the rendered image. Rendering without Adaptive Sampling helps keep these "sub-pixel" textures from "crawling" during an animation.

> **Note**
>
> Adaptive Sampling tends not to do so well when rendering text that is just a set of flat polygons. When rendering text, it is best to deactivate Adaptive Sampling and switch to an Enhanced level of antialiasing, which figures in almost twice as many samples per pixel.

● **Soft Filter** renders the objects in your scene with the "softness" of film (the background isn't affected by Soft Filter). This setting doesn't seem to be a "blur" of a kind that post-processing can mimic; it appears to actually change the way LightWave renders. If you're looking for a more "filmic" render, as opposed to something more "video-like," this, in conjunction with a Film Grain image filter, is your key to getting that look.

● **Motion Blur** becomes an option when you activate Antialiasing. With Motion Blur on, each antialiasing pass is not only rendered in its entirety, but each pass is also rendered from a slightly different point on LightWave's timeline. (Adaptive Sampling is *not* active when rendering with Motion Blur or Depth of Field, *even though the Adaptive Sampling box may remain checked*.) The result of this is an image that shows

the precise effect of your object's motion that would be too quick for LightWave's "shutter" to "freeze."

Because of the way this motion blur is calculated, factoring in a minutely different point on LightWave's timeline for each antialiasing pass, the more passes, the smoother and more "realistic" the render will be. So, the higher the level of antialiasing, the better your rendered image; this is why you'd want to use High or Extreme levels of antialiasing when rendering Motion Blur (or Depth of Field).

● The **Particle Blur** check box tells LightWave whether or not you want to blur single-point polys (particles) as well as "regular" objects.

● **Blur Length** is linked to the **Shutter Angle** and **Exposure Time** readouts, which tell you about your Blur Length setting in terms a cinematographer is familiar with. The higher the number, the longer the blur. (You can get some neat effects by having a Blur Length well over 100% or well under –100%.)

> **Note**
>
> The Motion Blur settings in the Camera Properties window give you the most accurate kind of motion blur, but they aren't the only way to have your objects blur in relation to their change in position over time. A huge factor in creating any art is to "give the illusion of" rather than "exactly recreating."
>
> Clever artists/programmers found out that they could "smudge" the pixels of an object based on its motion data available for that particular frame. And so came about a neat little plug-in called Vector Blur. You can find it under Scene | Effects | Image Processing | Add Image Filter. You can find out more about this plug-in in the LightWave manual, but in short, it is a way of quickly giving the illusion of motion blur without LightWave having to go through all the steps necessary to create good-looking exact motion blur.

• **Field Rendering**, at the bottom of the Motion Effects tab of the Camera Properties window, lets you render to the *scan-line fields* that make up an NTSC or PAL image. Think of every row of pixels as being numbered from 0 to 480. (Even First renders the even fields one frame before rendering the odd fields; Odd First does the opposite.)

> **Note**
>
> NTSC may run at 30 frames per second, but each frame is actually made up of two interwoven "frames," the even fields making up one of these "sub-frames" and the odd fields making up the other. When a TV set plays back a frame, it draws one field first. Then when those phosphors are "dying out," the scan-line goes back to the top of the screen and draws the second field. The result that our eyes perceive is 60 complete images per second, even though the data is only streamed through at 30 frames per second!

You use this setting when you want to get the absolute smoothest possible output on video and the tool you use to get your animation from your computer to video doesn't automatically separate your playback into fields or when you are compositing to "raw" captured video that hasn't been "de-interlaced."

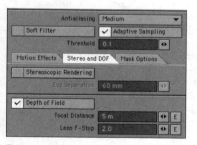

Figure 4-4: Under the Stereo and DOF tab, you'll find the tools that allow you to render your image in true "stereo" vision and recreate the depth-of-field effects you'd see when using a real camera.

• **Stereoscopic Rendering** will save your renders as *two separate images*, with the camera for each "eye" separated by the distance in the **Eye Separation** input field. (These can be combined into the kind of "red/blue" stereograph shown in Figure 4-5 using the Anaglyph Stereo: Compose image filter. See the LightWave manual for more information.)

Figure 4-5

• **Depth of Field** becomes an option when you have Antialiasing set to Medium or higher. As with Motion Blur, the higher the level of antialiasing, the better the final render will look.

• **Focal Distance** tells LightWave where you want to be "focusing." The **Lens F-Stop** setting tells LightWave how much area around your *focal distance* will be "in focus" (just like a real camera, the higher the F-stop, the larger the area that will be in focus).

Note

Depth of field is some pretty complex stuff to wrap your mind around if you're just starting out. If you really want to delve into this, the LightWave manual does a good job of explaining the details of the settings and how to make the most of them.

Also, be sure to check out the Digital Confusion image filter in the LightWave manual. Just as Vector Blur is a way of quickly approximating motion blur, the Digital Confusion plug-in is a way of quickly approximating depth of field.

# Rendering

So you know how to "twist the dials" of LightWave's camera. How do you snap a picture? You can think of <F9> as the shutter release.

## Hot Key Block

| | |
|---|---|
| <F9> | Render current frame |
| <F10> | Render all frames |
| <F11> | Render selected objects |

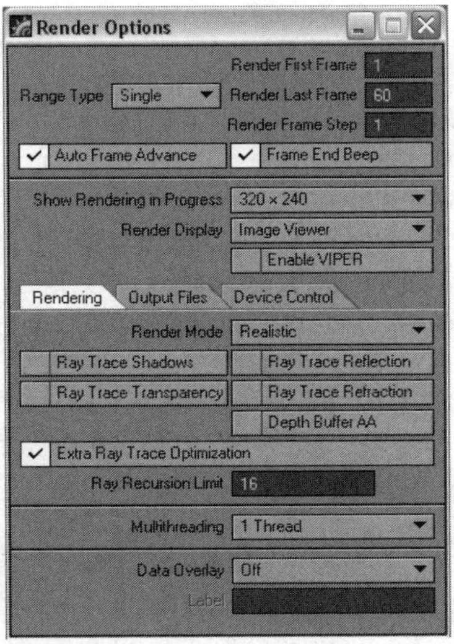

*Figure 4-6: The Render Options window.*

The Render Options window is accessed using **Render | Render Options**. In this window, you tell LightWave the frame range you want to render (which doesn't have to be the same as what you've set in the main

Layout window) by entering information into the Render First Frame and Render Last Frame fields. (You can tell LightWave to skip *n* frames as it renders by changing the value for Render Frame Step.)

●  **Range Type** allows you to specify which frames LightWave will render. In versions prior to 8.0, LightWave only had one range type: Single. Single allows you to specify a single sequence of frames to render. This is the most commonly used range type; however, 8.0 adds two new useful options. Arbitrary allows you to choose both ranges and individual frames (for example, frames 1-10, 15, 20, and 25-30). This is similar to the way ranges of pages can be printed from products such as Microsoft Word. Ranges are entered with a number followed by a dash and then another number. Individual frames can be added by separating them with commas. The Keyframe range allows you to render only the frames that have keyframes set for a particular object. This can be useful for creating animated storyboards by depicting only the key changes to a given object. When you choose the Keyframe range type, you are presented with the option to choose which object's keyframes LightWave will render, as well as the specific channel (such as movement, rotation, or scale) to watch for.

●  **Auto Frame Advance** tells LightWave not to stop and wait for your OK after

each frame renders
when rendering all
frames. (Though it
defaults to being
checked now, be sure
to verify this before
rendering your entire
scene. It's frustrating
to come back from
lunch expecting your
movie to be done and
finding "Click OK to
continue" sitting qui-
etly above your first
and only rendered
frame.)

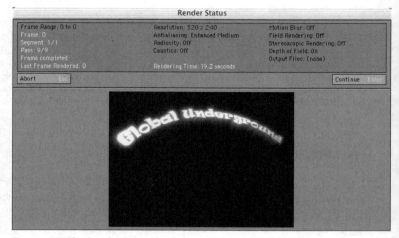

Figure 4-7: The Render Status window.

• **Frame End Beep** makes your computer beep after every frame is rendered.
(Though it can get annoying, when it is
active you know that when there's a long
period without the computer beeping, you
need to come back and check something.)

• The **Show Rendering in Progress**
pop-up menu lets you choose the size of the
window in which you watch your render
take shape. (Regardless of whether you are
watching the progress of the render, the
status information at the top of the window
shown in Figure 4-7 will always be visible
during a render.)

• **Render Display** lets you choose
whether or not you wish to have your render "held" for you in a window similar to
this after you're done rendering. (If you do
not have Render Display active and you
press F9, the Show Rendering in Progress
window is all you'll ever see of your
render.)

Render Display also lets you choose
whether the displayed frame you see will
be viewed in the "standard" 32-bit color
(24-bit "true" color plus an eight-bit transparency, or alpha, channel) by choosing the

"standard" image viewer. You can also view,
save, and balance your render display by
choosing Image Viewer FP, working with
the image data in LightWave's internal,
IEEE-compliant, floating-point color
buffers.

Using the pop-up menus on the Render
Display window in Figure 4-8, you can
manipulate the exposure of and/or save the
image (under the File pop-up), zoom in or
out, scroll through a list of renders (under
the Layer pop-up) done while that particular Render Display window was open, or
choose whether you are looking at the color
image or the alpha channel.

Figure 4-8

- The **Enable VIPER** check box (see Figure 4-6) stores information about your render to be used later with LightWave's Versatile Interactive Preview Render. We get into VIPER later on in this chapter, but in a nutshell, it is a way for you to get real-time updates of your render when you make changes to surfaces or volumetrics.

- **Render Mode** is a pop-up menu that lets you choose what kind of rendering style your image will use. Realistic is the render mode you will use most often because it looks, well, most realistic. Quickshade gives you something that looks like a smooth-shaded GL view *that obeys Anti-aliasing, Motion Blur, and Depth of Field settings*! Wireframe renders your image as a wireframe and, like Quickshade, it obeys what you have set for Antialiasing, Motion Blur, and Depth of Field.

> **Note**
>
> Because Quickshade quickly renders your scene *and* shows you what your Motion Blur and Depth of Field settings will look like, it is a great way to preview those complex, and sometimes confusing, time-intensive camera settings!

When rendering in Realistic render mode, you are given the options to have Light-Wave precisely calculate how light casts shadows (Ray Trace Shadows), reflects from polished surfaces (Ray Trace Reflection), and is bent through transparent surfaces (Ray Trace Refraction). You can also allow volumetrics to be seen through all transparent surfaces (Ray Trace Transparency).

- **Extra Ray Trace Optimization** asks LightWave to take a bit more time before it actually begins to render a scene to figure out just what is affecting the rays of light. This can significantly *reduce* the time a

ray-traced scene takes to render if there are a lot of objects casting shadows, reflecting other parts of the scene, or bending light. If there *isn't* a lot of this going on in a scene, the time up-front it takes LightWave to do this extra optimization may *make the render take longer*! (The only way to know for sure is to render a test frame with this setting active. Compare how long it takes for the same frame to render without it active. Then proceed with your final render with the setting that gets the job done quickest.)

- **Ray Recursion Limit** tells LightWave how many times you want light to be able to bounce off of reflective surfaces before LightWave stops keeping track of what that ray of light is doing. I like to keep this number low (like 1 or 2) unless I'm specifically going for that "hall of mirrors" kind of effect.

- **Multithreading** is a pop-up menu that allows LightWave's renderer to make use of multiple processors present in a single computer. (This can speed up a render, but some of the more complex or older plug-ins do not work well under multithreading.)

*Figure 4-9: Using the Data Overlay and Label options.*

- **Data Overlay** puts a "burn-in" on your final image of the contents in the **Label** box and the time format you select in the pop-up menu.

**101**

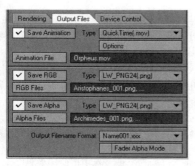

*Figure 4-10: The Output Files tab.*

The Output Files tab is where you tell LightWave to put the movies and frames you'll make when you select <F10> (**Render** [the entire] **Scene**).

- Under Save Animation, the **Type** pop-up lists several different animation formats, the most common being .AVI and QuickTime. The **Options** button opens an Options panel specific to the type of animation you are creating.

- The Save RGB **Type** pop-up presents a large number of file formats spanning many platforms. Choose your destination directory and type in your filename prefix under **RGB Files**, and LightWave does the rest.

Even though the RGB file type you've chosen may support alpha channels, you may wish to save your alpha separately.

- The **Save Alpha** options tell LightWave where you want the alpha

channels saved separately from the RGB images.

- **Output Filename Format** lets you choose from several numbering and naming conventions, just in case your files have to be read by a more pedantic picture processing program that needs its files named just the right way.

- **Fader Alpha Mode** affects *only the saved files*, not the Render Display window. With this active, the saved files will be saved with "straight mattes," as opposed to how LightWave normally saves its alphas as "premultiplied" with the background color — usually black. You use this most often when working with live, broadcast TV equipment or when rendering frames with lens flares or other delicate special FX that will be composited later.

> **Note**
>
> The Device Control tab is a bit of a holdover from when the *only* way to get your animations onto videotape was by using a single-frame VTR that supported external control. Though most people today use something like Video Toaster 4 to play their animations *directly* to their target tape media in real time, I'm sure the folks who stick by their old reliable single-frame VTRs are thankful that LightWave has not forgotten them.

# Lighting

Lighting is, beyond the shadow of a doubt, the most important factor in making anything look good in 3D. Because there are exceptional resources on lighting and lighting specifically in LightWave, such as

*LightWave 3D 8 Lighting* by Nicholas Boughen (Wordware Publishing), we're just going to blast through an application here and let books like Boughen's explain the "hows" and "whys" of it all.

## Note

Because lighting is so extremely important to how *every* form of visual art impacts its audience, it's a great idea to explore lighting in as many fashions as you can. Go through your art history books and see how masters like Rembrandt and Caravaggio handled lighting. Take a class on black-and-white photography (where the focus is *light*, not color). Take a class on theatrical lighting, or volunteer at your local community theater as an assistant lighting technician.

The more angles you can approach your work from, the better your work will look. (Besides, learning new things is fun!)

## Step 1: Load the Base Scene

Load **Scenes\Chapter_04\ StillLife_ 01_Lighting_Raw.lws** from where you have stored the companion files, and press <**F9**> to give it a render.

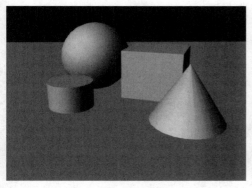

*Figure 4-11: The still life from the last chapter. Just as rendering it in pencil would help us to understand lighting in drawing, working with it here will do the same thing for 3D.*

## Step 2: Global Intensity

Clicking on the Global Illumination button in the Light Properties window (select the light and press <**p**> to activate the Properties window) brings up the Global Illumination window in which you can specify a variety of settings.

Using Global Light Intensity, you can *scale* every light in your scene at once. You can think of this as a way to adjust the contrast of your scene's lighting if you like. You can do the same thing with lens flares (the stars and sun dogs you see when you aim a film or CCD camera at a light) with the Global Lens Flare Intensity setting. (Used with *subtlety*, lens flares can be great tools; used garishly, they can make an image look cheap.) You can also disable and enable all flares, shadow maps, and volumetric lights (lights where you can see the beam of light, like sun filtering through a window).

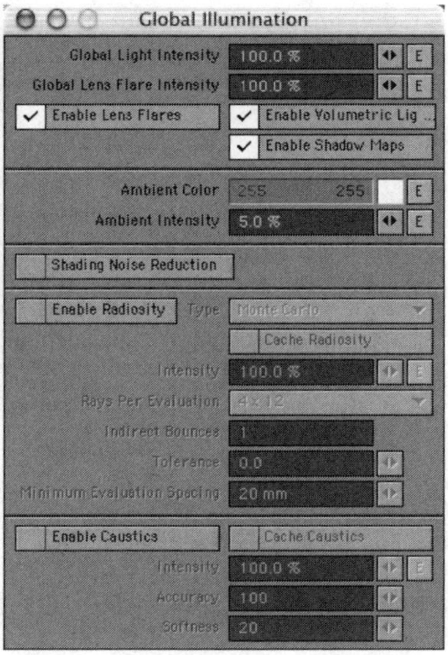

*Figure 4-12: The Global Illumination window.*

The setting we're interested in right now is Ambient Intensity, which is currently set at 5% by default.

LightWave's Ambient Intensity generates a pervasive, directionless light source. What does that mean in plain English? Well, if Global Intensity can be thought of as a contrast adjustment, Ambient Intensity would be a brightness adjustment. The more ambient light you pour into your scene, the brighter everything will become.

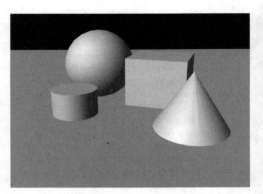

Figure 4-13: Everything has gotten a bit brighter than it was in Figure 4-11.

> **Note**
>
> When LightWave implemented radiosity (the ability for light to be bounced off objects and the environment), ambient lighting began to actually take on the qualities of "real" ambient light. When you're working with radiosity, as we will toward the end of this section, turn the Ambient Lighting setting up.

LightWave's default of 5% Ambient Intensity is a good base setting. But just to illustrate its use, change this to 25% and do another F9 test render.

The effects of the increased ambient light can be seen in Figure 4-13.

Once you've seen the effects of Ambient Intensity, change this setting to 0%.

> **Note**
>
> Something I do with ambient light when I don't want to get rid of it entirely is to set Ambient Color to a color that is *complementary* (opposite on the color wheel) to the primary light color used in my scene and change Ambient Intensity to something between 8% and 12%. This adds a nice bit of "richness" to the shadows, like the way shadows on snow on a sunny evening are a rich blue-violet.

## Step 3: Spotlight

Next, we're going to change the main light in the scene from the default distant light to a kind of light we'd have in the real world. Let's try a spotlight first and see how that looks.

a. With the light selected (by clicking on it or selecting it from the Current Item pop-up menu when Lights are the active Item type), press <**p**> to bring up the Light Properties window, as shown in Figure 4-14. (The viewport in the top left is set to Light View, which shows me what the light is seeing — the shaded circle around its outside shows me where the spotlight's light doesn't reach.)

Figure 4-14

**Note**

Remember, you can change your viewport layout to match my "2 Left, 1 Right" layout through Display Options | Viewport Layout.

b.  I've changed the light's color from 255, 255, 255 (white) to a bit of a bluish tint and changed Light Type to **Spotlight**. Something else I'd like us to do is bring the Spotlight Soft Edge Angle up to **30.0°**, the same as the Spotlight Cone Angle. This means that the spotlight will fade in intensity evenly from

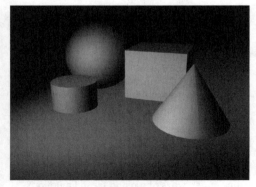

Figure 4-15: The still life looks a little more realistic now, but it's too dark, and without shadows, the objects look like they're "floating" over a nondescript plane.

its center to its outer edge. (The dashed line in the Light View viewport responds when I change this input, showing me where the light begins to fade from its base intensity.)

c.  As shown in Figure 4-16, increase Light Intensity to **125%**, and click on the **Shadows** tab so we can make the objects feel like they're "sitting" on something.

d.  I'm not a fan of the sharp, hard-edged shadows that ray tracing "casts" from spotlights, so I'm not even going to go there. We're going to start right off with a Shadow Type of **Shadow Map**. Shadow maps are quick to calculate, they look good enough under most circumstances, and they let spots cast soft-edged shadows.

How "good" a shadow map looks is directly related to how large it is. It is, after all, only a 2D "bitmap" created from the light's point

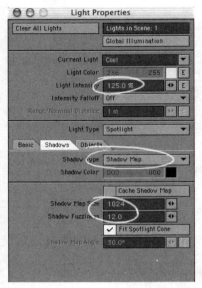

Figure 4-16

Figure 4-17: Not bad... sterile, but not bad.

## Step 4: Why Do Things Look "3D"?

What makes something look "3D"? Just the fact that it *is* 3D isn't enough; an actor's face can look flat if it's not lit well by the crew's director of photography.

The general rule of thumb for making something look 3D is to hit it with a warm (in terms of what color it is) light on one side and a cool light on the other side. One light should be much brighter than the other. And that's it — for the most extreme "basics" of lighting at least.

of view as to what it "sees" and what is "hidden" from it. For most of my video work, I generally use a Shadow Map Size of 1,024. It produces a good-looking shadow map for most instances, without eating a lot of my computer's physical memory while the scene renders.

The Shadow Fuzziness setting has always seemed a bit arbitrary to me. I've done a couple of quick test renders and found that 12 gives me the shadow softness I'm looking for.

You can save a little time in rendering a scene if a shadow-mapped spotlight doesn't move and nothing moves through its "beam" by activating Cache Shadow Map. This uses the shadow map data generated by the first frame rendered for all the other frames in that render.

You can manually change the shadow map's "view" by deactivating Fit Spotlight Cone and fiddling with the Shadow Map Angle setting. For all but the most "hackerish" circumstances, you'll want the shadow map to fit the spotlight's cone exactly.

### Note

One of the reasons I stress studying theatrical lighting so much is that a theatrical lighting director must make his set and actors look 3D, even to someone sitting in the cheap seats at the back of a 5,000-seat auditorium. All he has to do this with are spots in the auditorium aiming at the stage and banks of warm and cool lights hanging directly above the stage.

Challenging? Yes. But theatrical lighting directors, over many, many years, have developed ways of making these limitations work and work well. The best way to know what they know is to work a few shows with them.

We're going to be adding another light and moving it around, and the easiest way to move lights is to have them target something; that way you don't have to move, then aim, move, then aim again, etc.

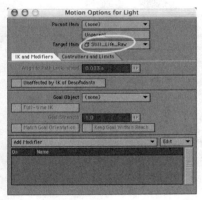

Figure 4-18: The Motion Options window.

a.  With your light still selected, press <m> to bring up the Motion Options window for that light.

b.  In the Target Item pop-up menu, select **Still_Life_Raw**. The light will always have that item's pivot point centered directly in its field of view.

c.  Since the settings for our current light are pretty okay, rather than start from scratch for the new light, let's clone this light so the new one is an exact replica of the old. **Items | Add | Clone** brings up a little window where you can tell LightWave how many clones of that item you want. Let's just go for one at the moment.

**Note**

If you have more than one light set for Max OpenGL Lights in your Display Options, you immediately see the effect of the new light in your shaded view(s).

d.  Before we do anything else, let's make it easier for us to distinguish between these two lights. LightWave automatically tacks on a parenthetical number to items with the same name in a scene, but we can do more.

Change your view type to Schematic. We'll use Schematic view to rename our lights and change the way they are depicted in Layout.

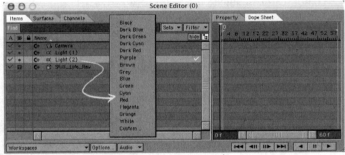

Figure 4-19: The Schematic view.

The Schematic view may seem scary at first, but it actually provides a fun, powerful way to organize and view the contents in your scene. Every item is represented by a small colored bar. These bars can be moved around to your liking without affecting the actual object's position within Layout. While other organizational tools such as the Scene Editor provide you with a highly structured means for managing content, the Schematic view takes a more free-form approach, allowing you to arrange items as if they were strips of paper laid out on a large table.

**107**

e.  We'll save the organization for another time. For now, simply right-click on the light labeled **Light (2)**. From the pop-up menu, choose **Rename** and change its name to **Warm**. Then right-click it again and use the Set Color option to change its Sketch Color (the color with which it is depicted in Layout) to **Orange**.

f.  After changing Light (2)'s name, the parenthetical after the first light went away; there weren't two items of the same name for you to keep track of. Still, let's change that light's name to **Cool** and its Sketch Color to **Blue**.

g.  Bring up the Light Properties window if it's not already open. For the light named Warm, change its Light Color to a soft, warm ochre (**252, 218, 154**) and change its Light Intensity to **42%**. I've also set its Shadow Fuzziness to **24** to add a bit of visual variety and to give a bit of a visual cue to viewers that the lights on either side are not identical.

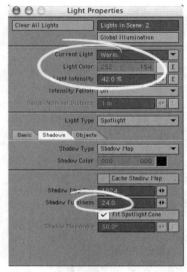

*Figure 4-20*

h.  As shown in Figure 4-21, move Warm to the right of the still life and up (in Y) just a little.

> **Note**
>
> The finished scene for this step is: Scenes\ Chapter_04\StillLife_02_Spot_F.lws.

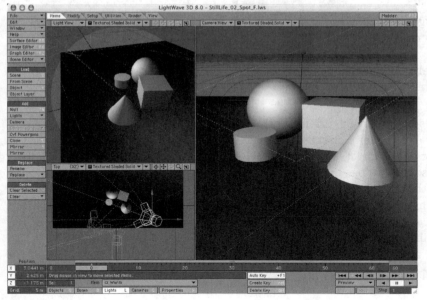

*Figure 4-21*

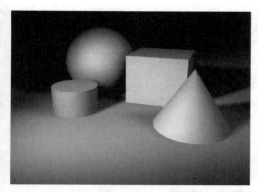

Figure 4-22: Rendering what we've got, the still life is beginning to show both depth and warmth.

## Step 5: Ray-Traced Soft Shadows

What if you want things to look more realistic? (Figure 4-22 looks neat, but it still has a flavor of 3D-ish-ness to it.) LightWave gives you area and linear lights to have it figure out *exactly* what the shadows would look like when cast from a light that has some surface area to it, like a fluorescent tube or a light with a diffusing screen in front of it.

a.  In the Light Properties window, set the Light Type of both your lights to **Area Light**. Because area lights tend to be a lot brighter than other kinds of lights, change the Light Intensity for Cool to **50%** and for Warm to **18%**. Double-check both lights to make sure Shadow Type is set to **Ray Trace**.

> **Note**
>
> Setting the Shadow Type to Ray Trace tells the *lights* that you want them to calculate exact shadows. LightWave's rendering engine still needs to know that *it* needs to pay attention to Ray Trace Shadows. *Be sure this is active under the Rendering Options.*

b.  Area lights cast light away from their surface, so the larger the surface, the softer the shadows. I want the Warm light, the least intense of the two, to cast very soft shadows. With Warm selected, activate the Size tool under **Modify | Transform | Size**. In the numeric input panel (in the lower left of LightWave's window), enter **2 m** for all axes of the item's scale.

Give things a render.

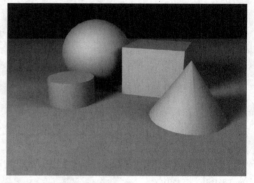

Figure 4-23: The light in this render behaves more like it does in the real world.

> **Note**
>
> Area and linear lights can have a "graini-ness" to their shadows. You can reduce this by increasing the Linear/Area Light Quality setting in the Light Properties window. You can enter values from 1 to 5, 1 being fast but not so good and 5 being slow but very polished. (The default value is 4.)
>
> You can also reduce the graininess of all shadows by activating Shading Noise Reduc-tion, accessible in the Global Illumination window. This adds a Shading Noise Reduc-tion pass to every antialiasing pass of your render. It does slow things down, but what it does for the quality of the output is worth the wait in a final render.

> **Note**
>
> The finished scene for this step is: Scenes\Chapter_04\StillLife_03_Area_F.lws.

# Step 6: Falloff (Atmosphere)

Even in a small room, the air absorbs "wavicles" of light, so the area of a wall nearest a lamp is significantly brighter than the wall on the opposite side of the room. One of the tools that we have to recreate this is the Intensity Falloff setting in each light's Light Properties window.

When Intensity Falloff is set to Linear, the light's intensity falls off in a smooth, linear fashion, falling to 0% at the distance set in the Range/Nominal Distance field.

When the Intensity Falloff is set to Inverse Distance, the light's intensity falls off in a parabola, and the value in Range/Nominal Distance shows the place where the light's intensity *will be what you set it at in the Light Intensity field*. (*Inside* that "nominal distance," the intensity of the light will *increase* along the same parabola of Intensity = –1 * Distance to Light.)

When the Intensity Falloff is set to Inverse Distance ^2, the formula creates a much steeper curve for the light's intensity (the effect of there being lots of stuff in the atmosphere to absorb the little wavicles of light).

a. Set both lights to have an Intensity Falloff of **Inverse Distance**.

b. In a Top viewport, adjust the slider buttons (to the immediate right of the Range/Nominal Distance field) so the dotted ring for the light passes through the approximate center of the still life (see Figure 4-24).

Render away!

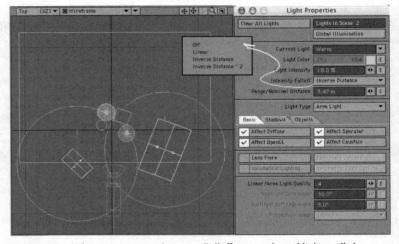

Figure 4-24: When you activate Intensity Falloff, your selected lights will show a dotted ring around them in orthogonal views, giving you a visual for the setting in the Range/Nominal Distance field.

Figure 4-25: The difference is subtle but significant. This render looks even more "realistic."

> **Note**
>
> When talking with clients who are new to 3D, I've found the best analogy to familiarize them with the process of zeroing in on the look of the piece is by saying this is like chiseling a sculpture out of marble. You can hew the rough form out of the block pretty quickly, and it looks okay. But each step toward that final polish takes exponentially more time than the last, and the visible differences to the untrained eye get smaller and smaller.
>
> So, when you psyche yourself up for doing something strictly for yourself in a realistic vein, just know that to get things perfect will take a lot more time, both for you and for the computer to calculate, than the early, rough strokes.
>
> This is why I lean toward using 3D and LightWave as an artistic tool — to make a comment *about* reality rather than try to recreate it exactly. Knowing how to run an airbrush so well that you can make a painting of glass look photo-real (or hyper-real) is good for developing your skill set, but if doing that doesn't fill your soul with passion, don't feel that it's a prerequisite to being "good."

In the opening paragraph to this step, I mentioned that Intensity Falloff is only *one* of the ways you can simulate the effect of atmosphere on light. The other way is by using LightWave's fog functions, which are found under **Scene | Effects | Volumetrics.**

In the Volumetrics window you can choose the Fog Type, which amounts to basically the same settings as you have for the light's Intensity Falloff. Here, they're labeled Linear, Nonlinear 1, and Nonlinear 2. (The little box on the left shows a visual interpretation of the "falloff" curve.)

Most of the settings are self-explanatory, except perhaps for Use Backdrop Color. This check box lets you "fog" your scene with whatever you set in the Backdrop tab

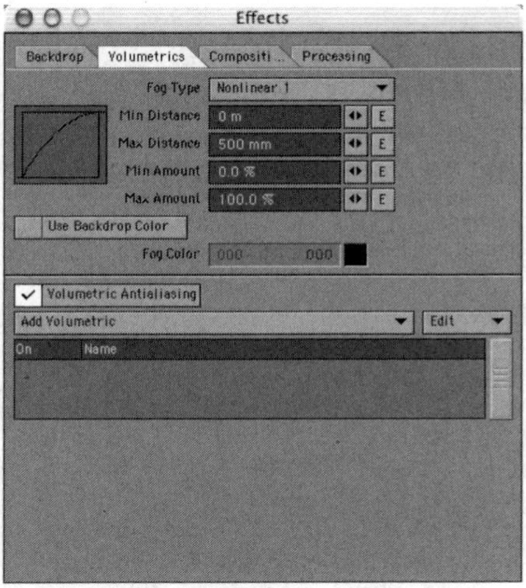


*Figure 4-26: The Volumetrics window.*

(just to this tab's left), which can be a texture, image sequence, or movie. This combination of "backdrop" fog and using a "gaseous" animated backdrop is a good, *fast* way of heightening the impression that your scene takes place underwater or in a nebula.

When you're working on a scene, regardless of it being an exterior or an interior shot, a little *hint* of fog almost always adds to the feeling of it being a real place. Only in desert places where there is no humidity, including the arctic tundra when it's –40° C/F, or in the vacuum of space does light travel unhindered. Everywhere else you have at least *some* atmospheric perspective going on. You might not notice it, but it's there. Your "realistic" scene will benefit from that little bit of "unnoticeable" fog.

> **Note**
>
> The finished scene for this step is Scenes\Chapter_04\StillLife_04_Falloff_F.lws.

# Step 7: Radiosity

You want even *more* "real?" Okay. Light-Wave's radiosity lets light *bounce* off surfaces, illuminating those nearby.

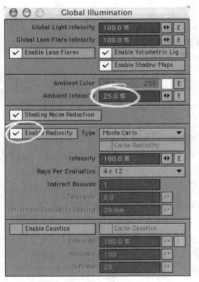

Figure 4-27

a. Leaving everything else as it is, open the Global Illumination panel again and choose **Enable Radiosity**, leaving it at its default Type, Monte Carlo. Don't forget to increase Ambient Intensity to **25%**.

Render away!

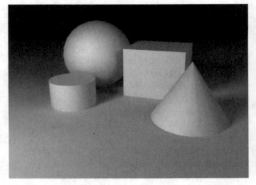

Figure 4-28: The differences are subtle but powerful. With light now able to "bounce" from surface to surface, this looks even more like a snapshot of something from the real world.

**Note**

The finished scene for this render is: Scenes\Chapter_04\StillLife_05_Radiosity1_F.lws.

Now, if you're saying, "Looks good, but *dang*, that took a long time," I totally hear you. With radiosity, as with just about everything else in LightWave, you have the choice to do things real or do things that approximate real.

Figure 4-29

b. Go back into the Global Illumination panel, and change the radiosity Type to **Backdrop Only**. Change its Intensity to **69%** as well.

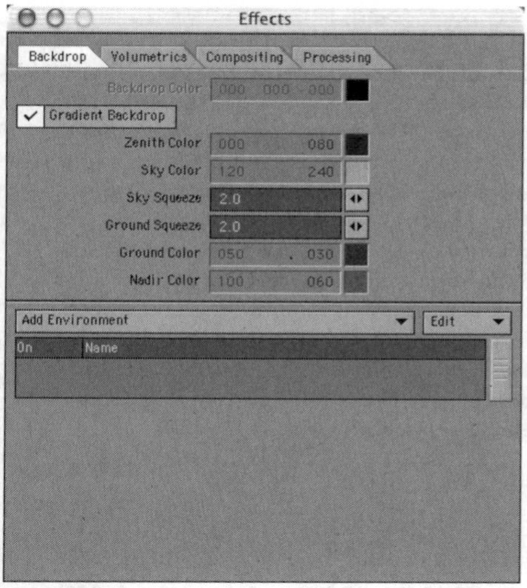

Figure 4-30

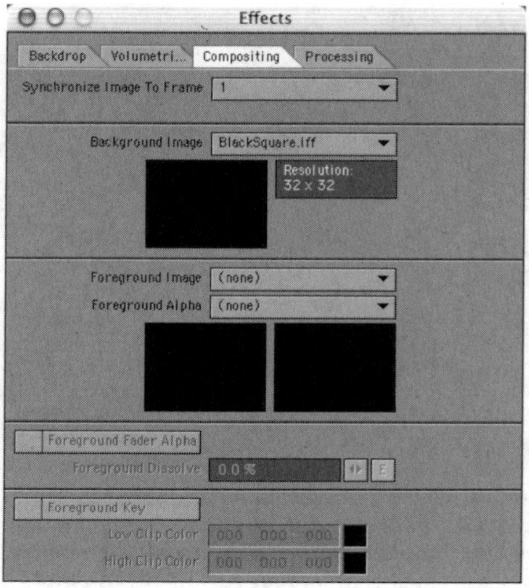

Figure 4-31

c.   <Ctrl> + <F5> brings up the Back-drop tab of the Effects window. Activate **Gradient Backdrop**, and accept the default colors and settings.

---

**Note**

*Zenith* is the part of the sky that is directly overhead. *Sky* refers to the sky color at the horizon. *Ground* refers to the ground color at the horizon. *Nadir* is the ground color directly below the horizon.

(Zenith and nadir are points on the "celestial sphere," an imaginary, infinitely large sphere with the Earth at its center and all the heavenly bodies appearing to be "painted" on its inward-facing surface.)

---

d.   Now, if we were to render at this point, we'd see a bit of the gradient back-drop's color peeking up above the back of the ground plane of our still life. Here's a trick I use when I want to use Backdrop Only radiosity for generating elements to be composited later onto a photographic plate, which requires me to keep the background of my rendered image black:

Switch to the **Compositing** tab in the Effects window, and under the Background Image pop-up menu, choose **(load Image)**. In the requester, choose **Images\Black-Square.iff**.

You'll notice that BlackSquare is only 32 pixels by 32 pixels. However, it is all black (0, 0, 0), and as the background image, it will be automatically stretched to perfectly fill the entire back of the Camera view of your scene, no matter what resolution you render.

---

**Note**

The trick of using tiny solid-colored swatches of colors as opposed to full-sized images for background, texturing, or whatever came about in order to save memory during complex renders. The less memory LightWave has to reserve for the images in a scene, the more it has available to calculate before it has to hit virtual memory.

---

**113**

Render away!

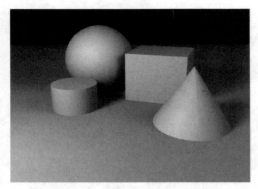

Figure 4-32: *For being a "fake," it doesn't look bad at all. The fact that it took one-quarter the time "real" radiosity took makes it look even better (from a production manager's point of view, that is).*

Note

One of the coolest uses of Backdrop Only radiosity is to use the image, sequence, or movie you'll be compositing your work onto (either in LightWave or in a compositing program like Video Toaster 4, Digital Fusion, After Effects, Chalice, Flint, Flame, or Inferno) as a texture environment (Window | Backdrop Options | Add Environment | Texture Environment) to light your entire scene! This quickly lets you get an *exact match* for the lighting in your "live-action" plate, using only one or two other lights in your scene for generating shadows.

Note

The scene for the above render is: Scenes\ Chapter_04\StillLife_06_Radiosity2_F.lws.

## Advanced Surfacing

The first thing that comes to most people's minds when they think of computer graphics (CG) is those chrome spheres floating over infinite chessboards done in the early '80s or some other long-past concept of what 3D is capable of doing. Today, using just LightWave's lighting and surfacing features, you can create models that even the sharpest expert can't tell from real life.

Whether your aim is to make something look real or just make something look good, there are two main things you've got to keep in mind when working on surfacing: *subtlety* and *layering*. Things that look good rarely make a big show of looking good (subtlety). Things that look good generally have many levels of things about them that hold your eye (layering).

Note

As an artist, you will need to be able to sort out what things "really" look like, what you "think" they look like, and what people in general "expect" them to look like.

Let's take a look at a chrome sphere for our first example.

## Step 1: Chrome Sphere

a. Load **Scenes\Chapter_04\StillLife_ 07_Surfacing1_Raw.lws** to get us all started at the same point.

b. With the StillLife_Raw object selected, use **File | Save | Save Current Object** to save the object as something you can work with, preserving the "raw" version for later, if you ever need it.

### Note

Surfaces, textures, shader settings, and the like are saved with the objects. All the movements of all the items, the lights, and the camera settings are saved with the scene file. When you make any changes to the surfacing of an object you don't want to lose, *save the object!*

This may seem a strange way of doing things if you are coming to LightWave from another package that saves the whole shebang in one gargantuan file. This keeps scene file size down to almost microscopic

proportions in comparison. It also allows for a production pipeline where modelers and animators can be evolving the scene toward "final" together, at the same time (by simply updating the models the scene references).

If you want to leave yourself a way to backtrack to an earlier version, you've got upward of 60 to 90 revisions of a scene before you call it done. LightWave's small file size means that saving the scene takes almost no time and no server space!

c. Open Layout's Surface Editor as shown in Figure 4-33. (Notice how it's identical to what we were looking at in Modeler.) Select the **Sphere** surface.

d. What's the first thing that comes to your mind when you think of "chrome"? It's super-*reflective*, right? Turn Reflection up to **100%**, turn on **Ray Trace Reflection** under Render Options, and do a test render.

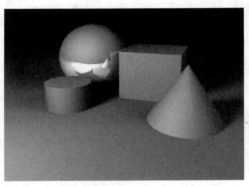

Figure 4-34: Cool! And yes, it's reflective — but it looks like we're on a soundstage of some sort.

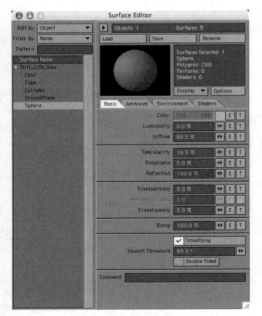

Figure 4-33: The Surface Editor.

We associate a certain look with chrome because, more often than not, it is photographed outside, on a mostly clear day, with blue sky, maybe a few clouds, and perhaps a bit of a tree line in the background to reflect. Well, guess what? We don't have that in this scene. If we were to try to build all that geometry just to reflect in a silly little test sphere, we'd be candidates for some serious therapy afterward.

Instead of racking our brains trying to build something to reflect in the sphere, we can apply a *reflection map*, which is like a texture map, only LightWave makes it "move" around the surface of the object as if it were actually being reflected. It is a

**115**

cheap, quick way of *approximating* the *look* of a reflective surface.

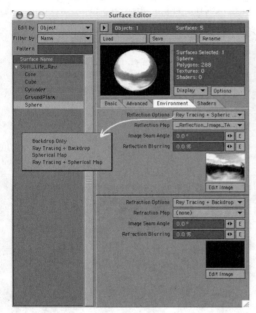

Figure 4-35

e.  Under the Environment tab, select **Ray Tracing + Spherical Map** from the Reflection Options pop-up menu.

The options under Reflection Options are:

● **Backdrop Only** "fakes" reflections by making *only* the *backdrop* appear to "reflect" from the surface.

● **Ray Tracing + Backdrop** adds "true" reflections to this (when you have Ray Trace Reflection active under the Render Options).

● **Spherical Map** "fakes" reflections using *only* the image used as the *reflection map*.

● **Ray Tracing + Spherical Map** adds "true" reflections to whatever image you are using as a reflection map. (If you have no reflection map image specified, this is just ray tracing over black.)

f.  Under Reflection Map, choose **(load image)** and select **Images\_Reflection_Image_TA.iff.**

Render away!

Figure 4-36: Somewhat less than excellent, huh? We've got to go into the Basic settings and tone some things down. (Subtlety.)

g.  Items that *reflect* light cleanly do not generally also *scatter* it as well. So, knock the Diffuse down to **30%**.

h.  I've found that even the most reflective of real-world things don't reflect as well as LightWave's 100% Reflection setting calculates. Change the Reflection setting to **55%**.

Render again.

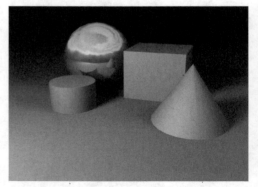

Figure 4-37: It looks a lot more like the chrome sphere is sitting in among the other objects now. Even though we can't really see the things the sphere is reflecting, we've been trained to think of chrome looking something like this.

## Note

When you have a surface that you're moderately happy with, right-click on it and copy it before you go making changes. You could go so far as to save it or add it to your presets if you wanted to, but *always* give yourself the ability to go back to something you know was acceptable, lest you find yourself having buggered up something that at one time was perfectly fine.

# Step 2: "Realistic" Reflections

Let's get rid of the chrome sphere. (I've never been one for chrome spheres, but as homage to those who have gone before us, we did one.) Copy and paste the surface from the cone onto the sphere, and let's move on to something a bit more subtle.

Many things reflect in real life, but most of them do so with such subtlety that we aren't even aware of it. Not just the obvious things, like an inactive CRT, but things like tabletops, book covers, a Wacom pad, whatever. These objects don't reflect very cleanly; you usually only see reflections in them when another object is very close. We don't usually pay any attention to these subtle reflections, as they just make up part of the *layering* that makes the real world seem real.

a.  Select the **GroundPlane** surface and set its Reflection to **9%**.

b.  Make sure that Reflection Options on the Environment tab is set to **Ray Tracing + Spherical Map** and that you have *no* reflection map specified. (If you load this object, or surface, into a scene that has a pronounced backdrop, it won't reflect it unless you tell it you want the backdrop reflected by changing this to Ray Tracing + Backdrop.)

Give 'er a render!

Figure 4-38: Notice how prominent the reflections are for only having a setting of 9%. For a surface in real life to reflect that well, it would have to be supremely buffed and polished.

c.  Click on the little **T** button next to the Bump field on the Basic tab of the Surface Editor to open the Texture Editor window. (All Texture Editor windows are basically the same, whether for Bump or Color or any other surfacing channel.)

d.  Change the Layer Type to **Procedural Texture**.

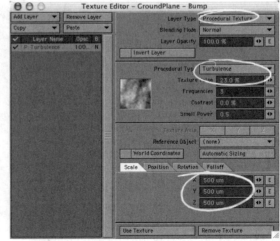

Figure 4-39

e.  Make sure the Procedural Type is set to **Turbulence**.

f.  Set the Texture Value to **23%** (leaving Frequencies, Contrast, and Small Power alone).

g.  Set the X, Y, and Z Scale for this texture at **500 um** (.0005 meters).

h.  Click on **Use Texture** to close the Texture Editor window if you want to get it out of your way. (There's no harm in leaving it open.)

Render away!

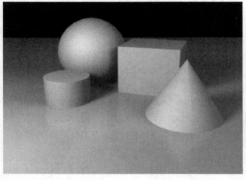

*Figure 4-40: The "micro" bump map that we added causes the reflection to be dispersed as it gets farther away from the surface it is reflecting — just like in real life.*

> **Note**
>
> Remember, in order for smaller and smaller textural details (like the "micro" bump we just added) to be properly interpreted by LightWave's renderer, you need to increase the antialiasing level. The smaller the detail, the greater the level of antialiasing needed in order for it to be properly rendered.

The render in Figure 4-40 is pretty good, but I want to see it look better. What's bothering me about it is that we can see the little pieces of reflection that the bump map is dispersing. I've tried making the bump map even smaller, but it doesn't give me

the softness I want in the reflection without setting Antialiasing to an amount that takes much longer to render than I care to wait. (Which is also the reason I'm not quite fond of the Reflection Blurring setting under the Environment tab — it takes tons of AA to get it to look good.)

Luckily, there's an image filter that LightWave ships with that softens reflections. Image filters are applied after everything else is done and then access the data LightWave generates as it renders, using that as a map to modify the final, rendered image.

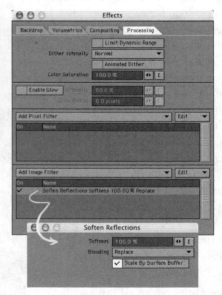

*Figure 4-41: Soften Reflections will take the edge off any reflections in the render.*

i.  Click on **Add Image Filter** under the Processing tab of the Effects window (via Window | Image Processing or by pressing <Ctrl> + <F8>) and choose **Soften Reflections**.

j.  Double-click on the newly added image filter to get the properties for the filter.

Leave Softness at **100%** and Blending at **Replace**.

Render away!

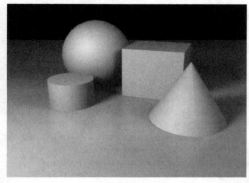

*Figure 4-42: The reflections of the other objects in the ground plane now look like something you'd see in real life.*

Save your still life object, and let's move on!

---

## Note

Notice in Figure 4-41 that there's a check box labeled Scale By Surface Buffer. With this checked, the amount of softening applied to a surface is multiplied by whatever number you enter into the Special Buffers 1 field of the Special Buffers Options window (accessed through Surfacing | Advanced | Special Buffers).

To the best of my knowledge, the softening effect won't go beyond what it does at 100%.

## Step 3: Exploring a Surface Preset

Let's take apart a surface that looks good to figure out what makes it tick. Let's also continue to use the scene from the previous step — it gives us a good-looking base to work from.

a.  With the **Sphere** surface selected, browse through the Presets and double-click on **Rock_2** once you've found it (see Figure 4-43).

*Figure 4-43*

---

## Note

*Subtlety...*
The thing about getting into any new area of art is that you are exposed to so many new visuals that it is easy to make broad gestures about what you're seeing. A master doesn't really care if someone sees his mastery or not. But it's there for those who wish to see.

Like the subtlety of "good acting," the reflection we created in Figure 4-42 gives us the feeling of being real because it quietly makes a statement we are familiar with in our daily experience in the real world. ("Bad acting" is often just "big acting.")

With your art, and this is very much an art, explore making the minimum statement possible about a thing in order for it to be read by an observant audience. The reflection of the other objects on the ground plane isn't something you notice right away, but it is there, and it feels "right" in its *subtlety*.

b.  Reducing the Diffuse on your sphere to **69%** (from the 80% Diffuse Rock_2 preset comes in with), render a frame and take a look at what the settings give us.

*Figure 4-44*

The sphere now looks like a very realistic, roughly hewn sphere of some kind of sedimentary rock that has seen a bit of wear and tear. There are no image maps used in generating this complex, real-world feel, only mathematical formulae. How does it do it? (More importantly, how can we do the same thing?)

The main, driving force behind this rock texture is what is in the Bump channel. Opening the Texture Editor window for the Bump channel, we find that it is being generated by the procedural texture Crumple (see Figure 4-45).

> **Note**
>
> The settings of procedural textures have always seemed a bit arcane to me. To help me understand what does what, I make mental notes about the settings in procedurals that look good, and then try those settings first in my own procedurals.
>
> There are a few conventions that hold true:
>
> • The higher the Texture Value, the more "contrasty" the texture will be.
> • The higher the Frequencies, the more detail there will be in the texture.
> • The higher the Small Power, the "sharper" the detail will be.
>
> I've also found that for an object of about 1m in diameter, using a Scale setting of between 100 and 250 mm creates a good look that's not too small and not too big.

That explains the "bumpiness" of the surface's appearance but not its rich, detailed coloring. Looking at the Basic tab for the surface again (Figure 4-43), we see that the only other place there is a texture is under the Color channel.

*Figure 4-45*

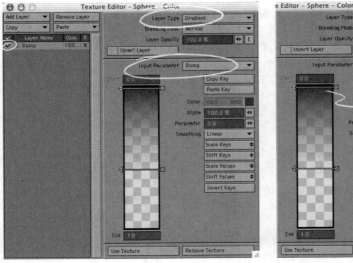

Figure 4-46

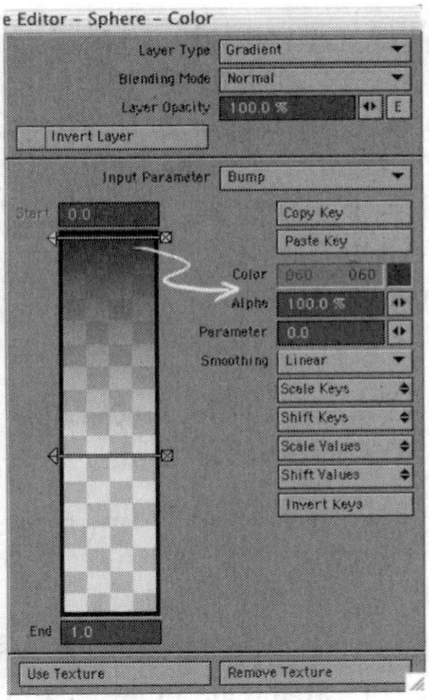

Figure 4-48

Entering the Texture Editor for the Color channel, we see that the Layer Type is set to Gradient and that its Input Parameter (what it is referencing) is the surface's Bump channel.

So what does it all mean? Well, the best way to get a handle on finding out is to take it away and see how things look then.

c.   Deactivate the Texture layer by clicking to remove the check next to "G: Bump" (the only Texture layer listed).

Figure 4-47: Quite a difference and not nearly as interesting as with the Gradient color texture active.

Let's take a closer look at the Gradient settings.

When Input Parameter is set to Bump, that means that whatever settings are on this layer are spread out between where the Bump channel is at its lowest (Start 0) and where it's at its highest (End 1.0).

### Note

Looking back at Figure 4-45, notice that Invert Layer is checked, meaning that the values generated by that layer are *inverted*. That's why, in Figure 4-48, the dark coloring we see in the key where the bump should be at its lowest (*Start* 0) is actually applied where the sphere's bump is highest.

Making sure the top key (the bar-like thing with the arrow on its left and the "x" box on its right) is clicked, we see the Color, Alpha, and Parameter settings reflect the attributes that key represents.

●   The **Color** is a dark gray, so where the Bump channel is at its lowest, the surface is also this dark gray color.

- The **Alpha** is set to 100%, so the color is opaque.

- The **Parameter** is 0, saying that we're looking at the point where the Bump channel is at its lowest. (The starting parameter is usually "locked" in place, though you can change the parameter for all the other keys.)

The other buttons below the input fields let you modify the values in real time.

- **Smoothing** is a pop-up menu that lets you choose how you want the values to be interpolated.

- **Scale Keys** is a drag button that lets you compress or expand all the keys in real time.

- **Shift Keys** is a drag button that moves the keys (except for Start) in real time.

- **Scale Values** leaves the keys right where they are and lets you compress or expand the values on the keys.

- **Shift Values** also leaves the keys where they are, adding values to or removing values from the keys.

- **Invert Keys** is a quick way for you to flip-flop the keys.

Starting with the **Input Parameter** field, we see that wherever the Bump channel is about midway from its lowest to its highest, these settings are in effect.

- The **Color** to be applied is 255, 255, 255 (white).

- But the **Alpha** is only 68.5%, so this color will be only 68.5% opaque (or 31.5% transparent, however you'd prefer to look at it). The "checkerboard" pattern is there to show that you are "seeing through" the color because the alpha's setting is making it transparent.

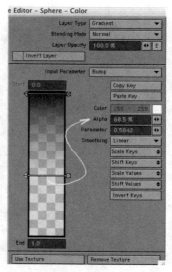

Figure 4-49: Clicking somewhere in the middle of the bottom key's bar makes the input fields reflect its attributes. (Clicking on the little "x" box will delete the key.)

That's it for the coloring! Using only references to how high or low the Bump channel is, the Gradient texture is able to give us more detail than if we had a huge, painted texture to provide the coloring for our surface.

### Note

If you want to move one of those bars on the gradient, just click and drag. If you want to add one, just click in an "empty" area of the gradient's span. If you want to remove one, just click in the little "x" box on the bar's right side.

Layer Opacity lets you tell LightWave how much of the layer's effect you want figured into the surface's overall look. You can use Invert Layer to keep all your settings as is and yet reverse the effect of your layer (in this case, what was dark would be light and vice versa).

Check out the LW manual for ways to use the different Input Parameter settings and ways of layering textures using Blending Mode to, among other things, let one layer serve to displace or be used as an alpha for another layer.

### Note

When you start playing with your own procedurals and come to something you kind of like, but still want to explore different settings, copy that layer (or layers) and paste/add them to the layers, turning "off" the old layer. You can noodle to your heart's content, knowing that all you have to do is delete (or deactivate) the new layer(s) and reactivate the old to get back to where you were.

*Figure 4-50*

What if we wanted the bumps to go *in* instead of *out* (making the sphere look like freshly chiseled sandstone)? One way would be to use the Invert Layer check box on the Bump channel, which would change the positioning of the darks and lights generated by the gradient on the Color channel. Another way would be to change the Bump field on the Surface Editor's Basic tab from 100% to –100%, which leaves the lights and darks where they are.

## Step 4: More Gradient Tricks — "Realistic" Metal

Another neat thing gradients can do is change a surface attribute based on its angle toward the camera — its *incidence angle*. (This is good for something like silk, which looks one color when seen from one angle and another color when seen from a different angle.)

a.  Select the **Cone** surface and give it a yellow, brassy color (251, 187, 68 works well).

b.  Give it a Diffuse of **49%**.

c.  Change its Specularity to **200%**.

d.  Set its Glossiness to **53%**.

e.  Its Reflection should be 50%. Additionally, Reflection Options should be set to **Ray Tracing + Spherical Map** with **_Reflection_Image_TA.iff** as its Reflection Map and Reflection Blurring set to **7%**.

*Figure 4-51: Doing an F9, it looks like we're having even more of a lack of realism than we had with the chrome sphere.*

f.  Open the Texture Editor for the Color channel.

g.  Set the Layer Type to **Gradient**.

h.  Set the Input Parameter to **Incidence Angle**.

**123**

i. Set the Color of the first key to **0, 0, 0** and its Alpha to **69%**.

j. Create another key anywhere on the gradient bar. Leave its Color at **0, 0, 0**, but change its Alpha to **79%** and its Parameter to **50**.

k. Create another key *below* the key you just created. Set its Color to **121, 23, 23**, its Alpha to **50%**, and its Parameter to **78**. (You can't move a key past any key immediately before or after it.)

l. Create another key *below* the key you just created. Set its Color to **95, 37, 54**, its Alpha to **0%**, and its Parameter to **90**.

*Figure 4-52: A new render shows that we're getting closer...*

m. Going into the Texture Editor for the Reflection channel, assign a gradient with the Input Parameter of **Incidence Angle**.

n. For the first key (representing polys facing *perpendicular* to the camera), set the Value to **0%**, and change its Alpha to **90%**. (Polys facing *perpendicular* to the camera will *almost* be non-reflective.)

o. Create another key, leaving its Value at **0%** but changing its Alpha to **0%** and making its Parameter **90**. (Polys facing *toward* the camera will retain their Reflection setting from what it is under the Basic tab of the Surface Editor.)

*Figure 4-53: A new render shows that things are continuing to look more realistic.*

p.  On the Advanced tab of the Surface Editor, set Color Highlights to **42%**. This will blend 42% of the surface color into the specular highlights. ("Metallic" surfaces tend to have their hot spots heavily influenced by their base colors.)

*Figure 4-54: Now it's starting to look like metal.*

There's one more thing I want to do to this before I call it "good enough," and that is sculpt the highlights a bit, getting Light-Wave to figure out what they would look like if the surface were to have the micro-fine, *anisotropic* look of "brushed metal." To do that, we have to add a special *shader*, a bit of code that LightWave uses in addition to (or in some cases completely replacing) its own rendering engine.

q.  Under the Shaders tab in the Surface Editor, choose **BDRF** (Bi-directional Reflectance Distribution Function) from the Add Shader pop-up menu.

r.  Double-click on the newly added shader to open its Properties window.

s.  In the Layer 1 tab, set Specular Reflection 1 to **Antistrophic II**. Set its Color to **255, 244, 187**.

t.  Set its Specularity to **51%** and its Glossiness to **42%**.

u.  Its Anisotropy should be **23°**, and its Direction should be **50°**.

v.  Set its Mapping to **Cylindrical** and its Axis to **Y**.

That will "shape" the *first* specular highlight. Now we're going to add a *second*, very subtle highlight to color the metal just a bit.

w.  Under Layer 2, choose **Anisotropic** for Specular Reflection 2. Its Color will be **103, 205, 73**.

x.  Specular should be **60%**, and Glossiness should be **20%**.

y.  Anisotropy should be **42°**, and Direction should be **45°**.

*Figure 4-55: In this render, the brass cone is good enough to call it done. Save all objects.*

## Step 5: VIPER

Anisotropy may look nifty, but it's not an easy thing to understand. How do you know what things will look like without wating for render after render? VIPER gives you a close approximation of what your stuff will look like every time you make an adjustment to your surfacing or volumetric settings.

To preview your surfaces with VIPER, you must fill its "info buffers" by rendering a frame once VIPER has been activated. VIPER can be activated by opening its preview window from the Render | Utilities

menu. (VIPER will remain active whether its preview window is open or closed. To shut down VIPER, deselect the Enable VIPER button on the Render | Utilities menu or in the Render Options panel.)

> **Note**
>
> As you can tell from Figure 4-56, what you see in VIPER isn't always what you get in a full-on render, but it's close enough to be a huge time-saver.

With VIPER active, anytime you make a change to a surface, you will see that change reflected in the VIPER window as soon as you let go of the mouse button.

You can even click on a surface in the VIPER window, and that surface will be selected in the Surface Editor window.

> **Note**
>
> The Preview pop-up menu will let you build a preview of textures that change over time (surfaces and volumetrics). No geometry will move, nor will the camera, but this is a great way to check out surfaces that "crawl" over an object (by assigning an envelope to their scale and/or position) or volumetrics that evolve through time.

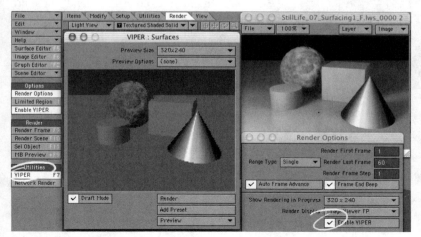

*Figure 4-56: The VIPER window.*

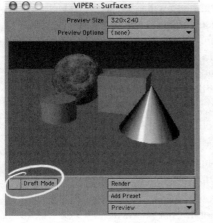

Figure 4-57: You can get a "cleaner" preview by deactivating Draft Mode, though the VIPER render will take longer to draw.

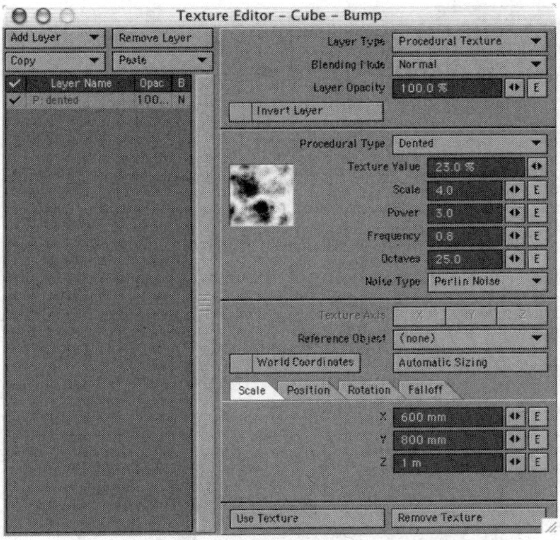

Figure 4-58: Dented gives very organic patterns that don't look like they were generated on a computer.

## Step 6: "Building" a Surface — Rusted Steel

When you look at something in real life, it doesn't *just* have a color *or* a specularity *or* a bump. Most things have a smattering of all of the above. Most of these "channels" *reference each other*!

One of the places this is most obvious is on rusting metal, where you still have parts of the surface that are shiny and polished but other parts are beginning to be eaten by "iron moths."

a. Select the **Cube** surface, and change its color to the base color for the rust: **155, 91, 49**. (Diffuse and Bump should be left where they are, but Luminosity, Specularity, Glossiness, Reflection, Transparency, and Translucency should all be set to **0%**.)

b. Next, go into the Texture Editor for the Bump channel and set the Layer Type to **Procedural Texture** and the Procedural Type to **Dented**.

c. Using Figure 4-58 as a guide, set the Texture Value to **23%**, Octaves to **25** (for lots of nice, crisp detail), and the Scale to **X=600 mm, Y=800 mm,** and **Z=1 m**.

d. Under the Position tab, set the texture's center at **X=9.5 mm, Y=53.5 mm**, and **Z=0 m**.

Figure 4-59: This is the bump we use to "drive" the rest of the surfacing for "rusting" this cube.

## Mac-Specific Info

At the time of publication, the Dented procedural texture looked *vastly* different between Macintosh and PC (though it does appear to be homogenous among different brands of PCs). The hypothesized reason for this is that there is a processor-based random seed used to "grow" the Turbulent (layered Fractal) Noise. (Whatever the reason, it's not good — it's a pedantic pain in the posterior.)

For Dented's Position, Mac users should enter **X=0, Y=0, Z=–720 mm.** This will give you some "rust" on the surface of your cube, but *it will look like this ... not like the following illustrations!* (Hey, that's what problem-solving is all about — do the best we can with what we've got. *Improvise, baby!*)

(Special thanks to Robin Wood!)

e. Our cube will have some reflective surfaces on it, so under the Environment tab, choose **Ray Tracing + Spherical Map** for Reflection Options, and choose **_Reflection_Image_TA.iff** for Reflection Map.

f. Now, enter the Texture Editor for Reflection under the Basic tab.

g. Choose **Gradient** for the Layer Type and **Bump** as the Input Parameter.

h. Where the bump is "flat" (0%), we want that part to be the still gleaming metal. That part will be reflective, so enter **23%** for the Value for the first key.

i. Next, create a key, and drag it down to the bottom, so the Parameter field reads **1**. This is the place in the bump texture where the surface is rusty and no longer reflects. Change its Value to **0%**.

j. Copy this layer (so we can save some mouse clicks on the other texture channels) by choosing **Current Layer** from the Copy pop-up menu.

*Figure 4-60: The cube looks pretty darn cool as it is . . .*

k.  Enter the Texture Editor for Specularity, and choose **Replace All Layers** from the Paste pop-up menu. (We should now be seeing a gradient that looks exactly like what we had in the reflection layer.)

l.  Just as with the reflectivity of the surface where it isn't "rusted," we want the "smooth" part to have the specularity of metal. So, enter **80%** for the Value of the key at Parameter 0 (the top key).

m.  Where the surface is "rusted," we want a very *low* specularity, so change the Value of the key at Parameter 1 to **2%**.

n.  Now, go into the Texture Editor for Glossiness, and **Paste | Replace All Layers**.

o.  Change the top key to a Value of **30%**, and double-check the Value of the bottom key, making sure it is **0%**. (The "rusted" metal will have a very low gloss like, well, rust. The "clean" metal will have a gloss of 30% — all this *layered* detail is still being driven by the Bump channel!)

Figure 4-61. The "rust" is really beginning to stand out from the "metal."

p.  Next, enter the Texture Editor for the Diffuse channel and once again **Paste | Replace All Layers**.

q.  With Diffuse, we want the opposite of the values we've been entering. The "clean" part of the metal will have a low Diffuse, so enter **58%** for the Value of the top key.

r.  The Diffuse of the "rust" will be very high, like paper or … rust. Enter **100%** as the Value of the bottom key (which should still have a Parameter of 1).

Figure 4-62: It looks like some red clay got thrown onto a block of copper.

s.  Now we're going to take care of the coloring. Enter the Texture Editor for the Color channel and once again **Paste | Replace All Layers**.

t.  Set the End field to **3** (see Figure 4-63) and delete the lowermost key (so you only have the key at Parameter 0).

u.  Set the Color for your one and only key to **129, 135, 150**, and make sure its Alpha is **100%**.

v.  Create another key, leaving everything the same, only set its Parameter at **0.33**.

**129**

w. Create a key just below the new one, and set its Color to **151, 97, 64**, its Alpha to **100%**, and its Parameter to **0.82**.

x. Create a new key just below that one, and set its Color to **106, 53, 40**, its Alpha to **0%**, and its Parameter to **2.66**.

y. Create another key just below that one, and set its Color to **209, 136, 101**, its Alpha to **42%**, and its Parameter to **2.91**.

z. Using Figure 4-63 as a guide, click and make *three* new keys in the general area indicated (exact placement isn't crucial).

Figure 4-63: Exact placement of these keys isn't crucial, but do try to get them close. The outer two will hold the colors we're getting from the gradient in place, while we use the center one to make a darker band through one level of the bump's height.

aa. Set the Alpha of the topmost of those three new keys to **32%** and its Parameter to **1.75**.

bb. Set the Color of the next lowest key to **0, 0, 0**, its Alpha to **12%**, and its Parameter to **2**.

cc. The lowest of this set of three new keys should have its Alpha at **17%** and its Parameter at **2.25**.

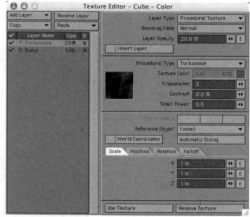

Figure 4-64: Each added texture layer adds another level of detail to your surfaces.

dd. Select **Add Layer | Procedural**, make sure the Procedural Type is **Turbulence**, and set the Texture Color to **141, 71, 71**.

ee. Change the Layer Opacity to **20%** so this adds just a *hint* of "irregular" color to the "clean" metal.

Figure 4-65: The completed, rusted steel block.

Save all objects!

# Step 7: "Found" Textures

One of the cool things about being a 3D artist is carrying a small, digital camera around with you wherever you go and really *looking* for things to photograph! It's the Digital Texture gang that walks down a street and really *sees* the way bricks are hanging in an old, dilapidated building or the way someone has covered an old shed in cedar shingles. The way light plays off nooks and crannies, the patina that years of being exposed to the elements has touched upon an aged surface, the "gnarling and snarling" that only real life can create — this stuff is *exciting!* (Yet most of the rest of the world just walks on by, oblivious.)

Part of the job of a texture artist is to "see it and save it!" You can either use it directly or have it help you paint details in textures you might never have thought of otherwise.

*Figure 4-66: This old building had the coolest shingles on it. It's part of my texture library now!*

Just because what you shot was one thing doesn't mean you can't use it for something entirely different. We're going to use the shingles in Figure 4-66 to make the cylinder in our little still life look like a segment from an old castle turret.

a. Select the **Cylinder** surface in the Surface Editor, and load onto it the Rock_2 preset (just like we did for the sphere.)

b. Go into the Texture Editor for the Bump channel, and select **Add New Layer | Image Map**. Remove the Crumple procedural layer.

c. For Projection, choose **Cylindrical**.

d. For the Texture Amplitude, enter **8**. (This will really show us every nook and cranny in the not-so-contrasty image of the shingles.)

e. Under Image, choose **(load image)** and load **Images\Shingles_white-top.jpg**.

f. Set the Height Tile to **Edge**, which will simply repeat the pixels on the edge of the image to infinity when the mapping reaches the image's top or bottom edge. (Other options are for areas outside the image to reset or to zero and for the image to be mirrored or repeated.)

> ### Note
> The reason there are two Shingle jpgs in the Images directory and the reason we choose "white-top" is that it has a line of white at its top edge. With the Height Tile set to Edge, that line of white will be continued onto the top of the cylinder, giving us a nice, smooth top.

g. The Texture Axis should be set to **Y**. (Think of the Texture Axis like a spindle onto which the texture is skewered.)

h. Click on **Automatic Sizing** to have LightWave calculate the exact scale and center for the texture to precisely fit the surface.

That's it. Render away!

**Note**

As a cool aside: The World Coordinates check box makes it so that the texture (or image map or procedural) *doesn't follow the object when the object moves*. With this box checked, the texture stays rooted to the "world." What's neat is that when you move an object with World Coordinates checked, the object appears to move *through* the texture! (Keep this in mind for when you find yourself doing special effects.)

Figure 4-67: *Using found textures and blending them with another surface, we quickly got something that looks like a slice right off of someone's model of a castle.*

**Note**

You can find out more about the different kinds of mapping types that LightWave offers — spherical, cubic, front, and planar — in the LightWave manual. The other type of mapping LightWave offers, *UV mapping*, is best explained through example, which we get into in the next chapter.

**Note**

The finished scene for this step is: Scenes\ Chapter_04\StillLife_07_Surfacing1_F.lws.

• • •

Not bad for just being "foundation material," eh? Remember, *we're only scratching the surface!* There's more to LightWave than I think anyone realizes. Every day, I look through periodicals or web sites that focus on LightWave and am constantly amazed at what people are doing. There are no limits for the passionate, creative soul, for the imaginative, explorative mind.

Now, go play! I'll see you in the next chapter. But until then, start using what you've learned and start having some fun!

# Chapter 5

# Modeling 2: Additional Tools

Now we're going to expand your modeling skills by adding a few more tools. Nothing all that intense — mostly they're just quick and easy things you'll probably find useful, even early in your path as a 3D artist. These are the kinds of things professionals often use on a daily basis — and couldn't get by without.

## EPS Import

What do you do if a client hands you a logo in Encapsulated PostScript (EPS) format and wants you to do a "tag" for a TV spot? Or what if you've created a great logo for yourself, using something like Macromedia's Flash? How do you get that 2D *vector-based* format into something you can render in LightWave?

> ### Note
>
> If you are working with a piece that has its lettering as part of the artwork, as is the case with Figure 5-1, be sure to *convert* the lettering to *curves* before importing. Modeler won't "see" the text otherwise.
>
> This is especially important when receiving a logo from an outside company. If it uses a font you don't have, and the letters of that font haven't been converted into raw curve information, *your system will substitute one of its own fonts for the missing one.*

Figure 5-1: A logo for an imaginary company (drawn on paper, auto-traced in Flash, and lettered in Freehand).

**File | Import | EPSF Loader** brings up the EPSF Loader interface. (The panel's settings are explained on the following page.)

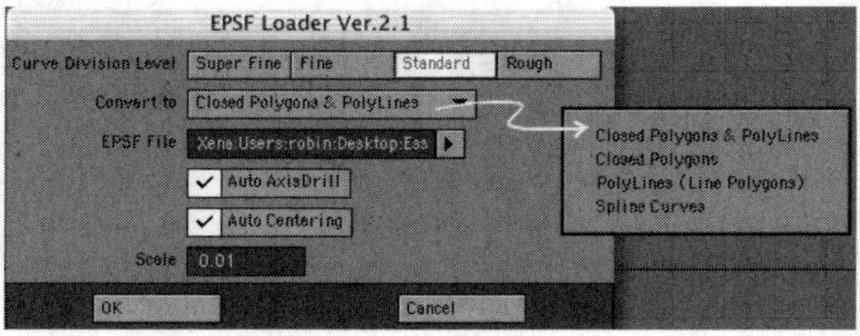

Figure 5-2: The EPSF Loader window.

- **Curve Division Level** allows you to determine the relative number of points that Modeler will use when converting curves in the EPS file into polygons in LightWave.

- **Closed Polygons & PolyLines** turns any closed shape into a polygon and every line ("stroked" path) into a connected series of two-point polygons (*polylines*).

- **Closed Polygons** turns everything into polygons, even open-ended lines.

- **PolyLines** turns everything into systems of two-point polygons.

- **Spline Curves** turns all the lines of both open and closed shapes into LightWave's default spline curves. (Notice how the sharp point at the peak of the open-ended triangle is no longer sharp when imported as a spline curve.)

- **Auto AxisDrill** will automatically find the open shapes within an EPS file and drill openings in the polygons it creates.

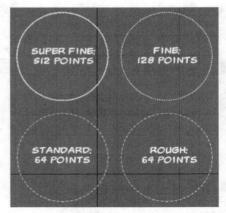

Figure 5-3: The differences in the loader's settings for Curve Division Level can be seen here, using the different settings to import a simple, filled circle.

- **Auto Centering** automatically centers the imported geometry.

- **Scale** resizes the imported geometry to LightWave's conventions of measurements. (With the default setting of 0.01, an 8.5" x 11" EPS file comes in at just over 2 m tall.)

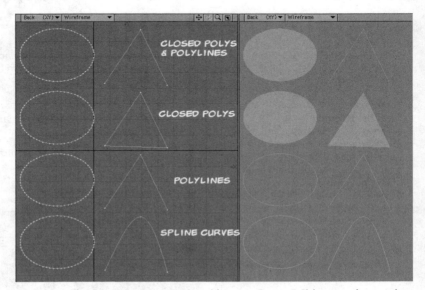

Figure 5-4: The Convert to pop-up menu (shown in Figure 5-2) lets you choose what form the imported geometry will take once inside Modeler.

*Figure 5-5: The imported EPS logo. (Auto AxisDrill was used to maintain the open spaces within the antler, the nose, and the top of the caribou.)*

## Note

Remember LightWave's self-imposed limitation of *1,023 points per polygon* when you're importing Encapsulated PostScript files!

If you're having problems with things coming in as a "cloud" of points instead of as polygons, it means that LightWave is trying to create more points on a poly than it will "allow" itself to have. You can decrease the Curve Division Level, or, in your vector-based illustration program, cut your image up into a series of different-colored bands (Flash is the quickest for doing this). *Each color in the illustration will import as a separate polygon.*

*Figure 5-6: A quick treatment of the imported EPS. (The only tools used in this render that we haven't already explored are Lens Flare and Glow Effect.)*

## Note

*Not all EPS files are created equal.* LightWave's EPSF importer requires Illustrator files in version 8.0 or earlier. Directly exporting an Encapsulated PostScript file from Freehand 10 generated something Modeler couldn't interpret. (Flash couldn't figure that file out either.) I had to export as an Adobe Illustrator .AI file in order for Modeler (and Flash) to make sense of it.

## Note

Should you wish to explore the scene and objects, load **Scenes\Chapter_05\World-WildAdventures_F.lws.**

This scene requires the Shades plug-in, available with the companion files, for the woven grass mat effect on the dome's surface. See Appendix A for more information about Shades and the other plug-ins and programs included with this book.

# Bridge

The Bridge tool allows you to connect points or polygons by creating new geometry to "bridge the gap" between them. The Bridge tool can be used for everything from tunneling through objects to connecting the hands and feet to a character's arms and legs.

1. Drag out a box in the Top viewport. Then, holding the <Ctrl> key down as a constraint, drag in the Back viewport to create a perfect cube. The exact size isn't important.

2. Press <D> (capital letter) (or go to **Multiply | Subdivide | Subdivide**) to activate the Subdivide tool. Subdivide is used to add geometry to low-resolution objects by dividing larger polygons into smaller ones. For now, just select **Faceted** and leave Fractal at 0%. This divides each poly into four new ones. Run the Subdivide tool again with the same settings to break the object up even further.

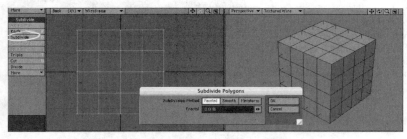

Figure 5-7: Subdivide a perfect cube twice to add extra geometry.

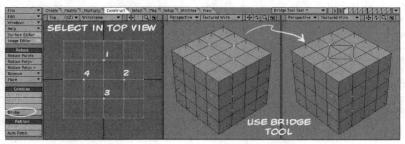

Figure 5-8: Running the Bridge tool "connects the dots" and cuts a diamond shape in our cube.

3. In the Top viewport, select the points as shown in Figure 5-8. When used with points, the Bridge tool attempts to "connect the dots" in the order in which they were selected. We'll use the Bridge tool to cut a diamond shape into the top and bottom of our cube. From the **Construct | Combine** menu choose the **Bridge** tool (or use the <1> keyboard shortcut).

4. You'll notice that the points are now connected to form a diamond shape. Let's Bridge the top and bottom diamonds to create a tunnel through the center of our cube. Move your mouse to the Top viewport, hold the <**Shift**> key down, and select the point at the center of our diamond. Go to the **View | Selection | More** menu and choose **Select Polygons**. This transforms our point selection into a polygon selection.

5. Run the Bridge tool once again. Lastly, select the lone point at the center of the diamond (it's no longer attached to anything) and delete it.

This is just a quick sample of what the Bridge tool can do. Once you get a feel for it, you'll find that the Bridge tool can be used for a variety of cool effects.

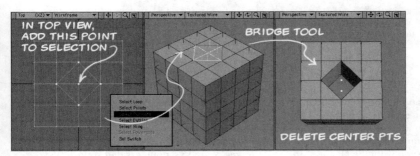

Figure 5-9

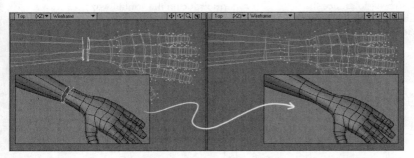

Figure 5-10: Connecting a character's hand and arm can be easily accomplished by creating a poly at the end of the arm and hand, then running the Bridge tool.

# Lathe

The Lathe tool lets you take something you've created and "spin" it around to create an object. It creates geometry from either polygons or curves. (Lathe is sometimes called Sweep in other 3D packages.)

1. Create a two-dimensional disc somewhere to the *left* of X=0.

2. Select **Multiply | Extend | Lathe** to activate the Lathe tool. Click in the Back viewport, as shown in Figure 5-12, and drag straight down. (The axis you are creating defines the angle around which your disc will be "lathed.")

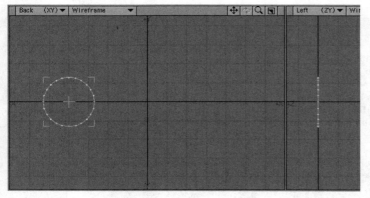

*Figure 5-11*

---

### Note

In addition to using the Numeric window to change the Lathe settings, you can drag the root handle around to move the center of the effect. You can drag the rotation handles to specify where you want the "lathing" to start and stop.

Press the <Left Arrow> to *reduce* the number of segments; press the <Right Arrow> to *increase* the number of segments.

---

### Note

Sometimes Lathe creates the new polys with their normals facing the "wrong" way. Be sure to check this every time after lathing and flip the polygons if necessary. (Even if you're using a double-sided surface on your polys, it's always a good idea to have your normals facing the "right" way.)

---

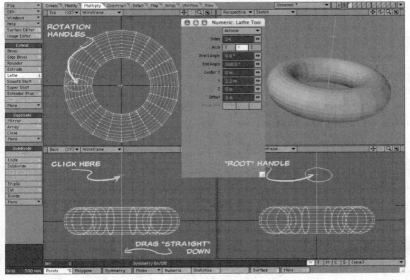

Figure 5-12: **Multiply | Extend | Lathe** activates the Lathe tool.

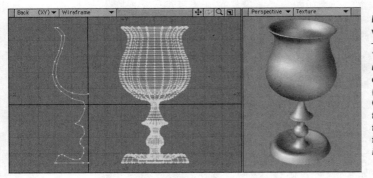

Figure 5-13: Lathe also works with splines (curves — also known sometimes as "rails") to quickly create rather neat-looking chalices and other "turned" objects. (The Sketch tool (**Create | Curves | Sketch**) was used to quickly draw the curve that was then lathed with the same settings as the disc in Figure 5-11.)

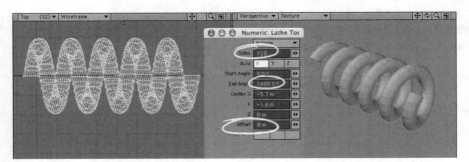

Figure 5-14: The Offset field lets you "skew" the lathe operation, letting you create springs and other nifty doodads! (Remember that you can enter a mathematical formula into any of LightWave's Numeric input fields. So, if, as in this illustration, you didn't quite know what five complete revolutions would be in degrees, just enter **360 * 5**, and let LightWave come up with 1800.0° for you.)

# Taper

Under the **Modify | Transform** menu, LightWave offers two kinds of tools that taper your geometry. Taper lets you control the amount of effect on each axis of the taper, depending on how much you move your mouse up and down or left and right. Taper Constrain, on the other hand, affects your geometry in both directions of your taper at once (for instance, if you wanted a Doric column to evenly taper as it rises).

With a Taper tool active, click in a Top viewport to taper your selected geometry

as it extends along the Y axis. Drag left or right, up or down to taper your object. (Technically, the Taper tool successively scales the selected geometry relative to the distance of the selected geometry's bottom.)

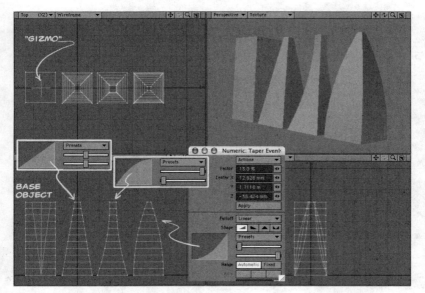

*Figure 5-15: The Taper Constrain tool in action.*

Pressing <n> opens the Numeric window for Taper and activates a little gizmo (seen on the "Base Object" in Figure 5-15) to give you a visual interpretation of the Taper tool's effect. Right-clicking and dragging the gizmo's ends will let you exactly position and angle the tool's effect.

Through the Numeric window, you can adjust the falloff of the effect to "sculpt" how Taper affects your selected geometry.

● The **Falloff** pop-up menu lets you choose from several complex ways of letting the taper effect dissipate through space. (We use Linear because it is what you will most often use. However, through this pop-up menu, the tool can even reference the settings on a weight map that you've created. To find out more about these falloff settings, explore the Light-Wave manual.)

● The **Shape** buttons let you *invert* the effect (so the bottom tapers instead of the top), have the taper affect both ends at once, or affect just the middle of the selected geometry.

● The **Presets** pop-up menu gives you quick access to four combinations for the sliders below it that shape the *curve* of the linear falloff. (You can see examples of the effect of changing these sliders in Figure 5-15.)

● The **Range** of the effect defaults to Automatic. However, by right-clicking and manipulating the gizmo, you are telling LightWave that you want to specify a fixed angle and/or position for the effect. Clicking on Automatic releases your specified, fixed settings.

## Twist

The Twist tool is something I don't use all that often, but when I need it, there's nothing else that can fit the bill like this tool can. Technically, it spreads out *rotation* through your selected geometry in relation to how far each bit is away from the effect's root. In layman's terms, it *twists* stuff. The Twist tool is accessed through **Modify | Rotate | Twist**.

Twist also obeys the same kind of falloff rules that Taper does. By shifting the falloff sliders, the twist in Figure 5-16 (on the following page) begins gently from the bottom, increasing as it reaches the top of our stack of segments.

You can move and angle the area of effect for the twist by right-clicking and dragging on the gizmo in the viewports. This sets the Range to Fixed, just like in Taper. Click on Automatic to revert to LW's automatic settings.

### Note

Twist is a cool tool, but it is notorious for creating many non-planar polys. Check your work for non-planars after using Twist.

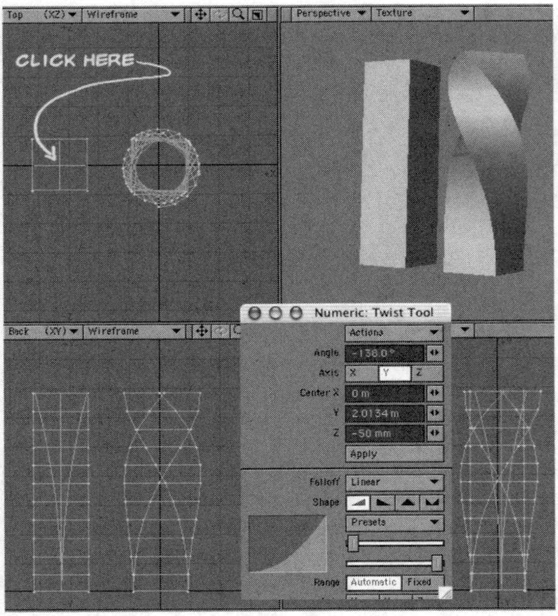

Figure 5-16: The twist axis is established by clicking in a viewport, "spindling" the effect directly away from you in the viewport in which you clicked. (Think of the axis around which you'd twist a tall stack of napkins, playing cards, or saltine crackers. You establish this axis by looking straight down at the stack.)

## Bend

We used Bend when making our flying text logo in Chapter 3. It follows along the same rationale as Taper and Twist.

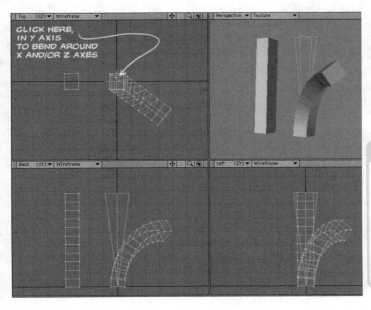

Figure 5-17: Click and drag in a viewport to bend your selection as if it were a car's radio antenna and you were looking straight down the antenna at the effect's axis.

### Note

Unlike Twist, Bend is usually very good about not creating non-planars, *if* you bend a poly only once. After hitting a selection more than once with Bend, check to see if it's created any non-planar polys.

# Smooth Scale/Move Plus

Smooth Scale *pushes* your selection *out* along each individual polygon's normal by the distance you enter in its input window. (It will *pull* your selection *in* if you enter a *negative* value.) Unfortunately, Smooth Scale has no real-time interface, which makes its use less than intuitive. That's why the Move Plus tool is such a welcome addition to LightWave 8. Move Plus features all of the functionality of the traditional Move tool when using the left mouse button. However, when used with the right mouse button, it performs a real-time smooth scale.

What if we wanted to make ThinGuy (one of the characters in *LightWave 3D 8 Character Animation*) into "PlumpGuy"? (Hey, anything can happen in production, right?)

I select the polys I want to push out and then select **Modify | Translate | More | Move Plus**. By right-clicking and dragging up, I can push the polygons out along their normals, essentially puffing it up. Dragging down pulls them back in. I often use the Move Plus tool on a character's fingers to make them fatter or thinner.

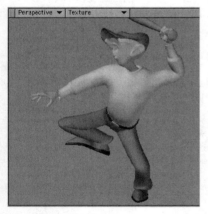

*Figure 5-18: ThinGuy.*

> ### Note
> Due to the way Smooth Scale and Move Plus operate, they can break the symmetry on your object. Be sure to check symmetry after working with one of these tools.

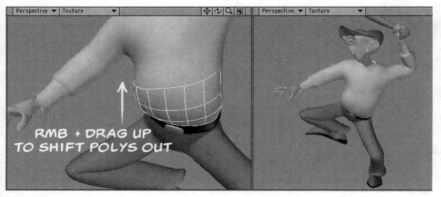

*Figure 5-19*

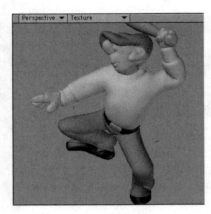

Figure 5-20: Using Smooth Scale or Move Plus on an entire object can produce some interesting results. (Remember Dig Dug?)

# Rail Extrude — Single Rail

Rail Extrude is a little like those "Leatherman" tools that are a combination screwdriver, pliers, scissors, awl, penknife, and so on. Rail Extrude is one little tool, but it does a whole lot of things. Let's start with one of its simple uses and move on from there.

Have you ever wanted to create one of those "tunnel fly-throughs"? Follow these steps:

1. Grab the Sketch tool, and draw a rail (curve) you'd like to have your tunnel follow. (You can load mine, if you like. It's had some points cut from it to help

smooth it out: **Objects\Chapter05\ RailExtrude_Raw.lwo.**)

### Note

Notice the funky little diamond thing at one end of the curve in Figure 5-21. That is the end I started sketching first. This is the *start point* of the curve, as far as LightWave's Rail Extrude is concerned. The circle we create in just a moment should be right at this place if we want the extrusion to follow this curve as we intend.

You can switch the end LightWave thinks of as its start point by flipping the curve the same way you would flip a polygon (**<f>**).

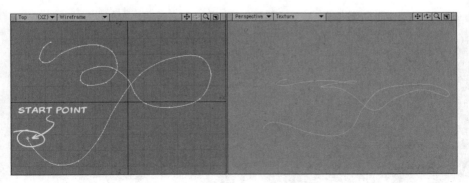

Figure 5-21

2.  With the curve in a background layer, create a disc and move it to the curve's *start point*. In order to have it orient properly along the curve, you will also need to rotate it so that its *normal* is like an extension of the curve's line. ("Spinning" around the Perspective viewport and touching up the rotation where the normal is most out of alignment is the quickest way to get it aligned well.)

> **Note**
>
> Carl Meritt's AlignToRail plug-in, available on the companion CD, will automatically line up your polygon to the start of the background curve, making quick work out of an otherwise time-consuming process.

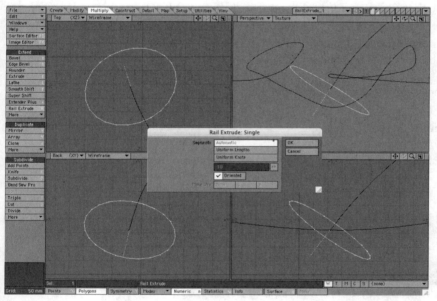

*Figure 5-22*

> **Note**
>
> If you want the extruded geometry to have its normals facing *out*, then you want to have the soon-to-be-extruded poly's normal facing *away from* the curve.
>
> If you want the new geometry to have its normals facing *in*, then the poly's normal should be facing *toward* the curve.

3.  Once you've got the polygon aligned, **Multiply | Extend | Rail Extrude** opens the Rail Extrude: Single window. It has the following options:

    •   **Automatic** segmentation will let LightWave make its best judgment as far as how many "slices" to make and where they should be so the extrusion most closely follows the curve.

    •   **Uniform Lengths** lets LightWave distribute its specified number of segments so they are all *equidistant* along the curve's length.

    •   **Uniform Knots** tells LightWave to distribute its specified number of segments with relation to the placement and number of *knots* (points) on the curve.

    •   **Oriented** tells LightWave to *rotate* the poly, *aligning* it to the curve as it is extruded.

4.  Accept the default settings shown in Figure 5-22. The disc is extruded along the curve (looking a little like the ductwork from *Brazil*).

5.  Save your object. (Mine is **Objects\ Chapter05\RailExtrude_1.lwo**.)

6.  With the layer that has the curve in it in the foreground, select **File | Export | Path to Motion**. Save the motion somewhere where you'll have intuitive access to it (**Motions\Chapter5\ TunnelFly-Through.mot** is what I used). *You will need to add ".mot" (without the quotes) to the end of the file for Layout to see it; Modeler doesn't do this automatically when you use Path to Motion.*

7.  Now, use **Send Object to Layout** so we can make a movie of our quick example here.

8.  While in Layout, use <[> and <]> to adjust the grid size so your extruded object fills the screen nicely.

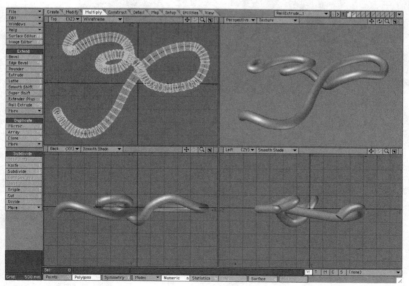

*Figure 5-23*

9. Select the camera and use **File | Load | Load Motion File**. Choose the motion file you created in Step 6 of this exercise.

10. Change the end frame of the Frame Slider to **160**, and "scrub" the Frame Slider along the timeline. You will see your camera move along the tube (even though it won't be "looking where it's going" yet).

11. Under Display Options, give yourself a Viewport Layout of **2 Left, 1 Right**. Set the Top Left viewport to **Camera View** and the Right viewport to **Top View** and have it **Center Current Item**. (You can set the Bottom Left viewport to whatever you'd like.)

12. With the camera still selected, press **<m>** to bring up the Motion Options window for the camera. (See Figure 5-24.)

13. Under the Controllers and Limits tab of the Motion Options window, set both Heading Controller and Pitch Controller to **Align to Path**. You can then go back to the IK and Modifiers tab and adjust how much your camera "anticipates" its motion by setting the Align to Path Look-ahead field. (It's easiest to use the slider button to the field's right and "scrub" through your scene, making little adjustments so the camera gives you what you want.)

If your polygon normals are facing in, your Camera viewport should be showing you what it's like to be looking down that tunnel. (If they aren't, just switch back to Modeler, flip them, and return to Layout; if you're working with the Hub active, when you get back to Layout, the polys will be flipped!)

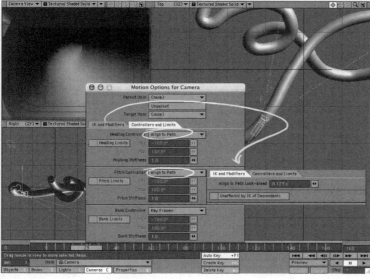

Figure 5-24

**Note**

Align to Path is a controller available *only*
for heading and pitch. You will want to go
through your movie and, with **General
Options | Auto Key Create | Modified
Channels** selected, rotate your camera on
bank where it seems fitting. (You can always
reload the motion file onto the camera if
you don't like what you've done — so
explore and experiment!)

*Figure 5-25: Just a quick F9 of the tunnel we just made.*

14. Open the Surface Editor, and onto your
    tunnel's surface, load in a preset with
    some bump to it so you can see some
    "nurnage" (that's the industry's techni-
    cal term for "neat-bumpy-detail") as
    you're flying down the shaft. (I wasn't
    happy with any of the presets that
    came with LightWave, so if you want to
    use one of mine, load in **Surfaces\
    GrungyCement.srf.**)

Spend some time lighting and surfacing
your tunnel scene. Render a movie and see
how things look.

If things move too quickly or too slowly,
you may have to change the end frame of
your movie and enter the Scene Editor to
scale your keys.

*Figure 5-26: You can scale the keyframes for objects in your scene using the Dope Sheet in
LightWave 8's Scene Editor. Click on the first keyframe for your camera (denoted by a green
bar), then, holding the <Shift> key, click on the last keyframe. You can drag the yellow bars on
either side of your selection to scale interactively or right-click and choose Numeric Time Scale
from the pop-up requester to scale your selection by a specific percentage. If you're unhappy
with the results, simply right-click again and select Undo.*

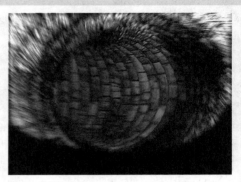

*Figure 5-27: A frame from my take on the fly-through.*

# Rail Extrude — Multiple Rails

Now how about "lofting"? Can LightWave do *lofting*? Absolutely.

**Note**

*Lofting* is a term from CAD/CAM programs that work almost exclusively in splines and NURBs (non-uniform, rational B-splines). In short, lofting is using splines to guide the creation of a NURB surface.

LightWave will let you guide the extrusion along *multiple background curves*. You can use this to create any level of mesh density, from things that can be used as *sub-patches* (very low density) to extremely high-density meshes (for use in slowing even a Cray supercomputer down to PC Jr. speeds).

Say you wanted to create a strangely ergonomic hilt for some alien blade. (See Figure 5-28.)

1. You would first create *two* curves that "outlined" the shape of the desired form. (The start points should be where you intend to put the geometry that will be extruded.)

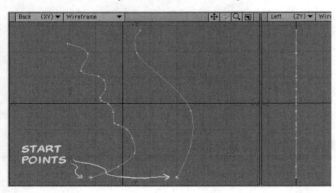

*Figure 5-28*

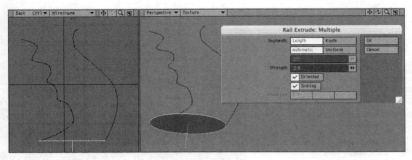

Figure 5-29

2. Next, with the curves in a *background layer*, create a shape you wish to be extruded. In this case, it is a standard disc that is wider in X than it is in Z. Position it at the curves' start points with its normal facing *out*.

3. Activate Rail Extrude to bring up the Rail Extrude: Multiple window. It has the following options:

   • The **Segments** section allows you to control how "dense" the extruded mesh is (just like Rail Extrude with only *one* curve in the background).

   • **Strength** is a factor of how "tightly" the extrusion will follow the curves.

   • **Oriented**, as when rail extruding with only *one* curve, "angles" the extrusion as it follows the curves.

   • **Scaling** lets your extrusion "expand" on all three axes in relation to the distance between the two curves.

> ### Note
>
> Using the Knots setting to determine segment placement means you must be a lot more careful when creating the curves you will be "lofting" along. LightWave will try to distribute *segments* and *orient* them knot for knot. If your object's silhouette must meet an exact shape, have all your curves made with the same number of knots, and know that from the first knot to the last on all curves, LightWave will use them to determine exact placement and angle of the extruded segments.

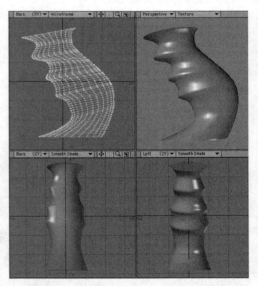

Figure 5-30: Using just the default settings for Rail Extrude: Multiple (shown in Figure 5-29), we get our funky handgrip.

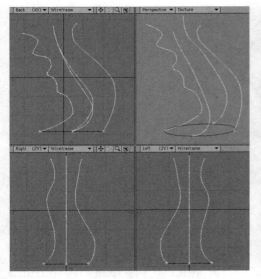

Figure 5-31: You can use more than two curves to shape your extrusion to get even more "organic" shapes.

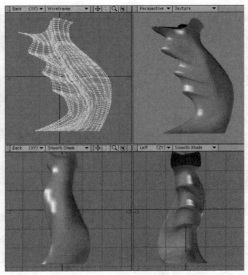

Figure 5-32: Again, using just the default settings, we get something that looks even more like it was "grown" than "machined."

> **Note**
>
> Rail Extrude: Multiple can create a lot of non-planar polys. Check your work after using this tool.

## Rail Bevel

Rail Bevel? Yep. It's a cool tool that lets you specify the shape of the bevel. (It's easier to show what it does than to try to explain it in words.)

1. Make a simple rectangle.

2. With your rectangle in a background layer, use **Sketch** to quickly doodle a shape that could be a molding joining the ceiling and walls of a house.

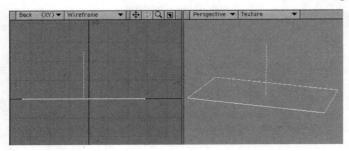

Figure 5-33

151

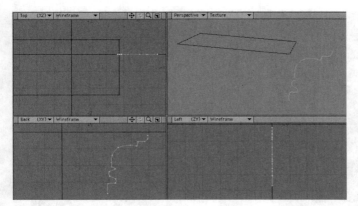

Figure 5-34

> **Note**
>
> The points of the background layer are used to guide Rail Bevel, not the curve itself. So, while you may be tempted to add points to smooth things out, don't. Rail Bevel is guided by the *point order*, the order in which the points were created. If you need more detail in an area, put your curve in the background and create new points in a "dot-to-dot" fashion along the *entire curve*, adding in the new ones you need as you go.

3. With the curve in the background layer, use **Multiply | Extend | More | Rail Bevel** to turn the simple polygon into an instant cornice piece. Dragging *up* and *down* in a viewport will make the bevel *wider* or *narrower*; dragging *right* and *left* will make it *taller* or *shorter*. (This seems backward to me, so I just use the Numeric window for my real-time rail bevels.)

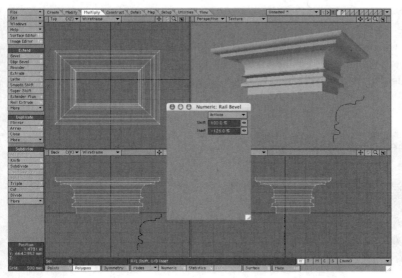

Figure 5-35

If you need some serious smoothing on your rail bevel, you can select your curve and freeze it (Construct | Convert | Freeze).

Freezing a curve turns it into a polygon with a level of detail relative to the Curve Divisions setting under General Options.

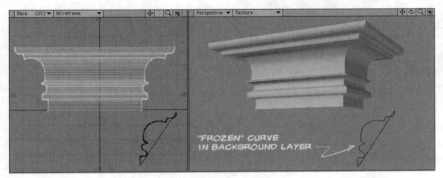

Figure 5-36: Only the points created by the Freeze operation matter to Rail Bevel, so even if your curve ends up looking inside out after freezing, the bevel will still look fine.

# Edge Tools

Does LightWave have any tools for working with edges? You bet! And once you start using them, you'll wonder how you ever got along without them. If you've ever modeled with another 3D package, the next few tools will make you feel right at home.

Note

In the real world, edges occur at the physical boundaries of an object, such as the edge of your desk. But in 3D, edges occur at the boundaries of every single polygon. When we talk about edge tools, we are talking about tools that add, reduce, and delete these boundaries. To this effect, the edge tools are like advanced, interactive versions of the BandSaw and BandGlue tools.

## Add Edges

The Add Edges tool (**Detail | Edges | Add Edges**) lets you draw new edges onto your object. *How cool is that?!* The blue dots that appear when you run this tool are control points. Adding a new edge is as simple as playing "connect the dots." The control points can be dragged along their existing edges to adjust the new edge's shape (Figure 5-37).

- **Position, Distance from Start**, and **Distance from End** are all methods of determining the placement of the currently selected control point. You can adjust these interactively by clicking on one of the control points and dragging it along its existing edge.

- **Grid Snap** enables you to constrain the motion of the control points. Without Grid Snap, they will freely move along their existing edge.

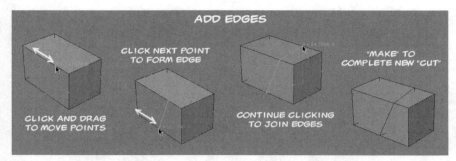

*Figure 5-37: Adding edges to create a non-uniform "cut" around an object.*

● **Grid Unit** allows you to select a method of constraint for the motion of your control points. You can snap to a ratio or a distance.

● **Ratio** looks at the edge on which the control point lies and lets you constrain its movement based on a percent of the source edge's length. Setting Ratio to 50% will constrain your control point to the very center (50% of the current edge's length) or either end.

● **Distance** allows you to determine an exact size for the grid snap. You can enter any size you'd like; however, if the size is larger than the length of the edge on which the control point lies, the control point will jump to either end of that edge.

● **Stopper** allows you to restrict the motion of the control point to a limited area. The settings used to define that area are similar to those used to define the Grid Snap.

● **Unit** allows you to choose a method for defining the Stopper area.

● **Ratio** sets the restriction area to a percentage of the length of the source edge on which the control point lies. At 50%, this will lock the motion of the control point entirely.

● **Distance** allows you to set a distance from the beginning and end of the source edge to restrict the control point's motion.

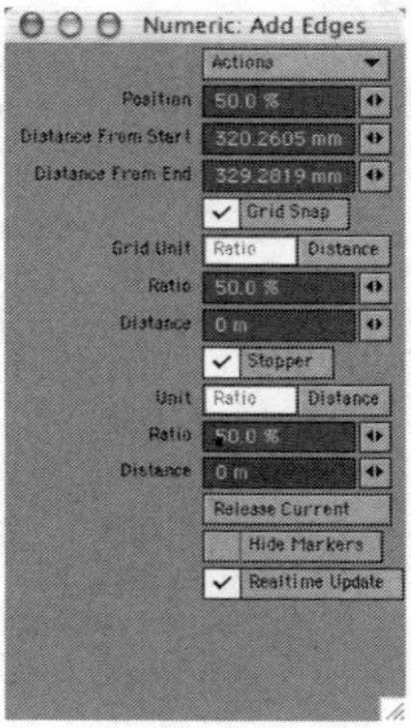

*Figure 5-38: The Add Edges Numeric window.*

● **Release Current** clears the most recently created edge.

● **Hide Markers** turns off the control points. This can make it easier to see the new edges you've created.

● **Realtime Update** shows the creation of your edges in real time. If your graphics card is a little older or begins to bog down, you can turn this off to get better feedback.

> **Note**
>
> The settings in the Numeric window are there to give you a greater degree of control over the edge tools, but don't let the myriad of options intimidate you. You can use all of the edge tools quite effectively without ever opening the Numeric window. Just know these options are available should you need them.

# Reduce Edges

The Reduce Edges tool (**Detail | Edges | Reduce Edges**) will remove the selected edge and collapse the edges that support it. (The supporting edges are those that run perpendicular to the edge you're reducing.) This tool works wonders for cleaning up problematic areas of your mesh.

To reduce an edge, select the control point on the edge that you'd like to remove. You'll see a preview of the effect. To accept this, right-click or press the <Return> key.

> **Note**
>
> Reducing and removing edges can easily lead to non-planar polygons. Be sure to keep a watchful eye on your Statistics panel when using these tools.

> **Note**
>
> If you right-click, the Reduce Edges tool will remain active, allowing you to quickly reduce multiple edges in your object.

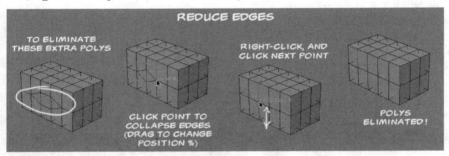

*Figure 5-39: Cleaning up our geometry by reducing edges.*

# Remove Edges

The Remove Edges tool (**Detail | Edges | Remove Edges**) does exactly what its name implies — it removes edges from your object.

To remove an edge, simply click on its associated control point. As with the Reduce Edges tool, right-clicking allows you to accept the elimination and continue removing edges from your object.

> **Note**
>
> The Remove Edges tool will remove edges, but in certain cases it won't remove the points associated with those edges. Switch to Wireframe view to ensure that no stray points are left in your object.

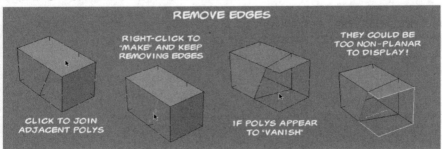

*Figure 5-40: Removing edges.*

# Rounder

Have you ever wanted a magic wand that you could wave over your objects to make them look more realistic? Well, you're in luck! That magic wand exists. It's called Rounder, and it can be found under the Multiply | Extend menu. You see, in the real world, the corners and edges of every single object (no matter how sharp they might appear) are slightly rounded. This rounding produces a glint along the object's edge when the light catches it. Unfortunately, 3D software makes it easy to create corners and edges that are infinitely sharp. While technically accurate, they don't catch the light like real objects do and when rendered, they look fake. Rounder takes care of this by adding multi-step bevels to the corners and edges of your objects.

*Figure 5-41: Rounder turns an average object into a great one.*

Rounder has two modes. You can toggle between them at any time during the tool's use. In the first mode, Rounder bevels points (called a chamfer in some 3D applications). In the other mode, it rounds edges. Using either mode is easy. Simply select the points or polys you wish to round, then click in any viewport and drag your mouse. Dragging up and down increases and decreases the bevel size. Dragging left and

right increases and decreases the number of bevel segments.

> **Note**
>
> Rounder only works on edges shared by exactly two polygons. It will not work on single, isolated polygons. When working with Boolean objects, make sure that you have merged points first or Rounder will give you an error!

In addition to adding the subtle bevels that make objects look more realistic, Rounder can be used to solve otherwise complicated modeling tasks.

The pegbox for this lute is a pretty complex shape, but you can make it very easily, in just a few steps, with Rounder.

*Figure 5-42: Robin Wood's lute object.*

1. First, make the basic shape, bevel the top poly in, then down, and use the Knife tool to determine where the sides will become straight, between the second and third pegs. Then select the four points that belong to the rounded edges (Figure 5-43).

2. Run Rounder. Robin used the settings shown in Figure 5-44. Rounder will instantly round the edges and simultaneously form the half-circles where the round and straight edges meet (Figure 5-45).

3. All you have to do after that is use the Stretch tool to give the curve the desired shape (with, perhaps, a bit of tweaking with the Rotate and Drag tools to line everything up) and you're done. Just like that (Figure 5-46).

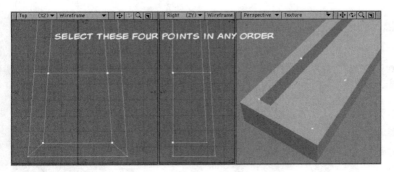

*Figure 5-43*

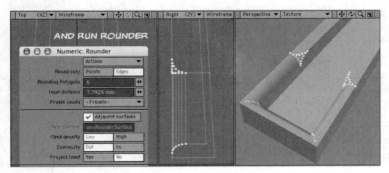

*Figure 5-44*

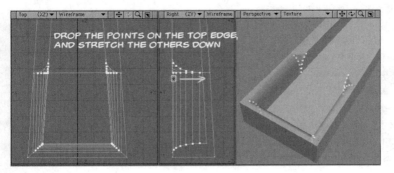

*Figure 5-45*

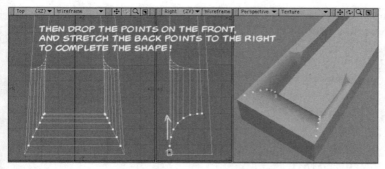

Figure 5-46

The Rounder Numeric window provides the following options.

- **Round Only** allows you to toggle between point rounding and edge rounding modes.

- **Rounding Polygons** determines the number of bevel segments to use. Higher numbers will result in a smoother-looking bevel.

- **Inset Distance** determines the size of the bevel.

- **Adjacent Surfaces** tells Rounder to apply the surface from the surrounding polygons to the new geometry. If you uncheck this box, you can specify a new surface name in the New Surface field.

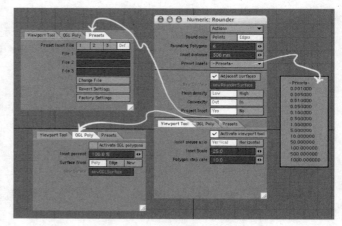

Figure 5-47: Rounder's Numeric window.

- **Mesh Density** determines the resolution of the mesh at the corners of your object. Low uses a minimum number of polygons; however, the rounding effect is compromised. High creates a wonderfully smooth corner but generates more polygons in the process (Figure 5-48).

- **Convexity** determines whether the corner bevel pulls the new polygons in or pushes them out. You won't see this in Edge mode as often as you will in Point mode (Figure 5-49).

- **Project Inset** uses a complicated set of algorithms to determine how the rounding will occur at the physical edge of your object. There is no "right" setting for this. In practice, if you find that the rounding is giving you unsatisfactory results, try turning this setting on and off (Figure 5-50).

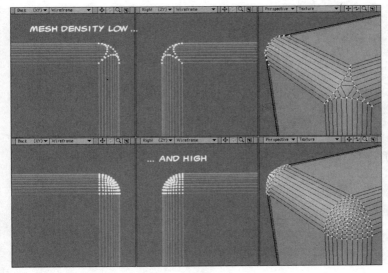

*Figure 5-48: Mesh Density settings at Low and High.*

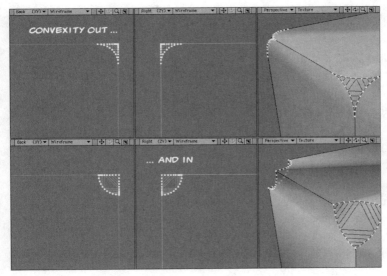

*Figure 5-49: Convexity settings set to In and Out.*

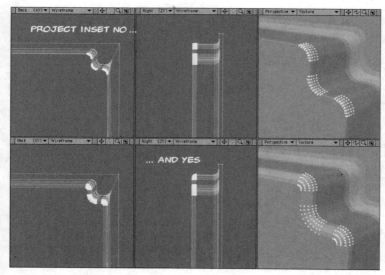

*Figure 5-50: Project Inset set to No and Yes.*

At the bottom of the Numeric window are three tabs: Viewport Tool, OGL Poly, and Presets.

- **Viewport Tool** allows you to adjust settings that deal with Rounder's interactivity controls.

- **OGL Poly** provides settings for correcting OpenGL rendering errors.

- **Presets** allow you to store and recall your favorite settings.

Let's take a look at how easy it is to round your polys and add realism to your objects.

For this exercise, we'll make a simple lava lamp.

1. Select the Ball tool. Holding the <Ctrl> key down, create a perfectly round disc in the Top view. The actual size doesn't matter, but for this example, I'm using a disc with a 122mm radius. Switch to the Extrude tool. Place your mouse over the Back viewport and holding the <Ctrl> key, pull down to form a tube. Give this object a new surface called **Glass** and turn Smoothing on. Check to make

sure that Action Center is set to **Selection**, then select the top disc polygon and use the Size tool to scale it in a bit, resulting in a slight taper. This forms the glass portion of our lamp in which all the goopy wax will flow. Finally, center the object by hitting the <F2> key.

## Note

We're using the Ball tool to create the disc in Step 1 rather than the Disc tool. That may seem a little confusing, but here's what's going on. When you work in two dimensions, the Ball tool and Disc tool produce the same results. It's only when you step into the third dimension that the differences between these tools become apparent. Now, just in case you were wondering, the Disc tool is the right tool for creating a tube. However, it doesn't have a keyboard shortcut. That means you'll have to navigate to the Create tab just to activate it. Most professionals find this process time-consuming and tedious and prefer keyboard shortcuts whenever they're available. As such, we're using the Ball tool followed by the Extrude tool since they both have easily accessible keyboard shortcuts.

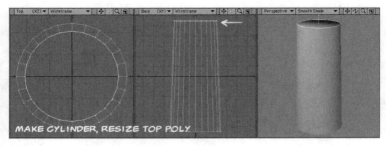

*Figure 5-51: The glass portion of our lava lamp.*

2. Copy the top and bottom disc polygons and paste them into a new layer. Flip the polygons (**Detail | Polygons | Flip**) so that their normals are facing the opposite direction. Place the glass object in the background layer and extrude each of these discs as shown in Figure 5-52. (Remember to use the <Ctrl> key (or middle mouse button) when extruding to constrain the action.) This forms the cap and base for our lamp. Give each a new surface, calling the top **Cap** and the bottom **Base**. Finally, move the base down slightly and the cap up slightly so that they are

not touching the polygons in the background layer. (This will make it easy to select their points for rounding.)

3. Select the top of the cap. Using the Size tool, scale it in slightly to taper the object. Repeat this process on the bottom of the base (Figure 5-53).

4. Go to a new layer and place the glass portion of our lamp along with the cap and base layers in the background. In the Top viewport, drag out a disc that is a bit larger than the diameter of our background object. Extrude it down as shown in Figure 5-54. This forms the

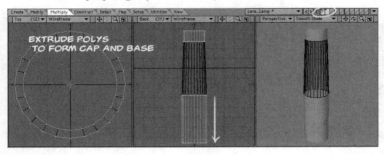

*Figure 5-52: The cap and base of our lava lamp.*

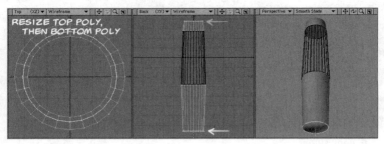

*Figure 5-53: Sizing the top and bottom discs tapers the cap and base objects.*

**161**

stand for our lamp. Give it a new surface called **Stand**. Press <**F2**> to center the object and then use the Move tool to move it into position.

5. Using the <**Shift**> key to select multiple layers, place the cap, the glass portion, the base, and the stand in the foreground. Press <**Ctrl**> + <**c**> to copy them. Go to a new layer and press <**Ctrl**> + <**v**> to paste them.

That's it for the basic modeling. Take a look at your object. It's not bad, but it's not good either (Figure 5-55). Let's use

Rounder to transform this average model into a great one!

6. Select the points at the top of the cap and press <**A**> to zoom into the selection. Activate Rounder by selecting it from the **Multiply | Extend** menu and hit <**n**> to bring up the Numeric window. Check to make sure that Activate viewport is turned on and Inset Mouse Axis is set to Vertical. Click in the Perspective viewport to activate the tool and drag up and down to adjust the size of the inset until it creates a nice, medium-sized edge. If you find that

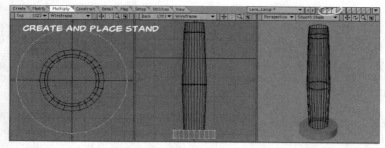

Figure 5-54: Creating the stand for our lamp.

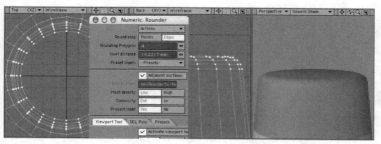

Figure 5-55: The basic lava lamp.

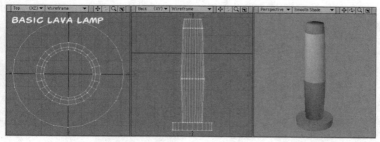

Figure 5-56: Rounding the top of the cap.

your edge isn't tapering enough, set Project Inset to **Yes** (Figure 5-56).

7. Repeat this process for the bottom of the cap, but instead of the medium-sized edge, reduce the size of the Inset Distance to create a small, tight rounded edge. Finally, select the polygon at the very bottom of the cap and use the Bevel tool to bevel it up, forming the inside of the cap object (Figures 5-57 and 5-58).

8. For the base, round its top and bottom with the same type of small edge you used on the bottom of the cap. (Simply activate the Rounder tool and it will utilize its previous settings.) After rounding, select the disc at the top of the base and use the Bevel tool to bevel it in and down slightly to form an inside lip. Then use the Bevel tool again to bevel it down, forming the inside of the object (Figure 5-59).

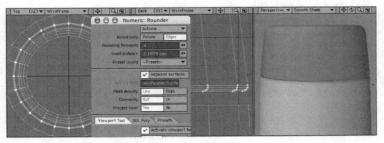

Figure 5-57: Rounding the bottom of the cap.

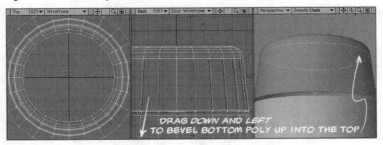

Figure 5-58: Beveling the bottom poly to form the inside of the cap.

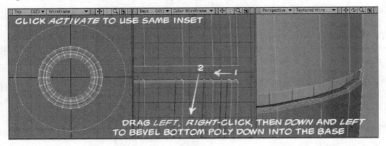

Figure 5-59: Rounding the base and beveling the top poly to create the inside geometry.

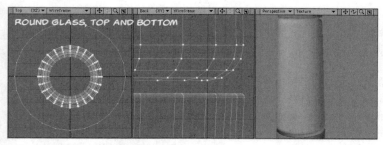

Figure 5-60: Rounding the glass portion.

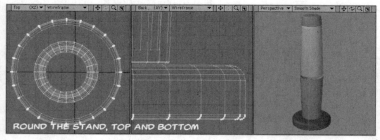

Figure 5-61: Rounding the stand.

9.  Round the top and bottom of the glass portion, giving it a slightly larger edge than you did on the top of the cap (Figure 5-60).

10. We're almost done! Select the points at the top of the stand and round them with a medium-sized edge. Then select the points at the bottom of the stand and give them a small- to medium-sized edge (Figure 5-61).

11. Finally, move the cap down so that its sides touch the glass. Move the base up so that it does the same. Then move the stand up so that it rests just below the base.

From here you can surface the lamp and use metaballs to create the blobby wax objects (which is what I've done). If you want to animate the lava, you can use HyperVoxels. (For more information about HyperVoxels, see Chapter 18.) The final textured lava lamp is available on the CD for your inspection.

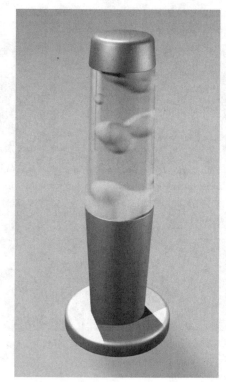

Figure 5-62: The final lava lamp.

# UV Texturing

UV texturing (U and V being the different axes attributed to an object's *surface*) is just a way of nailing down exactly what texture goes where on your model. It came about because planar, cubic, cylindrical, and spherical mapping coordinates didn't fit all applications — and had serious difficulties when "painting" the complex forms in characters.

Let's create a UV texture map.

1.  First, you must have the Texture button active (the "T" button in the lower-right corner). The pop-up menu to its right displays "Texture" and through it, you can choose **new** to access the Create UV Texture Map window. Be sure the Initial Value box is checked so you have access to the controls that actually take your selected geometry and make a UV map from it.

2.  Choose **Planar** as the Map Type, select the **Z** axis onto which we will "spindle" our 2D image, and let LightWave use its automatic settings to size the UV map it generates. This gives us the map shown in the UV Texture viewport.

The UV texture map in Figure 5-63 looks just like the sphere when seen (orthogonally) from the Z axis. (This is exactly what a *planar image map* is!) You see that the sphere in the UV Texture window perfectly fills the square 5x5 grid, which represents the *exact* extents of the texture map.

> **Note**
>
> You can load any size image as the texture map (square or rectangular), and LightWave will interpolate it to fit within this 5x5 grid.
>
> Any points that go off the edges of this 5x5 grid aren't "lost" to the texture. LightWave *tiles* the image (repeats it infinitely) when it reaches the edge of this grid.

Once you have created your UV texture, you can load an image to be seen in the backdrop of your UV Texture window. (Notice how the original dimensions of the image are now "squished" to fit the 5x5 UV Texture grid.) If the image "overpowers" the light colors LightWave uses for its points and polys, you can use the Display Options | Backdrop tab to adjust the brightness, contrast, and image resolution (see Figure 5-64).

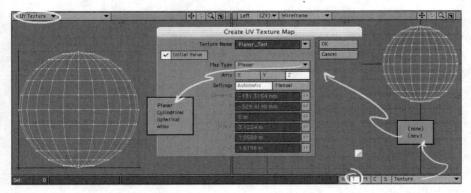

*Figure 5-63: In its simplest form, UV texturing is just a very specific way of looking at planar, cylindrical, and spherical mappings.*

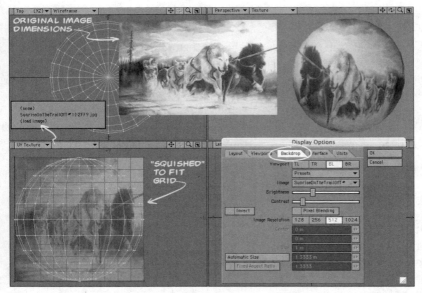

*Figure 5-64: Sunrise on the Trail of the Yukon Quest. Copyright 2002, Timothy Albee and the Yukon Quest. Used with permission.*

3. To get a surface to use your UV texture, you need to assign it to one of your Texture channels for your object's surface.

The Texture Editor offers these options:

- **Layer Type** is set to Image Map (UV texturing is just another way of using an image to define some part of your surface).

- **Projection** is set to UV.

- **UVMap** is set to the name of the UV map you have created for your geometry.

- **Image** is set to the image you want to have mapped onto your geometry.

- **Width Tile** and **Height Tile** tell LightWave how to tile the image when it reaches the edge of its 5x5 grid. It can be repeated or mirrored, have its edge pixels continue on indefinitely, or reset to the surface's base attribute (what it would be without the map applied).

- **Pixel Blending** smoothes the pixelation that can happen if you get the camera too close to a surface.

- **Texture Antialiasing** will help eliminate "pixel crawl" when you have more

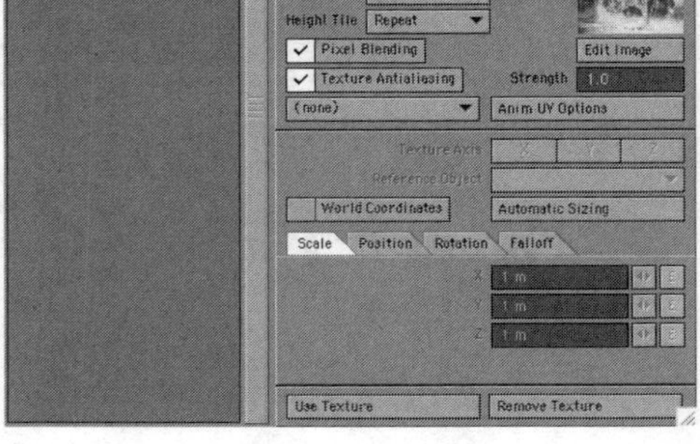

*Figure 5-65*

detail in your texture than can fit in a single pixel of LightWave's rendered image. Strength is a level of how much of an effect Texture Antialiasing will have on the texture map (the default value of 1 works well for most cases; higher levels can cause the texture to look blurry). Pixel Blending and Texture Antialiasing are the same for all image mapping types.

All this is interesting, but when most people in "the industry" think of UV mapping, they're thinking of *atlas UV mapping*. This is where you break apart your object into sections, like in a geographic atlas, so you can more easily wrap your mind around the geometry for which you are painting texture maps.

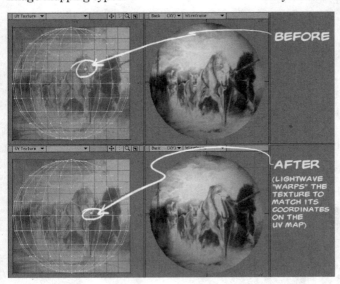

Figure 5-66: Point(s) selected on the model will also show up as selected in the UV Texture viewport. Moving a point in the UV Texture viewport will not alter its position on the model; LightWave will use its position on the image map to "warp" the image map's position on the geometry. (Similarly, moving a point on the geometry will not alter its position on the UV map.) This is how you tweak a map to fit the "landmarks" of your model — eyes, noses, cheeks, whatever!

Creating a UV texture of the Map Type Atlas "lays out" the faces of this cube so each one is easily accessible.

- **Relative Gap Size** tells LightWave how much space you want between the groupings on the atlas UV map.

- **Segment by Surface** will make sure that polys of different surfaces are separated on the atlas map, even if they are on the same relative plane.

Figure 5-67: The Create UV Texture Map window for an Atlas map type.

- **Segment by Part** does the same thing but with the polygon groupings (parts) you've got set up.

An odd thing with atlas maps is that on the map itself, not every polygon has points to drag around. When two or more polygons *share* a point, only *one* polygon has that point represented on the atlas map! This would mean trouble when tweaking an atlas map or laying one out by hand, if it weren't for Unweld.

**Detail | Points | Unweld** takes any point shared by more than one polygon and "breaks it apart" into as many exact copies as there need to be so each polygon "owns" one of the copies. After using Unweld on a selection, no one point (of that selection) is "owned" by more than one polygon. (So,

after doing this, forget about using Select Connected until you reunite all the points again.)

> **Note**
>
> After using Unweld to tweak your UV map, you use Detail | Points | Merge Points with the Range set to Automatic to "re-fuse" all the points that are in *exactly the same position*.
>
> This could cause smoothing problems where the surfaces of a Boolean operation meet (and you have purposely not merged those points). If you know you're going to want to make an atlas UV map for an object that for whatever reason has points sitting *exactly* on top of one another, and they need to stay that way, set these points as part of a Point Selection Set so you can unweld them again after merging everything back into one piece after adjusting your atlas map.

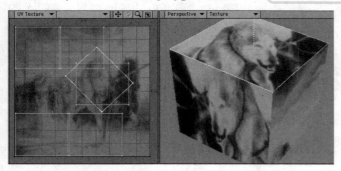

*Figure 5-68: After having used Unweld, the faces of the cube can be moved, rotated, scaled, and generally "pushed about," so you get the exact look on your object you are trying to achieve.*

How do the default settings for creating an atlas map work for something complex, like a character? Not too well for this artist's tastes. Here is a quick and simple way I would set up Wolfie's head for an atlas map:

1. Load **Objects\Chapter05\Cartoon-WolfHead.lwo**.

2. Select **Merge Points | Automatic** — just to see if there are any points lying

*exactly* in the same space that we will need to watch out for after we tweak our atlas map layout. The Information window that comes up after we merge points tells us that there were "no points eliminated," which means no points were in exactly the same space. We can proceed without worrying about messing something up when we merge points later.

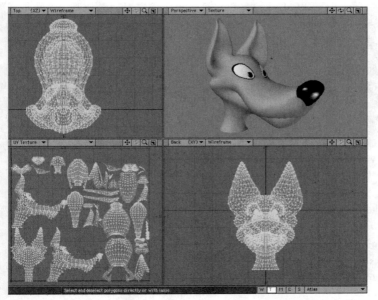

*Figure 5-69: This character's head belongs to Wolfie, one of the characters that ships, ready to animate, with* LightWave *3D 8 Character Animation.*

3. Select the surface **Wolf** (which is the only surface that we'll be applying the map to), and hide everything else.

4. Activate **Symmetry** so we know that when we select a poly on one side of our mesh, we're not leaving out the poly on the other side; Wolfie is *symmetrical*.

5. Set your Perspective viewport to **Sketch** so we can really see where the "bands" of polys lie, and so we can see the sketch colors that we'll be applying to polygons as another way of us being able to quickly select them when it comes time for tweaking our atlas map.

6. Using a combination of lassoing and direct polygon selection, select only Wolfie's ears.

7. Hide the polys you've got selected, and then clean up any strays that might have been missed before. (Remember the trick of using Hide Invert to see

what you've got hidden. You can treat what you've got *visible* and what you've got *hidden* as if they were two separate groups of polys. Hiding a poly from one group makes it "belong" to the other group.)

8. Using **Detail | Polygons | Sketch Color**, assign the sketch color for this part of Wolfie to **Black**. (This way, we'll be able to select them easily, without messing up the parts I already have assigned to differentiate between his upper and lower jaws.)

9. Select **Hide Invert**, and then select just the *front* of Wolfie's ears.

10. Once you have the *insides* of Wolfie's ears selected, assign them a sketch color of **Dark Blue**. (See Figure 5-70.)

11. With all of the polys of the insides of Wolfie's ears selected and set to **Dark Blue** as their sketch color, hide them. Then select the *backs* of Wolfie's ears,

**169**

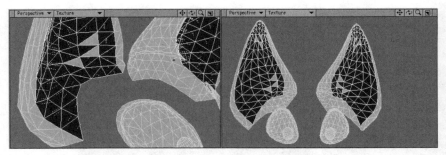

*Figure 5-70: With the Display Type set to Sketch, the "stray" polygons easily stand out when you assign your sketch color.*

setting them to a sketch color of **Yellow**. (See Figure 5-71.)

12. When you know you're not missing any polys from the *backs* of Wolfie's ears, unhide and save your work so far.

13. Deactivate **Symmetry**.

> **Note**
>
> I've found that Symmetry mode doesn't quite work as well with unwelded objects. Symmetry also doesn't work well when manipulating UV maps.

14. Unweld and, using the Polygon Statistics window, select just the polys with a

sketch color of black; hide everything else.

> **Note**
>
> If you're not sure if the Unweld command did its thing, you can always check the Point Statistics window. All of Wolfie's points should fall under the category "1 polygon."

15. Create a UV texture map using **Planar** mapping along the X axis. (This gives a profile of Wolfie, where each map poly from his left is in exactly the same place on the map as the map poly on his right.)

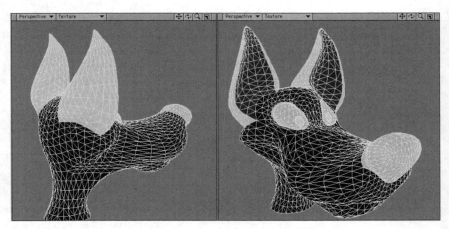

*Figure 5-71*

Figure 5-72

16. Using the Stretch tool, resize the UV map's polys so Wolfie doesn't look quite so dorky.

17. Next unhide everything. Select just the dark blue sketch color (assigned to the *insides* of Wolfie's ears), and select **Map | Texture | Make UVs**. This assigns a planar map type to the selected geometry along the Z axis.

18. Using Scale and Move, orient these polys on the UV Texture viewport so that the right ear-inside fits nicely in the upper-right corner of the map. (Don't worry about the left ear-inside; just leave it selected as you work, so it is the same size and shape as the right.)

19. Deselect the polys of the right ear-inside, and then use **Map | Texture | Flip UVs**. With Flip U active, clicking **OK** *flips* the map polys for the left ear-inside along the U axis, as shown in Figure 5-76.

20. Now move the map polys for the left ear-inside to exactly cover the map polys of the right. (You may want to use the Maximize icon on the UV Texture viewport to maximize that viewport so you can zoom in extremely close while you're doing this.) Figure 5-77 shows

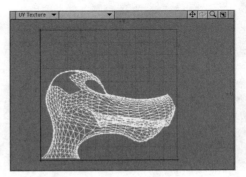

Figure 5-73

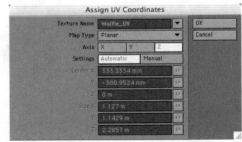

Figure 5-74

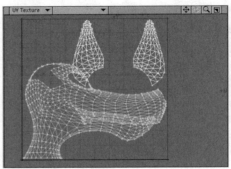

Figure 5-75

*both* ear-insides selected but occupying the same UV texture map space.

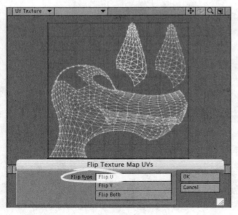

Figure 5-76

Figure 5-76

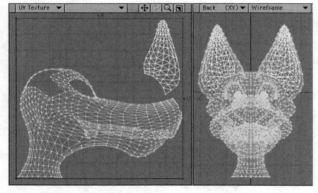

Figure 5-77

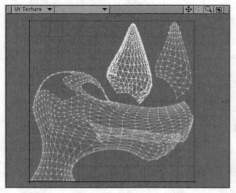

Figure 5-78

21. Repeat what you did for Figures 5-74 through 5-77 for the ear-outsides.

22. Merge points to get your model back to being one contiguous mesh again.

23. Now you can save a screen capture and bring the image into your favorite paint program, making sure your painted texture's size *exactly* matches the outer area of the UV grid. You now have a template to precisely paint anything you want on your models.

### Note

Now that we have both ear-insides occupying the same UV texture map coordinates, we can paint one area of the texture map and have it applied to *both* ear-insides!

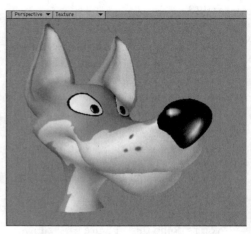

Figure 5-79: Wolfie, with a quick, painted UV texture map.

172

## Note

Another great way to get your UV map into your paint program is to export it as an EPS file. Go to the File | Export menu and select the Export Encapsulated Postscript option. You can determine which viewports Modeler will export (in this case, we'd simply use the Texture UV view). You also have options for rendering the background grid and the points of the object. Since EPS files are resolution independent, they can be placed into most paint and illustration programs at any size the user desires without sacrificing image clarity. That's just the type of flexibility you want when working on high-resolution image maps for television and film.

## Note

It is *vitally important* that you not move, rotate, or scale the pieces of your object's actual geometry while it is *unwelded* and you are adjusting sections of map polys. If you do, your model will *not* go back together again when you merge points. (Sifting through a character's many points to find the ones that are micrometers off is a torture I'd not wish on anyone.)

One way to "CYA" in this respect is to create a "junk" endomorph (see the LightWave manual) to have active as you work your mapping placements. Having an endomorph active won't affect the placement of the texture polys within a UV Texture viewport, but any accidental nudging or bumping to your actual geometry polys in the regular viewports can be easily gotten rid of using Map | General | Clear Map. Clearing the map must be done *while* you have the "junk" endomorph "map" active! It should be done *before* merging points; otherwise, points that are no longer in the same position on the endomorph will not be merged, even if they are in exactly the same position on the object's "base" state.

Be aware: If you have your UV texture map active instead of the "junk" endomorph, Clear Map will *erase* what you have selected from your UV map!

Obviously, it is important to have a good, clear working knowledge of using maps (weight, texture, morph, color, and selection) before using a technique like this if you don't plan on saving a revision of your work. But I want you to be aware of this technique — it's what the pros do.

· · ·

You've added some cool, powerful tools to your "bag-o'-tricks." They're things the pros use every day to get their jobs done *well* and done *fast*! Now they're a part of what *you* can do as well! With practice, they'll become so second nature, you won't ever want to work without them.

Yet, we're *still* just scratching the surface of what you can do in Modeler. So, when you're done exploring the things you've just learned, clear your desktop! In the next chapter, we're going to put some of what you've learned to work.

# Chapter 6

# Architectural Modeling Exercise: Interior Set

Now we're going to use what you've learned to actually build something. We may even pick up a new tool or two along the way! Most of what we'll be doing fits with how you've probably imagined a particular tool to be used. But some of it may leave you thinking, "Oh! I hadn't thought of using that *that* way!" And that's great! If it gets the job done, and done well, there's no such thing as using it wrong.

*Use the tools you've got to do the job you do!*

> ### Note
>
> In the exercise in this chapter, if you find yourself getting stuck somewhere, go back and carefully reread the instructions for that and the previous step(s). The book was examined by some very good tech checkers, so we know everything does indeed work. Don't be afraid to have the LW manual open beside you as you work. I've been using LW since 1989, and my LW manual *still* occupies a place of honor within arm's reach on my desk at all times.
>
> Being a professional often means that you are unafraid to do whatever it takes to get the job done — regardless of anyone else's opinion of what you need to do to achieve your goal.

## Floor Plan

Believe it or not, I find the most grinding part of doing an architectural interior to be making the floor plan. This is because in order to get all the rest of the stuff to go smoothly, including shadow casting in rendering, the floor plan can't be haphazardly laid down. It has to be built in such a way that doors and windows can be Booleaned out of it. The floor plan will also be used to "trim" the carpeting or whatever flooring will be laid in later. The floor plan, in the way I work, is used in shaping every other element of the structure.

> ### Note
>
> Bear in mind that this is just one way of working. This is the way I've found that works most smoothly with the way I think. You'll have to take this information with a grain (or a gram) of salt. It is by no means the only way to work. It is just the process I've developed to go from the uncarved block to having a completed, interior set with as little stress as possible.
>
> I encourage you to find out all you can about how other modelers work as well. Put all this together, throw out what doesn't work for you, and keep the rest!

Even though I am a big fan of the metric system, when I build interior sets, my mind seems only to function in the English system of measurements. To me, ceilings are most easily thought of as being eight or ten feet high. It's just the way I've been trained, and I haven't retrained my mind for metric units. So, my apologies to those of you who are more comfortable thinking in metric units, but for the sake of everyone being on the same page, here's how to change your settings to English units:

1. Set your Unit System to **English** (**Display Options | Units**) and your Default Unit to **feet**.

2. Next, set your Grid Snap to **Fixed** and your Snap Value to **1'** (one foot).

With a sizable, fixed grid snap, we can more quickly and accurately lay foundation. All our dragging around of walls, windows, and whatnot will now perfectly adhere to being at one-foot intervals, no matter what level of zoom we are using to inspect the detail of our set. (We'll change this value as we work, depending on what we're doing — sometimes snapping to half-foot intervals, sometimes to one-inch intervals.)

3. Maximize the Top viewport by clicking on its Maximize icon or by placing your mouse over the viewport and pressing **<0>** on the numeric pad.

## Two-Point Polyline Work

I lay out the walls of my set with two-point polylines. They're easy to work with, quick to resize, and easily transform into what I need later on.

1. Make two points on the same axis (X or Z) and press **<p>** to make a two-point poly out of them. (You should be aiming for a straight line along either the X or Z axis — no diagonals.)

2. With Polygons as your selection mode, the polyline you just created should be selected. (If it isn't, select it now.)

3. Press **<Ctrl>** + **<c>** and then press **<Ctrl>** + **<v>** to copy the polyline and paste a new, *unselected* copy of it right in its place. (The polyline you have selected *stays selected*.)

4. Press **<r>** to rotate your selection 90° clockwise.

5. Press **<t>** to move your selection so that it forms a right angle with the end of your *unselected* polyline. (See the left side of Figure 6-1.)

6. Repeat Steps 3-5 to mimic what is shown in Figure 6-1.

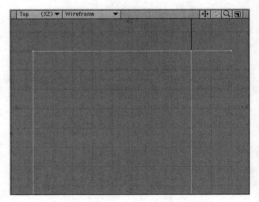

*Figure 6-1: What if we don't quite have the end of one of our walls where we need it to be? There's a cool tool that lets you click and drag any point of your selection: Drag.*

Drag, like all of LightWave's tools, only works with the points, polys, or volumes that are *selected*. You can use this fact to your advantage if you have two points almost on top of each other and you want to move only one. If you can select the polygon that owns the point you wish to move, by *selecting* the poly, you can *isolate* its point from the other!

*Select the poly. Drag the point!*

This is an extreme help when working with character modeling when there's a lot of information filling the screen. By *selecting the polys* that contain the *points* that you want to tweak, *you are temporarily isolating them from the rest of your model's points.*

7.  Press <Ctrl> + <t> to activate **Modify | Move | Drag**.

8.  Drag the "offending" point of the polyline that extends past the end of our "room" onto the point two grid squares to its left. (See Figure 6-2.)

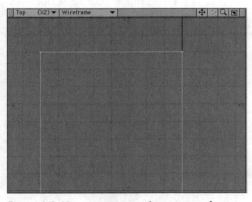

*Figure 6-2: You can continue this process of "Copy-Paste-Rotate-Move-Drag" to complete any right angle-based floor plan.*

Note

Again, so that we're all working from the same place, as we're doing something rather complex and precision focused, let me save you the trouble of laying out a floor plan and point you to **Objects\Chapter06\ Floorplan_Root.lwo**.

Load this object so we're all working from the same framework.

9.  Select the polyline shown in Figure 6-3, and press <**K**> to bring up **Multiply | Subdivide | Knife**.

Note

The Knife tool will *slice* any selected polygon that its *line of action* comes in contact with, creating *two connected polys*. You click and drag to create and position this *line of action*.

Because we have Grid Snap set at 1', the way we've positioned our walls makes them fall on these 1' grid lines. Knife will also obey the 1' Grid Snap, so slicing our long wall into segments that meet up exactly with the intersecting walls is just a matter of clicking and dragging the Knife tool's line of action as if it were an extension of the *intersecting* wall.

10. After using Knife to cut the long wall into segments where it intersects the other walls, double-check that all your walls are *segmented* where they *intersect* the other walls as well. (The quick way to do this is to select the entire floor plan and, one by one, click on the walls to deselect them segment by segment!)

11. Return to a Quad layout and verify that your floor plan is lying on the ground plane by pressing <v> and entering **0** feet for the Y axis.

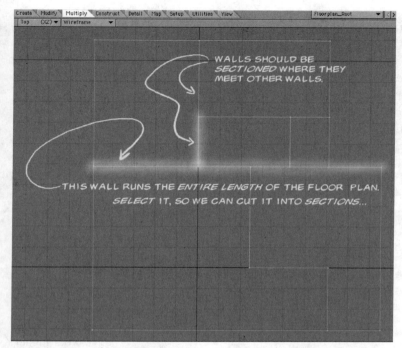

Figure 6-3: Our base floor plan. For the way we'll be working here, wherever two walls meet, you should Copy-Paste-Move-Drag to create another section so that all your walls have a "break" in them where they touch. (In Floorplan_Root.lwo, I've purposely left one wall "incorrect" so that it spans the length of the entire floor plan.)

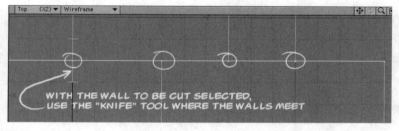

Figure 6-4: The quick way to accept your knifing and move on to another place you want to knife is to just right-click.

12. Now, merge points, and use a Fixed Range with a Distance of **0.9**". With our Grid Snap settings, we shouldn't have any points within a *foot* of one another,

but with the Distance setting of 9/10ths of an inch, we'll be able to use these settings for our later, more detailed work as well.

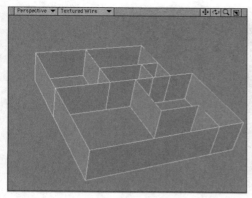

Figure 6-5

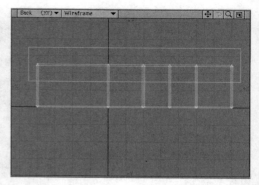

Figure 6-7

13. Extrude the floor plan *up* about five feet. (No, we're not building a hobbit-sized house. We just need to get some room to work to prepare for transforming our polylines into walls with thickness.)

14. Activate the Bevel tool and its Numeric window. Enter **1"** for both Shift and Inset.

15. Using Volume Select: Include (click the **View | Selection | Volume** button twice), drag a selection box around the top of your model and press the **Delete** key to delete it. You are left with only its bottom (see Figure 6-8).

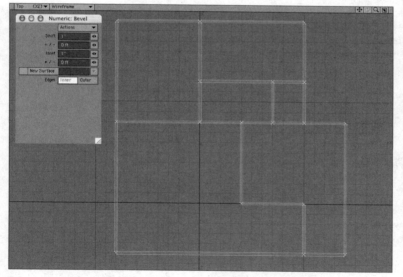

Figure 6-6: When we extruded the two-point polys, the "walls" became sets of two polygons back to back. So, beveling each "face" by 1 inch gives a total wall thickness of 2 inches. (Using the same value for the Inset as we used for the Shift means that where walls meet at right angles, the new points lie directly on top of one another — it saves us a little bit of time when merging points a bit later.)

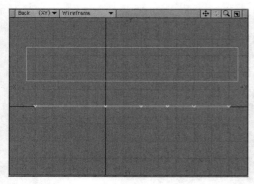

Figure 6-8

**Note**

You can cover great distances by using the <g> hot key to center your viewport around where the tip of the mouse's cursor is.

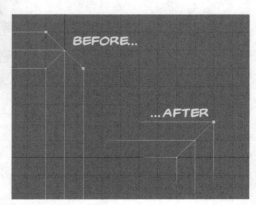

Figure 6-10

16. Now deselect everything (</>) and set the value for the Y axis to **0'** (zero feet), so all these points and polys once again lie flat on the ground.

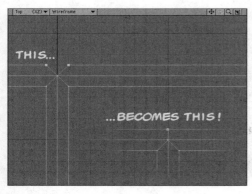

Figure 6-9

17. Now, from a Top viewport and with a Grid Snap Value of **1"** (one inch), go around the walls, and anywhere you see a gap like that shown in Figure 6-9, drag the points together so they meet. (Points are shown selected in the figure so they can be seen easier — this step is quickest to do with *nothing* selected.)

18. Do the same for every corner as well.

19. Merge points, again with a Fixed Distance of **0.9"**. You should get a message telling you that 44 points were eliminated. (If you're working with this floor plan and you get some other number, *go back and check your work*! Working from the *same model* and going through the *same steps*, we should get the *same results*.)

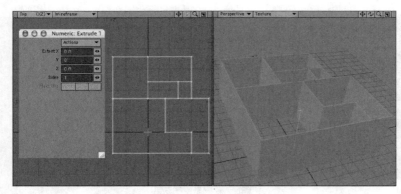

Figure 6-11

20. Now, using the Numeric window, extrude this version of your floor plan *up* **8'**. You'll see your walls have some thickness to them.

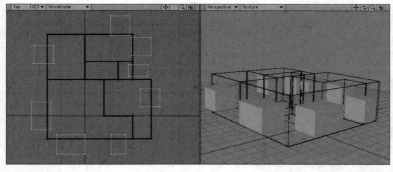

Figure 6-12

21. Now, create some boxes on a background layer where you'd like your windows to be. Place them in positions similar to those shown in Figure 6-12 so that they can be used as Boolean "cookie cutters" for our floor plan. (Make sure you have at least five inches between window boxes.)

**Note**

There are a couple of ways to do this quickly.

One way is to create one cookie cutter, select it, and copy and paste it, moving it to its new location and using <r> to rotate it 90° if necessary.

Another way is to get one window cookie cutter sized the way you want it and then right-click and drag on the "+" in the center of the box to drag a new one to a different location.

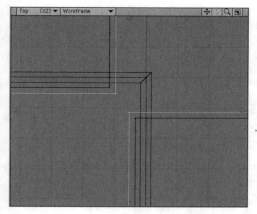

Figure 6-13

22. Now, copy and paste those "window boxes" into a fresh layer and Smooth Scale them **2"**. This will have the effect of making these boxes one inch larger all the way around (shown in Figure 6-13 with both the "old" window boxes and the floor plan in the background layers). We will be using these "new" boxes to stencil an area we will use later as a molding around each window.

23. With the new boxes created in Figure 6-13 in the background layer and your floor plan in the foreground layer, **Solid Drill | Stencil** a new surface with the name **Window_Molding** onto your floor plan. (You may want to go into the Surface Editor afterward and adjust the color of this new surface so it stands out from the default surface on the rest of the model.)

24. With the old window boxes (the smaller ones) in the background layer and your floor plan in the foreground layer, **Boolean | Subtract** the holes for your windows.

25. Merge points using the same fixed settings we've been using, and delete both the window boxes and the new boxes.

26. Next, with a Grid Snap Value of **6"**, create two boxes that will be used to Boolean the walkways that will not have doors in them, as shown in Figure 6-15. They should be three feet wide, extend just below the ground plane,

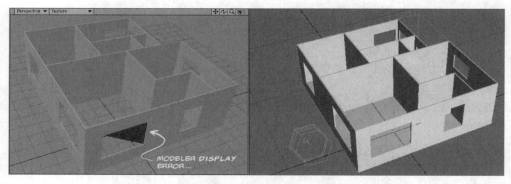

Figure 6-14: I'm not sure why, but sometimes Modeler doesn't quite know how to display a Boolean that is completely inside a large, flat surface like this wall. In Layout's Shaded preview, the Boolean looks fine; more importantly, it renders correctly. This little display error is just one of those things where, after testing to be absolutely sure, you have to be content with knowing that you're right and the computer is wrong.

and have their tops at 6'9". (Use **Set Value** for the tops of the walkway cutters.)

27. Boolean the walkways out of the floor plan, and merge points again (still with the same settings). You'll want to keep these walkway cutters on a background layer, out of the way, for use later when cutting the other doors.

28. Next, make a polygon that extends beyond the boundaries of our floor plan, as shown in Figure 6-16. It should be surfaced with the name **Ceiling**. Its Smoothing Threshold should be set to **23°**, its normal should be facing *down*, and you should use Set Value to put it exactly at **7'** high on the Y axis.

29. With Ceiling in the foreground layer and the floor plan in the background layer, use **Solid Drill | Tunnel** to cut the *exact* shape of the floor plan into the ceiling. (See Figure 6-17.)

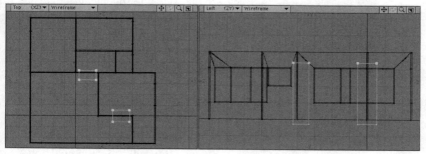

*Figure 6-15*

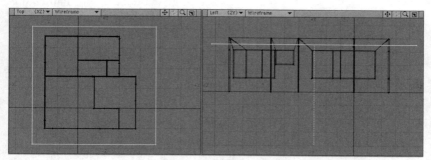

*Figure 6-16*

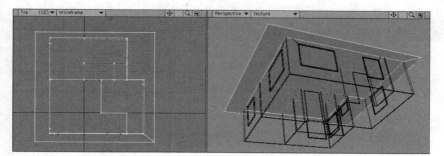

*Figure 6-17*

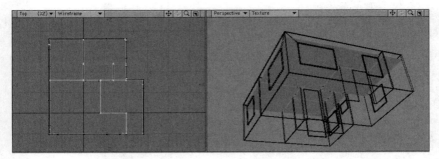

*Figure 6-18*

30. Delete the edge that extends outside the floor plan (Figure 6-18). Then delete all points from those polygons that do not fall directly on a *corner* of those polygons.

31. Now we're going to do the cornice work on the ceiling. You could draw a cornice yourself, but a cool thing about Rail Bevel is that you can save neat bevels for later. Load **Objects\Chapter06\Cornice_SubtleElegant.lwo**.

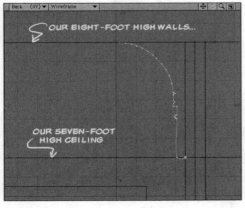

*Figure 6-19*

32. Copy and paste this into a clean foreground layer of your model with the floor plan *and* the ceiling in the background layers. Press <A> to zoom in on the cornice rail in the foreground layer. We can see that the cornice rail starts where we put our ceiling polys (at seven feet) and "does its thing," ending up gracefully blending to the height of the top of our walls at eight feet (where one would normally expect an eight-foot ceiling to be).

33. Now, with *only* our ceiling in the foreground layer and *only* our cornice rail in the background layer, activate **Rail Bevel**, and in the Numeric window, enter **–100%** for the Shift (pushing it up 100% of the distance outlined by the cornice rail) and **–140%** for the Inset, so our bevel's points line up directly with the cornice rail that we can see in the background layer. *Instant cornices!* (See Figure 6-20.)

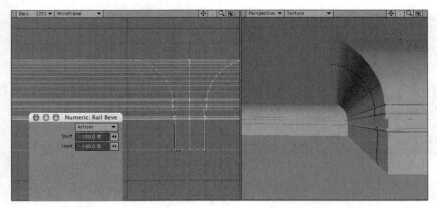

Figure 6-20

> **Note**
>
> Something to be aware of is that currently the Rail Bevel tool will only work properly with a shape defined by points that sculpt their curve when looking at them along the Z axis, as the cornice rail's points do. Rail Bevel won't work properly if the shape reads as a flat, straight-up-and-down line when viewed from a Back or Front viewport.

34. Leaving your cornice and ceiling in their layers, bring up an empty foreground layer, put the floor plan in a background layer, and create another polygon, just like you did in Figure 6-16. This polygon should be surfaced with the name **Floor**, its Smoothing should be **Off**, its normal should be facing *up*, and you should use Set Value to position it at exactly 4" "high" on the Y axis.

35. Use **Solid Drill | Tunnel** to have the floor plan cut the exact shape of your flooring into your polygon (shown in Figure 6-22 with the "excess" polygon around the edge already removed).

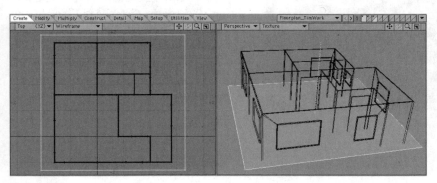

Figure 6-21

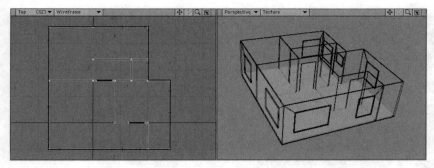

*Figure 6-22*

36. Once again, we're going to load in a prefabricated piece to use in rail beveling the floor molding. Load **Objects\ Chapter06\Molding_Rail.lwo.** Copy and paste it onto a blank foreground layer of your floor plan work-in-progress. With it alone on the foreground layer, select **View | Viewports | Fit Selected** so you'll have a clear view of it when you do your rail bevel.

## Note

You don't necessarily have to work with these prefab rails for rail beveling. It's just that I've already built them to fit the dimensions with which we're working; the values in the Numeric: Rail Bevel window shown in Figure 6-23 will give you *exactly* what you're looking at in this book.

If you find the ornamentation that these prefab rails produce too staid for your tastes, by all means feel free to create your own rails to rail bevel. When building your own rails, it's best if they span the distance you want the actual ornamentation to cover, so the value you enter for Shift is +/–100% (depending on an obscure combination of the poly's normal and the rail's start point). The rail should also be positioned along the X axis so that it silhouettes the shape you want to create (the Molding_Rail file with the flooring in the background touches the right edge of one of the flooring sections). With the rail in the side view and positioned along the X axis, adjusting the Inset value will make the geometry generated by the Rail Bevel tool "push" more and more to conform to the rail in the background layer. If you've already approved the shape of the rail, you know the new geometry has an appropriate height/depth ratio when the Inset value makes the new geometry line up perfectly with the rail's profile in the background layer.

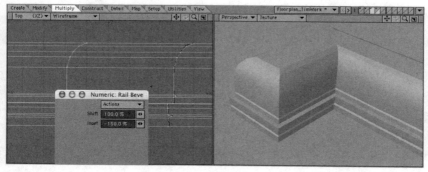

Figure 6-23

37. With the molding rail in the background
    layer and the flooring in the foreground
    layer, Rail Bevel with a Shift of **100%**,
    and an Inset of **–150%** — we have
    instant molding!

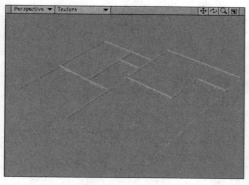

Figure 6-24

38. Select just the four polys that make up
    the actual "floor" and hide them, so
    you're just looking at the molding that
    you've created. Assign it a surface
    named **Molding** with a Smoothing
    Threshold of **42°**, and cut and paste it
    onto the layer on which you've got the
    rest of your floor plan. Select **Merge
    Points | Automatic** to clean up any

oddities the rail beveled molding may
have (be sure you use Automatic settings when merging points here, *not*
the settings we've been using up to
this point). We're leaving the actual
floor on its own layer, separating the
floor from the molding for the moment.

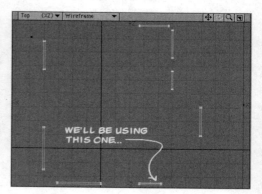

Figure 6-25

39. With the floor plan in the foreground
    layer, use the Polygon Statistics win-
    dow to select only the surface
    **Window_Molding**. Hide everything
    else.

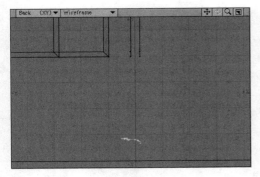

*Figure 6-26*

40. Put the window moldings in the background layer and the Molding_Rail (from creating the floor moldings) in the foreground layer. Zoom in on the Molding_Rail in a Back viewport, and with your mouse near the top of the rail, press <r> to rotate that rail 90° clockwise around the mouse's position. (This will get the window moldings to have the same basic shape as the floor molding. To rail bevel, the rail's placement in relation to the polys to be rail beveled doesn't matter, but its *orientation does*. I'm not quite sure why the Molding_Rail has to be angled this way in order for the window moldings to be the same basic shape as the floor moldings, but if it works, go with it!)

> **Note**
>
> We're about to make the window moldings. Instead of doing all of them at once, I want us to just do one, which we'll copy and paste to where the others should be. The reason for this is that we're about to see a situation where Rail Bevel doesn't quite work perfectly.
>
> When you have a polygon that has a hole cut out of it, that poly has a "seam" — a bit of a slice where the poly meets itself coming from the other direction. (Think of taking the ends of a U and bending them around to make an O.) When Rail Bevel encounters this, it splits those points apart by the same distance it is *shifting* the rest of the bevel.
>
> You'll probably encounter this problem at some point in your modeling career. The following step shows how to fix it.

41. With your reoriented Molding_Rail in the background layer and the highlighted Window Molding shown in Figure 6-25 selected in the foreground layer, activate Rail Bevel, using **50%** for the Shift and **–15%** for the Inset. (See Figure 6-27.)

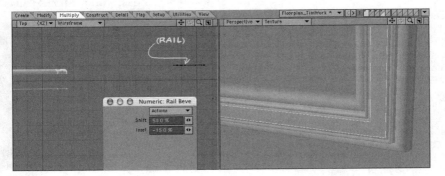

*Figure 6-27*

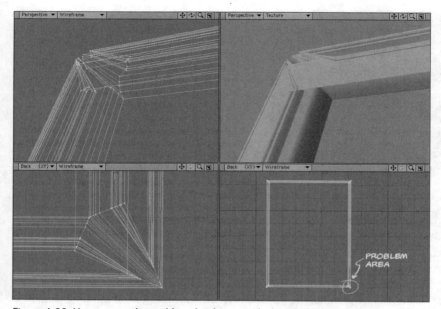

*Figure 6-28: You can see the problem that happened when Rail Bevel tried to bevel the seam. (It looks terribly mangled, but it'll take less than a minute to fix.)*

### Note

In addition to Merge Points, LightWave has two other ways of fusing multiple points into one: Weld and Weld Average.

• Detail | Points | Weld combines all the points you have selected into one point at the location of the *last point selected*.

• Detail | Points | Weld Average combines all points you have selected to a *new position* exactly in the *center* of the points you had selected.

My own preference for setting a hot key for this is <Shift> + <F12>. This way, I can have <Shift> held down for the almost-surgical single-click selecting of points inside a dense mesh and then, still holding <Shift>, just swing a finger over and tap <F12>.

Both kinds of Weld are good reasons to move your Alert Level to Intermediate or Expert. This way you're not clicking OK after every single weld. (Intermediate just brings up a "Press OK" when an error occurs. Expert *never* brings up a "Press OK"; all information, good and bad, appears in the little readout line above the Modes, Numeric, and Statistics buttons.)

42. Set your Perspective viewport to a good angle and zoom in on the problem area. Then select *two* points that are mirror copies of each other. (Once selected, orbit your viewport around a bit to make sure these two points really do go together!) Select **Weld Average**, and the *two* points become *one*, exactly between them! (See Figure 6-29.)

43. Repeat this process, working point-pair by point-pair, up from the base of the molding to its top. Then, when you've got the first side done, swing your viewport around and start again at the base of the other side of the molding. (You may want to make sure you have a sizable number of Undos set under your General Options just in case.)

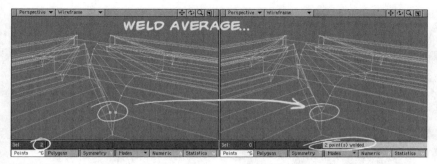

*Figure 6-29*

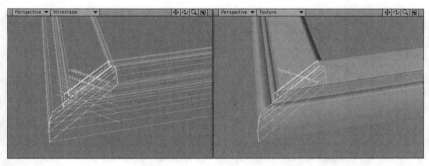

*Figure 6-30*

44. When you are done welding points, the corner of your molding looks like it should, but in the process of welding, the polys that made up the erroneous edges have been "buried" within the corner. Select these and delete them.

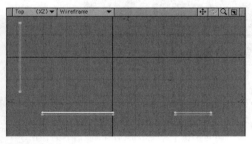

*Figure 6-31*

45. Merge points (just to be sure), and then cut the polygons for your completed window molding, separating them from the wall. Paste them first to a blank

layer (which we'll use later for making the door moldings), and then, with the moldings layer again in the foreground, paste the completed window molding *back to where it started*. Select the completed window molding again, and begin copying, pasting, moving, and rotating it to align with the other windows. (Grid Snap makes it a lot easier to get the alignment spot-on.)

> **Note**
>
> When you need to *stretch* the molding to fit a new size of window, just select the points on one side of the molding and move them to align with the new size, keeping the proportions of the strips of molding the same for all sizes of windows.

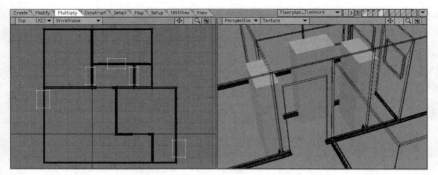

Figure 6-32

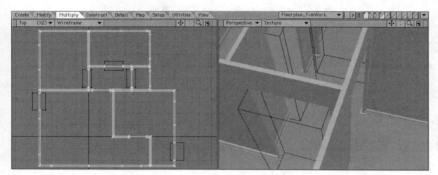

Figure 6-33

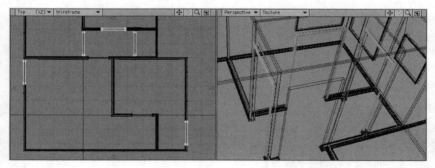

Figure 6-34

46. Now, using the "door cutters" that we have stashed on a background layer, move and rotate them to Boolean the openings where the doors will be. (See Figure 6-32.)

47. After **Boolean | Subtract**, we've got the places for our doors to go. Merge points! (Figure 6-33.)

48. Working with the copy of the window molding we put on a background layer, use the Knife tool to cut off the bottom part of it, and then move its points to fit the size of the door openings. Copy, paste, move, and rotate the door moldings to edge all the doors. You'll probably want to set your Grid Snap value to **1**". (See Figure 6-34.)

49. Once you've got your door moldings done, copy and paste them so you've got them on the same layer as your floor plan.

50. Copy and paste one of your door cutters onto a clear layer, and resize it to be **1"** thick (I find selecting and moving points in a Top viewport with a Grid Snap of 0.5" to be the quickest way to do this). Then **Set Val** for its *bottom* points to be **Y=0**.

51. On a blank layer, create a rectangular box (its exact size isn't important) and bevel *one* of its sides (the specifics of this bevel aren't important, but keep it shallow). (See Figure 6-36.)

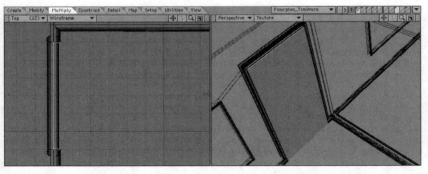

*Figure 6-35*

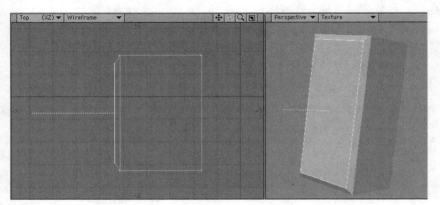

*Figure 6-36*

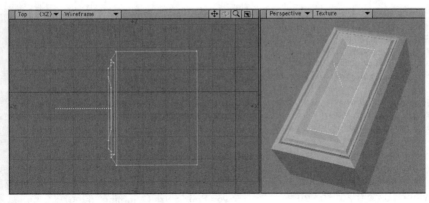

Figure 6-37

52. Keep beveling until you have a neat shape to be used as a Boolean cookie cutter to add some surface detail to the door. (Oooh, look! Pez!)

53. Move our little cookie cutter so it will "bite into" the door, then size and position it so we have *three rows* of *two* of these designs on the door. Make a point *above* and *beside* it that will tell LightWave how much distance to put between the copies, and bring up **Multiply | Duplicate | Array**. For a door in the same orientation as mine, enter **3** for the Y Count and **2** for the Z Count for the Rectangular Array, leaving the rest of the settings at their defaults. (The points are shown selected in Figure 6-38 just to help them stand out. You'll want to deselect everything for your own Array operation.)

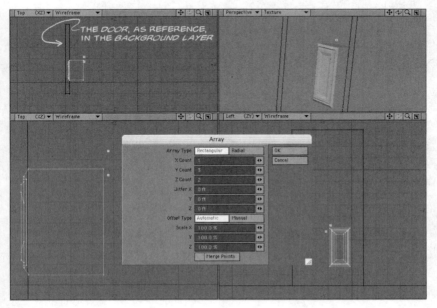

Figure 6-38

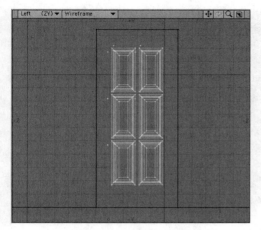

*Figure 6-39: The Array function's Automatic settings reproduce our selected geometry with respect to its original extents (which is why we added the "floating" points, specifying how much distance to keep between the copies).*

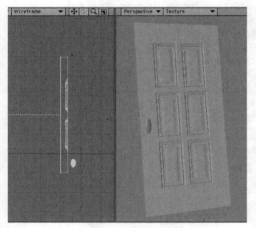

*Figure 6-40*

54. Use **Boolean | Subtract** to imprint the shape of our cookie cutters into the door and add a doorknob. Cut the back poly from the door and mirror it to create its other side, merging points to make the body of the door a complete unit. (See Figure 6-40.)

55. Copy, paste, move, and rotate the doors into position in the rest of the house, as shown in Figure 6-41.

56. Bring up the flooring polys (which we left alone on their own layer when we relocated the floor molding to the floor plan layer). Press <k> to **Construct | Reduce | Remove | Remove Polygons**. Then, select *only the outside corner points* (shown in Figure 6-42) and **Make Polygon** (getting rid of the stray points afterward). You'll need to reset the surface of this poly to **Floor**.

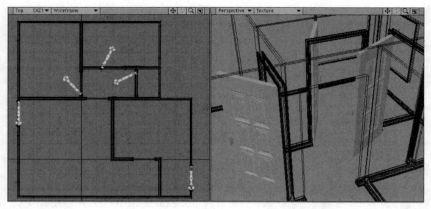

Figure 6-41

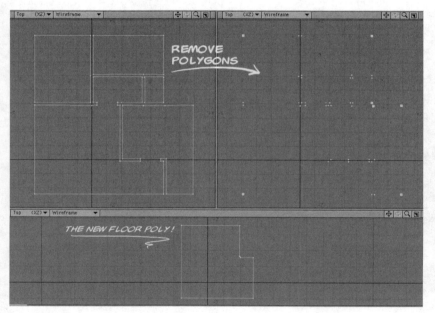

Figure 6-42

57. Cut and paste the new flooring onto the main floor plan layer. Do this with the ceiling and the doors as well, so you have your entire, finished house on one layer. Get rid of any extraneous "building supplies" hiding out on other layers, and have some fun surfacing, lighting, and rendering this quaint little place! (See Figure 6-43.)

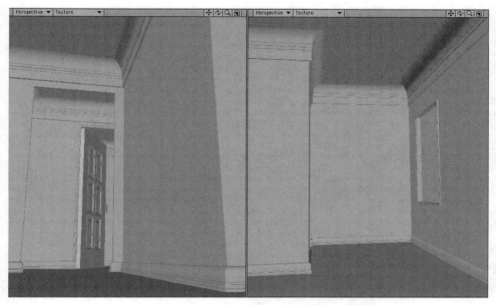

Figure 6-43

Figure 6-44: Just a super-quick surfacing job to see how the house looks in Layout.

*Figure 6-45: Another angle of the house model.*

• • •

After this exercise, I imagine you're feeling a lot more confident about your skills as a modeler. You've used many of the tools we explored in Chapter 3 and you've seen how they apply to *actually building something*.

My hope is that the wheels in your mind are already turning, working out how you can use this stuff to bring into being the things whirling about in your own imagination!

# Modeling 3: Sub-Patch Organic Modeling

A *sub-patch* is just a regular four-sided polygon that has been subdivided into smaller, four-sided polygons. How many depends upon the number set for Patch Divisions (*level of detail*) in the General Options window. (A three-sided poly will also work as a sub-patch but not quite as well.)

Saying that a sub-patch is "just" a polygon diced into tinier ones in no way, shape, or form gives even an inkling of how totally, awesomely *cool* a sub-patch is (in all its splendor and glory). The "magic" of the sub-patch lies in the fact that each of the component polys tries to make itself conform to a spherical shape (or a discoid shape, if the main poly is two-dimensional).

Pressing <**Tab**> activates **Construct | Convert | SubPatch**, which tells LightWave to handle all your quads as sub-patches. (I hesitate to say that the polys are "converted" into sub-patches because the polys technically *remain exactly as they were and are directly referenced in the interpreting of the sub-patch surface*. Pressing <**Tab**> again turns the sub-patches right back into the polys you were looking at before.)

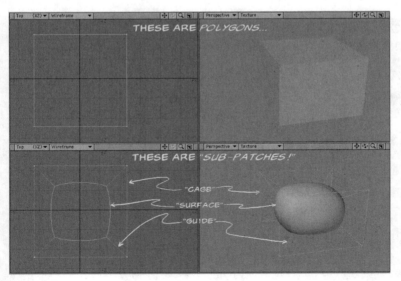

*Figure 7-1*

By default, LightWave viewports show a sub-patch's:

- **Cage** — The "ghosted" representation of the *poly* that is defining the *sub-patch*.

- **Surface** — What will actually be rendered in Layout.

- **Guide** — A ghosted line drawn from the surface to the point on the original poly that "controls" (influences) it.

Not quite sure what all the fuss is about? Each of the points of the original poly exerts *influence* over how the subdivision surfacing algorithm creates the smooth

surface of the sub-patch. The sub-patch surface behaves a lot like stretchy, digital clay.

Even so, you still may be inclined to think, "It's a neat gimmick, but what can it really do for me?" The upshot of this real-time application of **Multiply | Subdivide | More | Metaform Plus** is that you can model extremely dense meshes using a very light polygon "cage," *and* you can do it with the tools with which you're *already* familiar!

Sub-patch surface models can have their resolution dialed up or dialed down, not just while you're modeling but while you're

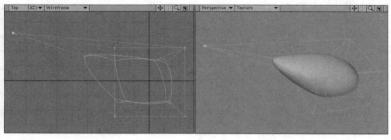

Figure 7-2

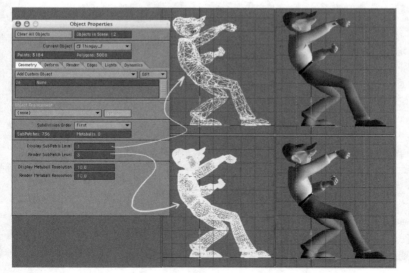

Figure 7-3

animating as well! Under Layout's Object Properties window, you set the resolution at which your sub-patch model will be displayed and the resolution at which it will be rendered. (In Figure 7-3, that's a difference of 24,064 polygons!) You can *animate* with a very speedy, low-poly mesh and *render* with the ultra-polished 27,072 poly mesh without having to change a single setting when it's time to render!

Now that I've got your attention, how do you turn that sub-patch "blob" in Figure 7-2 into the character in Figure 7-3? You use the Smooth Shift, Bevel, Drag, Move, and Rotate tools.

That's it? Yep. That's basically it. There are a couple of other tools I use to make things a little easier or to fix things when my work shows me I'm lacking in the foresight department, but for the vast majority of my character modeling, those five tools (always with a healthy helping of the Symmetry mode) are the main tools I use when modeling *organic* models.

> **Note**
>
> You can also use what you have sub-patched as a kind of quick, temporary "grouping" as you work. Leaving part of your model as sub-patches and part as faces as you work, you can quickly select what you want to work on through the SubPatches and Faces headings in the Polygon Statistics window.

## Smooth Shift

Smooth Shift works with sub-patches just the same as it does with polys. (In truth, you're better off thinking of your sub-patch *not* as some arcane, spline-based "mysticism" but as polys that just happen to be nice, soft, and "roundy" and are never considered "non-planar," no matter how you push their points.)

However, as nice as the real-time workings of Smooth Shift are with planar, polygonal faces, it often "splits" the mesh apart at its points with sub-patches (similar to what happened with the window moldings when we rail beveled them in the last chapter). There is a quick and easy fix to this, though: Let Smooth Shift handle making the new geometry, and *you* handle shaping and sizing it.

Smooth Shift with an Offset of 0 and a Max Smoothing Angle of 0° is the best way to work with sub-patches. A simple way to do this is to activate the Smooth Shift tool (<**F**>) and then click *without* moving your mouse. (You can also achieve the same

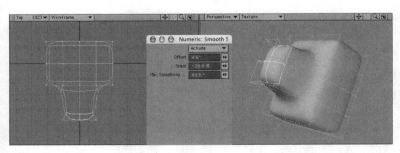

*Figure 7-4*

effect by using the Super Shift tool mentioned in Chapter 3.) After smooth shifting, position and shape the new geometry by hand. (It's good to get in the habit of smooth shifting your sub-patches with these settings. The tiny bit of extra time it takes more than makes up for the headache of finding a half-buried, "dismembered" set of points much later on in your work, the results of an erroneous Smooth Shift operation you didn't catch.)

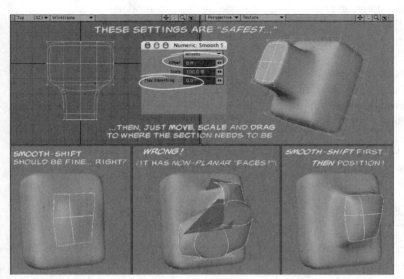

Figure 7-5

# BandSaw

The best characters are made up of loops (or bands) of four-point polygons. The BandSaw tool can be used to subdivide these loops into smaller bands. You can think of it as knifing along the path created by the band of the polygons.

When you have Enable Divide active in the BandSaw window, the tool not only *selects* the band of polys (along the U or V), it also creates more *segments* in that selected band with respect to the *band markers*. You create and position these

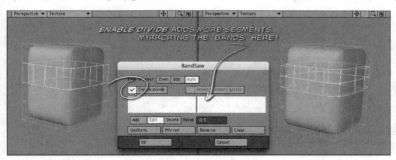

Figure 7-6

markers in the white area of the interface, which represents the top and bottom of the band of polys that will be selected/cut.

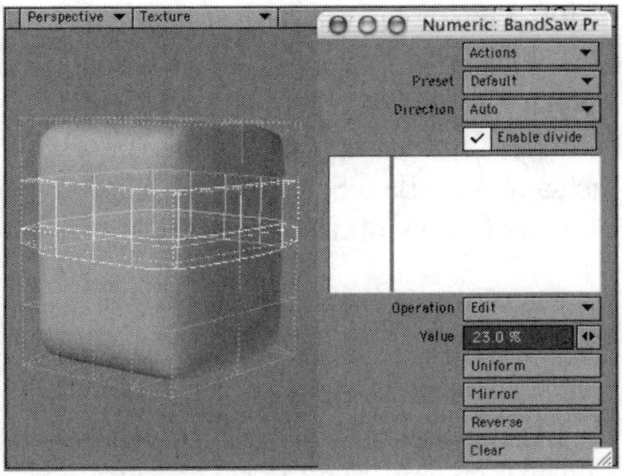

> **Note**
>
> A good way to determine the path that BandSaw will take as it cuts through your polys is to use the Select Loop tool (discussed in Chapter 3) first.

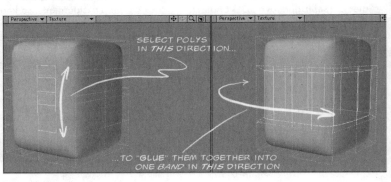

Figure 7-7

- **Add** puts more of these band markers wherever you click your mouse in the white area.

- **Edit** lets you click and drag the band markers.

- **Delete** removes any band marker you click on.

- **Value** lets you enter a specific position (0 to 1) along the white area for the selected band marker.

- **Uniform** repositions the band markers you have, spreading them all out evenly.

- **Mirror** creates a new band marker that mirrors your currently selected one.

- **Reverse** flip-flops the band markers.

- **Clear** removes all but one of the band markers, placed exactly in the center.

**Multiply | Subdivide | More | Band-Saw Pro** does the same thing as BandSaw but with a real-time Numeric window interface that lets you still interact with your viewports while open. The cool upshot of this, other than being able to orbit your model to see if the segmenting is working as you'd like, is that it *doesn't require* you

to use its interface window. It "remembers" the last settings you used with it and applies them immediately when activating the tool. (I've mapped this tool to a hot key and assigned it to my Quick-Tools menu tab, so when I want to select a band of my mesh, I just tap its hot key and keep right on working!)

> **Note**
>
> The Preset pop-up menu in the BandSaw Pro Numeric window will remember the settings in ten different presets. Just choose one, do your thing, and the next time you choose that preset, your previous settings will be ready and waiting for you!

Figure 7-8

What if you want to *remove* segments from your mesh? LightWave has **Construct | Reduce | More | BandGlue**, which "stitches" bands of polys together in much the same way BandSaw cuts them apart. The tool has no interface (just click its button, and away it goes). The one big difference between it and its counterparts is the direction in which you select the polys to be glued. Just remember that you're selecting the polys that will become *one band* around your model.

---

## Note

### "Elegance" in Modeling

Something that takes most folks a while to pick up on is an overriding concept of elegance in whatever it is you're doing in 3D. This applies to modeling, animating, texturing, lighting — all aspects of working in 3D.

*Your best work will come from using the absolute minimum number of "whatsits" needed to hold your "schiznit" in place — no more and no less.*

Tools like BandSaw can let you really load up your mesh with lots and lots of segments, and it's very tempting to do so. But the best modelers build their meshes with the barest minimum number of these *isoparms* necessary to keep the exact shape they're going for. Sometimes a good modeler will spend half the time it took to create the mesh just going through it again and again, looking for places he can optimize it and removing anything that isn't absolutely necessary to hold its shape.

This optimization not only makes for a model that's quicker to refresh when working in both Modeler and Layout, but when working with characters, it means that it is a lot easier to *rig* (set up for character animation). It also means that the bones that drive its deformation will create shapes that look a whole lot better than on a mesh that has a lot of segments. (See *LightWave 3D 8 Character Animation* for complete information on character rigging.)

To help us use as few segments as possible in making our mesh do what we need it to, we can adjust the *weight* by which the sub-patch is controlled by its cage. This information is stored on each individual vertex as the Sub-Patch Weight. *Positive values* increase the pull of the *control vertex* on the sub-patch surface, where 100% makes it touch its *control vertex*. *Negative values* relax the sub-patch's pull toward its control vertex. Map | General | Airbrush is a tool that lets you modify the values of your currently selected weight map in real time.

It's important to note that the vertices in your object are not inherently assigned to any given weight map, including SubPatch Weight. While Weight Shade will show your vertices as having a value of zero, until you actually assign a map value to them, they have no value whatsoever. You can directly enter values for selected points under the Information window for your selected points, or you can use Map | General | Set Map Value. While this information may not be of immediate use as you're learning the software, higher-end functions such as Dynamics do utilize vertex map assignments, so keep this bit of information in the back of your head.

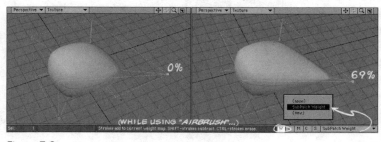

Figure 7-9

# Magnet

**Modify | Translate | Magnet** is a great tool for working with your sub-patch surface model as if it were a lump of digital clay. It's a tool I use *extensively* to rough in my basic forms when sculpting anything organic (characters, heads, artifacts, whatever).

With the Magnet tool active, you right-click and drag in a viewport to set its "sphere of influence" and then left-click and drag to move your mesh around. Points closer to the center of the sphere of influence will be affected more than those at its outer edge in accordance with the falloff. This is very similar to what we've seen already with the Bend, Taper, and Twist tools.

If you establish (and continue to manipulate) the Magnet tool's sphere of influence in a *single* viewport, the sphere will be more like a cylinder, extending infinitely through space.

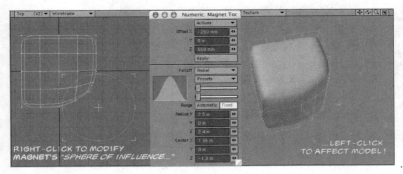

*Figure 7-10*

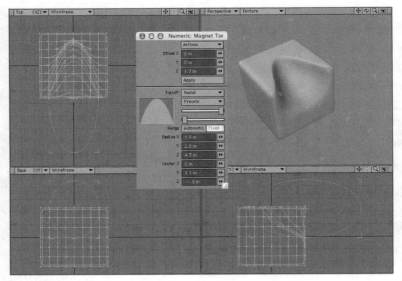

*Figure 7-11*

When you manipulate the Magnet tool's sphere of influence in *multiple viewports*, it becomes a true ovoid that can be used like a traditional sculptor's tool, pressing and pulling at a mass of Super Sculpey. (The Perspective viewport in Figure 7-11 shows how I usually like to work with my sub-patch models, with Independent Visibility active and choosing *not* to show cages, guides, or the grid.)

## Pole

**Modify | Transform | More | Pole** takes Size (Pole Evenly tool) and Stretch (Pole tool), and blends them with the sphere of influence of the Magnet tool. This is an underrated tool that is very helpful for organic modeling — especially "futuristic" design.

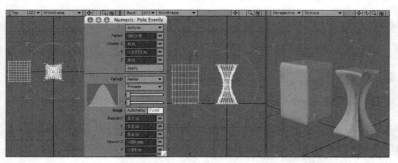

*Figure 7-12*

## Vortex

**Modify | Rotate | More | Vortex Tool** takes the Rotate tool and blends it with the sphere of influence of the Magnet tool. This also is an underrated tool that is very helpful for *quickly* creating graceful, fluid curves.

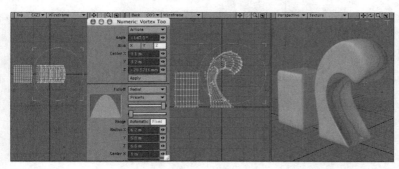

*Figure 7-13*

## Subdivision Order

Does the order in which your sub-patch surface model is diced up into its tinier pieces matter? It matters a whole lot — and one of the best ways to show this is by using a variant on the old "single-poly mountain" trick.

1. Start with a 5x5 sub-patch grid.

2. Bring the 5x5 sub-patch into Layout, and set its Display SubPatch Level to **42**. Then under its Deform tab, click on the **T** button next to Displacement Map

to enter the Texture Editor, and set up the dented texture shown in Figure 7-16. We get a very cool "insta-mountain," strongly reminiscent of the artwork of Roger Dean, the artist for the Yes album covers.

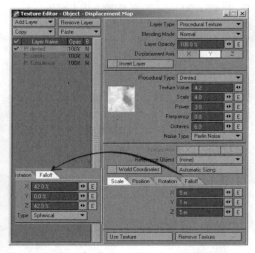

Figure 7-16: A displacement map actually moves the points of the mesh, whereas a bump map just "fakes" it by working with how the light plays across the surface. These are the settings used to create the mountain in Figure 7-15.

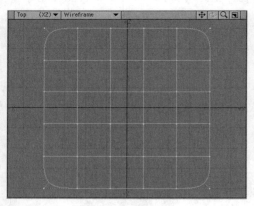

Figure 7-14

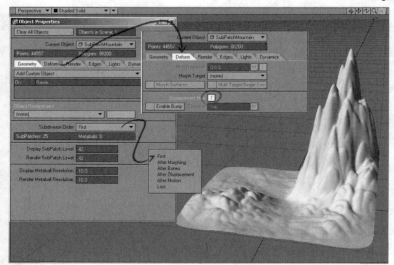

Figure 7-15

(Do you want to see something neat? Activate World Coordinates for your displacement map, remove your falloff values, and then move your object about. You'll see your object flow *through* the texture! It's a neat way to understand more about the workings of textures in general. Be sure to try this in *all three axes*.)

The two inactive textures in Figure 7-16 are other examples of different kinds of terrain.

### Mac-Specific Info

Because of the current weirdness with the Mac version of Dented, Mac users will have to use a Texture Value of **20.2**, instead of the 4.2 shown in Figure 7-16, and play with the texture's position in order to get decent mountains. (But it's worth it — no other procedural does mountains like Dented.)

(Special thanks to Robin Wood!)

Load **Scenes\Chapter_07\Subdiv_ Order.lws**, activating each layer in turn, so only one is active at a time, to see other nifty settings.

Subdivision Order tells LightWave when to apply its subdivision surfacing algorithm to the polygonal cage. If you tell it to apply its smoothing *last*, the displacement map is only displacing the 36 points of our 5x5 cage. If the smoothing is applied *before* the displacement map, the displacement map has all 44,557 points to push about.

Subdivision Order can really come into play when you're working with animating a character. The quickest, most reliable animation comes from subdividing your character using the After Motion or Last options. This way, the bones are only having to calculate their influence on, say, 7,000 points instead of the sometimes astronomically high number of points in even a Display SubPatch Level setting ("animation resolution") character's mesh.

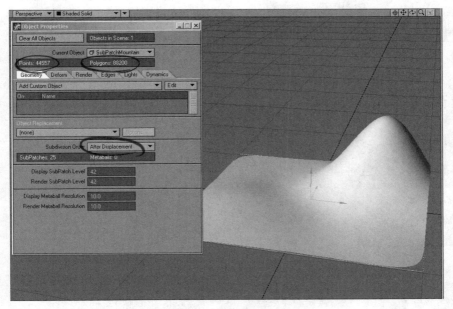

*Figure 7-17: Modifying the Subdivision Order setting.*

**Note**

If you want to freeze your mountain's deformations in place for use as a prefab object,
File | Save | Save Trans Object will save your
object as it exists on its current frame of LW's
world-space — transformations, displacements, bone movements, and all. (Be sure to
choose a name different from your original
object; otherwise, you'll replace the original
with the object as you're seeing it right now in
Layout's viewports!)

Save Transformed Object also respects the
Display SubPatch Level setting. "Exporting" our
mountain as it exists in Figure 7-15 will give us
a mesh with 88,200 polys! If you want to save
your transformed object as an object you can
still use as a sub-patch model, set Display
SubPatch Level to 0 before using Save Transformed Object.

. . .

Sub-patches open up a whole new level for
both modeling *and* animating. Modeling
complex meshes can now be done in a fraction of the time it would take to noodle all
those minute polys. Animating with a cast
of sub-patch characters means once we
choose our Display SubPatch Level and
Render SubPatch Level settings, we can
enjoy the speed of low-resolution *animation
meshes* and the beauty of high-res *render
meshes* without having to think about or do
anything more than just press <F9>.

Just remember the credo of good 3D
modelers and animators everywhere: *Your
best work will come from using the absolute
minimum number of "whatsits" needed to
hold your "schiznit" in place.*

**Note**

I can't stress enough how cool it is to have a
crowd of SubPatch Level 0 characters all on
screen at once *and still have screen-refresh
rates that are actually conducive to animating.* (In 1996, by contrast, three low-res
characters in Softimage slowed an R10K
down to a mind-mangling crawl!)

## Chapter 8

# Organic Modeling Exercise 1: "One-Minute" Spaceship

This chapter shows how to create one of those "one-minute wonders" that you'd see at trade shows and the like. It's not supposed to be spectacular; it's just meant to get you more comfortable with using sub-patches to actually do something.

1. Create a box with dimensions similar to the one in Figure 8-1 (the Numeric window is shown just in case you

would like to reproduce it exactly). The important thing is that the box is centered on the X axis and has two segments along the Z axis.

2. Activate Symmetry mode, and then check that your model is indeed centered by clicking on some polys (or points) on one side. If your model is centered, the corresponding geometry

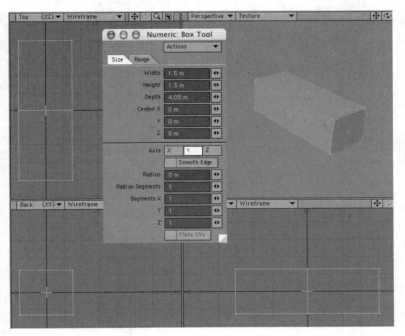

Figure 8-1

on the other side will also be selected. (If your box isn't centered, with Symmetry inactive, use **Modify | Translate | Center** to center it on all axes, and then reactivate Symmetry mode.)

3. Select the rear two polys at the sides. (See Figure 8-2.)

4. Apply Smooth Shift with an Offset of **0 m**, a Scale of **100%**, and a Max

Smoothing Angle of **0°**. (You will see no visible change in your model at this time.)

5. Using the Stretch and Move tools, position these polys similarly to what you see in Figure 8-4. Don't move them off the sides of the ship; just "squish" them a bit — these are the bases for what will become the wings.

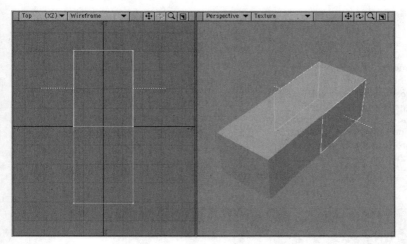

Figure 8-2

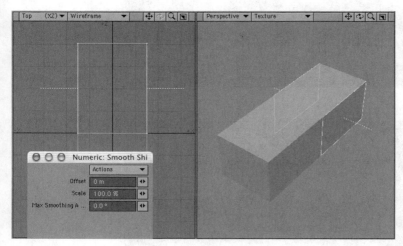

Figure 8-3

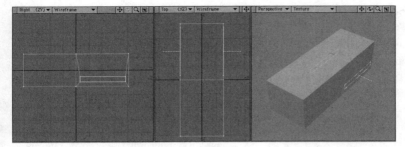

Figure 8-4

6. Next we're going to use Bevel on *only* the top rear poly. Apply only an Inset (we're exploring using a different tool to do the same job). This poly is the base of the tail. (See Figure 8-5.)

7. Use Stretch and Move to get this poly the rest of the way to where it needs to be. (Remember, with Symmetry mode active, you need to do your mouse work on the positive side of the X axis!)

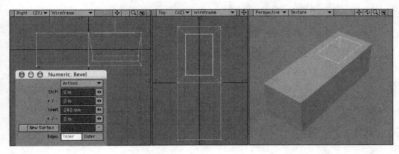

Figure 8-5

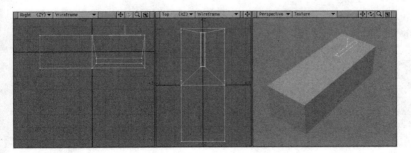

Figure 8-6

8. Now for the moment we've all been waiting for — deselect everything and press <Tab> to activate sub-patch surfaces. (It's not much to look at, but it'll start looking better in a moment.)

9. With the tail poly selected, use Smooth Shift as you did before for the wings and then position the new poly as you see in Figure 8-8, making the tail fin. Once you've got your model matching the figure, use Smooth Shift on the poly again, and move it just the barest of micrometers so its points aren't directly on top of the points from which it originated.

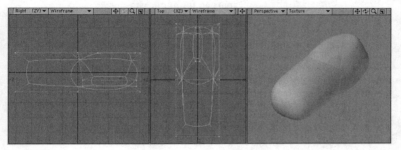

Figure 8-7

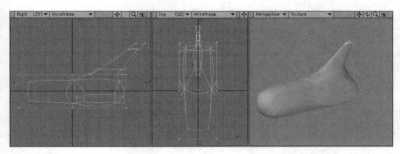

Figure 8-8

### Note

A trick you will eventually pick up on is the "Space, two-tap." (But why wait?)

Modeler has two primary selection modes: Points and Polys. You use <Space> to toggle between them. If you're working with polys in Polygon selection mode and want to view your model as sub-patches without "letting go" of the polys you currently have selected:

• Press <Spacebar> (you'll be in Points selection mode).
• Press <Tab> to activate sub-patches (if you have no selection defined for your points selection).
• Press <Spacebar> again.

You'll be right back where you were, in Polygon selection mode, with the same polys selected. Only now, your model is being viewed as sub-patches.

(This has the effect of "flattening" the top of the smooth shifted area, making the edge of it nice and sharp. This is one of the ways you can make a sub-patch model have "crisp" areas of definition. It's not quite as elegant as setting a value of +100% for the SubPatch Weight setting for the desired geometry, but it is a popular trick. Moving it just that little bit means that the points won't get eliminated if you were to do a Merge Points somewhere down the line.)

**Note**

For the rest of the book, whenever we smooth shift a sub-patch, let it be understood that it is with an Offset of 0, a Max Smoothing Angle of 0, and a Scale of 100% — just as we've done for all the smooth shifts so far in this chapter.

10. Next, use the Smooth Shift and Move tools on the two wing polys to get the preliminary shape of the wings.

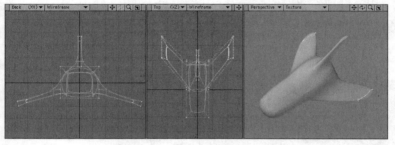

Figure 8-9

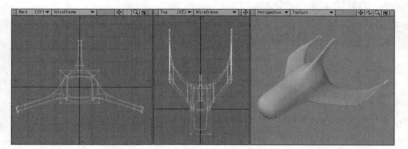

Figure 8-10

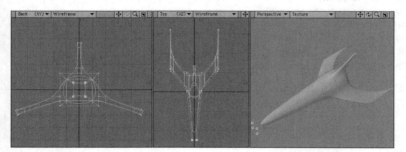

Figure 8-11

11. Now, just to add some "nifty-ness" to the ship, use Smooth Shift on the tips of the wings again. Leaving the front of the new polys very close to where they were, use Stretch to pull the back of the polys away from the ship to get an avian effect (Figure 8-10).

12. Move and stretch the points of the ship's nose, as shown in Figure 8-11, and you're done!

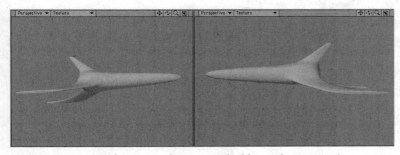

Figure 8-12: Not bad for a spaceship you can build in under a minute!

. . .

What we did here isn't earth-shattering or ground-breaking, but it *does* get you started thinking about how you can use sub-patches to build whatever you desire. You can see how quickly you can rough in a shape that you can work back into, using BandSaw, Smooth Shift, and Bevel to continue to layer in detail — honing... refining... perfecting.

A suggestion from my own experience is to use LightWave 8's Save Incremental to save multiple revisions of your work as you go. For example, if I've got my "whatsit" to a point where I'm pretty happy with the "doohickey" section of it, before starting work on the "snarf-blat" section, I'll save "Whatsit_ w22.lwo" and then save as "Whatsit_w23.lwo." This way if I totally botch the "snarf-blat" section, I can always go back to the way the "whatsit" was before I started (unintentionally) mangling my masterpiece!

Don't be afraid to cut your losses when you're modeling, reverting to an earlier state. When you tackle a troublesome section again, you'll be coming at it from the experience of having been there before. Not only will you finish that section *more quickly* than if you had stuck it out, you'll finish it *markedly better* almost 100% of the time!

# Chapter 9

# Organic Modeling Exercise 2: Character Body

Now, using the same basic techniques we explored in the previous chapter, we're going to model a character's *body*. In following along, you'll see how quickly you can get the job done by *roughing-in* first *and then* going back and adding detail later.

I've found that it's easy for artists to get swept away in the minutiae of the work, not wanting to move on until what they've done looks "perfect." There are three issues I have with this way of working. One, it makes for a very slow working process. Two, human perception is *referential*; we can't easily tell what's "right" and what's "wrong" without something with which to compare it. Three, when you come back to a piece, even after only half an hour, you see things that you missed before. By letting the rough forms have time to air out a

bit, you are allowing yourself the ability to see where you can make things better.

> ## Note
>
> As with everything (in this book, out of this book, as you move through life), this is only one way of working. This is not the "be-all and end-all" of anything. There aren't hard-and-fast rules as to how a character should be built. You just do what is most forefront in your focus. Let this chapter serve to give *suggestions* to you to *inspire* your own ways of working. Push, pull, play! Let your creativity be your guide! (Save multiple, incrementally numbered revisions of your work, so you know you can get back to where you were, wherever that happens to be!)
>
> "The man who makes no mistakes does not usually make anything." — Edward J. Phelps

## Torso

1.  Create a box (centered along the X axis) that is three segments high, four segments wide, and two segments deep. Surface it with the name **Shirt**, and let's get going.

2.  Set Val of all the points along the box's center to **X=0** to make *doubly sure* that they are indeed in the center of our virtual world. With Symmetry mode

active, lasso all of the points on the right side of the object to check its symmetry. If the points on the left side get selected as a result, you know that your object is truly symmetrical. (It's easier to fix something slightly out of alignment *now* than it is to fight with it later on down the road.)

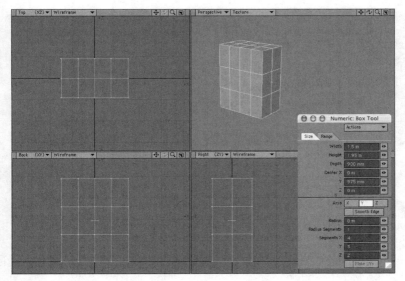

Figure 9-1

3. Next, with sub-patched surfaces activated and Grid Snap set to None, use Magnet to push the box around until it becomes "torso-ish." (Here's where knowledge of anatomy and drawing comes in handy — you know what the viewer needs to see to have him associate it with what you have in mind.)

4. Then, using Drag, move some of the corner points in toward the center of the model to take some of the sharp edges off the piece. (See Figure 9-3.) Just use your best judgment. You don't have to get things perfect here; we'll go back and really refine things once we can use the completed character for reference as to what needs to be done.

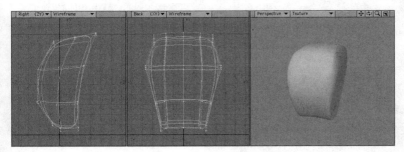

Figure 9-2

"Sooner is better than later!" — Joan, *The Messenger*

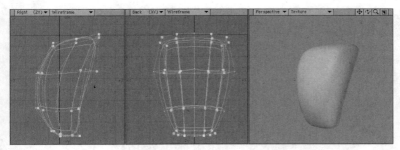

Figure 9-3

# Arms and Hands

Let's add the arms and hands to the torso created in the previous section.

1. Select the four polys shown in Figure 9-4 (Symmetry will select the four on the other side) and use Smooth Shift (as always when working with sub-patches, with an Offset of **0 m** and a Max Smoothing Angle of **0°**), moving and stretching them to just outside of where the deltoid would be.

2. Now hide everything else and turn your selection back into polys so we can more easily see its defining shape. Drag the points around until the segment is roughly more circular. Perfection isn't necessary.

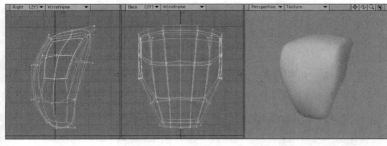

(Try not to move any point too far from where it started. We're just making our character's arms come from something "round" rather than something "rhomboid.")

Figure 9-4

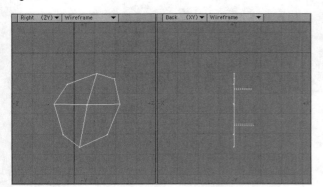

Figure 9-5

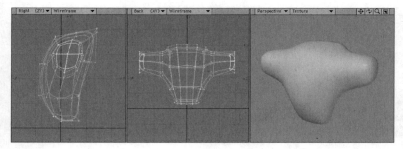

*Figure 9-6*

3. With the rest of your model visible again and your selection returned to sub-patches, use Smooth Shift, Move, and Stretch so that the segment is now right where the character's elbow will be. (You will probably want to put in more detail segments later, using BandSaw, but for now, for the ease of us being able to tweak our character's base forms and proportions, build him with as few segments (*isoparms*) as possible.)

4. Use Smooth Shift, Move, and Stretch again, positioning the selection just inside where the shirt's cuff would be.

5. Now, smooth shift and stretch the segment so it just reduces the size of the tube (like where the sleeve meets the cuff on a baggy sweatshirt). Then move it into the sleeve just a bit; this will help us more easily get at its points later, and it will also give us a nice "bump" where the cuff and sleeve meet (shown in Figure 9-8 as polygons to better illustrate what we're talking about).

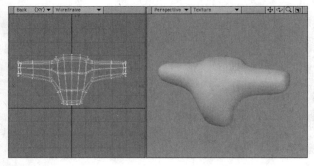

*Figure 9-7*

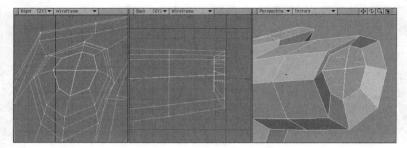

*Figure 9-8*

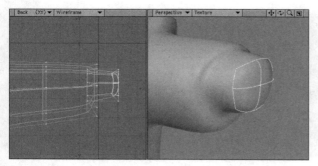

Figure 9-9

6. Smooth shift, move, and stretch the segment to make the cuff.

7. Smooth shift and stretch the segment, defining the *thickness* of the cuff (shown as polygons in Figure 9-10 to give a clearer picture of what crazy things I'm asking you to do).

8. Next, smooth shift, move, and stretch that segment so it lines up with the base of the cuff we created in Figure 9-8. Make it smaller than the real

inside of a cuff would be so in case the camera gets a shot up the sleeve, the tapering will give the appearance of depth without us having to actually build more of the inside of the sleeve.

9. As shown in Figure 9-12, on a new layer, create a box on the positive side of the X axis that has **4** segments in Z, **2** in X, and **1** in Y. Position it so it is in the palm area of the right hand. Give it a surface named **Skin**.

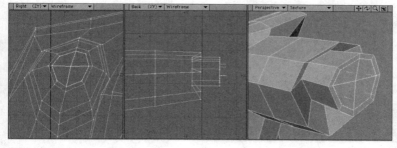

Figure 9-10

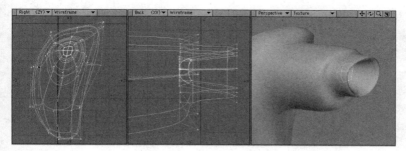

Figure 9-11

**218**

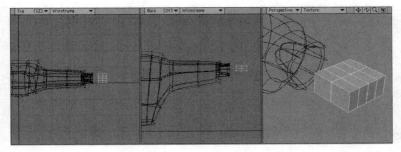

Figure 9-12

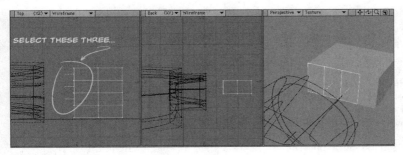

Figure 9-13

10. Select the three polys on the pinky side of the base of the palm, shown in Figure 9-13. (Even though I *always* animate with my characters facing toward the positive side of the Z axis, I've started modeling this guy with him facing toward the negative side of the Z axis. I'll rotate him around to face the "proper" direction when I'm done modeling him.)

11. Smooth shift, move, scale, and drag the segment so that it narrows, "wrist-like," coming out of the palm.

12. Smooth shift, scale, and move this section to the same place on the X axis where you terminated the polys for the cuff. (See Figure 9-15.)

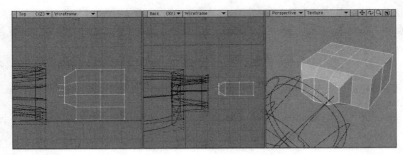

Figure 9-14

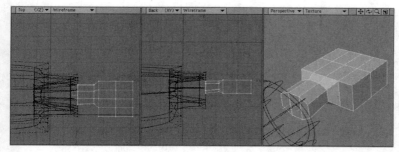

Figure 9-15

**Note**

I've always found it to be a good idea when modeling characters to have your segments line up along a plane on an axis like the segment we positioned in Figure 9-15. This makes it much easier later on when you are telling the character's vertices how much to follow each bone that makes up its skeleton (*point weighting*).

Remember to not add too much detail at this phase. We're just roughing in things to tweak later. We can add the little bumps and whatnot that make a character look really good *after* we've been able to view the model as a whole and make sure the proportions are correct.

13. Now smooth shift and move the section to where you terminated the inside part of the cuff.

14. Select each of the four polys, in turn, where the fingers will be. Assign each part names that correspond to the names of the individual fingers. When you've done that, select all four together. (This will allow you to select each finger by name under the Part heading of the Polygon Statistics window later when we're making this thing look like a hand.)

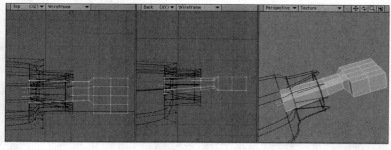

Figure 9-16

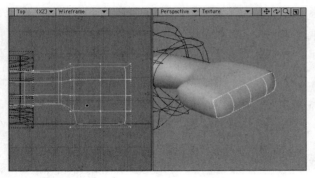

Figure 9-17

**Note**

You'll notice that in Figure 9-17, I've switched back to using sub-patches. You can work either in sub-patches or polys, whichever you feel most comfortable using. Feel free to switch back and forth at will.

15. Bevel the fingers with a Shift of about **2 cm** and an Inset of about **3 mm**.

16. Smooth shift this collection of four separate polys *three times* to make the segments of the fingers. (Cool fork, dude...)

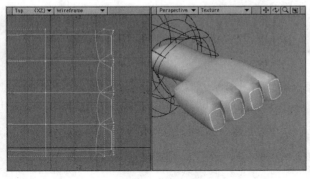

Figure 9-18

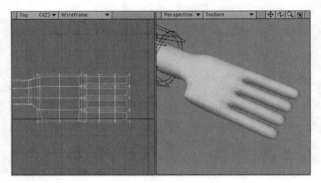

Figure 9-19

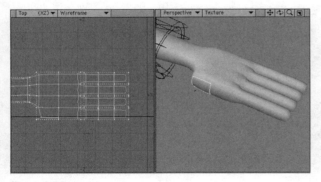

*Figure 9-20*

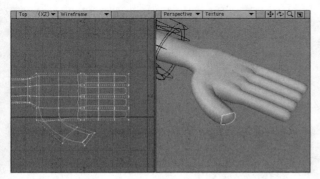

*Figure 9-21*

17. Select the one polygon shown in Figure 9-20 at the base of the thumb.

18. Smooth shift the poly out *twice*, moving, rotating, and stretching it to form something that looks vaguely like a thumb.

19. Just by using Drag and Magnet on various selections (using your own hand as reference), you can quickly make that dorky-looking fork-like thing look a lot more like the decent hand shown in Figure 9-22 with both the torso layer and the hand layer in the foreground.

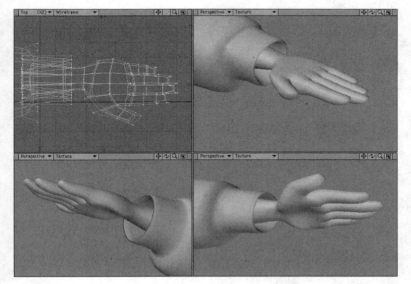

*Figure 9-22*

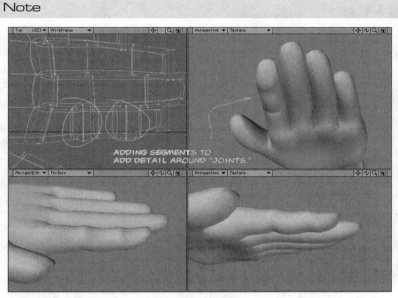

Figure 9-23: After the model's base form is finished, I like to add more segments to lock in more detail around the joints. You do this by sandwiching the joint segment between two other segments and moving the points of the joint segment up or down to create tucks and bulges. With a finger, this gives me the indication of knuckles and finger creases. (This figure shows the index finger handled in this manner.)

20. Mirror the hand along the X axis, and cut and paste the pair onto the same layer as the torso.

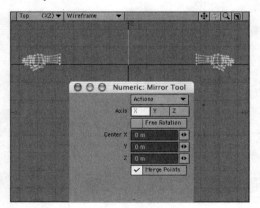

Figure 9-24

# Legs and Feet

In this section, we add the belt, legs, and feet of our character.

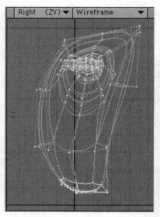

Figure 9-25

1. Select the *eight* poly-gons that make up the bottom of the torso.

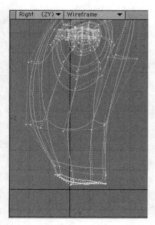

Figure 9-26

2. Smooth shift these polys, and then move them *down* about **4 cm** (the width of a belt).

3. Hide the polys you just smooth shifted, and select the polys that were created in the process of smooth shifting (shown in Figure 9-27 with Double Sided activated for the shirt's surface).

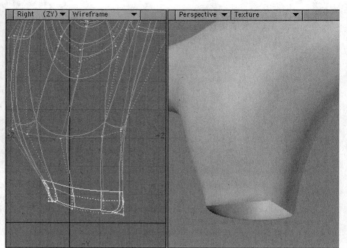

Figure 9-27

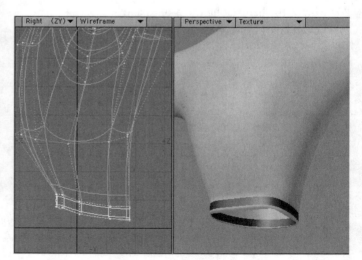

Figure 9-28

4. Smooth shift and then smooth scale the polys by about **2 mm** — just enough so the points of the belt don't sit directly on top of the points of the shirt and won't be eliminated if we Merge Points | Automatic at some point later on. (Smooth shifting here allows us to limit the color of the belt to being applied to the belt alone and not running over onto the shirt.) Surface the selected polys with something appropriate for a belt.

5. Smooth shift again and smooth scale by **0.5 cm** (or whatever thickness you'd like for your character's belt). Notice how only after smooth shifting again does the belt's coloring "expand" to fill the area between the segments we designated to be the belt in Figure 9-26. This may seem odd, but it is the way the subdivision surfacing logarithm works — and since *that's* the way it works, the "hoop-jumping" we just did is the way *we* must work.

6. Next, unhide everything, and then hide just the polys with the surfacing of the belt we just created. Then assign a surface to *all* the polys on the *bottom* of your model with something appropriate for pants.

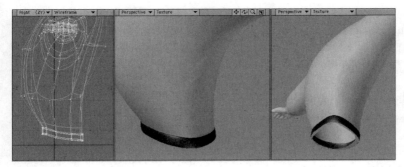

Figure 9-29

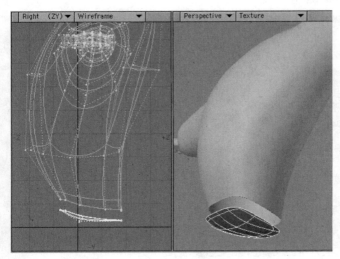

Figure 9-30

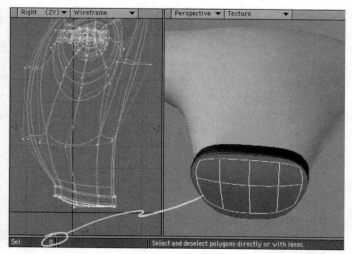

Figure 9-31

7. Unhide everything again. Then select just the *eight polys* on the *bottom* of your model that were smooth shifted back in Figure 9-26.

8. Smooth shift the eight polys and move them down *twice*, shaping and stretching them to form the curves of the pelvis.

9. *Temporarily* deactivate Symmetry. Select *only* the polys that will be the left leg and smooth shift them. Then, move them out from the body along the X axis by 1 mm, using only the Numeric window to do so. (Moving the polys, even this minute distance, moves the points that had been on X=0 away from that "center-line." Points on X=0 won't move away from X=0 when you have Symmetry mode active. Using the Numeric window to

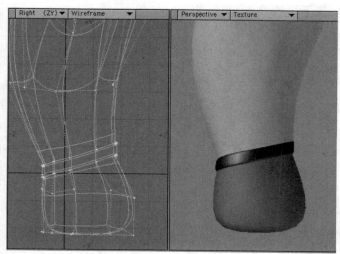

Figure 9-32

do the move, let's exactly mirror the move for the polys of the other leg. Then, when we activate Symmetry mode again, the geometry of the legs will still respond symmetrically.)

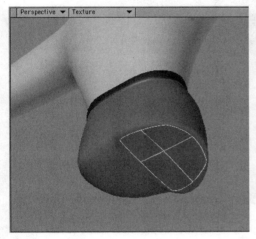

Figure 9-33

10. Repeat what you did in Figure 9-33 for the polys of the other leg, making sure that when you move these polys numerically, you invert (multiply by –1)

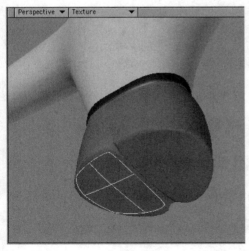

Figure 9-34

the value you used for the first leg. (You can enter mathematical expressions in the numeric input fields, and LightWave will calculate the answer for its input.)

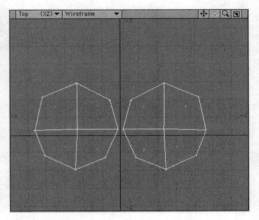

Figure 9-35

11. Reactivate Symmetry, and select only the *eight* polys you've just created for the legs. Hide everything else, and then drag their points around so the two sets are disc-shaped and will create cylinders when smooth shifted and moved to create the geometry of the legs. (I like to do this sort of thing while looking at the shapes as polys, not sub-patches. I find viewing them this way makes it easier to know if my shapes are accurate.)

**227**

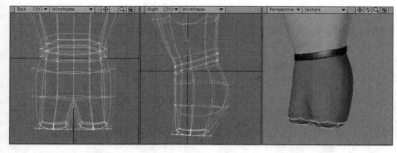

Figure 9-36

12. Smooth shift and then move the two sets of symmetrical polys *down* to begin to form the shape of the legs.

13. Continue smooth shifting and moving to create the rest of the geometry for the legs. You should have a segment at the knee and where the calf muscle (Gastrocnemius) bulges. Terminate the pants similarly to what we did for the end of the cuff — smooth shifting and

tucking the new polys inside the pant leg, with the new points lying along the same plane as defined by the calf segment.

14. On a new layer, create a box that is **2** segments in Y, **2** segments in X, and **4** segments in Z. Position this box on the positive side of X=0 where the character's foot should be.

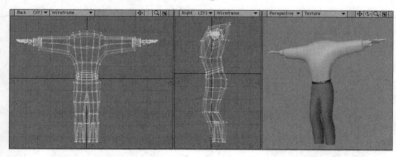

Figure 9-37

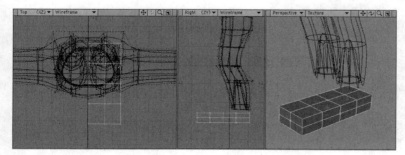

Figure 9-38

## Note

Here's where drawing training comes into play in a huge way. How do you know what proportions are right for a body unless you've trained yourself to see and understand what is right? Drawing is the cheapest, quickest, most portable way to *train* your eye to see what is right. (If you look at drawing simply as a *training exercise* for something you *really enjoy doing*, you'll get really good *really fast* and not even know you're doing it.)

Drawing is just understanding mathematical relationships. (Hello? What is modeling?) *Anyone* — and I mean *anyone* — can learn to draw and learn to draw *well*! It's just a matter of doing whatever it takes to trust that you will see from your own drawings the same quality of mathematical relationships that you see in "good" drawings.

*The Vilppu Drawing Manual* by Glen Vilppu (available through the Animation World Network, http:www.awn.com) is the *single most*

helpful book on getting someone from square one to having their work look like a master figurative artist in simple, understandable, achievable steps. (While working at Disney, I took Glen's life drawing classes and was dumbstruck when he was able to get production assistants to create life drawings that looked as good as a full-on animator's drawings in a matter of a couple of months!) To put it bluntly: If you want to learn how to draw figures well, get his book, read it, and do the exercises. It's as simple as that.

However, even if you're not a master figurative artist, you can still make sure your character's proportions are correct by loading into your backdrops images of characters in similar poses that you know *are* correctly proportioned. By working from something that *is* correct, you are training yourself to *expect* to see those same correct proportions in your own work. Pretty neat, huh?

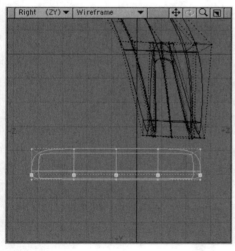

Figure 9-39

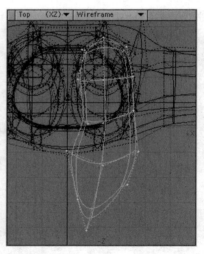

Figure 9-40

15. Select **Activate Sub-Patches** for the box, and move the points of its middle Y segment *down* to indicate the thickness of the shoe's sole.

16. In a Top viewport, drag the points around so the box begins looking like a shoe.

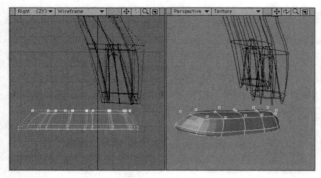

Figure 9-41

17. Having applied a surface that is "shoe-like," select the points of the shoe's top and stretch them *inward*, so the shoe becomes less "boxy" when viewed from the sides. Then, grab the center point for the toe area of the shoe, and move it *upward* to give us the good ol' "cartoon-shoe look," as shown in Figure 9-42.

18. Select the four polys that make up the rear of the shoe's top and smooth shift them. Then move them *up* just a bit to start creating the ankle.

19. Smooth shift and move the polys again, making the lower part of the calf and fitting it inside the pant leg.

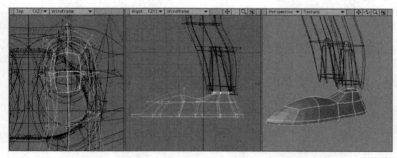

Figure 9-42

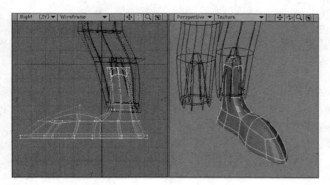

Figure 9-43

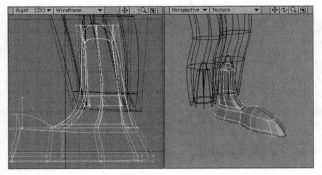

Figure 9-44

20. Now, select only the polys you've just created in making the calf/ankle (including the ones you've been smooth shifting, now at the top of the calf's "spike").

21. Smooth shift them. Then move them *down* to set them inside the shoe.

Apply a "sock-like" surface to them, and you've got some "loafer action" going on.

22. Start pushing points until you've got a nice cartoony form for the shoe/foot/ankle.

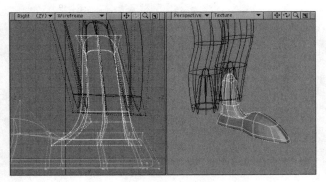

Figure 9-45

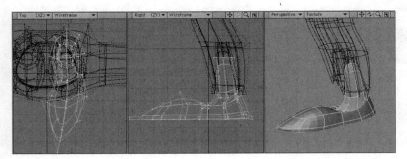

Figure 9-46

**231**

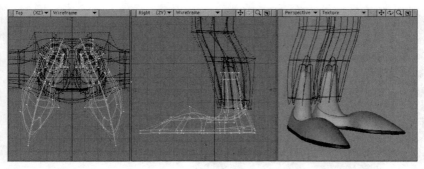

*Figure 9-47*

23. Apply a sole-like surface to the bottom layer of the shoe, rotate the whole thing outward a bit, and mirror on the X axis.

You've given this guy some neat feet! (When you're done, cut and paste them onto the main layer for your character.)

## Finishing Touches

This section describes a few finishing touches you can make to your character.

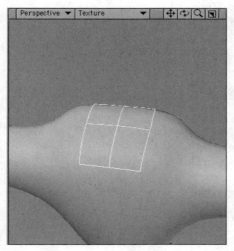

*Figure 9-48*

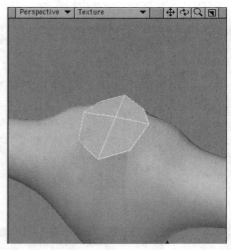

*Figure 9-49*

1. Select the four polygons that make up the neck area at the top of your character's torso.

2. Select **Deactivate Sub-Patches** for the polys, and push their points so you've got something more discoid than the rectangle they originally formed.

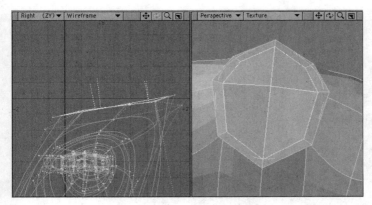

*Figure 9-50*

3. Continuing to view your selection as polygons, smooth shift and then stretch them to create a bit of a "lip" for what will become the shirt's neck.

---

**Note**

I find that when working in a Perspective viewport, LightWave's tools conform to a plane described by the viewport's "point of view." So, to scale something that doesn't lie along a simple X, Y, or Z plane, you can *angle* your Perspective viewport so you're looking "directly down" at your selection. Working from this angle, your tools will work more or less as they do when manipulating something in an isometric view lying "flat" on an X, Y, or Z plane.

---

4. Smooth shift, and then move and stretch those polys *in* and *down* to become the inside of the shirt's neck, returning all your polys to sub-patches. (See Figure 9-51.)

5. Go back through your model and adjust anything that needs tweaking. You now have a base you can use as is or, using Smooth Shift and BandSaw, you can add as much detail as you'd like, making nearly any kind of humanoid character imaginable.

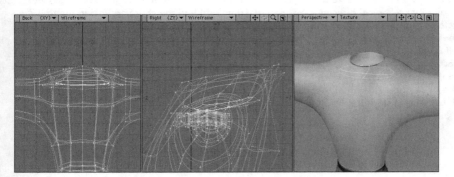

*Figure 9-51*

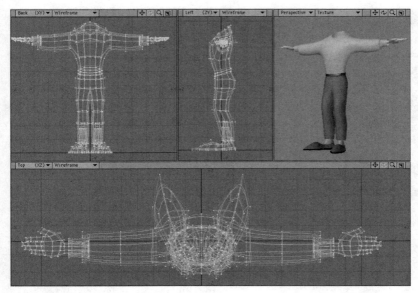

Figure 9-52

If you'd like to load the character I modeled for this exercise, he can be found in **Objects\Chapter09\Character_F.lwo**.

If you load him in, you'll notice that he's facing along the positive Z axis (versus "looking" along the negative Z axis, as he was while modeling him). When I'm modeling, I don't get all concerned with which way my character is facing — I'm all about getting the job done well and quickly. However, when I'm *animating* a character, I *always* have him facing along the positive Z axis (as do 98% of all other technical directors). So, for Character_F.lwo, I've already rotated him 180 degrees around his Y axis at X=0, Z=0, so he's still perfectly symmetrical but facing the "proper" way.

How did this convention of characters facing along +Z get started? I can only speak for myself, but when I started animating vehicles, I found that when you use Align to Path in Layout, the object gets aligned with its "front" being whatever is facing down the +Z axis. (It didn't take more than a couple of times of mucking about with parenting my already-surfaced-the-way-I-wanted model to a null and having the null Align to Path before I started just modeling things "right" to begin with.)

Then when I started getting into rigging some complex character setups, I found that I could "trust" IK more readily for what I was doing if I had the character facing along +Z. With the improvements to how LW handles rotations and pivots, this isn't quite as important as it was then, but I stick with the convention because it has come to make sense to me — I don't have to think about it when I'm working; I *expect* things to be a certain way.

. . .

Nearly all character modeling follows the same basic steps that we followed here. When building my own characters, I *always* start with a base like this — something that has only as many segments as needed to hold the geometry in place. Often, I'll save my base for later, just in case I want to have a "stand-in" model if my scene becomes so thick with objects that animating slows to a crawl.

For making my final, "super-mega-ultra" high-res models, I take this base, whose proportions I know are correct, and start working at it like a sculptor chiseling away at a rough-hewn marble likeness. Because I know the *proportions* are good, I can lose myself in the *details* for days, knowing that what gnarly stuff I've done won't have to be scrapped because I wasn't paying attention to the rest of the character.

I suppose what we're doing here could be called "deductive modeling" — modeling from the *general* to the *specific*, just like Sherlock Holmes' reasoning to solve a mystery. Because we've created such general forms to work with, with only a few more hours of working, you can quickly turn this base into nearly any bipedal, humanoid character imaginable!

# Chapter 10

# Organic Modeling Exercise 3: Head Modeling

Modeling a human face and head is one of the most challenging things you can model (if you're not used to modeling human heads, that is). It isn't *difficult*; it is just very, very exacting. If you give yourself the time you need to get it done and have someone show you a path you can follow, it can be a fun, relaxing, explorative process. If you're one of those people who really enjoys falling into the details and noodling to your heart's content, head/facial modeling can be one of the most enjoyable areas of 3D modeling.

How can something be "challenging" and yet "not difficult"? Well, we are all experts on the geometry and landmarks of the human face. Every day, from the time we get up in the morning to the time we go to bed at night, we are surrounded by human faces. Faces tell us 90% of the things about a person he doesn't say with his voice. Our survival on a day-to-day basis depends on being able to identify the subtle *landmarks* that exist as commonalities to all human faces and being able to extrapolate the underlying thought/feeling processes that alter these landmarks from their "at-rest" positions. (In industrial design terms, the "tolerances" of the human face are measured in hundredths of millimeters.)

We all get gut feelings when something on a face isn't quite right. While we spend

so much time *looking* at faces, we don't spend much time at all really *seeing* and *understanding* the structures that create the complex shape of the human facial mask.

So, to become skilled at modeling human faces, we must become skilled at understanding the layers, landmarks, and multiple planes that create its complex system of interrelationships. A human face can look *completely* different when seen from a slightly different angle. This is because of the relationships of the many planes that make up the human face. As the head turns, these planes create an ever-shifting flow of silhouettes. In short: We must let go of the *symbolism* of what we *think* we are seeing and begin to truly *understand* what we are seeing.

In this simple tutorial, there is little space for me to do more than show you how to "stretch" a polygonal mesh over an imaginary structure. This tutorial will indeed result in a completed human head, but it will not leave you with the understanding of why the head looks the way it does. If you find you enjoy the process of facial modeling (and there are modelers in studio environments who specialize in faces and facial shapes for animation), then let this be a first step for you — let it be a tool for you to translate your future studies of facial anatomy into a 3D environment.

The method that is outlined in this chapter represents only *one* way to work. It is known as the detail-out approach. It begins by modeling a small, detailed area of the head (typically the eye) and then working out from there. The detail-out approach is arguably the most popular way to build a head, but it's not the only way. There are two other approaches that artists typically use: box modeling and spline modeling.

Box modeling rivals the detail-out approach in its popularity. This method begins with a large, generic shape (typically a box) and works the details in from there. The third major approach, spline modeling, is in many ways a hybrid of the other two approaches. Spline modeling involves the creation of a low-resolution cage to generate the overall form. After that the details are modeled in. We'll take an extensive look at the process of spline modeling a head in Chapter 14.

I encourage you to try the different approaches and find the one that works best for you. Each approach has its advantages and disadvantages. But be prepared — there is no quick and easy way to do head modeling. There are very few shortcuts, and there is much that must be done by hand.

The advantage of the detail-out approach is that it gives the artist complete control (quite literally) right from square one. There is nothing that gets left to chance. Anything that is out of place is that way because of what the artist has done. Having learned what to expect in this process, I can now put a head model together in about two to three hours (with the right music to jam to as I work), whereas my first head took nearly two days to build.

**Note**

While this exercise isn't necessarily complicated, it does require that you follow the instructions *carefully*. If you find yourself struggling for whatever reason, make sure you are following the instructions *exactly*. (Yes, it is pedantic, but it is the best that can be done without having me actually be there with you.) If you have to backtrack to a point where you know things were on track, that's okay. Usually, getting off-track is a simple matter of slipping past some simple bit of detail.

**Note**

Actually, there *is* an easy way to do facial modeling. Take an existing head you know is modeled well, and start pushing points.

To this end, Objects\Chapter10\Head_Base_F.lwo is the finished model of what we create in this chapter. You may find that while you need a human head for this or that, you have no desire to sit down and actually build one yourself. That's fine! Take this guy and start "pushin' dem points!"

**Note**

**Industry sayings:**

There is no "Animate" button on a computer's keyboard.

There is no "Model Human Head" button on a computer's keyboard.

**Note**

**Industry joke:**

Q. What's the easiest way to do facial modeling?
A. Pay someone else to do it for you.

# Reference

The detail-out approach to facial modeling requires that you have something to reference as you work. When you're directly referencing something, as we do here, it's a lot easier to get a result that looks decent.

Figure 10-1: The reference figure.

To work in the way that is outlined here, we need a front and a side view of the face we are modeling, as shown in Figure 10-2.

1. Under **Display Options | Backdrop**, set the Backdrop Image for your Front viewport to **Reference\ch10\Head_ Frontal_Ref.png** and the Image for your Left viewport to **Reference\ ch10\Head_Profile_Ref.png**. The Size for both images will need to be set to **33.3375 cm**. You'll want to set the Image Resolution to **512** so when you get in close, the image won't get all pixelated on you. So the images don't overpower your points and polys in the viewports, you'll want to reduce the contrast of the backdrops. Some people like to have Pixel Blending on to make the images even smoother (I, personally, am not fond of this). The rest of the settings should be left alone.

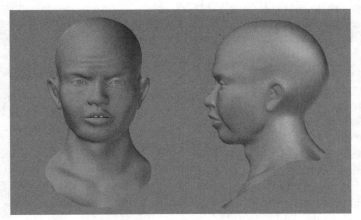

Figure 10-2: The head underneath the musher in Figure 10-1.

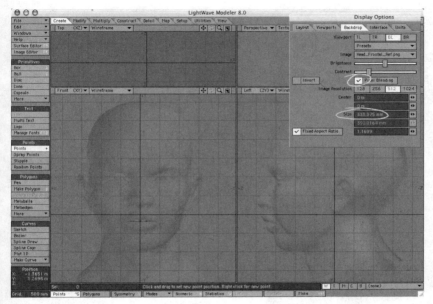

Figure 10-3

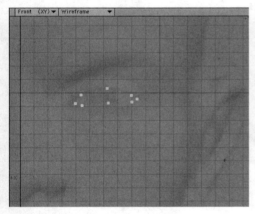

Figure 10-4

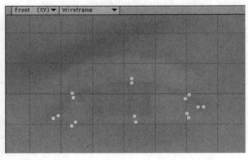

Figure 10-5

2. Zoom in tight on the reference model's eye in a Front (or Rear) viewport. Create eight points, outlining the eye where the lid meets the eyeball, as shown in Figure 10-4. (You don't have to worry about point order as we work.)

3. Create another "ring" of eight points, just outside the first, where the lid begins to "turn" to meet the eyeball.

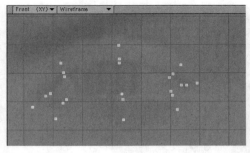

*Figure 10-6*

4. Create one more ring of eight points, as shown in Figure 10-6.

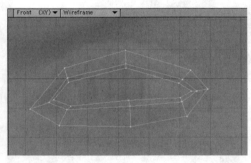

*Figure 10-7*

5. Manually select each set of four points, creating quad-polys from them and making two rings of quad-polys around the opening for the eyeball. (Connecting points clockwise will make a poly with its normal facing one way; connecting them counterclockwise will make the normal face in the opposite direction.)

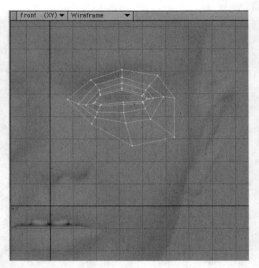

*Figure 10-8*

6. Having added two more rings, following the same theory used in the making of topographical maps (where more rings indicate more changes in altitude), we have something that looks a little like Locutus of Borg.

7. Next, we do something similar for the area around the mouth. Notice how the area at the corner of the mouth is handled. We want to always try to envision a "Spider-Man-like webwork" radiating out from major landmarks on our character, flowing smoothly around and over the "topography." Sometimes, this isn't possible when we are trying to work only with quads, so we do our best to improvise, as we have with the corner of the mouth. (See Figure 10-9.)

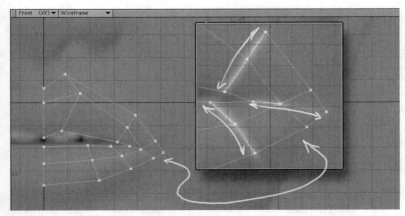

Figure 10-9

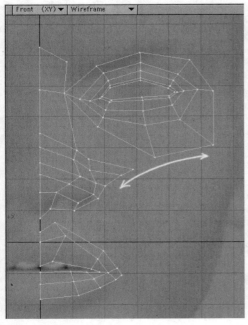

Figure 10-10

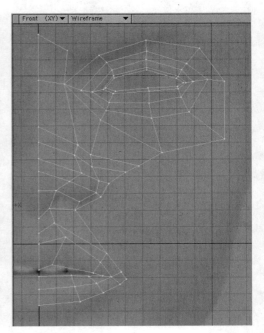

Figure 10-11

8. Do the same thing for the nose, planning out how the radial segments will connect.

9. Create the polys from the existing points, bridging the mouth, nose, and eye socket.

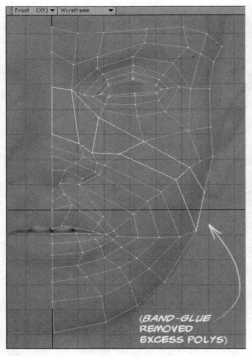

Figure 10-12

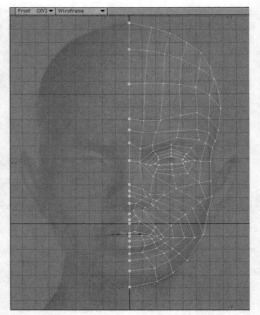

Figure 10-13

10. Continue expanding the "webwork topology" across the face. Let's face it, it's difficult to plan out everything you're going to do and everything you'll need. You may need to add segments or, like in this work-in-progress in these figures, remove segments. With BandGlue, I was able to remove a band of polys I didn't really need.

11. Continuing to work in similar fashion around the topography of the head, establish one half of the "facial mask." (Make sure that all the points that are in the center of the work actually do fall on X=0, using **Detail | Points | Set Value** if necessary.)

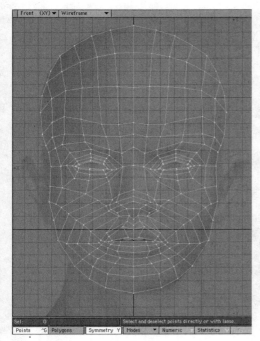

*Figure 10-14*

12. Mirroring along the X axis and merging points gives us a completed, two-dimensional facial mask.

13. Now take the points along X=0 and move, drag, and magnet them so they roughly fit the silhouette of the reference face in the Left viewport. (Remember that when we sub-patch this mesh, the sub-patch will be slightly "inside" the points that define it.)

### Note

When you're moving your points to conform to the reference profile, to help make sure that you're only moving them in Z, hold down <Ctrl> before moving your points. Your movement will be restricted to the axis in which your selection is moved *first*.

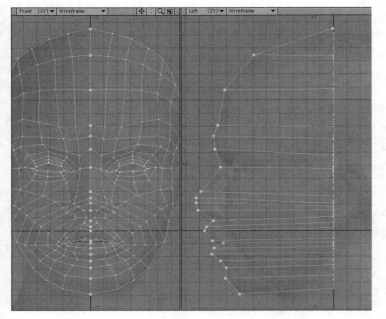

*Figure 10-15*

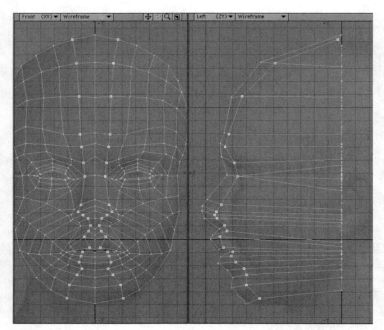

*Figure 10-16*

14. Work your way outward from the
    mask's center, using the visual cues
    from both backdrops to make your best
    guess as to where the points should be.
    (Right now, all we are concerned about
    is getting close.)

### Note

Don't forget about the power of making
point selection sets to help you quickly "sift"
through the points of a complex model. (See
Chapter 3, Figures 3-17 through 3-19.)

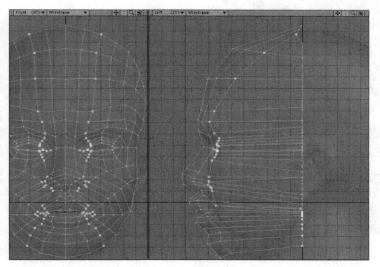

*Figure 10-17: The third "row" out from the center — a "work-in-progress."*

**Note**

Don't worry yourself with checking your work in a Perspective viewport. Getting all nitpicky about the details before you've got everything roughed in is a sure way to let time get away from you. Once all the points are in their rough positions, we can then go in and start noodling.

15. Once all the points have been "pushed" using our best judgment, take a look at the results of our labor in a Perspective viewport. (If your work is anything like mine, it looks pretty creepy!)

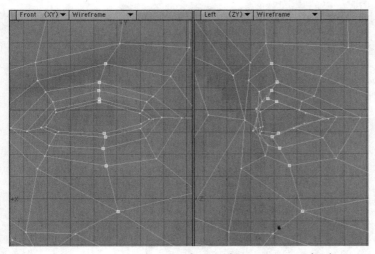

*Figure 10-18: You can use selections of points that you can see clearly in one viewport to help you make sense of complicated areas in another viewport.*

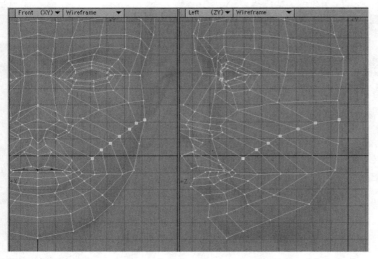

*Figure 10-19: Try to get your radial segments as smooth as possible in both viewports.*

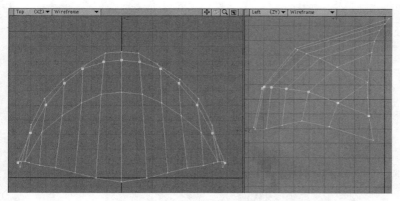

Figure 10-20: When working on the forehead, switch to a Top viewport so you can more clearly examine the arc that the points define (seen here with the extra "clutter" of the rest of the face hidden).

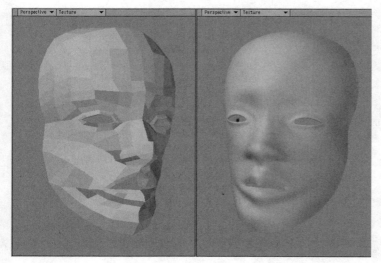

Figure 10-21

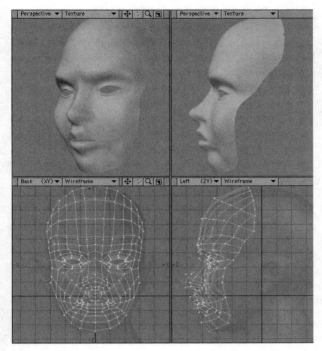

16. Continue to push points *only along the Z axis*, referencing all four viewports until you have something that looks a little less like a prop from a B-grade horror film.

*Figure 10-22*

### Note

There may be times when no matter how you tweak your points, the sub-patches just seem to refuse to give you the contour you are looking for. This is because of the way the radial segments are defining the topography of your face. Now, you could scrap what you've done, reworking based on a stronger knowledge of what your topography must be in order to get the forms you want (not fun). Or you could use Detail | Polygons | Spin Quads to rework your radial segments without having to tear down anything

(much better).

When you select *two* adjacent quad-polys and use Spin Quads, Modeler "reworks" those two polys based on the different ways of "connecting the dots" to make two quadrilateral polygons (leaving the "dots" right where they were).

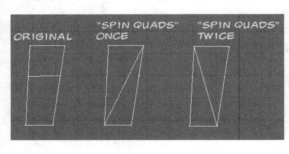

You can use Spin Quads to completely restructure your radial segments. (Spin Quads works with Symmetry active too!)

*Figure 10-23*

Note

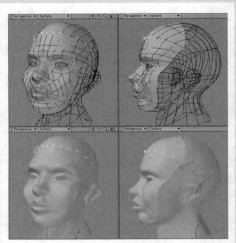

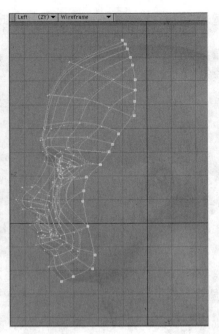

Figure 10-24: A huge help, whenever you're modeling something complex that you've never modeled before, is to have a reference model in a background layer as you work. (You can also assign a transparent surface to the mesh you are referencing so both objects are in the foreground. If you do this, remember that you must select the geometry of your work object first so you don't alter your reference mesh.) When your work object starts to push through your reference mesh, you know you've got things right.

Figure 10-25

17. Now, select all the points that make up the back edge of your facial mask, and copy them.

18. Paste them into an empty layer, move them toward the back of the head just a bit, and then paste again to get two sets of points.

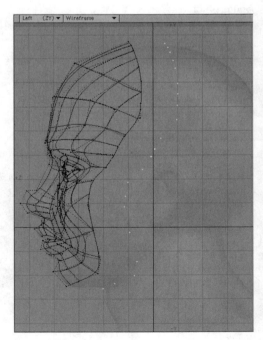

Figure 10-26

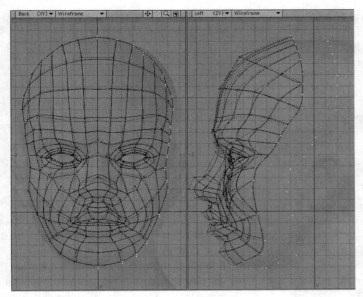

*Figure 10-27*

19. With Symmetry deactivated, delete the points on the negative X side of the model (leaving the points at X=0).

20. In a side view, connect the points four at a time to create a new row of quad-polygons. (If you start connecting the dots in one direction, be sure you connect all the new polys in the same direction as well; this ensures that all your new polys have their normals facing in the same direction. Even if they all need to be flipped, they can be flipped as a unit, rather than having to ferret out the errant normals.)

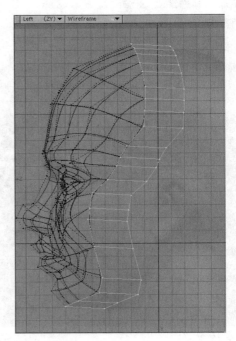

*Figure 10-28*

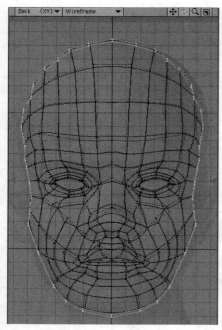

*Figure 10-29*

21. Mirror these new polys along the X axis, merge points, and make sure that all their normals are facing outward.

22. Cut those new polys, paste them onto the layer with the rest of the facial mask, and merge points. (Since you didn't move the second set of points you pasted in Figure 10-26, they should still be sitting *exactly* on top of the original points of the facial mask you selected in Figure 10-25.) Activating sub-patches for these polys, we now have an "extension" to our facial mask that we can BandSaw!

23. Setting BandSaw so it divides very close to the rearmost edge of this mask will give you another segment with its points almost exactly where your previous segment's points were, preserving the shape you've defined as you continue to "stretch" the mask around the form of the head. Match the shapes we've got going on in Figure 10-31 with the new "back edge" of the mask meeting right under where the neck and the chin meet, stretching up and around the front of the ear and then extending off the back of the head.

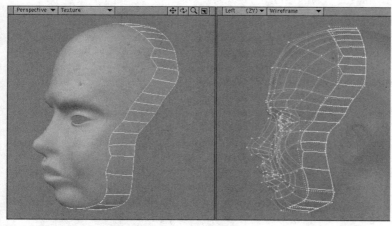

*Figure 10-30*

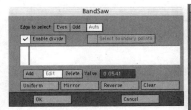

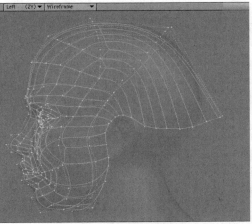

Figure 10-31

## Note

I don't know about you, but I can't look at half a face and imagine what it would look like were it a whole face. So, when I'm "pushing points" to make the facial mask look like a decent face, I need to see both halves at once.

But when I don't need to see the model as a complete, 3D unit, I often find it easier to just cut away the polys on the negative X half of the model, mirroring them later when that portion of the work is done. This makes it a lot easier to manually create polys, as we did in Figure 10-28 and as we will in Figure 10-32. (When looking at your model from the side, you don't have the points from the left and right sides of the model appearing in the same Y, Z space — this makes it easier to "stitch" new quads onto your model.)

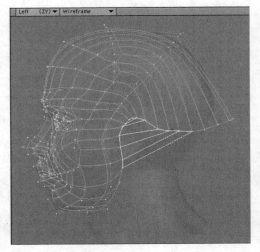

Figure 10-32

24. Delete the negative X half of your model, leaving the points that exist along X=0 and with Symmetry deactivated, just as we did with the points in Figure 10-27. Selecting sets of four points to create new polys, "stitch together" six rows of segments (as shown in Figure 10-33). Make sure these new polys have their normals facing outward, then turn them into sub-patches.

**251**

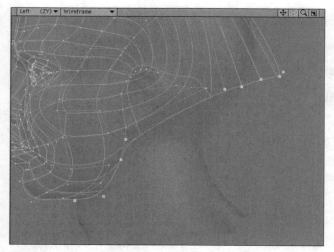

Figure 10-33

25. Now select the new back end of your mask (which, thanks to having "stitched" those six rows together, now has 12 fewer points) and copy them.

26. We're going to do the same thing with these points as we did with the ones

back in Figure 10-26. Paste the points into a blank layer, moving them a short distance from their origin. Then paste again to give yourself another row of points in exactly the same positions as the "original" points on the mask.

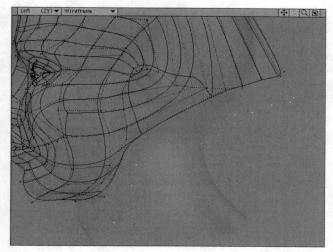

Figure 10-34

27. Create quad polys from these points, making sure their normals are facing outward. Then cut and paste them back to the layer where the rest of your mask is.

28. Sub-patch those new polys, and drag their points so the sub-patch surface conforms to the silhouette of the head.

29. BandSaw (as we did in Figure 10-31) to create a new row of points. Select and drag the bottommost row to new positions along the silhouette, down about 1.5 cm from where they were. You may have to invert your settings for BandSaw in order to have the new band at the bottom of the original polys. See Figure 10-37.

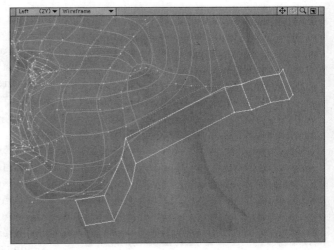

Figure 10-35

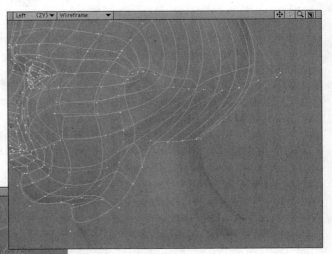

Figure 10-36

Figure 10-37

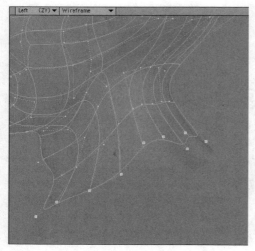

*Figure 10-38*

30. Repeat this process, adding another row/segment, and work back into the other rows of points to get the sub-patch surface to closely "adhere" to the contours of the silhouette's profile.

31. Now here comes the fun part. Mirror and merge points to get your model back to being a complete whole again. Then, with Symmetry active, work back into the points you've created while you've been "stretching" the sub-patch surface over the profile of the skull (like a caramel-apple wrap) and tweak the subtleties of their positioning until the surface describes the relatively smooth forms of a head and neck.

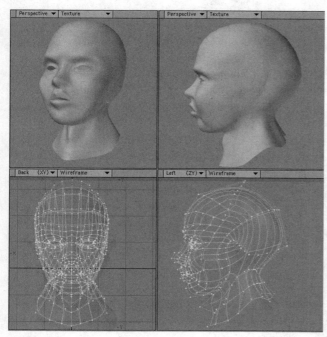

*Figure 10-39*

## Note

It is always a good idea, *before* you use Mirror and Merge Points (as in Figure 10-39), to first grab all the points that should lay along X=0 and manually set the value of their X position to 0. It may seem like a bit of extra work, but it is so easy to slide a point off of X=0 when working in the Perspective viewport and not even realize you've done it.

This will ensure that your model "seams" correctly in the center when you Mirror/ Merge Points and will make it a *lot* easier working in Symmetry mode; points exactly on X=0 cannot be moved off of X=0 when you have Symmetry active.

## Note

Avoid huge movements as you tweak the points here. You'll get your skull looking better quicker if you sneak up on the point's proper positions.

"Small moves, Ellie. Small moves." — Ted "Sparks" Arroway, *Contact*

32. Select the top five polys you made while "stitching" the mask together around the ear in Figure 10-32. (We're going to make the ear by smooth shifting these polys, so just select the polys that are close to where the ear attaches to the skull.)

33. Smooth shift and then stretch these polys to create the relatively small base of the ear where it is attached to the skull. (You will want to group these polys now as **Ear**, so you can quickly select just the ears should you ever need to isolate them from the skull.)

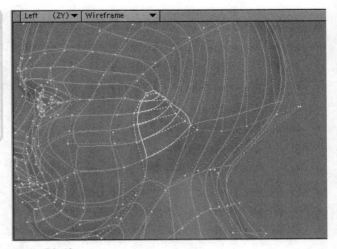

*Figure 10-40*

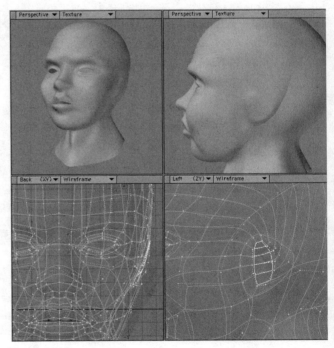

*Figure 10-41*

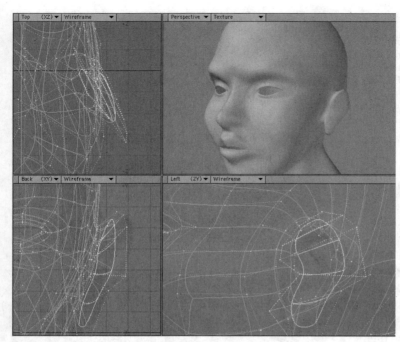

Figure 10-42

34. Smooth shift, move, stretch, and drag the new polys to create the side of the actual ear that is closest to the skull.

35. Smooth shift, move, stretch, and drag the new polys to create the side of the ear that faces away from the head.

36. Smooth shift, move, stretch, and drag one more time, "tucking" these new polys inside the forms created by the other two Smooth Shift operations for

the ears (Figure 10-43). Select just the polys of the ear, isolating them from the rest of the skull so you can tweak their points until you have something that looks like an ear (shown in Figure 10-44 with the two polys where the nostrils are already smooth shifted and moved to create their openings).

You have just modeled a notably "realistic" human face and head!

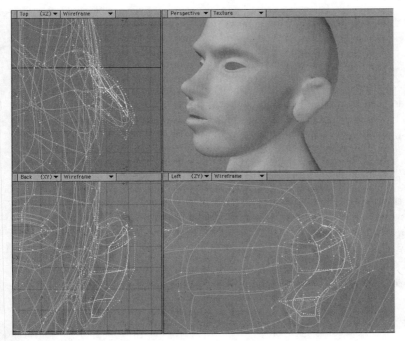

*Figure 10-43*

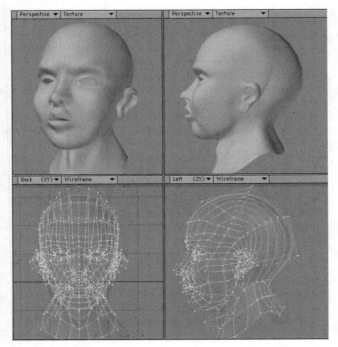

*Figure 10-44*

. . .

That's all there is to it! It just takes *time* and *patience*. (With *practice*, the time requirement drops considerably — though the patience allocation must always remain high if you're going to enjoy doing anything.) When broken down into "next logical steps," even someone who is relatively new to 3D can model heads with the best of 'em.

Remember that the finding of the "next logical steps" is the single, most important key to doing *anything* (3D or otherwise). If you're not sure how to get to your ultimate goal, just figure out what you can do that moves you a little way *toward* that goal.

Do that thing, and then figure out what you can do next! Now, granted, it is much easier to have a guide to show you the trail, pointing out where to step and where not to step, but that doesn't mean that you really need one.

Your creativity is your single most important asset; it allows you to be your own guide.

Learning is a skill (just like any other skill). By practicing this skill, you learn *how* to learn. Problem-solving is also a skill. You can learn how to use *what you already know* to get you *where you want to be*!

It's as simple as that.

# Organic Modeling Exercise 4: Modeling a Wolf's Head

This chapter presents another take on modeling a face and head. It's the technique I use when I'm asked to model an animal. We create a very simple, basic sketch in this exercise, one that you can "work back into" with BandSaw, Spin Quads, and Smooth Shift to create a model of incredible detail.

1. Start with a symmetrical box centered along the X axis. Under the Segments setting, set X to **4**, Y to **4**, and Z to **5**.

## Note

You may notice that I'm leaving more and more up to your own artistic sensibilities. If you compare your confidence level before reading this book with how you feel about what you can handle now, you will sense a pronounced evolution.

I am going to continue to leave more and more of the artistic decisions up to you, helping you to expand and trust your own sensibilities and judgment.

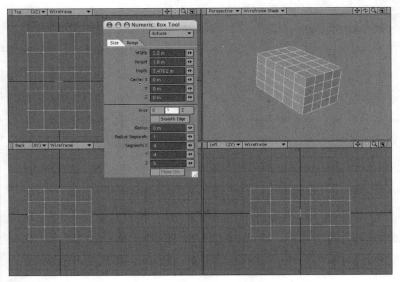

*Figure 11-1*

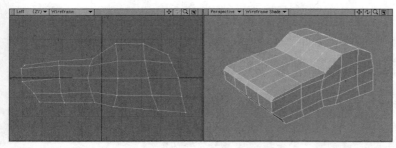

Figure 11-2

2.  In a Left viewport, use Magnet and Drag to get the rough shape of a wolf's profile.

3.  Now, working from a Top viewport with Symmetry active, use Magnet and Drag to get something that looks like a top-down view of a wolf (or a bicycle seat — bet you won't ever think about a bicycle seat in the same way again!).

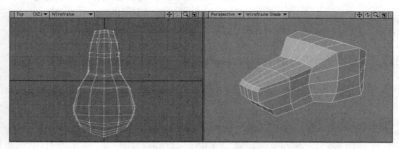

Figure 11-3

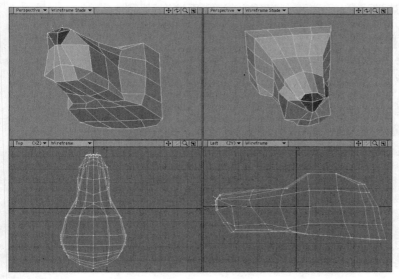

Figure 11-4

4. Working our way from the tip of the nose backward, start pushing points to give some roundness to the front of the muzzle. Surface the four polys that we smooth shift into the nose with something "nose-like."

5. Having smooth shifted the nose to give it some definition, activate sub-patches for your model and tweak the points of the muzzle to define the smooth, rounded masses of a wolf's snout.

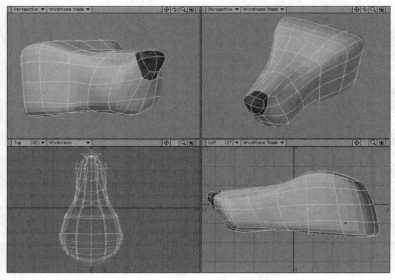

Figure 11-5

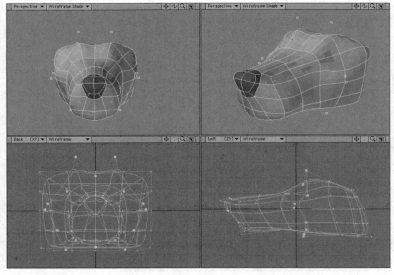

Figure 11-6

6. Now, working with the first "ring" of points that defines the skull mass of the wolf, push points to create the eye ridges, cheekbones, and jawline.

7. The next "ring" of points back sees the crown of the head rise above the eyebrow ridges, while the sides of the head angle down to the receding cheek line.

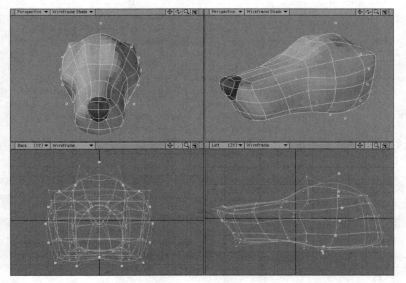

Figure 11-7

**Note**

As someone who has drawn many wolves and spent a lot of time around them, I'm familiar with the "shorthand" that defines a lupine form. You'll probably want to surround yourself with as many photographs of wolves from *as many different angles as you can find* as you work. Whatever way you tilt your Perspective viewport to evaluate your work, you should have reference material in a similar angle to compare and contrast.

You may also want to load my wolf sketch model from the CD: Objects\Chapter11\ WolfHead _F.lwo.

8.  Using Magnet (almost exclusively), shape the points that make up the back of the wolf's head. (Notice how I've indicated the back of the skull as a bit of a bump, where the neck goes.)

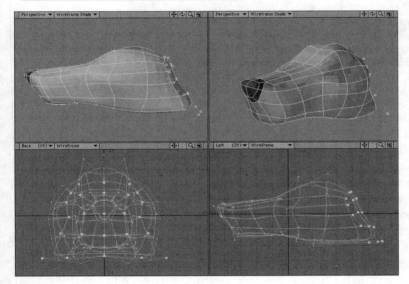

*Figure 11-8*

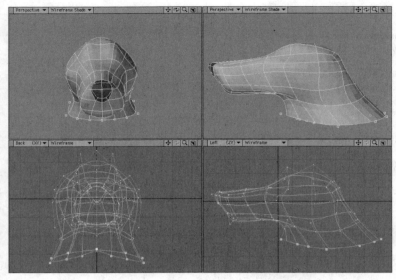

Figure 11-9

9. Next, select the eight polys at the rear of the underside of the skull and smooth shift and move them downward, reshaping the points of the neck, muzzle, and throat as you do to create the beginnings of the neck. (I've deleted the polys I smooth shifted after positioning them to create the sharp, clean line for the bottom of the neck in Figure 11-9.) You'll want to work a little with the underside of the muzzle where it meets the skull to suggest the esophageal area rather than just leaving it flat and "boxy," as it is after smooth shifting.

10. The thing about canine and feline ears that surprises so many people is how far down on the skull they actually start. (They aren't just these little "tabs" that are stuck on top of the head.) Select the seven outer rear polys on each side of the head, as shown in Figure 11-10. (You'll want to group these polys now, setting their Part Name to **Ear**, so you can select them quickly later on if you need to isolate them from the rest of the points of the head.)

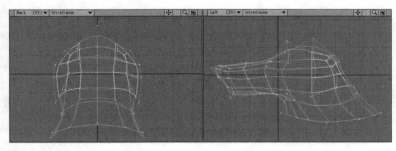

Figure 11-10

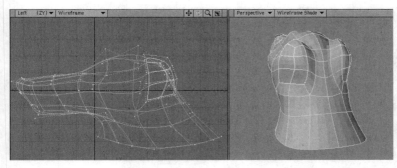

*Figure 11-11*

11. Smooth shift the ear polys, and move them upward just a bit.

12. Using Stretch, "squish" the ear polys down so they become more of a plane described by the X and Z axes (though not totally flat yet). The bottom row of points of the selected polys should be even with the top of the muzzle.

13. Smooth shift again, moving the polys upward just below where the tips of the ears will be. Use Stretch to "flatten" the selected polys so they are "flat" along the XZ plane, and drag the points around so the backs of the ears are rounded and the fronts are flat, as shown in Figure 11-13.

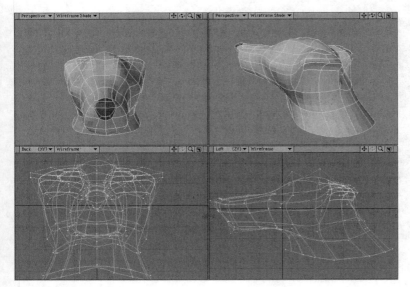

*Figure 11-12*

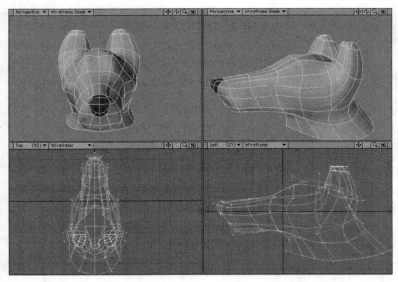

Figure 11-13

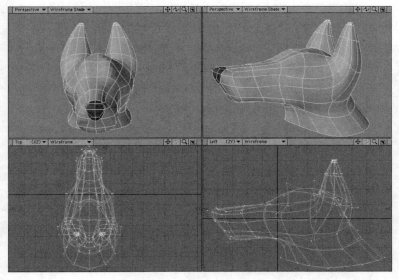

Figure 11-14

14. Smooth shift these polys one more
    time, stretching and moving them to
    become the pointy tips of the ears.

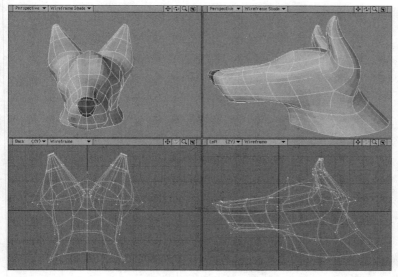

Figure 11-15

15. Now, selecting just the polys of the ears (so you can "filter" their geometry from the webwork of the rest of the wolf's head), push points so you have something that reflects the graceful angles of lupine ears.

16. Select the polys that make up the (currently flat) fronts of the ears. (For my model, this is nine polys for each ear, going right up to the edge where the ear turns toward the back of the head.) Smooth shift them, and then use Magnet to push points so the ears become little "cups."

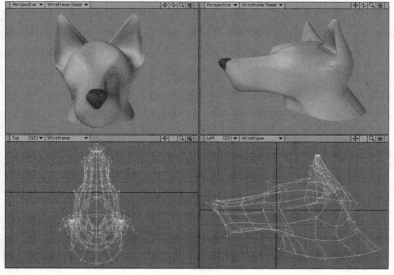

Figure 11-16

There is your completed sketch of a wolf's head! But this is much more than just a simple sketch exercise. You have a base form that you can "work back into" with BandSaw, Smooth Shift, and Spin Quads to create models of incredible detail.

(Just because this is a wolf's head doesn't mean it can only be used to create other canine forms — I once "pulled points" of a cheetah model of mine to quickly make a pug dog!)

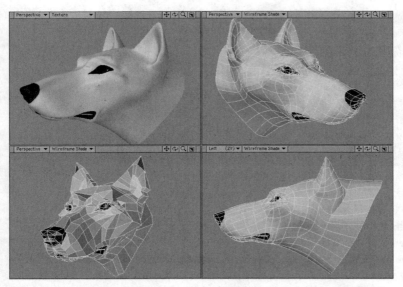

*Figure 11-17: "Working back into" a similar base form, this realistic wolf's head was modeled much more quickly than if it had been created from scratch.*

Figure 11-18: This is a detail of Reflections, showing what the wolf head from Figure 11-17 looks like in a final render. (Fur by Sasquatch)

. . .

There are many, many ways to model heads and faces. Now you know two of them. Continue to explore and find out as much as you can, picking and pulling what fits with your ways of thinking and problem-solving — and letting the rest be cast to the winds. There is no "right" or "wrong" way of doing this sort of thing — so long as you are happy with the result of what you've done (it does what you *intended* it to do), and it works with whatever animation you will be using on it.

When you are modeling animals for "furring" later on, with either Sasquatch or its free version, Sasquatch Lite, bear in mind that you are modeling the animal's *skin*. The fur rides on top of this skin, adding *thickness* and removing *detail*. If your ultimate goal for your model is realism, study anatomy books that show the structure of the animal's skin.

Nothing increases the power of your work more than working from a position of knowledge and understanding.

# Modeling 4: Spline Modeling Basics

*Spline modeling* is a way of *interpolating* a surface between three or four curves that define its boundaries. This allows you to define very complex surfaces — replete with complex, compound curves (curves that bend in more than one direction at once) — with "simple" spatial lines (splines). Spline modeling is big in the automotive and industrial design industries.

Alias|Wavefront's claim to fame is that it was a forerunner of spline modeling and heavily used in the automotive industries (back when it cost more than $60,000 for a single license of the software).

*Subdivision surfacing*, or *sub-patch modeling*, has long since surpassed spline modeling in the field of character modeling, but there are still many opportunities to use spline modeling; it is still a very handy thing to have as a part of your toolset.

> **Note**
>
> LightWave was one of the first software packages to implement subdivision surfacing. Back then, it wasn't real time, and in LightWave, it was called "metaforming."

## The "Rules of the Game"

**pe·dan·tic** *adj.* Characterized by a narrow, often ostentatious concern for book learning and formal rules. (*American Heritage Dictionary*)

When you look in the dictionary under "pedantic," you see "See spline modeling." (Just kidding — sort of.) Spline modeling adheres rigidly to a set of rules (covered in detail in Chapter 14). Deviate one iota from the rules, and you won't get what you were expecting — plain and simple.

> **Note**
>
> What I'm going to do here is lay out before you my understanding of spline modeling as it exists in LightWave. Your job, should you wish to integrate this powerful but pedantic modeling tool, is to take the information from the next three chapters, understand it, and make it your own. I'm just getting you started — where you go from there is up to you!

The rules are:

- Spline modeling in LightWave is not real time. You must use your splines to create polygonal "patches," which, if General Options | Polygons is set to Quadrangles, you can use as sub-patches later, if you wish.

- Spline patches can *only* be generated from areas defined by three or four curves.

- The ends of each curve that define an area must be welded to the ends of its neighboring curves. (When you have one curve selected and you use Select Connected, your *entire* area to be patched will become selected — if you've done things right!)

- Knot placement (the points that define a curve) is *excruciatingly* important. (Precision modeling is achieved by Modeler doing a "connect-the-knots," as it were. So, when making defining areas with your curves, be precise and aware of your "knotwork.")

- The *order* in which you select the curves to be patched affects how Modeler creates the patch.

- "Automation" can *rarely* be trusted.

## Three-Curve Patches

Just to keep us all on the same page while we're working with these tools, I've created a couple of examples for us to work from. Load **Objects\Chapter12\SplinePatch-Examples.lwo**. On the first layer, you'll see the spline "cage" shown in Figure 12-1.

Notice that the ends of the curves in Figure 12-1 have all been welded to one another and the two long, smooth curves both have the same number of knots.

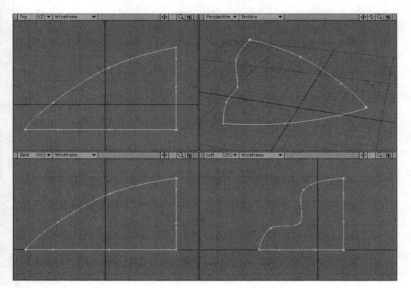

*Figure 12-1*

**Note**

When patching areas that are defined by three curves, Modeler "fans out" its geometry from the point where the first two curves selected meet. (So, by selecting your curves in a different order, you can be presented with completely different patch shapes — see Figures 12-2 through 12-4.)

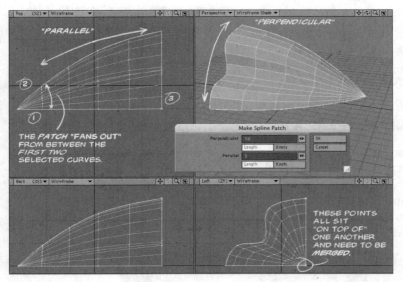

Figure 12-2

Selecting the curves in the order shown in Figure 12-1 and then using **Construct | Patches | Patch** (or the <Ctrl> + <f> keyboard shortcut) brings up a window where you control aspects of the patch to be created.

• **Perpendicular** refers to the number of polygonal rows that will be created, like the "ribs" of a fan, radiating out from the point where the first two selected curves join.

• **Parallel** refers to the rows of polys that stretch between the first two selected curves.

• **Length** specifies that the entered number of polygonal rows are to be evenly spaced along the length of the curves that define it.

• **Knots** specifies that the entered number of polygonal rows be weighted relative to the points that hold the shape of the curves. (More knots means more polys; this is a way of letting areas of more detail get more of the rows than other areas.)

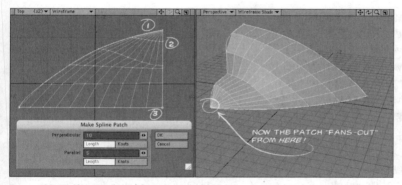

Figure 12-3: Altering the order in which the curves are selected changes where the patch "fans out" from, making a marked difference in how the patch looks.

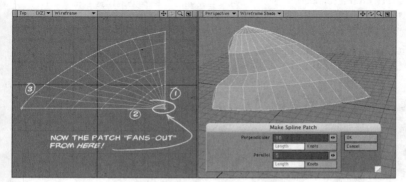

Figure 12-4: Same settings, different order, different patch.

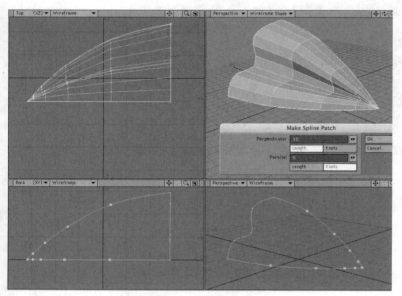

Figure 12-5: Using Knots for the Parallel setting.

By changing the setting for the parallel segments to Knots (and selecting the curves in the same order as we did in Figure 12-2), the "long" curves now have their segments weighted according to where the curve's knots are. (This preserves the subtle slope of the tip of our dingus.)

> **Note**
>
> You add points to a curve or a polygon by selecting it and then activating Multiply | Subdivide | Add Points. A new point will be added wherever you click on the selected curve(s) or polygon(s).

By altering the positioning of the knots and using the Knots setting for defining our

parallel segments, we can "sculpt" the ways our segments lay over our surface. (LightWave interpolates its segmentation in a "connect-the-knots" fashion.)

> **Note**
>
> You've probably noticed that the direction in which you select the curves (clockwise or counterclockwise) determines whether the normals of the polys that are created will be facing toward or away from you. You've probably also noticed that the convention established by selecting points to make polygons is reversed here when selecting curves to make patches.
>
> It's not really a big deal — just something to be aware of.

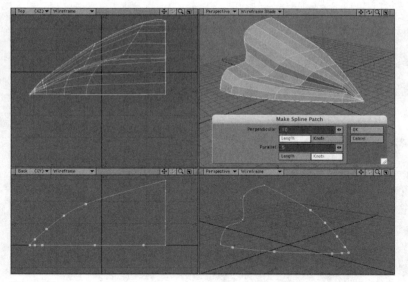

Figure 12-6

# Four-Curve Patches

Patches defined by four curves work almost exactly the same as ones defined by three curves. The endpoints of each curve must be welded to the endpoints of its neighboring curves, and the order in which the curves are selected still controls what the Make Spline Patch interface thinks of as parallel and perpendicular. The one thing that really differentiates four-curve patches is that the segments don't "bunch up" in a

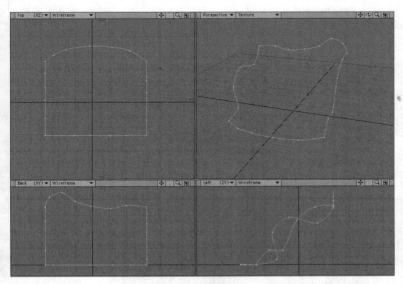

*Figure 12-7: Layer 2 of SplinePatchExamples has this neat, little funky shape to play with.*

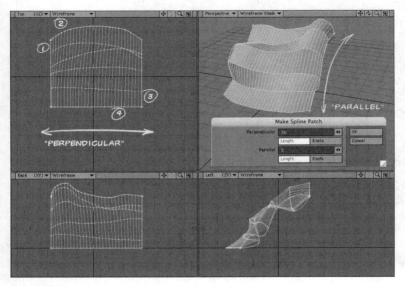

*Figure 12-8*

**275**

corner. They all spread themselves across to the opposite curve (like the threads of the warp and woof of a loom).

Selecting the curves in the order shown in Figure 12-8, Perpendicular refers to the rows of polys that are created that extend away from the first curve selected, and Parallel refers to the rows of polys that run along the axis defined by the first curve selected.

Selection order, the number of segments, and *how the segments are distributed* really begin to matter when you want to actually make something with patches. The selection order of the defining curves of these patches was different, and thus the points along the center don't line up. Merge Points can't be used to create a single, contiguous mesh.

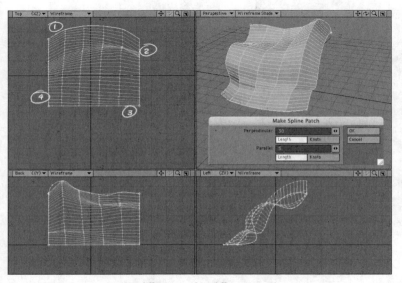

Figure 12-9: Same settings, different order, different patch.

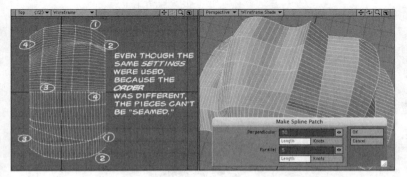

Figure 12-10

> **Note**
>
> Because patches are intended to be merged together to form more complex shapes, the curves themselves are sometimes called *seams*. The process of merging points to create objects from the patch sections is sometimes called *seaming*.

> **Note**
>
> Under the Patches pop-up menu, you may have noticed Auto Patcher MK. This is a tool that is supposed to automatically patch all the curves in your spline cage at once. As I'm sure you can see with even the simple applications we've gone over so far, spline patch modeling can have a lot of variance in its outcome, even when patching the most modest of cages.
>
> Spline modeling requires your input to tell LightWave what you want it to do. As the documentation in the LW manual says, when using Auto Patcher MK, "To insure success, never have more than four knots in a curve."
>
> Remember that you can often spend much more time fighting with the automation than it would have taken to just do the task right manually from the start.

Patches created with the same settings and order can be seamed into a single, contiguous mesh (shown in the Perspective viewport in Figure 12-11 as sub-patches).

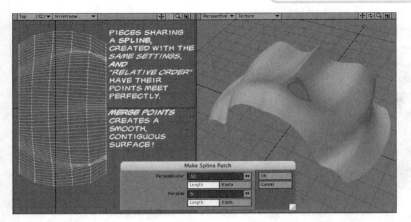

*Figure 12-11*

• • •

So those are the basics of spline patch modeling. You may never need it. Then again, for what you may want to do, you may find it to be the greatest thing since sliced bread. The important thing is that now you know how to use it (in its simplest form), so should you ever need it, you will know that it exists and what it can do for you.

# Chapter 13

# Spline Modeling Exercise: Kayak

Modeling a kayak may not be as exciting as modeling a BMW R1200C, but it'll help you become familiar with how all that stuff in the last chapter comes together to make something you can use. In this chapter you're going to get your feet wet with spline modeling in order to prepare you for the next chapter where we'll use splines to model another human head.

Figure 13-1 shows the spline cage we use to create our kayak. It looks simple enough — and that's exactly the point of spline modeling! However, if you wish to skip the construction of the splines, load **Objects\Chapter13\KayakSplines.lwo**, and go to Step 10.

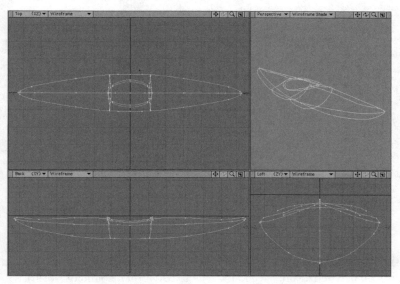

Figure 13-1: The spline cage we work from to create our kayak.

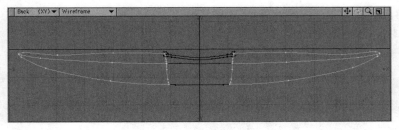

*Figure 13-2*

We model the splines in three sections: the front and back of the kayak (which are identical, mirrored across X=0) and the center piece that has the hole in which the person sits. In doing things this way, we've broken down the kayak into the simplest, largest sections that can be easily defined with either three or four curves.

1. Using **Create | Points**, manually create five points in a Back viewport in a shape somewhat like that in Figure

13-3. This represents the underside of the "nose" of the kayak. Then, use **Create | Curves | Make Curve | Make Open Curve** (remembering that LightWave will "connect the dots" in the order in which the points were created/selected — so, if you get something weird but your points look right, undo, reselect the points in a linear order, and then hit Make Open Curve). This curve needs to lie along Z=0.

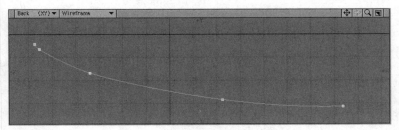

*Figure 13-3*

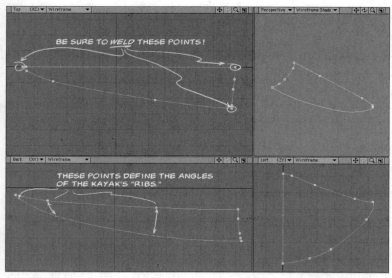

Figure 13-4

2. Next, create curves for the side "seam" of the kayak and the seam where it will connect with the center section. (To keep the "ribs" of the kayak from bunching up, the curve for the side seam should have the same number of points (knots) as the one for the bottom.) Be sure to weld the points of the ends of each curve to its neighbor; otherwise, Modeler will refuse to create a patch from them!

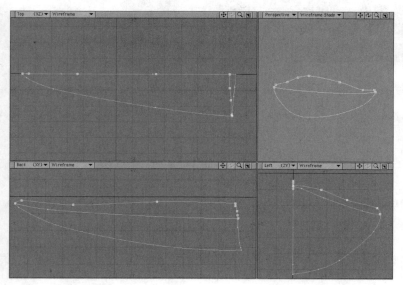

Figure 13-5

3. Next, create the seam for the top of the kayak. (It's easiest to select the bottom seam, copy it, hide it, and then paste to create a new curve that has its end-points in exactly the same position. Drag the middle points of this new curve up to make the silhouette of the top.) Make the seam that connects the top and side seams. When you're done, double-check that all your curves' end-points are welded to their neighboring curve's endpoints.

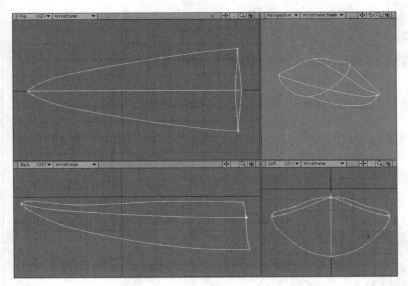

*Figure 13-6*

4. Select all the curves except the top and bottom seams, and mirror them across Z=0, merging points. You have the "nose" of your kayak all ready to be patched!

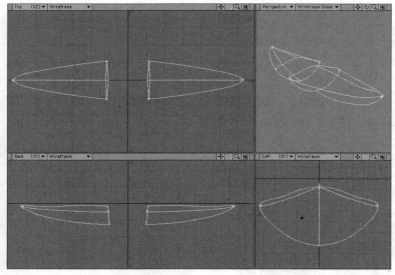

Figure 13-7

5. Mirror everything across X=0, and you'll have your kayak's "tail" too! (If it looks like you'll need more room for the center section of the kayak after this operation, just temporarily activate Symmetry and move your kayak's curves to give yourself the room you need.)

6. Next, create the curves that join the bottom seams, side seams, and top seams (shown in Figure 13-8 with the already-created curves in the background solely for the sake of being easy to see — all these curves should be on the same layer). The curves joining the top seams are actually *two* curves that

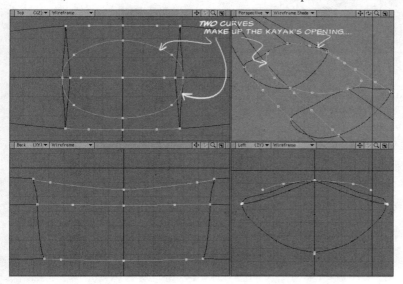

Figure 13-8

create an elliptical opening, each having five points. (See the following Note.) The points of these two curves defining the kayak's opening should be welded together where they meet at Z=0. (Symmetry mode will help as you're tweaking these curves, if the points you created them with were mirrored across the X axis.) Be sure to weld all the endpoints of your curves that meet up with one another.

> **Note**
>
> In creating the top seams (curves) for the kayak's opening, it is easiest to just make one curve with five points all lying along Z=0. Then, using the Top and Left viewports, drag the points so you have the shape of one half of that elliptical opening. Then, making sure the endpoints are at Z=0, mirror the curve across the Z axis and merge points.
>
> You may need to tweak what you get to make the ellipse nice and smooth, but this is the quickest way to create this kind of spline shape.

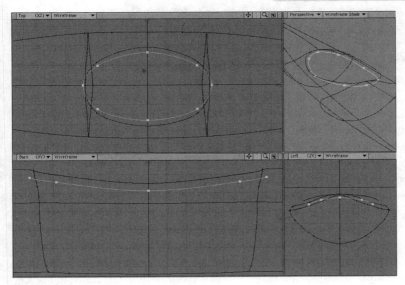

*Figure 13-9*

7.  Copy and paste the top two curves that form the kayak's opening onto another layer, move them down "inside" the kayak, and stretch them — they will create the bottom of the rubberized bumper that keeps a kayaker from banging up against the thin, hard plastic walls of the kayak's opening. When you've got these curves the way you want them, cut and paste them back onto the main layer of your kayak.

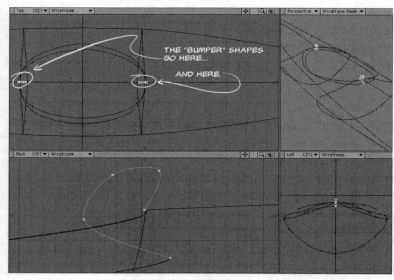

THE "BUMPER" SHAPES
GO HERE...

AND HERE.

*Figure 13-10*

8. Next, with the curves of the rest of your kayak in the background as reference, create a little shape that will be the profile of the rubberized bumper that rings the opening of the kayak. It should lie along Z=0 and be mirrored across X=0, as shown in Figure 13-10. When you've got these doodads done, cut and paste them onto the layer with the rest of your kayak, and weld their endpoints to the ends of the top seams and to the ends of the curves we created in Step 7.

9. Double-check to make sure that all your curves' endpoints are welded and/or merged to their neighbors' endpoints.

Now that you've got the "spline cage" built, we can patch it to create geometry we can render in Layout.

10. Select the curves that enclose the top front of our kayak's spline cage in the order shown in Figure 13-11. (The rest of the kayak is hidden to keep screen clutter to a minimum as we work.) In the Make Spline Patch window, set Perpendicular to **5** segments distributed WRT (with respect to) **Length**, and set Parallel to **10** segments distributed WRT **Knots**. You should get a patch that looks like the one shown in Figure 13-11. (When you select the curves in this clockwise order, you'll have to flip your polys in order to get their normals facing the right way.)

Note

Using the Perspective viewport's ability to orbit your model is a great help in selecting elements within a complex object.

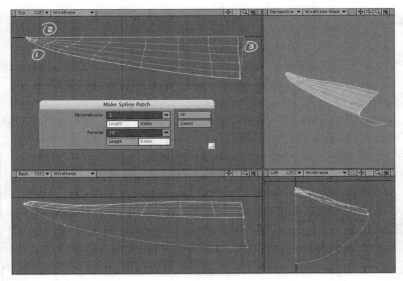

Figure 13-11

11. Cut and paste the polys that were just created onto a blank layer, where we assemble them into our actual kayak.

12. Selecting the curves of the bottom front of our kayak in the order shown in Figure 13-12, using the same settings for Make Spline Patch as in Step 10, gives us the polys for the bottom front of our kayak. Cut and paste them onto our "assembly" layer, and we'll see if their segments line up.

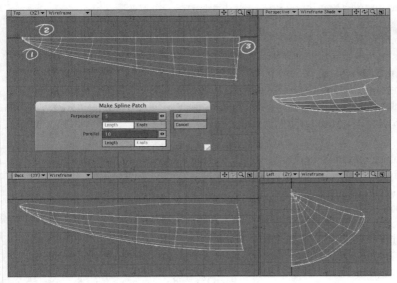

Figure 13-12

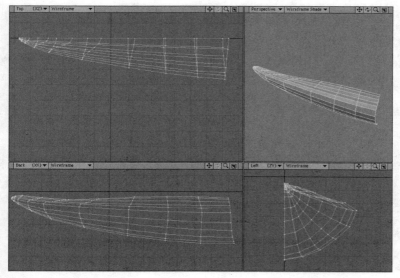

Figure 13-13

13. Examining the two patches together, it looks like our seams match perfectly! (You can use Merge Points now if you'd like to see that the points along the seam actually do go together. If you've followed the steps correctly, they do! Remember, though, that the tip of the kayak has all its points meeting at one spot — the point from which the lengthwise segments fan out — so if you merge points, you'll see that more points have merged than you might expect.)

14. Now, working on the middle section of the kayak's body (not yet working with the rubberized bumper curves), select the four curves of its top in the order shown in Figure 13-14. In the Make Spline Patch window, set Perpendicular to **5** segments distributed WRT **Length**, and set Parallel to **5** segments distributed WRT **Knots**. Cut and paste the resultant patch onto your assembly

layer. (You'll have to flip the polys to get their normals facing outward.)

> **Note**
>
> Some of you may be wondering, "Why don't you select your curves counterclockwise so you wouldn't have to flip the patch-polys?" Doing things in a clockwise fashion is a habit I picked up a long time ago. I find it much quicker to simply follow this habit, flipping polys if necessary, than to have to ponder the direction in which to select the curves to get the normals facing out before even selecting my curves.
>
> For me it's quicker to just "muscle through" what it is I need to get done than to try to do things strictly by the book.

> **Note**
>
> *Don't* merge points when you paste this section onto your assembly layer. We'll need to keep the middle separate from the nose of the kayak until Figure 13-18.

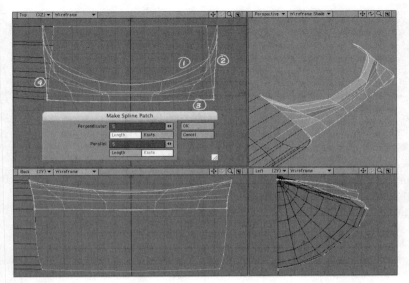

Figure 13-14

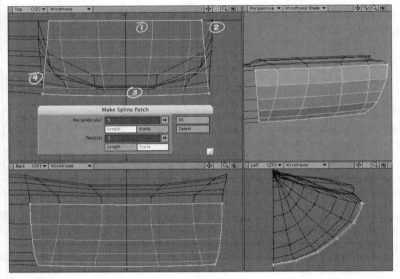

Figure 13-15

15. Select the four curves of the bottom of
    the middle section in the order shown
    in Figure 13-15. Fill in the Make Spline
    Patch window with the same settings
    as in Step 14. Cut and paste the resul-
    tant patch onto your assembly layer.

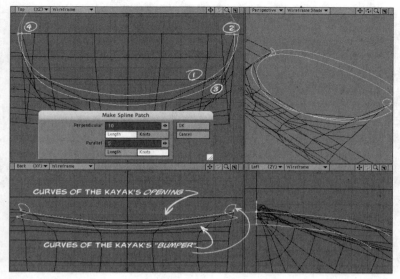

Figure 13-16

16. Now, working with the curves that define the rubberized bumper and the opening on top of the kayak, select the curves in the order shown in Figure 13-16. Fill in the Make Spline Patch window with Perpendicular set to **10** segments distributed WRT **Length** (for a nice, soft feel to its silhouette) and Parallel set to **5** segments distributed WRT **Knots** (so the bumper's segments will line up perfectly with the segments of our kayak's opening).

17. The resultant patch may look pretty angular as it skirts the rim of the kayak's opening, but I'm planning on using this as a sub-patch model, so it'll be fine. (Notice how the segments of the bumper and the opening line up perfectly.) Assign these polys a surface

appropriate for a rubberized bumper, and copy and paste the bumper onto your assembly layer.

### Note

Wouldn't it be nice to be so brilliant that you know exactly what every setting does at every turn? I'm pretty far away from that myself. To get the above settings correct to match the bumper up with the kayak's opening, just like anyone else, I had to play around with it a bit until I found the right settings. Still, I didn't trust it just *looking* right. I tested it, copying both patches to a "junk" layer and using Merge Points to see if it fused the two sections together.

No one's perfect. Don't bust your chops if you're not.

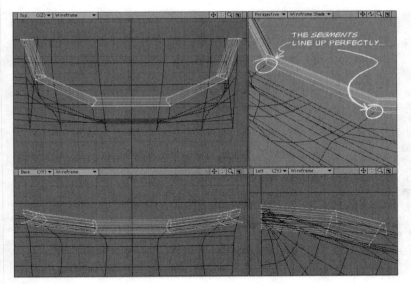

Figure 13-17

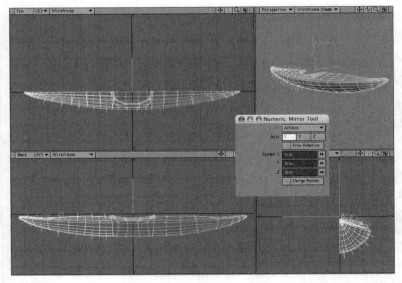

Figure 13-18

18. Selecting a few polys from the nose sections of our kayak and using Select Connected quickly selects all the polys we'll need to mirror to become its tail. Mirror those polys across X=0. (You may merge points if you like. I don't because I like to get the numeric info of just how many points were eliminated when I merge points manually.) Because our spline cage was created by mirroring, our patches should fit perfectly by mirroring as well.

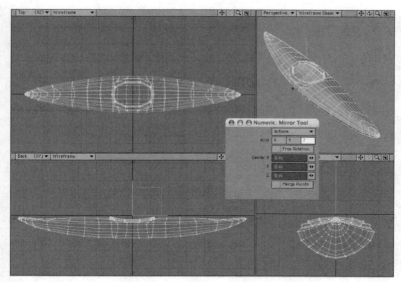

*Figure 13-19*

19. Mirror the entire kayak across Z=0, and then merge points.

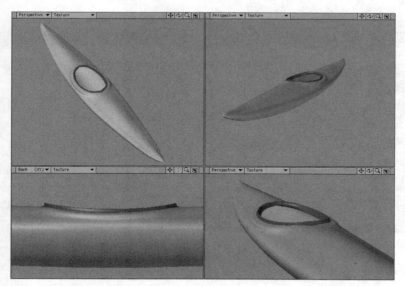

*Figure 13-20: Our completed kayak, surfaced and viewed as sub-patches!*

. . .

That wasn't so hard, was it? There are many applications where using spline patches can be pretty nifty.

The hardest part about spline modeling in LightWave is juggling the settings in your mind so your patches end up seaming properly. (It's a little like that children's game of memory — but it's not cheating if you want to use pencil and paper.) Just know that it may take a couple of tries to get things to line up.

Also, remember that you've got to watch the distribution of your knots. You can do some pretty fancy tricks through creative placement of those little things. Be sure to weld all your endpoints. (This is a simple thing, but it still slips by me from time to time.)

There you go. To quote Obi Wan Kenobi, "You've taken your first step into a larger world." At the time of publication, only an estimated 4% of LightWave users said that they understood spline patch modeling. You can take pride in knowing that you're actually *ahead* of the pack! And to solidify your position there, we're going to exercise your knowledge of splines by using them to model a human head. Flip the page and let's begin!

# Chapter 14

# Spline Modeling Exercise 2: Modeling a Human Head

Splines are a wonderful tool and I hope you're beginning to see just how powerful they can be. Splines are most often used to model objects with large complex surface areas, such as vehicles and aircraft. In this chapter, we'll be looking at a more esoteric use of splines, namely for the creation of a realistic human head model.

This chapter will provide a detailed explanation of the process. It is a long chapter, but don't let that intimidate you. Each step is broken down and discussed in detail, making it easy to follow, even for new users. That said, however, I expect you to have already worked through the previous modeling chapters and to have a basic understanding of the spline modeling rules outlined in Chapter 12.

We'll get into the actual modeling shortly, but first let's talk about the things that make a good head model.

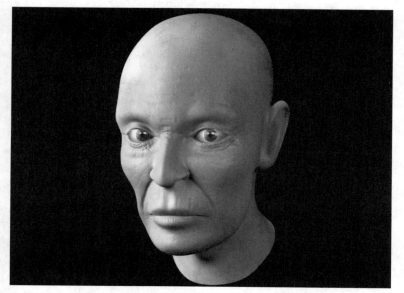

*Figure 14-1: The head model built in this chapter with textures applied.*

## Poly Count and Flow

I've seen hundreds of head models and dozens of tutorials showing how to build them. There are as many techniques for building a head as there are people building them. But regardless of how the head is constructed, there are two inherent qualities it must possess in order for it to be "successful." Contrary to what you might think, looking good is not one of them. Rather, the most successful head models are those with a reasonably low polygon count and an ideal polygon flow.

### Poly Count

The best modelers are always striving to create their objects with the fewest number of polygons possible. This isn't just an obsessive-compulsive drive. It's a practical quest. The more polygons an object has, the longer it will take to render. Even with the most modern processors, a high-poly sub-patch object will hit the render engine harder than a low-poly object. But the quest for minimal polygons isn't just about render time. It's much more practical than that. You see, when you sub-patch an object, you are actually interpolating geometry between each point in your object. Take a look at Figure 14-2, which shows two sub-patched objects.

The object on the left is a simple box with a single cut running down the center. Moving the points at the center of this box creates a smooth arc from one end of the object to the other. This arc is caused by the interpolation of geometry that occurs when an object is sub-patched. Now take a look at the object on the right. It is the same box, but in this case, there are six more cuts running through it. Moving the middle points on this object still results in an interpolation of geometry; however, since the points on either side of those being moved are now closer together, the arc is tighter and more pronounced. Understanding this

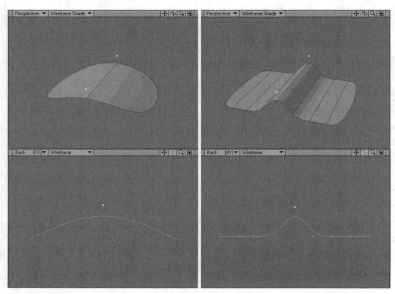

*Figure 14-2: Low poly count enables broader changes to your model.*

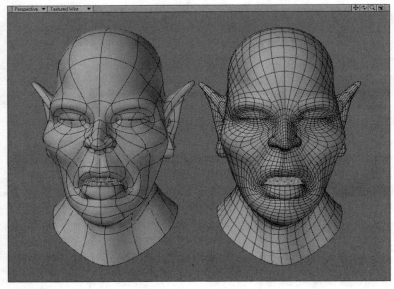

Figure 14-3

simple truth is the key to effective subpatch modeling. The more polygons you have in a given area, the more pronounced the effect on the movement of points in that area.

Take a look at Figure 14-3. Keeping in mind what you saw in Figure 14-2, you can imagine what would happen if you moved the points on either of these objects. Undoubtedly, the object on the left would enable you to make broad changes (similar to the object on the left in Figure 14-2). Small movements to the points on this object would not have a drastic impact on its overall shape. That's not true for the object on the right. Even minor adjustments to this object's points would result in a noticeable change to its form.

Learning to control the poly count and understanding where and when it's appropriate to add more geometry is a skill that takes time to develop. But suffice it to say that as you model, you should strive to keep your poly count as low as possible.

## Poly Flow

The other quality that makes a good head model is proper polygon flow. Flow is a difficult concept to grasp, especially for beginners. In essence, it is the deliberate layout of polygons into overlapping bands or loops that, when fully realized, mimic the natural flow of muscles under the skin.

Keep in mind that as you model, you are simulating reality. Whether it's a wineglass, a sports car, or a human being, you are building a simulation of a real-world object. In the case of organic models such as animals and people, you are simulating the features that make up their outward appearance, typically muscle and bone. It is important, then, to study in great detail the forms you are attempting to simulate. Amazing character models aren't created by accident. The best character modelers are those who have a solid grasp of human anatomy.

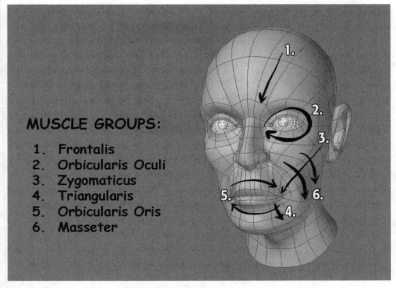

MUSCLE GROUPS:

1. Frontalis
2. Orbicularis Oculi
3. Zygomaticus
4. Triangularis
5. Orbicularis Oris
6. Masseter

Figure 14-4: Basic muscle flow of the human head.

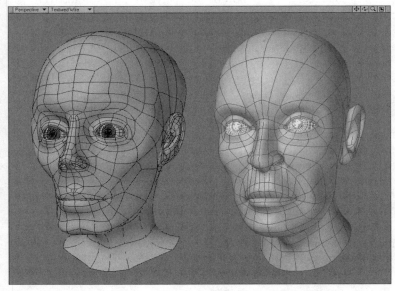

Figure 14-5: Bad polygon flow (left) compared with good flow (right).

Unfortunately, an introduction to anatomy is beyond the scope of this chapter, but I would encourage you to pick up an anatomy book or attend a figure drawing class if you intend to pursue character modeling. And I would encourage you to visit http://www.fineart.sk and http://www.3d.sk. These two sites offer the most comprehensive set of resources for character modelers that you can find.

The need for ideal polygon flow doesn't stem from a purist compulsion. Like polygon count, it is a practical requirement. Consider this: Character models are rarely built to hold a single pose or a solitary facial expression (like Michelangelo's sculpture of David). On the contrary, they are built to be animated and posed in a variety of fashions. A real face can make expressions (e.g., smiling or frowning) because of the layout of muscles in the face. Therefore, if your 3D model's polygons do not mimic the flow of

muscles in a *real* face, it will be difficult to create realistic expressions in a *simulated* face. You will find yourself fighting the model to get so much as a smirk. It becomes imperative, then, to build a model with great flow.

In Chapter 10, we built a head model using the detail-out approach. The advantage to the detail-out approach is that it is a WYSIWYG process. You have immediate feedback on the model at each stage of development. The problem with the detail-out approach is that poly-by-poly construction makes it frustratingly difficult to develop good flow (especially for beginners) and it often yields objects with a high poly count. Spline modeling, however, avoids these pitfalls, allowing you to visualize the flow of your polygons and to selectively adjust the resolution of each patch for optimal poly count.

## Spline Modeling Pitfalls

Spline modeling, while elegant and efficient, is not without its problems. As we've seen in previous chapters, there are rules that need to be followed. And even when the rules are followed, the occasional "Curves Do Not Cross" error will appear (seemingly for no reason at all). Moreover, spline modeling's greatest strength can also be its biggest weakness, especially when dealing with organic models. While splines make it easy to visualize the flow of your polys, you must have a solid understanding of flow in the first place to build them correctly. You also have to be extremely careful when

specifying your Perpendicular and Parallel patch settings to avoid creating polygons that do not line up properly from patch to patch. And as if all of that weren't enough, the cold hard truth is that some objects are not well-suited for spline modeling. These drawbacks cause many modelers to steer clear of splines altogether. But you're in luck — I'm going to show you several tricks to work around these pesky problems.

## Spline Modeling Tips and Tricks

The major pitfalls of spline modeling can be avoided by following these simple tips and tricks.

● **Tip 1**: Use splines for their strengths, not their weaknesses. It sounds obvious, but you'd be surprised at how many people don't get this. Splines work best as a visualization tool, allowing you to establish the overall form of your object quickly and easily. They do not work well for creating intricate details, but I see people attempting this all the time. They build spline cages with an incredible amount of detail and expect to simply patch it and be done. It sounds great in theory, but it rarely works out in practice. So rather than using splines as a be-all and end-all, use them for what they're good for — namely building the overall form of your object. Then use the other tools at your disposal to model in the details.

● **Tip 2**: Build quad cages. It's best to build your cage so that every region is bounded by four splines. I call this a quad cage. It consists of splines for the top, bottom, left, and right for each area in your cage, both large and small. Building a quad cage is perhaps the most critical component of spline modeling, and I'll be teaching you more about it as we proceed.

● **Tip 3**: Use simple patches. One of the most time-consuming aspects of spline modeling is determining the proper Parallel and Perpendicular patch settings. Figuring this out is like some sort of twisted game.

You have to remember which spline you selected first in order to establish how the perpendicular and parallel patches are constructed. And then you have to ensure that the patches line up properly to those around them. It's a hassle, but here's a simple solution: Use the same patch settings for the whole object. If you construct your splines properly (by making sure your patched areas are roughly the same size), you can use the same patch settings for your whole object. This can save you loads of time and frustration down the line.

Keep these simple tricks in your back pocket and they will make your spline modeling job much easier.

Now that we've covered the basics, we're ready to start modeling. Here's an outline of what we'll be doing:

1. First we'll build the spline cage. I'm going to show you how to construct a cage with great flow using the tricks outlined above. Once built, this cage can be saved and used over and over again to quickly knock out other head models.

2. Next, we'll patch the splines, add a few details, and learn how to reduce the number of polygons to obtain an optimal poly count.

3. Lastly, we'll construct the remaining details using tools you're already familiar with.

Fire up Modeler and let's get started!

# Creating the Cage

As was the case with the detail-out approach, it's helpful (and often necessary) to use a reference image when building your spline cage. You can find the images for this chapter on the companion CD under Images\Chapter14. In the Setup\Chapter 14 folder, there is a Backdrop config file. Bring up the Display Options window (<d>) and click on the **Backdrop** tab. From the Presets pop-up menu, select **Load Backdrop** and load the **Spline_Head_Backdrop.cfg** file.

Once your images are loaded, zoom in on the eye on the right (which is the character's left eye). Oftentimes, finding the best place to start a spline cage can be difficult. I chose the eye as a starting point because it

can easily be divided into four sections (top, bottom, left, and right), and that provides a good starting point for building a quad cage (see Tip #2 above).

1.  Begin by laying down three points over the top of the eye in the Back viewport. Then, with the points still selected, use the **Create | Curves | Make Curve | Make Open Curve** tool (or press <**Ctrl**> + <**p**>) to generate your first spline. Finally, use the Drag tool (or a similar tool for moving points) to adjust the spline in the Right view. Keep in mind that the eye bulges out in the center, so your middle point should stick out farther than the points on either side.

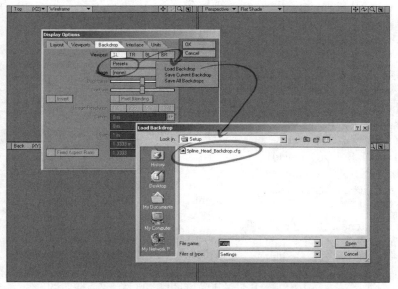

*Figure 14-6: Load the Spline_Head_Backdrop file that we'll use as a reference for building the spline cage.*

## Note

Don't feel that you have to adhere to my particular workflow. I find that laying down points and then converting them into splines gives me the control that I want, but if you're more comfortable using the Sketch, Bezier, or Spline Draw tools, go right ahead. It's not important how you arrive at the end result so long as you are comfortable with the process used to get there.

## Note

The most basic curve consists of a starting point, an ending point, and a control point somewhere in between. You can build your splines with as many points as you like, but keep in mind that the more points you have, the more difficult it will be to adjust the overall shape of the spline.

## Note

As we build our splines, many of them will jut up against each another, creating harsh angles between them. This is nothing to worry about. There's no need to rebuild your splines. We'll be fixing these harsh angles *after* we've completely built our cage.

## Note

You'll notice as we proceed that the splines I lay down don't strictly adhere to the reference image. *Remember Tip #1!* At this stage, we're only interested in getting the basic form. We'll be doing plenty of fine-tuning to the model after we patch it. So do yourself a favor: Don't waste time trying to precisely match the reference image. Focus on the overall form. Getting it close is good enough *for now*. The actual refining stage comes later.

Notice that this spline does not extend over the top of the entire eye. Rather, it covers about 70 to 80% of the total area. This is done to ensure that the splines on either side of the eye are roughly the same size as those on the top and bottom. Remember Tip #3. We want to create patches that are roughly the same size. If they are significantly smaller, the polys created by patching this area will get crammed together, resulting in an unpleasant pinching effect that's difficult to remove in the final object.

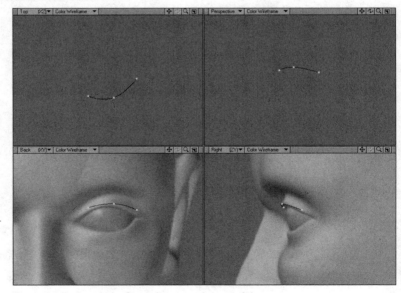

*Figure 14-7: Create the first spline over the top of the eye.*

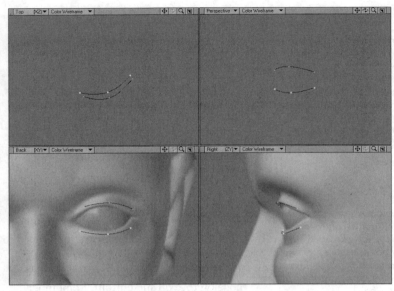

Figure 14-8: Create the second spline along the bottom of the eye.

2.  Create three more points in the Back viewport along the bottom of the eye and press <**Ctrl**> + <**p**> to convert them into a spline. Then shape the spline in the Right viewport as you did in Step 1. The middle point on this spline should stick out farther than the endpoints but not as much as the middle point for the top of the eye.

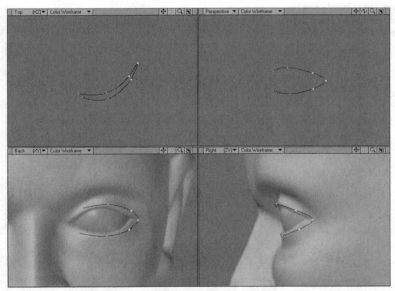

Figure 14-9: The third spline is created by using the two existing points from our other splines and a new point at the outside corner of the eye.

3. Create a single point at the outside corner of the eye. Then deselect it. Now select the outside point on the top spline, followed by the point you just created, and finally the outside point on the bottom spline. Press <Ctrl> + <p> to create a new spline.

4. Create a single point at the inside corner of the eye. Then deselect it. We're going to repeat the procedure in Step 3 for the left (inside) part of the eye. Select the point on the inside top spline, the point you just created, and then the point on the inside bottom spline. Then create a new spline by pressing <Ctrl> + <p>.

You've just completed the outline of the eye using four separate splines. Take a moment to spin around in your Perspective view and check for anything that looks out of place. The outline should bulge out at the center and taper in and back on the sides. Inspecting your splines like this is a habit you should get into. Check it from multiple angles and don't be afraid to move points that seem out of place. Oftentimes you'll find that the Perspective view will reveal problems that would be difficult to identify in the orthographic views alone.

Now that we've got an initial outline, it's time to branch out.

5. Create three more points over the top of the eyebrow and convert them into a spline.

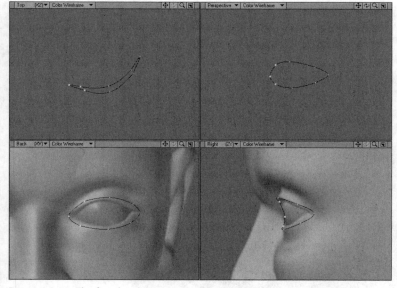

*Figure 14-10: The fourth spline is created in the same manner as the third by using two existing points and a third new point at the inside corner of the eye.*

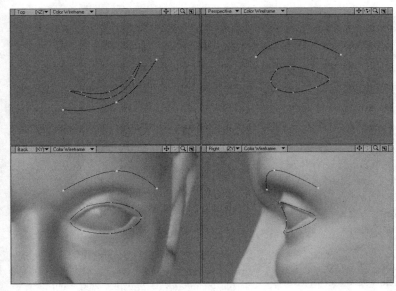

*Figure 14-11: Create a new spline over the eyebrow.*

6. Create three points under the eye (about the same distance below as the eyebrow spline is above). Then convert these into a spline. The inside point for this spline should rest at the base of the nose and the outside point should rest on the cheek bone.

7. Add a new point where the top of the nose and the eyebrow meet. Move it back slightly on the Z axis, then deselect it. Select the inside point from the eyebrow spline, the point you just created, and the inside point from the spline below the eye. Press <**Ctrl**> +

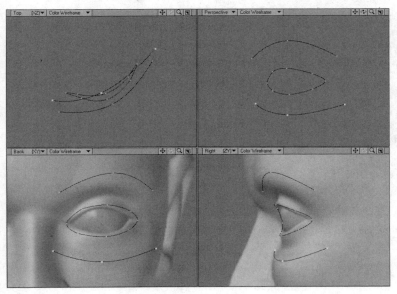

*Figure 14-12: Create a new spline under the eye.*

<p> to create a new spline and adjust its shape as needed.

8.  Add a new point at the outside of the eye behind the eye socket cavity. Deselect this point, then reselect the point on the outside of the eyebrow, the new point you just created, and the point on the outside of the cheekbone spline. Press <Ctrl> + <p> to create a new spline.

As we did before, spin your view around in the Perspective viewport to check for anything that looks out of place.

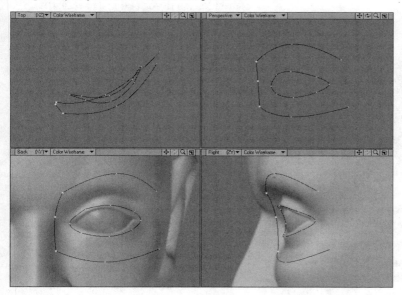

Figure 14-13: Create a new spline running along the inside of the eye.

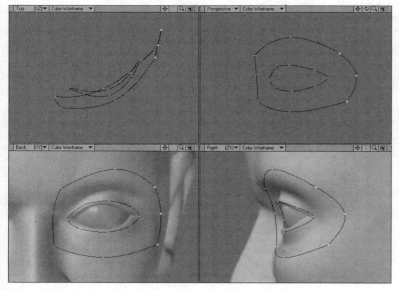

Figure 14-14: Create a new spline along the outside of the eye.

We've now got two sets of splines radiating out from the eye of our model. The area enclosed by these splines forms a loop, known as an *edge loop*. When we patch the splines in this loop, the resulting polys will follow the basic musculature of the orbicularis oculi shown as the dark polys in Figure 14-15.

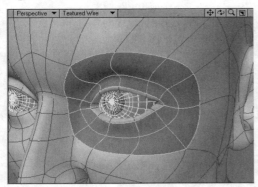

Figure 14-15: The orbicularis oculi edge loop.

Let's go ahead and patch them now. Select the splines of the outer loop in a counter-clockwise fashion and press **<Ctrl>** + **<f>**. Accept the defaults of **10** Parallel and **10** Perpendicular and press **OK**. If you get a "Curves Do Not Cross" error, press **<m>**

to ensure that the points in your splines are merged together properly. Figure 14-16 shows the results.

Wait a minute. This is just a grid-like mesh. We were expecting a nice clean edge loop. What happened? Well, here's the problem. Even though we built our splines with four sides (as described in Tip #2), the *outer* splines have no way of knowing that they should be bounded by the *inner* splines. When we patched the outer splines, they generated polys that ran right over the inner splines. That's *definitely* not what we want. In order to resolve this, we need to link the outside splines to the inside splines so that we can patch the region *between* them.

Go ahead and undo the spline patch.

9. Add three points in a roughly horizontal line about the center of the eye. They should mimic the points in the splines above and below them. In other words, the middle point should stick out farther than the ones on the left and right. Deselect these, then select the points shown in Figure 14-17 and create a new spline.

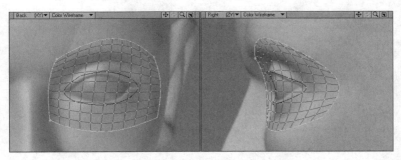

Figure 14-16: The results of patching the outside splines.

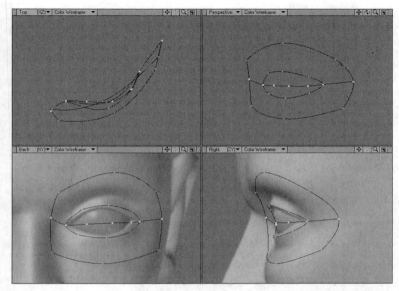

*Figure 14-17: Create a new spline that runs from the bridge of the nose to the outside edge of the eye.*

10. Select the points shown in Figure 14-18 and create a new spline.

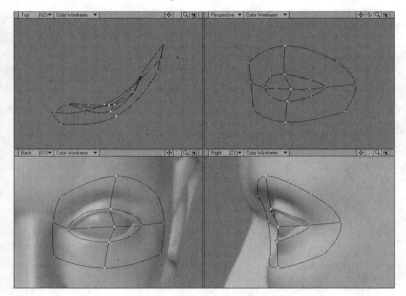

*Figure 14-18: Create a new spline from these existing points.*

> **Note**
>
> Technically speaking, you don't need the points running through the center of the eye that you created in Step 9. But like sub-patches, splines are directly affected by the points around them. I had you add these extra points to provide a subtle element of control to the splines extending out either side of the eye.

Let's take a look at what we've got. By adding these two extra splines, we've partitioned off sections of this edge loop. That's

good. But we no longer have a quad cage. That's bad. It may *look* like we have a quad cage, but in reality, each area is made up of six separate splines.

We can resolve this by partitioning our edge loop with a few more splines, and in the process we'll begin to expand our cage.

11. Zoom out and create a new point in the center of the forehead, just a bit above the bridge of the nose. Select the remaining points as shown in Figure 14-20 and create a new spline.

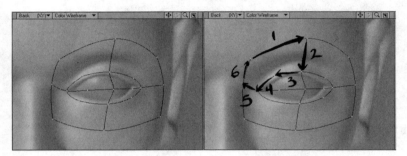

Figure 14-19: It looks like we've sectioned our edge loop with four splines, but in reality, each area is made up of six separate splines.

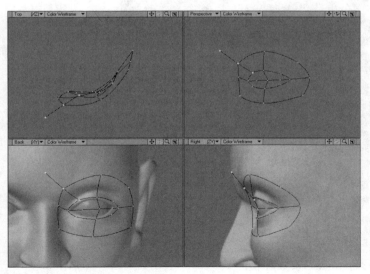

Figure 14-20: Expanding the spline cage

12. Create a new point at the center of the nose, about the same distance from the bridge as the point you created in Step 11. Then create a second point slightly off to the right and down a bit. This second point will act as a constraint, allowing us to shape the spline better to fit the nose. Finally, select the remaining points shown in Figure 14-21 and create a new spline.

13. In the Right viewport, create two more points as shown in Figure 14-22. The first should be placed in the temple region of the head and the second should be placed above and in front of the ear. Deselect these points, then reselect them in the proper (sequential) order and create a new spline.

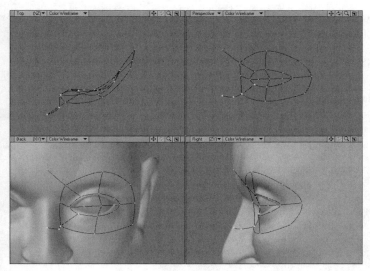

Figure 14-21

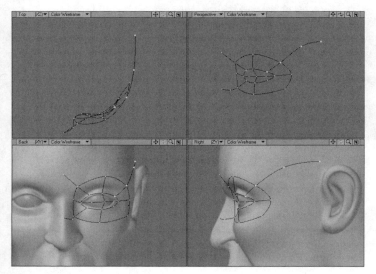

Figure 14-22

14. Again, in the Right viewport, create two more points as shown in Figure 14-23. The position of these points should loosely mirror those created in the previous step.

Go ahead and inspect your cage in the Perspective viewport, correcting anything that looks out of place.

Let's talk briefly about what we've just done. The primary purpose of these four splines was to partition our edge loop into a quad cage. We've successfully done that. But we've also used them to expand the entire spline cage and set new boundaries. The two additional splines on the inside reach to the center of the nose and forehead. The two on the outside reach to the edge of the face. As we proceed, we'll continue to build the spline cage around half of

the face. Once the face is complete, we'll build the cage out to encompass the back of the head and neck. Then we'll patch the cage and mirror it across the X axis to create a full head. It sounds like a lot of work, and if you're new to the art of modeling, it will certainly seem so. But trust me when I tell you that with practice, the process becomes second nature and can be done in a snap.

Let's get back to expanding our spline cage. We already have splines extending from four of the points in our edge loop. Let's continue building splines off of the rest of the points in the loop.

15. Add one point at the center of the bridge of the nose, then select the point to its right and create a new spline.

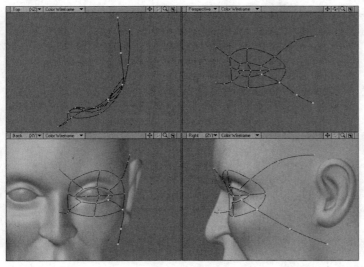

*Figure 14-23*

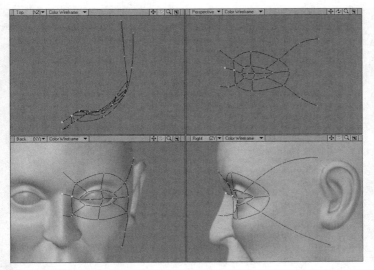

Figure 14-24

16. In the Right viewport, add two points between the splines created in Steps 13 and 14. Select the points as shown in Figure 14-25 and create a new spline.

17. Create two more points as shown in Figure 14-26, then select the three points shown and create a new spline. Note that the spline does not run straight up the forehead, but rather it veers off to the right and back. We are doing this in order to space our splines evenly apart (see Tip #3).

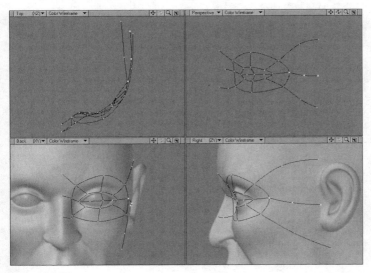

Figure 14-25

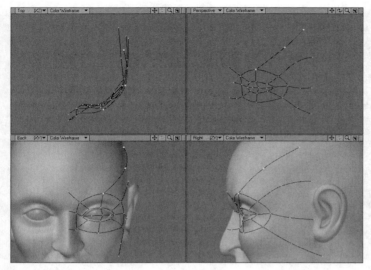

*Figure 14-26*

18. Now for the tricky spline. Add three points as shown in Figure 14-27. The first gets placed below the center of the eye and slightly to the right of the nostril. It also gets placed out farther on the Z axis to account for the bulge of the cheek. The next point gets placed below and slightly behind the first one (as seen in the Right viewport). The third point gets placed just above the lip.

Spin your model around in the Perspective viewport and check for anything that appears to be out of place.

At this point the cage may seem a little unruly. Don't panic! Keep in mind the simple tips I gave you. Tip #2 says that we

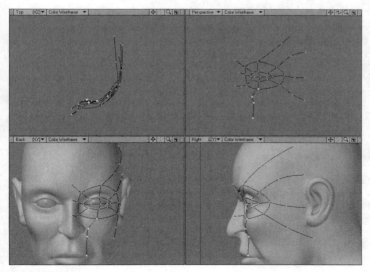

*Figure 14-27*

should build quad cages. We did that at the start by creating an edge loop out of four distinct splines and then expanding and dividing the cage from there. We now need to create an even larger edge loop that encompasses most of what we've built so far. We'll do this by building a new quad cage.

19. In the Right viewport, create a number of points along the profile of the background image. These points should run from the top of the forehead to the top of the upper lip. Select the points in sequence and create a spline similar to the one shown in Figure 14-28. This will become the left spline of a quad cage (see Tip #2).

20. Add a single point as shown in Figure 14-29. Place it above the eye and in between the profile spline and the spline extending from the center of our eye edge loop. Then select the points in order and create a new spline. This will become the top of our quad cage.

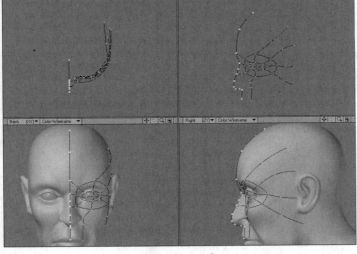

*Figure 14-28*

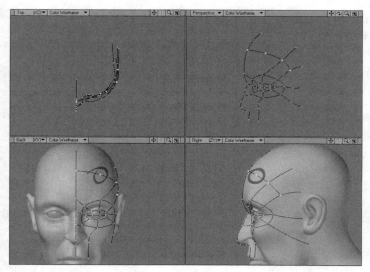

*Figure 14-29*

21. Add three more points over the top of the lip. Be sure to adjust the points in both the Back and Right viewports so that they follow the curve of the lip back toward the cheek. Select all of the points shown in Figure 14-30 and create a new spline. This will become the bottom of our quad cage.

22. Finally, add the three points circled in Figure 14-31. The first should be placed above and behind the corner of the mouth. The second should be placed slightly above, to the right, and behind the first. And the third should be placed above, to the right and behind the second. Once you've created these

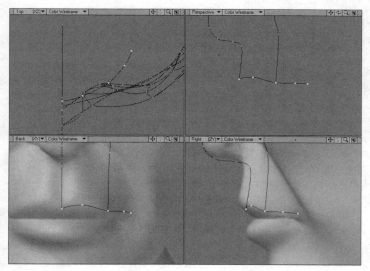

*Figure 14-30*

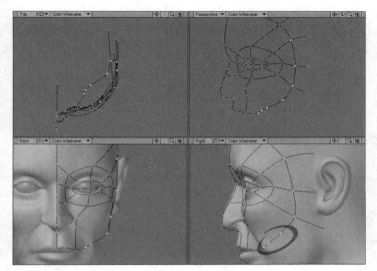

*Figure 14-31*

three points, select all of the points shown in Figure 14-31 and create a new spline. This will become the right spline in our quad cage.

Check your model by spinning it around in the Perspective viewport and correct any errors you might find.

We're making good progress. We've built a quad cage with four new splines (top, bottom, left, and right) that forms a new edge loop. This loop runs over the brow, behind the eye, down across the cheek, and over the upper lip and tip of the nose. Of course, we now have a number of regions bounded by more than four splines (violating Tip #2). It's time to correct this.

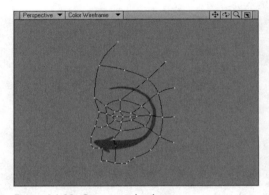

*Figure 14-32: Our new edge loop.*

23. Create a new point at the top of the forehead between the first point in the profile spline and the first point in the spline to its right (see Figure 14-33). Select the remaining two points in Figure 14-33 and create a new spline.

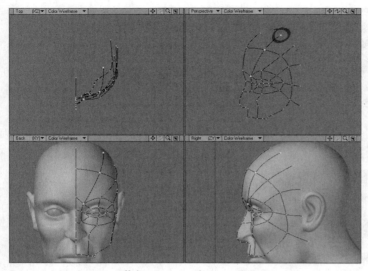

*Figure 14-33: Partition off this region with a new spline to create a quad cage.*

24. Take a look at Figure 14-34. This next spline is a little tricky, but don't let that intimidate you. We're going to create a spline that runs from the outside edge of the nose, down over the nostril, and ends at the upper lip. As was the case when creating our profile spline, the number of points we use isn't extremely important so long as you have enough to define the general shape. In my example, I'm using five new points (and two existing points) to define the spline. The first gets placed on the outside of the nose, just above the nostril. The second gets placed toward the front of the nose just above

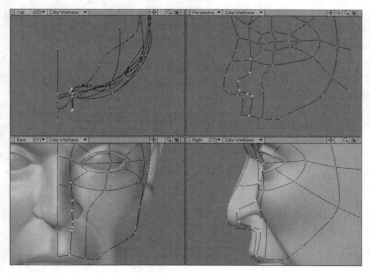

*Figure 14-34*

the nostril. The third is placed toward the front of the nose just below the nostril. The fourth goes right under the nostril and the fifth is positioned right on the lip toward the back of the nostril. As always, select the points in order (including the existing points shown in Figure 14-34) and create a new spline.

**Note**

If you find that a spline needs an extra point or two in order to properly partition off an area, don't hesitate to add one. Just be sure to inspect the spline afterward to account for the shape change that can occur when you add extra points.

25. Create three more points as shown in Figure 14-35. The first should be placed at the outside of the cheek bone, and the second and third should be placed toward the inside of the cheek.

Step back and take a look at what you've got. It's starting to come together! We've successfully partitioned the cage so that each area is bounded by four splines, making a quad cage. Now it's time to add splines around the outside edge of the face.

26. Select the three points that run over the top of the forehead as shown in Figure 14-36 and create a new spline. Keeping Tip #2 in mind, this will become the top spline in a new quad cage.

27. Select the four points running down the side of the head as shown in Figure 14-37 and create a new spline. This becomes the right spline of our quad cage.

Spin your model around in the Perspective viewport and check for any problem areas. Since the cage is starting to take shape, it will be much easier to spot areas where the splines don't curve naturally.

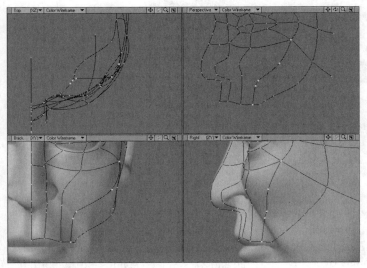

*Figure 14-35*

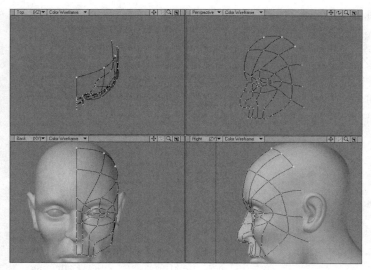

Figure 14-36

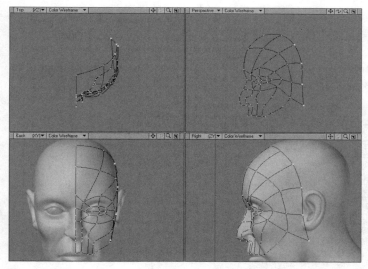

Figure 14-37

We've now completed the upper portion of the face. You can see that the splines we created in Steps 26 and 27 are beginning to form a new edge loop running over the forehead and down the side of the face. Unfortunately, the lower part of the face (consisting primarily of the jaw and lower lip) has yet to be defined.

We already have splines for the top and right sides of a new quad cage. In order to complete the quad cage we started in Steps 26 and 27, we need splines for the bottom and left sides of the face. There's just one problem: If you look at the Right viewport, you can see that the jaw actually runs farther down the side of the face than our current right side spline does. In other words, our right side spline is not long enough. We could create a bottom spline that runs up to the side, but that would violate Tip #2. Therefore, we need create a *second* right side spline.

28. Create two more points as shown in Figure 14-38, select all the points

shown in the figure, and create a new spline.

29. Create two more points as shown in Figure 14-39. The first should be placed at the center of the chin (as shown in the Back viewport) and underneath the jaw (as seen in the Right viewport). The second should be

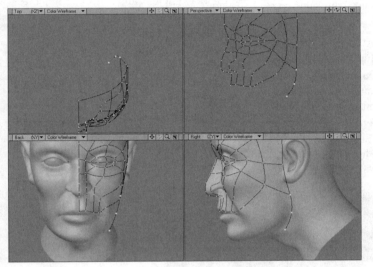

Figure 14-38: Add a second right side spline to define the rest of the jaw.

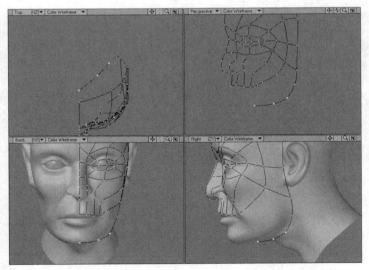

Figure 14-39: Note the placement of the points, especially in the Right viewport.

placed straight down from the corner of the mouth (when looking in the Back viewport) and centered between the first point and the last point of the spline created in Step 28. Create a new spline. This will act as the bottom of our quad cage.

Since we now have top, right, and bottom splines, we need to complete our quad cage with a left spline.

30. In the Right viewport, create four new points as shown in Figure 14-40. These should start at the lower lip and run down the profile, ending at the center of the chin. The points should be positioned at the very center of the head in the Back viewport. Select all of the points shown in the figure and create a new spline.

Spin your model around in the Perspective viewport and check for anything that looks out of place.

We've expanded our spline cage, but the area around the mouth is still open. Let's close that off. Considering that we already have a top spline (created in Step 20), it makes sense that we should create splines for the bottom, left, and right to complete a quad cage. However, there's no need to patch the region inside the mouth, and thus there's no need for a left spline. You can create one if you like, but it won't be used. Hence, we simply need splines for the right and bottom.

31. Create two new points as shown in Figure 14-41. Select all three points as shown and create a new spline. This will be the right side of our quad cage.

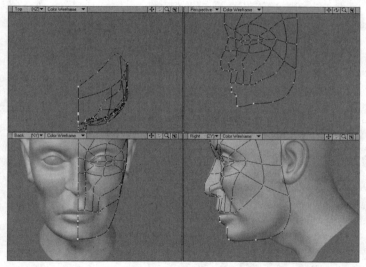

Figure 14-40

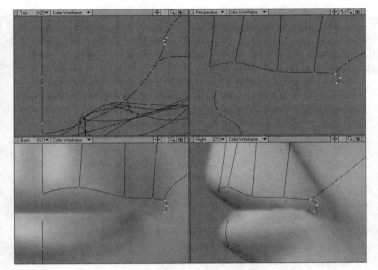

*Figure 14-41: This small spline defines the corner of the mouth.*

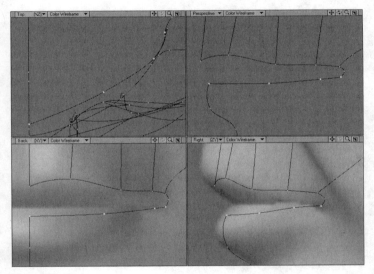

*Figure 14-42*

32. Create two additional points as shown in Figure 14-42. Then select the points shown and create a new spline. This will be the bottom of our quad cage.

By adding these two splines, we've created the inside boundaries for our face, but we're now in violation of Tips 2 and 3. The area over the nose and cheek is much larger

than the other regions in our cage, and the area around the jaw consists of more than four splines. We need to address each of these issues.

33. Select the existing points under the nose and over the cheek as shown in Figure 14-43 and create a new spline. (If you don't have the points needed to

create this spline, you can add them by selecting each spline and using the **Multiply | Subdivide | Add Points** tool.) This becomes the top spline of a new quad cage.

34. Create two more points as shown in Figure 14-44. Select all of the points shown and create a new spline. This becomes the right spline in our quad cage.

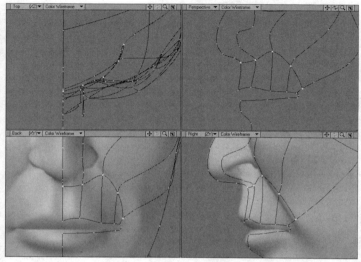

*Figure 14-43*

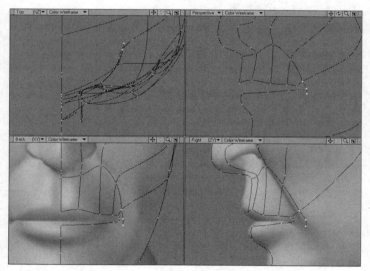

*Figure 14-44*

35. Create two points along the bottom of the lower lip as shown in Figure 14-45. Select all of the points shown and create a new spline. This becomes the bottom spline in our quad cage. And since the profile spline already exists, it will act as the left spline, completing the quad cage for this area.

We've partitioned off the area under the nose and around the cheek, but it wouldn't hurt to break the entire area into smaller sections.

36. Create a single point at the top of the nostril where it indents and joins the tip of the nose. Then select the existing points as shown in Figure 14-46 and create a new spline. This becomes the top of a new quad cage.

You'll notice that this new spline is not evenly spaced between those around it. As a result, we have created a narrow region running over the tip of the nose and down the side of the face. This narrow region violates Tip #3, but the tightly spaced polygons we'll get by patching this region are necessary to properly define the muzzle region of the face.

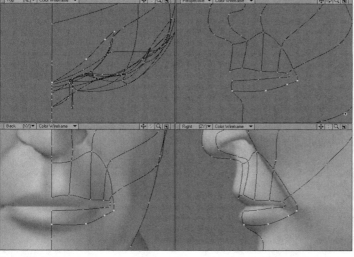

Figure 14-45

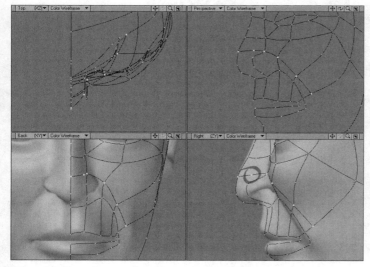

Figure 14-46

37. Create two more points radiating out from the corner of the mouth as seen in Figure 14-47. Select all of the points and create a new spline. This becomes the right side of our quad cage.

38. Create two more points below the lower lip as shown in Figure 14-48, then select all of the points in order, and create a new spline. This becomes the bottom spline in our quad cage. Once again, with the profile spline acting as the left spline, this completes our quad cage.

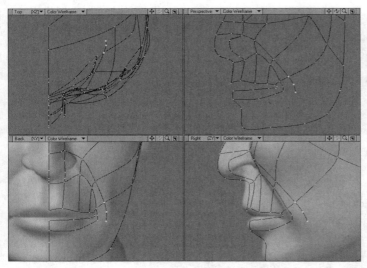

*Figure 14-47*

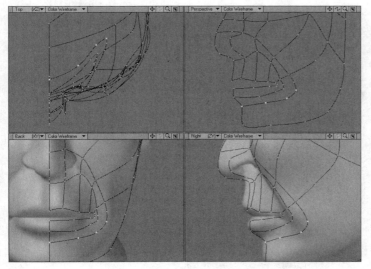

*Figure 14-48*

If you haven't done so recently, now would be a good time to spin your model and check for anything that looks out of place. It would also be a good time to *save* your model.

You can really see the face starting to take shape! But we still have areas that consist of more than four splines (specifically around the jaw and chin areas), so we must partition these to create a quad cage.

Looking at Figure 14-49, we can see that two distinct edge loops converge at the jaw. We need to section off the jaw so that each of these loops can continue along its own distinct path.

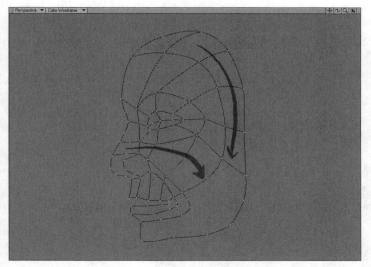

*Figure 14-49: Two edge loops converge at the jaw, requiring us to divide the area with a new spline.*

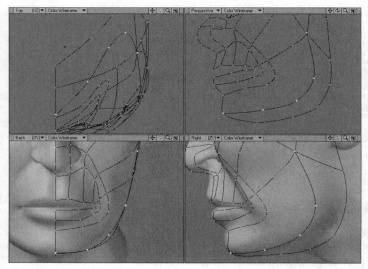

*Figure 14-50*

39. Create three new points that follow the jaw line as shown in Figure 14-50. Select each of the highlighted points shown in the figure and create a new spline. You can see that each loop from Figure 14-49 now has its own path to follow.

Spin your model and check for anything that appears to be out of place. Looking at the cage, two things are pretty clear. First, we're almost done with the face. And second, we're violating Tip #3. Although the jaw now consists of a quad cage (where each region is bounded by four separate splines), the areas to be patched are much larger than those around them. We'll finish the face by partitioning these areas.

40. Select the existing points shown in Figure 14-51 and create a new spline.

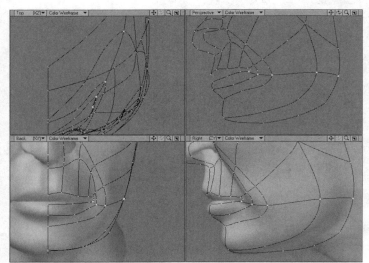

Figure 14-51

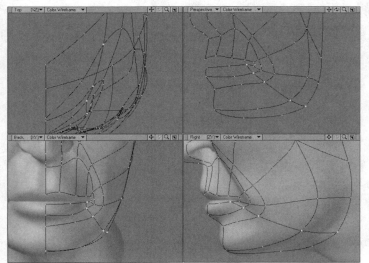

Figure 14-52

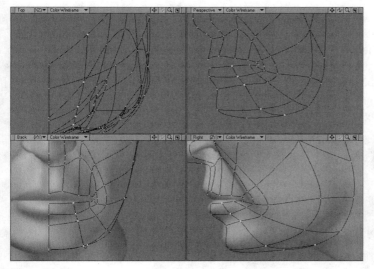

*Figure 14-53*

41. Select the existing points shown in Figure 14-52 and create a new spline.

42. Select the existing points shown in Figure 14-53 and create a new spline.

Zoom out and take a look at your spline cage, correcting anything that seems out of place. The face is now complete. All that remains is to build splines for the back of the head and neck, but if you've made it this far, that will be a piece of cake.

We can use the existing cage as a starting point for building the remaining splines. But with no ending point to guide us, it's difficult to determine where each spline should go. Therefore, we must develop a basic framework to help guide the placement of each new spline. This framework can be created from an outline of the head and neck.

Take a look at Figure 14-54. The head and neck can be broken down into one large quad cage. There are distinct top, bottom, left, and right sides. At this point, most of the left side and part of the top already have splines in place. We simply need to complete the remaining splines to form a quad cage around the entire region.

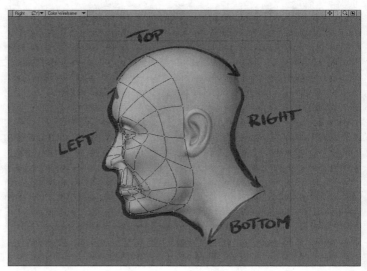
*Figure 14-54*

43. Create three more points at the center of the head that run over the top toward the back of the skull. Deselect these points. Select the four points shown in Figure 14-55 and create a new spline. This completes the top spline in our quad cage.

44. Create five more points running down the back center of the head. Select all of the points shown in Figure 14-56 and create a new spline. This becomes the right spline in our quad cage.

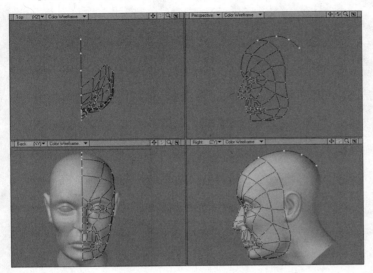

Figure 14-55

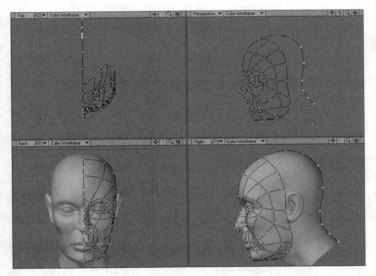

Figure 14-56

45. Create six new points around the neck running from the back to the front. Then select all of the points as shown in Figure 14-57 and create a new spline. Make sure that you adjust the points for this spline in both the Back and Right viewports to ensure that the spline forms a semicircular shape. This becomes the bottom spline in our quad cage.

46. Create a single point about halfway up the center of the neck. Then select the points shown in Figure 14-58 and create a new spline. This becomes the left spline, completing our quad cage.

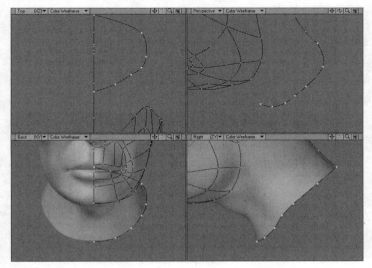

Figure 14-57

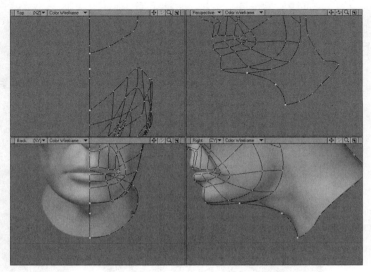

Figure 14-58

Having completed the framework, we can wrap up our spline cage by playing "connect the dots." The existing splines on the face end at an edge loop that runs over the forehead, down the side of the head, and under the chin. Each of these splines can be connected to the framework created in Steps 43 through 46. (See Figure 14-59.)

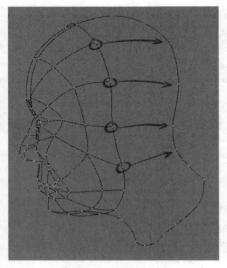

*Figure 14-59: The remaining splines can be created by connecting those in the face to those outlining the head and neck.*

We could build each of these splines as we've done in the past by creating "in-between" points, then selecting the points in order and pressing <**Ctrl**> + <**p**>. However, our spline cage has become fairly complex and this will make it difficult to position the in-between

points on the back of the head. As a result, we're going to use a different technique for building these splines.

47. Select the *two* points shown in Figure 14-60 and press <**Ctrl**> + <**p**> to create a new spline.

I mentioned at the beginning of this tutorial that the most basic spline consists of three points. Two act as endpoints, and the third acts as a control point that allows you to adjust the shape. We've just created a two-point spline which, if you examine carefully, is perfectly straight. It needs a *third* control point to alter its shape.

48. Switch to Polygon Select mode. The spline you just created should be highlighted. Navigate to the **Multiply | Subdivide** menu and select the **Add Points** tool. Click on the center of the spline to add a third point. Then use the Drag tool (<**Ctrl**> + <**t**>) to adjust the shape of the spline. Make sure you rotate your object in the Perspective view to check the shape of this new spline. (See Figure 14-61.)

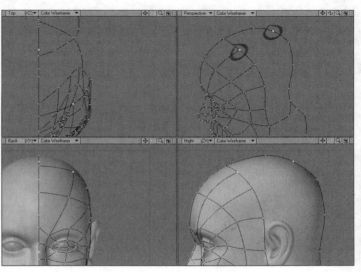

*Figure 14-60*

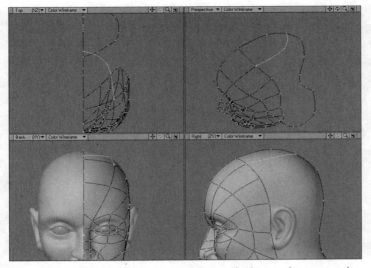

*Figure 14-61: Add a third point to this spline and adjust its shape using the Drag tool.*

### Note

You probably noticed that the region we defined in Steps 47 and 48 has only three sides (see Figure 14-62). Sometimes, no matter how hard you try, it's impossible to create a quad cage. This is one of those times. In circumstances like this, you should do your best to position the three-sided cage in a part of the model that will rarely be seen (as we've done here).

49. Continue connecting the dots and adding control points to create four more splines as shown in Figure 14-63. Be sure to check your model in the Perspective viewport after you shape each new spline. Remember that the back of the head is rounded at the top but tapers as it approaches the neck. Your splines should reflect this. If you feel that you need additional control points to help maintain the shape of the splines, feel free to create them. (I've added extra points to two of the splines shown in Figure 14-63.)

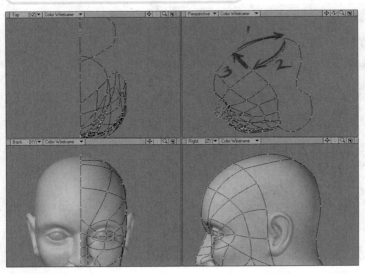

*Figure 14-62*

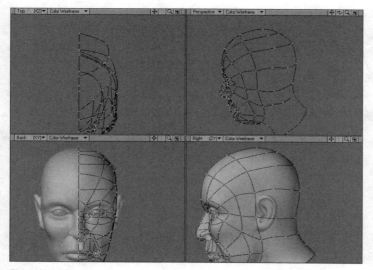

Figure 14-63

## Note

You'll notice that we are skipping over the ears at this point. Ears can be created with splines, but the process of linking them into a larger spline cage can be tricky. As such, we're following Tip #1 by using splines to create the overall form. The detailed process of creating the ears will be covered in the final section of this chapter using traditional modeling tools.

At this point, we have another instance where two edge loops converge at a large empty space. (See Figure 14-64.) We need to partition this space just as we did before so that each loop can continue on its own path.

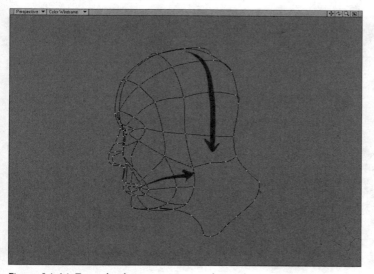

Figure 14-64: Two edge loops converge at the neck, requiring us to divide it with a new spline.

50. Select the two endpoints shown in Figure 14-65 and create a new spline. Then use the Add Points tool to add a central control point. Use the Drag tool in the Back viewport to move this point to the left slightly, creating a subtle arc in the neck.

We have a nearly perfect quad cage, but the back of the head and the neck are comprised of areas that are much larger than the rest of our cage. We must not forget Tip #3! These areas should be divided into smaller sections so that the same patch settings can be used on the entire model.

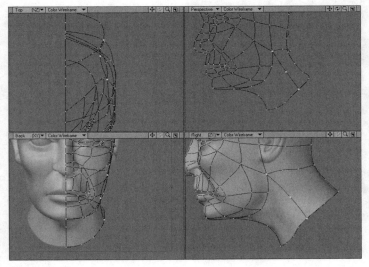

Figure 14-65

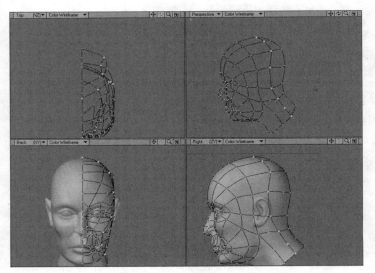

Figure 14-66: Keeping Tip #3 in mind, we must section off these large areas by creating a new spline.

331

51. Select the existing points shown in Figure 14-66 and create a new spline running down the back of the head.

52. Create the three remaining splines shown in Figure 14-67 using the techniques you learned earlier.

53. The last thing we need to do is section off the neck so that its surface area is not so large. Select the existing points shown in Figure 14-68 and create a new spline.

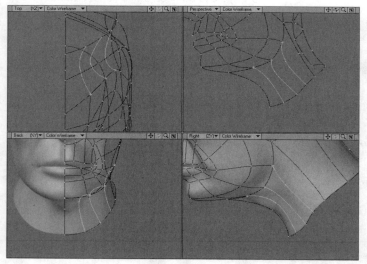

Figure 14-67

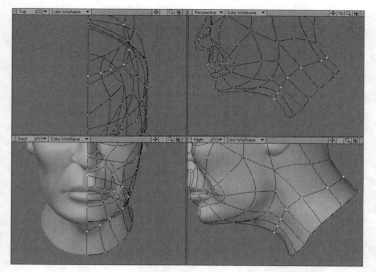

Figure 14-68: Divide the neck area into two halves with this new spline.

Spin your model around in the Perspective viewport and move any points that seem out of place. If you feel that you need more control over your splines, you can add points to help adjust their shape. When you're finished, save a new version of your model.

Before we wrap up this section, there are two more things we should do.

The first is to run a Merge Points operation on our model. As I mentioned earlier, the number one cause of the "Curves Do Not Cross" error is splines whose points are not welded together. By running a Merge Points operation, we can ensure that any stray points are fused together and pre-emptively ward off this infamous error message.

Press the <m> key to bring up the Merge Points window. Accept the default settings and press **OK**.

The second thing we should do is merge a few of these splines. Take a look at Figure 14-69.

The image on the left shows two splines that follow the same path from the top of the eye to the back of the head. At the point where these splines meet, there is a sharp dip. This dip isn't a major problem and won't affect our ability to patch this region, but it will have a subtle effect on the overall shape of our model. As such, it's a good idea to merge these splines together.

With the two splines selected, press <Z> to merge them into a single spline. The image on the right of Figure 14-69 shows the effect of merging these splines together. Note that the slope is now much more gradual.

You can continue working through your spline cage at this point, merging splines which, like those mentioned above, follow the same basic path but meet at sharp angles. The splines highlighted in Figure 14-70 are just a few of the ones I would recommend merging.

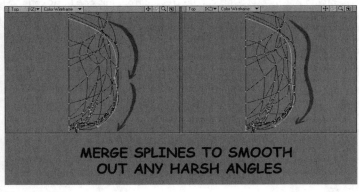

Figure 14-69

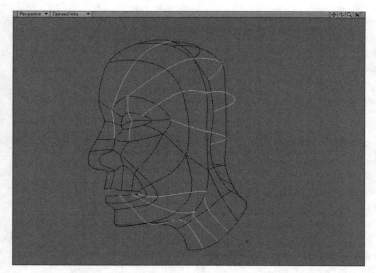

*Figure 14-70: Merge these splines to refine their overall shape.*

**Note**

Merging splines can be beneficial to the overall shape of your cage, but it can also be detrimental if taken too far and can ultimately affect your ability to patch the cage. For example, merging the profile splines that run from the front of the head to the back will cause havoc when you try to patch your cage. As you merge your splines, keep in mind Tip #2: Build quad cages. Try to keep the top, bottom, left, and right splines distinct from one another. Merging a Top spline with a right or left spline could have adverse effects. If you find that you are getting erroneous patches (or patches that don't fit the area you're attempting to fill), try splitting large splines into two or more parts. You can do this by selecting the spline, then switching to Points mode, selecting the point where you'd like the split to occur, and pressing <Ctrl> + <I>.

**Note**

At this point, I recommend saving your object with a name such as "Generic Spline Head Cage." One of the great things about modeling with splines is that a basic cage can be used over and over to create similar objects. In this case, a variety of head models can be created from this one basic cage.

Congratulations!! Using the tips and tricks outlined earlier in this chapter, you've built a very complex spline cage. This cage is not only efficient, but it has exceptional flow — one of the most crucial factors of a good head model.

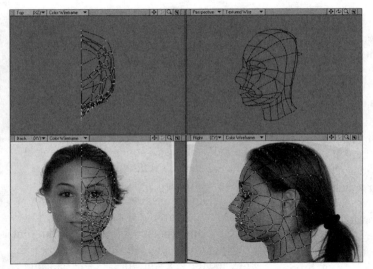

*Figure 14-71: The cage we've just built can be quickly modified to create other head models.*

Later in this chapter, we'll patch the cage and modify the results to ensure optimal poly count. When you're ready, save your object with a new name and let's begin by learning about patching.

## Patching Tips and Tricks

We've done a lot of work to get to this point, but this is where our initial investment really pays off. Under normal circumstances, patching our cage would involve the tedious and painful process of determining how many perpendicular and parallel divisions to use for each section of our cage. No more! Since we've built a quad cage and partitioned it into similarly sized segments, we can use the same patch settings for the whole object, making it a relatively easy procedure. *Easy*, however, does not mean *foolproof*. There are a number of problems that can plague the patching process. Therefore, before we get started, I'm going to share a few more tips and tricks with you.

● **Tip 1**: Patch in the Perspective viewport. Trying to select splines in one of the orthographic viewports can be cumbersome. To make your life easier, I suggest working directly in the Perspective viewport. Click the Maximize Viewport button to work full-screen within this view.

● **Tip 2**: Patch in Wireframe mode. As you patch your cage, each region will be filled with polygons. Unfortunately, Modeler treats *splines* as polygons. If your view type is set to one of the shaded views (i.e., Smooth Shade, Flat Shade, or even Textured Wire), Modeler will attempt to select the polygons on top first and will skip over the polygons on the bottom. As such, it can be particularly difficult to select your splines, especially as you get further along in the process. Therefore, I suggest working in the Color Wireframe mode. When in the wireframe modes, Modeler does not respect polygon order and will select everything your mouse moves over, not just the polygons on top.

● **Tip 3**: Use contrasting sketch colors. The biggest pitfall of working in one of the wireframe modes is that it can be difficult to distinguish between your splines and your polygons. To make this process easier, give your spline cage one color and your polygon wireframes another. To do this, go to the Detail menu and under the Polygons heading, click on the Sketch Color tool. From the pop-up menu, select Black as the sketch color and click OK. Changing the sketch color here will cause our spline cage to be black when viewed in the Color Wireframe mode. Now bring up the Display Properties panel by pressing the <d> keyboard shortcut. On the Layout tab, change Default Sketch Color to White. By changing the default sketch color, we are telling Modeler to use white wireframes for all of our newly created geometry. This division of color will help us determine which polys are splines and which are patches when viewed in a wireframe render style.

● **Tip 4**: If At First You Don't Succeed, Patch, Patch Again. The number one problem that people run into when spline modeling is the enigmatic "Curves Do Not Cross" error. Often this results from splines whose points aren't welded together properly. *But sometimes it happens in spite of the fact that everything has been done correctly.* I see questions like this posted online all the time: "My points are welded but I'm still getting the 'Curves Do Not Cross' error... What's wrong?" I honestly don't know. Sometimes Modeler is weird like that. But I can tell you this: If you go back and select your splines in a different order (even reverse order), it will often work. I've run into a number of cases where selecting top (1), left (2), bottom (3), and right (4) will give me an error, but selecting in a different order, for example, left (2), bottom (3), right (4), and top (1), will work. I can't explain it. I can only tell you that it works. It's very likely that you'll be seeing the "Curves Do Not Cross" error when you patch your head model. If that happens, refer back to this tip.

● **Tip 5**: Don't worry about spline selection order. To get the normals of your polygons facing out, you must select your splines in a counterclockwise order before you patch them. But as we've seen in Tip #4, there may be times when this results in a "Curves Do Not Cross" error. Therefore, don't worry about the order in which you select your splines. It's easy to correct polygons whose normals are facing the wrong direction after the fact. For now, simply patch and have fun.

## Patching the Cage

Let's begin patching the cage. Make sure that you've set your spline color to Black and your default sketch color to White as described in patching Tip #3. Then maximize the Perspective viewport and change the view mode to Color Wireframe. Hit **<a>** to "fit all" so that our cage fills the screen as shown in Figure 14-72.

You can begin anywhere you'd like, but the area around the eye is a nice place to start.

1. Select four splines in a clockwise or counterclockwise order and press **<Ctrl>** + **<f>** to bring up the Make Spline Patch window.

> **Note**
>
> You can access the Make Spline Patch window from the Construct | Patches | Patch menu item, but I recommend using the <Ctrl> + <f> keyboard shortcut as it will save you a good deal of time.

2. The default for a spline patch is 10 Perpendicular and 10 Parallel divisions distributed over the Length of the splines. However, 10 is far too many for the cage we've built. Change each of these to **2**. Leave the distribution set to its default (Length) and click **OK**. The

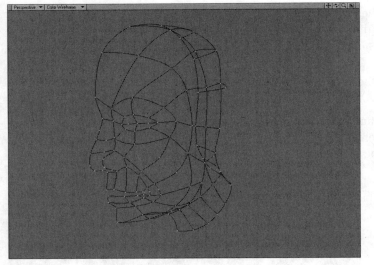

*Figure 14-72: We're ready to begin patching!*

*Figure 14-73: The proper patch settings.*

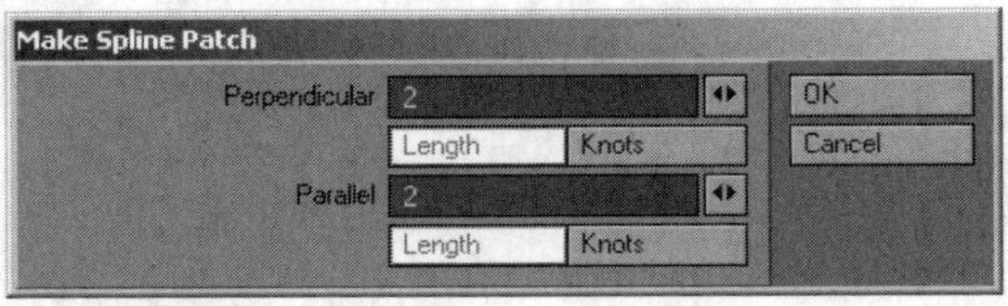

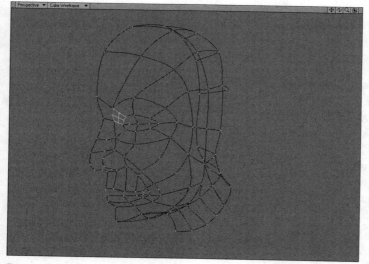

Figure 14-74: Our first patch.

splines will be patched with four new polygons. Deselect the splines. Figure 14-74 shows the results of this new patch.

3. Continue patching the edge loop around the eye.

If, as you select your splines, you happen to select a few polygons from one of your patches, don't worry. The Make Spline Patch tool will ignore any non-spline objects. If you get a "Curves Do Not Cross" error at this point, there are several things you should do:

a. Make sure that you have four splines selected (press <i> to bring up the Info window and count the number of curves listed).

b. Make sure that you've selected your splines in a clockwise or counterclockwise order.

c. Double-check that the points of each spline are welded together.

If this doesn't resolve the problem, see Tip #4 above.

The results of patching this area are shown in Figure 14-75.

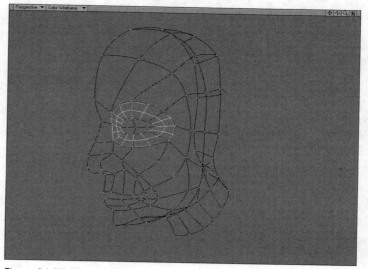

Figure 14-75: The patched edge loop.

4. Continue working around the face of your cage, adjusting your view as needed in the Perspective viewport.

> **Note**
>
> Don't patch the inside area of the eye. We'll build the inside of the eye with regular modeling tools later in the chapter.

5. When you've finished with the face, start patching the neck.

6. Finally, work your way up the back of the head.

Take a look at Figure 14-78. I've nearly completed patching the head model, but the region shown on the left side of the figure is giving me a "Curves Do Not Cross" error

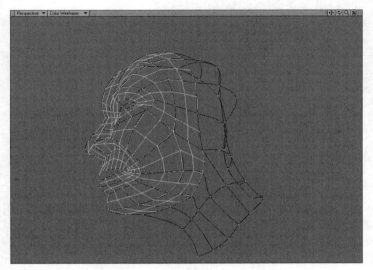

*Figure 14-76: Continue patching the face section of the cage.*

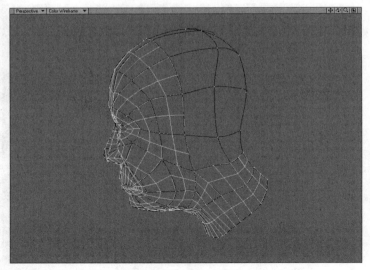

*Figure 14-77: After you finish with the face, patch the neck.*

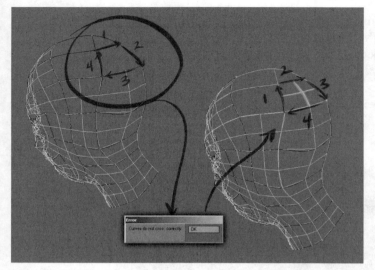

Figure 14-78: This region will not patch properly, but following patching Tip #4 enables me to work around the problem.

when the splines are selected in the order shown. I checked to make sure that four splines were selected in a counterclockwise order and that all their points were welded together properly. Having worked through the obvious solutions, it's now time to try patching Tip #4. By selecting the splines in the order shown on the right side of the Figure, I no longer get an error message.

The last area to patch should be the triangular region at the top back of the head shown in Figure 14-79. Since there are only three splines here, the order in which these splines are selected will affect the polygon layout of our patch. In all honesty, you can select them in any order you desire, but to be consistent with the work we'll be doing throughout the rest of

this chapter, select them in the order shown in the figure.

Spin your model in the Perspective viewport to check for any unpatched areas in your cage. When your whole cage has been patched, bring up the Statistics window by pressing the <w> keyboard shortcut. If any splines are selected,

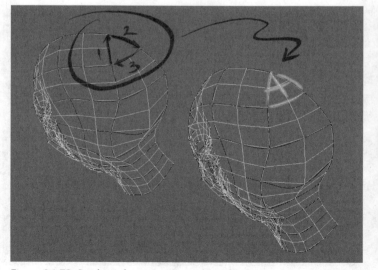

Figure 14-79: Patching the triangular region in the order shown on the left yields the polygon layout on the right.

deselect them. Then press the "+" icon to the left of the word "Faces." This will select all of the polygons in your head model. Cut these and paste them into a new layer, leaving just the spline cage in this layer. Then save your object.

Exit the full-screen Perspective view and return to Modeler's normal quad view. Then change your Perspective view type from Color Wireframe to Textured Wire. If you see any blank or incorrectly colored areas in your model (and you know that you successfully patched those areas), it's likely that the normals for the polygons have been flipped. Select these errant polygons and from the **Detail | Polygons** menu select the **Flip** command (or press the <f> keyboard shortcut).

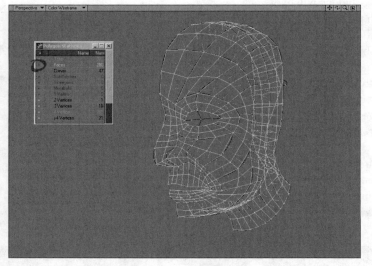

Figure 14-80: Select the polygons created by patching the cage, then cut and paste them into a new layer.

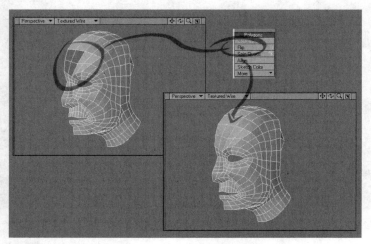

Figure 14-81: Flip any polygons whose normals are facing the wrong direction.

Congratulations on successfully patching your spline cage! We can now mirror the object to complete the basic head, but before we do so we need to run the Merge Points command again. As it stands, each individual patch is a separate object. You can see this for yourself by selecting any single polygon and tapping the <]> (right bracket) key to select the connected polygons. No more than four polygons will ever be selected because each patch is its own distinct object. In order to fuse the patches together into one large object, we need to merge points.

Press the <m> key to bring up the Merge Points window. Accept the defaults and press **OK**. A message should appear saying that roughly 300 points have been eliminated.

Let's go ahead and mirror our object. To successfully mirror the head, we need to ensure that the points running down the center are positioned *exactly* at 0 on the X axis.

1. Click the **Maximize** button for the Back viewport. This takes us to a full-screen view. Tap the <a> key to fit the object in our viewport as shown in Figure 14-82.

We need a way to select all of the points running down the center of our object, but as you can see, there are a lot of points in this region. Selecting them all by hand would be a nightmare. To remedy this, we'll use Modeler's Volume Select tools.

2. Press <Ctrl> + <j> *twice* to activate *Inclusive* Volume Select mode. (Pressing <Ctrl> + <j> once would activate *Exclusive* Volume Select mode.) Volume Select mode enables us to drag a bounding box around the polys or points we want affected. The Inclusive option means that anything partially inside the bounding box will still be selected. Drag out a bounding box as shown in Figure 14-83.

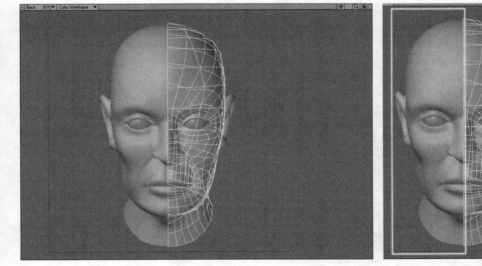

Figure 14-82

*Figure 14-83: Using the Inclusive Volume Select tool, drag out a bounding box that reaches just inside your model.*

3. From the **Detail | Points** menu select the **Set Value** tool (or press the <v> keyboard shortcut). Set Axis to **X** and Value to **0**. Then press **OK**.

The points at the center of your object should now rest at 0 on the X axis. To check this, select several of the points along the center of the head and press <i> to bring up the Point Info window. The Y and Z values should say "(mixed)" but the X value should be 0. (See Figure 14-84.) Press **OK** to exit the Point Info window and deselect your points. Then exit full-screen mode, returning to Modeler's default quad view.

We'll wrap up this section by mirroring our object to complete the basic head model.

From the **Multiply | Duplicate** menu, select the **Mirror** tool. Then press the <n> keyboard shortcut to bring up the Numeric panel. (If the Numeric panel is already open, select the Activate button from the Actions pop-up menu.) Bringing up the Numeric panel automatically

activates the tool with the settings shown in Figure 14-85. With your head model successfully mirrored, you can now close the Numeric window and press the <**Spacebar**> to drop the Mirror tool.

Figure 14-85: The Numeric window with the proper settings for the Mirror tool.

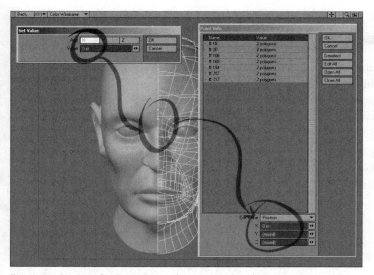

Figure 14-84: Use the Set Value tool to ensure that the points in our Volume Select region are positioned at 0 on the X axis. You can check these points using the Point Info window.

**Note**

If any of your points were not aligned to the 0 mark of the X axis, you may notice "tears" in the object when we activate sub-patch mode. If you find that this is the case, you will need to isolate the problem points and weld them together.

Violá! You're now looking at a completely spline-patched head model! Granted, it still needs a bit of work, but at this point you have successfully spline patched a head. Take a bow!

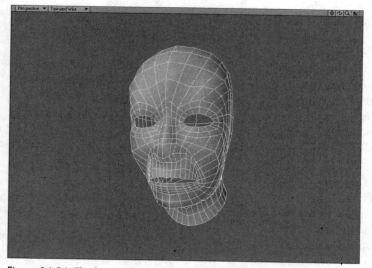

*Figure 14-86: The basic spline-patched head, ready to be detailed.*

# Basic Detailing

Our head model has great flow, but it's lacking a number of details. In this section, we'll start adding some of those details. We'll also do some basic refinements so that our head model looks less like an alien and more like a human. Once we have the necessary geometry in place, we'll move on to the process of optimizing our mesh.

**Note**

Up until now, we've used a number of tips and tricks to help guide us through the construction of our spline cage. But at this point, we must rely on the power of observation to determine the proper course of action. I cannot teach you to see. I can only tell you what I am seeing. As you grow in your modeling skills, you should cultivate the power of observation. Knowing *what* to change is just as important as knowing *how* to change it.

Let's set up our workspace by making it more conducive to modeling a sub-patch object. We no longer need white wireframes to distinguish polygons from splines so let's change the color to something with more contrast, such as black. Deselect any polys that may be currently selected. From the **Detail** tab, locate the **Polygons** menu and choose the **Sketch Color** tool. Set the sketch color to **Black**. Then bring up the

Display Options window by pressing the <**d**> keyboard shortcut. Since we'll be creating new geometry, we should change the default sketch color here so that the wireframe color for all new geometry will match our existing model.

While we're in the Display Options, let's also set up our viewports. I've found over the years that the best way to refine a sub-patch object is to have two Perspective viewports open at the same time. One of these should have a wireframe shaded view of the model and the other should have a smooth shaded view. The wireframe shaded view enables you to see the underlying mesh and easily make changes. The smooth shaded view gives you an unencumbered picture of the model (free from distracting wireframes), allowing you to clearly see the changes you are making to your mesh.

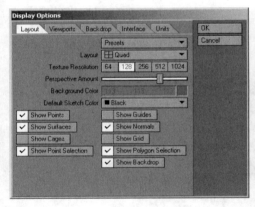

*Figure 14-87: Use the Display Options window to customize your workspace.*

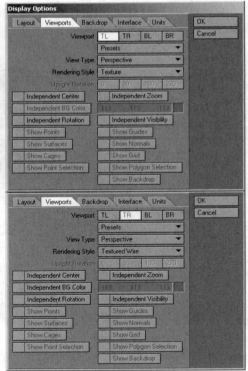

Click on the **Viewports** tab of the Display Options window. Click on the **TL** button to affect the top left viewport. Change View Type to **Perspective** and Rendering Style to **Texture**. Uncheck all of the Independent options as shown in Figure 14-87, then click on the **TR** button to change the top right viewport. View Type should already be set to **Perspective**. Change Rendering Style to **Textured Wire** and make sure that the Independent options are deselected (again as shown in Figure 14-87). Press **OK** to exit the Display Options window.

Until now, our model has been a standard polygonal object. At this point, we are going to activate Modeler's sub-patch mode, which will smooth out the rough edges and enable us to easily adjust the mesh.

Press **Tab** to enter sub-patch mode. We're now ready to begin modeling.

Take a look at Figure 14-88. The smooth shaded (no wireframes) view on the left shows a number of areas with problems.

The region between the brows is pinching too much. Also, the area where the nose meets the upper lip needs to be defined more so that we can build the nostrils. Let's start by addressing these problems.

1. Activate Symmetry mode by pressing <**Y**> or click on the Symmetry button at the bottom of the interface. Using the Drag tool (or a similar shaping tool), adjust the points at the center of the brows so that they are flush with the points around them. Then select the innermost point on the brow and move it out slightly so that the crease in the forehead is smoothed out (see Figure 14-89).

2. Grab the points where the nose meets the lip and move them up to help define the bottom of the nose. Then select the two points around the nostril region and move them out and back slightly. Figure 14-89 shows the points to move (top) and the effect of moving them (bottom).

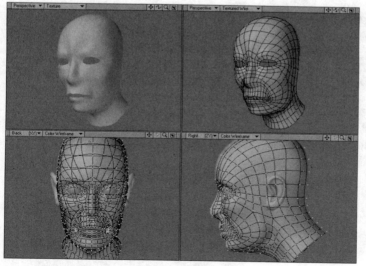

Figure 14-88: Our sub-patched head model.

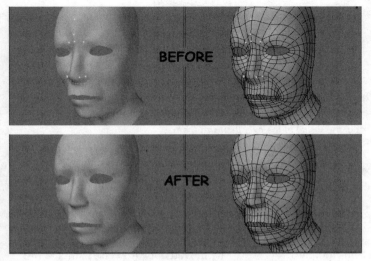

Figure 14-89: Smooth out the forehead and tighten up the bottom of the nose.

Let's add a little extra geometry to the eyes so they don't look like paper cutouts.

3. Select one or two of the points running along the loop at the inside of the eye. Then navigate to the **View | Selection | More | More** menu and choose **Select Loop**. All of the points around the inside of the eye will be selected.

4. Navigate to the **Multiply | Extend** menu and choose the **Extender Plus** tool. The geometry around the inside of the eye will automatically be extended.

5. Click the **Modes** button at the bottom of the interface and change your Action Center to **Mouse**.

6. Activate the Stretch tool (<**h**>) and position your mouse over the center of the eye on the positive side of the X axis in the Back viewport. (This is the left eye of the model.) Stretch the new points down and in slightly. Then activate the Move tool (<**t**>), and in the Right viewport move the points slightly back into the head. Figure 14-91 shows the results.

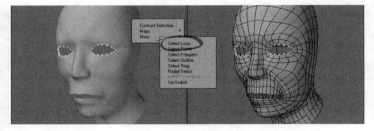

Figure 14-90: Select the points around the inner edge of the eye socket.

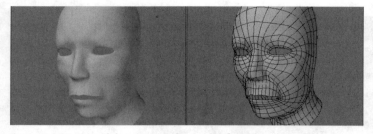

Figure 14-91: Extend the points at the inside of the eye, then size them down and move them back slightly.

Now let's work on the nose by adding a basic nostril. Select the four polygons (there will be a total of eight selected if you've got Symmetry turned on) shown in Figure 14-92.

1. Activate the Smooth Shift tool by pressing <F>.

2. Position your mouse over any of the viewports and click either the left or right mouse button. *Make sure you don't move your mouse when you click!*

The image at the bottom of Figure 14-92 shows the results of the Smooth Shift operation.

3. Sculpt the nose as shown in Figure 14-93. The points around the tip should be moved outward. The points at the top and bottom of the nostril should be moved up slightly. This will round the outside of the nostril and create a slightly concave shape underneath.

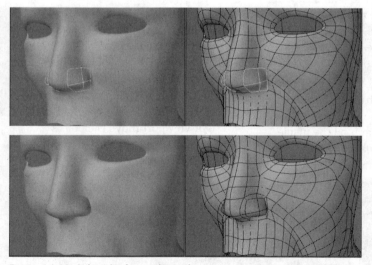

Figure 14-92: Select the four polys in the top image, then smooth shift to get the results shown in the bottom image.

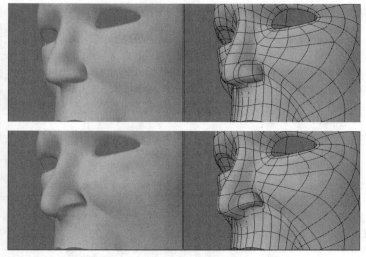

Figure 14-93: Sculpt the nose region and refine the nostrils.

Looking at our model again, it appears that the skull of our character no longer seems to fit the reference image. Let's fix that.

1. Select the polygons that make up the top of the head, shown at the top of Figure 14-94.

2. Activate the Stretch tool and position your mouse just above the center of the ear in the Right viewport.

3. Hold down the <**Ctrl**> key (or use your middle mouse button) and drag your mouse to the right, stretching the head horizontally about 107% or until it more closely fits the background image.

Zoom out and take a look at what you've done so far. These small changes have made big improvements. In order to make the rest of our changes, however, we're going to need a serious reduction in polys.

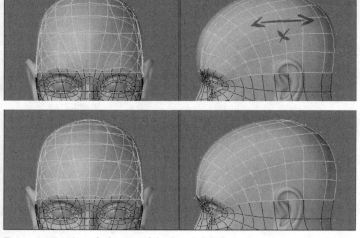

Figure 14-94: Stretch the top of the head slightly so that it more closely matches the reference image.

**349**

## Polygon Reduction

So far, we've achieved the first goal of head modeling, namely, developing good flow. But the second goal of minimal polygon count is still unmet. You may have noticed as you worked through the steps in the last section that even minor adjustments to the vertices of your model had a serious impact on its overall appearance. Trying to work with this number of polys can be a real nightmare and often makes the detailing process unnecessarily time consuming. In this section we'll work through the process of reducing the number of polygons, leaving us with an object that is easier to edit.

> **Note**
>
> Reducing the number of polygons will have a drastic effect on the appearance of our model. Don't panic when you see that the reduction is making things look *worse* rather than *better*.

Modeler has several automated polygon reduction tools, but frankly, they don't work that well. I've found that I can get much better results by simply merging key bands of polygons. The primary tool for this is BandGlue, found under the Construct | Reduce | More menu.

Click the **Maximize** button in the top right Perspective viewport to enter full-screen mode. Press the <a> key to fit your model to the viewport. If you spin your model, you will see consecutive bands which, if merged together, would not cause problems to the mesh. Figure 14-95 shows arrows running down the center of several of these bands.

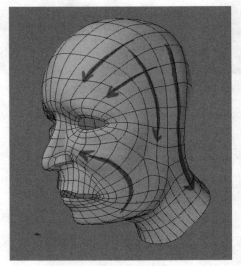

*Figure 14-95: The polygons on either side of these arrows can be merged together to create one new band.*

Select the two polygons shown on the left of Figure 14-96 and activate the BandGlue tool. The result of this operation can be seen in the image on the right of the figure.

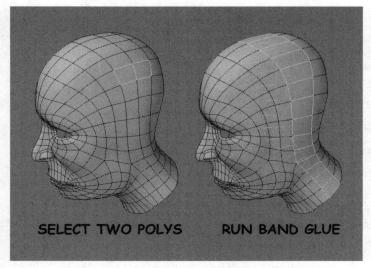

*Figure 14-96: Select the two polygons on the left and run BandGlue to merge them together. The image on the right shows the results.*

Continue running BandGlue on the groups of polygons shown in the next 13 illustrations.

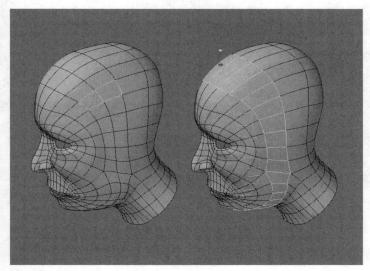

*Figure 14-97*

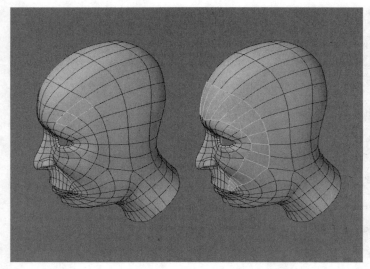

Figure 14-98

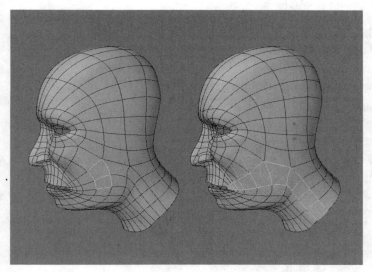

Figure 14-99

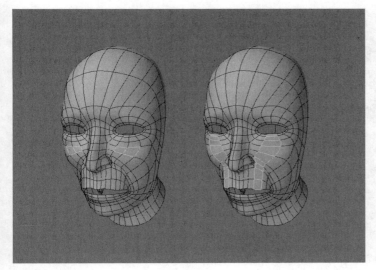

Figure 14-100

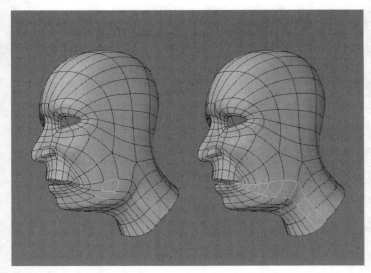

Figure 14-101

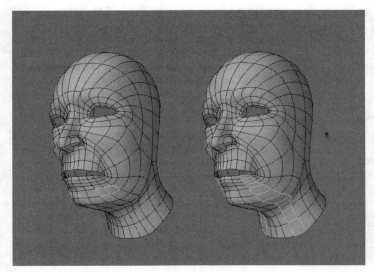

Figure 14-102

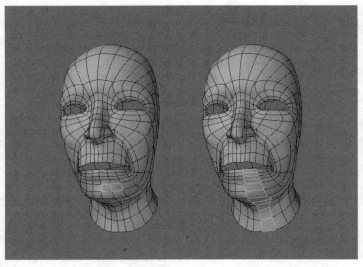

Figure 14-103: Be sure to turn off Symmetry when selecting these polys.

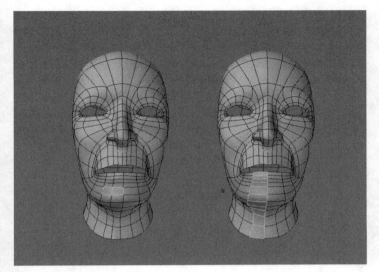

Figure 14-104

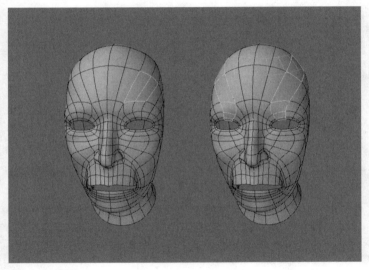

Figure 14-105

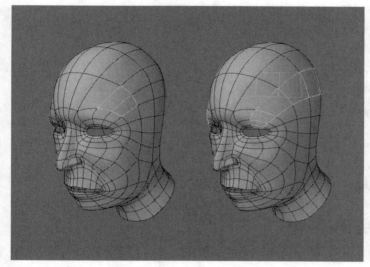

Figure 14-106

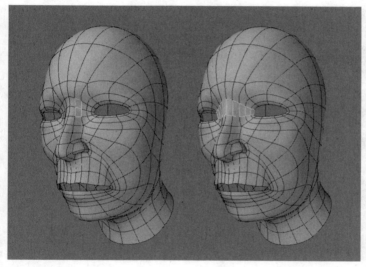

Figure 14-107

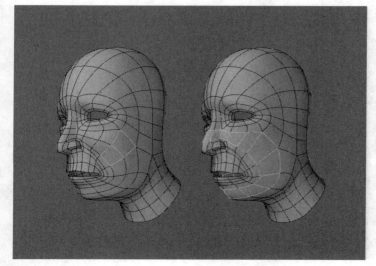

Figure 14-108

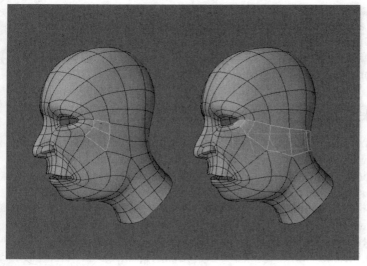

Figure 14-109

The last step is to eliminate the triangles at the top of the head. You should have already turned Symmetry off when selecting the polygons in Figure 14-103. Select the polygons shown in the upper-left corner of Figure 14-110. Since there are only four points on the outside perimeter of these two polygons, we can safely merge them into one single quad.

Press <Z> to merge the polygons as shown in the upper-right corner of Figure 14-110. Now repeat the process for the two polys on the opposite side of the X axis shown at the bottom of the figure.

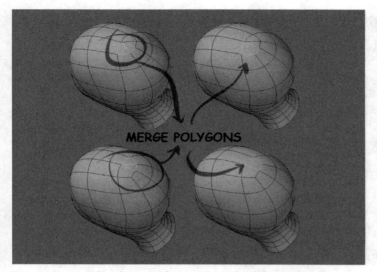

Figure 14-110: Select the two polys on either side of the X axis and merge them together.

Zoom out and take a look at your model. It's kind of ugly. But this is where the fun really begins! You've done the hard work and achieved the two most important goals in head modeling: great flow and minimal polygons. Now it's time to play. Save your model and move on to the final phase: advanced detailing.

## Advanced Detailing

One of the hardest concepts to grasp for those new to organic modeling is that most models look awful until they're about 93% complete. It shouldn't be surprising, really. When you think about it, people all over the world share identical features (eyes, nose, mouth, ears), but the subtle differences in size and shape determine whether one person is considered ugly and another beautiful. Nevertheless, I frequently see people in online forums asking for tips on how to improve their models when quite often, there's nothing wrong. At least, not technically. Oftentimes, the problem is that they've hit the 90% mark and given up in frustration. They've come to a point where all of the geometry is in place and they've developed a reasonable flow with an acceptable number of polygons, but their model

still looks bad. Almost without fail, the solution in these cases is to push past the 90% mark. You'd be surprised at how quickly things can come together, especially if you've done everything right from the start.

If you've followed the technical direction in this chapter, I can tell you that you've done everything right. You have created a head model with great flow and minimal polys that is 85% complete. In the next few minutes, we will bring that up to the 90% mark. The biggest challenge before you, then, is whether or not you're willing to push past the 90% mark.

We are nearing the completion of our head model and there is little left for me to teach you. It is up to you as the artist to take what you have learned and apply it in a manner that expresses your artistic vision.

As I mentioned earlier, this is where the fun really begins. This is where I let go of the bike and you begin to pedal on your own. I'll still be here to guide you, but I encourage you to begin making this model your own. Experiment and play, for that is the true joy of modeling.

Take a look at Figure 14-111. There is virtually no difference between the model shown on the top and the model shown on the bottom. They both have the same number of polygons and exactly the same polygon flow. Yet one looks markedly better than the other. This is due to the subtle difference in size and shape that I spoke of earlier. By simply moving points and sizing polygons, your model can go from "ho-hum" to "holy smokes!" Let's take a brief look at how to do that.

The four prominent areas of change are the eyes, mouth, cheeks, and jaw/chin. You should spend time working on each of these areas.

1. The eyes are currently too boxy. Begin by sculpting them with one of the

modification tools (I prefer the Drag tool, but you can also use the Dragnet, Magnet, or even Move tools). You should work toward creating a more almond-like shape. Be sure to turn on Symmetry so that the changes you make to one side of your model will be reflected on the other.

2. When you're finished shaping the eye, select the ring of points highlighted in Figure 14-112 and pull them back in toward the face. Doing this causes the inner two rings of points to jut out, giving the appearance of eyelids.

3. Grab the outside point also highlighted in Figure 14-112 and move it down and out slightly. This point acts as the upper support for our cheekbone. By moving this point around, you can make drastic changes to the shape of your character's face.

4. Continue refining the points and polygons around the eye to match the bottom two images shown in Figure 14-111.

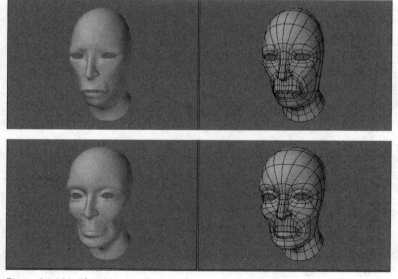

*Figure 14-111: There is virtually no difference between these two models.*

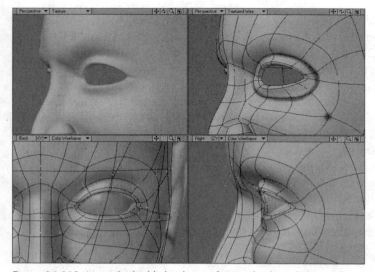

Figure 14-112: Move the highlighted ring of points back on the Z axis to create the appearance of eyelids. Then adjust the highlighted point for the cheekbone.

5. Reshape the three bands of points radiating out from the side of the nose as shown in Figure 14-113. The first (top) band should be moved up and out. This band defines the overall shape of the cheek and acts as the lower support for the cheekbone. The second (middle) band of points defines the outer muzzle of the face. The third (lower) band enhances the middle band. Adjusting the points in the third band determines how strong of a crease you'll get where the cheeks meet the muzzle of the face.

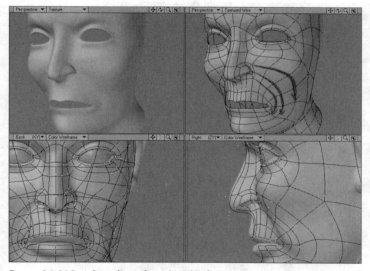

Figure 14-113: Adjust these three bands of points as shown, distributing them more evenly to define the cheeks and muzzle.

6.  Redistribute the points below the lower lip to shape and form the jaw, as shown in Figure 14-114.

7.  Select the lower set of points that form the upper lip highlighted in Figure 14-115. Activate the Stretch tool and position your mouse in the Back viewport over the lowest point in the group. Hold down the <**Ctrl**> key (or press the middle mouse button) to constrain the motion and drag down until the points are roughly in line with one another. Then, with the points still selected, move them up slightly so that the mouth region is open.

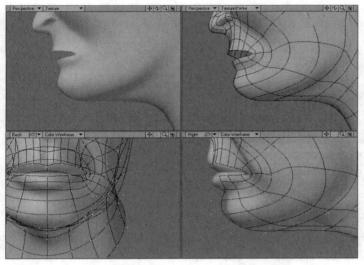

Figure 14-114: The points below the lower lip can be reshaped to form the chin and jaw.

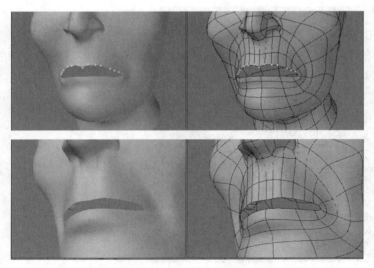

Figure 14-115: Even out the points of the upper lip and continue to shape the points around the mouth.

8. Continue to shape the points in and around the mouth so that they create the oval-like shapes seen at the bottom of Figure 14-115.

9. Select the innermost ring of points that make up the mouth and from the **Multiply | Extend** menu run **Extender Plus**.

10. Shape the points in the mouth region as shown in Figure 14-116.

11. Make sure that Symmetry is turned on and select the four polygons shown in Figure 14-117.

12. Activate the Smooth Shift tool and, making sure that you do not move your mouse, click either the right or left mouse button. A new band of geometry will be created.

13. Sculpt the nostril as shown in the bottom image of Figure 14-117.

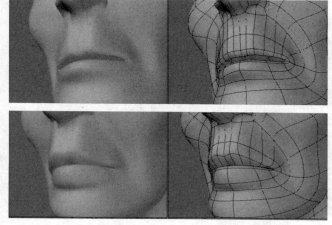

*Figure 14-116: Extend the ring of points around the inside of the mouth. Then shape the points as shown.*

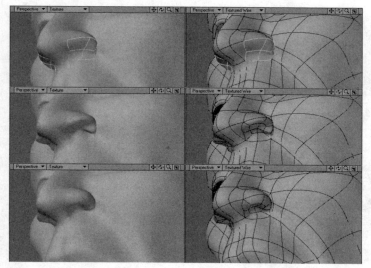

*Figure 14-117: Select these four polys, smooth shift, then shape the nostril as shown.*

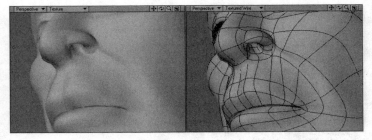

*Figure 14-118: Use Smooth Shift on the inner polys of the nostril and move them into the nose.*

14. Select the four innermost polygons from the nostril and smooth shift them again. With the four polygons still selected, activate the Move tool and move them up into the nose as shown in Figure 14-118.

Zoom out and spin your model. From here, you should continue adjusting the mesh, watching the changes that take place in your smooth shaded viewport. If your model doesn't look like the background image, don't be too concerned. The most important thing is that you resolve any issues with the overall appearance. If the model looks good to you, then it's a success. Continue refining until you're happy. Then continue reading to build the remaining details.

We're down to the last two details: the eyes and the ears. Let's start with the eyes.

1. Deactivate Symmetry. Then go to an empty layer and activate the Ball tool by pressing <**O**>. In the Back viewport, drag out a circle over the eye on the right side of the head. Hold down the <**Ctrl**> key to constrain the Ball tool. Position your mouse over the Right viewport and drag to create a perfect sphere. The size of this sphere should be roughly the size of the eye shown in the background image.

2. Select the polygons that make up the back half of the eye and press <**Delete**> to remove them. Since we won't ever be seeing the back of the eye, we can safely eliminate the extra geometry here.

3. Create a new surface for this object (<**q**>) called **Eye**.

The eye is covered by a transparent surface called the cornea. The cornea bulges out slightly at the center. It is this bulge that catches the light, creating a glint that gives the eye a "lifelike" appearance. Let's create the cornea.

4. Copy the Eye object to a new foreground layer and place the original in the background. From the Modes button at the bottom of the interface, change your Action Center to **Selection**.

5. Activate the Size tool and drag your mouse, resizing the eye by about 1% so that it is slightly *larger* than the original.

6. Select the two bands of polys at the center as shown in Figure 14-120. Activate Smooth Shift and click the left or right mouse button. Then use the Move tool to move the polys out slightly.

7. Use the Size tool to scale the polygons down by about 85%.

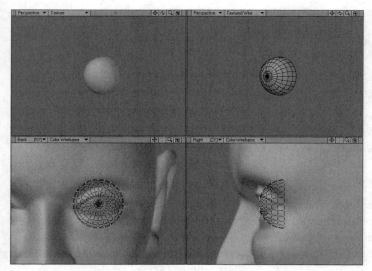

Figure 14-119: Create a sphere for the eye and delete the back half of the object.

Figure 14-120: Use the Smooth Shift, Move, and Size tools to create the cornea.

8. Give this object a new surface (<q>) and call it **Cornea**.

9. Cut the Cornea object and paste it into the layer with the eye.

10. Finally, use the Mirror tool to mirror the eye across the X axis.

At this stage, you will need to shape the area around the eye socket so that it fits snugly over the eyeball. Place your head model in the foreground and your Eye objects in the background. Activate Symmetry mode and then begin sculpting. If you can see the background layer poking through your mesh (as in Figure 14-121),

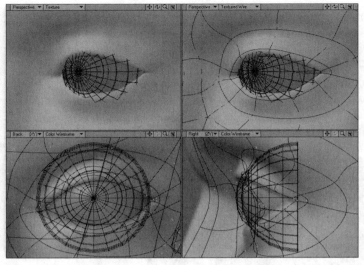

Figure 14-121: Reshape the eye socket to better fit the eye.

you need to either move the eye back slightly or reposition the polygons in the face to accommodate it. Sculpting this area can take time, so be patient and pay close attention to detail.

Before you finish with the eye, make sure that the points that make up the inner ring of the eye socket get pulled back into the eye, past the cornea. If these polygons do not pass through the cornea, you can end up with rendering errors.

With the eyes finished, it's time to move on to the ears. When new users are asked what they consider to be the most difficult part of the head to model, the ear is almost always at the top of their list. Ears are not that hard to model, as you'll soon see. They are, however, very detailed and require that

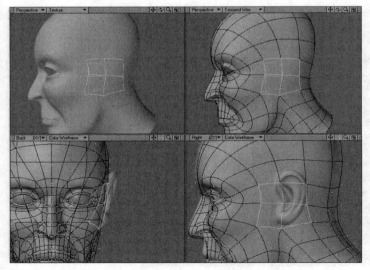

Figure 14-122: Select these four polygons to begin modeling the ear.

you pay close attention to the overall form. As you model, you should focus your attention on *what* you are modeling more than *how* you are modeling it. The most important question to keep in mind is not "Am I following the steps correctly?" but rather, "Am I making this look like an ear?"

Begin by selecting the four polygons shown in Figure 14-122.

1. Activate the Smooth Shift tool and, ensuring that you do not move your mouse, click the left or right mouse button.

2. Reshape the polys into the basic form of an ear. The back of the ear should begin to bulge out away from the head as shown in Figure 14-124.

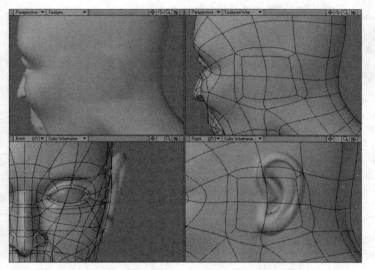

Figure 14-123: Smooth shift the polygons to add extra geometry.

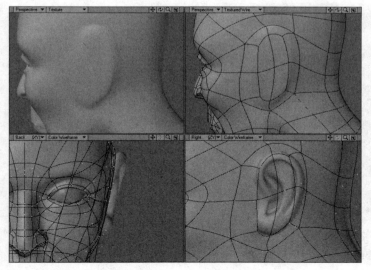

Figure 14-124: Shape the polygons to resemble an ear.

3. Select the four polygons at the center and the eight polygons forming the loop around them. Smooth shift these as you've done in the past.

4. Change your Action Center to **Mouse** and using the Stretch tool, resize the polygons that are still selected after using Smooth Shift in Step 3.

5. Use the Drag tool to continue reshaping the ear. The point at the very center of the four polygons should be dragged in to create a concave surface. Then drag this same point toward the back of the head slightly as shown in Figure 14-125.

6. Select the 12 polygons we smooth shifted in Step 3 and smooth shift them again.

7. In the Back viewport, use the Move tool to move these 12 polygons away from the head slightly. Then use the Stretch tool to resize them as shown in Figure 14-126.

8. Continue reshaping the ear as shown in Figure 14-127. The points at the center on the left side of the ear should lie flush with the rest of the head. The center point from our original four polygons should continue to be pushed back into the ear to form a concave shape.

9. Select the original four polygons at the center of the ear and use Smooth Shift again.

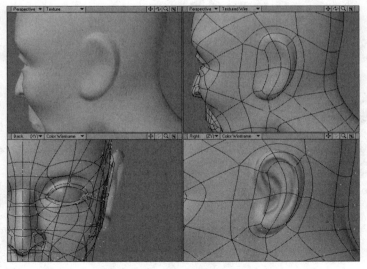

*Figure 14-125: Smooth shift the 12 polys that currently make up the ear, then size them and continue sculpting.*

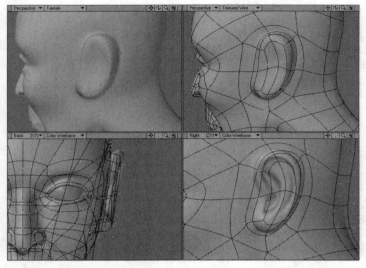

Figure 14-126: Smooth shift the 12 polys again, move them away from the head, and resize them slightly.

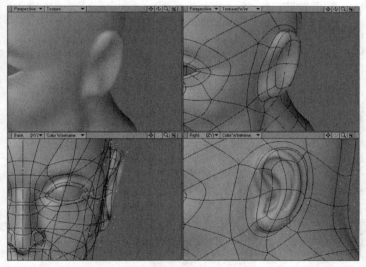

Figure 14-127: Continue shaping the ear.

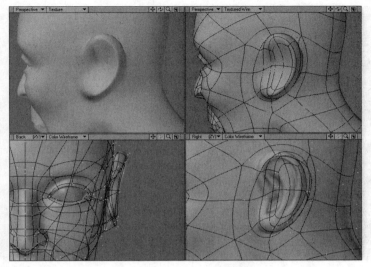

Figure 14-128: Smooth Shift the four polygons at the center of the ear.

10. Adjust the polygons that form the outermost loop around the ear. By dragging the points at the top of this loop down, you can begin to distinguish the ear from the rest of the head.

11. Resize the inner four polygons and move them up slightly. The points at the top of these four polygons should be pushed into the ear slightly. The points on the bottom should be pulled out as shown in Figure 14-130.

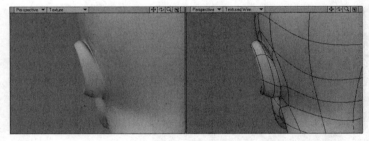

Figure 14-129: Move the points at the top of the ear down to separate it from the head.

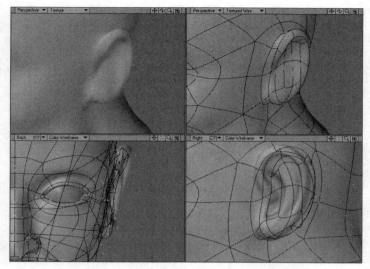

*Figure 14-130: Resize and reshape the inner four polygons as shown.*

12. Continue reshaping the entire ear as shown in Figure 14-131.

13. Select the four polygons shown in Figure 14-132 and smooth shift them as we've done in the past by simply

activating the tool and clicking the mouse button. Then, with these four polygons still selected, use the Drag tool to reshape them as shown in both the top and bottom images of Figure 14-133.

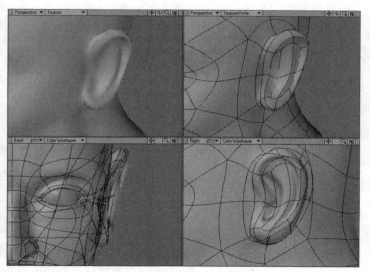

*Figure 14-131: Continue shaping the ear.*

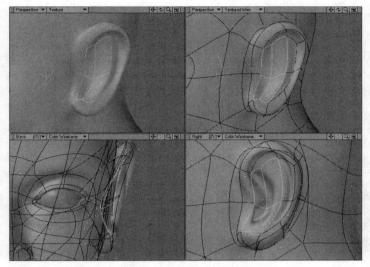

Figure 14-132: Smooth shift these four polygons.

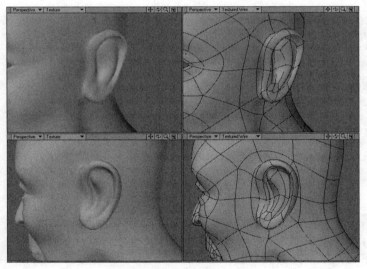

Figure 14-133: Spend time shaping the polygons you just smooth shifted to resemble the images shown here.

14. Continue shaping the ear as shown in Figure 14-134. Then select the two polygons highlighted in this image.

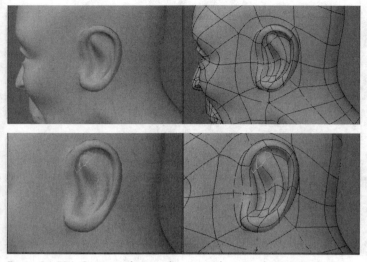

Figure 14-134: Continue shaping the ear as shown in the top image, then select the two highlighted polygons in the bottom image.

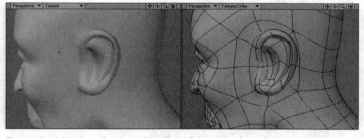

Figure 14-135: Run the Spin Quads tool once on the selected polygons. Then continue shaping the ear.

We're going to redirect the flow of these polygons to better fit the ear.

15. Navigate to the **Detail | Polygons** menu and press the **Spin Quads** button (or use <**Ctrl**> + <**k**>). Then continue shaping as shown in Figure 14-135.

16. Select the two polygons shown in Figure 14-136 and run Spin Quads on them as well.

17. Select the two polygons shown in Figure 14-137 and run Spin Quads on them.

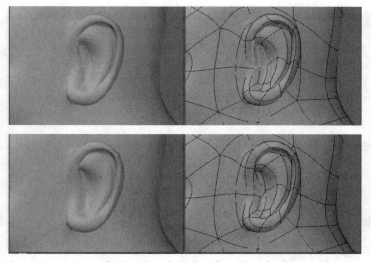

Figure 14-136: Run the Spin Quads tool on the selected polygons. The image on the bottom shows the results.

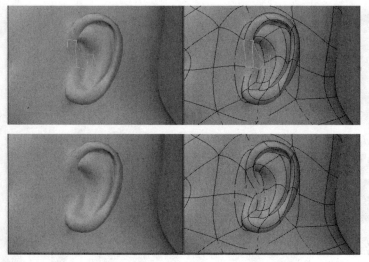

Figure 14-137: Run the Spin Quads tool on the selected polygons. The image on the bottom shows the results.

18. It's time to eliminate a few of these polygons. Select the two polys shown in Figure 14-138. Press <Z> to merge them.

19. Now select the two polygons shown in Figure 14-139 and merge them.

**373**

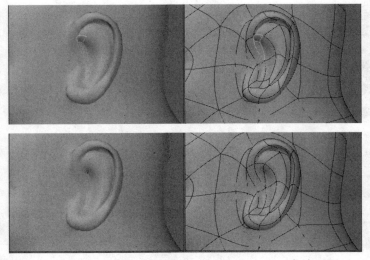

Figure 14-138: Merge the selected polygons. The image on the bottom shows the results.

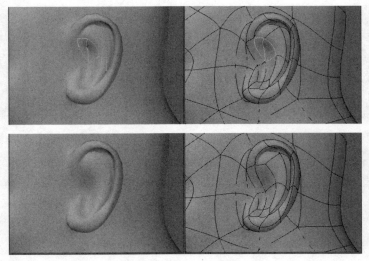

Figure 14-139: Merge the selected polygons. The image on the bottom shows the results.

20. Select the polygons shown in Figure 14-140 and smooth shift them.

21. Reshape the polygons you just smooth shifted as shown in Figure 14-141. By pushing them into the head slightly, you can begin to distinguish between the inner folds and outer folds of the ear.

22. Shape the polygons at the front of the ear in the places where they connect with the head as shown in Figure 14-142. By forming a small indention, we can begin the process of building the ear canal.

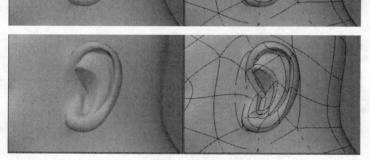

Figure 14-140: Smooth shift the selected polygons. The result of the Smooth Shift operation can be seen in the bottom image.

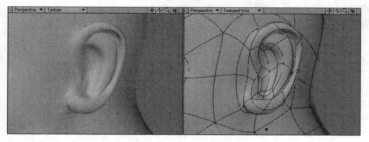

Figure 14-141: Reshape the polygons as shown.

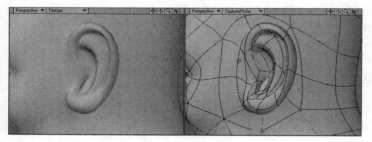

Figure 14-142: Reshape the ear as shown.

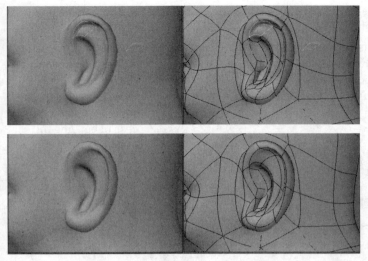

Figure 14-143: Merge the selected polygons. The results are shown in the image on the bottom.

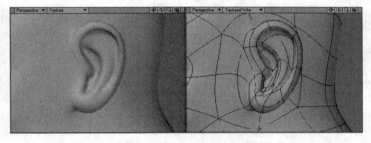

Figure 14-144: Reshape the ear.

23. Select the two polygons shown in Figure 14-143 and press <Z> to merge them.

24. Reshape the ear as shown in Figure 14-144.

We're just about through with the ear. The last few steps require quite a bit of sculpting work, so be sure to move about your Perspective viewport often to get a good look at what you're doing. Also, it may help to select the polys you wish to adjust and tweak them individually in the orthographic viewports.

25. Select the three polygons shown in Figure 14-145 and smooth shift them as we've done in the past.

26. Activate the Stretch tool and from the Modes button, set your Action Center to **Mouse**.

27. Position your mouse in the Back viewport just to the left of the selected polygons (still highlighted from the Smooth Shift operation). Hold down the <Ctrl> key and drag left to flatten out the polygons.

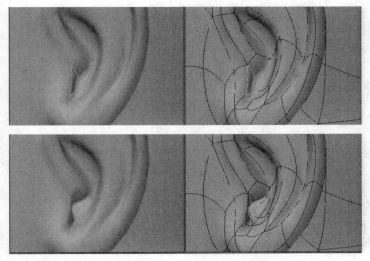

Figure 14-145: Smooth shift the selected polygons and reshape them as shown. Then push the selected polys slightly into the head.

28. Position your mouse in the Right viewport over the three selected polygons and resize them as shown at the bottom of Figure 14-145.

29. Move the three selected polygons back into the head slightly to form the ear canal.

30. Continue shaping the ear by rounding it and making sure that it stands out from the head properly. If you need to, change your upper-left Perspective viewport back to a Top view and rotate the ears slightly so they stick out a bit more.

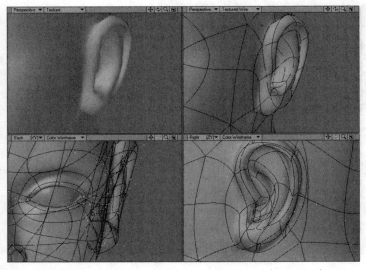

Figure 14-146: Reshape the ear as necessary to ensure that it stands out from the head.

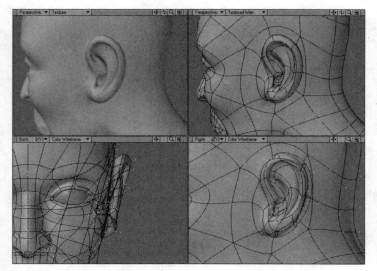

Figure 14-147: The finished ear.

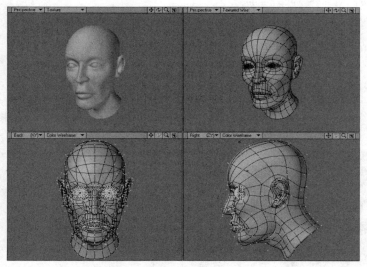

Figure 14-148: The finished head.

From here, you can continue to reshape the ear to your satisfaction. Figure 14-147 shows the completed ear.

Zoom out and take a look at what you've got. The head model should be at least 93% complete or better. If you find that it's not quite right, I encourage you to continue working with it. Being willing to push past the point of mediocrity is often what turns a good model into a great one.

## Closing Thoughts

We've covered a tremendous amount of ground in this chapter, from the proper techniques of building a spline cage to refining the mesh and adding in complex details. In the process, you've constructed a world-class head model. From here, I encourage you to continue on. Begin constructing morph targets for facial animation. Build the rest of the body and use the information in Chapters 15 and 16 to get started in character animation. Let the work you've done in this chapter be the start of great things as you continue to realize your dreams in 3D.

# Chapter 15

# Layout 2: Animation Basics

This chapter explores the basic tools that LightWave uses to control the movements of items within an animation. While these are the *tools* to control animation, they are not the *skills* to create great works of animation. There's an entire book (*LightWave 3D 8 Character Animation*) devoted to understanding these skills — inverse kinematics, bones, weight mappings, and the skills common to good animation, whether hand-drawn on paper or created in LightWave.

Here, I'll give you a taste of some of the things that are in store for you in the world of animation. These are things that are *integral* to animation, but they are no more animation itself than a cinema is the movies it shows.

## Keyframes (Keys)

The concept of *keyframes* comes from traditional animation (animation drawn on paper). The animator draws the *primary* poses — the ones that define the action — assigning the drawings positions on a *dope sheet* (a spreadsheet that shows the position in time of every drawing within a scene). After the animator is happy with the definition of the action, the scene goes on to other artists who fill in the drawings that come in between the key drawings (creatively called *inbetweens*).

A *keyframe* in LightWave is a record of the position, rotation, and/or scale of an item, whether it be an object, bone, light, camera, etc. A keyframe is recorded in LightWave when you change an item's scaling, rotation, or position (if you have Auto Key Create active) or by using Create Key to manually create a keyframe.

How do animators know how much time (how many frames) to put between their keyframes? We use a stopwatch to time either how long it takes for us to do an action physically or how long the action takes to play out in our imaginations.

The thing I never liked about stopwatches is that I could never find one that would give me the timings in frames (working in 30 FPS for NTSC or 24 FPS for film), feet/frames, SMPTE, or whatever. (I had to do all that "translation" in my head or on paper.) So, I wrote a little utility in Flash that serves as an animation timer and unit-conversion utility.

The Itty-Bitty Animation Timer looks simple but packs a lot of power. Click on the icon at the center to time how long you hold the mouse button down. Click **Frames**, **Feet/Frames**, **SMPTE**, or **Seconds** to see your time displayed in that format. You can manually enter any value for any field, and press <**Return**> to update the calculations (this is how you change your FPS or add a frame offset if you're timing part of an action that doesn't start on frame 0).

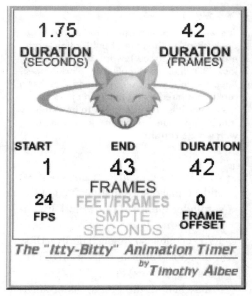

Figure 15-1: The Itty-Bitty Animation Timer.

### Note

You can find more information on The Itty-Bitty Animation Timer, along with a whole slew of other plug-ins, programs, and utilities, in Appendix A.

1.  Load **Objects\Chapter15\Anima-tion.lwo**. We'll be doing a little "flying logo" work with this bit of text.

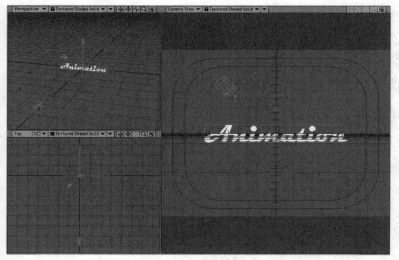

Figure 15-2

2.  We'll be working in 24 frames per second, so make sure that you've got this set under **General Options | Frames Per Second**. Our animation will be 1.75 seconds, so (using The Itty-Bitty Animation Timer to convert 1.75 seconds into frames) enter **42** as your End Frame in both the Frame Slider and the Render Options fields. Take a moment to make sure you have *both parts* of Auto Key Create *active*! (You'll have to develop your own preferences as to whether your moving an item will create keys on only the channels in which it is moved or on all channels at once.)

3.  Making sure you're still on frame 0, move the text along the negative Z axis until it is just a tiny bit "behind" the camera (as shown in Figure 15-3, the camera "sees" from an invisible point in the *center* of its icon). You will also want to move the text a little bit in the negative X axis so the camera is *between* the "m" and "a" in the word "Animation."

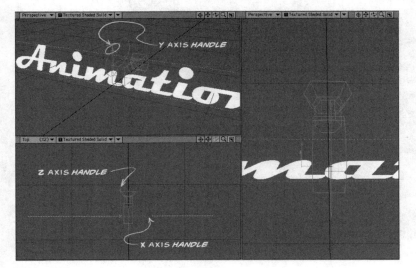

Figure 15-3

**Note**

Clicking and dragging on an item's handles will restrict movement, rotation, or scaling to one axis. It makes precise positioning much easier, especially when working in a Perspective viewport. (Make sure you have Display Options | Show Handles active.)

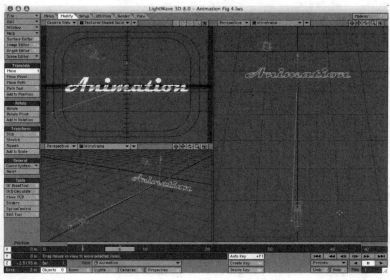

Figure 15-4

4.  Now, we're going to get into some actual animation. Moving the Frame Slider to frame 6, move your text toward the positive Z axis so it just barely fills the "title safe" area (see Chapter 2 if necessary) in a Camera viewport. You'll also want to move the text to X=0 so it's centered again. (Now you can move the Frame Slider back and forth between 0 and 6 and watch the text come zooming in from behind the camera.)

5.  Press <f> to bring up the Go to Frame dialog and enter **36**, as shown in Figure 15-5. Move the text toward the positive Z axis by about another meter at frame 36. (This will keep the text "alive" while the viewers are reading what it says.)

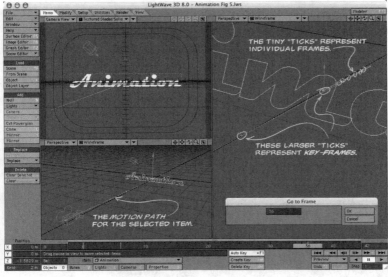

Figure 15-5

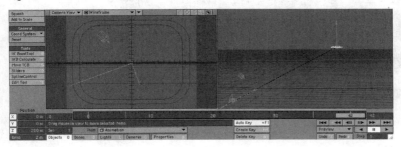

Figure 15-6

6. Now go to frame 42 (the end of our scene), and enter the value of **200 m** for that frame's Z position. (This will make the text "zoom off" into the distance.)

Hey! You're animating! (Well, you're starting to at least.) When you "scrub" the Frame Slider back and forth, you'll see that the text "bounces" backward, going "behind" the camera again between frames 6 and 36. It didn't do this before when we scrubbed through our frames in Figure 15-4. This is *not* what we want our text to do.

LightWave will *interpolate* (*inbetween*) from keyframe to keyframe smoothly with mathematical perfection. Its default mode of interpolation is a kind of *spline* (spatial line) known as a *TCB spline* (which stands for *tension*, *continuity*, and *bias*). This kind of spline is affected heavily by large, quick motions that come immediately before or after a *keyframe* (just like we've got between frames 0 and 6). The solution to our bouncing text is to either add more keyframes or manually adjust the interpolation to make the "inbetweening" exactly what we want for our motion. LightWave's Graph Editor will let us "sculpt" the *function curves* that control every aspect of an item's motion — and more!

# "Motion" Graph Editor

Below the File pop-up menu on the upper-left side of the Layout interface is the Graph Editor button. Clicking on it will open the "Motion" Graph Editor for your selected item. (The Graph Editor controls a lot more than just motions now, though at one time that's all it did, and so us "old-timers" still sometimes call it by its original name: "Motion Graph.")

Every aspect of an item's motion and every "envelopable" attribute is controlled through this interface. Press <a> to Zoom All and <A> to Zoom Selected. (There's so much here that I'm going to just hit the high points and leave the details to the LW manual.)

● On the left side, the **Channels** list shows all the aspects that LW is tracking for the currently selected item. Click on one channel to view and edit it in the Graph area, or Shift-click or Ctrl-click to select more than one channel to view and modify at once.

● Double-click on an item under the **Channels** tab (just under the Channels list) to change what item's curves you are viewing (without having to close the window,

select the new item, and reopen the Graph Editor). Shift-double-click to add an item's channels to the list you are currently viewing.

● The **Graph** area itself is where you right-click and drag to create a bounding box for selecting multiple keyframes or left-click and drag to modify them. (The same hot key and mouse combinations you're used to in Modeler will work here as well to zoom and scroll the view.)

● Just below the Graph area are the Graph Editor's tool buttons. From the left are **Move Keys**, **Add Keys**, **Stretch Keys**, **Roll Keys**, and **Zoom**. (Left-click and drag affects the selected keys' *value*, while Ctrl-left-click and drag affects the selected keys' *frames*.)

● **Frame** is an input field that shows the frame on which your currently selected keyframe is located.

● **Value** tells you the selected key on the selected channel's precise location. (In Figure 15-7, we are looking only at the "curve" for the Z position for the item named Animation. On the selected frame, 6, it is at precisely –2.3195 m along the Z axis.)

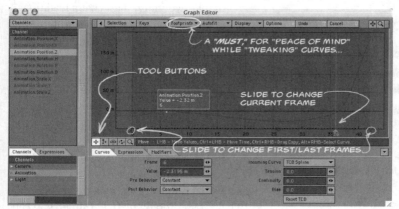

*Figure 15-7: The Graph Editor.*

385

• **Pre Behavior** and **Post Behavior** tell LightWave what to do *before* it reaches the item's first keyframe and *after* it reaches its last keyframe (respectively).

> • **Constant** (as shown in the figure) holds the value of the *first key* for "infinity" before the first keyframe begins and/or the value of the *last key* for "infinity" after the last keyframe.

> • **Reset** sets the value of the graph to 0 when it has no more keys with which to work.

> • **Repeat** plays the series of keys over and over again, *ad infinitum*.

> • **Oscillate** "ping-pongs" the animation set by the keys, reversing it when it reaches the end and playing it forward once again when it returns to the beginning.

> • **Offset Repeat** repeats the motion but with everything shifted by the difference between the first and last keys (this would make our curve here into an infinite set of "stairs").

> • **Linear** continues the curve infinitely, projecting it at an angle established by the last two keys (or first two keys, if we're talking about Pre Behavior).

• **Incoming Curve** tells LightWave how to handle the curve segment that is directly to the *left* of the selected key.

> • **TCB Spline** is LightWave's default setting, and it gives good results most of the time, without having to worry about tweaking the curves much. (Tension, Continuity, and Bias all affect the shape of the curve, based on values from –1 to +1. Of these, I have only ever found myself needing to use Tension, and then only to put in a value

of +1 to get an item to ease into or out of its keyed position.)

> • **Hermite Spline** gives you little "handles" that extend from the key, allowing you to visually control the shape of the curve. (It isn't quite as controllable as a bezier spline.) *Alt-dragging* on one of these handles will let you split it from its partner, so it is not a mirror of the handle on the other side of the key. *Double-clicking* on a handle that has been split will get it to once again mirror the angle of the handle on the other side of the key.

> • **Bezier Spline** also gives you handles, but you can move the position of these handles a great distance relative to their respective keys, giving you a lot more control. (*Alt-dragging* and *double-clicking* on these handles splits and reunites the handles with their partners, just as with Hermite Spline handles.)

> • **Linear** gives you a straight line inbetween from the previous keyframe.

> • **Stepped** holds the value of the previous key until the moment before the stepped key, so it goes right from one value to the next without any kind of inbetweening (like what a traditional animation "pencil test" looks like before it goes to the assistant animators who put in the "missing" frames).

• The **Footprints** drop-down (located along the top row of pop-up menus) lets you choose among several options: Leave Footprint, Backtrack Footprint, and Pickup Footprint. Leave Footprint places a bit of a "ghosted" image of how your curve looked when you left the footprint. You can use this as a visual reference to help you as you tweak. If you totally mangle things, you can use Backtrack Footprint to get back to the way things were. If you like how things are, you can choose Pickup Footprint. (Footprints only last until you close the Graph Editor window, use Pickup Footprint, or select a different item's curves.)

1. Let's go back to where we were at the end of the last section. With the text object selected, open the Graph Editor and select its **Position Z** channel. Right-drag a rectangle around *all* the keys, and set Incoming Curve to **Bezier Spline**. Double-click on the handles shown to get them to mirror their shorter partners.

**Note**

All these controls, buttons, and gizmos in the Graph Editor may seem like overkill, but believe me, everything here has a purpose, and though you may not need one of these bits of functionality much, when you do need it, you'll be thankful it's there. Bear in mind that this is *only scratching the surface.* The Graph Editor is the animator's most trusted and versatile tool. Its spline types, handles, footprints, you name it — all of it lets you have the minimum number of keys to hold your animation in place.

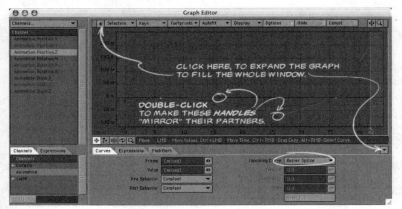

Figure 15-8

Figure 15-9

2.   Drop your selection. Then select *only* the keys on frames 6 and 36 (still working with the Position Z channel). Press <A> to Zoom Selected, and tweak the handles until you have a nice, smooth slope between the two keys. Minimize the Graph Editor window, and play your animation to see the difference.

Animation controls are available in the lower-right corner of the interface. (See Figure 2-82.) If the playback seems too fast or too slow, make sure you have **Play at Exact Rate** active under the General Options.

## Adjusting Timing

The animation we've just created looks good, but you may notice that the logo "pops" onto the screen a little too abruptly. Let's take a look at a few different ways in which we can tinker with timing to refine our animation.

The two primary tools for adjusting timing are the Dope Track and Dope Sheet. The Dope Track can be accessed from the main interface. Its cousin, the Dope Sheet, can be found in the Scene Editor. Both offer a similar, yet slightly different set of tools for adjusting the timing of your animations.

Let's do some fine-tuning using the Dope Track. Click on the textured portion of the gray bar just above the main timeline. This will open the Dope Track.

You'll notice that a second timeline appears, complete with a duplicate set of keyframes. The difference between these keys and the ones found in the main timeline, however, is that they can be dragged to different locations, cut, copied,

pasted, and "baked" to create keys for the inbetween frames.

Looking at our timeline we can see that the logo takes six frames to appear onscreen. At 24 frames per second, that's only ¼ of a second for the logo to appear. Let's give the "on" motion a little more time.

1.   Click on the key at frame 6 in the Dope Track. A white rectangle will appear around the top of this keyframe, indicating it has been selected.

2.   Click and drag left and right to move the keyframe. As you can see, the keyframe can be moved to any location on the timeline, even past existing keys. For now, drag the key to frame 10 and let go.

3.   Using the playback controls, take a look at the adjustments you've made. Those four extra frames make quite a bit of

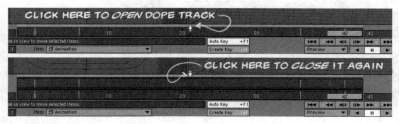

*Figure 15-10: Opening the Dope Track.*

difference! That brings me to my next point.

In animation, just as in film and video editing, timing is crucial. The difference of a few frames can literally make or break a scene. That's why features like the Dope Track are so vitally important. They make it easy for us to fine-tune the timing of individual elements in our scene. Let's take a look at some of the other features available in the Dope Track.

Keyframes can be added to the timeline simply by double-clicking. The values for the new key will be taken from those found at the location of the Frame Slider.

1. Move the Frame Slider to frame 42.

2. Now move your mouse over frame 20 in the Dope Track and double-click. A new keyframe will be created.

3. Play the scene using the playback controls. You'll notice that the logo now jumps back on the Z axis at frame 20.

Markers can be placed on the Dope Track to identify specific locations. They can even be labeled to provide greater clarity as to the purpose of each marker.

1. Holding the <**Shift**> key down, double-click the timeline at frame 20 where we just created the new key. A marker will be created.

2. Drag your Frame Slider over to frame 20. You'll notice that the marker turns yellow.

3. Right-click on the Dope Track and select **Set Marker Text** from the pop-up menu. In the requester that appears, type the name **ZoomZoom**. This will remind us that on this keyframe, the logo is zooming to the back. Press **OK** in the requester.

4. A marker label now appears in the info field to the bottom left of the timeline (see Figure 15-11).

At this point we can move our key away from frame 20 and still have a visual reminder of its original location. I don't really want the ZoomZoom keyframe, however, so let's delete it.

1. Click the key we created at frame 20 to select it. Now right-click. This brings up a context-sensitive pop-up menu.

2. Scroll down and select the **Delete Keys** option.

3. The logo will immediately jump forward again, as the key that pushed it back has been removed.

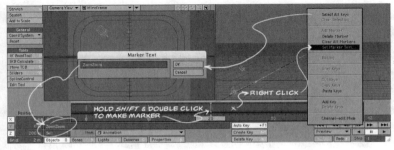

*Figure 15-11*

Since we deleted the ZoomZoom keyframe, we no longer need its marker either.

1. Move the Frame Slider to frame 20. The marker will turn yellow. This tells us that we can perform functions on this marker.

2. Right-click to bring up the pop-up menu. Choose the **Delete Marker** option.

Our animation is looking better, but there's still room for improvement. Let's make the logo's motion a little more dynamic.

1. Move the Frame Slider to frame 0. Click the **Rotate** tool from the **Modify | Rotate** menu or press the keyboard shortcut <**y**>. You'll notice that the Quick-Info display now shows controls for heading (H), pitch (P), and bank (B).

2. Click in the Bank field and replace the 0 with **10**. Then press <**Enter**> to accept the value. This rotates our logo 10° on its Bank channel (Figure 15-12).

Drag the Frame Slider or use the playback controls to see the result of this change. You'll notice that the logo is cocked at a constant 10° angle. Since the only keyframe for rotation was at frame 0, modifying it caused the change to remain in effect throughout the duration of the animation. This is nice, but not quite what we wanted.

1. Move the Frame Slider to frame 10. This is the frame at which the logo has moved completely onscreen and rests briefly before flying off.

2. Click in the Bank field and replace the 10 with a **0**. Press <**Enter**> to accept the results and play back your animation.

Ah! Much better! But there's still room for improvement. I want the rotation to end just before the logo comes to rest at frame 10. In order to achieve this, I need to move the keyframe for the Bank channel so that it is offset slightly from the logo's XYZ motion. If you look at the Dope Track, however, you'll notice that there's no way to adjust the rotation keyframe independently of the position keyframe. Or is there?

Right-click on the Dope Track and scroll all the way to the bottom of the pop-up menu. Select **Channel Edit Mode**. You'll notice that the keyframes on the Dope

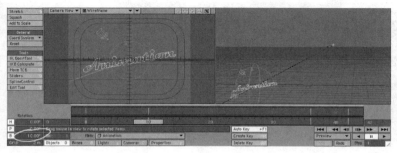

*Figure 15-12*

Track are no longer represented by solid yellow lines. Instead, they are made up of three small bars colored red, green, and blue. These correspond to the individual X, Y, Z or H, P, B channels of our object.

Take a look at frame 0. (You should still have the Rotate tool active.) The three bars tell us that there are keyframes here for heading, pitch, and bank. Now take a look at frame 10. Since the only adjustment to this frame was in the Bank channel, the red and green bars for heading and pitch are absent. Instead, we find a single blue bar representing our logo's bank depicted here.

Just as a quick comparison, select the Move tool by pressing the <t> keyboard shortcut. You'll notice that the keyframes changed. You see, the Channel Edit mode is context sensitive. When the Move tool is selected, the Dope Track will show keys for the X, Y, and Z position. However, when the Rotate tool is selected, it will show keys for the H, P, and B rotation.

Take a look at the Quick-Info display. Do you see the X, Y, and Z buttons? Even if a channel is present (i.e., keyframes exist for it), you can limit the Dope Track's ability to tweak it by deselecting its button in the Quick-Info display. Try turning on and off the different channels to see how it affects the Dope Track. When you're finished, turn on all of the position channels again. Then switch back to the Rotate tool. We're going

to adjust the Bank channel independently to refine the logo's "on" motion.

1. Make sure that the Rotate tool is active by pressing the <y> keyboard short-cut. Then click on the key at frame 10. This is the keyframe that we created to restore our logo's rotation to 0 degrees. By moving this keyframe, we can adjust the timing of that rotation.

2. Drag the key for this channel left and drop it at frame 8. Then, using the play-back controls, preview your animation. (See Figure 15-13.)

This is much better! The logo now moves onscreen and finishes rotating slightly before its "on" motion is complete. It hovers briefly, then shoots off out of view.

> **Note**
>
> Keep in mind that the settings I give you here are just a guide. Feel free to experiment with different locations for each keyframe. Remember, you are the artist. The look and feel of this animation is entirely up to you!

Our animation is just about finished. But before we wrap up this section, let's take a quick look at the Dope Sheet. Press <Ctrl> + <F1> or choose **Scene Editor | Open** from the main menu. The Dope

*Figure 15-13*

Sheet can be found on the tab at the right side of the Scene Editor.

The blocks in the Dope Sheet represent keyframes. By default, the blocks for objects appear in blue, the blocks for cameras appear in green, and the blocks for lights appear in magenta. You can click on any of these blocks to select it, or click and drag to define a range. Once a keyframe or range of frames is selected, you can move and scale it at will.

1.  Click on frame 10 of the animation object to select it. Yellow borders will appear around the left, right, and top of the frame. These denote the boundaries of the current selection.

2.  Click and drag to move the key to frame 20. You'll notice that a gray box has been left on the key's original frame. This gray box acts as a marker, making it easy for you to return the key to its starting position should you find the change unsatisfactory.

3.  You'll also notice that there are playback controls at the bottom right of the Scene Editor. Press **Play** to preview your animation. If needed, minimize the Scene Editor or move it out of the way, but *do not close it yet* (Figure 15-14).

Moving this keyframe didn't really help anything. Let's return it to its original position.

1.  Bring up the Scene Editor again. Since we did not close it, the frame we moved should still be highlighted.

2.  Click and drag the keyframe until it rests over the gray box at frame 10.

So far, we've been adjusting keyframes for all channels just as we did in the Dope Track. But it is possible to adjust the keyframes for individual channels as well. The C+ icon to the left of each item allows you to expand an object to see its individual channels.

The red, green, and blue blocks here are simply larger versions of the ones we saw in the Dope Track. The keyframes for individual channels can be moved, cut, copied, pasted, and scaled.

1.  Left-click on the animation object's Position X red key at frame 10.

2.  Hold the <**Shift**> key down and click on the Position Y key at frame 36. This selects the entire range of frames for the X and Y channels.

3.  Note the solid yellow bar on the far left and right sides of the selection. Dragging this bar allows you to interactively scale the selection.

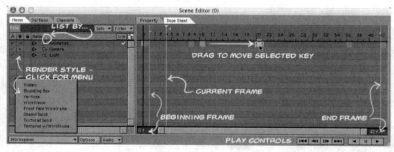

*Figure 15-14*

4. Click the yellow bar on the right side of the selection and drag it left until the two right channel keys rest at frame 14.

5. Clicking and dragging on one of the individual channels will allow you to move the entire selection.

6. Click and hold down your left mouse button over the Position X key at frame 10. Now drag to the right until this key rests at frame 20. Note that the gray blocks still show the original positions of your keyframes.

While scaling and moving the X and Y keys was a good lesson in the use of the Dope Sheet, it didn't really do anything to improve our animation, so let's put them back where they started. We could move and drag our keyframes back into place, but that would require multiple steps. An easier way to revert to our previous keyframe positions is to use the Undo command.

1. Right-click over any portion of the Dope Sheet and choose **Undo**.

2. Finally, click any portion of the Dope Sheet that does not contain an item (such as a camera, object, or light) to deselect the range.

If you haven't done so recently, this would be a great time to save your scene!

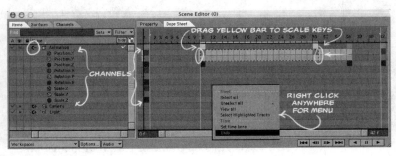

Figure 15-15

# Previews

If you've got a heavily complex scene, not like this simple flying logo we're working on but something really grindingly detailed, your scene won't look good at all when played using the animation controls. You'll have to make a preview first.

> **Note**
>
> Previews are built from whatever window is in the *upper-left corner* of the interface. That window can be any view LightWave has to offer (even Schematic view — though it'll be awfully boring).

*Figure 15-16*

With the upper-left viewport set to Camera View, select **Make Preview** from the Preview pop-up menu (next to the animation controls in the lower-right corner of the interface). A dialog box opens in which you

can tell LightWave to make a preview of part of your scene. When you press **OK** to accept the default values, LightWave "zings" through the animation, storing the image of each frame in memory and numbering it for easy referencing.

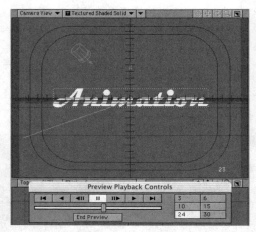

*Figure 15-17*

When LW is finished building the preview, a VCR-like control set pops up that you can use to step-frame or play your animation forward or backward, looping or stopping at the ends. You can play your preview at the frame rates listed, or you can use the little handle to scrub through your scene to your heart's content.

> **Note**
>
> Under the Preview pop-up menu, you can also save your preview as a movie format, using whatever *codec* (compression format) you set under Preview Options.
>
> Choosing Play Preview under the Preview pop-up menu, you can see your preview again for as long as it is held in memory.
>
> While LightWave is storing your preview in memory, it is storing it in a *lossless* format, which can take up a sizable chunk of memory. Under the Preview pop-up menu, you can also choose Free Preview to retrieve whatever memory is being used to hold the preview.

# Rendering an Animation

You might think this is a no-brainer, but there is something to point out about rendering your animations. If you're rendering to a *movie* format (Rendering | Render Options | Save Animation) and the power goes out (and you haven't got a UPS), or the machine crashes, or any of the other things that can go wrong do, guess what? *Your animation is more than likely irretrievable.* This may not be such a biggie if the whole render takes less than a minute to complete, but what if you're looking at a 120-frame scene that's taking *nine minutes per frame*? (Not uncommon…)

The solution? Cover your ASCII!

When you're rendering to an animation format (AVI, QuickTime, whatever), be sure to *render to frames as well*! If your computer dies while you're rendering, you can just go back and restart the render for the remainder of the frames, letting LightWave compile the rendered frames into an animation after everything's done. (See Figure 15-18.)

> **Note**
>
> Computer crashes *during* or *immediately after* renders are good reasons for *saving your scene before you render!* ("Hey! That finally looks the way I want it! Hey! What happened to the electricity?!!")

Under the Image Editor, you can tell LightWave to load in the *first* frame of a *series of* rendered frames; then under the Image Type pop-up menu, you can tell LightWave that it isn't a still frame but a *sequence*. LightWave will scan the directory, analyzing the sequence of frames, and fill in the rest of the information shown in Figure 15-18. You can then set the end frame of your movie (and render) to the Out point of the sequence (see the figure), and under Effects | Compositing, set Background Image to be the sequence you just loaded.

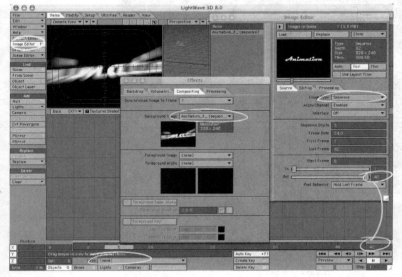

*Figure 15-18*

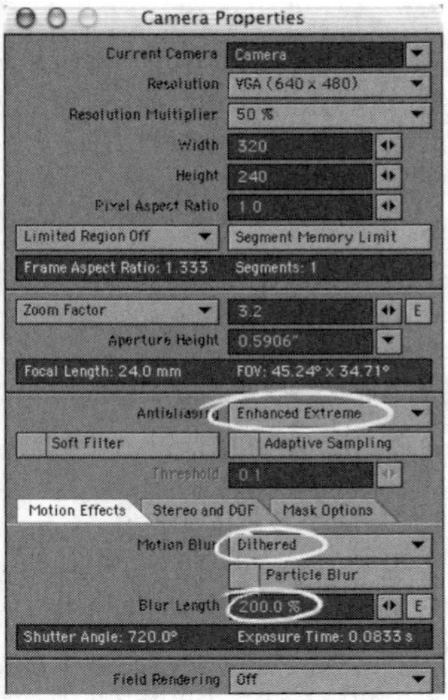

View Background set to Background Image).

To render the flying logo we did here, I recommend using some serious motion blur (more as a special effect than the simulation of film speed) since the text moves so fast. In order to get the effect looking as good as possible, we need to really crank up the Antialiasing setting (Enhanced Extreme will factor *33 passes into a single frame*) and set Motion Blur to Dithered (which will render every other pixel from a slightly different point on the timeline). To get the special effect I'm thinking of, set Blur Length to 200%. (See Figure 15-19.)

*Figure 15-19*

> ### Note
>
> If you'd like to see a movie of what we've gone over here, Renders\Chapter15\ Animation.mov will show you what Scenes\ Chapter_15\Animation_F.lws looks like when rendered.

Without any objects in the scene (and without the need to antialias), you can render a movie from your pre-rendered frames (shown with Display Options | Camera

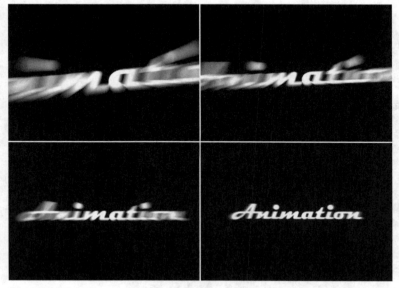

*Figure 15-20: Here are some frames from the finished animation to show what the "super-mega-ultra" motion blur looks like as the text settles. (The vector blur we used on our tunnel fly-through could be used here as well.)*

. . .

These are the basics of what LightWave uses to *control* animation. (Remember, these are the *"hows,"* not the *"whys."*) At its core, animation is simply manipulating an item's changes in *position, rotation*, and/or *scale* over time. All LightWave animations consist of moving, rotating, and/or scaling an object, bone, light, camera, or special effect, creating keyframes that record these changes over time, and using the Graph Editor to hone the shape of the curves that LightWave uses to store the motion data.

What you've learned in this chapter has shown you the basic tools used by *all* CG animators, whether they are creating spaceships flying through minefields or animating Mortal Kombats. It's *how* these tools are used that create the art we know as animation. The use of these tools defines an animator and the animations he or she creates.

# Layout 3: Character Animation

In the previous chapter we examined the basic tools used to create *any* type of animation. In this chapter, we'll look at the tools designed specifically for *character* animation. The principles of character animation are the same in every major 3D package.

We'll be discussing those here first. Once we've looked at the basics, however, we'll delve into more advanced topics such as using Joint Compensation, Muscle Flexing, and LightWave 8's powerful new IK Booster tool.

## A Brief Introduction to Character Animation

Computer animation has come a long way over the past 20 years. Those who've been working in this field from the start will tell you how difficult it was in those days to get a simple character built, let alone animated. But today, 3D programs such as LightWave offer a number of highly advanced tools, giving you everything you need to bring your characters to life. And by definition, that's what animation is: the illusion of life. You create this illusion through the use of highly advanced technologies. Chief among these are bones, forward kinematics, and inverse kinematics.

### Bones and Rigs

Nearly all computer-based character animation is accomplished through the use of bones. If this is your first experience with character animation, it's important to understand the difference between real

bones (such as those in your arms, legs, hands, and feet) and 3D bones. In the real world, bones act as the framework for your body. That framework determines your overall shape. Think about it: Without bones, you would be nothing but a large blob of skin sitting on the floor. But in the 3D world, that's not so. A character without bones does not go limp when it's taken out of Modeler and brought into Layout. That's because its overall form is determined by its polygonal mesh. So what purpose do bones serve in the 3D world? Well, here bones are used to deform a mesh by affecting its position, rotation, and scale.

Bones are created using the various tools available in LightWave. You can use a single bone to animate a character, or you can create a hierarchy of bones to allow for a greater range of motion. Generally speaking, the number of bones you'll need for any given character is directly proportional to the complexity of the animation you want to achieve. Sound confusing? Think of it this way: A single bone can be used to animate a hand waving back and forth. But if you want that hand to perform sign language, you'll need a lot more bones.

Complex character animation can often yield dozens (and in some cases hundreds) of bones. These bones can be arranged in any number of ways. The person responsible for their arrangement is known as a *rigger* and the set of controls used to manipulate them is known as a *rig*.

# Inverse Kinematics, Forward Kinematics, and IK Booster

Every character rig employs a form of motion control known as *kinematics*. So what the heck is a "kinematic" and why would anyone care whether it's "forward," "backward," or somewhere in between?

Kinematics refers to the study of mechanics concerned with motion. Where 3D animation is concerned, kinematics defines the way in which you manipulate a system of hierarchical (parent/child) items.

## FK (Forward Kinematics)

*Forward kinematics* (most often referred to simply as FK) is the "old reliable" way of animating. It is labor-intensive, but there are no surprises — everything that's in an animation must be put there, on purpose, by the animator.

With FK, if you wanted to make the tip of the character's "forearm" reach the null object (represented as the "+" in Figure 16-1), you'd have to first rotate the bicep and then the forearm, evaluate how close you got to your objective, and then refine.

As you can see in the figure, the tip of the forearm overshoots the null. I'd have to go back and tweak the rotations of the bicep and forearm again and again (and probably again).

As you can see, there are no surprises in this kind of animation — everything that's done must be done on purpose by the animator, and as such, it is a painfully slow way to work with a character's rig.

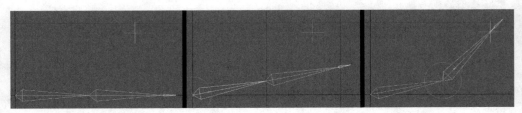

Figure 16-1: Forward kinematics. Here, you see a hierarchical set of bones that could easily be a character's bicep, forearm, and hand.

# IK (Inverse Kinematics)

*Inverse kinematics* (IK) uses a complex set of calculations to figure out the exact rotations that need to be applied to every item within a hierarchical system in order to have its *puller* remain in constant contact with its *goal*.

In practice, IK systems consist of chains of bones. The last bone in the chain acts as the *puller* for those higher up. The puller bone uses a *goal* object with which it strives to remain in contact. The goal is typically a *null* object, although it can be any object you choose.

## What Is IK?

IK allows the animator to focus on the broad strokes of a pose or gesture while the IK solver handles many of the small but important details. Using IK, you simply pose a character's hand control, and the character's arm bones do what they need to do to remain in contact with the hand's base.

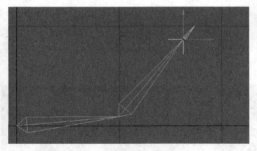

Figure 16-2: Inverse kinematics. With IK, you set the hand as the puller for the chain of bones and the null as the puller's goal, and the bicep and forearm automatically figure the perfect set of rotations that will keep the puller's base at the exact location as the goal's base.

> ### Note
>
> *Not all IK is created equal!*
>
> IK requires very precise calculations in order for it to work *dependably*. In this, LightWave's floating-point mathematics engine (which keeps its calculations accurate to many, many places to the right of the decimal point) makes it one of the best packages available for character animation.
>
> Don't be fooled. Other software may have great salesmen, but LightWave has got it where it counts. It is *dependable* and *predictable* in every situation. Thanks to LightWave's robust IK, I was able to do nearly ten times the amount of feature-quality animation per day as is expected from feature animators using other packages.

Figure 16-3: IK in action driving the positioning for a character's arm.

## "Standard" IK Basics

Let's take a look at the basics of "standard" IK. I'm saying *"standard"* here because LightWave 8's new IK Booster tool (which we'll discuss shortly) provides a system that is as much of an advancement on IK as IK *itself* was on character animation back in the early '90s. I've found that IK Booster works best when it's used as a supplement to standard IK, so we'll begin by laying the groundwork for how a traditional IK system works and how it is set up.

## Note

You may want to change your viewport layout to allow for multiple views on your project (as opposed to the single viewport that is LightWave Layout's default). I find this helps me get a better handle on the true position and rotation of items in 3D space.

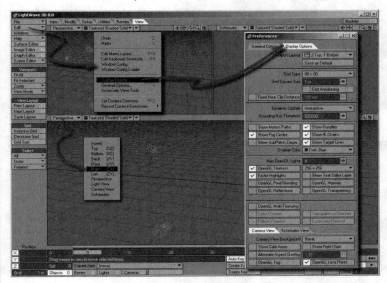

Figure 16-4: Under Edit | Display Options, you'll find the Viewport Layout setting. I've experimented with a lot of options and have settled on 2 Top, 1 Bottom as my current favorite.

Make sure you have one of your viewports set to Right by selecting **Right (ZY)** from the view's View Type list. (This will allow us to more easily work with the bones in this simple example.)

As I mentioned earlier, character animation is achieved through bones. We'll use them here to explore a standard IK setup. Bones in LightWave need to belong to an object, so we'll need to first create a null object to which they'll belong.

1. Click on **Items | Add | Null**, and a requester window opens up, asking what you'd like to name your new null object. Press **Enter** (or click **OK**) to leave the null object's name "Null." (See Figure 16-5.)

## Note

Null objects are the handiest little things in 3D CGI. They are "placeholders," treated by LightWave with all the respect of a "real" object (i.e., one that has geometry), without taking up any memory or hard drive space. Null objects don't show up in a render or cast shadows and, like vampires, don't show up in reflective objects either.

Nulls are super-handy when you want to have a "handle" to move a bunch of different objects, lights, and/or cameras at the same time, and they're perfectly suited for the job of being a *goal object* in an inverse kinematic system.

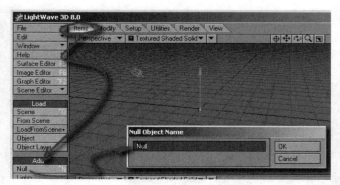

*Figure 16-5*

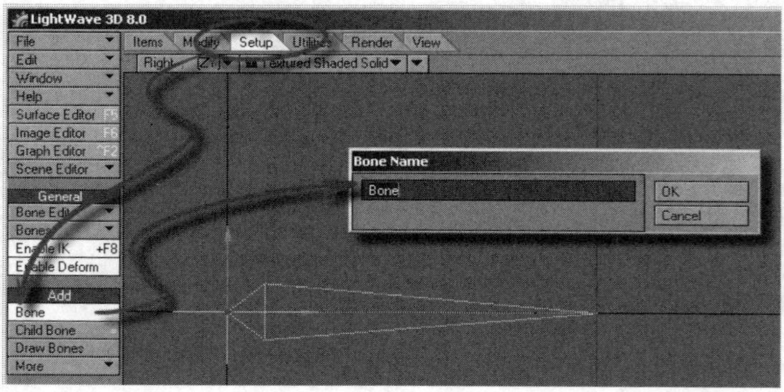

*Figure 16-6*

2. Click on **Setup | Add | Bone**, and a requester window opens, asking for the name you'd like for your new bone. Accept the default name of "Bone."

3. You can add a second bone that will automatically be ordered as the child of the first and positioned at the exact tip of the first bone by clicking **Setup | Add | Child Bone** (or by pressing the < = > key). Again, a requester window opens, asking for a name for this new bone. And again, accept the default name of "Bone." This new bone will be our *puller* for the IK chain.

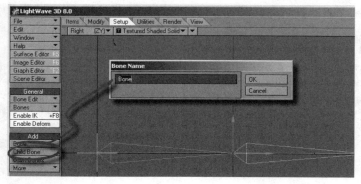

*Figure 16-7*

## Note

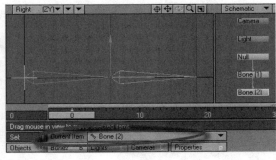

Figure 16-8

You'll notice that even though you accepted the name "Bone" as the name for the second bone, it shows up as "Bone (2)" in the Current Item list and in the Schematic views and Scene Editor windows.

When there are two similar items with the same name in a scene, LightWave automatically adds temporary, sequential numbers to the similarly named items. These numbers go away if/when you choose to rename the item (which you can do by choosing Rename from the right-click menu that opens when right-clicking on the item in a Schematic view or Scene Editor window, or by choosing Items | Replace | Rename).

4. Use **Items | Add | Null** to create another null object, but this time, name the null **Goal**. This will become the goal object (target) of our simple IK chain.

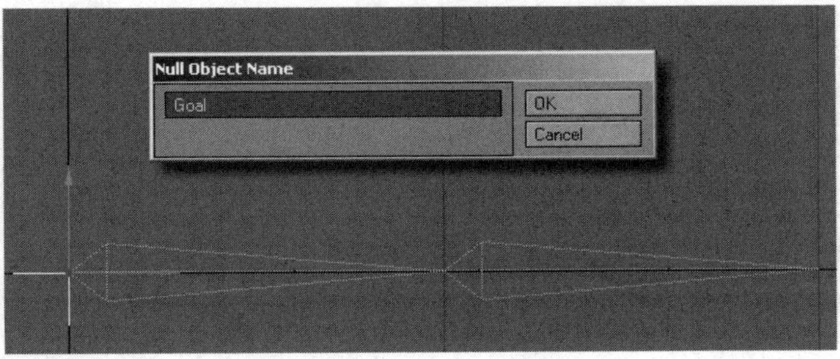

Figure 16-9

Note

If you're not yet familiar with animating in LightWave, here's a hint to make your life a lot easier. Have Layout automatically create keyframes for you whenever you move, scale, or rotate an item (as opposed to having to press Enter or click Create Key every time you want Layout to remember an item's scaling, rotation, or translation on a particular frame — *keyframe*).

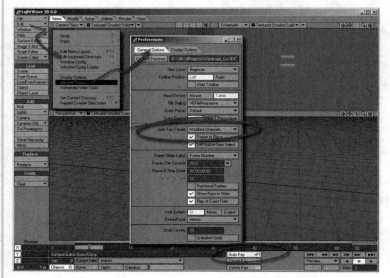

*Figure 16-10*

You activate Auto Key Create by *first* telling LightWave that you want Auto Key active by making sure its button is selected at the bottom of the screen.

Then you need to tell LightWave whether you want keys created for *all* channels (scaling, rotation, and translation), even when you only have modified only one of those channels, or if you want LightWave to remember changes specifically for the channel type that has been modified. You make this choice under Edit | General Options | Auto Key Create.

Both settings need to be active in order for LightWave's Auto Key Create function to be active.

---

We've got the basic components of an IK chain in place. Now it's time to get it working.

1.  In a Right viewport, move the null object called Goal up and to the left a bit as seen in Figure 16-11.

2.  Select **Bone (2)** by clicking on it (you'll find it easiest to select items by clicking on the item's node in a viewport set to Schematic).

3.  Press <m> (**Window | Motion Options...**) to open the Motion Options window for the selected item.

4.  Select **Goal** as the goal object for this bone, and check **Full-time IK**.

> **Note**
>
> If you have Display Options | Show IK Chains active, then the moment you set an IK chain's goal object, a teal-colored line appears along the length of the chain in Layout's windows. Even viewports set to Schematic show a line connecting the puller with its goal.

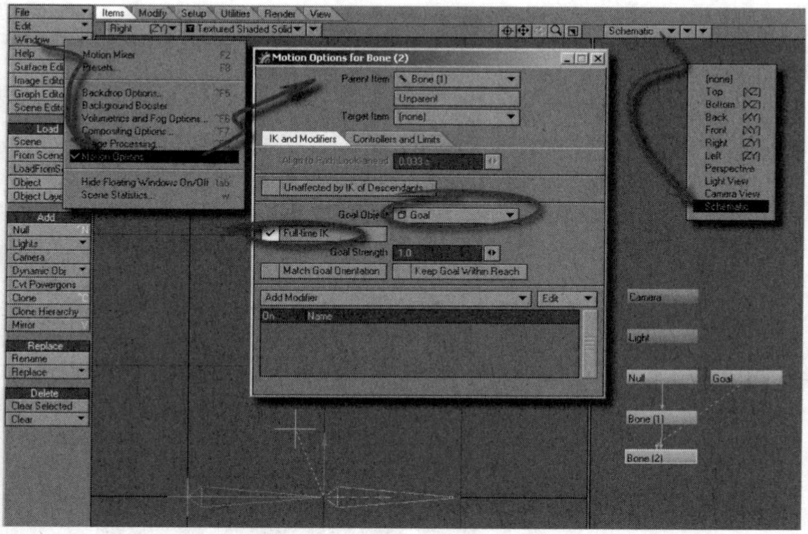

Figure 16-11

---

### Note

What's the difference between full-time IK and IK that isn't "full-time"?

Way back when IK was new, its calculations not yet streamlined, and 40 MHz was mind-bogglingly fast, the friendly folks at NewTek thought it would be a help for animators to have the option of only solving for IK when the chain's goal object was moved, requiring keyframes to be set by hand for the items in the chain. This saved the computer's CPU from constantly having to think about IK calculations, and in turn, sped up the process of animation significantly.

Nowadays, CPUs are so fast, and the calculations for IK so optimized, there's *almost* no reason to not have all IK chains full-time, all the time. I say "almost," because who knows...maybe you might find a need for part-time IK you can't live without that nobody else has thought of.

It's for those instances when something most people see as passé is the key to a solution of genius magnitude that NewTek still gives you these and similar options.

Similar thoughtful options have saved my job on several occasions. This philosophy of letting the users have all the options they might need, even if "mundania" may not be able to see the benefits, is one of the major reasons behind my strong respect for LightWave and for NewTek.

Setting the chain's goal object is just the first step in setting up IK. The chain will be pulled toward the goal, but only when the parent items in the chain are told that they can use IK to solve for their rotations.

1. Select **Bone (1)**.

2. Click on the **Controllers and Limits** tab in the Motion Options window.

3. Choose **Inverse Kinematics** for its Pitch Controller. The moment you do this, LightWave begins using IK to solve for the pitch axis for that item, and the bone swings upward, bringing the base of the puller item as close as it can get to the goal item.

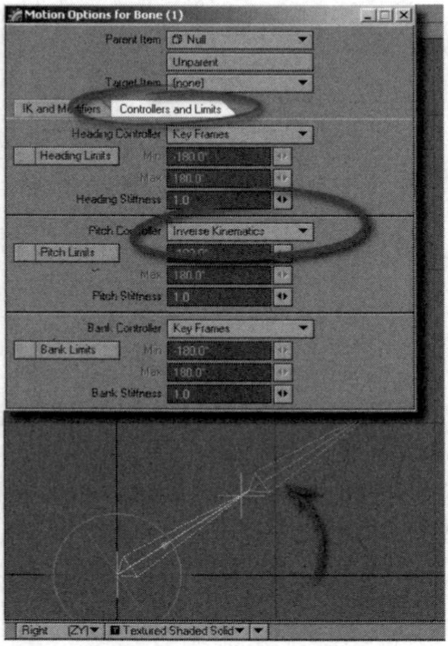

*Figure 16-12*

## Note

*Figure 16-13*

If you recall our discussion of rotation in Chapter 1, the best way to remember LightWave's conventions for its axes of rotation is to think of your hand like an airplane. *Heading* changes where the "plane" is heading (represented by a red circle in Layout). *Pitch* changes its altitude (green). And *bank* would be the amount of "roll" (blue).

Well, there you have it — a quick and easy explanation of standard IK and how to set it up. (That wasn't so painful, was it?) The same basic principles you've seen here also hold true as you add more parts to the chain, but keep in mind that as you do so, the math required of the IK solver grows ever more complicated for the computer. That can lead to a number of problems.

If you want your IK system to behave predictably in complex situations, you need to help the IK solver as much as possible. This means putting some restrictions on what you ask IK to do.

# "Standard" IK Hazards

Good, old-fashioned IK is a nifty and time-saving tool, but it's not perfect. Here are some things to bear in mind when working with IK.

## Pre-bending

An IK chain that has two (or more) joints laid out in a straight line (as was the case in our previous example) is as apt to swing the child item in the chain *up* as it is *down*. While this is good for things like whips and chains, it's not so pleasant for things like elbows and knees.

If you need a child item to favor bending in one direction over another, it is best to set up the IK chain so that it is "pre-bent" in the direction you want the item to favor.

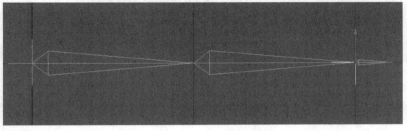

*Figure 16-14*

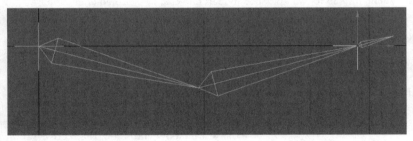

*Figure 16-15*

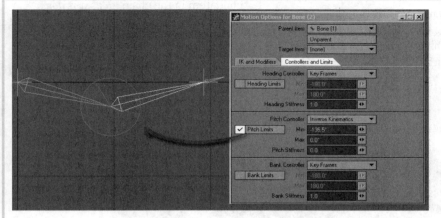

Figure 16-16

Some have had great success with using limits to restrict how far a bone will bend in a given angular direction. However, without the ability to "cushion" these limits, the resulting motion of an item as it reaches its limit is often sharp and inorganic. So I tend to shy away from using limits whenever possible, opting instead for well-planned models and cleanly executed animation.

## Number of Axes Solved

When you have two or more joints in an IK chain operating in 2D space, things tend to work quite well. But in three-dimensional space, the level of complexity of the calculations that IK must figure out rises dramatically. If you want things to work dependably, you're going to have to curb your demands on the IK solver.

If you take a look at your own arm or leg, you'll find that it's built much the same way as the above illustration. Your bicep and thigh can swing back and forth, and up and down (two axes: heading and pitch), while your forearm and calf move only around one axis of the elbow and knee, respectively.

I've found that referencing real life in building riggings helps more than nearly

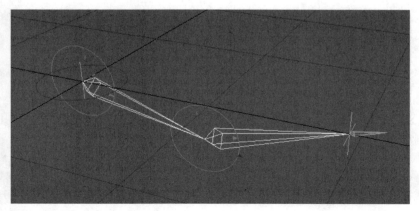

Figure 16-17

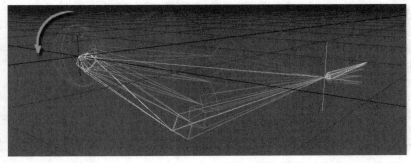

*Figure 16-18*

anything else in making character setups that do what you'd expect them to do.

While the desire to use IK on shoulder or hip joints in order to solve for all three axes (heading, pitch, and bank) is tempting, I find that often (though not always) this makes for a loose, "swively," hard-to-control arm or leg. Most often, character riggers will leave the bank axis to be controlled manually by the animator using FK. This lets you precisely control the position of the elbow or knee joint just by rotating the bicep or thigh.

So, the rule of thumb for good, solid IK chains in character riggings is: *The topmost item can use IK to solve for a maximum of two rotation axes, and the child item in a character IK chain should use IK for only one axis.*

> **Note**
>
> I don't recommend using standard IK on a bone chain consisting of more than two joints (such as for a character's tail). It creates too many opportunities for the complex math to give you something you neither expect nor want. IK Booster is the tool for the job if you have something like a tail, tentacle, whip, or rope you need to animate.

## Rotation Order

Character riggings are complex things. Riggings use a lot of heavy-duty math that we animators take for granted when we're doing our jobs. Usually, we don't care *how* something works, so long as it *does*.

But, if you're curious about the more complex details that make for a good, dependable character rigging, this section and the next one will fill you in on a lot of the stuff that goes on behind the scenes.

> **Note**
>
> The "Rotation Order" and "Joint Compensation and Muscle Flexing" sections are mainly for the technical directors and the heavy-duty math-oriented folks who really want to understand why things happen and why certain decisions are made in the crafting of riggings. If this isn't your cup of tea, don't worry (there won't be a quiz on this later); just skip to the section called "Flipping."

LightWave has a fixed order in which it calculates the rotation of an item:

1) Heading
2) Pitch
3) Bank

You can think of this rotation order as if your object ("Arrow" in Figure 16-19) were parented to a hierarchical series of null objects, each null handling *one* rotation axis. Rotating one null will cause all of its children to rotate right along with it.

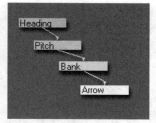

Using this logic, I've set up a scene in which we've got two arrows as children of a hierarchical series of nulls.

*Figure 16-19*

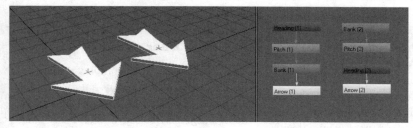

*Figure 16-20*

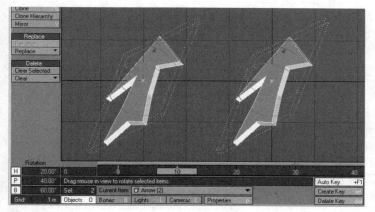

*Figure 16-21*

In Figure 16-21, notice I've selected both arrow objects and rotated them: H=20, P=40, B=60.

If an object is rotated H=20, it would make sense that to reset its *applicable rotation* to H=0, its parent object would need to be rotated H=–20 (0 = *n* + [–1 · *n*]).

When you want to "unwind" an object, reset its applicable rotation to 0, 0, 0. When

its rotation is being controlled by a system that solves heading first, then pitch, then bank, the order in which the rotations were applied must be *reversed*. (LightWave does this automatically when you simply reset an item's rotation to 0, 0, 0 — but if you have a hierarchical system creating Steadycam-like "floating head" movement, then rotation order becomes very important.)

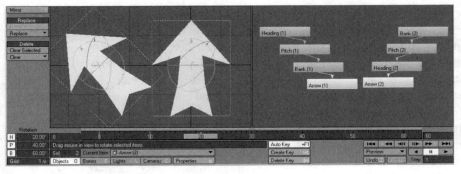

*Figure 16-22*

I've left the arrow objects at H=20, P=40, B=60, and I've rotated the parent nulls labeled Heading by –20, Pitch by –40, and Bank by –60. The only difference between the two hierarchies is the *order* in which the rotations are applied. The arrow on the right applies bank first, then pitch, then heading, essentially *reversing* the rotation order applied by LightWave.

Among other things, rotation order is responsible for the phenomenon known as "gimbal lock."

In each viewport, the left-hand arrow is rotated 0, 0, 0. The right-hand arrow is rotated 0, –90, 0. The bank axis is a *child* of the pitch axis, and so when pitch is rotated +/– 90°, the bank axis swings into exactly the same plane as the heading axis. In the top viewports of Figure 16-23, you see two concentric circles, representing the heading (larger) and the bank (smaller), around the right-hand arrow. The right-hand arrow is in a condition where rotating in heading and bank produce the same applicable results. This is *gimbal lock*.

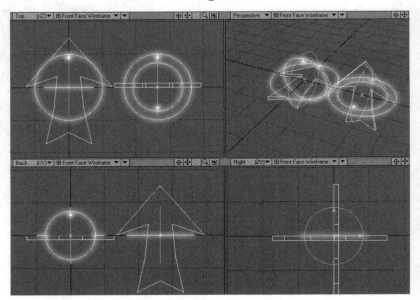

*Figure 16-23*

Now, if you feel you're having a hard time wrapping your mind around this problem, don't feel bad; you're not alone. Even the best IK solving engines have a difficult time with this.

When the rotation axis that is recorded *second* (pitch) nears/exceeds +/– 90°, IK can start to have problems. As the pitch angle nears/exceeds +/– 90°, the item can instantly "spin" around to face the opposite direction. Often, this will happen suddenly, over the course of a single frame. This is called *flipping*.

> **Note**
>
> There are as many ways of setting up a character rig as there are people to do the setups. Everyone will find his own sets of rules that work for him.
>
> Over the course of your career, you will hear many opinions as far as the "best" way of doing things. In my experience, there is no "best way." There are only ways that work more easily for the ways in which your mind solves problems. Try what sounds interesting, keep it if it works for you, and *always* keep your mind open to finding new and better ways of working!

## Joint Compensation and Muscle Flexing

> **Note**
>
> This section on joint compensation and muscle flexing gets into some pretty heavy-duty LightWave and mathematical concepts. If you're just starting out, or if you have little desire to get into the "hard-core" aspects of character rigging, please feel free to skip this section, moving on to the next section, called "Flipping."

At the bottom of the Bone | Properties window, LightWave has a set of Muscle Flexing and Joint Compensation settings for each bone. These help LightWave preserve the volume of the character's joints as bones bend and the object's mesh (or "skin") flexes.

| | | |
|---|---|---|
| ✓ Joint Compensation | 100.0 % | ◀▶ |
| ✓ Joint Comp for Parent | 100.0 % | ◀▶ |
| ✓ Muscle Flexing | 100.0 % | ◀▶ |
| ✓ Parental Muscle Flexing | 100.0 % | ◀▶ |

Figure 16-24

Here, you see the difference between the character's hand when Muscle Flexing and Joint Compensation are active for the bones of the fingers, and when they are not.

The important thing to know about Muscle Flexing and Joint Compensation is that these functions *only work with the bones' pitch axis*!

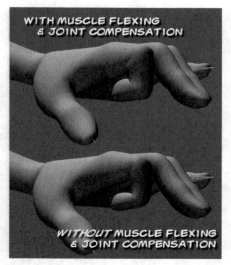

Figure 16-25

Okay, so what if you want to use Muscle Flexing and Joint Compensation with a bone that is only supposed to rotate in heading, as with the forearm?

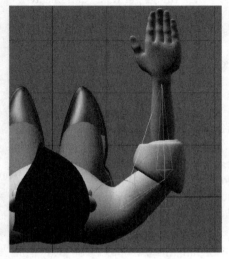

*Figure 16-26*

Under Modify | Rotate | Rotate Pivot, you can manually change the angle that LightWave Layout thinks of as that particular item's H=0, P=0, B=0. If you change the Bank setting of an item's pivot rotation

to +/– 90°, you essentially "swap" that item's heading and pitch axes.

> **Note**
>
> LightWave allows you to set/record the pivot rotation for an item as a way of helping to combat gimbal lock.
>
> A character's thigh points more or less straight downward, meaning that by default its rotation is nearly P=–90 right from the start.
>
> By using Setup | Modify | Orientation | Record Pivot Rotation (the hot key for this is <P>; don't forget to use uppercase), you can tell LightWave to store that item's current rotation as the rotation setting for that item's pivot.
>
> The result of the Record Pivot Rotation tool is that the value of the item's previous rotation is stored as the *pivot's* rotation. Because the item's pivot now assumes the previous rotation information, the item itself now lies along that particular set of angles when it is set to H=0, P=0, B=0. So, the item's *rotation* is then set to 0, 0, 0, and a keyframe is created to hold the change in rotation data.
>
> In short, using Record Pivot Rotation means that a bone can still *look* like it's pointing straight up or straight down (P=+/– 90°), but it will animate from the perception that that direction is H=0, P=0, B=0.

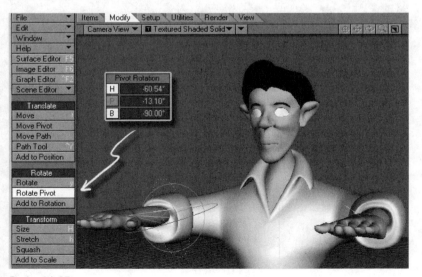

*Figure 16-27*

**Note**

In changing the rotation of an item's pivot, you must do so on that item's rest pose, the frame where your character exists without any changes to his default rigging position whatsoever.

**Note**

You can also use this technique of altering the Bank setting of an item's pivot rotation to help control IK instabilities, which happen most often when an item using IK to solve for both heading and pitch approaches or exceeds +/– 90° in its pitch axis.

If you notice that your character requires a greater range of movement in the pitch axis of an item that uses IK for both heading and pitch, and you're getting headaches from the IK misbehaving, you can set the item's pivot rotation for its bank axis to +/– 90°, so then the greater range of movement occurs on the heading axis, which now falls in the same plane that used to be pitch!

## Flipping

IK relies on a heavy-duty set of calculations. Even the best IK solvers still have issues when things get really complicated.

The biggest problem with even the best IK is *flipping*, where a joint will spin 180° over the course of one frame.

Foresight and planning in both your rigging and animation, coupled with a strong IK solver such as LightWave's, will usually keep flipping to a minimum.

I find that I can avoid most flipping by:

- Keeping the goal object at a distance of at least one-third the length of the bicep or thigh away from the bicep or thigh's point of rotation (the shoulder or hip, respectively).

- Keeping the bicep or thigh from nearing/exceeding +/– 90° in the pitch axis.

- Keeping the goal object well away from the area *behind* the bicep or thigh as that bone would lie in its rest pose.

- Not trying to have my character assume a pose that would be painful to do in real life.

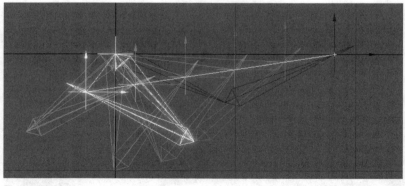

*Figure 16-28*

Figure 16-29

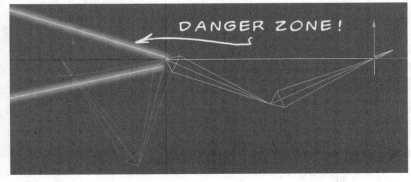

Figure 16-30

### Note

I find that if I'm having problems with flip-ping, I'm usually trying to put the character into a pose that my *own* joints would com-plain about.

If you find you absolutely, positively have to have a particular, "painful" pose, you can save a lot of time by making a "special-pur-pose" rigging that can more easily move through that pose.

## "Standard" IK Rules

These *rules* are more like *guidelines*. They can be bent and broken as you see fit to suit the needs of your particular IK setup.

However, that being said, these rules have kept my characters moving smoothly

and predictably through many productions. It's always best to learn the rules well before you start seeing what happens by breaking them.

● IK is only dependable when solving rotations for a maximum of *two items* within an IK chain.

● On any item controlled by IK, let IK solve for a maximum of two axes.

● In a chain of two items, the child item should only use IK to solve for one of its axes.

● Always give your two-item IK chain a little "suggestion" in knowing which direc-tion it should bend by pre-bending those items.

**415**

# IK Booster

As stated earlier, IK Booster is as much of an advancement to the art of character animation as IK itself was back in the early '90s.

What is IK Booster? It's a whole lot of things all wrapped up in a nice, neat little package. But with respect to character rigging, it's best to think of it as something that can be used to add even more ease, power, functionality, and stability to the IK systems we've been talking about already.

IK Booster enables us to overcome many of the limitations imposed by standard IK. For example, in the standard IK rules, I said that it's best not to use IK on a chain consisting of more than two joints. But with IK Booster, we are no longer bound by this rule. Let's take a look at how this works.

## Applying IK Booster

IK Booster can be applied to any object that has bones set up in a hierarchy.

Start with a fresh scene, and add a null (as described earlier in this chapter). We're going to create a chain of five bones. We could do this by adding a bone and then adding four more child bones, but there's an easier way.

Make sure that your null is selected and then go to the Setup tab.

1. Click **Add | Bone**.

2. Further down on the Setup tab is the Detail section. Click on the **Bone Split** tool. A window will pop up asking for the number of new bones.

3. Enter **5** for the number of bones and leave the Fracture Mode at Collinear. Then click **OK**. Your existing bone will be broken into a hierarchal chain consisting of five bones.

Activate the IK Booster tool by clicking on **Modify | Tools | IK BoostTool** or (**<Ctrl>** + **<b>**). Then, right-click on the null that is the *root* for the chain of bones we just created. A pop-up window will appear. Click the **Apply IK Booster** option.

After clicking on Apply IK_Booster as shown in Figure 16-32, you'll notice a few changes to the appearance of your object. So long as you have IK BoostTool active, you'll see a *control icon* for your currently selected item within your IK Booster-enabled object(s). You'll also see *handles* that default to the tips of all the bones within the "IK-boosted" object.

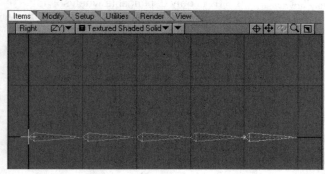

*Figure 16-31*

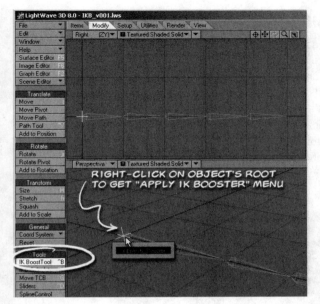

Figure 16-32

Figure 16-33

<br>

> **Note**
>
> IK Booster is a custom object function applied to the object itself. To remove it from an object, you'll need to open the Object Properties for that particular object, and remove the IK_Booster custom object under the Geometry tab.

That's it! That's all you need to do to apply IK Booster and start animating this chain of bones far more reliably than IK alone would let you. (Read on!)

## Long Chain Dependability

With IK Booster, you don't have to assign any goal objects or tell LightWave to use IK for any rotation axes; you just grab any of the handles and move them around!

IK Booster handles "long chains" of hundreds of bones with speed and reliability. If you've got a whip, tentacle, or tail you need to animate, IK Booster lets you confidently use as many bones as you need to get the smoothest deformations possible.

You probably noticed that when you dragged your IK-boosted chain around, you dragged the whole thing around, root and all. If you want to have the root stay in place, make sure you have the root bone (or the object itself) selected, right-click on the item's control, and check **ikstop**. This causes the IK movements of all child bones to have no effect on any items higher up the IK-boosted chain.

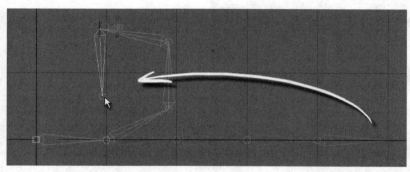

Figure 16-34

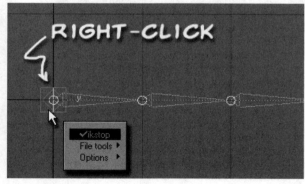

Figure 16-35

## IK Booster and Movement

IK Booster is a *mode* of movement unto itself. Selecting Modify | Translate | Move or Modify | Rotate | Rotate or Modify | Transform | Size (or Stretch — or any other tool) will deactivate IK BoostTool.

Movement within the IK Booster system isn't the same as you may have gotten used to thus far in LightWave; the handles are different, and you can essentially move and rotate without having to change tools.

You've already seen how you can click and drag a handle to move the IK-boosted chain. If you need to rotate an item, select it, then click and drag on the numbers that

appear beside its control. The top is heading (green), then pitch (red), then bank (blue).

## IK Booster and Keyframes

IK Booster creates its own keyframes whenever you move or rotate an item in its chain (regardless of your Auto Key Create settings). And because IK Booster pushes beyond LightWave's normal way of working, the usual ways of creating and deleting keyframes (by pressing Enter and Delete) don't apply *when you have the IK BoostTool active*.

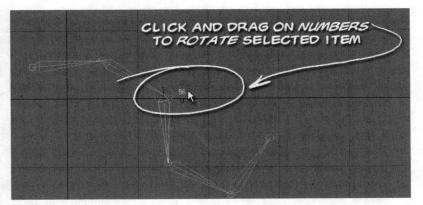

Figure 16-36

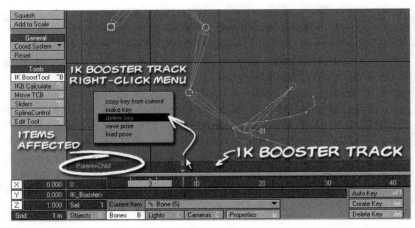

Figure 16-37

When you have IK Booster active (and the Dope Track is *inactive* — see Chapter 15, "Layout 2: Animation Basics"), a darkened area appears above the timeline at the bottom of Layout's screen. This is the IK Booster Track. There's a lot of power packed within that little track.

The display at the left of the IK Booster Track tells you what items within the IK-boosted chain will be affected by what you're doing with the chain. In this case, all the parents and children of the selected item will have keyframes created whenever I move a handle. (Clicking on this display cycles you through the different modes — you can choose to affect only the current item, only the selected item's children, only its parents, both that item's parents and children, or all items within the IKB chain.)

Right-clicking on the IK Booster Track opens up the right-click menu for that particular frame. It is from this right-click menu that you can choose to delete a keyframe or create one arbitrarily (without having to move or rotate an item). (Remember that the action you choose is applied to the Items Affected choice at the left of the IKB track!)

Now, what if you had a whole lot of frames you wanted to delete at once?

Right-click drag-select an area within the IK Booster Track to select a *range* of frames. You can then choose Delete from the right-click menu that opens when you release the right mouse button.

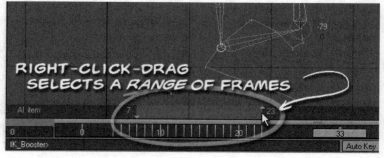

Figure 16-38

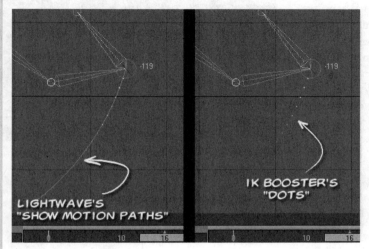

*Figure 16-39*

When you have IK Booster active, if you turn off LightWave's Show Motion Paths, you'll more clearly see IK Booster's "onionskin" dots that represent the selected handle's position on surrounding frames that fade out the farther a frame is from the current one.

## Pose and Motion Saving and Loading

When you have IK Booster applied to a character rigging (even if you are using none of the other IK Booster features), you can save and load poses and motions for *some* or *all* of your rigging!

Clicking on the IKB Menu button on the right side of the IK Booster Track (which, as mentioned earlier, is visible when the Dope Track is inactive) brings up a menu in which you can choose to save and load the motion of your entire rigging.

From the IKB Menu | Motions menu, you can also choose to copy the motion of your entire rigging, storing it to be swapped with the

current motion by choosing Motion Rollback. This is very handy when you want to quickly compare two motions without

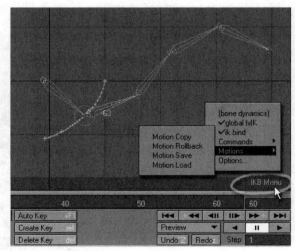

*Figure 16-40*

421

having to bother going through the extra step of saving and loading the different motions.

Right-clicking on the control for any item in an IKB chain also brings up a menu that you can use to save and load *both* motions *and/or* poses for that item and its children in the chain. (Be sure to right-click on the control, not the numbers. Right-clicking on the numbers will open a different set of menus that allow you to lock and/or limit motion on the clicked-upon number's axis.)

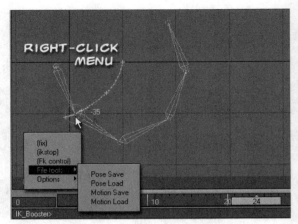

Figure 16-41

### Note

Using this item-based way of saving/loading poses and motions, you can quickly load complex shapes onto, say, your character's hands (clenched fists, martial-arts hand shapes, etc.). Being able to load complex poses onto parts of your characters means you can really take your time to get those complex poses perfect, knowing that you'll only have to create those poses once!

It's a good idea, though, to put the name of the item you had selected when you created that pose in the name of the pose and/or motion file you create. IK Booster will let you load a pose or motion onto a different item in your hierarchy than the one you had selected to save its motion and the motion of its children, which can create some unpredictable results.

## Quaternion Rotations

If you followed the information in the section on rotation order in the first part of this chapter on inverse kinematics and the problems with flipping that can occur because of gimbal lock, you may find it interesting to know that LightWave 8's IK Booster now allows for a new kind of angular mathematics that can help with the problem of gimbal lock: quaternion rotations.

You activate quaternion rotation for an item within an IK Booster chain by selecting Options | Quaternion from its controller's right-click menu.

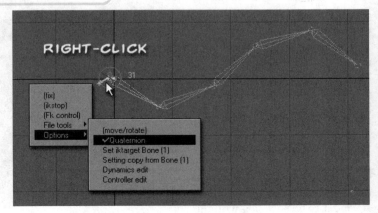

Figure 16-42

To you, the animator, you won't notice much more than a little "Q" appearing inside the controller icon, and that certain problem poses for your rigging *may* not be such a problem anymore. (Quaternion rotation only *helps* in dealing with the issues of gimbal lock; it is not a "magic bullet.")

## Keyframe Move Mode

IK Booster also gives you the ability to quickly move your keyframes about without ever having to leave Layout's main window.

> **Note**
>
> General Options | Show Keys in Slider turns on and off LightWave's representation of keyframes for the current item as light, vertical lines in the background of the frame slider at the bottom of Layout's window.

In Figure 16-43, I'm starting off with keyframes on frames 0, 10, 20, and 30 for all the items in the IKB chain. Clicking on the IKB Track on frame 15 sets the center mark of the Move mode. Dragging in the

IKB Track on the right-hand side of this center mark moves all the keyframes to the right of the center mark (for the currently selected Affected Items choice) by the distance dragged. (The little triangles in the IKB Track to the right of frame 15 show the start and end positions of my drag.)

In Figure 16-43, because Child is the currently selected Affected Items choice (displayed on the left-hand side of the IKB Track), only the selected item and its child item(s) will have their keyframes moved.

When you're done moving keyframes in relation to that particular center mark, simply click on the center mark and it will disappear.

> **Note**
>
> Using IK Booster's Move mode with the parent or child Affected Items choice is a great way to quickly add the "whip-like" action known in character animation as the "successive breaking of the joints" after you have made sure your character hits the key poses you want.

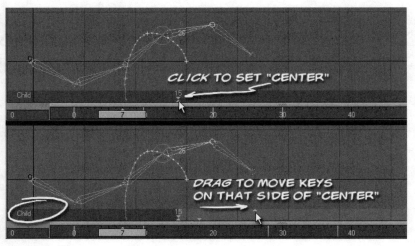

Figure 16-43

# Newbie Sensory Overload

I can imagine that if you're new to IK and/or IK Booster, all the information in this chapter may seem a bit overwhelming. Don't worry. In time, you'll find yourself talking about IK, FK, and IKB as if they were the most natural things on earth. The important thing is not to be overwhelmed by the tools and options available.

You may not at first completely understand *why* things are done a certain way, but you will find that once you've gone through the process, a lot more of it will make sense in retrospect.

And once you start actually *using* a rigging you've made, you'll experience a whole lot of "Ah, now I see why we did that."

So, remember not to worry. None of us came into this world already knowing how to pontificate on the intricacies of inverse kinematics — we *all* had to pick up this information somewhere on our journeys.

Your greatest asset, throughout your entire life, will be your ability to find the solutions you seek yourself.

Every question or problem can be broken down into ever more simple bits that you can more easily master.

If you find yourself feeling stuck, take a step back to where you *do* feel confident about what you know. Seek out the resources that can help you understand the smaller component parts of what you are seeking to learn (books, online resources, and exploring functional examples where these elements are used well).

Knowing you can find the way to get yourself to where you want to be is one of the most powerful realizations you can come to in a lifetime.

# Chapter 17

# Layout 4: Special FX

When people in the industry talk about *production value*, they are referring to whether the work looks like it was done "professionally." Is *each* and *every* part of its process brought up to the highest level appropriate for the story?

"Low budget" does not have to look low budget. Just because you're filmmaking on a shoestring doesn't mean it has to look that way! There are hundreds, if not thousands, of simple, little things you can do to "kiss the details" and make your work read with a high production value.

In this chapter, we go over some of Layout's special effects that can be used to greatly increase the level of professionalism that your work exudes.

> **Note**
>
> Some adjectives used to describe a high production value are: lush, luscious, juicy, deep, rich, polished, slick, and tasty.

## Glow Effect

Glow Effect is something I use in almost every single one of my renders. Most of the time it is handled so subtly you wouldn't know it was there; it's a general soft, "atmospheric" sort of thing that is hard to put one's finger on. Glow Effect is *this* artist's *first* step in making something look "not CG."

Glow Effect isn't something to be restricted to "recreations of reality." Glow Effect cranks up the cool factor on flying logos, web graphics, and all kinds of design-oriented applications. It can even be used to imitate volumetric lighting.

> **Note**
>
> A way of looking at using Glow Effect is like imagining the way light bounces around inside a practical camera's exposure chamber. If there's too much light coming in on a certain spot (like a pinpoint of sunlight on a chrome bumper), that light "bleeds" out, exposing the film around it as well as the actual spot of film where the light really falls.
>
> Lens flares (explained later in this chapter) simulate the way light *scatters* on the *defects* of a lens. (Those nifty "star-thingies" around lights and whatnot were first considered flaws.) Together, lens flares and Glow Effect can increase the level of "realism" in your renders. They have a *multiplicative* effect on one another, so plan on spending some time testing and tweaking to get things right.

Figure 17-1: Using Glow Effect.

The only difference between the two lines of text in Figure 17-1 is that the bottom one uses Glow Effect.

## Glow Effect Basics

1.  Load **Objects\Chapter17\Glow_01.lwo**.

Figure 17-2

2.  A quick **<F9>** render (with the camera's Antialiasing level set to **Enhanced Low** in the Camera Properties window) shows us what we've got to start with. (See Figure 17-3.)

Figure 17-3

3.  Glow Effect is a two-part process. It must be activated both on the Surface Editor | Advanced tab (a percentage that acts as a "multiplier" for the global settings — and need not be restricted to 100% as its maximum) and on the Effects | Processing tab, where **Enable Glow** must be active and the global Intensity and Glow Radius values must be set (see Figure 17-4).

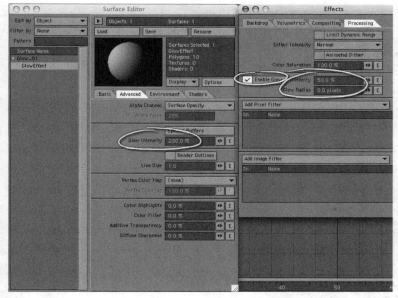

Figure 17-4

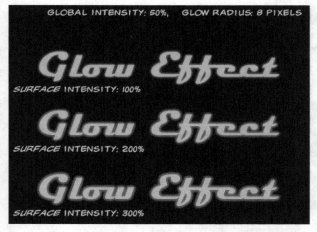

Figure 17-5: As you can see, while Glow Intensity for individual surfaces can be set above 100%, it may not always be a good idea. (The bottom version, with Intensity set at 300%, looks pretty crummy to me.)

## Note

Remember that the Glow Radius value is in *pixels*. This value represents the number of pixels the glow will extend when the Camera | Properties | Resolution Multiplier is set to 100%.

If the Glow Radius is 16 pixels, and you change the camera's Resolution Multiplier to 50%, the Glow Radius will be "scaled" to affect only 8 pixels for that render. (Change the Resolution Multiplier to 400%, and the Glow Radius will affect 64 pixels!) This results in you being able to see the exact effect of the glow when you're rendering at "test" resolutions, without having to go in and change your Glow Radius setting.

However, if you manually change the Width and Height values for your camera's resolution, leaving the Resolution Multiplier at 100% regardless of whatever size image you are rendering, your Glow Radius will only affect the number of pixels you have set in its input field.

427

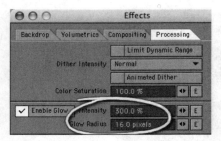

Figure 17-6

Figure 17-7

4. Select **Enable Glow**, set Intensity to **300%**, and set Glow Radius to **16** pixels (for an NTSC-size frame). This is an old trick I picked up a long time ago. I started using it because at first, you *couldn't* set individual surfaces' Intensity above 100%. I still use it because it yields both "tasty" effects and lots of diversity among the glowing surfaces in a single scene.

5. With the global glow settings cranked to the level we've got them in Figure 17-6, we need just a touch of Glow Intensity on the surface to make it start doing its magic. Set Glow Intensity for the object's surface to **10%**. Do an <**F9**> render, and see what you've got!

Figure 17-8: The settings in the previous two figures give us something that looks fairly "luscious" (especially when compared with the rather pallid renders of Figure 17-5).

Figure 17-9: Using this trick of "over-cranking" the global glow settings, you can get a vast amount of diversity among the glowing surfaces in your scene.

# Fake "Volumetric Lights"

LightWave incorporates the ability for lights to appear to illuminate particulate matter in its virtual atmosphere (like morning light streaming in through a misty forest). This effect is called *volumetric lighting*. While this effect can be stunning, I find that I use it only rarely because of the time needed for the volumetrics to calculate. More often than not, I use the old tricks of faking this effect that LightWavers had to resort to before it implemented "real" volumetrics. (Not only does it render much faster, I find that for the way my mind works, I can more quickly get the look I want of wisps of fog catching in the light's beam.)

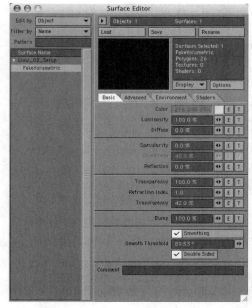

Figure 17-11

1. Load **Scenes\Chapter_17\Glow_ 02_Setup.lws**. I've created a 1 m tall cone-like object to be our "shaft of light" and thrown a bit of animation on it (so it'll swing from right to left over the course of our scene). But everything else is "default" and up to us to put into effect.

2. The first thing we've got to do is change the default surface on that "cone of light" to something that looks a bit less like automotive primer. Change the following settings for the surface:

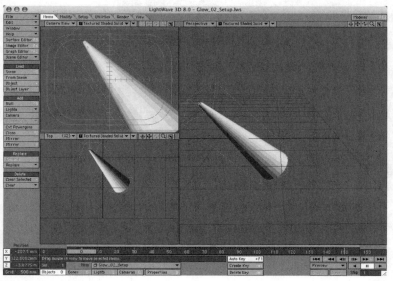

Figure 17-10

- Set Color to **216, 240, 254**.
- Change Luminosity to **100%** (It's a shaft of "light," right? It's supposed to be "perfectly lit" under all lighting circumstances.)
- Set Diffuse to **0%**. (If it's "perfectly lit," it doesn't need to scatter light from its surface.)
- Transparency should be set to **100%**. (Won't this make it impossible to see? Yep. But we're going to do some special "tricks" with its Texture channel, so hold tight.)
- Activate **Set Smoothing** and **Double Sided**.

(Don't worry about setting Translucency to 42 — I'm just doing my habitual homage to *The Hitchhiker's Guide to the Galaxy*. Because our Luminosity is set to 100% and we're using a color that is very close to "pure" white already, any value here won't have much effect at all.)

3. Now, we're going to make our "shaft-o'-light" visible. Open the Texture Editor window for the Transparency channel, and set the Layer Type to **Procedural Texture**. Set the Procedural Type to **Value** (this is a procedural texture that is just a flat, featureless expanse of whatever value we enter for it), and enter **42%** for its Texture Value. Under its Falloff tab, enter **125%** for its Y axis, and set Type to **Spherical**. (This will force the effective value for the surface's transparency to be 42% at the object's origin, that value falling off to the setting we entered in the previous figure at a rate of 125% per meter. So, in just under a meter from its origin, the shaft will be 100% transparent!) Doing a quick <**F9**> shows us what we've got. (Figure 17-12.)

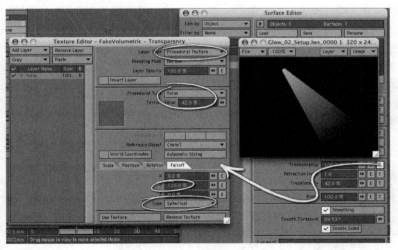

*Figure 17-12*

4. Now, very few light beams (other than a laser) are as "hard-edged" as the render in Figure 17-12. So, let's soften the edge of our cone by adding the **Edge_Transparency** shader under the Shaders tab. Set its Edge Transparency to **Transparent** and its Edge Threshold to **1.0**. (Effective values for this shader range from –1 to 1. While an Edge Transparency of Transparent is good for things like shafts of light, Opaque is handy for creating things like soap bubbles and similar things that are more opaque around their edges.) This time our <**F9**> looks like a faint beam cutting through the mists of night.

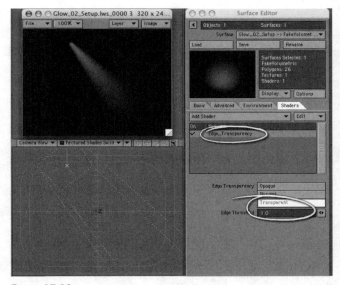

Figure 17-13

5. Now, activating **Glow Effect** with an Intensity of **300%** and a Glow Radius of **16** pixels and then setting the Glow Intensity for the surface to **18%**, we crank up both the *intensity* and *realism* of our shaft of light.

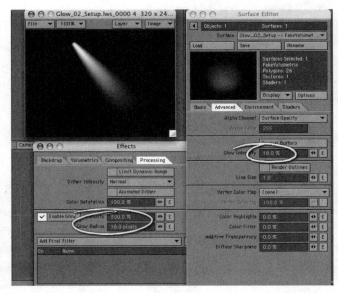

Figure 17-14

**431**

Now, because I pride myself on being an unabashed smart aleck (and can never leave anything well enough alone when there's the possibility of making something *better*), I want us to go back into our Transparency Texture channel and add some "niftyness" that will make it look like our beam is catching little puffs of moisture.

> "A) You can never go too far..." — Ferris Bueller, *Ferris Bueller's Day Off*

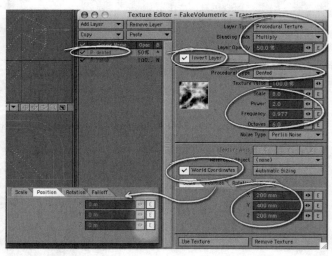

*Figure 17-15*

6. Going back into the Transparency channel's Texture Editor window, select **Add Layer** and set the new layer's Layer Type to **Procedural Texture**.

- Set Blending Mode to **Multiply** (which will *multiply* the values generated with the *layer(s)* below it in the Layer list).

- Set Layer Opacity to **50%**. (It'll have *half* the effect it would were this set to 100%.)

- Check **Invert Layer**. (This will flip-flop the effect of this texture, reversing the lights and darks.)

- Set Procedural Type to **Dented** (my personal favorite "mathematical playground" that at the time of publication produces different results on Macs and PCs; PC users should be aware that their shaft-o'-light won't match the figures in this section).

- Set Scale to **8**, Power to **2**, Frequency to **0.977**, and Octaves to **6**. (I've read the manuals, and I still don't fully understand what effect each of these settings has on the *exact* result of the texture. Mostly, I just fool around until I find something I like, watching the effect on the "render ball" on the main surface window and doing quick renders using **Rendering | Render Selected Objects**.)

- Check **World Coordinates**. (This will "lock" the texture to the "world," which means that when the beam moves, it will appear to pass through smoke that is hanging in the air, *completely independent of the beam*.)

- On the Scale tab, set X and Z to **200 mm** and Y to **400 mm**.

- Now, on the Position tab, click on the little **E** button to open the Graph Editor where we will create an "envelope" that will let this texture *move through space over time*!

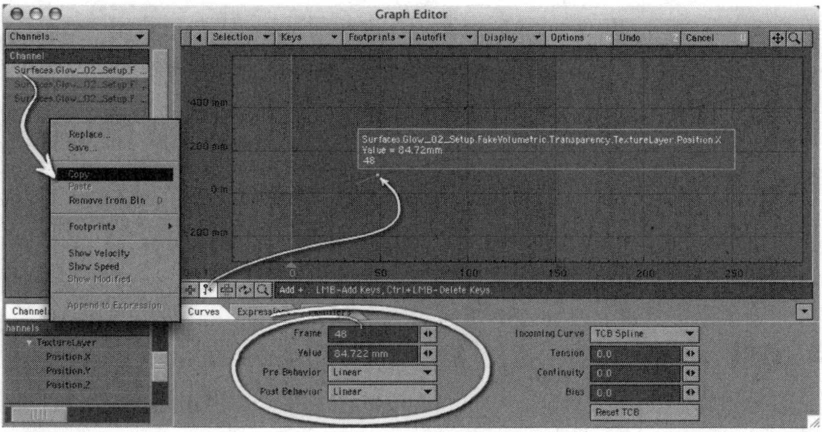

Figure 17-16

7. With one of the Position channels active (it doesn't matter which one, as we'll be copying and pasting it to all the others), activate the **Add Keys** button and click somewhere near frame 50. (My click just happened to be on frame 48; precision isn't really important right now.)

● With the newly created keyframe still selected, enter **48** for Frame and **84.722 mm** for Value. (From frame 0 to frame 48, the texture's position along the X axis will change by +84.722 mm.)

● Pre Behavior and Post Behavior should both be set to **Linear**, so rate of change defined by the keys at frame 0 and frame 48 continues *indefinitely* both *before* and *after* our two keyframes.

● Right-click on the channel you have been working on, and choose **Copy**. Then, right-click on the other two channels, in turn, and choose **Paste** to get the texture moving along *all three axes*.

Figure 17-17: A render of what we've done now shows our shaft of light catching some vaporous clouds. (The scene that has all this work already done for you can be found at Scenes\Chapter_17\ Glow_02_F.lws.)

## Lens Flares

As soon as computer software, both 2D and 3D, began to produce lens flares, the industry saw a flood of flares. After a while, even the lay public could tell which program was used to generate a particular lens flare. Don't get me wrong — lens flares are most definitely cool and can do a lot to increase the production value of a render, but because our audience is more educated, we must be more *subtle* in the application of our tricks.

Lens flares assume their base coloring from the color you have set for the light itself. You activate a flare for an individual

light by checking Lens Flare in its Item Properties window, and you change its settings by clicking on Lens Flare Options to open the window seen in Figure 17-20. You can see lens flares real time in Layout by having OpenGL Lens Flares active under the Display Options, but be aware that if you don't have a "full GL" graphics accelerator, even a single GL lens flare will make graphics updates dreadfully slow. (For Figure 17-19, I've just moved the one light in the scene to X=0, Y=0, Z=0 and activated Lens Flare with an Intensity of 100%.)

*Figure 17-18: This is the standard, out-of-the-box lens flare from LightWave. Most people can spot it a hundred miles away.*

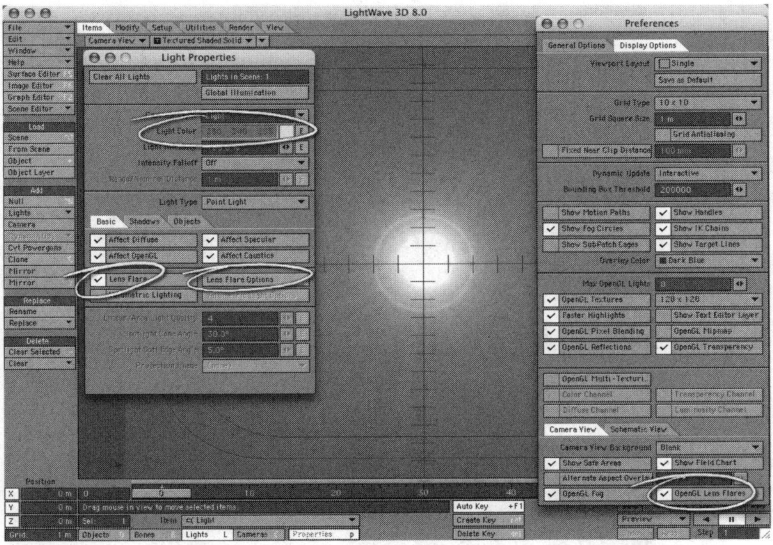

*Figure 17-19*

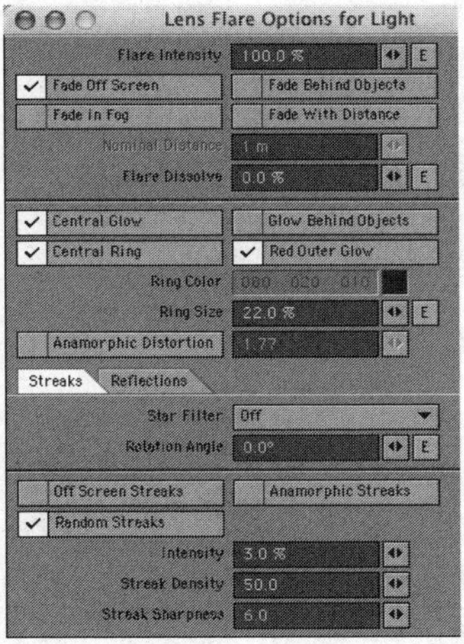

*Figure 17-20: The Lens Flare Options window.*

The Lens Flare Options window is where you set the options that affect the look and feel of your lens flares. (Central Ring and Red Outer Glow are the two default settings that most clearly identify a flare as coming from LightWave.)

- **Flare Intensity** is a measure of how "overpowering" the flare is. (A setting of 450% nearly obliterates everything else on the screen.)

- **Fade Off Screen** will let your flare "ramp up" as it gets closer to being on screen for an added touch of reality.

- **Fade Behind Objects** will reduce your flare's intensity when it goes behind objects.

- **Fade in Fog** will reduce your flare's intensity when it is "submerged" in LightWave's fog effects.

- **Fade With Distance** will let the flare diminish in intensity the farther it gets away from the camera, with the **Nominal Distance** being the distance from the camera where the flare is at the intensity set in the Flare Intensity field.

- **Flare Dissolve** will let your flare become more and more faint without reducing its *size*, as does reducing its intensity.

**435**

- **Central Glow** is the soft glow of the flare, colored by the light's base color.

- **Glow Behind Objects** sets the glow of the flare *behind* any object that comes *between* the light and the camera. Using this setting, you can simulate atmospheric glows at some distance from the camera. (Without this checked, the flare is rendered on top of everything in the scene, *regardless of its relative Z position from the camera.*)

- **Central Ring** and **Red Outer Glow** are the two things that just scream, "Hi! I'm a LightWave lens flare!" They make a ring around the flare and tint the flare with a ruddy hue. (**Ring Color** and **Ring Size** control the hue and size of the Central Ring, respectively.)

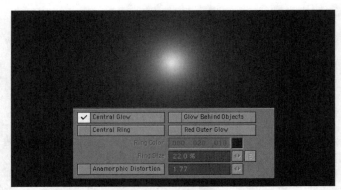

*Figure 17-21: Central Glow.*

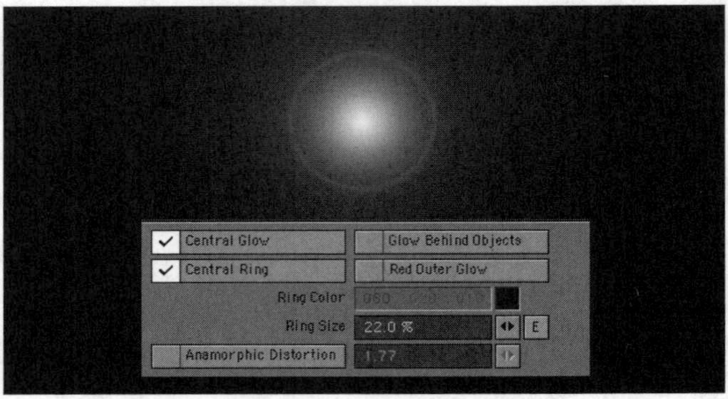

*Figure 17-22: Central Ring.*

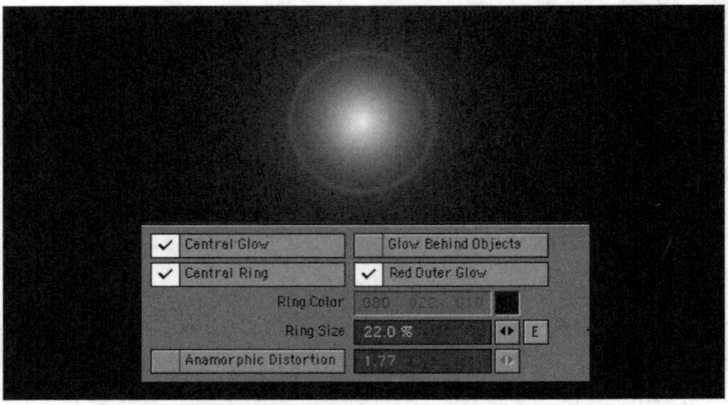

*Figure 17-23: Red Outer Glow.*

• **Anamorphic Distortion** "stretches" the whole flare along the camera's X axis, respecting what happens when lens flares are recorded while shooting on film with an anamorphic lens. (In a nutshell, *anamorphic lenses* "squish" a "wider" field of view onto a "narrower" strip of film. They are often used when filming a movie to be seen in 2.34:1 aspect ratio on 35mm film, which normally records in 1.85:1.)

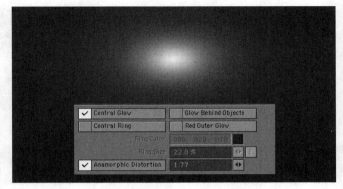

*Figure 17-24: Anamorphic Distortion.*

• **Star Filter** behaves as if you'd screwed a "star filter" onto your camera (for those misty, dreamy high-school prom type photos). Its pop-up menu gives you access to many different starring effects, all controlled by the (envelopable) **Rotation Angle**.

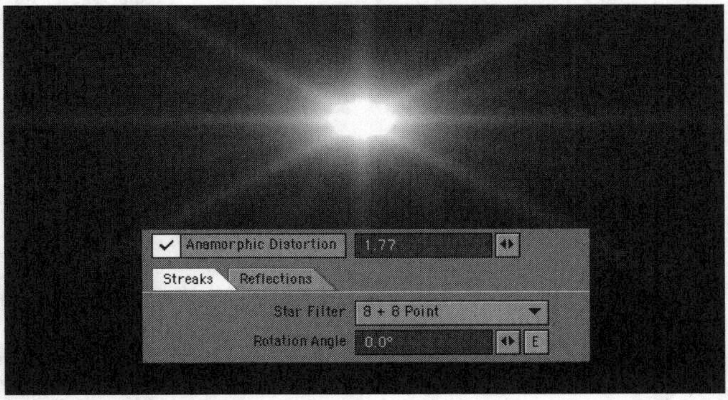

*Figure 17-25: Star Filter.*

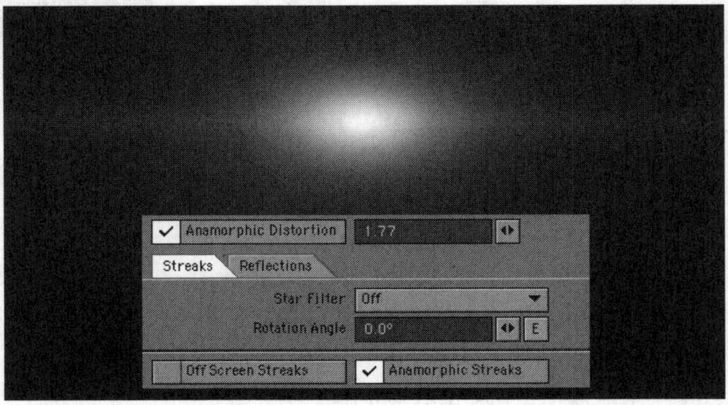

• **Off Screen Streaks** lets the "streaks" that your flare casts be seen, even when your flare is off-screen. (This is, of course, affected by your Fade Off Screen setting.)

• **Anamorphic Streaks** gives you those blue horizontal line streaks you've seen in *Aliens* when the plasma cutter opens Ripley's escape pod and in *The X-Files* when the flashlights shine.

*Figure 17-26: Anamorphic Streaks.*

- **Random Streaks** are the fine, numerous "spiky streaks" that help give the impression of something being painfully bright.

- The **Reflections** tab offers access to a multitude of settings to recreate the sun dogs that appear when light catches within the multiple layers of camera optics. (I'd suggest using this setting sparingly, creating your own custom combinations of elements instead so this effect doesn't look canned.)

*Figure 17-27: Random Streaks.*

Let's go back to the fake volumetric light scene we were working on in the previous section of this chapter, as shown in Figure 17-29.

1. Set the light's Parent to your "shaft of light" object, and move it numerically to X=0, Y=0, Z=0. (I've changed my light from a distant light to a point light, but this doesn't really matter.)

2. Activate **Lens Flare** for the light, and open the Lens Flare Options window. Deactivate Central Ring and Red Outer Glow. Activate **Anamorphic Distortion** and **Anamorphic Streaks**. (Leave everything else as is.)

3. An <F9> gives you something you might see hovering over a rural landscape on *The X-Files*. (See Figure 17-29.)

One of the best ways to use lens flares is to work them into your scene in such a way that the viewer isn't even aware that a lens flare is being used. (Huh?) That's right! When you have a flare that is just a Central Glow with a high Intensity and a fairly high

*Figure 17-28: The Reflections tab.*

Flare Dissolve, the flare serves more to add a bit of "light bloom" to the entire scene, giving the same feel that lights do when "catching" in a faint hint of haze. This faint hinting is indicative of the elusive quality of subtlety that runs through all I try to convey to an up-and-coming artist. Anyone can tell the difference when shown a render "with" and a render "without," but on its own, it doesn't jump out at the viewer because it just looks good.

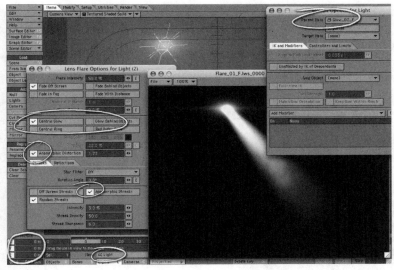

Figure 17-29

Lens flares aren't just for "realistic" works. The addition of *two* lens flares in the *center* of the work in Figure 17-30 makes the version on the right much more intense, *all over*! I had to use *two* flares because I wanted a soft, "all-over" glow and another, much more pinpoint focus for the "consciousness seed" at the center of the work. Flares render very quickly, so don't be afraid to use as many flares as it takes to get the exact look you're trying to create.

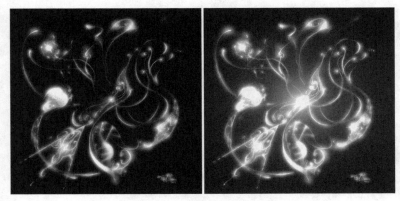

Figure 17-30: The Formation of Consciousness.

# Compositing

LightWave lets you composite CG elements right into live-action plates without having to open up another piece of software. It's quick, it's easy, and it opens up a whole new world of possibilities to a filmmaker. Let's take a look at an example.

## CG Elements onto a "Live-Action Plate"

Figure 17-31: A deserted country road — the perfect place for a trio of alien probe 'droids! (Insert maniacal laughter here.)

1. Load **Scenes\Chapter_17\Compositing_01_Setup.lws** — the layout of the three 'droids — and we're ready to go!

Figure 17-32

## Note

The 'droids use the FI's_PatchyR procedural texture.

**PC crowd:** You'll have to make sure you add the fisptxtrs.p plug-in. (More info on FI's procedural textures can be found in Appendix A.)

**Mac crowd:** Using Surface Baker (see the LW manual for more information on this très cool shader that is currently hard-coded as a part of LightWave — it can't be used over ScreamerNet just yet), I've created a Mac version of the probe 'droid for these next exercises. Be sure to work with the _Mac versions of the 'droid and his scenes.

If you're wondering how to "bake" a procedural bump channel when Surface Baker doesn't have this as one of its options, see the LW manual to get up to speed on the "whos" and "whats" of Surface Baker. You copy the texture layer(s) you're using for the bump channel to replace all layers of your color channel and with 100% Luminosity, 100% Diffuse, 0% Specular, 0% Transparency, and 0% Bump, render a frame with the Surface Baker shader active and set to create an appropriate UV texture map. The image the Surface Baker shader generates can be used as a bump map for machines that don't have access to your procedural shaders!

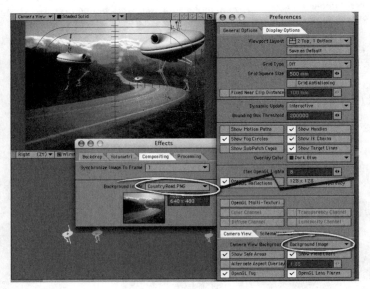

*Figure 17-33*

2. The first step to getting these guys *composited* onto a live-action plate is to load that plate into Effects | Compositing | Background Image. (Either select the plate, if CountryRoad.png is already in the list, or choose **(load image)** and select **Images\Chapter17\CountryRoad.PNG** if it isn't in the list.) You can get a really good feel for how this composite will look by choosing **Background Image** in the Display Options | Camera View Background — your camera viewports will show your objects over your background image.

*Figure 17-34: Doing an <F9> shows us what we've got so far. It's not bad and could probably pass as okay in some lower-end productions. But something is amiss: The lighting on the 'droids is coming from a completely different angle than where the sun obviously is in our plate!*

## Note

One of the first things you learn as a painter is that no matter how many *visible or implied* lights there are in an image, *there is only one primary light source*. Unless you have a darn good reason for breaking this convention, all things in a scene should show the effect of the *primary light source;* all other light sources should be handled with such subtlety that they go almost unnoticed to the untrained observer. (When in doubt about complex lighting, or when you have a limited time to ray-trace, shadows are cast *only* from the primary light source.)

These conventions have worked for hundreds of years. But even so, you still don't have to take it as "law," just as an idea to help make your own work better, *faster!*

3. Let's change our light to an area light so it will cast realistic shadows. In its Motion Options window, set Target Item to **ProbeDroid (1)** (the middle 'droid in our scene), so when we move our light, we don't have to worry about aiming it as well. Move it to where the sun would be *relative to our 'droids,* based on what we're able to surmise

from our live-action plate (I found X=1.63, Y=15.88, Z=−240 mm to work well). Set Light Intensity to **125%**. (I always have a value of over 100% for sunlight; it gives harsher lights and darks — chiaroscuro — and *feels* more like outdoor lighting.) Make sure Shadow Type is set to **Ray Trace**, activate **Trace Shadows** under Rendering Options, and do an <**F9**>.

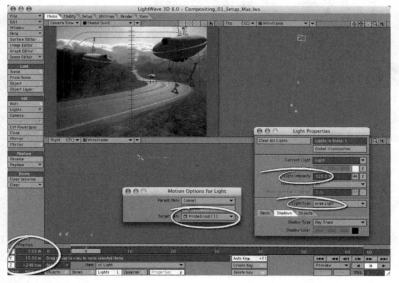

*Figure 17-35*

Figure 17-36: Hmm... Well, the light is coming from the correct direction, but the scene is dark. We could spend a lot of time "hanging" other lights to mimic the light reflecting off the ground, pavement, sky, and all that, or we could use our live-action plate to light our scene!

Figure 17-38: Hey! Not bad! Not bad at all! As a matter of fact, pretty darn passable! But something I'd like to see is to have the lens flare effect in the live-action plate carry onto our 'droids just a touch.

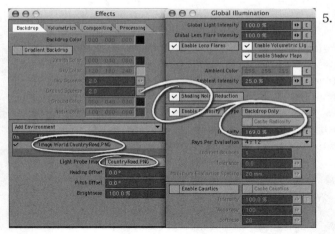

Figure 17-37

4.  Under **Effects | Backdrop**, choose **Image World** from the Add Environment pop-up menu, and then choose our backdrop image, **Country-Road.PNG**, in the Light Probe Image box. Then, on the Global Illumination panel, select **Enable Radiosity**, select **Backdrop Only** as the radiosity type, and activate **Shading Noise Reduction**. Change Intensity to **169%**, and do an <F9> to see what we've got.

5.  As shown in Figure 17-39, add a point light, naming it **Flare**. Set its Position to X=**890 mm**, Y=**7.269 m**, Z=**–69 mm**. Set Light Intensity to **0%**, and activate **Lens Flare**. Set Flare Intensity to **200%**, deactivate **Fade Off Screen**, set Flare Dissolve to **69%**, and set it so that only **Central Glow** is active. Set Star Filter to **4 Point** and the star filter's Rotation Angle to **45°**. (You can do an <F9> if you like; I've already tested it and know the effect is what I'm looking for, but it is so *subtle* as to not really merit a figure of its own.)

What's the big thing that stands out as being "wrong" when you look at Figure 17-38? *The 'droids aren't casting any shadows*! Compositing shadows onto things seen in photographic plates is a bit of a multi-part process with the tools that are a part of LightWave's basic toolset. (Other plug-ins exist that streamline shadow

**443**

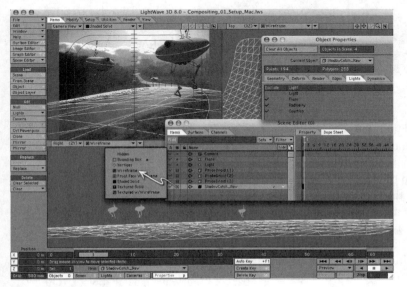

Figure 17-39

compositing — most notably Worley Labs' G2, which does many other things for your rendering as well, including letting you see changes to your render in real time.)

But here, we're going to show you how to composite shadows using the basics of LightWave *right out of the box*, without

having to own a separate compositing program or buy additional software or anything!

First, we've got to have something that "catches" the shadows cast by the 'droids. This "shadow-catcher" is just a simple bit of geometry that *mimics* the general shape

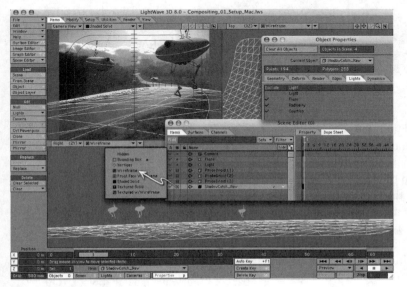

Figure 17-40

and position of the things seen in your plate. (You'd be surprised at how general this "shadow-catcher" can be and still look good.)

6. Load in **Objects\Chapter17\Shadow-Catch_Raw.lwo**. This object has been presized and positioned to simulate the curvature of the road where the 'droids may cast their shadows. Under its **Object Properties | Lights** tab, check to exclude **Radiosity, Caustics**, and the light named **Flare** from being calculated for that object; it'll save lots of time when rendering. (The only light that needs to interact with our shadow-catcher is our primary light: Light. You may find it easier to match your shadow-catching objects to their respective landmarks on the plate when they're viewed as wireframes and not as opaque, solid objects. This can be set through the Scene Editor.)

Figure 17-41

When you first load ShadowCatch_Raw.lwo, it has a *default* surface on it, with its Transparency bumped up to 80%, so it will receive shadows *and* still show the background image through it. This lets me fine-tune the positioning of both the shadow-catcher and the objects that are casting the shadows. When everything is as it should be (and everything should be fine in our scene with our prepositioned objects), move on to the next step where we'll get everything ready for a final render.

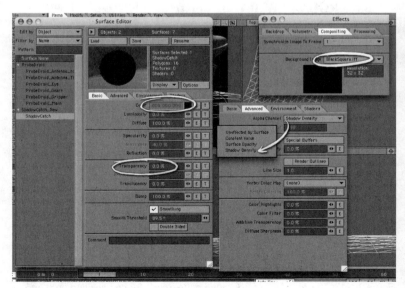

Figure 17-42

7. As shown in Figure 17-42, set the ShadowCatch surface Color to **0, 0, 0** (black) and its Transparency to **0%**. On the Advanced tab, set the Alpha Channel to **Shadow Density** (which is what will let us composite the black of the object's surface color onto our plate). As final preparation for generating an image that can be composited onto the plate, we need a completely *black* background. ("Premultiplying" our *foreground image* with black helps the computer deal with the rather touchy process of seamlessly blending the edges of our foreground image into that of our background.) Replace your **Effects | Compositing | Background Image** with **Images\BlackSquare.iff**.

8. Figure 17-43 shows our completed foreground plate, ready for compositing onto our background plate. To work with a single frame, as we are here, once you have hit **<F9>**, under the Render Display's File menu, choose **Save RGBA | LW_PNG32 (.png)**. Portable Network Graphics files are the most compact file type that holds

both the image channel (24 bits) and its alpha channel (another 8 bits), making a total of 32 bits per channel in a *single file*. If you wanted to save a *series of frames*, perhaps if you were doing this for a movie, you would set Save RGB to a 32-bit file format under Rendering Options (and possibly even save out the alpha separately, just in case your compositing application needs the alpha as a separate file).

Figure 17-44: The alpha channel for our plate.

Looking at Figure 17-43, you may be wondering where the shadows are. They're there, but they're 0, 0, 0 (black), the same

Figure 17-43: The completed foreground plate, ready for compositing onto our background plate.

color as our background image. When we take a look at our alpha channel, which is what is used to "cut out" our foreground elements, we see that the shadows are there — but they're *white*! (See Figure 17-44.) In a LightWave alpha channel, what is *white* is *opaque* and what is *black* is *transparent* (some programs have this reversed).

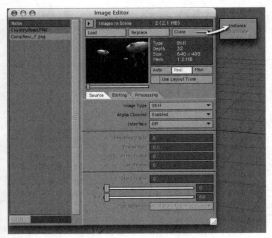

*Figure 17-45*

So, the white shadows on the alpha channel will make the black of the foreground plate's image channel opaque where the shadows are!

9. Now, to piece the background and foreground together, save your scene, and then clear your scene (or start another process of LightWave), so we can have a completely "virgin" space in which to work our "magic." In that empty scene's Image Editor, load **Images\ Chapter17\CountryRoad.PNG**. Also, load the *render* of the foreground elements that you saved in Figure 17-43 (you can use mine, if you wish: **Renders\Chapter17\CompRaw_F.png**). With your foreground "plate" selected, choose **Clone | Instance** to create a "referential copy" of the image. (See Figure 17-45.)

10. Then, with the *instance* selected, choose **Alpha Only** for Alpha Channel. (This "splits" the 32-bit image into one

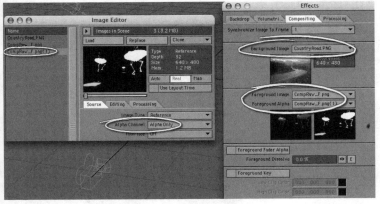

*Figure 17-46*

image that has the colors of the foreground elements and another image that has their alpha "mask.") Then, under **Effects | Compositing**, choose **CountryRoad.PNG** for Background Image, choose your (original) foreground image for Foreground Image, and choose your instanced image that has been set to Alpha Only for Foreground Alpha.

*Figure 17-47: It takes but a moment to render the pieces together. When you do, you'll see the probe 'droids hovering over and casting shadows onto a deserted country road, a freak incident that a hapless traveler managed to catch on film!*

## Note

It's times like this, when you're compositing your render onto something shot on film, that you'll want to render your foreground elements with the camera's "filmic" soft filter. You may also want to add some "film grain" to the foreground elements using either the Wave Filter or Virtual Darkroom image filters (found under Effects | Processing | Add Image Filter).

Virtual Darkroom is an amazing piece of software. It does much more than add film grain. It actually *simulates* the ways that certain films, processing techniques, and photographic papers would record the image that LightWave renders. I've found that because Virtual Darkroom offers such a plethora of presets, it's best to use this filter on a prerendered series of frames (saved using an image format like Flexible Format, Radiance, SGI 64-bit RGBA, SGI 48-bit GRB, or Cineon formats that support LightWave's ability to create images in IEEE floating-point accuracy, higher-than-film-color-depth quality, rather than in 24-bits-per-channel, television-color-depth images).

Virtual Darkroom can even be used (to a degree) to "color grade" your footage, giving it the unearthly feeling of *Minority Report* or the look of footage shot in rural America in the '70s (the Kodak Gold 100 preset gives this look quite nicely). It even has settings for black-and-white film, letting you make your work look like it was unearthed from some esoteric, archive film vault.

*Figure 17-48: Summer Vacation (undisclosed location), 1953.*

# Basic Explosions

What do you do if you want to make things go "boom"? There are just as many ways of doing this as there are ways of doing anything else in 3D. The "trick" of mapping an image sequence of an explosion onto a polygon that sits between the object that goes "boom" and the camera is ancient (in computer terms at least). But, ancient though it may be, it still works beautifully and is used today in productions big and small.

The first thing we need when compositing an explosion this way is an image sequence of an explosion. The very best explosions are the ones that are actually *filmed* with the camera going faster than its usual 24 FPS to give the impression that what you've got is a gigantic fireball, not a smallish "pop."

### Seriously Important Note

Filming (or "taping" — see the following note) explosions requires a *lot* of experience, expertise, and training! No matter how much of a "fire nut" you may fancy yourself, *don't shoot your own explosions until you can get someone who honestly knows what they're doing to train you properly!*

### Note

*Filming* refers to when you're shooting on *film; taping* refers to when you're shooting on *videotape*. As nitpicky as this may seem, using these terms correctly shows other industry folks that you know what you're talking about. Besides, it's always best to *mean* what you *say*, and to *say* what you *mean*, right?

There are videotapes and CDs available containing image sequences of explosions, of which Artbeats and Pyromania are two of the more popular sources. Alternatively, Wondertouch's Particle Illusion provides a real-time WYSIWYG particle system with dozens of great-looking preset explosions. But remember, as with lens flares, *popular* and/or *easy* often means that your viewers will be able to identify the umpteen different places they've seen that particular explosion. (A solution to this is to use several explosion polys in front of one another to make something that looks slightly different from the stock footage.)

*Figure 17-49*

However, with LightWave, you can make a simple explosion in a matter of minutes. (You don't believe me? Just take a peek through the first bit of the next chapter — the explosion we'll be using is the result of the HyperVoxel explosion exercise. It's not the best explosion in the world, but for something that can be done, start to finish, in about ten minutes, it's decent enough.)

The next thing we need to composite an explosion is a scene in which to put our "blazing blossom." I've taken the liberty of putting our little probe 'droid adrift in space, with just enough resources to trigger its self-destruct mechanism. (Hey, filmmaking is a dirty job; get used to it.)

1. Load **Scenes\Chapter_17\Compositing_02_Setup.lws**, and you'll see something like what is shown in Figure 17-50.

2. Next, load **Objects\Chapter17\ExplosionPoly_Raw.lwo**. Open the object's Object Properties window, and deactivate **Self Shadow**, **Cast Shadow**, and **Receive Shadow** (it's a rare thing for a ball of fire to either cast or receive shadows).

3. Then, using the Scene Editor, set the explosion *poly* to be viewed as a **Wireframe** or **Bounding Box**. This

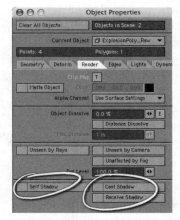

Figure 17-51

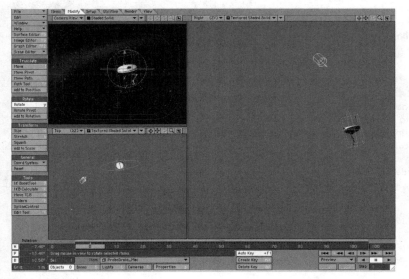

Figure 17-50

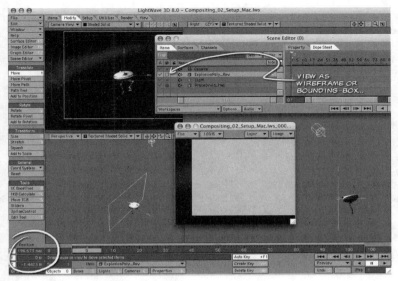

*Figure 17-52*

will help you considerably when you're positioning and scaling it, centering it directly in front of the derelict 'droid. An <F9> reveals that I've left all the wonderful work of applying the explosion for you. (Hey! How else are you gonna learn?)

4. Next, enter the Image Editor, and load the first image in the **Images\HV_Explosion** sequence. Then, set Image

Type to **Sequence**. (Most explosion sequences you'll buy will come with an alpha channel so you can "cut" the explosion onto a transparent poly. I'm not a big fan of this because it leaves the explosion looking flat. So, set Alpha Channel to **Disabled**.) Instead of the explosion sequence starting right at frame 0, I want the audience to have some time to register what's going on

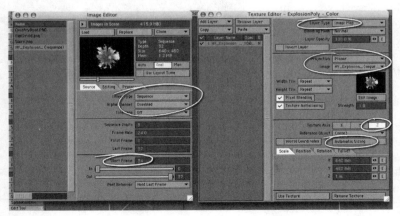

*Figure 17-53*

in the scene, so set Start Frame to **34**. (This just pushes the whole thing ahead to start at frame 34. Don't mess with the In or Out points; they will "trim" (shorten) the footage.)

> **Note**
>
> In the Image Editor, you can use the slider directly below the image window to scrub through the frames of an image sequence. Or you can check Use Layout Time to link the image displayed in the window to your scene's current frame.

5. In the Surface Editor for the explosion poly, enter the Texture Editor for its Color channel. For the Layer Type, choose **Image Map**. Set Projection to **Planar**, Image to the **HV_Explosion_(sequence)** we just loaded, and Texture Axis to **Z**. Click on the **Automatic Sizing** button to have LightWave calculate the correct scale and position for the image to perfectly fill the poly. Close the Texture Editor window.

6. In the Surface Editor's Advanced tab, set the Additive Transparency for the surface to **100%**. This means that it will *add* the value of whatever its surface is to whatever is *behind* it. If the surface is black, then 0, 0, 0 gets added to the pixels behind it (meaning there is no change). If the surface is white at a certain point, then 255, 255, 255 gets added to the pixels behind it (and thinking in terms of 255, 255, 255 being the highest values a pixel can have, white is the highest value a pixel can have; in short, it's like having a layer set to Screen in Photoshop). The end result

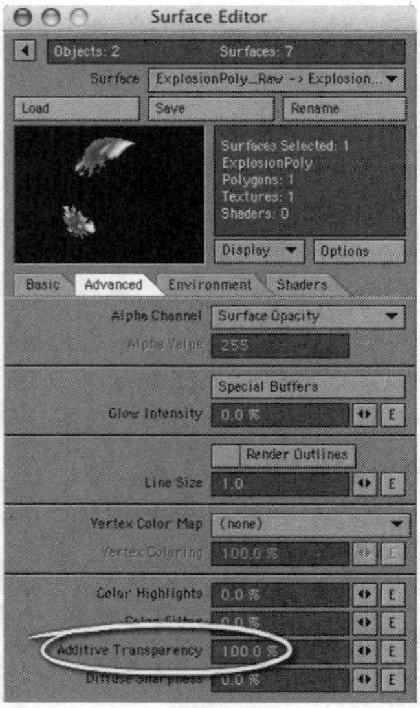

*Figure 17-54*

of this is that the black background of the explosion will be completely transparent, and the lighter the explosion gets, the more opaque it'll be.

*Figure 17-55: Doing a quick <F9> (around frame 50) shows something that doesn't look half-bad. But an explosion is light, not just color. Let's add a lens flare to simulate a lot of light flooding our camera's exposure chamber and to give us something to hide our removal of the 'droid.*

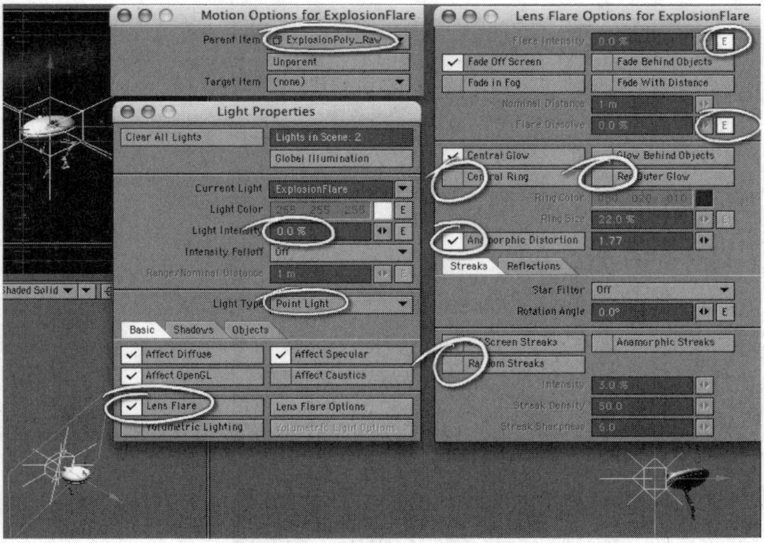

Figure 17-56

7. Add a point light named **Explosion-Flare**, and set its Parent Item to **ExplosionPoly_Raw**. Then, set its Light Intensity to **0%**. Activate **Lens Flare**, and enter the Lens Flare Options window. Deactivate **Central Ring**, **Red Outer Glow**, and **Random Streaks**. Activate **Anamorphic Distortion**, and then click on the **E** button for Flare Intensity so we can tell this flare to "ramp up" with our explosion.

8. For the Flare Intensity envelope, we'll need to have a total of four keyframes. Set the values and frames for the keys as shown in the upper half of Figure 17-57. You'll want to select the *last two*

keys, set their Incoming Curve to **Bezier Spline**, and play with their handles a bit to get the smooth ramps you're seeing with the curve in the figure. When you're done setting the envelope for Flare Intensity, close the Graph Editor.

9. Next, click on the **E** button next to Flare Dissolve to edit its graph. The Flare Dissolve envelope needs only two keyframes. Set their values and times as shown in the lower half of Figure 17-57. (The default TCB Incoming Curve settings are fine for these two keys.)

**453**

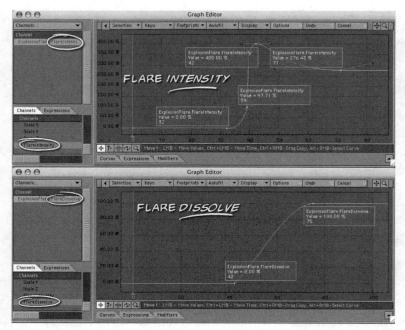

Figure 17-57

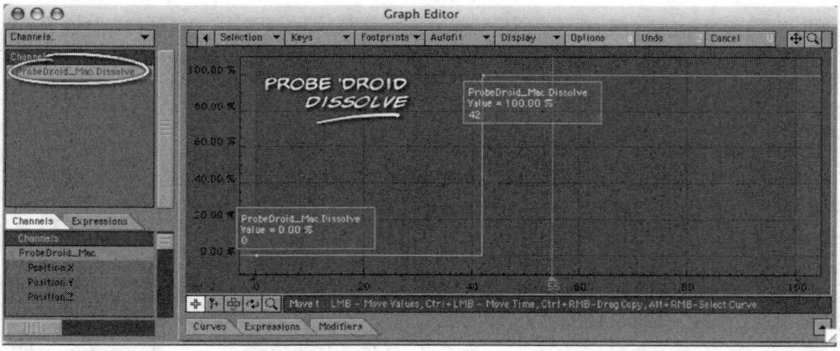

Figure 17-58

10. Now, under the cover of the explosion flare's "blinding radiance," we're going to make our 'droid disappear. (If you wanted to be really "filmic," you would dissolve in charred, short-circuiting debris the *moment* the 'droid dissolves out, but for the sake of brevity, we'll just let the tutorial suffice with the 'droid simply vanishing.) Under **Object Properties | Render | Object**

**Dissolve**, click on the **E** button, and enter the Dissolve Envelope for the ProbeDroid. It only needs two keys, with values and times as shown in Figure 17-58. With the key at frame 42's Incoming Curve set to **Stepped**, the 'droid remains visible (0% dissolved) until that frame, whereupon it "bipps" out of existence.

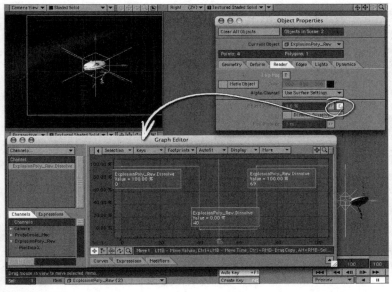

*Figure 17-59*

11. Lastly, so we don't slow down our render by asking LightWave to draw our explosion poly while it is transparent before the sequence *starts* (and after the sequence *ends* and its image is all black once again), set this stepped envelope for the Object Dissolve for your explosion poly.

12. Before we render a movie of our little 'droid going "boom," press <**Return**> with your frame slider on frame 0 to create a keyframe for him on all position, rotation, and scaling axes, but enter **42** for the Create Key At option, so the keyframe is created at frame 42 instead of at 0.

*Figure 17-60*

**455**

Figure 17-61

13. Now, with your frame slider still on frame 0 (and Auto Key Create active), move and rotate the 'droid so between frames 0 and 42 he'll drift just a bit (keeping him "alive" until he, uh... "dies"). Move and rotate the 'droid, scrubbing the frame slider to see if what you've got is appealing. If not, go back to frame 0, and tweak. Repeat if necessary.

When you're done fiddling with the 'droid's animation, render your scene to a movie, and see how it looks. My version can be found at **Renders\Chapter17\ExplosionComp.mov**. (I added a couple of arms spinning off after the explosion just as an idea of where to start when adding debris.)

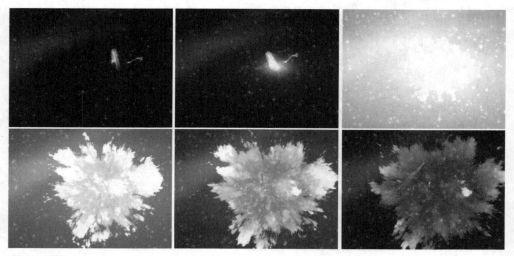

Figure 17-62

**Note**

A strange phenomena about things in space blowing up is that no matter where you place the camera, at least one large piece of debris seems to just narrowly miss it. (The Star Furies on *Babylon 5* did the same thing.) I don't know why — maybe it's a design flaw or something.

If you'd like to see my scene to explore my quick answer to the question of making a 'droid go "boom," load **Scenes\Chapter_17\Compositing_02_F.lws**. (I also added a touch of "camera shake" at the spike of the explosion using Bob Hood's Jolt! motion plug-in. It's a simple, effective plug-in similar to Colin Cohen's Vibrate plug-in that adds temporal random motion to an item in your scene. It's perfect for adding realism to scenes where large objects move close to the camera, such as asteroids or dinosaurs or, in this case, explosions.

**Note**

Now, generally I like to refrain from having you "parrot" my work as I asked you to do when copying the timing and values that made the flare bloom in relationship to the explosion beginning its animation at frame 34. Deciding what happens when is a matter of taste that develops over time as you begin to learn animation. As I've mentioned before, this isn't a book on *animation*; it's a book on the *basic essentials* of driving LightWave. (It's just what I consider to be the "basic essentials" needed for you to get up and start making your dreams may be a bit less "basic" than what someone else might have in mind.)

But still, I don't want to leave you scratching your head as to why I chose the timing relationship that I did between the flare and the explosion. So in brief: I'm a big fan of animé (Asian animation). And I love the way animé explosions build just a bit before going off the charts. So, the flare spends two frames building enough for the viewer to register it and

extrapolate its assumed growth. (The flare is like the "energy" of the explosion building.) Then I just ramp the snot out of the flare so it practically obliterates everything on the screen. It's at this point that the explosion poly is dissolved in, so as the flare begins to recede, there's the explosion, and everything "makes sense" from that point on.

(It takes a *minimum* of two frames at 24 FPS for a viewer to register something. Something that is on screen for three frames is seen by *most* viewers.)

What this is doing is playing with modified timings (which is covered in some depth in *LightWave 3D 8 Character Animation*). The effect the viewer feels from watching an explosion handled this way has a lot more punch than an explosion that just ramps up in a linear fashion, with the explosion itself visible right from the start. (Go ahead and shift the keys for the flare back so they match up with the dissolving in of the explosion poly, and you'll see what I mean.)

. . .

So you've picked up some techniques to make your work look polished, slick, and professional — just like the pros use. (Heck, these techniques *are* what we use!) I imagine you're pretty darn excited, thinking of all the doors these techniques can open up for you. (I know I'd be!) Honestly, I think you're absolutely right to be excited! You're now standing on a knowledge base where you can see that all you'd hoped to accomplish with LightWave is indeed within your range of ability. The really awesomely cool thing about this is knowing just how much more is still out there, *just waiting to be discovered by you* — and shared with others!

The true understanding of knowledge is to know just how much is out there for you to know. That's the really friggin' exciting thing about this whole 3D gig! "Learning to learn" means that everything out there that you *don't* know is an adventure just waiting to be explored! That's exciting as heck! You're *never* going to know all there is to know about LightWave (not anymore — it's just too big). There will always be new things to explore and learn and help you create visions of things you've always wanted to see and no longer will wait for someone else to create for you!

# Chapter 18

# Simulations 1: HyperVoxels and Particles

Working with simulations is a lot like working with watercolors. The best-looking work comes from careful, exacting planning and then letting yourself be pleasantly surprised by what the media does "all by itself." Sure, if you really fixate on things you can get the mathematics that *shape* the simulations to be exactly what you had in mind, but it doesn't mean that it's going to be as good as it can be. What I've found is that the stuff that really leaps off the screen (or page) is the stuff I've evaluated as to whether or not it is *good*, not whether it is what *I* had preconceptualized.

It is the *unknown*, the *random factor*, that makes things *really interesting*! The same is true with *life* and *art* as well as *3D*.

> **Note**
>
> Some of the best traditional matte and background painters in the industry will often wad up plastic wrap, dip it in paint, and dab it over an area of their painting. While it's drying, they'll sit back and figure out how they can work with the "randomness" generated by the crinkles of the plastic wrap. The result is something that feels as richly random as something that has been shaped by "real life."

## HyperVoxels

What the heck is a *voxel*? Why, it's a pixel with *volume*. *HyperVoxels* are tools for rendering gases, fluids, or solids based on *volumetrics* rather than on building things out of polygons. What in the world are *volumetrics*? In plain English, it's the math/science/study of how stuff moves within and fills a certain space (aka volume).

These little doodads known as HyperVoxels are pretty darn *powerful* and *versatile*. We're just going to hit the high points, but those high points are enough to keep you going for some time. The first thing we're going to do is make the explosion you used in the previous chapter.

## HyperVoxel Explosion

As nifty as this 10-minute explosion might seem at first, from an *industry* standpoint, it is no great shakes. It is a *starting point* for creating explosions (and it is only *one* approach — there are many others). Using what you'll learn about the other functionalities of HyperVoxels (particles and the like), put everything together and create some explosions that are the equal of what you see on your favorite games, TV shows, and films.

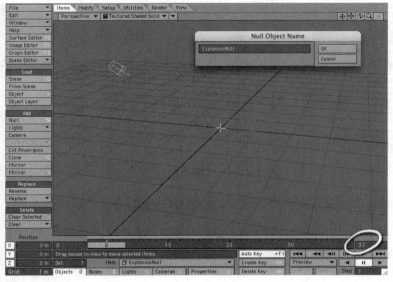

Figure 18-1

1. Start with a blank scene in Layout. Set End Frame to **37**. Then select **Items | Add | Null**, and name the null **ExplosionNull**.

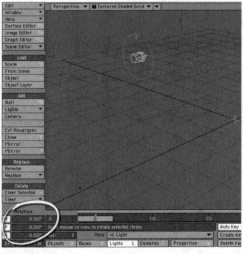

Figure 18-2

2. Next, set the light's rotation to **H=0, P=0, B=0**. This will give us flat, even lighting on our explosion, letting us manually "sculpt" its shading. (The default light in a scene is a *distant light*. Its position doesn't matter, only its *rotation*; all the rays are parallel to each other, like a light a very long distance away. Having it oriented the same direction as the camera means that we will have flat lighting on our explosion.)

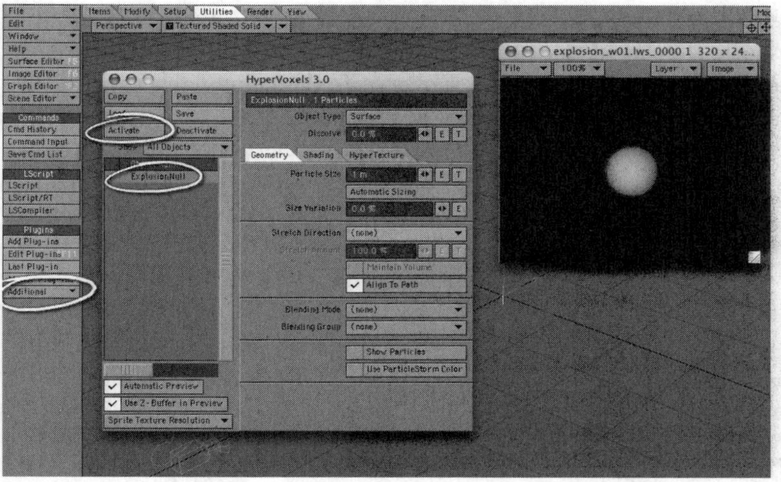

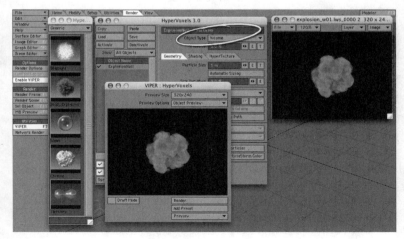

Figure 18-3

3. On the Utilities tab, click on **Additional | HyperVoxels** to open the HyperVoxels interface. Select **ExplosionNull** and click on **Activate** to make HyperVoxels active for that object. (A check mark will appear next to an *active* HyperVoxel object in the list, as seen in Figure 18-3.) In an <F9>, we see that our null object now shows up as a sphere.

Note

The HyperVoxels interface is also accessible through the Effects window, which can be found under the Window | Volumetrics and Fog Options pop-up menu, or by pressing <Ctrl> + <F6>.

4. HyperVoxels can be calculated as a solid *surface* (as in Figure 18-3), as a *volume* (the "gaseous cloud" in Figure 18-4), or as a *sprite* (a "slice" of that

Figure 18-4

cloud). We'll examine each of these in turn. For our explosion, we need to have our voxel interpreted as a gaseous cloud. So, set the Object Type for ExplosionNull to **Volume**. An <F9> shows that we've "instantly" changed that sphere in Figure 18-3 into a lumpy cloud.

> **Note**
>
> The VIPER window is a great tool to have open when you're working with Hyper-Voxels. Any change you make is reflected in the VIPER window the moment you accept a change. (With HyperVoxels, VIPER doesn't require you to do a preliminary <F9> to set up its buffers.)
>
> There are many helpful starting points in the presets for HyperVoxels. Let these serve to stir your imagination and show you ways of handling HVs you may not have thought of before.

*Figure 18-5*

5. Set the Particle Size for ExplosionNull to **2 m**.

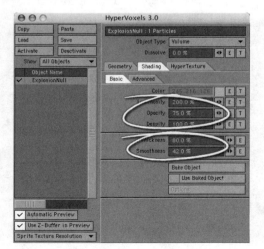

*Figure 18-6*

6. In the **Shading | Basic** tab, set your voxel's Color to **245, 216, 126** (we overwrite this color with a texture gradient in Step 7, so *technically*, setting the color here is optional). Set its Luminosity (how well it catches light) to **200%**, its Opacity (how well you can "see *into* and/or *through* it") to **75%**, its Density (how much "stuff" exists within its volume) to **100%**, its Thickness (a refinement of "how much stuff" exists within its volume) to **80%**, and its Smoothness (how "crinkly" the details within it are) to **42%**.

> **Note**
>
> A really *groovy* thing NewTek implemented in LW 7.5 is the ability to "bake" your volumetric "cloud(s)." This means that LightWave takes all the time it needs to figure out how the cloud looks in its entirety only once during "baking," not on every single frame! The result of this is a "frozen cloud" that renders in a mere fraction of the time it would take for LightWave to figure out all its details normally. When you use a baked volumetric, you can see it, in real time, in your Layout viewports. (Because we've got work to do that doesn't involve baking, turn to your LW manuals when you want to find out how to bake your HyperVoxel volumes.)

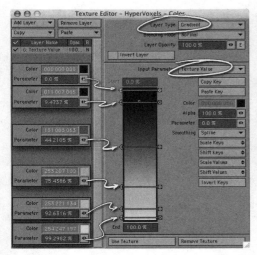

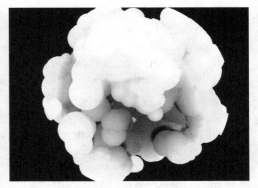

Figure 18-8: An F9 shows us something pretty weird, like the way a lava lamp looks when the wax inside it just starts to get going. It's neat but not very explosion-like.

Figure 18-7

7. Now, enter the Texture Editor for the voxel's Color channel, and set the Layer Type to **Gradient**. Set the Input Parameter to **Texture Value**. (The Texture Value is a lot like the Bump Value for the surface gradients that we explored back in Chapter 4.) Then, using Figure 18-7 as a guide, set a total of six keys with the color and parameters shown. (All Alpha values are **100%**.) The *darker* colors, starting at 0%, will be applied where the volume is closest to its origin. The other colors are applied as parts of the volume move farther and farther away from its "core" to where its texture is at 100% of its effect.

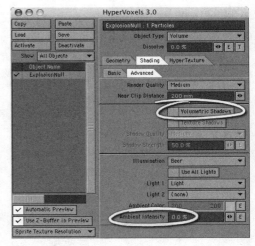

Figure 18-9

8. By the way, if you did the <F9> for Figure 18-8, did you notice that it took an awfully long time to render? That's because LightWave is actually calculating the *paths* of the rays, "marching" them *through* the area defined by the volume. (So, ray tracing *through* a volume is thought of as *ray marching*.) This is where volumetrics can really bog down a scene. We don't really *need* to have the light's shadows define the areas of lights and darks for our

volume, as we've already defined that with the texture we assigned to the Color channel in Figure 18-7. So, deactivate **Volumetric Shadows**, and set Ambient Intensity to **0%**.

Now, let's make our "blob" look like an explosion by assigning a *mathematical set* that will define the "stuff" inside the volume in a manner that will give us the look of what we've all come to think of as an explosion. (Just think how *cool* math class would be if they let you create formulae that actually did stuff like this.) We can't enter formulae ourselves, but we have access to the groovy "mathematica" that someone else thought of.

9.  On the HyperTexture tab, assign **FBM** as the Texture. Set Frequencies to **6**, Contrast to **–50%**, and Small Power to **0.5**. Texture Amplitude should be **33%**, Texture Effect should be **Billowing**, and Effect Speed should be **25%**. (Texture Effect tells LightWave how to apply the texture, and the Effect Speed of 25% gives us a nice, slow "roll" common to large explosions.)

Figure 18-11: Just making the changes to the HyperTexture transforms our "lava lamp" into something that looks for all the world to be a single frame from an explosion sequence. Pretty cool, huh?

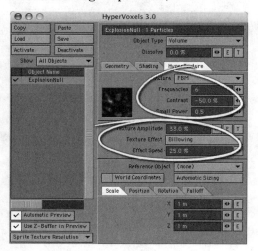

Figure 18-10

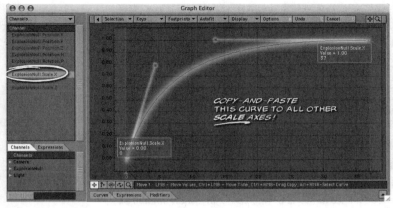

*Figure 18-12*

10. Now we've got to make this thing expand like compressed gas and plasma just "aching" to escape. (Otherwise, what we have in Figure 18-11 would just sit there and "roil" pleasantly, which is neat but not very explosion-like.) So, enter the Motion Graph Editor for your ExplosionNull object, and on its ScaleX channel, set two Bezier keys, as shown in Figure 18-12. Adjust their handles so the curve "ramps up" quickly from frame 0 and then slowly "settles" into frame 37. When you've got this curve looking good, right-click on its name in the list on the left, and copy and paste it onto ScaleY and ScaleZ (so the null will expand exactly the same on *all three axes*).

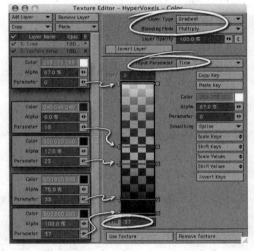

*Figure 18-13*

11. Now, we're going to apply another layer to the voxel's Color channel that will make the explosion start off lighter and fade to black at its end. Enter the Texture Editor for the voxel's Color channel, and select **Add Layer | Gradient**. Set its Blending Mode to **Multiply** and its Input Parameter to **Time**. Since our scene ends at frame 37, set the End of our gradient to **37**. Then, referencing Figure 18-13, assign a total of five keys with the Color, Alpha, and Parameter settings as

> **Note**
>
> In the creation of your own explosions, remember that *not all explosions are symmetrical or even*. If a part of the thing that explodes stays intact while other parts give way, it'll create channels that will *focus* the expanding plasma and gases. So there will be times that you *won't* want all three axes of your ExplosionNulls to be exact copies of each other.

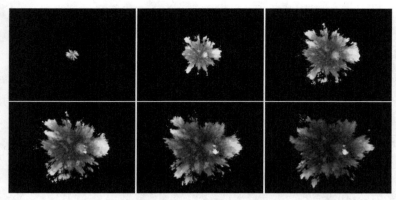

Fig 18-14: Render a frame sequence or movie of your scene. In a short amount of time, you've created from scratch a very respectable-looking explosion.

indicated. (As our voxel progresses through time, the settings of these keys will be multiplied with the coloring defined on the layer below it.) If you'd like to load my scene, it is **Scenes\Chapter_18\HyperVoxel-Explosion_F.lws**.

## HyperVoxel "Surfaces"

HyperVoxels can also use their mathematics to generate a "skin" with the possibility of holding much more displacement detail than we could model, even with subpatches. Thus, whereas a bump map on a "regular" surface would never affect the object's silhouette and a displacement map is limited by the *density* of the displaced geometry, a HyperVoxel surface is as "detailed" as the mathematics used to define it. Meaning you can have "*nurnage* from Hell" (Hell being a small town in central, rural Michigan).

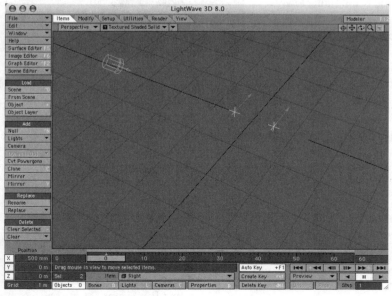

Figure 18-15

1. Start with a fresh, clean scene, and add two null objects. Name the first one you create **Left**, and move it numerically to **X=−.5 m**. Name the second one **Right**, and move it numerically to **X=.5 m**. Move the camera numerically to **Z=−3 m**.

2. Open the HyperVoxels interface, and activate both nulls. For the Right null, set its Particle Size to **1.5 m** (the Left null should stay at 1 m). Check **Show Particles** for both nulls, and you will see representations of them in Layout. The outer, dashed line represents the extent of their "influence" — more on

this in a bit. The solid, inner line shows where the core of the HyperVoxel surface is. (See Figure 18-16.)

3. Under the Shading tab, you'll see another set of tabs almost identical to the tabs under the Surface Editor. Set the Color for the Left null to **238**, **158**, **70** and the Right null to **131**, **121**, **242**. Set *both* nulls to have Specularity of **23%**, Glossiness of **42%**, and Reflection of **23%**. Set *both* nulls to have **Spherical Map** for their Reflection Options and **Images\_Reflection_ Image_TA.iff** as their Reflection Map. (See Figure 18-17.)

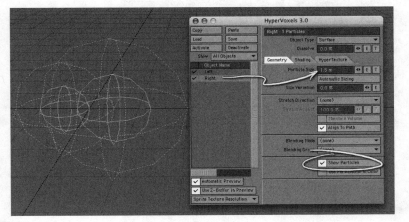

*Figure 18-16*

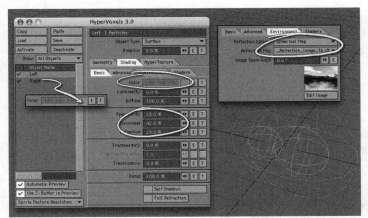

*Figure 18-17*

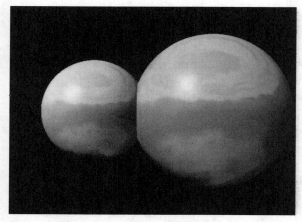

Figure 18-18: An <F9> shows two different colored spheres that slightly intersect.

4. Back under the Geometry tab, set the Blending Mode for *both* nulls to **Additive**. Then, under Blending Group, you'll need to create a new group. Name this group **Mix**, and set it as the Blending Group for *both* nulls.

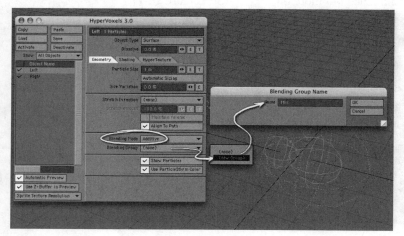

Figure 18-19

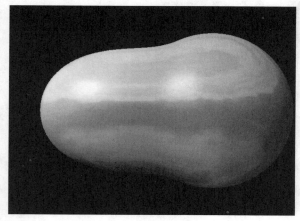

Figure 18-20

An <F9> shows that the two spheres now "blob" into one another! (Wherever the dashed lines representing the influences of the HyperVoxel surfaces, seen in Figure 18-16, come in contact with another whose Blending Mode is also set to Additive and which is also a part of the same blending group, the "surfaces" begin to "reach toward" one another — behaving like a viscous liquid.)

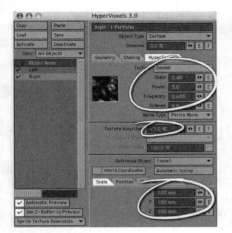

Figure 18-21

Figure 18-22: The HyperTexture actually affects the silhouette of the HyperVoxel surface. You can see it smoothly blending into the left voxel, which doesn't have a HyperTexture assigned.

5. How does the HyperTexture work with HyperVoxel surfaces? For the Right null, click to the HyperTexture tab, and set its Texture to **Dented**, its Scale to **2.45**, its Frequency to **0.605**, and its Texture Amplitude to **–7%**. (Power and Octaves should already be at **3** and **6**, respectively.) Set the Scale for *all three axes* to **100 mm**. (See Figure 18-21.)

### PC-Specific Info

Since we're using Dented, PC results will vary from the results shown here, which are rendered on a Mac.

6. Clear your scene and load the Voxel-Ground object from the companion CD (**Objects\Chapter18\Voxel-Ground.lwo**). Move your camera in so that it matches Figure 18-23 and then press **<F9>** to do a test render. Your results will look a lot like Figure 18-24. Not very interesting, huh?

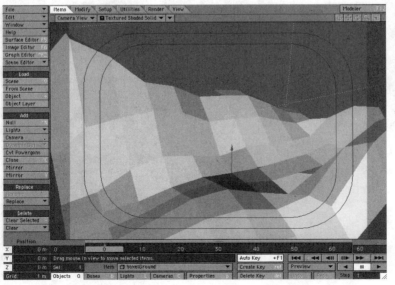

Figure 18-23: An application of all this can be explored by loading Scenes\Chapter_18\HV_Landscape_Setup.lws.

7.  Bring up the HyperVoxels interface, and activate **HyperVoxels** for VoxelGround. Then open the Presets window and select the **Rock** library. Double-click on **Rocky** to load its settings onto your HyperVoxel object. When LW asks if you'd like to keep your current particle size when loading the settings for Rocky, click **No** since after we load the settings, we need to change Particle Size to **3 m** anyway. Set Size Variation to **5%** (this will make each particle deviate by a fixed-random number of between +/– 5%). (See Figure 18-25.)

*Figure 18-24: Doing an <F9> reveals pretty much what one would expect, given the scene in Figure 18-23.*

8.  Press <**F9**> to do another test render. While the render takes quite a bit longer, the results are well worth it. Take a look at the change shown in Figure 18-26.

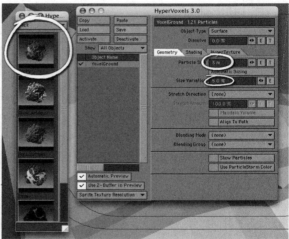

**PC-Specific Info**

The Rocky preset uses Dented as its HyperTexture, so once again, this will look different on a PC than what you're seeing here.

*Figure 18-25*

(**Scenes\Chapter_18\HV_Land-scape_ F.lws** is the scene used to create Figure 18-26.)

*Figure 18-26: When you render this time, what you see is a "whole other story." Every point in the object is handled as a HyperVoxel particle! Because all these particles are in the same object, they all blend smoothly into one another.*

# HyperVoxel "Sprites"

Something you can do that greatly reduces the time LightWave needs to render Hyper-Voxels is to not render the *whole* volume but to render only a "slice" of it. LightWave doesn't need to calculate the whole volume, only a tiny fraction of it — a *plane* that runs directly through its *center*, always aiming at the viewer (*camera* or *viewport angle*).

This is similar in its result to "mapping" our explosion sequence onto the *plane* in the last chapter, except LightWave takes care of all the details for us. All we need to do is use the reduced HyperVoxel controls to set how our sprite looks, and LightWave does the rest!

1. Start with a new scene running at 24 FPS. Set the End Frame to **120** (for *both* the scene itself and within the Rendering Options). Add a null, naming it **HV_Sprite**. Set its Y position to **800 mm**. Then, under the camera's Motion Options, set the camera's Target Item to **HV_Sprite**. To give us

something a bit more exciting in the "background department," under **Effects | Backdrop**, activate **Gradient Backdrop** and set the Zenith Color to **20, 0, 47**, the Sky *and* Ground Colors to **98, 92, 169**, and the Nadir Color to **176, 182, 200**. (See Figure 18-27.)

2. Next, activate HyperVoxels for **HV_Sprite**. Bring up the presets for HyperVoxels, and open the **Generic** library. Double-click on **Sand_Explosion** to load in its settings, changing its Particle Size to **2 m** and its Object Type to **Sprite**. When you check **Show Particles**, you get much more than a linear representation of the voxel — you get a real-time image of the sprite, *complete with OpenGL transparency*. (See Figure 18-28.) (To increase the detail of the sprite, choose a higher resolution from the Sprite Texture Resolution pop-up menu; this will impact your graphics accelerator, however.)

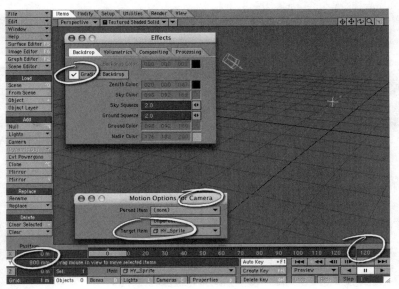

*Figure 18-27*

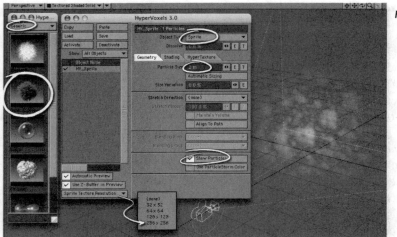

*Figure 18-28*

Figure 18-29: A render of what we've done shows us a "slice" of our voxel.

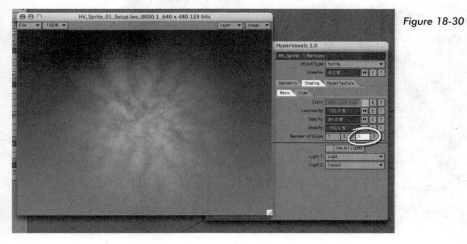

*Figure 18-30*

3. You can increase the quality of your rendered voxel by *increasing* the number of slices (found on the Shading | Basic tab). Comparing Figure 18-30 with Figure 18-29, there is a marked increase in detail, and the render time is still light-years away from the lengthy render we would have were we to set our Object Type to Volume.

4. Now, let's do something really cool. Under the Geometry tab, set the Particle Size to **20 m**, the Stretch Direction to **Y**, and the Stretch Amount to **4%** (this will "squish" our voxel down to 4% of its natural spherical shape along the Y axis). You may as well deactivate **Show Particles**, since the effect we're creating isn't "captured" by the Show Particles engine. Under the Shading | Basic tab, set Color to **200, 200, 200**, Luminosity to **100%**, Opacity to **0%**, Density to **80%**, and Number of Slices to **1**. Then, under the HyperTexture tab, set Texture to **Dented** (*double-check* that Scale is 4, Power is 3, Frequency is **0.8**, and Octaves is **6**). Set

Noise Type to **Gradient Noise** (just a different kind of "fractal engine" powering our Dented procedural texture). Set Texture Amplitude to **150%**, Texture Effect to **Turbulence**, and Effect Speed to **50%**.

(*Double-check* your settings against the above text and Figure 18-31. If your settings don't match mine, your render won't either.)

Figure 18-32

A render shows something that looks like high-altitude clouds. What we've done is *quickly* fake volumetric ground fog (the misty, wispy stuff that hovers in quiet hollows on nights when the moon is full). You can move *through* this ground fog, and you can set the fog's *exact* position above the ground by positioning the null. It won't "catch" shadows very well, but if you ever try "real" volumetric ground fog, you'll appreciate the time-in-render-land this hack provides.

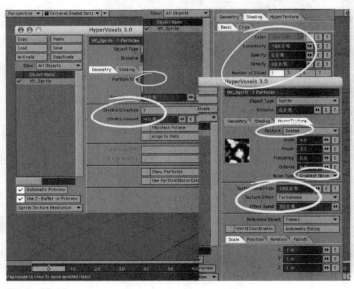

Figure 18-31

But *wait*! There's *more*! If you *act now* and render this scene to a movie, you'll see that you've not only created some nifty fake ground fog, but you'll see that this hack can also be used to recreate the way clouds roil in time-lapse photography! (Effect Speed is the setting that controls the speed of the roiling.)

Scenes\Chapter_18\HV_Sprite_ 01_F.lws is the scene that created Figure 18-32 and the following movie: **Renders\ Chapter18\RoilingClouds.mov**.

1. Now, there's something else Hyper-Voxel sprites can do that is *most excellent*. Load in **Scenes\Chapter_18\ HV_Sprite_02_Setup.lws** to get us ready to go with a *null object* "flying" into frame from behind the camera.

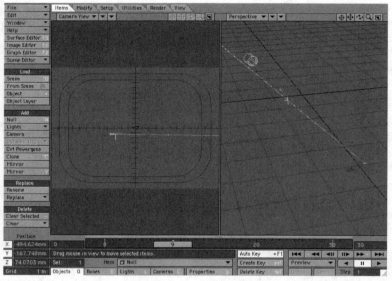

Figure 18-33

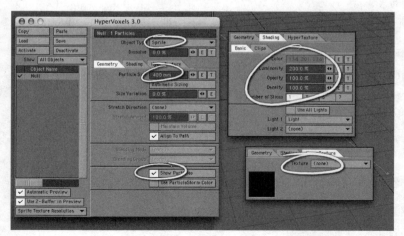

Figure 18-34

474

2. Activate HyperVoxels for the null. Set its Object Type to **Sprite** and its Particle Size to **400 mm**, and check **Show Particles**. On the Shading | Basic tab, set Color to **134, 201, 234**, Luminosity to **200%**, Opacity to **100%**, Density to **100%**, and Number of Slices to **1**. Under the HyperTexture tab, set the Texture to **(none)**. (See Figure 18-34.)

*Figure 18-35: The obligatory <F9>. (Oooh, a blue dot. How nice.)*

3. I've created a sequence of frames that looks something like a science-fiction "torpedo." In the Image Editor, load **Images\TorpedoFrames\Torpedo_000.jpg**. Then, set its Image Type to **Sequence** (LightWave's default handling of the image sequence is shown here). Then, on the Shading | Clips tab of the HyperVoxel interface for your null, select **Torpedo_(sequence)** from the Add Clip pop-up menu. Make sure Alpha is set to **Luminosity** and that **Use Color, AntiAliasing**, and **Solid** are all checked. Select **Fixed Random** for the Frame Offset. (See Figure 18-36.)

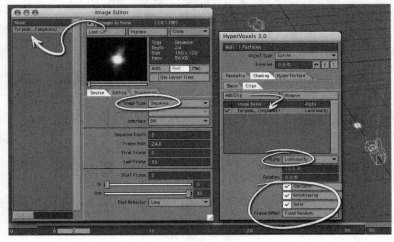

*Figure 18-36*

4.  When rendering a movie of this scene, I recommend using **Enhanced Low** Antialiasing (without Adaptive Sampling), **Dithered** Motion Blur, and a Blur Length of **100%**. (**Scenes\**

**Chapter_18\HV_ Sprite_02_F.lws** is the finished scene of this example, and the movie of the final render is **Renders\Chapter18\ Torpedo.mov**.)

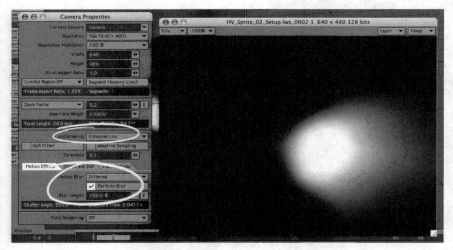

Figure 18-37: (Yet another <F9>.) Our "blue dot" is now a glowing "bolt" of plasma that renders extremely quickly.

Figure 18-38

A *really* cool thing about HyperVoxel sprite clips is that you can load in *more than one clip* onto an HV object. Each clip will be assigned, in turn, to the next point of the HV object's point order.

So, assuming you have a few nice clips of some flame and smoke sequences, you could (using *particles*, which we touch on next) create the same fire effect as seen on the Balrog in *Lord of the Rings: The Fellowship of the Ring*.

And (just to plant ideas in your head) using Particle Age as the clip's Frame Offset and LightWave's ability to have collisions "spawn" new particles, you could have *non-looping*

*clips* of explosions "do their thing" when a projectile impacts its target! (For something even more complex, if you have clips of splashing water and create a particle simulation of water flowing where "splash" particles are spawned when the "water" particles collide with objects, you will have recreated the "two-and-a-half-D" used to create the breathtaking water effects seen in feature films from *Tarzan* to *The Road to El Dorado*.)

To find out how to have particles react with one another and with objects in your scene, dive into the LW manuals. It's all there for you, just waiting to be unearthed!

# Particles

As you may have guessed from the previous parenthetical, I'm not going to show you *everything* there is to know about LightWave particles here. (That would be a complete book unto itself.) As with the rest of this book, I'm going to show you the essentials. You'll have enough to start exploring and learning on your own — where you go from there is up to you!

1. Start with a fresh, new scene. With **Objects** selected, choose **Items | Add | Dynamic Obj | Particle**. Accept the name **Emitter** and the Emitter Type of **HV Emitter**. (A little box will appear when you click **OK** that represents the place where the particles will be

emitted. A little Properties window will also open when you add an emitter this way.) Under the Generator tab of the emitter's Properties window, assign a Birth Rate of **300**. This means that 300 particles will be created each *second*, as set in the Generated By pop-up menu immediately below it. Set the X, Y, and Z of the Generator Size to **100 mm**, and set the Particle Limit (the maximum number of particles on screen at any one time from this particular particle producer) to **300**.

When you're done with all that, set the End Frame to **120**, and then move the camera to **–3 m** in the Z axis.

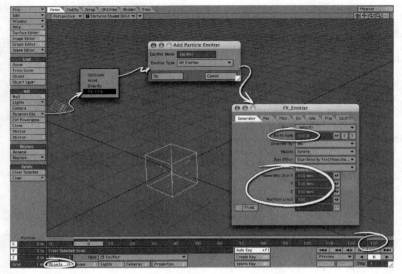

Figure 18-39

## Note

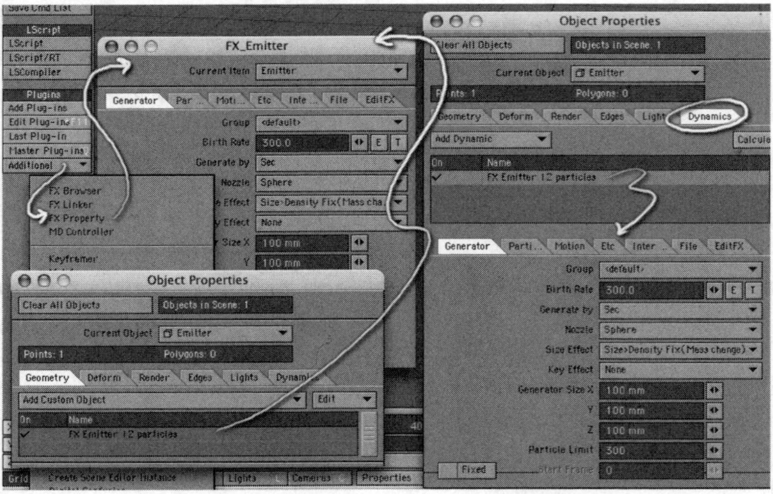

Figure 18-40: There are a few ways to get to the Properties window for a PFX (Particle FX) item. With the object selected, you can choose FX Property from the Plugins | Additional pop-up menu. You can also open the Object Properties window and double-click on the FX Emitter custom object entry on the Geometry tab. Or if you'd rather not open a separate window, you can make all of your adjustments right in the Object Properties window by double-clicking the Effects Emitter in the Dynamics tab.

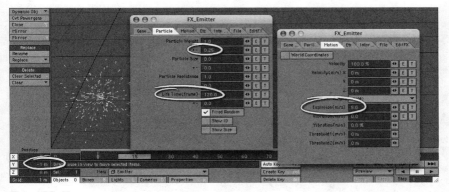

Figure 18-41

2. On the Particle tab of the FX-Emitter window, set Particle Weight +/– to **0.25** (which will make our particles "weigh" between 0.75 and 1.25 units). Set the Life Time (frame) to **120**, which will make each particle "live" 120 frames (the length of our scene) before "dying" and being "reborn." Then, on the Motion tab, set Explosion(m/s) to **5** (meters per second). Move our emitter to **–1 m** on the Y axis. When you scrub the frame slider, you see particles "exploding" from our emitter. (See Figure 18-41.)

3. Select **Items | Add | Dynamic Obj | Gravity** (leaving it at X=0, Y=0, Z=0). Set Gravity Mode to **Point**, Fall-off Mode to **OFF**, Radius to **10 m**, and

Power to **–100%**. Now, when you scrub the frame slider, you see your particles "falling into" this "singularity" that you've created. Although, unlike a "true" singularity, the particles continue falling right on *through* the gravitational central point, accelerating out the other side. (Maybe that's the way black holes really do work — we have no way to prove one way or the other.)

4. Let's have a little bit of fun here. Before we do any rendering, add **Textured Environment** under **Effects | Backdrop | Add Environment**. Click on the **Texture** button to open the Texture Editor window, and assign a **Procedural Texture** to the Layer Type. Set the Procedural Type to **Underwater**, Texture Color to **151, 0, 0**, Wave Sources to **6**, Wavelength to **1**, Wave Speed to **0.02**, and Band Sharpness to **1**. (This will make the background of our render a little more interesting....) (See Figure 18-43.)

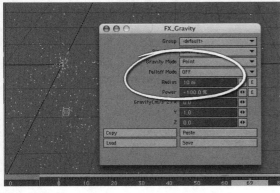

Figure 18-42

**479**

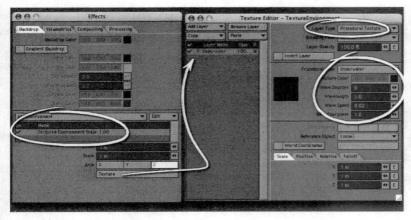

Figure 18-43

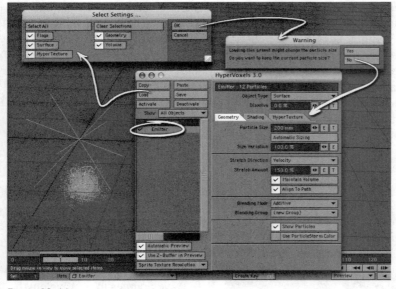

Figure 18-44

5.  Activate **HyperVoxels** for the Emitter. Then click on **Load** and choose **Surfaces\HV_Surface_ch18.hv**. The Select Settings window will appear. Leave everything *checked*, click **OK**, then choose **No** when LightWave asks if you'd like to keep your current particle size. Doing this replaces the entirety of the HyperVoxel settings. (See Figure 18-44.)

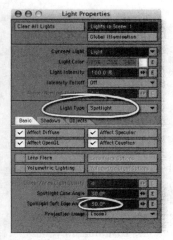

Figure 18-45

6. Lastly, before we render our scene, set Light Type to **Spotlight** and Spotlight Soft Edge Angle to **30°**. This will give our scene a little depth as the particles move through the spotlight's "beam."

Frames from the final render have a kind of surrealist, expressionistic feel to them. The rendered movie of the scene (**Renders\ Chapter18\Particles.mov**) looks like it would fit right in with the music of Kimball Collins or Judge Jules.

Figure 18-46

# Conclusion

We've covered quite a bit of ground in this chapter. I'm sure you'll agree that Hyper-Voxels and particles are powerful tools for creating special effects. By exploring these simulations and appreciating the levels of detail their mathematics create, details no one person could ever envision in their entirety, you have hopefully touched upon one of the greatest truths: Knowing the answer is not important. Knowing how to solve the question is.

# Chapter 19

# Simulations 2: Dynamics

One of the most highly touted features of LightWave 8 is the new Dynamics system, consisting of hard and soft body simulators, particle emitters, natural force generators, collision objects, and effect linkers, each with the ability to interact with one another. The attention given to these tools is well deserved. Dynamics allow you to imbue your objects with real-world physical properties such as weight, air resistance, and gravity. They allow you to create everything from realistic-looking clothes to debris-filled explosions. Complex effects that would take hours to animate by hand can now be done in a matter of minutes. In this chapter, we'll look at these incredible tools and cover the essential information you need to get started using them.

## An Introduction to Dynamics

dy·nam·ic *Noun* 1. An interactive system or process, especially one involving competing or conflicting forces.
—Dictionary.com

When we talk about dynamics, we are referring to the simulation of real-world physical properties within an artificial 3D environment. As strange as it may seem, to a 3D application such as LightWave, a leaf is just as heavy as a car and concrete is as permeable as water. That's because 3D applications cannot differentiate between objects. It's all just points and polygons in the eyes of the program. Therefore, if we want to simulate real-world phenomena, we have to tell our software about the unique characteristics of each object. We have to tell LightWave that a leaf is light, a car is heavy, water is permeable, and concrete is not. We do this by adding a dynamic property to the object. This can be done by opening the Object Properties panel and clicking on the Add Dynamic pop-up menu on the Dynamics tab.

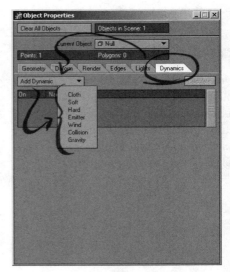

Figure 19-1: Dynamic properties can be added from the Object Properties panel.

There are seven types of dynamic properties. The first four are what I call "personal dynamics." They directly affect the *individual* object to which they are applied. The last three are what I call "social dynamics." They affect the behavior of *other* dynamic objects within the scene.

## Personal Dynamics

### Cloth

Don't let the name fool you: ClothFX isn't just for clothing. This is LightWave's full-featured soft body dynamics engine, capable of simulating everything from the billowing of a superhero's cape to the violent splash of water on the surface of a pool. ClothFX is the evolution of Motion Designer, the soft body simulator found in LightWave 7.5.

### Soft

New to LightWave 8, SoftFX is a soft body simulator well suited to producing "secondary animation" for your objects. For example, you could animate a character running, then apply SoftFX to get the stomach to jiggle and bounce in response to the motion.

### Hard

HardFX is LightWave's new rigid body dynamics engine. It allows you to simulate hard objects such as metal and stone. You can use HardFX to create the explosion of a spaceship or the breaking of a window as a baseball crashes through it.

### Emitter

The Emitter dynamic turns your object into a particle emitter. Adding this dynamic property to your object gives you more options than stand-alone emitters, such as

the ability to generate particles from the object's points or to cover the entire surface of an object with particles.

## Social Dynamics

### Wind

The Wind dynamic allows you to apply a repelling force to your object. As a social dynamic, Wind does not affect the object to which it is applied. Rather, it affects the other dynamic objects around it. For example, you could add Wind to the model of a fan, causing any hard, soft, or particle objects to be pushed away when they pass in front of it.

### Collision

The Collision dynamic operates as an indicator to other dynamic objects. It tells hard bodies, soft bodies, and particles that they cannot pass through the polygons of the Collision object. For example, if you applied HardFX to a ball and dropped it onto a ground plane, it would simply pass through the ground and continue falling. However, adding the Collision dynamic to the ground would cause the ball to bounce off its surface.

### Gravity

The Gravity dynamic is similar to the Wind dynamic. It is a force that can be tied directly to an object. But where Wind is generally used as a repelling force, Gravity is used as an attracting force. It causes personal dynamic objects to be pulled toward it.

## Relational Dynamics

In addition to the personal dynamics and social dynamics, there are also "relational dynamics" called Effect Links. Effect Links work on the *children* of dynamic objects, allowing them to inherit the properties of their parent. They are applied from the Add Displacement pop-up menu in the Deform tab of the Object Properties panel.

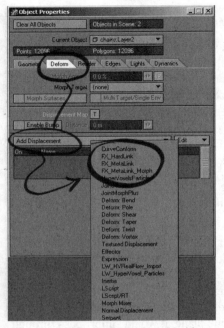

*Figure 19-2: Effect Links can be added from the Deform tab of the Object Properties panel.*

While not true Dynamics in and of themselves, Effect Links are often used to apply the dynamic properties of a simple object to a higher resolution mesh. This not only speeds up the calculation of complicated simulations, but it also opens the door for effects that would otherwise be difficult to achieve.

### HardLink

HardLink applies the dynamic properties of a parent object to its child using rigid body qualities. The obvious question to ask is, "Why would you want to do this?" Here's an example: If you wanted to animate a

chain, you might think of adding HardFX since chains are hard. But HardFX would only see the object in one of two ways: as an entire (solid) chain or as individual links. It would not understand that the links are actually connected to one another. Therefore, HardFX would not work for this simulation. ClothFX would keep the links together and allow the chain to dangle, but it would deform every point in the mesh, causing your links to stretch like rubber. What you need is a way to get the motion of ClothFX with the properties of HardFX. HardLink allows you to do this.

### MetaLink

MetaLink functions similarly to HardLink, but rather than applying rigid body qualities to your child object, it applies soft body qualities. MetaLink is useful for those instances where you want to maintain the volume (or shape) of an object but still give it a degree of flexibility. For example, if you wanted to animate a rope rather than a chain, you could use ClothFX on a simple object (such as a two-point polygon chain) and apply MetaLink to the rope object. ClothFX will give you the motion you want, and MetaLink will help the rope to keep its basic shape.

## The Dynamics Community

When you add a dynamic property to an object, you are telling it what behavioral tendencies it will have. In essence, you are giving it a personality. Taken this way, the process of building a Dynamics simulation can be seen as a form of social engineering. You begin by building a community — a Dynamics Community — where each object is given a personality and told how it should react to the other objects within the community.

Knowing the difference between the various dynamics properties (or personalities) is important. But knowing how they work *together* is equally (if not *more*) important. You see, when you assign a dynamic property to an object, you are really asking LightWave to perform a simulation of physics on the object. Physics is the study of matter (hard objects, soft objects, particles) and energy (wind, gravity, collision). But more specifically, physics deals with the *interaction* between the two. Assigning a dynamic property to your object is not enough. You need to understand how each of the properties work together in order to produce a successful simulation.

Think about Newton's Third Law of Motion. It states that for every action there is an equal and opposite reaction. In terms of the Dynamics Community, we would say: *For every personal dynamic, you should also have a social dynamic to which it is accountable*.

Consider this. When you place a can of soda on your desk, the can doesn't fall straight to the ground because it collides with the desk. To build this as a Dynamics simulation, you would apply HardFX to the can of soda and Collision to the desk. One without the other would cause the simulation to fail, but together they produce the desired results. You should keep this rule in mind as you build your Dynamics Community. When you add a personal dynamic, make sure that you have a social dynamic somewhere in your scene to which it is accountable. This brings me to the most important issue of them all: When is it right to build a Dynamics simulation and, more to the point, when is it not?

## Dynamic Decisions

Dynamics can be incredibly powerful, but they are far from foolproof. Just as people can be temperamental, so can Dynamics. There have been numerous occasions where making a single adjustment has sent my entire simulation into chaotic fits. And since every simulation is different, it can be difficult to troubleshoot. The important thing to consider, then, is whether or not it's worth the time to set up a Dynamics simulation. You must ask yourself, "Can I do this by hand faster or easier than the time it's going to take to set up and tweak a simulation?" If I'm animating a basketball player shooting hoops, it would be easier for me to animate the ball by hand than it would be to set up a simulation. But if I were animating a pool hall junkie shooting a game of 8-ball, that would be a different story. Animating the complex interaction of each ball on the pool table while accurately replicating its rotation and constantly changing velocity would be time consuming to say the least. But it can be done with Dynamics in a matter of minutes. So let this serve as sage advice to you. Dynamics are a

*Figure 19-3: Animating a pool table is the perfect job for Dynamics.*

lot of fun and can produce incredible results. But you don't want to find yourself in a production environment about to miss

your deadline because you opted to use Dynamics on an animation that could be done just as easily by hand.

## Applied Dynamics

In the next few sections we're going to look at four of the most commonly used Dynamics properties: HardFX, ClothFX, SoftFX, and Collision Effects. We'll be setting up simulations that will give you a taste of the power these tools offer. The manual and online help system provide detailed information on each of these tools and you should refer to them when you need more information on a specific setting. The knowledge you gain over the next few pages can be expanded upon to create many of the complex animations that you see in movies and on TV.

Bring up Layout and we'll begin.

## Collision Effects

Collisions are perhaps the most frequently used social dynamic, and it's not uncommon to have more than one of them in a simulation. Let's set up a simple scene to see how they work with other dynamic objects.

1. Add a **Particle Emitter** from the **Items | Add | Dynamic Obj** menu. From the Add Particle Emitter window that appears, accept the defaults and press **OK**. A new Particle

Emitter will appear and the FX_Emitter properties window will open. Change Birth Rate to **500** (so that the particles appear more quickly), then switch to the Etc tab and change Gravity in the Y axis to **–9.8** meters (which simulates real-world gravity). When you're finished, close the window.

> **Note**
>
> You'll notice that the Particle Emitter has its own gravity setting. In fact, each of the personal dynamics (except SoftFX, which we'll talk about later) has its own internal gravity setting. Adding internal gravity applies the effect to the object globally throughout the scene. This eliminates the need for (and differentiates it from) the social dynamic of Gravity, which is typically used to apply the effect to a limited region of your scene.

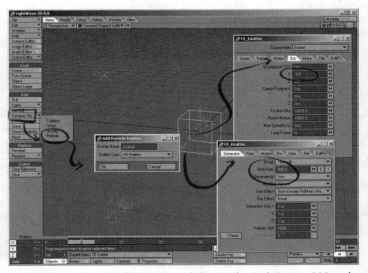

Figure 19-4: Add a Particle Emitter, and change the Birth Rate to 500 and Gravity in the Y axis to –9.8 meters.

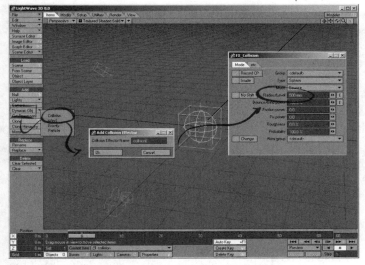

*Figure 19-5: Add a Collision object and set its size to 500 mm.*

2.  Now let's add a Collision object. From the **Items | Add | Dynamic Obj** menu, choose **Collision**. The Add Collision Effector window will appear. Accept the defaults by pressing **OK**. You will then be presented with the FX_Collision window. Change Radius/Level to **500 mm** and leave the remaining settings at their default.

    We now have one personal dynamic and one social dynamic, forming a simple but complete Dynamics Community. Let's see how these two Dynamics interact.

3.  At frame 0, move the Collision object back about **5** meters on the Z axis. At frame 20, reset the Collision object so that it's at **0** on the Z axis. Set

    another key at frame **40** with the same settings as frame 20. Finally, at frame 60 move the Collision object back to **5** meters on the Z axis.

    Switch to a full-screen Perspective view and then press the **Play** button. Spin around in the Perspective view as the animation plays and check the results.

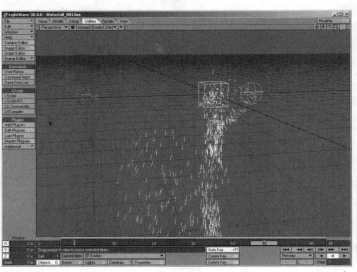

*Figure 19-6: The Collision object impacts the Particle Emitter.*

**487**

Even though this is a very simple simulation, it's still quite impressive! The Particle Emitter begins generating a virtual waterfall at frame 0. Then at frame 20, the Collision object rams into it, sending particles flying. At frame 40, the Collision object passes through the Emitter again, causing particles to bounce off as it returns to its starting point. You can see that the initial impact of our Collision object causes the particles to scatter farther than the second impact. It's important to note that the speed at which your Collision object moves has a tremendous effect on the object it collides with, just as it would in real life. Stop for a moment and think about how long it would take you to animate each of these particles by hand. You'll begin to realize just how powerful Dynamics can be!

The settings for a Collision object play a large part in determining how it interacts with other dynamic objects in your scene. As we examine the remaining Dynamic types, we'll spend more time talking about Collision objects and their various settings. For now, however, we'll wrap up this discussion with a few helpful hints.

● A collision occurs when the *points* of an object come in contact with the *polygons* of another object. If the *polygons* (or *edges*) of an object collide with the *polygons* (or *edges*) of another object, the collision detection will fail. For this reason, it's best to have more points in the object that collides (often a personal dynamic) and less

points in the object it collides with (the Collision object).

● The Collision property works best when the object it's applied to is made up of quads. If you find that the collision detection is failing, even on simple geometry, try rebuilding the collision surface so that it is comprised of four-point polygons.

● Collision detection works differently depending on the type of object you're using. When the Collision dynamic is applied to a regular polygonal object, a *bounding box* will be used to determine the collision area. This works well in some cases, but not so well in others. Take, for example, Figure 19-7. You would expect the ball to fall through the hole in the ground, but it won't. Instead, the ball will fall *onto* the hole and bounce. To remedy this, we need to convert the ground into a subpatch object. Collision detection for subpatch objects is determined by the *actual shape* of the polygons in the object.

If you follow these hints, you should be able to avoid most situations that cause collision

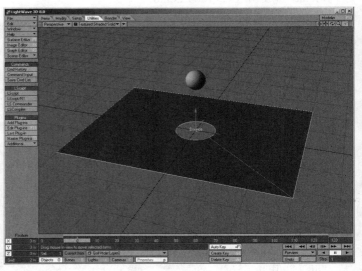

*Figure 19-7*

detection to fail. Let's move on to HardFX and see how a simple collision can be used to knock a hole in a brick wall.

## HardFX

HardFX is a personal dynamic that gives your objects a rigid structure. You should apply HardFX to objects that need to interact with other objects and must retain their basic shape throughout the simulation. For example, HardFX can be applied to a set of bowling pins. Each pin must be able to interact with the bowling ball and the other pins, but they must also retain their shape (i.e., not bend or stretch as a result of collisions).

In this section, I'll show you how to use HardFX to knock a hole in a brick wall. Navigate to Renders\Chapter 19\Bricks.avi on the CD. This shows the completed animation we'll be creating.

1.  Open the **Bricks.lws** scene file from **Scenes\Chapter_19** on the CD. This scene contains a simple brick wall, a ground plane, and a large ball. The ball has been parented to a null object that has then been animated to simulate the motion of a demolition ball. Switch to the Perspective viewport and press **Play** to see the animation before the simulation.

> **Note**
>
> The Brick Wall object uses the TB Edge Bevel shader. This shader enhances the look of the rendered bricks, but it is not necessary for the following tutorial. If you'd like to download a copy of the shader, one is available from http://home.att.ne.jp/omega/tabo/3dlabo/p_lwp.html.

Let's add some excitement to this animation using Dynamics. To properly build a simulation, we must create a Dynamics Community by assigning personalities (Dynamics types) to our objects. We determine which personalities to use by analyzing the role that each object will play in the scene. We have three objects that will be used: the ball, the ground, and the brick wall.

The ball is used to impact the wall and break it into pieces.

The ground acts as a resting place for the bricks that break off the wall.

The brick wall is our star. It breaks apart on impact and collides with the ground.

Let's begin by analyzing the function of the ball. It has but one purpose — to impact

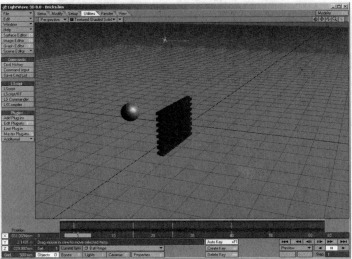

*Figure 19-8: The basic Bricks scene.*

**489**

the wall. Since the ball is being used to affect another object, it must be given one of the social dynamics. It is not attracting or repelling the wall, so we can effectively rule out Gravity and Wind. That leaves us with Collision as the correct choice.

> **Note**
>
> It may seem like a lot of work went into determining the correct dynamic personality for the ball when it was fairly obvious that it needed to be a Collision. However, determining the correct Dynamic type won't always be so easy. For this reason, it's good to get in the habit of analyzing the function of your objects as it can help narrow down the choices when building more complicated simulations.

2.  Select the **ball** and open the Object Properties panel. Click on the Dynamics tab, and choose **Collision** from the Add Dynamic pop-up menu. The Collision property will be added to the Dynamic Properties list.

Now let's analyze the ground. The ground has a much more passive role than the ball, but it is still used to affect another object (in this case the wall). Since we do not want the bricks of the wall to fall through the ground, we will give it a Collision property as well.

3.  With the Object Properties window still open, click the Current Object pop-up menu and choose the **Ground** object. Then, from the Add Dynamic pop-up, choose **Collision**.

We now have two social dynamics in our scene. That means that we must add a personal dynamic to our final object in order to complete the Dynamics Community. Since we do not want the wall to deform (e.g., bend or stretch) during the simulation, we can rule out Cloth and Soft Dynamics. That leaves us with Hard Dynamics.

4.  Select the **Wall** from the Current Object pop-up and then add the **Hard** dynamic property to it.

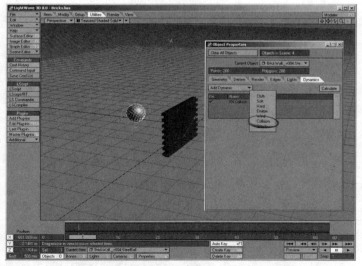

*Figure 19-9: Add the Collision property to the ball.*

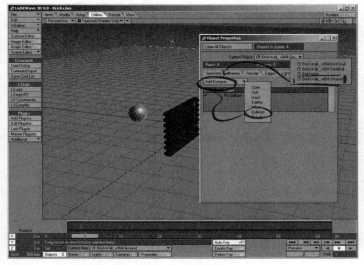

Figure 19-10: Add the Collision property to the ground.

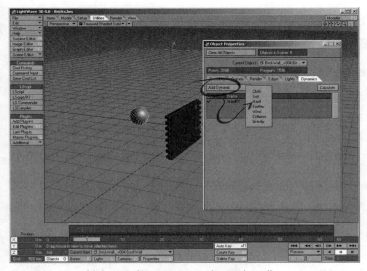

Figure 19-11: Add the HardFX property to the Brick Wall.

5.  Our Dynamics Community is now complete. Click on the **Calculate** button in the upper-right corner of the Dynamics tab to begin the simulation. When the calculations are completed, press the **Play** button. Figure 19-12 shows the results.

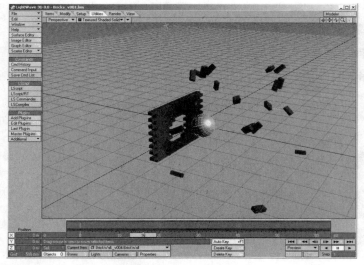

*Figure 19-12: The initial results of our simulation.*

Wow! Using just the default settings, we've created a fairly impressive animation. But it's far from perfect. If you zoom out, you'll notice that the initial impact causes the bricks to fly into the air as if they're weightless. As odd as it might seem, that's not far from the truth. Although the bricks do have a small amount of weight, they currently exist in a vacuum because we have not told them that gravity exists. Let's do that now.

We can add gravity as an independent social dynamic to our scene, but we only need it to affect our brick wall, so we can use the internal gravity setting found in HardFX.

6.  With the brick wall selected, click on the **HardFX** listing in the Dynamics tab. A new set of options will open below the Dynamic Properties list. Click on the **Basic** tab and enter **–9.8** in the Gravity field. Hit **Calculate** to see the results.

Whoa! The brick wall now collapses on itself! Let's fix this.

7.  Navigate to the Collision tab of the HardFX settings. From the Start by

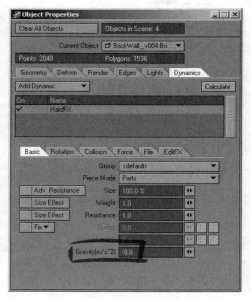

*Figure 19-13: Add Gravity to the HardFX settings.*

Collision pop-up menu, choose the **Start by Collision** setting (Figure 19-14). Then press the **Calculate** button to check the results.

That's much better. The Start by Collision option tells our HardFX object not to act

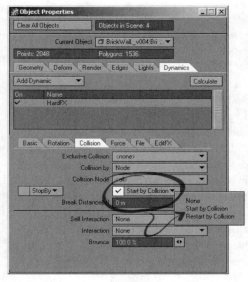

*Figure 19-14: Activate the Start by Collision setting.*

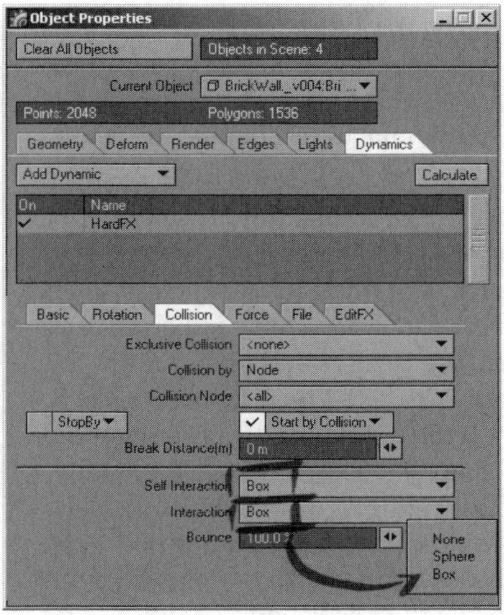

*Figure 19-15: Activate Self Interaction.*

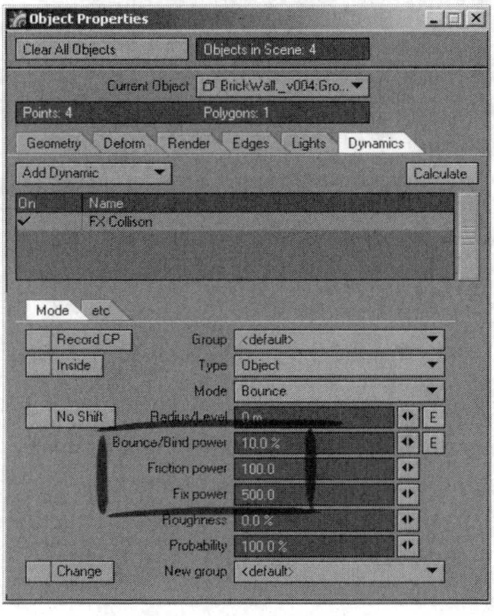

until it has come in contact with a Collision object. While this setting stopped our wall from collapsing onto itself, we now have other issues to deal with. Most notably is the fact that certain bricks are falling *inside* the wall. This is caused by three things:

- First, collision detection is active between the wall and other objects in the scene, but it is not active between each individual brick. Activating Self Interaction in the Collision tab of HardFX will help (it will also make the calculation process slower), but it won't completely solve the problem (see the first tip in the Collision section earlier in this chapter for further explanation). Still, we should turn this setting on. From the Collision tab, change the Self Interaction and Interaction pop-up menus to Box as shown in Figure 19-15.

- Second, when the bricks fall inside the wall, they continue to bounce in place. You can control this by changing the Bounce/Bind power, the Friction power, and the Fix power in the Collision settings for the Ground object. Switch to the Ground object

and click on the FX Collision setting in the Dynamics list. From the Mode tab, change Bounce/Bind power to **10%**. This reduces the bouncing effect of the bricks hitting the ground. Change Friction power to **100**. This reduces the ability of the bricks to slide

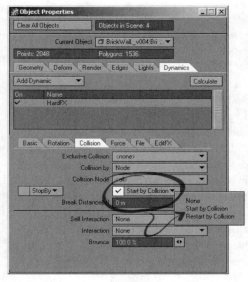

*Figure 19-16: Lower the Bounce and increase the Friction and Fix Powers for the Ground object.*

along the surface of the ground. Finally, change Fix power to **500**. This helps prevent the bricks from jittering as they come to rest on the ground.

- Third, the simulation is not accurate enough. The accuracy of the simulation is controlled by the Resolution setting on the File tab of the HardFX parameters. Higher numbers allow for a greater margin of error. Currently, the Resolution is set to 100 mm. Change this to **50 mm**. Increasing the accuracy of the simulation (by lowering the resolution number) will have a direct impact on the calculation time. The default setting is often a good starting point, but will need to be adjusted if you see obvious errors in the calculation.

> **Note**
>
> If you find that the calculations are taking too long, you can hold down the Ctrl key to cancel them.

To help speed up the calculation, we can tell LightWave not to waste time calculating collisions until the Collision object is close to the HardFX object. Just how close is determined by the Break Distance setting in the Collision tab of the HardFX properties. Currently it is set to 0. Increasing this number will allow the Collision object to get closer to the object before calculations take place. If the number is too high, it will cause inaccuracies in the calculations. For now, change this to **50 mm**.

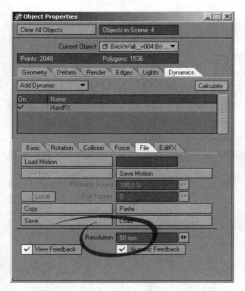

Figure 19-17: Lower the Resolution to reduce the margin of error in the calculations.

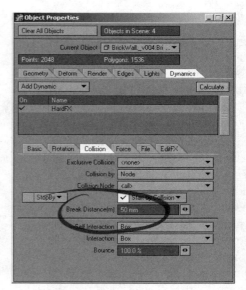

Figure 19-18: Increase the Break Distance to help speed up calculations.

Press the **Calculate** button. You'll probably notice that the calculation time is now excruciatingly long and while it did fix *some* of the problems, it didn't fix *all* of them.

Press the **Calculate** button again. You should see a significant reduction in the calculation time. When the processing is complete, switch to the Camera view and play the animation.

Our simulation is starting to take shape but it still needs work. Currently on impact, the bricks go flying past the camera, leaving only a few in the camera's field of view. I want more of the bricks to land in front of the camera. The movement of the bricks is caused by two factors. The first is the speed of the Collision object and the second is the Collision parameters. We'll leave the speed as it is, but we will change the parameters.

8. Switch to the **Ball** object and click on **FX Collision** in the Dynamics tab to bring up its settings. From the Mode tab, change Bounce/Bind power to **100%**. We still want the ball to have a decent impact, just not so extreme. Lowering the Bounce/Bind setting will do this. We also want the ball to have a slight bit of friction so that the bricks don't slide so much when they come in contact with the ball's surface. Increase Friction to **5**. Finally, we will increase the Fix power to help resolve any issues with the bricks colliding with the ball. Change Fix power to **50**.

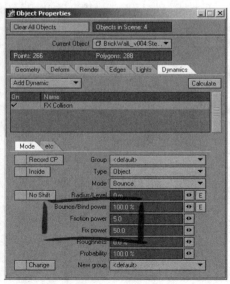

*Figure 19-19: Change the Bounce/Bind, Friction, and Fix powers.*

9. Press **Calculate** to see the results. That helped quite a bit! But there are still a few annoying problems. It appears that the bricks are much too light and that they bounce and roll a little more than I'd like. Bring up the HardFX properties for the brick wall and we'll change that.

10. From the Basic tab of the HardFX properties, change Weight to **250** and Resistance to **10**. Finally, activate **Adv. Resistance** and the **Size Effect** boxes next to Weight and Resistance.

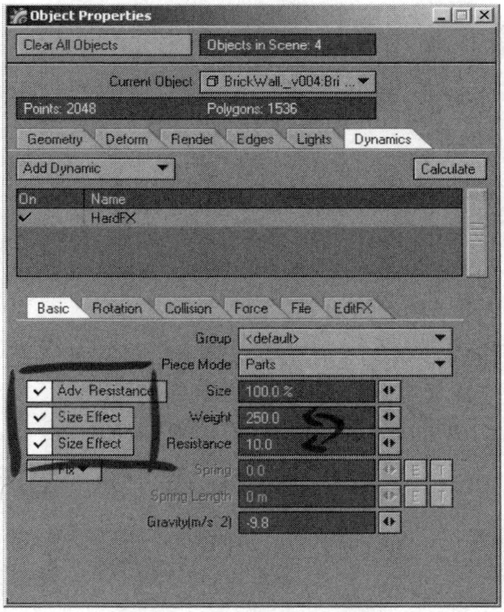

*Figure 19-20: Increase the Weight and Resistance and activate the Adv. Resistance and Size Effects.*

Increasing the weight makes the entire wall heavier. Activating the Size Effect to the left of Weight tells HardFX that the weight is determined by the size of the individual objects, in this case, the bricks. If the wall were made up of various sized stones, the Size Effect would make the larger stones heavier than the smaller stones. Increasing Resistance added an element of air resistance to the bricks. The Size Effect option for Resistance works the same as it did for

**495**

Weight. Activating Adv. Resistance tells HardFX that the shape of each brick has an effect on its air resistance.

11. Hit the **Calculate** button and play back the results. Our bricks now have more weight, but they still bounce too much, causing them to scatter. Switch to the Rotation tab of the HardFX properties. Change Torque Min to **0%** and Torque Max to **20%**. Then activate **Size Effect** to allow the size of each brick to impact its rotation. Recalculate and play back the results.

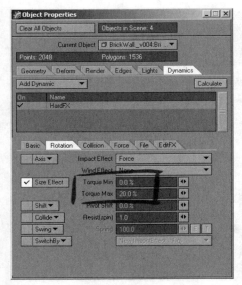

*Figure 19-21: Decrease the brick rotations by lowering the Min and Max Torque.*

This looks great and we could probably call it complete, but it still seems like the bricks rotate too much, giving them a less weighty feel. We could correct this with the Torque settings, but there's another way.

12. Click on the **Force** tab of the HardFX properties and select **Rotation Control** from the Force Mode pop-up menu. This will help constrain the rotation of our bricks based on the impact of the ball. Since we know that the ball

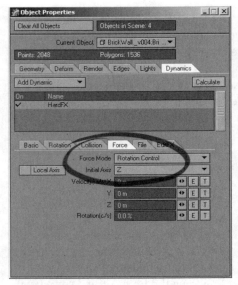

*Figure 19-22: Set Force Mode to Rotation Control and Initial Axis to Z.*

is hitting the wall along the Z axis, let's also change the Initial Axis pop-up to **Z**.

13. Hit the **Calculate** button and then play back the animation. Everything looks good, but it appears that the bricks "jitter" after they've landed on the ground. This type of error can often be resolved

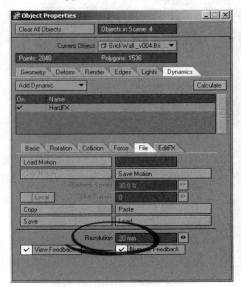

*Figure 19-23: Lower the Resolution to 20 mm.*

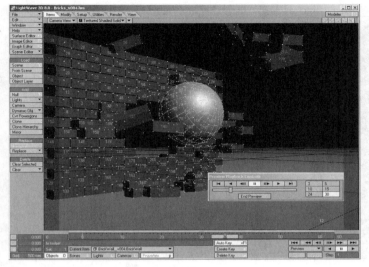

*Figure 19-24: Create a preview animation.*

by increasing the Fix Power for the Collision object. But we already have a fair amount of Fix Power on the ground. In cases like this, jittering typically means that our calculation resolution needs to be adjusted. Switch to the File tab of the HardFX properties and change Resolution to **20 mm** as shown in Figure 19-23. Then recalculate and play back the results.

14. This looks terrific! Go ahead and create a preview animation by clicking **Make Preview** from the pop-up menu in the lower-right corner of the main interface.

At the default 30 frames per second, the animation is much too fast. We could go back and tweak our settings all over again, but that would

ruin the look that we worked so hard to achieve. Fortunately, there's an easier way.

15. Make sure the **Wall** object is selected. Click on the **HardFX** item in the Dynamics tab of the Object Properties panel to bring up its settings. Click on the **File** tab. The options here allow you to save your settings, but they also allow you to save the actual motion of

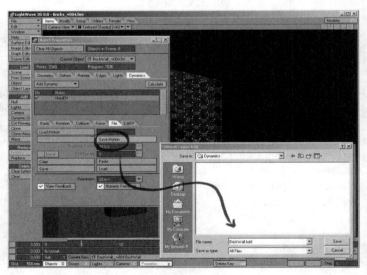

*Figure 19-25: Save the motion of the bricks.*

**497**

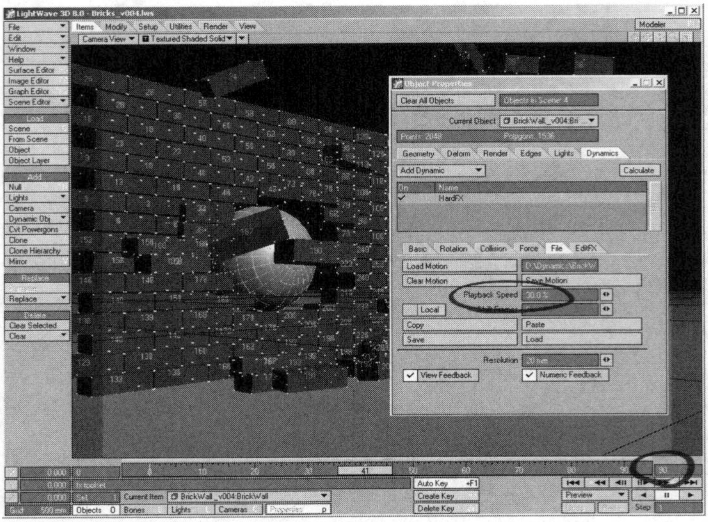

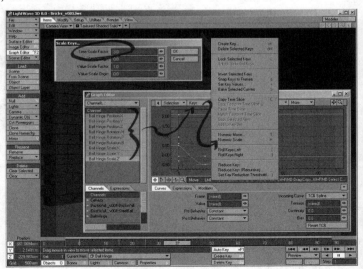

Figure 19-26: Change Playback Speed to 30% and the end frame of your animation to 90.

the object. Click on the **Save Motion** button and save the object's motion to a location on your hard drive.

16. Once you've saved the motion file, you gain the ability to adjust the speed of the simulation. Change Playback Speed to **30%**. The animation will now play at one-third of its regular speed. In order to see most of the effect, we need to change our end frame from 60 to **90**. Once you've done this, create another preview animation.

The bricks now look great at 30 frames per second, but the ball no longer moves with them. That's because we've only changed the playback rate for the brick wall. Let's adjust the timing of the ball to match.

17. The motion of the ball is controlled by the **Ball Hinge** null object. Select this object from the Current Item pop-up menu (just below the timeline) and press <**Ctrl**> + <**F2**> to bring up the Graph Editor. Select the first channel on the left, then hold the <**Shift**> key down and select the last channel so that all of the channels in between are

Figure 19-27: Scale the keys of the Ball Hinge object by a factor of 3.

selected. Using your right mouse button, drag a bounding box around all of the keys in the main Graph Editor window to select them. Then, from the Keys pop-up menu, select the **Numeric Scale** option. The Scale Keys window will appear. Change Time Scale factor to **3** and press **OK**. The motion of the ball now matches up with our brick wall.

At this point, you can continue tweaking with the animation to make it truly exceptional. Try adding Colin Cohen's Vibrate plug-in (available on the CD) to the camera for realistic camera shake as the ball impacts the wall. Play with the tools in the EditFX tab to alter the motion path for errant bricks (look closely and you'll see them). Allow this introduction to HardFX to serve as a launching pad as you continue to explore LightWave Dynamics.

## ClothFX

ClothFX is a personal dynamic that gives your object elastic qualities. You should apply ClothFX to objects that you want to

deform naturally and organically. For example, ClothFX can be used to simulate clothing that stretches and folds over a character's body. But ClothFX isn't just for clothing. It can be used to leave footprints on the ground where a character walks. It can be used on the surface of a pond to create ripples and waves. It can even be used to simulate the motion of hair. ClothFX is an extremely powerful tool that can yield an impressive array of results.

In this section, I'll show you how you can use ClothFX to simulate clothing for your characters. Navigate to Scenes\Chapter_19 on the CD and load the Skirt scene.

The object in this scene is a simple tube. The points at the center of the tube were extended out to form the skirt and Band-Saw was used to slice it into smaller segments. The points at the top and bottom of the tube, along with those at the point where the skirt connects to the tube, were placed into a selection set called Fixed. Finally, the skirt itself was converted into a sub-patch object. It may not look like much, but that's the beauty of it. ClothFX can turn a ho-hum object such as this into something great.

Before we begin tweaking the settings for ClothFX, let's talk briefly about the scene. The tube object already has three keyframes, which give it a slight spin to its right. You should make it a rule to set up and refine your motions *first*, then apply ClothFX for the soft-body simulation. The order here is important. If you set up your dynamics first, then tweak the motion of your

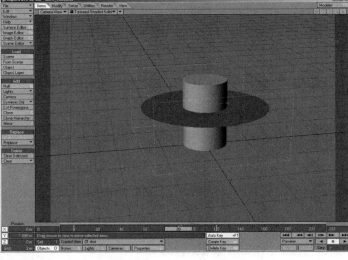

*Figure 19-28: Our simulated Skirt object.*

object, you will have to rework the simulation all over again.

You'll notice that the tube is the only object in the scene. Technically speaking, this violates the principal law of the Dynamics Community, as there are no opposing dynamics to which this object is accountable. Under normal circumstances, we would correct this by adding a social dynamic such as Gravity. But in this situation, we can avoid the extra trouble of setting up an independent Gravity object and simply use the Gravity setting available in ClothFX.

1. Bring up the Object Properties panel for the Skirt. Click on the **Dynamics** tab and choose **Cloth** from the Add

Dynamic pop-up. Then click on **ClothFX** in the Dynamics list to bring up its settings.

Due to a bug in ClothFX, I cannot walk you through the *individual* application of each setting, but I can walk you through the *group* application of specific settings. And again, keep in mind that these settings are described in detail in the manual and online help system.

2. In the **Basic** tab of the ClothFX properties, select the Fix pop-up menu and choose the **Fixed/pointset** option. The Fix option allows you to choose the points that will *not* be affected by ClothFX. All of the points in the object *except* those in the skirt were added to the Fixed selection set. By choosing that selection set here, we are telling ClothFX to ignore the rest of the object and focus solely on the skirt.

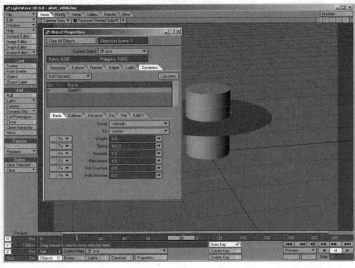

*Figure 19-29: The default ClothFX settings.*

3. Change the Spring and Sub Structure settings to **750**. Spring deals with the ability of a point to move closer to or farther away from those directly *in line* with it. Sub Structure deals with the ability of a point to move closer to or farther from those directly *across* from it. (See Figure 19-31.) Increasing these settings makes it more difficult for the points of our object to move from their original positions and will help simulate a more sturdy cloth like cotton rather than a more flimsy one like silk.

### Note

The settings used to get the "right" look for each Dynamic object are greatly dependent upon the size, shape, and number of polygons in the object. The settings we're using in this tutorial will work well for this object, but they may not work for a different object. It's important, then, to pay close attention to what each setting does. Learning the role of each setting will help you troubleshoot problems in the simulation and enable you to make intelligent decisions about what changes need to be made when those problems arise.

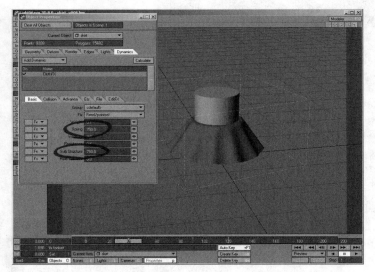

Figure 19-30: Change the Spring and Sub Structure settings to 750.

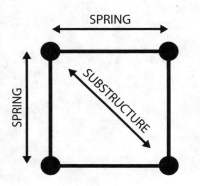

Figure 19-31: Spring and Sub Structure as they affect quad polygons.

4. With Spring and Sub Structure set, switch to the Etc tab and change Gravity to **−9.8 m**. Changing gravity here eliminates our need for an independent social dynamic in our Dynamics Community.

5. Press **Calculate** and take a look at the results.

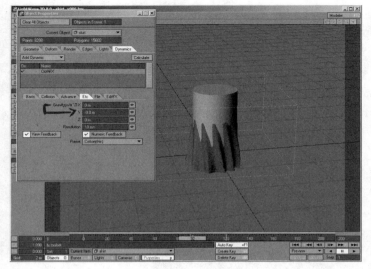

*Figure 19-32: Set Gravity to –9.8 m.*

6. The object now has a sense of weight (having activated Gravity) and is beginning to look more like cloth; however, it's colliding with the tube object. Let's fix this. Switch to the **Collision** tab and set Collision Detect to **<all>**. This opens up a variety of options. We can leave most of these at their default, but change Collision Offset to **30 mm**. Adjusting the offset helps keep the skirt from penetrating the surface of the tube by creating a 30 mm invisible barrier between the two. Finally, set Self Collision and Double Side to **<all>**. This will ensure that the skirt can interact with itself.

7. Press **Calculate** and check the results again.

Adding collision detection certainly helped, but it didn't completely solve the problem. We can increase Collision Offset to compensate, but there's a larger issue here. The skirt is stretching in ways that pull the polygons *into* the tube. We need to resolve the stretching.

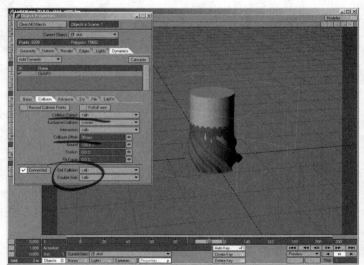

*Figure 19-33: Adding Collision detection helps keep the skirt from passing through itself and other objects.*

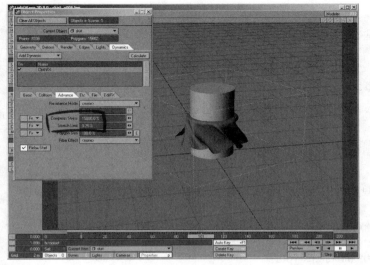

Figure 19-34: Boost Compress Stretch and reduce Stretch Limit.

8. Click on the **Advance** tab. Increase Compress Stretch to **15000%** and reduce Stretch Limit to **0.25%**. Compress Stretch limits an object's ability to stretch. How far it is allowed to stretch is determined by Stretch Limit.

9. Press **Calculate** and check the results.

These changes helped constrain the skirt and are keeping it from penetrating the tube surface, but the cloth now looks like it's suffering from a bad case of static cling. There are several reasons for this. One is that the cloth is too heavy. When it swings around, it hits itself and gets caught in its own self-collision routines. Another is that the cloth is a little too responsive to the object's motion. We could increase the Spring and Sub Structure settings to make it stiffer,

but there's another setting we can use to resolve this.

10. Switch back to the **Basic** tab. Decrease Weight to **0.1**. This will make the cloth lighter and a little less responsive to the skirt object's motion. Then increase Viscosity to **3**. Viscosity operates as a dampening effect, making the

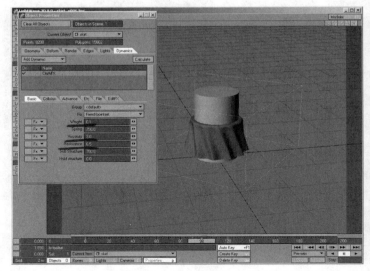

Figure 19-35: Change the Weight, Viscosity, and Resistance settings.

**503**

motion of the cloth less severe. Finally change the Resistance setting to **0.5**. This will make the cloth less resistant to wind and help its overall motion.

11. Press **Calculate** and check the results.

Making these last few changes really helped, and our skirt is now looking much better. But it seems to be puffing out at the point where it connects to the tube object. To fix this, we can tell the Sub Structure setting to only pay attention to the Skirt surface.

12. From the Fx pop-up menu to the left of Sub Structure, select the **Skirt/sur-face** option. Calculate and check your results.

That did it! We now have a great-looking skirt that responds well to the motion we've set up in our animation. ClothFX is an incredible tool and can produce amazing results. From here, you should continue to experiment and play with the settings. The more you work with ClothFX and become

familiar with it, the more it will reward you with outstanding results that would be impossible to create by hand.

## SoftFX

SoftFX is a personal dynamic that gives your object elastic qualities similar to those in ClothFX. The primary difference is that SoftFX is designed to be used on objects that need to return to their original state (meaning their size, shape, and orientation). ClothFX is not. For example, SoftFX can be used on the branches of a tree, allowing them to bend and sway in the wind. When the wind dies down, the tree will return to its original shape. SoftFX also has features that enable cyclical deformations, making it possible to automate many effects, including the expanding and contracting of your character's chest as he breathes.

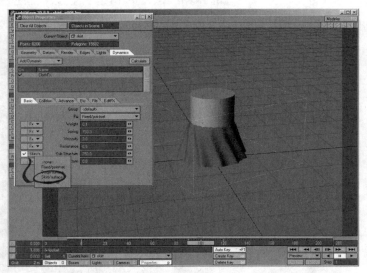

*Figure 19-36: Limiting the Sub Structure to just the skirt gives us just the look we want.*

In this final section, we'll be looking at several of the options available in SoftFX.

1. Bring up Layout and load the **Bendy.lwo** object from the Objects\ Chapter 19 directory. The Bendy object is a simple tube that was sectioned off with BandSaw. It was then converted into a sub-patch object. It has two weight maps. One is a gradient from 0% at the bottom to 100% at the top. The other is localized to the blue surface around the tube's blue center.

2. Let's set a few keyframes to give this object some motion. At frame 10, move Bendy **–200 mm** to the left. At frame 20, move him **200 mm** to the right. And at frame 30, move him back to **0**.

3. Play back the animation and take note of the motion.

4. Now bring up the Object Properties panel and from the Dynamics tab, add **SoftFX** from the Add Dynamic pop-up menu. There are a number of options here, but before we change any of

them, click **Calculate** to see what the default settings do to our object.

You can see that the original motion has been exaggerated and the object appears to be bound by a large rubber band. Even when the object reaches the final keyframe, it continues to move back and forth, its motion dampening over time.

As a personal dynamic, SoftFX is subject to the laws of the Dynamics Community. And in the Dynamics Community, every personal dynamic must be accountable to a social dynamic. However at this point, we only have one personal dynamic in our scene. There are no social dynamics. Only a bit of motion. Ah, but there it is. You see, motion *is* a social dynamic. It's a user-defined social dynamic that every personal dynamic will respond to. SoftFX still responds to collisions, gravity, and wind, but it's uniquely designed to respond to motion. Let's take a look at the SoftFX options.

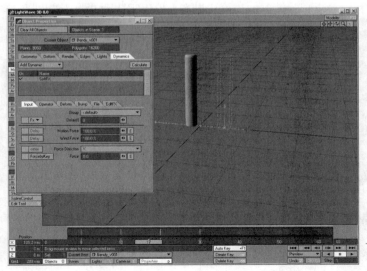

*Figure 19-37: Set your keyframes, then calculate SoftFX with the default settings.*

5.  Click on the **Input** tab of the SoftFX properties. Change the Motion Force setting to **500%** and recalculate.

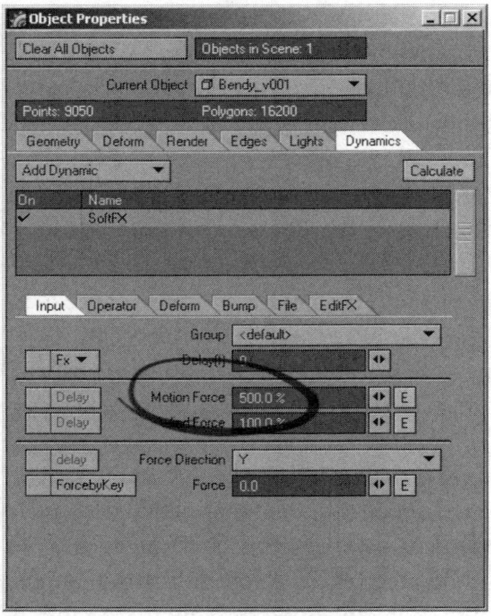

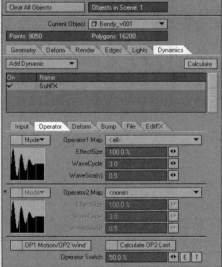

*Figure 19-38: Change Motion Force to 500%.*

6.  You can see that the object is now much more responsive to its motion.

*Figure 19-39: The Operator tab allows you to fine-tune the effects of motion on your object.*

Return Motion Force to **100%** and click on the **Operator** tab. The Operator tab fine-tunes the effect of motion (or optionally wind) on the object. There are two Operator maps. At this point, the top one is set to <all>, meaning that the motion will affect the entire object.

7.  The wave graphic to the left is a visual indicator of the falloff that will be applied to your object's motion. Change the EffectSize to **0%** and recalculate. The residual motion has been severely reduced and it now looks as if SoftFX has not been applied. The EffectSize setting works hand in hand with the Motion Force setting to determine the extent of the object's reaction to motion. Change EffectSize back to **100%** and change WaveCycle to **1**. Calculate and check the results. The number of times the object moves after it reaches its final keyframe has been reduced. Change WaveSize(s) from 0.5 to **3** and calculate again to see the results. The time it takes to complete the motion after the object reaches its final keyframe has been extended.

8.  This motion isn't very realistic so let's change the settings to something more "natural." Keep EffectSize at **100%** and change WaveCycle to **5**. This will create more motion after the last keyframe has been reached. Change WaveSize(s) to **0.1**. This will shorten the time needed to complete the residual motion. Press **Calculate** and check the results.

The object now appears to have come to a hard stop. As you can see, the Operator settings greatly affect your object's response to motion. Up to this point, we've only affected our object's position in response to

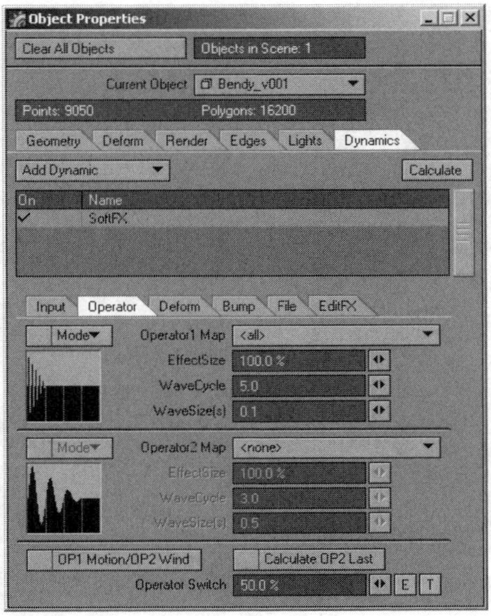

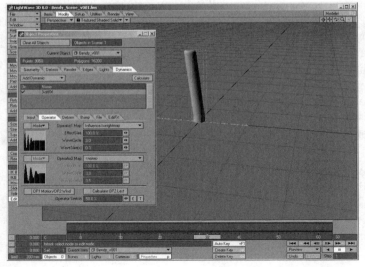

Figure 19-40: Creating a "hard stop" type of motion.

its motion. However, by using an influence map (such as a weight map, selection set, or even a surface), we can alter our object's shape as well.

9. Click on the **Operator1 Map** pop-up menu and choose the **Influence/**

**weightmap** option. The Influence weight map (described at the beginning of this section) is a graduated weight map with 0% influence at the bottom and 100% at the top. Leave EffectSize at 100%, but change WaveCycle to **3** and WaveSize(s) to **0.3**. Then calculate to see the results.

10. You can see that the object sways back and forth as if made of rubber. But if you look closely, the deformation is completely linear and the object appears to slant, giving it a slightly unnatural quality. What if we want the deformation to be a little more natural? We can affect the application of the deformation by applying a mode. From the Mode pop-up menu, choose **Square** and recalculate.

Square does not refer to the shape of the motion (as in square, rectangle, or triangle). Rather, it describes the application of the deformation. Square here is a mathematical term, as in $E=mc^2$. It amplifies the deformation of our object by multiplying the

Figure 19-41: Assigning an Operator map allows us to deform our object based on its motion.

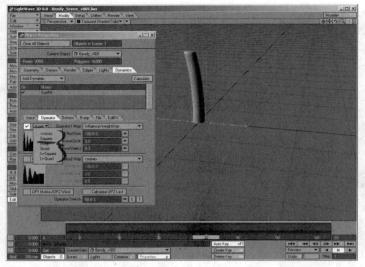

*Figure 19-42: The modes affect how the deformation is applied.*

Weight percentage by itself. This causes the top to receive significantly more deformation than the bottom. You can change the Mode setting and get immediate feedback on the results without having to recalculate. Feel free to try out the different modes to see how they affect the model. When you're finished, set Mode back to **Square**.

11. The deformation of our object now looks good. Let's make one last adjustment to this animation. Click on the **Bump** tab. The Wave settings at the bottom half of this tab allow you to define cyclical deformation. When restricted by an influence map, it opens the door for a variety of effects. We'll use it to make our Bendy object breathe.

12. Change the Make Wave By option to **<all>**. This applies the Wave deformation to the entire object. We can then use the Fx pop-up menu to specify the strength of the deformation. Choose

the **Chest/weightmap** option. The Chest weight map is localized to the blue section (or chest) of the Bendy object. The wave effect will have a strength of 0 outside that area and will gradually increase toward the center of the chest. Change WaveSize(s) to **0.01**. This affects the size of the deformation. You can leave LoopCycle at its default of **5**. LoopCycle determines the number of wave deformations, but since we've restricted the deformation by a weight map, this setting does not apply here. You can also leave LoopSpeed at its default of **2**. LoopSpeed determines the speed of the deformation. The default of 2 will produce a "rapid breathing" effect on this model. You can reduce this setting for a more natural motion or increase it for hyperventilation. Press **Calculate** and check out the results.

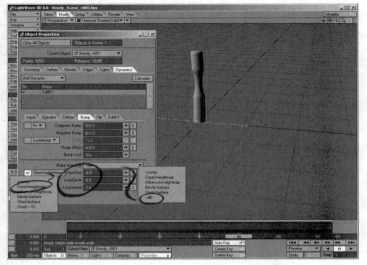

*Figure 19-43: Automated breathing, complements of SoftFX.*

Our Bendy object now responds frenetically to his motion and breathes hard from the rapid pace. It's worth noting that the settings for WaveSpeed and WaveSize can be keyframed with an envelope by pressing the E button. This will enable you to increase or decrease these effects over time, causing the breathing to start slow and pick up after the basic motion is complete.

. . .

As usual, we've covered a lot of ground in this chapter, but in reality, we've only scratched the surface. Dynamics are incredibly powerful tools. They are also a lot of fun to work with. Now that you've been introduced to the characters in the Dynamics Community, I encourage you to spend time becoming well acquainted with them. It's a relationship that will reward you greatly for the investment.

# Chapter 20

# Simulations 3: Fur and Hair

In this chapter, we'll take a detailed look at the tools needed to simulate hair and fur through the use of LightWave's SasLite plug-in. SasLite is the younger brother to Sasquatch, a comprehensive hair and fur simulator developed by Worley Labs. The focus of this chapter will be on the capabilities of SasLite, but we will also examine the differences between it and the full version of this amazing utility.

> **Note**
>
> Robin Wood is the artist who wrote the documentation on SasLite for the LightWave [8] manual. She is an expert on SasLite and has been kind enough to share her knowledge with us by authoring this chapter.

## An Introduction to SasLite

SasLite is a wonderful tool that allows you to add fur and hair to your objects. It works as both a displacement plug-in and a pixel filter. As such, you need to enable it in two different places in LightWave in order to see the effect.

Let's jump right in and see how it works.

1. Make a 1 meter sphere in Modeler, and bring it into Layout (or simply load objects\Chapter20\1MeterBall.lwo from the CD).

2. Open the Object Properties panel by tapping <p>, and click on the **Deform** tab, where the displacement plug-ins are stored. Click on **Add Displacement**, and choose **SasLite** from the list. (See Figure 20-1.)

3. Double-click on **SasLite** to open the Sasquatch Lite options panel. For now, just change Fiber Color to something

you like, and leave everything else at the default values. (See Figure 20-2.)

> **Note**
>
> I won't be going into great detail about what each of the SasLite options does, because I've already covered that in the LightWave 8 documentation. If you don't yet have LightWave 8, you can find that portion of the documentation on the companion CD in the Sas Settings folder.

4. Tap <**Ctrl**> + <**F8**> (or go to **Window | Image Processing...**) and open the Processing tab of the Effects window. You'll see places to add two kinds of filters to your rendered image: pixel filters and image filters. Since SasLite is a pixel filter, that's the one you want. Click on **Add Pixel Filter** and choose **SasLite** from the list. (See Figure 20-3.)

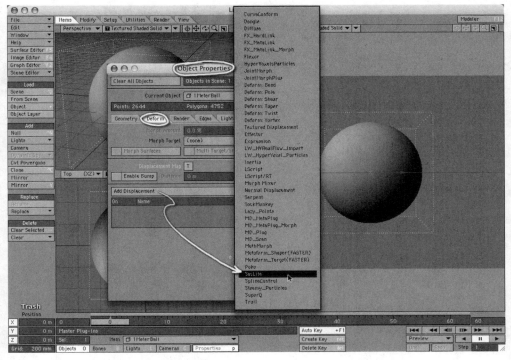

Figure 20-1: SasLite in the Add Displacement menu.

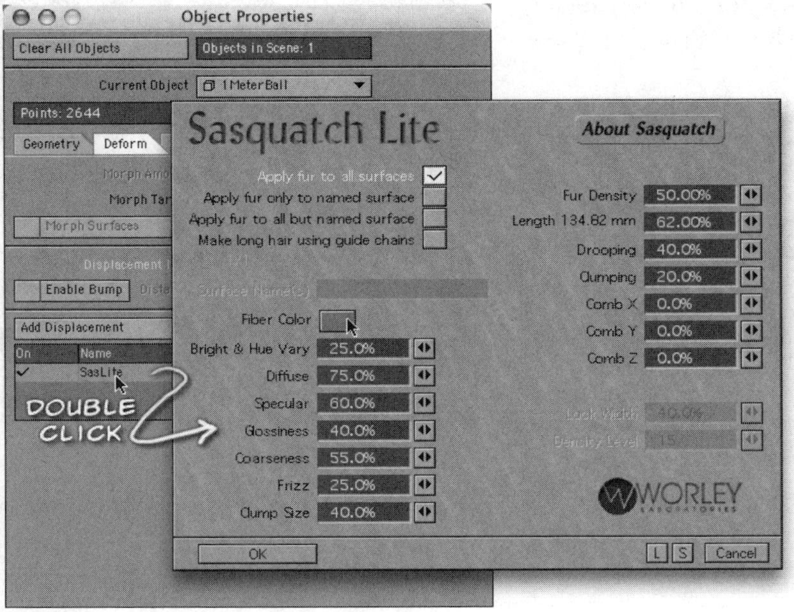

Figure 20-2: The Sasquatch Lite panel.

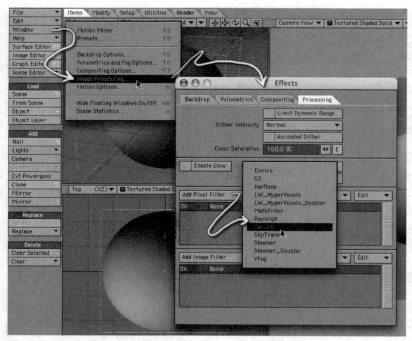

*Figure 20-3: SasLite in the Add Pixel Filter list.*

5.  Double-click on the filter name to open
    its options. Click **Self Shadowing** to
    enable it, and close the panel by click-
    ing **OK**.

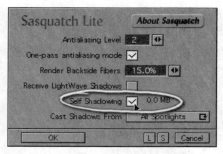

*Figure 20-4: Enable Self Shadowing in the
Sasquatch Lite panel.*

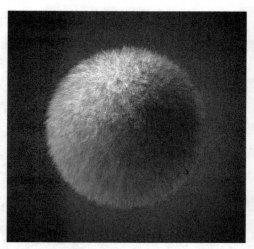

*Figure 20-5: A lovely fur ball!*

6.  Tap <**F9**> to render a single frame.
    Congratulations! You've used SasLite
    and made your first fur ball!

7.  But we're not going to stop here,
    because I want to show you something
    else. Tap <**L**>, then <**p**> (or click on
    **Lights** and then **Properties**) to open
    the Light Properties panel. Change

Light Type from Distant Light to **Spot-light**. You should see some difference in the OpenGL shading of your sphere, but not a whole lot.

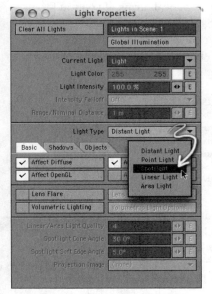

Figure 20-6: Change the Light Type to Spotlight in the Light Properties panel.

8. Tap <F9> now, however, and you'll find that the sphere is considerably darker. This is because the fibers are now self-shadowing.

SasLite, like its older brother Sasquatch, works best with spotlights. That's something that you will want to remember. (If you need to prove it to yourself, turn off Self Shadowing in the Pixel Filter options (<Ctrl> + <F8>) and do another <F9> render. You'll find that the fibers look almost exactly the same as they did when

Figure 20-7: Same fur ball, but now the shadows are working!

we were using a distant light. In other words, even though we had Self Shadowing selected in the SasLite Pixel Filter options, the fibers weren't really shadowing themselves because we were using a distant light.)

So, to sum it up, if you want to use SasLite, you'll need to do these things:

1. Choose **SasLite** from the Add Displacement menu in the Object Properties panel.

2. Choose **SasLite** from the Add Pixel Filter menu in the Processing tab of the Effects window.

3. Change the lights in the scene to **Spotlights** so that SasLite can shade the fibers properly.

Remember these three simple steps and the rest of the work is simply tinkering with the options!

# Beyond the Basics

So much for a fur ball. What if you want to make something other than tribbles or dust bunnies? Well, there are a few limitations in SasLite that require you to do a bit of extra work. But it can be done, and done quite effectively.

Say that you wanted to make a rug. No, not a toupee, although we will be doing that a bit later. I mean a flat rug, like the kind you find on the floor. Are you surprised that SasLite can be used to create a rug? Don't limit yourself to thinking of this as merely a "hair and fur" generator. SasLite makes fibers. It can simulate anything that's composed of strands — rugs, grass, seaweed, peach fuzz, centipede legs, cobwebs — anything that consists of one or more filaments.

The full version of Sasquatch can color the fibers according to maps (such as texture maps or weight maps) so the possibilities are endless. SasLite, however, can't; whatever color you choose for your fiber applies to that entire instance of SasLite. (There is a percentage variable for color,

but it varies both brightness and hue, and is entirely random in its application.)

So, in practical terms, if you want to use more than one color on an object you have to assign different surfaces to that object and different instances of SasLite for each surface.

> **Note**
>
> Be aware that you are limited to eight instances of SasLite in a given scene, so if you need more than that, you'll have to make several renders and composite them in post.

Since surfaces are applied on a per-poly basis, all you need to do is make the pattern for your rug using polys, and assign different surfaces and different instances of SasLite for each color.

This is really quite simple to do, especially if you want the fibers to be similar all over the object. Let's take a look at how it works using a rug with a very simple design as an example.

# Creating a Rug

Find the **StarRug.lwo** object on the companion CD (Objects\Chapter20), and load it into Modeler. (Yes, SasLite only operates in Layout, but this model needs some work. If you want to skip this part, you can. The StarRugEnd.lwo object doesn't need these modifications.)

When SasLite puts fur on a poly, it won't reliably follow concave curves. In other words, if you can draw a straight line between any two points of a poly, and part of that line falls outside the poly, the fur may follow that line. You can see what I mean by looking at Figure 20-8.

Figure 20-8: SasLite can't follow the outline of this poly, which results in undesirable ruggage.

1. To fix this, it's necessary to split the poly so that you can't draw such a line. So, in Polygon mode, select the central star by clicking on it in the Perspective viewport.

2. Then tap the **<Spacebar>** to toggle to Points mode. (The star remains selected, although you can't see that.) Select two inside points that aren't next to each other, as shown in Figure 20-9. Then tap **<Ctrl> + <1>** (or go to **Multiply | Subdivide: Split**) to split the poly.

3. Tap **</>** or click in any open area to drop the points. (If you have a mouse with extra buttons and you can assign keystrokes to them, you'll save a world of time if you assign the **</>** key to one of those buttons, by the way.)

4. Go to **Multiply | Subdivide: Add Points**, and add a point to the "split" line you just made. It should be near the center of the star. (See Figure 20-10.)

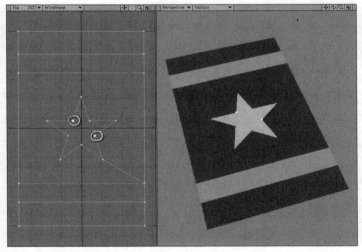

Figure 20-9: Select these two points, and split the poly.

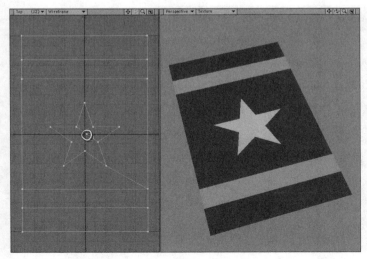

Figure 20-10: Add a point to the polys, as shown.

5. Tap the <**Spacebar**> to drop the Add Points tool, and select one of the inside star points and the new, central point. Split the poly again, (<**Ctrl**> + <**l**>) as shown. (See Figure 20-11.)

6. Drop those points, and repeat Step 5 for each of the remaining two inside corner points of the star. When you're finished, you should have a line going from each of those points to the middle point.

7. Select that point, and tap <**F2**> (or go to **Modify | Translate: Center**) to center it. Then tap <**Ctrl**> + <**t**> (or go to **Modify | Translate: Drag**), hold down the <**Ctrl**> key to constrain the movement, and drag it down until the five polys that make up the star look about the same size. (See Figure 20-12.)

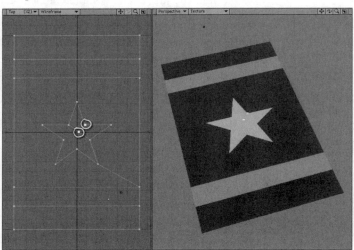

*Figure 20-11: Split the poly again, using these two points.*

*Figure 20-12: Center the middle point for symmetry.*

8. Now SasLite will read the star correctly, but it will still render fur over the entire ground that the star sits on. So, once again, select the large poly that makes this background, and split it into smaller polys that have no concave curves.

9. When you're finished, send the object to Layout (or if you skipped the previous steps, load the **StarRugEnd.lwo** file from the CD). Change the light to a spotlight. (Lights (<**L**>), Properties (<**p**>), and change the light type.) Select the rug and rotate it so that you can see it in a Camera viewport. Make sure it's well lit by the spotlight.

10. Open the Surface Editor. When you're assigning fur to surfaces in SasLite, you need to type in the exact name of the surface. It's easier to do this if the Surface Editor is open and you can see the name. (See Figure 20-15.) (By the way, if you are wondering why there's not just a drop-down list, it's because you can use a wildcard character, "*" (asterisk), to select several surfaces at once. So "*hair" would apply the displacement to Leghair, Chesthair, Tailhair, and Backhair (but not FaceHair, as it's case sensitive), which saves time.)

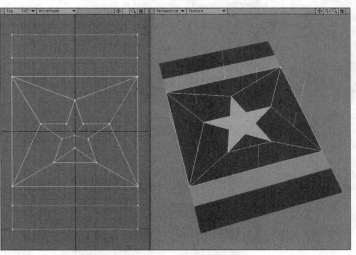

Figure 20-13: Split the ground into polys that will render correctly.

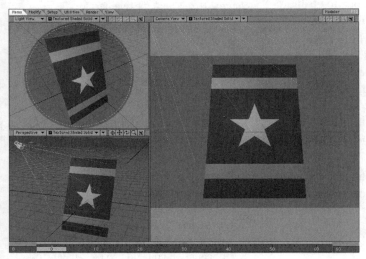

Figure 20-14: Set the rug up for easy rendering.

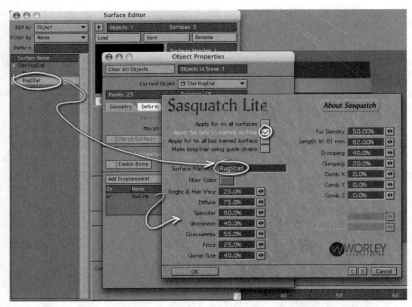

Figure 20-15: With the Surface Editor open, it's easy to pick which surface you want the fur applied to.

11. Open the Objects Properties panel. Click on the **Deform** tab and choose **SasLite** from the menu. Double-click on it to edit the parameters. The first thing we need to do is make sure that this instance will only be applied to one of the colors (surfaces) on the rug. So, at the top, click in the box to enable **Apply fur only to named surface**.

12. When you do, the Surface Name(s) text field will be enabled. Pick a surface from the Surface Editor, and type that name into the field. I'm going to use **RugStar**. If I type it correctly and hit the <**Tab**> key, the little green numbers will now read 1/3. If they say 0/3, check your typing.

(The first number tells you how many surfaces are using this instance of SasLite. The second tells how many surfaces there are in this object.)

Figure 20-16: Check the numbers to make sure that you typed correctly.

13. Pick a Fiber Color that goes with the star. I'm choosing yellow. (If you pick a color that's similar to the surface color, you can get away with less density, which saves rendering time.)

14. Now it's time to tweak the fibers in the rug. I'm setting Bright & Hue Vary quite low (**5%**) because I don't want much variation in the yarn colors used. Diffuse is high, and Specular and Glossiness low because it's yarn, and I don't want it to be shiny. Coarseness is high, because yarn tends to be fairly thick.

Frizz is low, because I want the fibers to be straight. Clump Size is low, because I want the rug to look fairly new.

15. Fur Density is fairly high, because I don't want to see "holes" in the fibers of the new rug. Length is around 15 mm, because I'm making the rug "real size" and that's the length of the fibers on the rug I have here. Drooping and Clumping are very low, because of the "new" look I'm going for. Finally, I've set Comb Y to **90%** so the fibers will stand up tall.

> **Note**
>
> The Comb values are relative to the model orientation in Modeler, not the way it's sitting in Layout, so the fibers will grow away from the polys, even though we've rotated the rug.

16. You can match the numbers shown in Figure 20-17, or you can choose your own, of course.

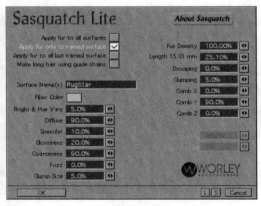

*Figure 20-17: The settings used for the rug pictured.*

17. When you're finished, click **OK**. You should see "SasLite Seen on RugStar" in the Add Displacement area of the Object Properties panel.

*Figure 20-18: SasLite applied to a surface.*

18. Tap <Ctrl> + <F8> (or go to **Window | Image Processing...**) and open the Processing tab of the Effects window. Click on **Add Pixel Filter**, and choose **SasLite** from the list, as you did before. Make the fibers self-shadowing, so you can see them in the test renders. You know how to do that.

19. Tap <F9> (or go to **Render | Render Frame**) to see what you have. (It may take several moments to apply SasLite, depending on the speed of your computer.) If you like the results, then move on to the next step. If you don't, then feel free to tweak the settings until you do.

20. Once you're happy with the fibers, you need to assign the same settings (except for color) to the other two materials. To do that, just click the **SasLite Seen on RugStar** line with the RMB (right mouse button) and choose **Copy** from the drop-down menu that appears. Click again, and choose **Paste** to create another instance with the same settings. **Paste** again, so you have three instances. (See Figure 20-20.)

21. Then simply click on each setting to open it, type in the name of the surface, and choose a new color. The rest of the settings can remain the same. When you're finished, you should have three instances, each showing a different surface (Figure 20-21).

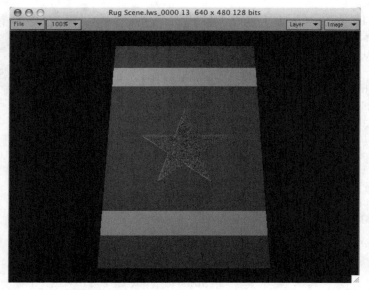

Figure 20-19: Fibers on the star!

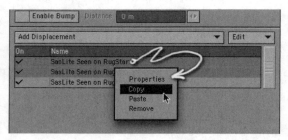

Figure 20-20: Copy and paste the displacement, one per surface.

Figure 20-21: Three colors, three instances.

22. Render (<**F9**>), and you'll have a rug with three colors of fibers. You can, of course, obtain textural variation by adjusting any of the other parameters.

You might also want to enable **Receive Shadows**, as was done here, in the SasLite Pixel Filter panel. Play with it some, and have fun!

Figure 20-22: Finished rug, in its natural habitat.

## There's Nothing Plain about This Grassy Plain

In the previous example, we used a separate instance of SasLite for each surface. You can also use multiple instances of SasLite on the *same* surface to add extra punch to your renders. For instance, you can easily make a field of mixed grass and weeds.

1. Load the **GrassyPlain.lws** file from the CD (Scenes\Chapter_20), and let's see how that's done. Everything is set up and ready for you here; all you need to do is add the plug-ins. So, choose the **Pixel Filter** plug-in from the

Processing tab in the Effects window, and the **Displacement** plug-in from the Deform tab of the Object Properties, as always.

Open the filter, and let's make grass.

2. There's only one surface, so we can just leave it on the default (**Apply fur to all surfaces**) for application. Choose a grass color, and set the parameters. You can see what I used in Figure 20-23.

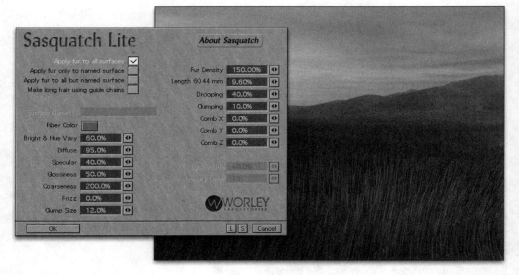

*Figure 20-23: Settings for the grass.*

As you will notice, you can push some of the parameters beyond 100%. In this case, I chose 200% Coarseness and 150% Density.

> **Note**
>
> Coarseness is linked with Length internally; as you make the fibers shorter, such as the grass here, they automatically become finer, as well. (Think of them scaling in all three dimensions.) You won't see the numbers change, but it's happening, and those wispy grass blades won't give you good coverage. The answer, of course, is to crank up the Coarseness value. In SasLite, the maximum coarseness is 400%. (The full version can go to 750%.)

If you decide to overdrive the Density as I did, that increase will cost you in render time. Often, you can get the appearance of denser fibers by using the same surface color and fiber color. You can see that in the image, where the distant hills have some green areas and some brown areas. The grass looks thicker where the ground is green.

3. It still looks rather sparse and homogeneous. It's easy to give it more coverage and more variety, however, by adding another instance of SasLite. Copy and paste the plug-in, as you did with the rug, and choose slightly different parameters for the second instance. Figure 20-24 shows what I used.

You can keep going, making more interesting and realistic grass, up to the eight instances that SasLite allows. I'll leave that for you to do. Have fun!

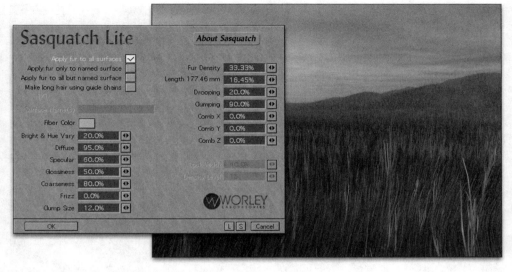

Figure 20-24: Settings for the second instance.

## Hair's Where It's At!

Of course, you might also want to use SasLite to make fur and hair!

Say you wanted to add a beard and mustache to the head that you made in Chapter 14. As you know, there is no mapping of any kind in SasLite; the entire surface that the displacement is applied to will have exactly the same length, density, combing, and everything else.

So how can you make something like a beard, which needs a smooth variation in hair length? Simple — you don't apply the fur to the skin polys at all. Instead, you copy and paste those polys, put them under the skin, and apply the fur to them. It will grow

right out through the skin with no problem, since it doesn't care in the least if there's another surface beyond the polys it's assigned to.

Shall we see how it's done?

1. Open the head, and save it with a new name, something like **HeadSasLite.lwo**. Then copy all the polys where you would expect the beard to grow, and paste them into a new layer. Put that layer in the foreground and the head in the background. Name the new layer **Beard** and make it the child of the Head layer.

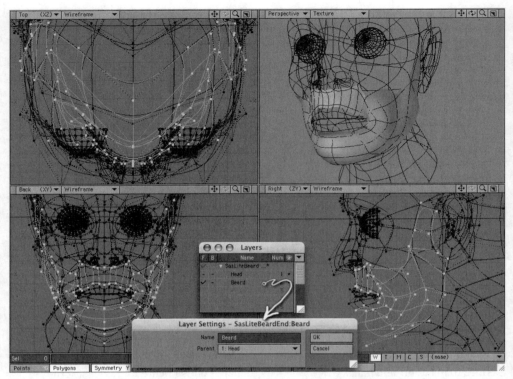

Figure 20-25: The beard polys in the foreground, with the head in the background.

2. Trim up the beard polys; in other words, split them, remove points, or whatever you think you should do to shape them as much like a "beard wig" as possible. The hairline will exactly follow whatever you make here, so take your time and be careful with it.

3. When it looks pretty good, assign it a new material (<q>), call it **Beard**, and make it a color that will contrast with the skin color. Tap <H> to get the Size tool (or go to **Modify | Transform: Size**) and make it a little smaller, so it lies under the head polys. Put both

layers in the foreground, and check from all angles to make sure that you can't see any of the beard through the skin. When you are satisfied with it, save it, and send the object to Layout, so you can start making test renders.

4. In Layout, apply the SasLite displacement and pixel filter, as you've done in the past. Leave the settings for both at the defaults for now; you'll have plenty of time to tweak them in a moment. Tap <F9> to get a quick render, so you can see how the basic shape looks.

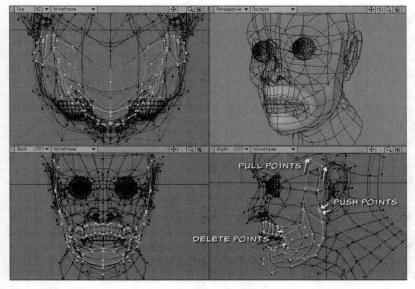

Figure 20-26: Reshape the polys so they have the line you want the beard to have.

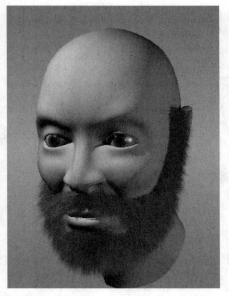

Figure 20-27: First test render; the beard with the default settings.

Now, most men trim their beards around the sideburns, so they won't grow straight out like this. You can't vary the length of SasLite fur, but you can pull the polys deeper into the head, so that the hair will appear to be shorter near the sideburns.

5. Return to Modeler, make sure that **Symmetry** is active, put the head in the background once more, and begin to pull those points away from the surface. I use the Drag tool (<**Ctrl**> + <t> or **Modify | Translate: Drag**) to do this, but you can use any method that you prefer. You are aiming for something like what you see in Figure 20-28.

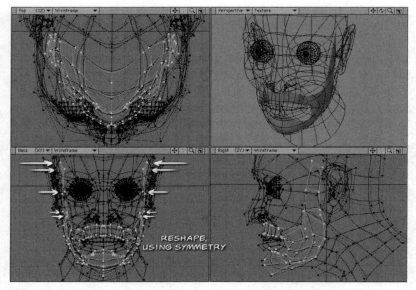

Figure 20-28: Pull the polys into the head where you want the hair to be shorter.

6.  When you think it's right, return to Layout and do another test render. Continue this process until you have the basic shape of a beard as shown in Figure 20-29.

7.  Now, it's time to tweak the settings. Begin by checking **Apply fur only to named surface**, because even though we only have one surface now, we're going to be adding more. That will enable the Surface Name(s) field. As always, you need to remember exactly what you named the surface. This time it's easy, so type **Beard** into the field. (Case does matter, by the way.) When you do, the little green numbers should change to say 1/1. If they don't, then you've made a spelling mistake.

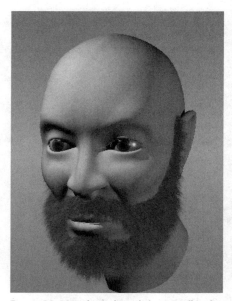

Figure 20-29: A basic beard shape, still with default settings.

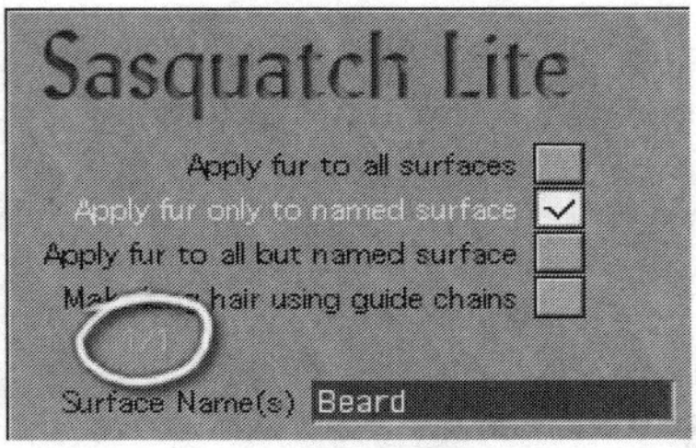

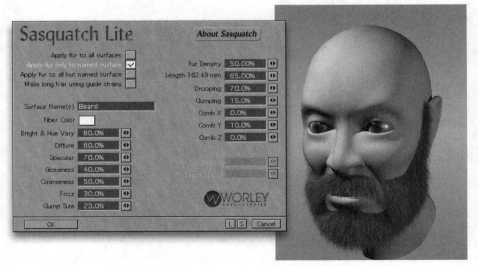

Figure 20-30: Check the numbers here to make sure the plug-in is being applied to the correct number of surfaces.

8. SasLite doesn't give you separate control of the hue and brightness; it's all one control. So, if you want a lot of variation in the brightness, choose a low saturation. Otherwise, you're likely to get very different colors, as well. (Which may be what you want. If that's the case, go for it!)

9. Human hair, even beard hair, tends to be fairly glossy. So leave the Diffuse value low, pump up Specular, and give it a medium Glossiness value. Beards are fairly coarse, so make that on the high side. Choose the Frizz that seems best (more for a wilder beard, less for one that's more groomed). The same goes

for Clump Size. The lower the value, the more the beard will look like it's been combed recently. The higher it is, the more you'll be making a Wild Man of the Mountains!

10. Give it medium Density and Length, with quite a bit of Drooping (otherwise, it's likely to look too spiky). Clumping, like Clump Size, will make it look clean or less than clean, depending on the value. (Higher for matted, lower for a neat beard.)

11. Combing influences the direction the hair grows. (It's also dependent on the Drooping value and the direction of the poly normal.) We're using quite a bit of Drooping, so the hair will leave the face and head downward. Let's use a small amount of combing on the positive Y axis to give the hair a bit of a lift and make it just a tiny bit bushier. Think of it as backcombing. (Giving it a negative value will make it less bushy, if that's what you would prefer.)

The values I used are shown in Figure 20-31 if you want to copy them.

Figure 20-31: The values used for the beard shown, with Self-Shadowing enabled.

**527**

12. Render this, and see how it looks. (You may want to add shadowing, so you can see what you're really getting, if you intend to use it in the finished render.

Fur can look very, very different with and without it.) If you're reasonably happy with the results so far, it's time to refine it further.

## Refining the Beard and Mustache

Mustache hair tends to grow out from the philtrum (the groove in the center of the upper lip), often leaving the middle without hair at all. Since you can't vary the combing on a surface with SasLite, the only way to achieve that is to separate the Mustache surface from the Beard surface, and divide it into two pieces. So we'll do just that.

1. In Modeler, select the polys that form the mustache and hide the rest (tap the <=> key). Then select the half on the positive X axis, and give it a new surface, say **lMustache**. Tap the <"> (<**Shift**> + <**Quote**>) key to invert the selection, and name the other side **rMustache**. (These correspond to the model's right and left side, not yours.)

2. Return to Layout and open the Object Properties panel if you've closed it. Right-click on the line that says **SasLite Seen on Beard**, and choose **Copy** from the drop-down menu that appears. Right-click again, and choose **Paste**. That will give you two identical copies of the displacement.

3. Open one of them and change the Surface Name(s) to **lMustache**. Leave everything else the same, except for the Comb X value. Make it pretty high. (I used **80%**, and also lowered the Comb Y value to **5%**.)

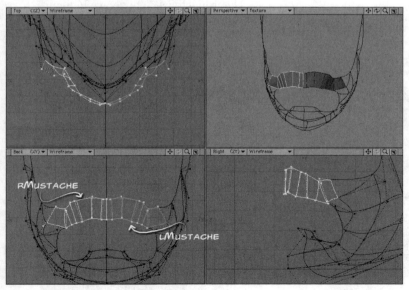

*Figure 20-32: Divide the surface into three — the beard and two halves of the mustache.*

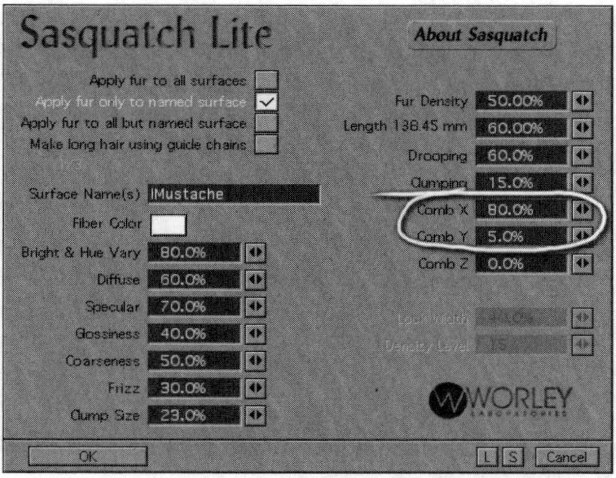

Sasquatch Lite | About Sasquatch

Apply fur to all surfaces ☐
Apply fur to only to named surface ☑
Apply fur to all but named surface ☐
Make long hair using guide chains ☐

Surface Name(s) |Mustache
Fiber Color ☐
Bright & Hue Vary 80.0%
Diffuse 60.0%
Specular 70.0%
Glossiness 40.0%
Coarseness 50.0%
Frizz 30.0%
Clump Size 23.0%

Fur Density 50.00%
Length 138.45 mm 60.00%
Drooping 60.0%
Clumping 15.0%
Comb X 80.0%
Comb Y 5.0%
Comb Z 0.0%

Lock Width 4.0%
Density Level 15

OK | L | S | Cancel

*Figure 20-33: New values for the left half of the mustache.*

4. Click **OK** to close it, and use the copy/ paste trick again to make a copy of it. Change the parameters of the copy so that it's applied to the **rMustache** sur-face, and put a *minus* sign in front of the Combing value (for instance, **–80%**). That will send the hairs along the –X axis, or toward the right cheek, and away from the center of the face.

Render to see what you have now.

5. If the break along the philtrum is too pronounced, go back into Modeler, select the points on either side of the center line, and bring them closer to the center. You might also want to split the mustache so it can conform better to the shape of the lip. (I used the Edge tools to do that here.)

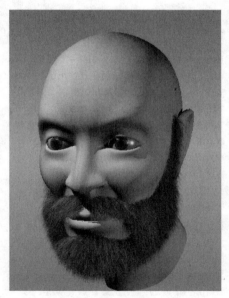

*Figure 20-34: The beard and mustache.*

**529**

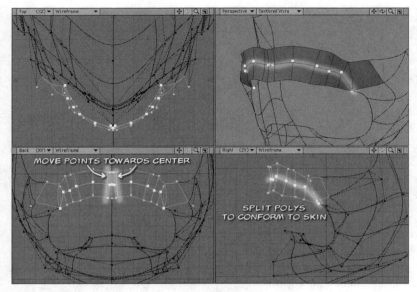

Figure 20-35: Modify the beard geometry further, if need be.

6. Keep refining and making test renders until you have the beard and mustache you are looking for. Don't be afraid to add another couple of surfaces, blend the density, put in streaks of a different color, etc. You can have up to eight instances of SasLite in a scene. (If you want more, you can render your scene in a couple of passes, and put them together in post.)

7. For this beard, I added a **BeardThin** surface on either side of the lower lip (just a couple of very small polys) and a **BeardWhite** surface to give him a couple of gray streaks. If you want to dissect what I've done, you can go through the SasLiteBeard.lwo file on the CD in Objects\Chapter20. Each step listed here corresponds to a layer in the model.

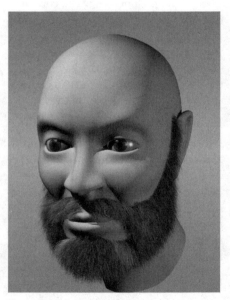

Figure 20-36: Finished beard.

8. When you're finished, and it's just what you want, you can cut the beard polys, if you desire, and paste them inside the head. (The SasLite displacements will be on the "Beard" object, not the "Head" object, so you'll have to copy/paste them to the head if you do this.) The extra polys make it a bit trickier to animate the head (you'll have to include them in your endomorphs), but if you can't afford the full version of Sasquatch, they will let you add believable hair, beards, mustaches, fur, etc., to your models.

You can use the same principles anytime you want to vary the length of SasLite fibers. If you want grass to grow higher on the bank of a river, if you want a werewolf's fur to bristle along his back, if you want to model a soldier with a crewcut — all you need to do is make sub-surface polys, and pull them back for shorter fibers or push them toward the surface for longer ones. (Or, really, just get the full version, and do it the easy way with maps and effectors.)

You can do the same thing for eyebrows, eyelashes, and the hair on a character's head, but there's another way to accomplish these effects that we have yet to explore. Instead of using subsurface fur patches, we can use long hair guides, which are also supported, in a limited fashion, in SasLite.

# Creating Hair with Long Hair Guides

Long hair guides are two-point poly chains (two-point polys that share a point with another two-point poly) that direct the flow of the fibers. To work in SasLite (or Sasquatch, for that matter), it's necessary for the point on the "root" end to have a different surface than the rest of the chain. (That's how the plug-in determines which end is which.) They are usually named "Hair" and "Root" to keep things simple.

SasLite will generate a lock of hair that follows the general direction of the guide. The number of hairs in that lock, their length, and how closely they follow the guide is determined by the number and placement of polys in the chain and the settings in SasLite.

Let's start with the hair on his head. There are several methods to do this, the "point" of all of them being to spend less time creating the guides than it would take to actually grow the hair.

Making hair guides can be grueling, but it doesn't have to be. The more control you want or the more complex the hairstyle, the more guides you'll need. The process I'm about to show you isn't the easiest, but it will show you a way to make a whole lot of guides reasonably quickly, without using any third-party plug-ins. You won't normally need quite this many, but just in case you do, here's a good way to get them.

1. Begin by lassoing all the polys that could have hair growing from them. Then tap the < } > (right curly bracket) key to Select Connected and get the next ones, too. (Because of the way that subpatches work, the curve changes when polys are abruptly removed. By grabbing the polys next to the ones that you actually want, you can ensure that doesn't affect the polys you need.)

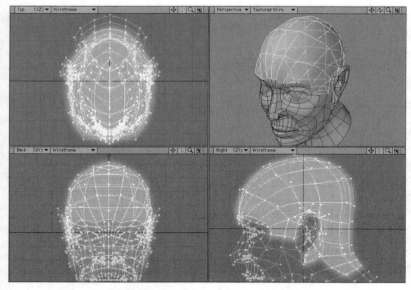

Figure 20-37: Select the scalp polys and the ones next to them.

2. Paste those polys into a new layer. For this particular method, we're going to use a lot of points to grow hair guides from, so tap <Ctrl> + <d> (or go to **Construct | Convert: Freeze**) and freeze the polys, which will make faces from the "virtual" polys in the subpatches. Tap the <Tab> key to subpatch those polys, and freeze again. (If you don't think you need as many guides, then you might want to freeze only once, or change the Subpatch level (in either direction) before freezing.)

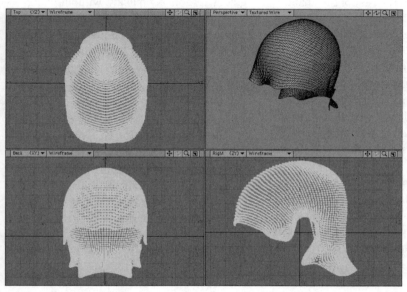

Figure 20-38: The poly-rich mesh that results from double-freezing.

3. We don't need the polys, just the points. So tap <k> (or go to **Construct | Reduce: Remove | Remove Polygons**) to "kill" the polys. That will leave you with a bunch of points that aren't connected to anything. Copy the whole bunch and paste them into another layer. Now begin to lasso and remove sections to form the actual hairline. As always, it helps if you have a reference. If you accidentally get too many, you can grab them from the previous layer, and paste them in here. Just tap <m> to merge the points, so you won't have to worry about multiple overlapping point problems. Keep going until you are happy with it.

4. When you're satisfied, tap <m> to merge points. (Even if you haven't copied points from another layer it's good to do this just to be safe.) Then reduce the size of the wig slightly so it fits

inside the scalp <H>, tap <J> (or **Modify | Transform: Jitter**), and jitter the points a tiny bit so it looks more like hair roots and less like transplants. Name this layer **Roots**. (You can name layers in the Layers window found under the Windows menu.) You can delete the points from the previous layer now, if you feel so inclined, or save them "just in case."

5. We're going to rail extrude the two-point polys, but right now, we've only got points. Rail Extrude doesn't work on points. Therefore, we must convert our points into polygons. Go to the **Create** tab and click on **Polygons: Points to Polys**. Give them the surface **Root** (<q>), copy the whole thing, paste it into another layer, and call it **Hair Building**. Tap <q> again, and change the surface to **Hair**.

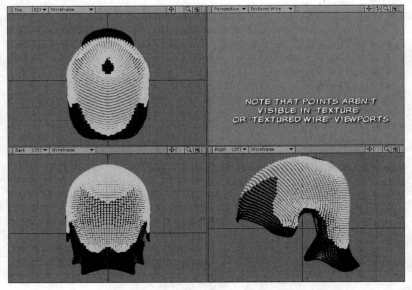

*Figure 20-39: Trim the extra points away from the hairline. (Original points shown in background for clarity.)*

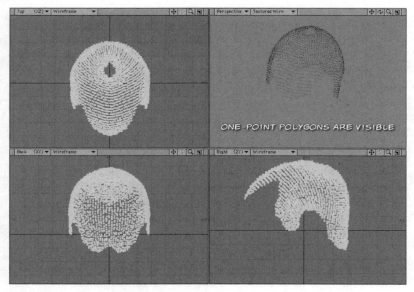

Figure 20-40: The Roots layer, all ready to grow hair!

6. Select the one-point polys around the hairline, including a good portion of the front, and place them into an empty layer called **Hairline**. We're going to style them more carefully in a few minutes, but it's easier if the bulk of the hair is done first. (Depending on the style of the hair, these points could be along a part, just in the front, on the side, or wherever the scalp shows.)

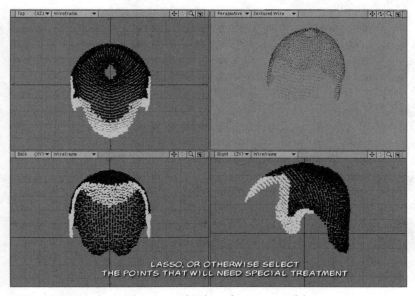

Figure 20-41: Put the Hairline in another layer for more careful treatment.

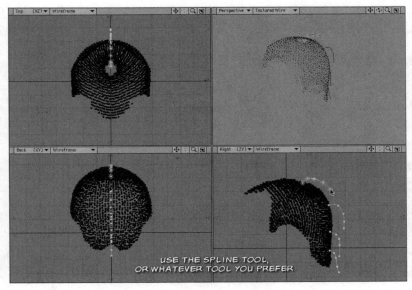

Figure 20-42: Begin to make curves to describe the bulk of the hair.

7. Open an empty layer, and put the Head and Hair Building layers in the background. Beginning at the center, or where the part is, start to make a series of spline curves (you can use whichever of the Curve tools you are most comfortable with).

8. We are going to use Rail Extrude to extrude the one-point polys, which will automatically make two-point poly chains from them. The spline curves we just created are the rails the polys will be extruded along.

In SasLite, the actual hairs may appear to be a little shorter than the hair guides, so keep that in mind while you are making them.

9. Work from the hairline at the collar to the front, so you can make each curve slightly overlap the one below it. This will keep the hair falling naturally, instead of having fibers diving under the ones below.

10. Make two to five curves, and then begin to copy/paste them, and move them around the head, rotating so that they will follow the line you want the hair to have. The more curves you use, the smoother the hair will be, but be aware that there are limits to how many splines Rail Extrude can handle before it simply tells you there are too many. (If you reach those limits, you can divide your hair into smaller sections to extrude, of course.)

11. When you have enough to describe the basic shape of the hair, somewhere between 5 and 20 or so, depending on the hairstyle, put the curves in the background, and the Hair Building layer in the foreground. Tap <Ctrl> + <r> (or **Multiply | Extend: Rail Extrude**) to open the Rail Extrude: Multiple panel.

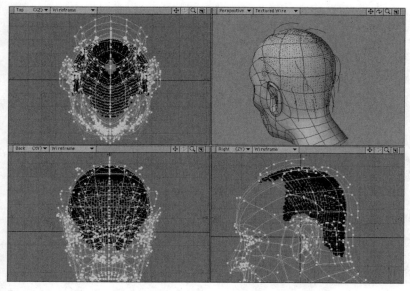

Figure 20-43: The head, with enough rails to describe the main hair mass.

12. Choose to make Segments according to **Length**, make them **Uniform**, and choose around **5** or **6** segments. (There are limits to how many vertices SasLite allows, and they add up quickly.) Leave the Strength at **2**, and disable both **Oriented** and **Scaling**.

13. Click **OK**, and you'll have a bunch of two-point poly hair guides! Name the

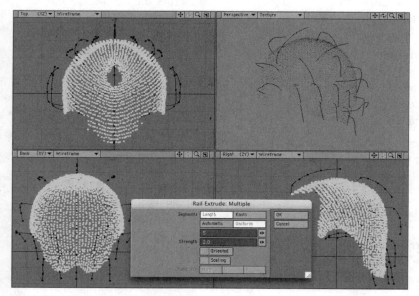

Figure 20-44: The Rail Extrude: Multiple panel.

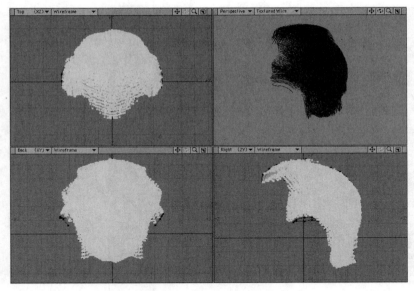

*Figure 20-45: The bulk of the hair guides, made in a snap!*

layer **Wig**. We'll be collecting the hair here as we build it.

Now, of course, there are things that can go a little weird at this step.

14. The most common problems are the guides swirling in odd directions, piling up in ridges, and/or leaving bald spots when viewed against the head. Most of these are caused by the same thing — not enough curves for the number of one-point polys being extruded. (I've found that sometimes, for some reason, you can also fix the swirling problem by undoing and deleting the last point on the curve. So if you're pretty sure there are enough, you might want to try that.)

To fix them, of course, either add some curves, or extrude a fewer number of one-point polys at once.

15. If a lot of the hair is below the surface, then your splines might be too close to the head. **Undo**, select all the points on the spline except the endpoints, and

use the Size tool <**H**> to make it all larger.

16. Now, if you want to shape it as you go, which is easier from my point of view (but also requires more steps), cut the hair. (That sounds like barber talk, but I really mean to cut using the <**Ctrl**> + <**x**> shortcut, of course.)

17. Open the **Roots** layer and paste the hair in. Tap <**m**> to merge points, and accept the defaults. That will merge each chain with its root. Select the Hair material (using the Statistics window <**w**>) and tap the <**]**> key (or go to **View | Select: Select Connected**) to get the roots, as well. Cut again, and paste back into the **Wig** layer. Now you can tweak the hair to your heart's desire, without any fear of the guides becoming disassociated from their roots. Go ahead and do that, shaping it until you are happy with it. The Magnet tool works well for this, but of course you can use any tool you are comfortable with.

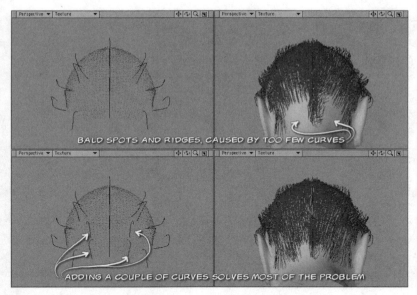

Figure 20-46: Ridges leaving bald spots, corrected by adding four curves.

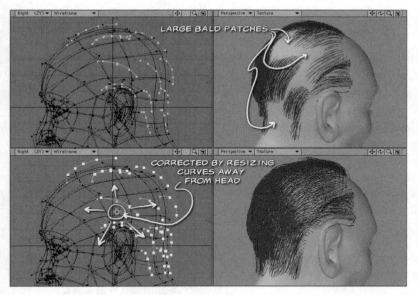

Figure 20-47: If the splines are too close to the head, the guides will be inside it, not outside.

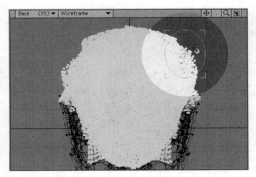

Figure 20-48: Styling the hair with the Magnet tool.

18. Once you are happy with that part of the hair, it's time to work on the front and the hairline. This is done the same way, except that you work on only a small section at a time, which gives you much better control and allows you to style the hair with (relative) ease.

By small, I mean small. The trick is to keep the sections to 20 or 30 of the one-point polys at a time.

If the portion of the hairstyle you're working on is symmetrical, select a group

from the **Hairline** layer in one of the Side viewports (Right or Left) so you get both sides, cut it, and paste it into an empty layer. Then make two or three splines, as if you were modeling the outermost hairs (and perhaps a middle hair) from that group. Mirror those splines across the X axis, and tweak the mirrored ones a tiny bit so it's not too symmetrical. (I use the Drag tool (<**Ctrl**> + <**t**>) for that, because I'm a control freak, but you might want to use Jitter.)

19. Then Rail Extrude the points, using more segments if you can afford it. If they haven't gone wonky (that's a technical term), put the guides and the head in a foreground layer, and take a look. If they don't penetrate anything they shouldn't (like the ears), and if they are standing out from the scalp, move on to the next step. You don't have to be exact, since you can style the section with the Modify tools. But the closer you are, the easier that will be. Just don't make yourself crazy with it.

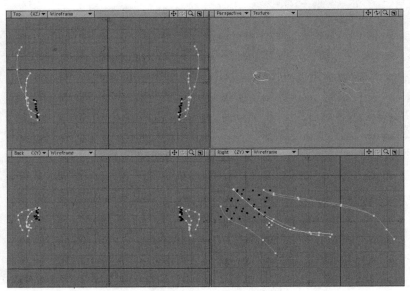

Figure 20-49: Symmetrical groups of one-point polys and rails.

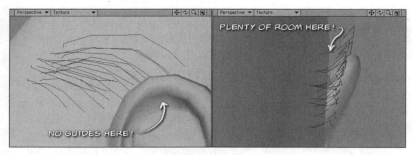

*Figure 20-50: Extruded guides, viewed against the head.*

20. If the style isn't symmetrical, it will take a little longer, because you'll have to grab the one-point polys one group at a time. You might find, though, that it's still easier to copy the curves and tweak them from group to group than it is to build a whole new set of curves.

Once again, I find it's easiest to work from back to front, with the finished hair piece and the roots you are currently working with in the background.

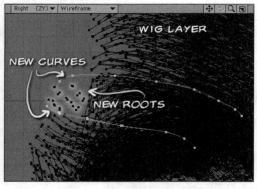

*Figure 20-51: Making the rails for another section of hair.*

**Note**

If you want to have the best, thickest hair you can have, then make sure you have more points at the tip than you do at the root, and extrude by knot, not length. SasLite uses the placement of points on the guide when it determines how to "grow" the hair. The more the points are concentrated at the tip, the thicker and longer the hair will grow.

21. As you finish each section, if you are using the style-as-you-go method, cut it and paste it into the **Roots** layer, merge the points, select the **Hair** surface, **Select Connected**, and paste it back into the **Hair Building** layer. Then, with that layer in the foreground and the Wig in the background, tweak the hair until you are satisfied with the shape. (Don't forget to add Minoxidil to make the hair healthy and strong.*) Once it looks good, cut it again, and paste it into the Wig layer. As I mentioned before, this method has more steps, and may take more time, but for me, it gives much better results (with a lot less stress).

(* Don't go looking for the Minoxidil button. It's a joke! If you didn't get it, take a break, right now.)

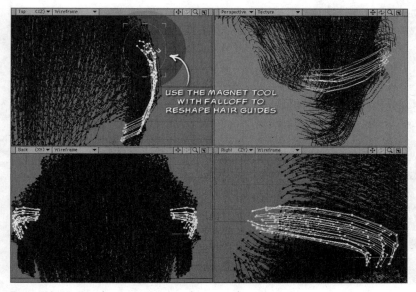

*Figure 20-52: Tweaking a section, working into the wig.*

While you are styling, remember that these are hair guides, not hairs. Every one of them will turn into multiple hairs when it's rendered with SasLite. *Complete coverage isn't necessary, or even particularly desirable*. It's better to make hairs that are a little offset, with an even amount of room between them.

22. If you aren't using the style-as-you-go method, then just cut each section as you finish it, and paste it into the **Wig** layer.

23. Once a section is pasted into the Wig, open the **Hairline** layer, cut the next section of roots, paste it into the **Hair Building** layer, and make curves for it. (You might want to save all the curves, or you might want to delete them. It's up to you.)

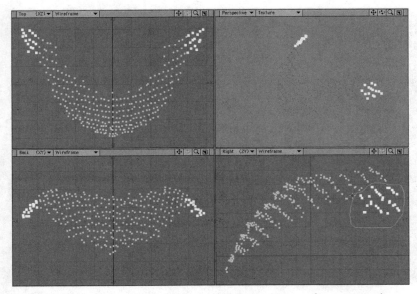

Figure 20-53: As each section is finished, select the next group of one-point polys.

## Note

When you're in the Wig layer, keep an eye on the number of points you have. Remember that SasLite will only allow *25,001 points per object* that has SasLite applied. If you exceed that number, you're going to have to break the wig into different layers. Since SasLite also allows only *eight instances of the plug-in per scene*, you'll need to keep the total below that number unless you want to render in multiple passes. Think about how many instances of SasLite you're using for eyelashes, eyebrows, hair, beard, mustache, etc., when deciding if you can afford to run over on the guides.

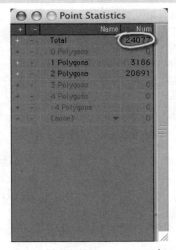

Figure 20-54: Keep an eye on this number in the Wig layer, so you don't exceed SasLite's limit of 25,001.

All of this will probably take a while, especially if you haven't done this kind of thing before. But eventually you'll have a full head of hair guides, ready to convert into realistic hair.

24. If you haven't used the style-as-you-go method, select all the one-point polys in the **Root** layer, paste them into the **Wig** layer, and merge the points now. If you decide that you want to style it, go ahead.

If you want to practice making the guides some other time and just want to use them for now, you can find the SasLiteHair-End.lwo model in the Objects\Chapter20 directory on the CD. (On the other hand, if you really want to dissect the procedure, there's a model called SasLiteHair-Guides.lwo there, too, which has layers for each step of the process.)

When you decide that your wig is as good as you can get it without a test render, then it's time to do exactly that! If your wig is too large for SasLite to handle (25,001 polys, remember), you'll have to split it.

## Splitting Hairs to Work with SasLite's Limits

Lasso the section you want to remove, and then tap the <]> key to select all the connected polys. (Anything without a root isn't going to work, remember, so you need to keep the whole length of each individual guide together.) Cut them and paste them into another layer. Both of them will need to have their own instance of SasLite. Good thing that you can copy/paste the options, huh?

How you split it, of course, is up to you. Since it's a wig for a balding man, I'm

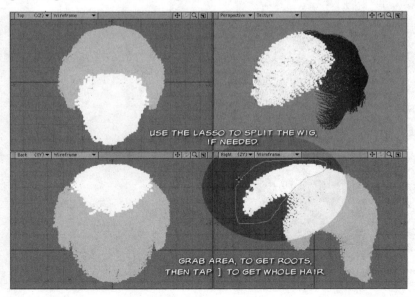

Figure 20-55: If you need to split the wig, try to do it so you get extra versatility out of it.

splitting it so that I have the possibility of an additional hairline, as shown in Figure 20-55. It's always a good idea to split it in some fashion that allows extra versatility, if you can.

When it's as ready as can be, save the head, and load it into Layout.

## Rendering the Hair

1. As always, you will need to apply the **SasLite** displacement in the Object Properties panel, as well as the **Pixel Filter** in the Processing tab of the Effects window.

2. Open the options for the Displacement plug-in, and choose **Make long hair using guide chains** from the list on the left. Once again, you'll need to type the name of the surface into the Surface Name(s) field. Unless you make a typing error, you should see the green numbers change, so the correct number of surfaces is displayed on the left. (In this case, 1 of 2. The second surface is the Root.)

3. Set your parameters however you want them. Figure 20-56 shows what I'm using for this particular model, if you want to copy them. Once again, I'm not going into detail about them, since I've done that already in the LightWave 8 docs.

4. Once that's done, you need to make a test render to see if your hard work is resulting in the hair you envisioned. But, if you render now, you'll see the polychain hair guides, as well as the hair. That's probably not what you want.

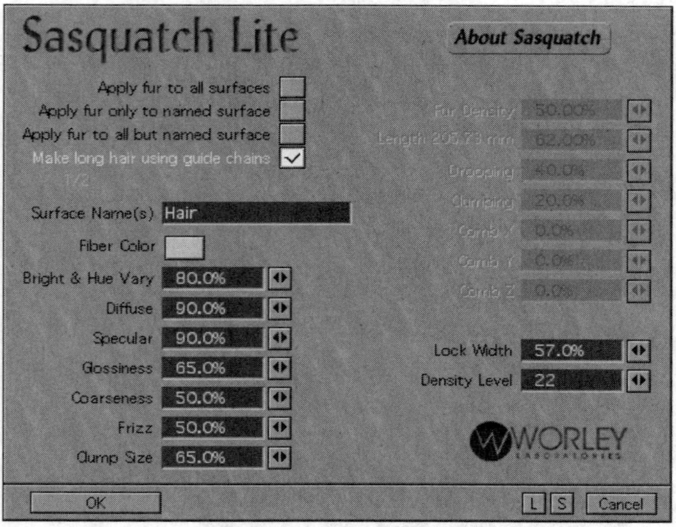

Figure 20-56: The SasLite panel when using long hair guides.

So, with the Object Properties window still open, click on the **Render** tab, and set the Object Dissolve to **100%**. That won't have any effect on SasLite, but it will cause LightWave to ignore the guides when it renders. (Don't forget to disable the shadowing as well to save render time.)

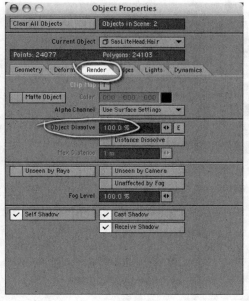

Figure 20-57: Set the Object Dissolve to 100% to hide the long hair guides.

5. Tap <**F9**>, and see what you've got. If you need to go back and tweak the guides, do that and make another render. Keep going, checking from all the sides that will be visible in your final render, until you have what you want. (Don't be afraid to copy and paste sections of guides to duplicate them if there's a thin spot in the hair. Just be aware of the SasLite limits when you do.)

The whole process can take an hour or more, but the results are well worth it. (Besides, if you get a nice wig, you can often reuse it for other characters with a minimum of restyling.)

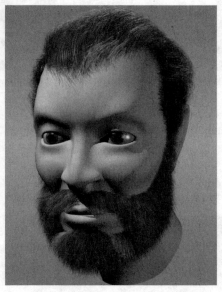

Figure 20-58: The finished wig-and-beard combo.

# Long Hair Guides, the Sequel!

We're going to use another method of dealing with long hair guides to give this guy some eyelashes. This one is a lot faster, at least for me, but it does use a couple of third-party plug-ins. The good news is that you can download them from the web for free.

1. Select a couple of polys from the eyelid where you want the eyelashes to grow. Then go to **View | Selection: More | Select Loop** to get the "rim" of the whole lid. Tap the <}> (right curly bracket) key to expand the selection to the loops above and below that, so that there won't be distortion when they

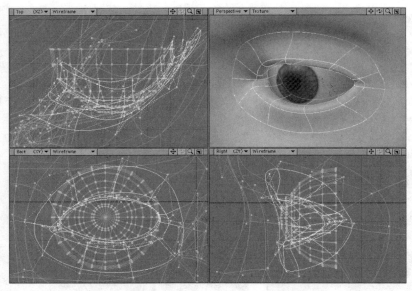

Figure 20-59: Select the polys for the lashes and the ones next to them.

are isolated (just like we did for the head). Copy and paste into a new layer.

2. Freeze the polys (<**Ctrl**> + <**d**>). Select two of the ones on the new edge, just as you did before, and **Select Loop** again. Then smooth shift the

whole loop (<**F**>), but don't resize or move it in any way. Just click in a viewport and drop the tool. Deselect the polys, then tap <**m**> to merge the points. That will leave you with a couple rows of two-point polys.

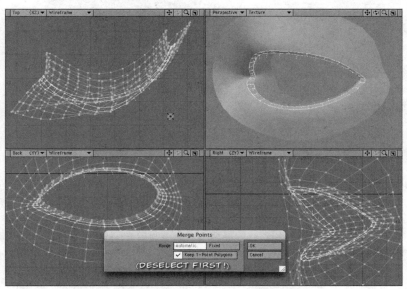

Figure 20-60: Select the edge loop, smooth shift, deselect, and merge points.

3. Usually, you just delete those polys; but we're going to use a free plug-in from D-Storm called **Polygon2Curve** to make them into a spline, which we'll then use to rail clone a lash. (You can download the plug-in from the D-Storm plug-in site at http://www.dstorm.co.jp/english\plugin\modeler.htm.)

4. Select the **2 Vertices** polys from the Polygon Statistics panel (click the + in the line), tap <"> (double quote) to invert the selection, and delete the polys. We don't need them any more. (It will look like you've selected everything, but you really haven't. Check the Statistics panel after deleting and you'll see the two-point poly chains are left.)

5. Select the "extra" one (whichever one you choose), and delete it. Then run the **Polygon2Curve** plug-in. (When you used Add Plug-ins (Utilities | Plug-ins), it probably went into the Utilities | Plug-ins: Additional menu. So check there for it.) That will make each poly into its own tiny little curve. Merge them into one long curve by tapping <Z> (**Detail | Polygons: Merge Polys**).

6. With the curve still selected, tap the <Spacebar> to toggle to Points mode, select the two points in the corners of the eyes, and tap <Ctrl> + <1> (**Multiply | Subdivide: Split**) twice to split the curve into two pieces.

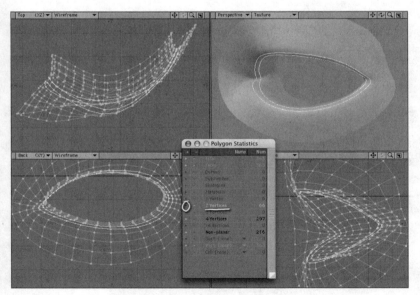

*Figure 20-61: Select the two-point polys from the Statistics panel.*

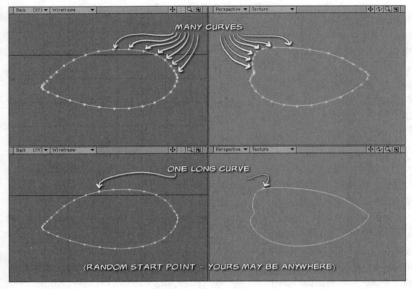

Figure 20-62: A string of little curves converted into one long curve.

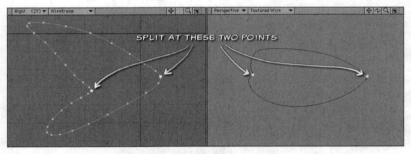

Figure 20-63: Select these points, and split the curve.

7. Use the <**Spacebar**> to toggle back; you should see three of the little diamonds that Modeler uses to show the

beginning of a curve: the two you just made and the one that resulted from merging the polys.

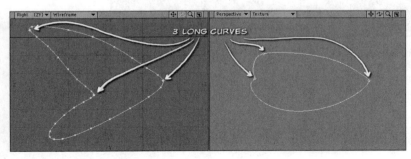

Figure 20-64: Three curves.

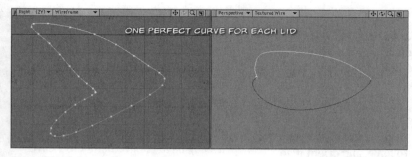

Figure 20-65: Merge the remaining two curves.

8. Click on whichever lid has only one spline to deselect it. That will leave both splines on the other lid still selected. Tap <Z> again, to merge those two splines, and you'll have two curves that perfectly match the eyelids, all ready to go!

9. Take the top eyelid curve and paste it into an empty layer. Delete any points that go too far into the corners of the eyes, where you don't want lashes to grow. Select the curve, copy it, and paste it back into the same layer, so you have two curves.

10. Reshape the curve that's still selected. I use the Stretch and Magnet tools, but you can use any tools you find most convenient. You're making a curve that describes the "trim line" you want the lashes to have. Remember that the actual hairs will look shorter than this, so make it a bit farther from the lid than the desired lash length. Make sure that both of these curves start at the outer edge of the lid. (The diamond should be at the outer corner when the curves are selected.) If they don't, tap the <f> key to flip them.

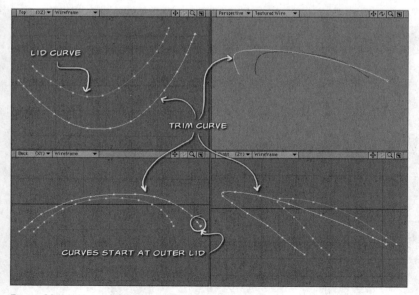

Figure 20-66: Upper lid, with eyelid and trim curves.

11. When you are pleased with them, put them in the background and open a new foreground layer. (The fastest way to do that is to click on another layer as the background, and then Invert Layers using the <'> (single quote) key.)

12. Draw a third curve, in the shape you want the lash to have, and orient it so that it appears to grow from the outer corner of the eyelid. Match it to the curves as closely as you easily can, with the diamond that shows where the lash curve starts placed *behind* the curve into the eyelid. (It doesn't have to be exact, but close is nice.) If you need to readjust the "trim" curve, then do so. (See Figure 20-67.)

13. After you are happy with all three curves, put the lash curve layer in the foreground, and the layer with the lid and trim curves in the background. Then go to **Multiply | Duplicate: More | Rail Clone…** to open the Rail Clone: Multiple panel. (See Figure 20-68.)

14. Choose whether you want to make clones by Length (evenly spaced) or Knots (weighted according to where the points are in the lid and trim curves), choose **Uniform** so you can determine how many clones there will be, and type in the number of lash guides you want, minus one. (You already have one, remember.) Leave **Oriented** and **Scaling** both enabled, so the lash will change orientation and size as it conforms to the rails, and click **OK**.

Presto! Perfect lashes, all set to go. But they are curves, and you need poly chains with roots. Fortunately, there is a plug-in for that called CurveToPolychain, written by Terry Ford. (In fact, there's more than one, but this is the best I'm aware of. It's available for both Mac and PC. Thanks to Richard Brak for compiling the Mac version, and to Terry for allowing us to use it in this book.) You can find it on the CD in Plugs_n_Programs. A number of other useful plug-ins are available at http://www.terryf.dsl.pipex.com/htm/frame plugins.shtml.

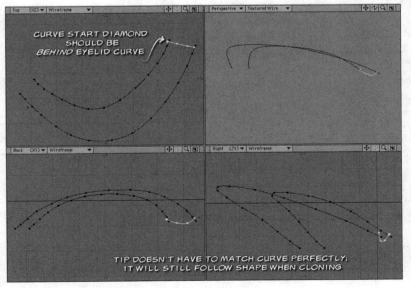

Figure 20-67: Position the first lash on the eyelid curve.

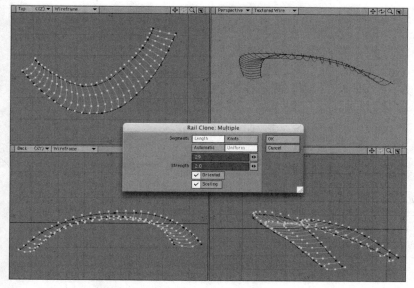

Figure 20-68: The Rail Clone: Multiple panel.

15. Run the **CurveToPolychain** plug-in. (If you haven't made a button for it, look in the Utilities/Additional menu.) Type in the name for the Chain surface, and one for the Root surface, or choose them from the drop-down menus. Then choose your segments and so on as you have for the last several plug-ins. Disable **Replace curves** if you want the poly chains to be made in a new layer (in case you want to preserve the original curves). Disable **Merge/Unify**

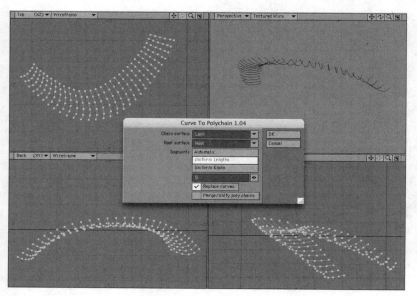

Figure 20-69: Curve To Polychain panel.

**poly chains** if you don't have any that overlap. (If there's nothing to merge and you leave it enabled, it's possible that Modeler will crash.)

16. Click **OK**, and there you go!

17. Repeat the process for the bottom lid, mirror both sets of lashes across the head, and you're done.

18. Take them into Layout, apply **SasLite**, and render to see how they look. Tweak if necessary. You know the drill by now!

# Eyelash Settings and Refinements

The values I used are shown in Figure 20-70. Coarseness and Frizz are high because these tiny chains make very fine hair and lashes look more realistic to me if they aren't too straight. A high Lock Width spreads them out more around the guides, both vertically and horizontally, so they don't have the all-lined-up look of artificial lashes.

For close-ups, or more realistic lashes, you can add points to the rails where you want them to grow more thickly. (Do this before you copy them to make the trim curves, of course, to save work.) Then clone using Knots, not Length, to get a more realistic distribution of lashes.

You might also want two sets of guides, one on top of the other, if you need extra-heavy lashes, such as in a glamour shot, where you want the model to appear "made up." That will enable you to control the length and clump size more easily.

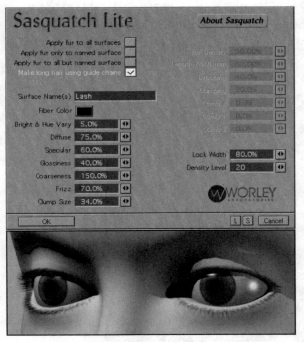

*Figure 20-70: The SasLite panel, and the lashes it makes.*

# Making Eyebrows

Eyebrows can be created using either fur or long hair guides. We're going to use long hair guides so that I can show you one more technique for creating them.

1. We are going to begin, once again, by selecting the area of the face that contains the polys the brow will grow from, and one poly out from that in all directions (<}>). Paste the selection into another layer. Tap <o> to open the General Options panel, and change the Patch Divisions to **5**. (That should give you enough points, without giving you too many.) Now Freeze (<**Ctrl**> + <**d**>) the polys.

2. Tap <**k**> to kill the polys so there's nothing left but points, and use the lasso to draw the brow in those points. The "brow" should light up, leaving the rest unselected. Take a look, and refine the selection if you are so inclined.

When it's perfect, tap <"> (double quote) to invert the selection. Take one more look, refine if necessary, and delete the selected points. That leaves you with just the brow points.

3. Mirror them, so you have brow points on both sides of the face, and give them a little jitter. (Very little in the Z axis, if your head is set up like most (facing down the Z axis). You don't want them to wander away from the skin.) **Hide** the points on your left (select and <–>).

4. Put that layer in the background, a new layer in the foreground, and draw an eyebrow hair in the middle of the brow. You just need one, but don't forget to shape it in all three dimensions. Mirror it, so you'll have a hair for the other brow, too. (If you're using the Numeric panel to make sure that your mirror is at 0 on all three axes, all you need to do is choose **Activate** and hit <**Return**> twice. The panel will use the same parameters as the last time.)

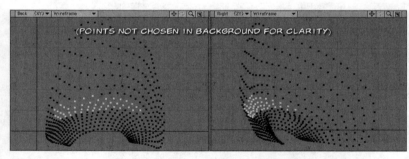

Figure 20-71: Choose the points for the eyebrow guides from the frozen group.

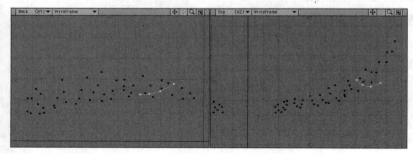

Figure 20-72: Make a single hair in the middle of the brow.

Point Clone Plus+

Random Rotation (Deg)

| Min H | -10.0 | | Max H | 20.0 |
| Min P | -10.0 | | Max P | 10.0 |
| Min B | -10.0 | | Max B | 15.0 |

Random Scale

| Min X | 1.0 | | Max X | 1.0 |
| Min Y | 1.0 | | Max Y | 1.0 |
| Min Z | 1.0 | | Max Z | 1.0 |

Random Size

| Min | 0.5 | Max | 1.5 |

Random Centering (Meters)

| Min X | 0.0 | Max X | 0.0 | X Axis | - | Center | + |
| Min Y | 0.0 | Max Y | 0.0 | Y Axis | - | Center | + |
| Min Z | 0.0 | Max Z | 0.0 | Z Axis | - | Center | + |

OK          Cancel

*Figure 20-73: The Point Clone Plus+ panel.*

5. Hide the hair on your left, make sure the points are in the background, and go to **Multiply | Duplicate: More | Point Clone Plus...** to open the Point Clone Plus+ panel. This allows you to make clones of the hair wherever you have a point in the background layer. (See Figure 20-73.)

6. Since this is an older man, I'm going to give him sort of wild brows. So, I'm setting a **Random Rotation** in all three axes. Not much, but some. Put negative values in the Min fields, and positive values in the Max fields. I don't want the scaling to change, so I'm leaving all of those at the default. But I do want some size difference.

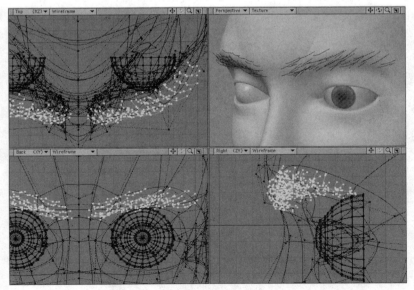

*Figure 20-74: Bushy eyebrow curves!*

The values are multiples of the size, so 1.0 is no change, 0.5 is half the size it was, and 2.0 is twice the size. (Think of them as percentages.) I'm going to go 50 percent (**0.5**) in both directions. Leave the rest of the settings at the default, and click **OK**. Instant hair curves!

7. Tap <**Shift**> + <\> to toggle hidden, so the curve clones are hidden and the lone curve isn't. Tap <'> (single quote) to invert foreground and background, and then <**Shift**> + <\> again so the left side points are visible. Invert again, to put the hair in the foreground and points in background, and run the plug-in once more.

8. It will remember the last settings used, so you don't have to. Unless you didn't use symmetrical settings, of course. In that case, you'll have to mirror the values. In other words, if you used a Min H of **−10** and a Max H of **20**, you'll need a Min H of **−20**, and a Max H of **10**.

9. There you go! Unhide everything. You should have two unique eyebrows that are similar but different enough to be realistic. Run **CurveToPolychain**, and you're ready to take it into Layout for testing.

## Tips for SasLite Eyebrow Settings

You should be familiar enough with the settings by now that you can choose your own parameters. You might want to push the Coarseness value beyond 100%. You might also want a very small Clump Size and a very large Lock Width so the hairs look like they are growing individually. If you are interested, you can see the parameters I used by checking the SasLiteHead.lws scene on the CD. You can also look at each step by opening the SasLiteEyebrows.lwo model and checking out the layers.

Those three methods should give you a good jumping off-point for deciding how you want to make long hair guides. You can mix and match them, of course; for instance, Rail Extrude using a handful of guides for a lower layer of hair (for coverage), and then get a spline from the head, and use Rail Clone to make the hairline hairs. Or use Point Clone Plus for a short, spiky style, or use the spline and several circles around the head to gather the hair into a ponytail.

Or you can make straight guides, take them into Layout, and use dynamics to shape them. (Things like wind, collision, and gravity allow the hair to flow naturally, without the drudgery of shaping each guide manually.)

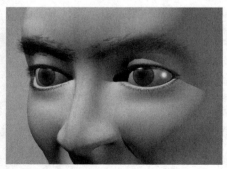

*Figure 20-75: The finished brows and lashes.*

The point is, you can do this. It's not as scary or difficult as you may have been led to believe, and the results can be fantastic.

Figure 20-76: The finished hirsute head.

# SasLite vs. Sasquatch

Now, you may be asking, "If I can do all of this with SasLite, then why shell out the cash for the full version?"

Ah, Grasshopper, because SasLite can only do a small fraction of what the full version of Sasquatch can do.

Let's start by looking at just the potential time savings, not the capabilities.

## Time-Saving Features

First, Sasquatch simply renders considerably faster than SasLite. You know the head you just finished with the SasLite hair and beard? On my machine, which is old and slow, that head takes about 10 minutes to render, with no AA, at 640x480. With Sasquatch, it takes a little more than one minute. Quite a time savings!

If you've noticed, once SasLite starts to render fibers, there's no stopping it. Even if you click on the Abort button, it takes a

while for the process to abort. You also have no idea how much longer you're going to have to wait for it to finish. All you get is a notice that says "Applying SasLite."

With the full version, there's a separate Sasquatch Rendering Progress window. It has a progress bar and an Abort button that instantly aborts the plug-in (but not the full render), once again potentially saving a lot of time.

You may have noticed that the SasLite window is in the middle of your screen, and there's no moving it. This isn't true of the Sasquatch window. It's as movable as any of the other windows you're used to. So if you have a test render that's behind the window, all you have to do is move the window; not close it, move the test, and reopen the window. This saves a little bit of time, and a large bit of annoyance.

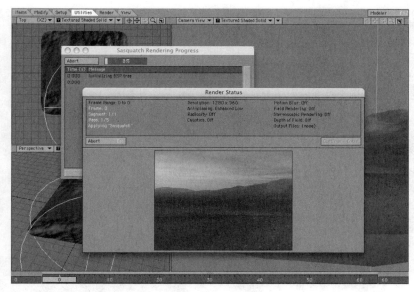

*Figure 20-77: Rendering in Sasquatch.*

When you are making test renders to check hair color, specularity, and so on in SasLite, you have to actually render the scene over and over in order to tweak things. This encourages you to stop at "good enough" instead of spending the extra time to get to "great!"

With Sasquatch, you can click the Preview Mode button in the Pixel Filter, and do one render. Then Sasquatch uses that render to allow you to play with the colors, mapping, and shading in very nearly real time, so you can tweak them until they're just what you envisioned, without spending much time at all. You can move from object to object, and instance to instance, and never have to do another preview render, while you tweak and balance everything until it's perfect.

Much like VIPER, the Sasquatch preview can't accommodate changes in geometry (length, clumping, combing, and so on), so it's not perfect. But it can still save you quite a lot of time over the course of a project.

In addition, if you are tweaking something other than the fibers, for instance the texture of the ground under the grass, you can freeze the Sasquatch render so that the plug-in will hold the fibers in memory, and just apply them, which only takes a moment. You can see what the ground will look like with the fibers on it, but without the render hit for those fibers. Once again, a great time-saver.

With SasLite, if there are enough polys that the plug-in decides to work in two (or more) pieces, it does. There's nothing you can do about it, no matter how much RAM you have. And, of course, splitting the render like that, although it uses less RAM per piece, takes extra time.

With the full version of Sasquatch, you can determine how large the RAM cache is (in MB) so if you have enough RAM, you can render any amount of fibers in a single pass, once more saving time.

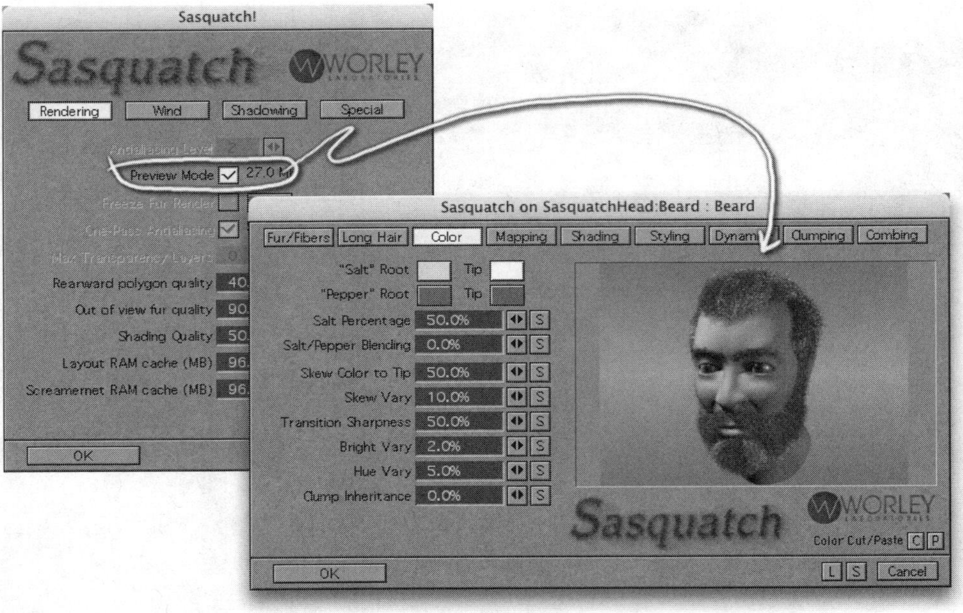

*Figure 20-78: The Preview window in Sasquatch is easy to set up, and a real time-saver.*

Both SasLite and Sasquatch render little straight lines when they make fibers. These look curved, but, like a polygon, really

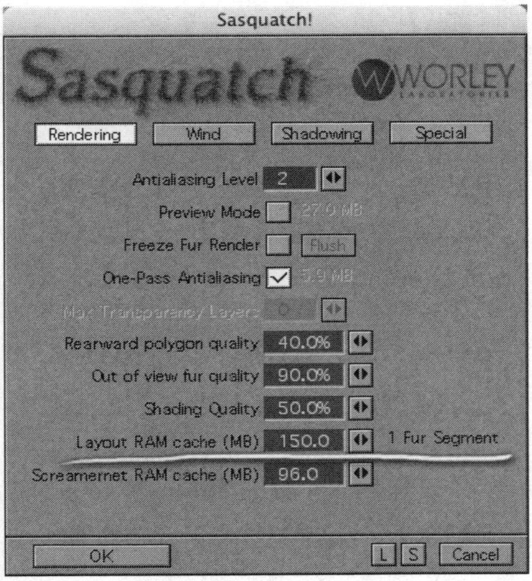

*Figure 20-79: The Rendering page of the Sasquatch Pixel Filter panel.*

aren't. In SasLite, the number of curves is fixed. If there aren't enough for the coarseness and frizziness you have chosen, you might see the lines. Much more commonly, there are many more than you need, especially if you are making fairly straight fibers. But you are going to render them all anyway because you can't change the number.

In Sasquatch, you can edit the Fiber Divisions number, so you aren't rendering any more segments than you need to. Once again, this can save quite a bit of time over a long animation.

In fact, Sasquatch can save you so much time that, if you have clients, and time is money, it will probably pay for itself in short order. And that's without all the extra capabilities!

However, let's talk about those for a few moments.

# Sasquatch's Valuable Extra Features

There are things that SasLite simply can't do that Sasquatch can.

For instance, SasLite can't cast shadows on anything, in any way, for any reason.

Sasquatch includes a surface shader, "Shadow of Sasquatch," that allows you to selectively cast shadows on any surface in the scene, in addition to controlling the opacity, colored highlights, and softness, among other things. It uses shadow maps, so it's fast. You can control the size of the map in the Pixel Filter panel, so you can use small maps for small or distant objects, and high-resolution maps for close-ups and detail work.

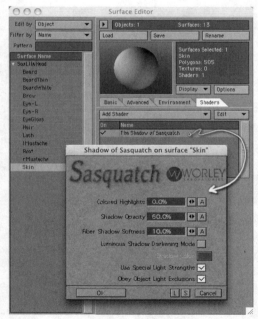

Figure 20-80: Shadow of Sasquatch Shader panel.

The SasLite displacement, as you know, has one panel of options. Sasquatch has nine, including dynamics; most of them can accept surface textures and some can be animated.

Surface textures are called by clicking a little "S" next to the name of the attribute. That opens a panel that allows you to choose whether to apply a map (image or weight), noise, spots, effectors, slope, or some variation of all of them to the attribute. Since you can also determine how much of each attribute will be applied in both the black and white pixels, you have a great deal of control.

This allows you to tweak the color, growth pattern, density, coarseness — virtually any of the parameters — in minute detail, and in very little time.

For instance, remember the grassy plain that we made in the beginning of this chapter? Those fibers were applied to the whole object, at the same length and density. There wasn't any way to tweak it so that there was more detail near the camera than on the distant hills.

But with Sasquatch, there is. Using an effector (usually a null object, set up in Layout), it's simple to put long, luxuriant grass near the camera, with the grass getting not only thinner but shorter (to increase the illusion of distance) farther away. In the far distance, where the fog takes over, you don't really need any fibers at all. With Sasquatch, you don't have to render them. And, of course, that again saves time.

While we're talking about grass, in SasLite, you have no control over the taper of the fibers. With Sasquatch, you do; you can grow fibers that are the same width from root to tip or fibers that taper to a point. So you can make blades that look more like an uncut field of grass in the first place.

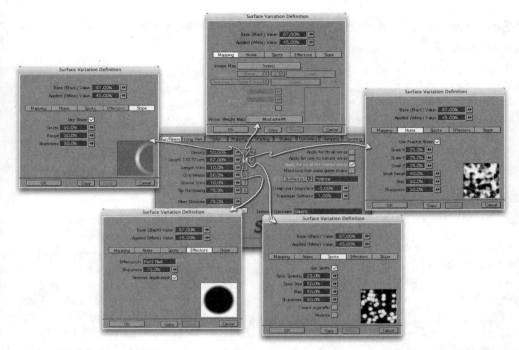

Figure 20-81: Sasquatch surface texture panels.

Figure 20-82: Using an Effector to control fibers in Sasquatch.

*Figure 20-83: SasLite grass vs. Sasquatch grass.*

Perhaps the biggest thing that Sasquatch can do but SasLite cannot is animation.

With SasLite, the fibers are the fibers. They don't respond to anything, and they don't change over time.

With Sasquatch, not only can they respond to wind, movement, and so on, but length and density can be independently animated. You can, quite literally, make fibers grow before your eyes.

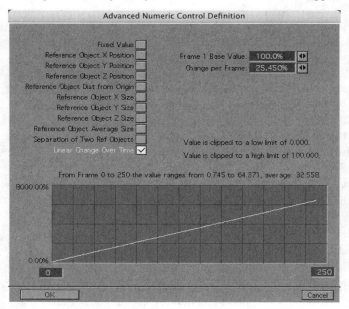

*Figure 20-84: Animating properties panel in Sasquatch.*

The differences in color are also enormous. In SasLite, as you know, the only variation in color possible is a single control, which randomly changes both the brightness and hue within a percentage range.

In Sasquatch, not only are those two things separated into two different ranges (one for each), but you also pick a "Salt" and a "Pepper" fiber, each of which has a different base and tip color (that's two colors per fiber, for every fiber). You pick how close to the tip the change occurs and how sharp the division is. Then you decide the percentage of "Salt" fibers, and the percentage of blend between "Salt" and "Pepper." (Is each fiber either black or white, for instance, or are there some that are gray?)

In addition, you can decide if the fibers inherit the dominant color from the clump they are in, if they keep their own color, or if they have some percentage of both.

Then you can put all of that on a map, too. (The colors blend much like Multiply in Photoshop. They can be darker than the map, but never lighter.)

Remember the rug we did? In Sasquatch, if you want a complex pattern in the rug all you have to do is choose pure white for the Salt and Pepper, root and tip, and use the map of the rug for the image under the Mapping button. Presto! A perfect, colorful rug.

*Figure 20-86: The head, redone with Sasquatch!*

*Figure 20-85: Mapping in Sasquatch, and the rug you can make with it.*

While we're talking about re-rendering using Sasquatch, remember the head? Well, in Sasquatch, you don't have to make separate parts for the mustache. Just choose a poly in the philtrum, and use Smart Combing, starting from that poly. The beard and mustache are automatically combed, just the way they would grow. (You can tweak this, if you like, but I didn't have to here.) This, again, saves both time and frustration!

If you want to match colors but not length, density, clumping, etc., in two instances of SasLite, you have to either make a note of the colors you used and

re-enter them in the second instance, or save the entire thing, load it into the second instance, and then tweak the non-color parameters.

In Sasquatch, you can copy each page of parameters separately. So moving just the color or just the shading or just the animation from one instance to another is a snap! (Sasquatch can also load saved SasLite files. So, if you have a wig you like in SasLite, you can use the same parameters in Sasquatch. There will be lots of thing missing, of course, that will simply have the default values, but it's a start.)

In fact, there's so much that Sasquatch can do that I'm not going to try to tell you all of it. Instead, I suggest that you go to the Worley Labs site at http://www.worley.com and download the plug-in from the Download page. You won't be able to open the interface or change the parameters if you don't buy it, but you can render things that use it.

Download the demo files as well, and render some of them, and the Sasquatch version of the files that I've included on the CD. Notice how much faster they render, and how much more information they contain. Then make up your own mind if SasLite will fill your needs or not.

I hope you enjoyed this chapter, and I encourage you to jump into Sasquatch or SasLite and have a ball.

# Epilogue

It has been a pleasure sharing with you these *essential* techniques of using LightWave as a tool for bringing the things you've got tucked away in your mind into a form that others can see as well. You've come a very long way in a very short amount of time. I hope the "ominous mystique" that may have prevailed before opening these pages has been replaced with an overwhelming sense of possibility and excitement. There is so much you *can* do with what you know *right now*! This is only the *beginning of your path*!

The things in these pages are the things that "the best of the best" have as part of their "toolboxes" that they use on a daily basis. (You'd eventually learn them in X number of years, but why wait?) All we've done is take some choice things from our own toolboxs and lay them out for you to play with, to test their "heft" and "feel." (These are things we couldn't work without, no one should have to try to work without them, unless they consciously decide they don't want to.)

There may be some other "hotshots" out there who may wonder why the heck we're doing this. Doesn't this threaten our positions as authorities? Let us make this *perfectly clear*: Beyond all shadows of doubt, *absolutely not*!

Consider the kind of *growth* in the field of 3D that has the possibility of happening when what was once considered the pinnacle of the exploration phase of LightWave is *now merely the beginning*. The things that *you* will discover should be far beyond what any of us already well along on our own journeys can imagine. All we ask is that you share what you learn, what you find out, with others. What you will be doing is raising the level that *everyone* will be able to achieve and what we *expect* of our achievements.

Just as every seventh-grader today understands, without even thinking about it, the theories that took Pythagoras almost a lifetime to develop, it is our hope that tomorrow we will all be able to work miracles with 3D, the likes of which are contemplated only by the wishful dreamers of today.

Where you go from here is limited only by what you *choose* to do. You now have the skill set that it takes most LightWavers many years to develop. You could explore character animation and the creation of your own short films. You could delve into special effects, even learning LScripting to create with mathematics things that can be neither modeled nor animated. You could find yourself working with other extremely dedicated and talented artists to create something even bigger than *Lord of the Rings*. Or you could find yourself living a pastoral life, as if on some remote colony-planet, making the films you have always wanted to see and helping others to achieve their dreams and goals as well.

Beginnings are wonderful things. Possibilities lay out before you like a never-ending webwork that connects where you are right now to everywhere you dream to be.

## Epilogue

Where will *you* choose to let your path take you now that it has begun?

When you think about just how far 3D has come in the few short years it has been actually possible, this beginning you are now a part of is itself a part of one of the more exciting things to touch this little planet in a long, long time.

Just remember, in *all that you do*, find the ways of making it *fun*. Find ways of letting what you do be more *play* than *work*. When you do that, the work that will come *through* you will look more and more like the work that *inspired you* to take this journey yourself!

Be well, and enjoy the journey!

Timothy
http://Timothy.ArtistNation.com

Steve
http://www.stevewarner.com

# Appendix A

# Plug-ins and Programs

Something that has always struck me about the community that has gravitated to LightWave is the amazing sense of, well, "community." I've used all the major software packages and *only* found this sense of openness, sharing, camaraderie, and support among the users of LightWave. These feelings of connection exist with LightWave artists from all areas of the globe, regardless of language, belief, or computer platform.

I'm not quite sure why this is so with LightWave — maybe it has something to do with the initial intent of Video Toaster as a "paradigm shift" or something. The point is that there are incredibly talented artists, programmers, and programmer/artists working with LightWave who have done some amazing things, and out of their own feelings of connection with this community have *chosen* to share what they've created with the rest of us. These are plug-ins, LScripts, and external programs that save *hours* of time or make you sit up and say, "Dude! That's *cool*! I never would have thought of that!"

As a firm believer in giving back, and someone who uses these additions to LightWave on a constant basis, I am very thankful and deeply indebted to the works of these honorable people. What they have created are things that would sell for hundreds, if not thousands, of dollars were we using Maya, XSI, or 3ds max. These are *incredibly helpful* tools. Once you start using

them, you won't want to work without them.

I am equally thankful to each of the artist/programmers who have let me include the plug-ins that I use most frequently on the companion CD. I encourage you, if you have a leaning toward programming, to make note of the things you've always wished existed in LightWave and code them, adding to the wealth of things that make the LightWave community the awesome "concept in action" it is.

This chapter outlines brief descriptions of the plug-ins and programs that are on the companion CD. These descriptions describe the basics of what they do, giving you an idea of whether or not they're something you want to add to your own toolbox. (Most of these are *free, full versions* of the software, while some are demos of commercial products. All are included with the permission of their authors.)

The directory structure for the plug-ins is *Plugs_n_Programs\Creator\Program Name\Computer Platform\*.

Each included plug-in (or program) has its own README file in either its *Program Name* or *Computer Platform* directories. The README files will get into much more depth about how to use and set up the plug-ins (or programs).

A snippet of the creator's web site is included under the *Creator* directory, as is a link to the web site itself. You'll be able to get the most recent versions of the files directly from there and see what new things those artist/programmers have created.

## Note

You will need to know how to add plug-ins in order to implement their functionality into LightWave. If you do not know how to do this, please see the LW manuals.

## Note

Most of these utilities are for both Intel and Macintosh. Some, however, have not yet been compiled for Macintosh (at the time of publication). I apologize for the frustration this may present to Mac users of LightWave.

With the aim of strengthening the ties of the LightWave community, if you are a Mac programmer and can offer your time to compile a plug-in for Intel-only LightWave coders, I'm sure they, as well as Macintosh LightWave users, would be grateful for your help.

# 3D Cybercorp

http://www.3dcybercorp.com/
Plug-in by Antony Scerri

## UV Imaginator

(Intel, Mac OS9, Mac OSX) *Full Version*

**What it is:** Modeler => Utilities | Additional | UV Imaginator generates a bitmap image of any UV map that you have assigned to a model, which you can use as a guide for when you are painting UV texture maps.

**What makes this cool:** Without this plug-in, you typically take a screen capture of your UV Map viewport and paste it into your paint program. Your resolution, then, is limited to that of your screen. UV Imaginator lets you create any resolution image of a UV map layout, even letting you generate the bitmap based on a current selection or surface!

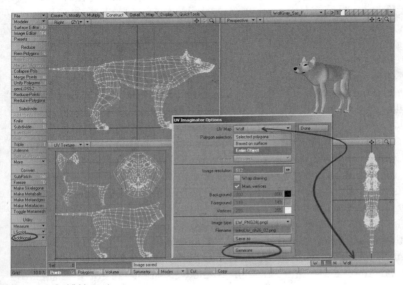

*Figure A-1: UV Imaginator.*

**Notes:** Once you have set the target image with Save As, be sure to click Generate. (*No bitmap is created unless you click Generate.*)

Figure A-2: The bitmap generated by the settings shown in Figure A-1, ready to be used as a template for your painted texture in your paint program.

# ASA

http://www.lw-fin.org/plugins/
Plug-ins by Juha Pinola

## ASA BufferSaver

(Intel, Mac OS9) *Full Version*

**What it is:** Layout => Effects | Processing | Image Filter | ASA_BufferSaver is a plug-in for advanced users that saves images containing the internal buffers that LightWave uses to create its images (Specularity, Shading, Raw RGB, etc.).

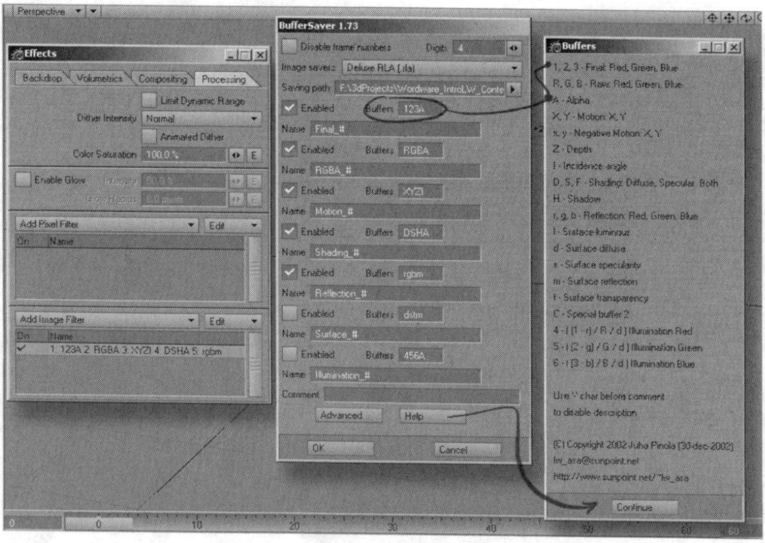

Figure A-3: ASA BufferSaver.

**What makes this cool:** By saving the internal buffers and then using a program like CinePaint or After FX to combine them *after rendering,* you can have amazing control over how the final image looks. You can adjust the darkness and tonality of base colors, shadows, and highlights. You can blur the Specular shading buffer, using Screen to create soft "bloom-like" effects. (The list of things you can do to control every aspect of the final image without re-rendering is nearly endless.) This is what the pros do.

**Notes:** Working in this manner is highly advanced, but it is something that you will want to get into when you want your renders to start taking on even more of a professional feel. The code-like information in the Buffers fields refers to which individual buffer channels (shown under the Help button) will be used to make up the R, G, B, and alpha channels of the *output* image. (The first entry in the Buffers field stands for the red channel, then the green channel, the blue channel, and finally the alpha channel.)

**Side Note:** If you're into random-dot stereograms, you can use this plug-in to save the depth buffer to the black-and-white image an RDS-generating program needs to work its "magic." (You can find RDS programs through TUCOWS.com, explored in Appendix B.)

## ASA ColorPicker

(Intel) *Full Version*

**What it is:** Layout => General Options | Color Picker | ASA_ColorPicker changes the tool you use to select colors in LightWave's interface.

**What makes this cool:** This opens up a whole new level of precision and ease for choosing your colors in LightWave. You can compare your original color with the color you are selecting in the upper part of its window and use the "ratchet-ring" around the color wheel to micro-adjust your color selection.

**Notes:** Using this plug-in makes selecting colors in other programs seem like a drag.

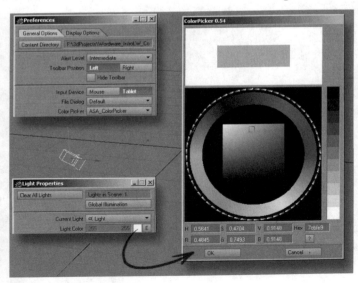

*Figure A-4: ASA ColorPicker.*

# Fake Irradiance Illumination

(Intel) *Full Version*

**What it is:** Surface Editor | Shaders | ASA_FakeIrradianceIllumination allows you to use a prerendered image to precalculate a very convincing "fake" radiosity.

**What makes this cool:** If you want to get the *look* of radiosity but don't have the time for even Backdrop Only radiosity, you need this plug-in.

**Notes:** See the README file for instructions on how to set up this plug-in and generate the image the plug-in needs to do its magic.

# Light Absorption in See-Through Items

(Intel, Mac OS9) *Full Version*

**What it is:** Surface Editor | Shaders | ASA_LASI is a shader that calculates the complex mathematics for the way light behaves when passing through transparent objects.

**What makes this cool:** This lets you have "glass" objects that more or less accurately recreate their real-world counterparts. While ray-tracing with this plug-in will very accurately recreate real life, you can render *without ray-tracing* and still have your surfaces show the coolness of light being absorbed as it passes through "see-through" items.

**Notes:** I've found this plug-in to be a little bit of a challenge to pick up at first, but when you do get the hang of its settings, it is well worth the time spent learning it.

Figure A-5 (Image by Juha Pinola — used with permission)

Figure A-6 (Image by Juha Pinola — used with permission)

## ASA RenderTarget

(Intel) *Full Version*

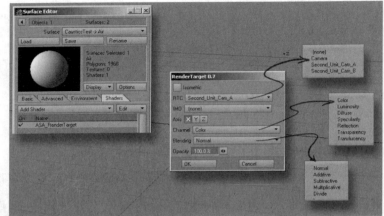

**What it is:**
ASA_RenderTarget
does a couple of
things, but what I
imagine you might
find most helpful is
its ability to render
what *any* camera in
your scene is "look-
ing at" onto a
surface. (In this
case, it is applied as
a shader.) You'll
probably find this

**Figure A-7**

extremely useful if you're doing
"vid-screens" that monitor an area from
several angles at once (or monitor the different parts of a spaceship's exterior).

**What makes this cool**: Using Surface
Editor | Shaders | ASA_RenderTarget lets
you do "in camera" things that would normally require you to prerender and then
map the prerendered image sequences onto
surfaces in your scene.

**Notes:** In the ASA RenderTarget shader
interface, RTC (Render Target Camera) lets
you choose which camera's view (already in
your scene) will be shown on the surface.
IMO (Isometric Object) lets an *object* be
your "camera" if Isometric is checked at the
top of the window. This plug-in only does
planar mapping at the moment, so be sure
your (Planar Mapping) axis is set correctly.

## Blochi

http://www.blochi.com/
Plug-in by Blochi

### Thickener

(LScript) *Full Version*

**What it is:** Modeler => Utilities | Utility
| Additional | Thickener will add *real thick-
ness* to a flat object, even sub-patch objects.

(As an LScript, it will work on *both* Intel
*and* Macintosh — regardless of Mac OS.)

**What makes this cool**: Try making a
couple of complex flat objects "thick" in the
same way by hand and get back to me.

**Notes:** Thickener is *more* than Extrude,
*more* than Smooth Scale. It *thickens* objects
along each poly's normal. Try it. I think
you'll like it!

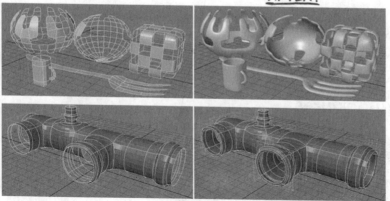

BEFORE...  AFTER!

Figure A-8 (Images by Blochi — used with permission)

# Faulknermano

http://thespread.ghostoutpost.com/
Plug-in by Lernie Ang

## RackFocusCF

(LScript) *Full Version*

**What it is:** RackFocusCF is a channel filter that you apply under the *camera's* Depth of Field | Focal Distance *envelope* (on the Graph Editor's Modifiers tab). It will make the camera's Focal Distance Curve automatically alter itself to keep whatever

object you set as the focus object right in the middle of that camera's depth of field.

**What makes this cool:** When you're using LightWave's *real* depth of field, once you set the focus object you no longer have to fiddle with envelopes to track a moving object.

**Notes:** If you are exploring depth of field, I highly recommend looking into LightWave's fast and good-looking DOF "faker" (Effects | Processing | Image Filter | Digital Confusion).

# FI

http://www.infoseek.livedoor.com/
~f_ichikawa/
Plug-ins by Fujio Ichikawa

## FI's Procedural Textures

(Intel) *Full Version*

**What it is**: fisptxtrs.p adds *seven* new procedural textures to choose from under your

Texture Editor | Procedural Type pop-up menu.

**What makes this cool**: Using *mathematics* to define a texture as opposed to *painting* one will more often than not give you a better-looking texture that uses far less memory and looks good both from a great distance and at close range.

**Notes:** The README and, more importantly, the sample scenes (under the Intel directory) will get you up to speed the quickest on how to use each one of these new procedurals.

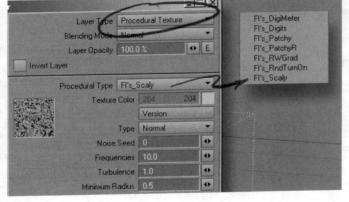

Figure A-9

## FI's Wrinkle

(Intel, Mac OS9, Mac OSX) *Full Version*

**What it is**: Modeler => Utilities | Additional | FI's_Wrinkle will "wrinkle" your model along a "seam" designated by your point selection. You drag your mouse left or right to change the depth of the wrinkle and up or down to change its width.

**What makes this cool**: You can quickly add detail to a mesh that holds up under scrutiny far better than any painted texture. The detail

FI's Wrinkle adds works perfectly with sub-patches and only adds the minimum amount of geometry to keep the detail in place.

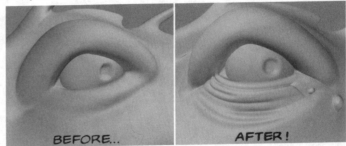

BEFORE...    AFTER !

Figure A-10: This model is the Peixe+Wrinkles.lwo that is found in each of the different computer platform directories for this plug-in.

**Notes**: With something that makes detailing as simple as this, it is easy to go overboard on how much you put into your model. Remember that the best details are the ones that look so natural, so much a part of the way the model "should" be, that you barely notice them until you look.

## Key Reducer

(LScript) *Full Version*

**What it is**: Scene | Utilities | Generics | KeyReducer will eliminate *all unnecessary keyframes* from TCB curves.

**What makes this cool**: This plug-in does its best to maintain the original shape of the curve, as seen in Figure A-11. If you work with motion capture data where there is a keyframe on every single frame (making changes to the animation an exercise in tedium), this will give you a curve that is much more easily animatable. (Or, if you find your curves getting sloppy with too many keys, you can use this to "clean" them.)

**Notes**: This plug-in will *only* work with TCB splines.

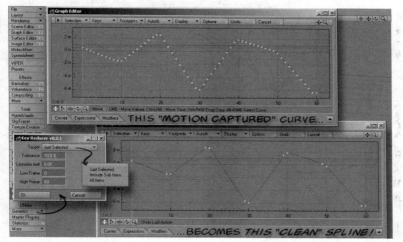

*Figure A-11: Key Reducer.*

# JettoCrack 3D

http://www.3dfightclub.com/~jettocrack/lightwave/plugins/index.htm
Plug-ins by Javier Gómez Cáceres

## JettoBevel

(Intel/Mac) *Full Version*

**What it is:** Modeler => Utilities | Additional | JettoBevel is an advanced all-in-one bevel tool.

**What makes this cool:** Combining the power of Bevel, Rail Bevel, and Rounder into one tool, JettoBevel makes it a snap to create complex bevels and works wonders in complex situations where power tools like Rounder fail. Its simple interface allows you to try out various bevels before committing to them and even allows you to assign new surfaces as you bevel.

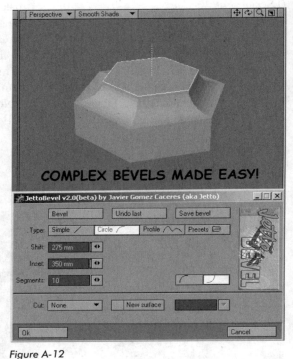

Figure A-12

## JettoFillet

(Intel/Mac) *Full Version*

**What it is:** Modeler => Utilities | Additional | JettoFillet rounds the sharp edges of individual polygons.

**What makes this cool:** LightWave's Rounder tool provides point rounding (also known as filleting in many 3D applications).

However, Rounder can only fillet points on 3D objects. JettoFillet augments Rounder's function by providing filleting on 2D objects.

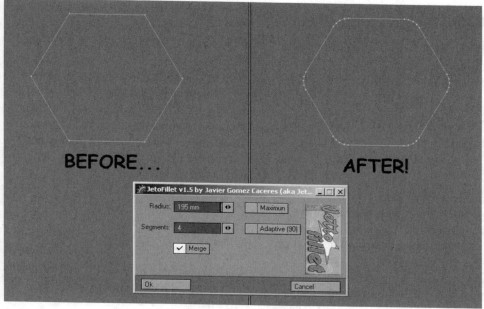

Figure A-13

## JettoLocal

(Intel) *Full Version*

**What it is:** Modeler => Utilities | Additional | JettoLocal allows you to define a local coordinate system in Modeler.

**What makes this cool:** By defining a local coordinate system, you can reorient an object so that any given polygon rests flush with the ground. This becomes critical when you want to align one object with another but find it difficult to do so due to the object's rotation. The local coordinate system can be saved with the object and restored to LightWave's native coordinate system at any time.

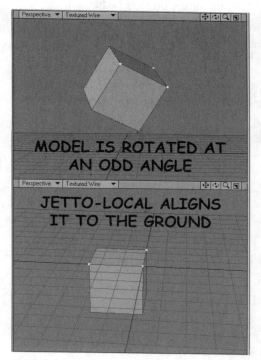

Figure A-14

## Landis

http://amber.rc.arizona.edu/lw/
newshades/
Plug-ins by Marvin Landis

# Shades for LightWave 7.5 and 8.0

(Intel) *Full Version*

**What it is:** The Shades project is an ongoing program to provide the LightWave community with a collection of shaders (procedural textures) written by artist/programmers from all over the world. Its original shaders were converted from RenderMan Shading Language. The beta of Shades for LightWave 7.5 and 8.0, included with this book, takes ten of the shaders written for the original LightWave Shades project and "ports" them to using the new functionality of LightWave 7.5 and 8.0's internal workings.

**What makes this cool**: Using shaders, you get more detailed, more "realistic," more interesting surface texturing than any one person could ever paint by hand. Plus, shaders let you get as close as you'd like to the surface of an object, and they never "break down" into pixels.

**Notes:** Shades for LightWave 7.5 and 8.0 comes with a directory of presets and settings that basically mirror each other's information. The subdirectories under Presets\, when copied correctly to your [LightWave_Directory]\Programs\Presets\ShaderHandler\ directory, gives you "preset examples" of the different shaders when you are within a particular shader's interface. The Settings directory gives you loadable versions of the same but without previews and having to copy anything anywhere.

If you're an artist, a programmer, or a combination of the two and have even the slightest interest in exploring using mathematics as the basis for creating surfacing more intricate than anyone could paint by hand, explore the LightWave Shades project's web sit at http://amber.rc.arizona.edu/lw/shades/.

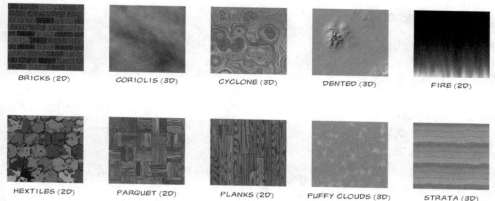

BRICKS (2D)   CORIOLIS (3D)   CYCLONE (3D)   DENTED (3D)   FIRE (2D)

HEXTILES (2D)   PARQUET (2D)   PLANKS (2D)   PUFFY CLOUDS (3D)   STRATA (3D)

Figure A-15

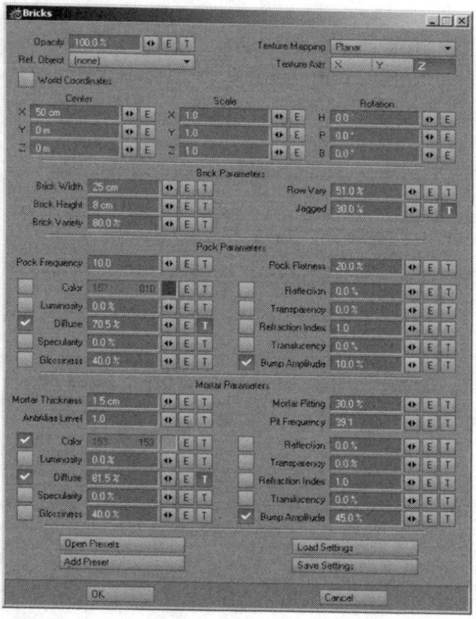

Figure A-16: This is the set of controls for the Bricks (2D) shader. Everything is envelopable to change over time, and most everything lets you assign textures to the individual controls (channels).

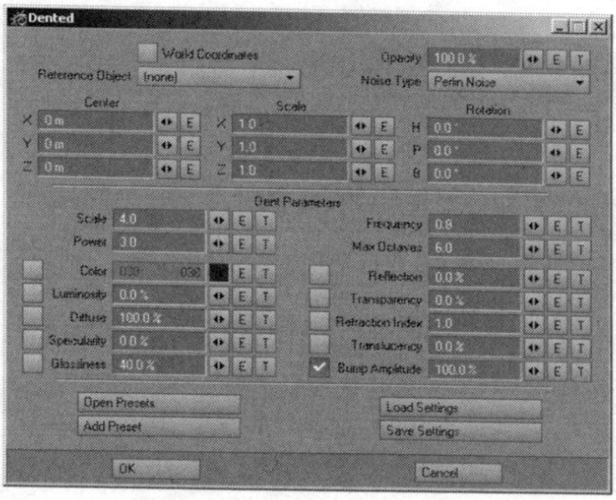

Figure A-17: Even for my personal favorite procedural texture, Dented, the Shades 7.5 version has some "roll up your sleeves and get dirty" advantages over LightWave's own Dented procedural — namely that you can assign the procedural to all channels at once, modified by individual textures and envelopes.

## m2e Studios

http://groups.yahoo.com/group/
CMAN_LScripts/
Plug-in by Carl Merritt

### Align to Rail

**What it is:** Modeler => Utilities | Additional | Align to Rail aligns your polys to the first point of your rail and then runs its own version of LightWave's Rail Extrude tool.

**What makes this cool:** Aligning your poly to the first point of a rail before extruding can be a tedious process. Imagine what would happen if you had to align polys to hundreds of rails. This plug-in automates the process and shaves hours (or in some cases *days*) off your modeling time.

## Mohh's

http://www.mohhs.com/lw/lwtc/
Plug-in by Martin Uribe

### LightWave Theme Creator

(Intel/Mac) *Full Version*

**What it is:** LightWave interface color adjustment visualization tool.

**What makes this cool:** The colors for many of LightWave's interface items can be customized to suit your needs by adding a set of parameters to the Hub config file.

Unfortunately, the process is not interactive, which means that you must enter the parameters, save the config, and launch LightWave to try them out. If you find that you don't like the results, you must start over from the beginning. Martin Uribe's LWTC is an ingenious Flash application that allows you to adjust the colors for the interface and preview the results in real time. When you're satisfied, you can simply copy and paste the data from the bottom of the LWTC into your Hub config file.

# Pictrix

http://www.pictrix.jp/lw/index2.html

Plug-ins by Masayuki Umezawa

**Note:** Pictrix has more than 50 free plug-ins available on this site, nearly every one of which does something unique and amazing. I highly encourage you to check them out. The site is in Japanese, so you'll likely need a translator utility to get the lowdown on each of these great tools, but the time you spend will be well worth it.

## C_Bend

(Intel/Mac) *Full Version*

**What it is:** Modeler => Utilities | Additional | C_Bend is a tool that allows you to bend your object based on a background spline (or curve).

**What makes this cool:** LightWave's native Bend tool is great for creating a single bend in an object, but makes complex bends tricky at best. Enter Pictrix's C_Bend. It will bend your object based on a spline, making it easy to create otherwise impossible deformations.

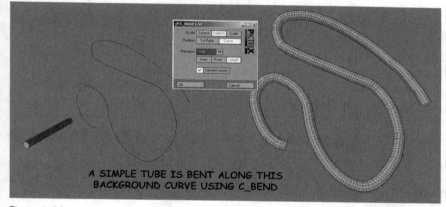

A SIMPLE TUBE IS BENT ALONG THIS
BACKGROUND CURVE USING C_BEND

*Figure A-18*

# Sininenplaneetta

http://koti.mbnet.fi/anttij77/
Plugins/Coffee.html
Plug-in by Antti Järvelä

## Coffee!

(Intel, Mac OS9, Mac OSX) *Full Version*

**What it is**: Coffee! is a shader that alters the transparency and coloring of a transparent object *based on thickness*. This is a quick and effective way of faking the look of things like glass, coffee, tea, or anything transparent that is less opaque or a different color around its edges.

Figure A-19 (Image by Antti Järvelä — used with permission)

**What makes this cool**: Used in conjunction with LightWave's own transparency and color filtering, you can quickly get the look of glass and other liquids. (Technically, glass *is* a liquid that at "normal" temperatures just moves *very slowly*.)

**Notes**: Coffee! is *not* the same as ASA_LASI. Coffee does *not* figure the complex mathematics of light absorption — and as such, you may find you understand it a lot more quickly.

LIGHTWAVE'S *TRANSPARENCY* AND *COLOR-FILTERING*

COFFEE'S *TRANSPARENCY* AND *COLOR-FILTERING*

LIGHTWAVE'S *TRANSPARENCY...* COFFEE'S *COLOR-FILTERING*

COFFEE'S *TRANSPARENCY, COLOR-FILTERING* AND *SURFACE COLORING*

Figure A-20

# Albee

http://Timothy.ArtistNation.com

Plug-ins by Timothy Albee

## 4-Point Lighting Setup

(LScript) *Full Version*

**What it is:** Layout => Scene | Utilities | Generics | 4-Point Lighting Setup creates a *basic* four-point lighting model in an instant.

**What makes this cool:** In addition to giving you a decent lighting model to test-render your models and whatnot, this script both *parents* and *targets* the camera and all lights to separate nulls. This makes it easier to move/scale the lights as a unit and orbit the camera about an object by simply rotating the "camera dolly."

**Notes:** I am no programmer, scripter, or coder. This script was created using LightWave's ability to record what you do and then turn it into a script (using LScript | LS Commander). So it's not perfect, but, so far, the only caveat in using it I've found is that *it is best run on a fresh, new scene*. (Running it on a scene with light names changed or the camera animated is not a good idea.)

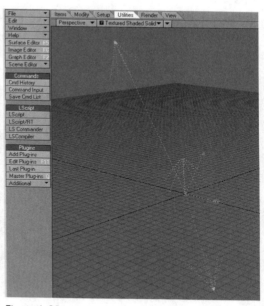

Figure A-21

Figure A-22: This image is of the probe droid loaded into a scene that has had its lighting gaffed with a four-point lighting setup.

# The Itty-Bitty Animation Timer

(HTML/Flash4) *Full Version*

**What it is:** The Itty-Bitty Animation Timer is a utility written in Macromedia's Flash4. It runs on any platform that supports Flash4 (Unix, WindowsCE "palm-tops," and, of course, Windows and Macintosh). To use it (if you have Flash4 installed), just open Animation Timer\AnimationTimer _v3.html — it will "run" the .swf file in your default web browser. (If you don't have Flash installed for your web browser, zip on over to Macromedia.com.)

**What makes this cool:** This animation timer/time-base conversion utility is not only versatile and easy to use, but it is so tiny, it's downright itty-bitty! At 17 KB, it fits easily on a floppy, USB keychain drive, or e-mail attachment so you can always have this cool tool with you.

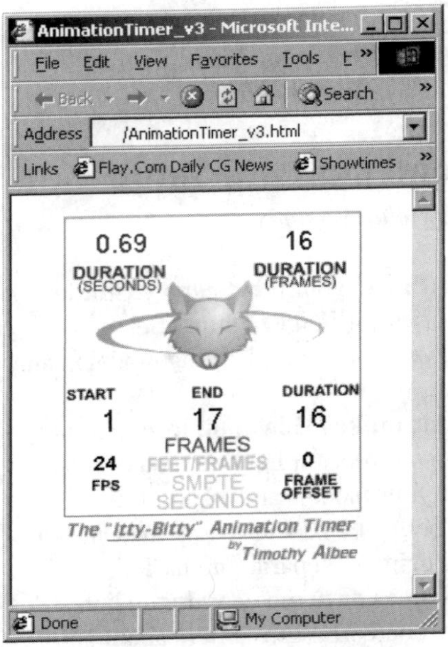

**Notes:** If you ever find yourself out on a job and you happen to have left The Itty-Bitty Animation Timer at home, just go to

*Figure A-23: The Itty-Bitty Animation Timer.*

my web site; I always keep the most recent version of it there.

> **Note**
>
> Now we get into the external programs. These are things that need to be installed and run separately from LightWave but are nonetheless integral to the magic we Light-Wave artists work.

# Dan Ritchie

http://www.squirreldome.com/
Program by Dan Ritchie

## Project Dogwaffle

(Intel) *Full "Free" Version*

**What it is:** Project Dogwaffle is a *paint program* (not to be confused with a photo-retouching program). It mimics the way "real" media handles so you can paint excellent-looking textures really quickly.

**What makes this cool:** Dogwaffle was created with one purpose in mind: *painting.* While the original idea for it may have been in creating digital matte paintings, its toolset is fantastic for painting texture maps.

**Notes:** Dogwaffle comes in two "flavors." What is included on the book's companion CD is the free version, 1.2. While this free version has a heck of a lot of functionality, Dan's newest version is available for $67 on his web site and adds a whole slew of new and improved features.

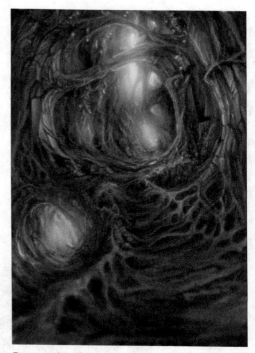

*Figure A-24: This image is courtesy of Dan, from Silver Squirrel.*

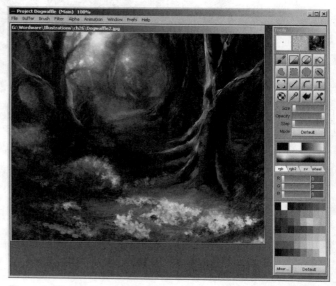

*Figure A-25: This is one of Dan's images created on Dogwaffle for the production Silver Squirrel; see Dan's web site for information.*

# CinePaint (Formerly Film GIMP)

(GNU Public License)
**http://cinepaint.sourceforge.net/**
Maintained by Robin Rowe

## CinePaint

(Linux, Mac, PC, Source Code) *Full Version*

**What it is:** CinePaint (formerly known as Film GIMP) is an *image manipulation* program that has been used on feature films, including *Harry Potter and the Sorcerer's Stone, Scooby-Doo, Cats & Dogs, Dr. Dolittle 2, Little Nicky, How the Grinch Stole Christmas, The 6th Day, Stuart Little,* and *Planet of the Apes*. It operates in 48-bit RGB color-space, so it can handle the increased color depth recorded by film.

**Notes:** For support and installation instructions, please refer to the CinePaint web site.

Within the CinePaint directory on the companion CD, you will notice that the installer for Win-Intel is named "CinePaint" while the installer for Macintosh is still "Film GIMP." It is highly recommended that you check the CinePaint web site for updates, especially since the included versions are early "ports" for PC and Mac platforms from the original Linux.

*Figure A-26: Image from the CinePaint web site.*

# Greenworks

http://www.xfrog.com/
Tools from Greenworks

## Xfrog

(Intel) *Demo*

**What it is**: Xfrog uses a component-based relational structure to create *organic models*. You don't actually push points as you do in LightWave; rather, you set up *associations* (guided by mathematics as precision-oriented as you have time to noodle), and Xfrog does the rest. You can achieve amazing detail in a short amount of time just by adding components and tweaking controls.

**What makes this cool**: Organic modeling of things that have fractal detail to them — trees, plants, shrubberies, alien cityscapes, and the like — requires the patience of a Zen master. If you aren't currently a devotee of "mindful meditation" and need to build trees or plants (or you are under a deadline and have to get things looking sharp *fast*), I recommend diving into this time-limited, fully-functional demo version.

**Notes**: Be sure to check out Xfrog Tune, Greenworks' polygon reduction program, if you want to populate a forest for your animation (Xfrog itself tends not to skimp when creating its geometry). When using Xfrog, be sure to work through the Xfrog_LW_Plugin (included on the CD). It is the easiest way to get Xfrog models and animations into LightWave. If you don't want to build trees for your animation yourself, check out Greenworks' Library CDs that have recreations of flora from around the world (approved by discriminating botanists).

Figure A-27

# Justice

http://www.joejustice.org/

Maintained by Joe Justice

## LightNet

(Intel) *Full Version*

**What it is**: LightNet is an external program that manages the bunches of networked computers that do nothing but await your bidding and render the scenes you send to them (known locally as a *render farm*). LightNet is the most widely used free render farm controller for LightWave.

**What makes this cool**: LightWave lets you have an almost unlimited number of "render nodes" for the purchase price of the software (unlike some other software packages). Using a render farm of only two machines (of equal processor speed and physical memory) will render your scene *twice as fast* as just one of the machines alone! Even if you only have one machine, you can queue a bunch of things to render and have LightNet set the CPU priority of the render node to Lowest, so you can still work while you're rendering. LightNet is much easier to set up and work with

than LightWave's built-in controller located under Rendering | Network Rendering (which fully occupies the instance of LightWave being used to control the network rendering).

**Notes:** Study *both* the LightNet Installation Guide and the LightWave manual section on network rendering to make setting up your render farm much easier. (If you are setting up a networked render farm, you will also need to understand basic network privileges and directory mappings. (Mac users can also find ScreamerNet controllers through Flay.com, discussed in Appendix B.)

*Figure A-28: LightNet.*

# Kaser

http://www.kaser.com/
Program by Everett Kaser

## Sherlock

(Intel) *Demo*

**What it is:** Sherlock is a game of logic — a lot like solitaire, only that with each and every puzzle you have the ability to be successful. *Your own mental ability*, not chance, is what determines whether you win or lose.

**What makes this cool:** This simple game will help *train* you to see how solving even the most seemingly complex puzzles is simply a matter of *doing what needs to be done in the moment* — eliminating the impossible and slowly resolving your way to the solution. This is training for 3D — and for *life*.

**Notes:** This demo version only contains five puzzles of each size (3x3 through 8x8). The full version ($19.95 + shipping) has over *65,000* puzzles of each size.

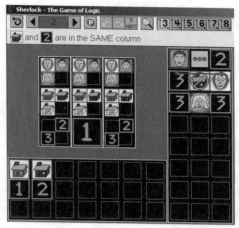

*Figure A-29: Sherlock.*

*Figure A-30: Sherlock.*

# Appendix B

# Resources

So, where do you go to find answers to the questions you come across as you go about your work? There are many resources, both online and in print. Some answer questions you may not even know you'll be asking yet. Some are just too cool to not jump in immediately and start scrounging around for neat bits and pieces that are the perfect fit for the things you have zinging about in your creative mind!

## Community

LightWave's *online community* is without equal. Just as some are gifted in programming (as are the artist/programmers who have contributed to the wealth of material described in Appendix A), some are gifted in teaching, organizing information, or connecting people from around the world. If you aren't sure where to find what you're looking for, or if you aren't quite sure what you're looking for yet, these places can help point you in the right direction.

## NewTek

http://www.newtek.com/products/lightwave/

One of the first places to go to find out "how" (as well as get updates, patches, and whatnot) is the NewTek web site. (Do you think this kind of community could exist for a package that doesn't stand with its users 100%?)

NewTek's web site has collections of tutorials, links, and information about "who's who" in the LightWave community. Check it out!

Figure B-1: NewTek web site.

# Flay

http://www.flay.com/

Flay is also a "first stop" for finding out just about anything that exists concerning LightWave. Here you will find up-to-date listings of news, jobs, tutorials, tips, and of course, my personal favorite: plug-ins. Each category is searchable so you can quickly find *exactly* what you're looking for.

Figure B-3 shows the plug-ins page, listing the latest 20 plug-in "spottings" and sporting a search engine that will find what you're looking for, even if you don't know its name — only what you want it to do for you!

Figure B-2: Flay.com web site.

Figure B-3: Flay.com plug-ins page.

# SpinQuad

http://www.spinquad.com/forums

SpinQuad is one of the leading LightWave forums on the web. Founded by industry legend William "Proton" Vaughan and populated by some of the most established LightWave users in the world, it is an excellent place to meet professionals, get answers to your questions, and hone your skills. With its friendly, small-town feel and an unwavering commitment to the user and his art, SpinQuad perfectly embodies the spirit of the LightWave community.

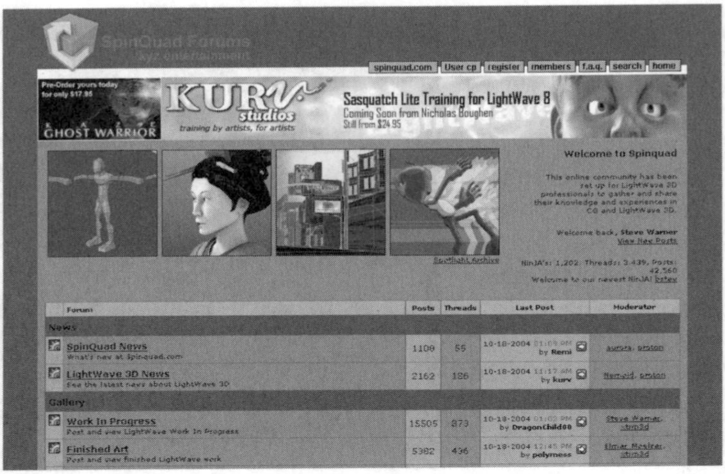

*Figure B-4: SpinQuad web site.*

# CgTalk

http://www.cgtalk.com/

CgTalk is the world's largest forum for computer graphics professionals. With almost 100,000 members, it offers support for nearly every major graphics application. Visitors can find focused critiques, contests, industry information, jobs, and, of course, discussions on more than a dozen 2D/3D applications.

*Figure B-5: CgTalk web site.*

# 3D Fight Club

http://www.3dfightclub.com/

There's nothing like a challenge to bring out the best in a person, and 3D Fight Club does a great job of providing users with just that. Born out of a desire to extol the powers of LightWave over Maya, the site now includes users of every 3D application. Members participate in a variety of challenges, ranging from several minutes to several hours in length. The idea is to work quickly toward your goal and produce better work than your competitors within the time allowed. If you really want to hone your skills, I highly recommend a workout at 3D Fight Club.

Figure B-6: 3D Fight Club web site.

# Friends of NewTek

http://www.friendsofnewtek.com/

Decades before the Internet made its debut, user groups functioned as the principal means of support for the computer-using community. While online forums now offer a chance to connect with people all over the world, they still lack the benefits that come from a local gathering. User groups frequently showcase new hardware and software, bring in special guest speakers, and offer personalized assistance to those new to the scene. The Friends of NewTek

site is a resource for connecting LightWave and Video Toaster users with established user groups in their area. If you've never had the privilege of being in a user group, you owe it to yourself to check one out.

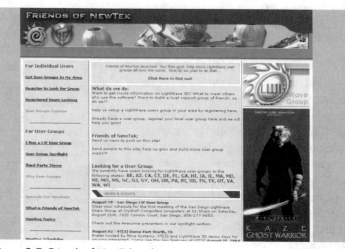

Figure B-7: Friends of NewTek web site.

# TUCOWS

http://www.tucows.com/

I had just sort of assumed that most people already knew about TUCOWS as *the* ultimate place on the net to download reviewed software for almost any and every computer platform. But I have found that a lot of people are still unaware of it. Plain and simple, it is the best place to search for programs you need, whether they be games, OS "fine-tuners," network "stuff," emulators, or whatever (IMHO). Almost every package is reviewed and scored in "cows" (five cows being the highest score). You can even *super search* on the kind of license agreement the package has (commercial, shareware, freeware, etc.).

*Figure B-8: TUCOWS web site.*

## Commercial

While the *quantity* of free materials available on the net is astounding, nothing can match the *quality* of dedicated commercial products. The following resources come from providers who have spent countless hours developing materials to assist in the development of your skills and abilities.

## Kurv Studios

http://www.kurvstudios.com/

Kurv Studios burst onto the scene in 2004 and has quickly become one of the leading suppliers of high-quality computer-based training material. Their LightWave series is hosted by industry-recognized artists and offers training on nearly every aspect of the software. But what makes Kurv Studios really stand out from the competition is not the quality; it's the price. Videos from Kurv Studios typically range from $24.95 to $49.95 and contain more than 10 hours of training material. That's less than $5 per hour, making them one of the most cost-effective sources of training you'll find.

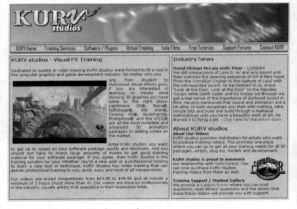

*Figure B-9: Kurv Studios web site.*

# 3D.sk

http://www.3d.sk/

3D.sk is the de facto supplier of high-resolution figure reference photos. The images range from male to female, young to old, clothed and nude. There are references for facial expressions, body poses, and even suggested poly-flow. If you're planning on developing 3D characters, a membership to this site should be considered essential. For less than $10 you can gain access to nearly 10,000 high-res images. If you've looked at the price of stock photos or the labor involved in hiring your own reference model, you'll quickly see why 3D.sk is an invaluable resource at an unparalleled price.

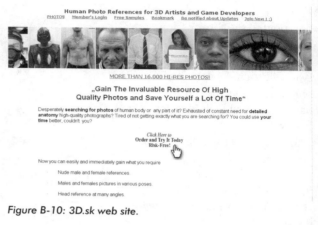

*Figure B-10: 3D.sk web site.*

# HDRI 3D

http://www.hdri3d.com/

*HDRI 3D* is definitely worth taking a look at. Each issue is filled with an amazing number of high-quality tutorials and articles on subjects from texturing and hair and fur shading to vehicular modeling and building cityscapes. It doesn't just touch on the "tried-and-true" uses of LightWave. The issues I've seen have also explored some really neat applications that I don't imagine a lot of people have thought of — yet!

*Figure B-11: HDRI 3D magazine web site.*

## Appendix B

# Worley Laboratories

http://www.worley.com/

Worley Labs is the company that contributed the Lite version of their Sasquatch Hair/Fur Shader to LightWave 7+. They also have two collections of very useful plug-ins bundled under the names Taft and Polk (yes, just like two former U.S. presidents). The really cool thing they've just come out with is the FPrime progressive rendering system. FPrime provides you with "real-time F9" rendering, allowing you to see changes to surfaces, lights, cameras, objects, etc., in real time. Without a doubt, FPrime is the most impressive product to hit the LightWave market in some time. There is simply not enough room to describe

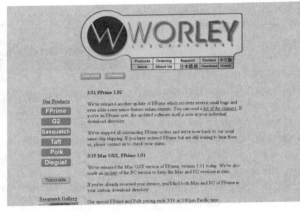

Figure B-12: Worley Labs web site.

everything that the plug-in does, but Worley's web site contains all of the details and nearly a dozen sample videos and I highly recommend you check it out.

# Colin Cohen: Freelance Programmer

http://cohen-plugs.tripod.com/

In the world of LightWave developers, there are an elite few who consistently produce high-caliber, extremely useful plug-ins. Colin Cohen is one of them. Colin is most widely known for his free plug-ins, but his generosity is not what makes him such a valuable asset to the community. Rather, Colin, who lives in the Los Angeles area, is one of the few programmers who make their exceptional skills available to

the public. His work as both an animator and a programmer (with over a decade of software development experience) gives him a unique insight into the needs that can arise during production. Keep Colin's information handy. There are a number of extremely talented programmers in the LightWave community, but very few of them are available for hire.

# Next Limit

http://www.nextlimit.com/

Next Limit makes two products that you'll definitely want to take a look at once you've got the basics of LightWave down. These products are RealFlow and RealWave. They create some of the best simulations of fluids (large and small) I've seen, and their fluid dynamics simulations equal work done on Houdini (which costs many, many, many times more). Fully functional time-limited demo

*Figure B-13*

versions of the software are available for download from their web site.

# Dynamic Realities

http://www.dynamic-realities.com

Dynamic Realities is the company that supplied the particle simulation Particle FX to LightWave. Their new version, Napalm, adds an exponential level of control to what you know in Particle FX. Pyro is a smoke and flame dynamics and

*Figure B-14*

rendering engine that greatly simplifies the creation of realistic fire and smoke in LightWave. Impact 3 is a solid body dynamics system for LightWave. NatureFX 2 realistically creates large bodies of water, wakes, clouds, and atmosphere effects.

Trees & Bolts creates lightning and other electrical effects with real-time OpenGL previews. LumeTools helps create realistic surfaces for your models and scenes. Demos are available from the Dynamic Realities web site.

## Electronic Rain

http://www.erain.com/

If you're into doing web graphics, Electronic Rain makes something I think will interest you. Swift 3D is a tool that exports LightWave stills and animations into Macromedia's Flash format. It fully supports gradients, transparency, reflections, specularity, and shadows. It'll render your LW scene to Flash's vector-based format as polygonal outlines, cartoon shading, or photo-realistic using multiple layers of transparency to get realistic specular highlights and shadows.

## Wordware Publishing

http://www.wordware.com/

Wordware, the publisher of the book you are reading, provides books on many different computer-related subjects, from its Game and Graphics Library to books on pixel shading and real-time graphics coding. Few publishers have books that actually teach you things you need to know. I don't want to get on a soapbox here, but I am fed up with books that talk a lot but don't say much. I choose to publish my LightWave books through Wordware because we share similar foci in our intent in *making a difference* and giving the community *things you can actually use, things you really want to know.*

## Safe Harbor

http://www.sharbor.com/

Safe Harbor is an online retailer that supports the 3D and graphics communities. While it is not my intention to single out one retailer from another, I call attention to Safe Harbor because they have served the digital content community for more than 16 years and consistently provide a high level of personal service and professionalism. If you're looking for 3D-related hardware and software and are having trouble locating what you need through other vendors, check out Safe Harbor.

# Recommended Reading

This section lists books I have found *essential* to getting to where I am in my career. With some of them, it will be immediately obvious as to how they relate to LightWave, animation, or filmmaking. With others, the connection may not be so obvious.

Art isn't something that can be quantified and put into a box. Every work of art, regardless of medium, is something that encapsulates the entirety of your emotional, mental, physical, and spiritual existence — whatever this summation happens to be. The more you know, the more you experience, and the more you live and can really "hold" the experiences you find, the better artist you will be.

## The Artist's Way
### Julia Cameron

Top on the list of books I recommend is this one. Why? Because if you're like most artists who find themselves *pulled* to 3D, you're not just good at one thing — you're good at a whole lot of things. How do you know what you really want to focus your time, energy, and *spirit* into? This book is made up of exercises that seem like play at first but really help you figure out what you want to devote your time as an artist toward. Perhaps even more valuable, it shows you how to experience the time you spend *creating your art* as "playtime"; this is the one true secret to letting your work soar to its highest heights more quickly than anything else.

## Letters to Strongheart
### J. Allen Boone

As an *artist*, you *see, feel, experience* life and the things that impact you in ways that leave much more permanent impressions on your spirit than do the travels of "everyday people." These things *have* to if you are going to be able to take these experiences and share them with others through your work. *Letters to Strongheart* is a collection of short letters detailing Boone's travels around the world. In a way I have not the skill to describe, Boone's experiences and *how he sees them* has done more to open my eyes to things in my own experiences that I never would have noticed before than nearly any other book (non-fiction or otherwise). I rank this on the same level as *The Artist's Way*.

## Film Directing: Shot by Shot
### Steven D. Katz

For anyone who is going to be successful in the art of visual storytelling, you *must* understand how to communicate within this medium. I've seen a few books come on the market that are seriously pale shadows of this book. This is what you study when you study filmmaking at the top schools in the country. (Need I say more? Okay, I will.) To illustrate its points as to how to *tell your story*, it has extensive storyboard sequences from *Citizen Kane*, *The Birds*, *Blade Runner*, *The Graduate*, and *Empire of the Sun*. It clearly shows you all the established filmic conventions (camera positions, ways of shooting dialogue, and establishing and maintaining narrative control) and *how to break them when you need to*.

### To the Actor
*Michael Chekhov*

This is the premier book for teaching actors the keys to "getting inside" their characters. Its exercises have been practiced by the best actors for generations. (It is what *directors* study to understand how to get the performances they need from the actors to tell the story they need to tell.) Plain and simple: If you plan on doing character-based work, either as an animator or director, the information in this book will be one of your greatest keys to success.

### LightWave 3D 8 Character Animation
*Timothy Albee*

This book takes you from where you are now and puts you on the path to being a feature-quality animator. Character rigging, inverse kinematics, posing, timing, silhouettes, squash-and-stretch, action, acting, facial animation, and taking a scene from start to finish are only a few of the items covered in depth within its pages. If you're not a modeler, don't worry; you can animate any of the characters that ship on the book's CD-ROM; they even come *fully rigged* if you have no interest in learning feature-quality rigging (setting up a character for animation). Exercises like "Life-Drawing in 3D" and "Moving Life Drawing in 3D" have proven themselves (in teaching promising young animators working for me at my studios) as the best, *fastest* ways of going from novice to feature-quality animator.

### Audition
*Michael Shurtleff*

This is another "must-have" for the character animation crowd. This book teaches you how to quickly understand the inner workings and dynamics between characters in a scene (and within a single character himself). In a nutshell, it teaches you the *quickest, most effective* ways of getting the clearest picture of *why* the scene is in the film (because in an audition, you frequently have less than thirty seconds from being handed the script to acting it out before director, producer, et al.). Then, *combining* what you find with Chekhov's "method," you can make the scene as moving to the audience as it possibly can be.

### Vilppu Drawing Manual
*Glenn Vilppu*

If you want to do figurative work — characters, humans, or otherwise — you need to get this book. As I mentioned earlier, Glenn's greatest gift is in being able to teach people (even those with little or no previous experience) an understanding of the human form such that they are able to create works that one would normally associate with a master figurative artist. It is the *understanding* of how the forms of the human body *work together* that make a model of a human look "good." The exercises in this book will give you that understanding.

## Alla Prima: Everything I Know About Painting

*Richard Schmid*

http://www.richardschmid.com

All arts pull from the same source. Having a strong understanding of drawing and painting is one of the *best* ways to make your 3D work excel. (It's *all art*! It doesn't matter what *tools* you use to create it!) I've been taught by teachers in some of the most respected art schools in the country. All of them together have taught me only a *fraction* of what I learned by reading Richard's book. Maybe the way in which he presents what he knows fits with how I need to have things presented to me in order to learn — or maybe he has a unique way of teaching that finally demystifies this gliding of paint on canvas. Regardless, reading his book, I finally *got it*. This is no "theorist" expounding about how things "should" be done or someone simply showing you moves to copy by rote. He talks about his *process of seeing* that leads his decision-making process. (I don't know how I can impress deeply enough the fact of how important this is in your actually becoming a good artist yourself — in every medium you touch!) Plus, Richard has this wonderful, light way of not taking himself or his art too seriously, and this is simply beyond refreshing — the book is a joy to read.

## Travels with Charley: In Search of America

*John Steinbeck*

If you ever find yourself getting entrenched in your element, don't just read this book — try your darnedest to follow in the author's footsteps. Steinbeck was in the same position — his solution was to pack up a pickup-camper, take his dog, Charley, and set off across the "blue highways" of America. He knew no one, and no one knew him, and through the book's pages, you can feel the excitement of the treasure of life and living flooding through author and text. (It is one thing to create art — it is another thing entirely to *live* it.)

# LightWave's Default Hot Keys

(Remember that all hot keys are CASE SENSITIVE.)

## Modeler

### Modeler: General

| | |
|---|---|
| Cut | Ctrl + x |
| Copy | Ctrl + c |
| Paste | Ctrl + v |
| Center around cursor | g |
| Rotate selection 90° clockwise | r |
| Undo | Ctrl + z |
| Redo | z |
| Point Selection mode | Ctrl + g |
| Polygon Selection mode | Ctrl + h |
| Volume Selection mode | Ctrl + j |
| Symmetry mode | Y |
| Numeric window | n |
| Statistics window | w |
| Point/Polygon Info window | i |
| Surface | q |
| Toggle full-screen viewport | Numeric keypad 0 |
| Help | F1 |
| General Options window | o |
| Display Options window | d |

### Modeler: Create

| | |
|---|---|
| Box | X |
| Ball | O |
| Manage Fonts | F10 |
| Text | W |
| "Open" curve from selected points | Ctrl + p |
| Points | + |
| Make Polygon | p |

## Modeler: Modify

| | |
|---|---|
| Move | t |
| Drag | Ctrl + t |
| Snap-Drag | G |
| DragNet | ; |
| Magnet | : |
| Shear | [ |
| Center | F2 |
| Rest on Ground | F3 |
| Rotate to Ground | F4 |
| Rotate | y |
| Bend | ~ |
| Size | H |
| Stretch | h |
| Jitter | J |
| Smooth | M |

## Modeler: Multiply

| | |
|---|---|
| Bevel | b |
| Edge Bevel | Ctrl + b |
| Extrude | E |
| Extend | e |
| Lathe | L |
| Smooth Shift | F |
| Path Extrude | P |
| Mirror | V |
| Array | Ctrl + y |
| Clone | c |
| Knife | K |
| Subdivide | D |
| Triple | T |
| Cut | U |

## Modeler: Construct

| | |
|---|---|
| Remove Polygons (Leave Points) | k |
| Bridge | l |
| SubPatch Activate/Deactivate | Tab |
| Freeze Polys | Ctrl + d |
| Spline Patch | Ctrl + f |

## Modeler: Detail

| | |
|---|---|
| Merge Polygons | Z |
| Merge Points | m |
| Unweld | Ctrl + u |
| Weld | Ctrl + w |
| Set Value | v |
| Flip | f |

| Spin Quads | Ctrl + k |
| Unify Polygons | I |
| Measure | Ctrl + e |

### Modeler: Map

| Clear Map from Selection | – |

### Moduler: Utilities

| Add Plug-ins | F11 |
| Edit Plug-ins | Alt + F11 |

### Modeler: View

| Zoom | Ctrl + q |
| Fit All | a |
| Fit Selected | A |
| Zoom In | . |
| Zoom In x 2 | > or Shift + . |
| Zoom Out | , |
| Zoom Out x 2 | < or Shift + , |
| Insert Layer | Insert |
| Delete Layer | Home |
| Swap Layers | ' |
| Next Layer Bank | Page Up |
| Previous Layer Bank | Page Down |
| Select Connected | ] |
| Invert Connected | ? |
| Expand Selection | } |
| Contract Selection | { |
| Invert Selection | " |
| Drop Selection | / |
| Hide Selected | - |
| Hide Unselected | = |
| Invert Hidden | | |
| Unhide All | \ |

## Layout

### Layout: General

| Save Scene | s |
| Save Scene As | Ctrl + s |
| Save Scene Increment | S |
| Show/Hide Floating Windows | Tab |
| Show/Hide Toolbar | Alt + F2 |
| Show/Hide SubPatch Cages | Alt + F3 |
| Show/Hide Motion Paths | Alt + F4 |
| Show/Hide Handles | Alt + F5 |
| Show/Hide IK Chains | Alt + F6 |

| Scene Editor | Ctrl + F1 |
| Graph Editor | Ctrl + F2 |
| Surface Editor | F5 |
| Image Editor | F6 |
| Display Options | d |
| General Options | o |
| Objects | O |
| Bones | B |
| Lights | L |
| Cameras | C |
| Item Properties | p |
| Auto Key Create | Shift + F1 |
| Create Key | Return |
| Delete Key | Del |
| Undo | Ctrl + z |
| Redo | z |
| Statistics | w |
| Help | F1 |

### Layout: Items

| Load Scene | Ctrl + o |
| Load Object | + |
| Add Null | Ctrl + n |
| Clone Selected Item | Ctrl + c |
| Mirror | V |
| Clear Selected Item | - |

### Layout: Modify

| Move | t |
| Rotate | y |
| Size | H |
| Stretch | h |
| Jump to Numeric Input Field | n |
| Coordinate System: World | Shift + F5 |
| Coordinate System: Parent | Shift + F6 |
| Coordinate System: Local | Shift + F7 |

### Layout: Setup

| Enter Bone Edit Mode | E |
| Exit Bone Edit Mode | D |
| Enable IK | Shift + F8 |
| Add Child Bone | = |
| Joint Move | Ctrl + j |
| Tip Move | Ctrl + t |
| Bone Twist | Ctrl + k |
| Record Pivot Rotation | P |
| Record Bone Rest Rotation | r |

| | |
|---|---|
| Unparent Bone | Ctrl + u |
| Mirror Hierarchy | Ctrl + w |
| Import Rig | I |
| Export Rig | J |
| Motion Options | m |
| Record Minimum Joint Angles | { |
| Record Maximum Joint Angles | } |
| Selected Bone Active/Inactive | Ctrl + r |

## Layout: Utilities

| | |
|---|---|
| Edit Plug-ins | Shift + F11 |
| Master Plug-ins | Ctrl + q |

## Layout: Render

| | |
|---|---|
| Render Frame | F9 |
| Render Scene | F10 |
| Render Selected Object | F11 |
| Render Motion Builder Preview | Shift + F9 |

## Layout: View

| | |
|---|---|
| Zoom In | . |
| Zoom In x 2 | > |
| Zoom Out | , |
| Zoom Out x 2 | < |
| View Mode: Back | 1 |
| View Mode: Top | 2 |
| View Mode: Right | 3 |
| View Mode: Perspective | 4 |
| View Mode: Light | 5 |
| View Mode: Camera | 6 |
| View Mode: Schematic | 7 |
| Previous View Layout | F3 |
| Next View Layout | F4 |
| Increase Grid | ] |
| Decrease Grid | [ |
| Select All Objects | Ctrl + a |
| Select Item By Name | ' |
| Select Next Item | down arrow |
| Select Previous Item | up arrow |
| Select First Item | Shift + up arrow |
| Select Last Item | Shift + down arrow |
| Select Next Sibling | Ctrl + down arrow |
| Select Previous Sibling | Ctrl + up arrow |
| Show/Hide Safe Areas | Alt + F7 |
| Show/Hide Field Chart | Alt + F8 |
| Toggle Fullscreen Viewport | Numeric keypad 0 |

# Index

4-Point Lighting Setup plug-in, 583

## A

action centers, 18
action modes, 17
Action Safe view, 6
Add Edges tool, 153-154
Align to Rail plug-in, 580
ambient light, 104
animation, rendering, 395-396
antialiasing, 96
area lights, 5
arms, modeling, 216-219
ASA
    BufferSaver plug-in, 569-570
    ColorPicker plug-in, 570
    Fake Irradiance Illumination plug-in, 571
    Light Absorption in See-Through Items
        plug-in, 571
    RenderTarget plug-in, 572
atlas mapping, 167-168
Auto Key button, 37
axes,
    protected, 45
    solving for, 408-409
axis, 1

## B

Backdrop tab, Modeler, 23-24
BandGlue tool, 202
BandSaw Pro tool, 201
BandSaw tool, 200-201
bank, 2-3
beard, creating with SasLite, 523-528
Bend tool, 142
    using, 77-78
Bevel tool, using, 88-89
body, modeling, 214-234
bones, 398-399
Boolean, 82
    using, 82-88
box modeling, 237
Bridge tool, using, 136-137

## C

C_Bend plug-in, 581
cage,
    creating, 298-335
    patching, 337-344
    tips for patching, 335-336
Camera Properties window settings, 94-99
camera, 6-7
caustics, 6
Center Current Item control, 33
Change Surface window, 16-17
character animation, 398-399
child items, 14
chrome sphere, creating, 114-117
CinePaint program, 586
ClothFX, 483
    using, 499-504
Coffee! plug-in, 582
Collision dynamic, 483
    using, 486-489
collisions, 488
color maps, 15
compositing,
    CG elements into live-action plate, 440-448
    explosions, 449-457
    shadows, 443-448
Configure Keys window, 27
Configure Menus window, 28-30
Construct tab, Modeler, 19-20
context menus, see quick menus
Contract Selection tool, 61-62
Create Key button, 36
Create tab, Modeler, 19-20
Current Item pop-up menu, Layout, 37
Current Object menu, 13
curves, selection order, 274, 276

## D

Delete Key button, 36
deselecting, in Modeler, 17
Detail tab, Modeler, 19-20
detail-out modeling, 237
Display Options tab, Layout, 44-45
Display Options window, Modeler, 22-25
distant light, 4